Holt Middle School Math

Are You Ready? Intervention and Enrichment

Course 1

HOLT, RINEHART AND WINSTON

A Harcourt Education Company

Orlando • **Austin** • New York • San Diego • Toronto • London

Printed in the United States of America

ISBN 0-03-067917-6

7 8 9 10 11 12   082   09 08 07 06 05

CONTENTS

CONTENTS, *CONTINUED*

CONTENTS, *CONTINUED*

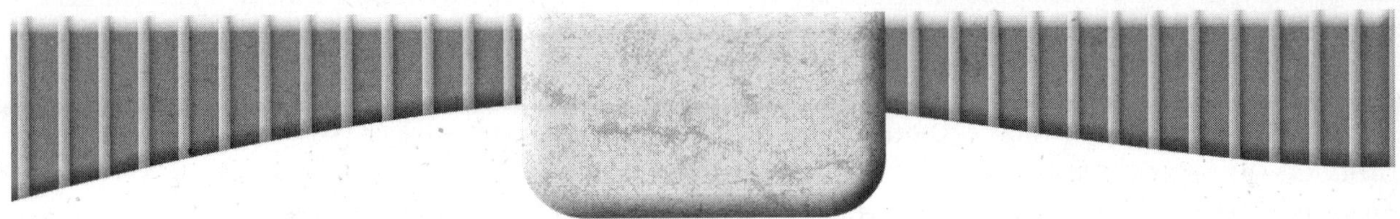

Using the Intervention Strategies and Activities in Your Class

The *Intervention Strategies and Activities* will help you accommodate the diverse skill levels of students in your class and will help you better prepare students to work successfully on grade-level content by targeting the prerequisite skills for *each chapter* in the program. The following questions and answers will help you make the best use of this rich resource.

How can I determine which skills or strategies a student or students should work on?

Before beginning each chapter, have students complete the "Are You Ready?" page in the student book. This page targets the prerequisite skills necessary for success in the chapter. A student's performance on this page will allow you to diagnose skill weaknesses and prescribe appropriate interventions. Intervention strategies and activities are tied directly to each of the skills assessed. A chart at the beginning of each chapter correlates the skill assessed to the appropriate intervention materials. The chart appears in the Teacher's Edition. A sample is shown below.

Are You Ready?
INTERVENTION • Diagnose and Prescribe

Prerequisite Skill	Items (Student Edition p. 151)	How to Help Options
Write and Read Decimals	6–11	Intervention Practice, Skill 15 CD-ROM Intervention Activities, Skill 15
Identify Sets of Numbers	12–19	Intervention Practice, Skill 6 CD-ROM Intervention Activities, Skill 6

In what format are the intervention materials?

Intervention materials are available in two different formats.

Copying masters—which provide the skill development and skill practice on reproducible pages. These pages in the *Are You Ready? Intervention and Enrichment* can be used by individual students or small groups. You can also allow students to record their answers on copies of the pages. This guide also provides teaching suggestions for skill development, as well as an alternative teaching strategy for students who continue to have difficulty with the skill.

CD-ROM—which provides the skill development and practice in an interactive format. Teaching suggestions and alternative teaching strategies are provided as printable PDF files.

Are manipulative activities included in the intervention strategies?

The teaching strategies in the teacher's materials for the *Are You Ready? Intervention and Enrichment* do require manipulatives, easily gathered classroom objects, or copying masters from the *Chapter Resource Books.* Since these activities are designed for only those students who show deficits in their skill development, the quantity of manipulatives will be small. For many activities, you may substitute materials, such as squares of paper for counters, coins for two-color counters, and so on.

How can I organize my classroom so that I have time and space to help students who show a need for these intervention strategies and activities?

You may want to set up a Math Skill Center with a folder for each of your students. Based on a student's performance on the *Are You Ready?* page, assign appropriate skills by marking the student's record folder. The student can then work through the intervention materials, record the date of completion, and place the completed work in a folder for your review. You may wish to assign students to a partner or assign a small group to work together, or you may wish to have a specified time during the day to meet with one or more of the individuals or small groups to assess their progress and to provide direct instruction.

How are the activities structured?

Each skill begins with a model or an explanation with a model for each skill. The first section of exercises titled *Try These* provides 2–4 exercises that allow students to move toward doing the work independently. A student who has difficulty with the *Try These* exercises might benefit from the activity for that skill described in this Teacher's Guide before they attempt the *Practice on Your Own* page. The *Practice on Your Own* page provides an additional model for the skill and scaffolded exercises, which gradually remove prompts. Scaffolding provides a framework within which the student can achieve success for the skill. At the end of the *Practice on Your Own,* there is a *Check.* The *Check* provides 3–4 problems that check the student's proficiency in the skill. Guidelines for success are provided in the teacher's materials.

Using the Diagnostic Assessment in an After-School or Summer School Program

The Diagnostic Assessment can be used as a tool to scaffold the instruction in the after-school or summer school program. Each test item ties directly to the same numbered skill in this intervention book. For example, students who fail to answer item 12 correctly may benefit from the instruction, alternative teaching strategy, and practice provided in Skill 12.

The assessment is set up by strand. You may want to test only one strand at time. Based upon students' performance on the diagnostic assessment, you may want to set up a folder for each student with a list of needed intervention skills. The student can then work through the intervention materials. You may want to work with small groups of students on specific skills.

Student's Name ______________________________

Individual Prerequisite Skills Checklist

Chapter	Prerequisite Skill	Prescription	Skill Mastered

Name ______________________________ Date ___________ Class ___________

COURSE 1

Diagnostic Assessment

Number and Quantitative Reasoning

1. Identify the place value of the underlined digit 6,70<u>4</u>,456.

A millions

B hundred thousands

C ten thousands

D thousands

2. Which is three million, two hundred fifty-two thousand, twelve written in standard form?

F 3,250,112

G 3,252,012

H 3,000,250,012

J 3,250,000,112

3. Round 48,529 to the nearest ten.

A 48,520 **C** 48,530

B 48,525 **D** 48,600

4. Which statement is true?

F $72,772 > 77,277$

G $84,563 < 84,653$

H $3,061 > 3,072$

J $3,245 > 4,999$

5. Which set of numbers is ordered from least to greatest?

A 83, 71, 53, 35, 17

B 17, 35, 53, 71, 83

C 17, 53, 35, 71, 83

D 35, 53, 17, 71, 83

6. Identify the number set that contains the number 15.

F counting, whole, even

G counting, whole, odd

H counting, whole, factor of 4

J counting, even

7. Which list contains the first three multiples of the number 7?

A 7, 8, 9

B 7, 14, 21

C 7, 17, 27

D 7, 70, 700

8. Which list contains all the factors of 16?

F 1, 16, 32

G 1, 2, 4, 8, 16

H 1, 16

J 1, 2, 4, 6, 8, 16

9. Which number is not prime?

A 7 **C** 17

B 11 **D** 21

10. Which number is prime?

F 25 **H** 61

G 39 **J** 72

11. Evaluate 15^2.

A 13 **C** 152

B 30 **D** 225

12. Find the value of 5^3.

F 15 **H** 125

G 53 **J** 1125

13. Find the next three numbers in the pattern.

16, 20, 24, 28...

A 30, 32, 34

B 32, 36, 40

C 31, 33, 35

D 46, 92, 184

Name ______________________ Date __________ Class __________

COURSE 1

Diagnostic Assessment

Number and Quantitative Reasoning, continued

14. What number is represented by the shaded portion of the grid?

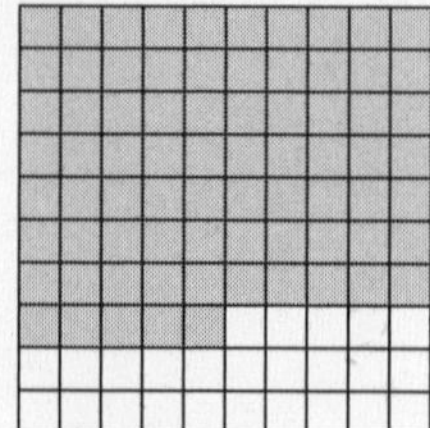

F $\frac{1}{4}$

G 0.25

H $\frac{4}{5}$

J 0.75

15. What is 92.15 in word form?

A nine, two, one five

B ninety-two and fifteen hundredths

C ninety-two and one-five thousandths

D ninety-two and fifteen tenths

16. Round 27.62 to the nearest whole number.

F 27

G 28

H 27.6

J 28.1

17. Which set of numbers is ordered from greatest to least?

A 14.2, 14.1, 12.3, 12.1

B 14.1, 14.2, 12.3, 12.1

C 12.1, 12.3, 14.2, 14.1

D 12.1, 12.3, 14.1, 14.2

18. Write the fraction for the shaded part of the circle.

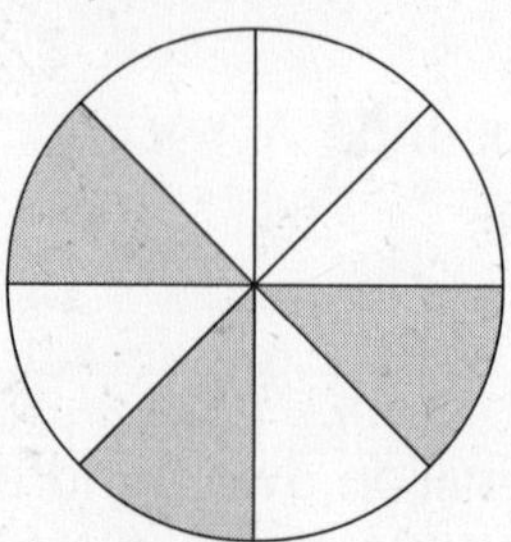

F $\frac{2}{3}$

G $\frac{1}{2}$

H $\frac{3}{8}$

J $\frac{3}{7}$

19. Simplify $\frac{12}{16}$.

A $\frac{1}{3}$

B $\frac{2}{3}$

C $\frac{1}{2}$

D $\frac{3}{4}$

20. Round $\frac{1}{9}$ to the nearest benchmark fraction.

F 0

G $\frac{1}{2}$

H 1

J cannot round

21. Write $\frac{13}{3}$ as a mixed number.

A $4\frac{1}{4}$

B $4\frac{1}{3}$

C $5\frac{1}{2}$

D $\frac{3}{13}$

22. Write an improper fraction equal to $2\frac{1}{4}$.

F $\frac{21}{4}$

G $\frac{9}{4}$

H $\frac{3}{4}$

J $\frac{9}{3}$

COURSE 1

Diagnostic Assessment

Number and Quantitative Reasoning, continued

23. Find a common denominator for $\frac{1}{8} + \frac{1}{12}$.

A 12 **C** 24

B 16 **D** 76

24. Which number should replace the question mark to make the statement true?

$\frac{2}{3} = \frac{?}{15}$

F 5 **H** 15

G 10 **J** 20

25. Compare $3\frac{1}{4} \square 3\frac{1}{5}$.

A > **C** =

B <

26. Change $\frac{7}{8}$ to a decimal.

F 0.07 **H** 0.875

G 0.78 **J** 7

27. Which is the ratio of pentagons to squares?

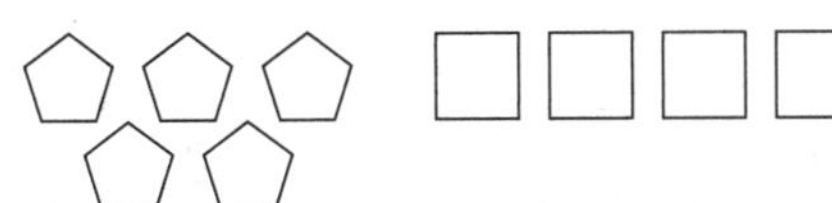

A 5:4 **C** 5:1

B 4:5 **D** 1:5

28. Simplify: 10 oranges to 2 lemons.

F 4:3 **H** 5:1

G 3:4 **J** 1:5

29. Which percent can be used to describe the shaded part of the grid?

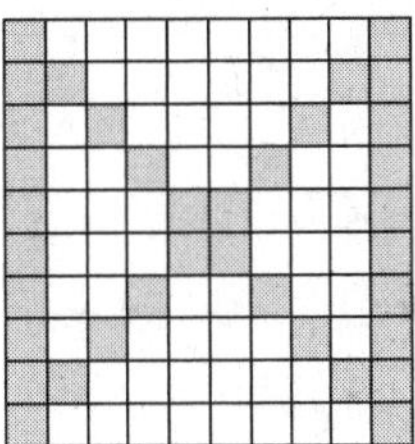

A 16% **C** 36%

B 32% **D** 64%

30. Change 0.15 to a percent.

F 0.15% **H** 15%

G 1.5% **J** 1,500%

31. Change $\frac{40}{50}$ to a percent.

A 20% **C** 50%

B 40% **D** 80%

32. Which statement is true?

F $\frac{1}{2} < 0.25$

G $75\% > \frac{3}{5}$

H $\frac{1}{2} < 25\%$

J $50\% = 5.0$

33. Which integer represents a loss of $12?

A −$12

B $12

C $0

D −$120

Name ______________________ Date ____________ Class ____________

COURSE 1

Diagnostic Assessment

Operations

34. Find the quotient. $6\overline{)70}$

F 10 r 4 **H** 11 r 4

G 10 r 10 **J** 12

35. Find the product. 4 × 4 × 4

A 12 **C** 176

B 64 **D** 444

36. Multiply. 9 × 8

F 17 **H** 72

G 64 **J** 98

37. $\frac{64}{100} = \underline{?}$

A 6.4 **C** 0.064

B 0.64 **D** 64

38. Divide. 92 ÷ 4

F 13 **H** 22

G 21 **J** 23

39. Divide $8\overline{)140}$. Write any remainder as a decimal.

A 16.3 **C** 132

B 17.5 **D** 1,120

40. Multiply. $\begin{array}{r} 6.8 \\ \times 0.5 \\ \hline \end{array}$

F 3.4 **H** 34

G 7.3 **J** 340

41. Multiply. 100 × 3.6

A 3.6 **C** 360

B 36 **D** 3,600

42. Add. $\begin{array}{r} \frac{5}{8} \\ +\frac{1}{4} \\ \hline \end{array}$

F $\frac{5}{32}$ **H** $\frac{3}{4}$

G $\frac{1}{2}$ **J** $\frac{7}{8}$

43. $\frac{3}{4} - \frac{1}{4}$

A 0 **C** $\frac{3}{4}$

B $\frac{1}{2}$ **D** 2

44. Multiply $\frac{1}{2} \times \frac{4}{5}$. Write the answer in simplest form.

F $\frac{2}{5}$ **H** $\frac{5}{7}$

G $\frac{3}{5}$ **J** 1

45. Multiply. $\frac{1}{4} \times 8$

A 1 **C** 4

B 2 **D** 32

46. What is 25% of 80?

F 20 **H** 60

G 40 **J** 75

47. Subtract. (−12) − 2

A −14 **C** 10

B −10 **D** 14

Name ______________________ Date __________ Class __________

COURSE 1

Diagnostic Assessment

Algebra

48. Identify the property shown.
$8 \times 1 = 8$

F Commutative Property of Multiplication

G Associative Property of Multiplication

H Multiplication Property of One

J Multiplication Property of Zero

49. Which is the correct use of the Distributive Property to find the product 3×11?

A $(3 + 10) \times (3 + 1)$

B 3×11

C $(3 \times 10) \times (3 \times 1)$

D $(3 \times 10) + (3 \times 1)$

50. Evaluate. $10 - (3 + 5)$

F -5 **H** 15

G 2 **J** 18

51. Evaluate. $3^2 + (9 - 1)$

A -2 **C** 16

B 12 **D** 17

52. $2(5.2)(3) =$ _____

F 10.12 **H** 26

G 13.4 **J** 31.2

53. Which expression represents the product of 6 and a number?

A $6w$

B $w + 6$

C $w - 6$

D $w \div 6$

54. Evaluate the expression $3x + 2$ for $x = 4$.

F 9 **H** 24

G 14 **J** 36

55. Simplify. $3x + 4x + 6$

A $12x + 6$ **C** $7x + 6$

B $13x$ **D** $13 + x$

56. Which algebraic equation describes the expression "6 plus a number is 8"?

F $6n = 8$ **H** $n + 6 = 8$

G $6 \div n = 8$ **J** $n - 6 = 8$

57. Use inverse operations to solve the equation. $n + 10 = 16$

A $n = -6$ **C** $n = 6$

B $n = 1.\overline{6}$ **D** $n = 26$

58. Solve. $a - 8 = 23$

F $a = 2.875$ **H** $a = 31$

G $a = 15$ **J** $a = 184$

59. Solve. $7x = 49$

A $x = 7$ **C** $x = 56$

B $x = 42$ **D** $x = 343$

60. Solve. $3h - 2 = 4$

F $h = -2$ **H** $h = 2$

G $h = 0.\overline{6}$ **J** $h = 3$

61. Identify the point graphed on the number line.

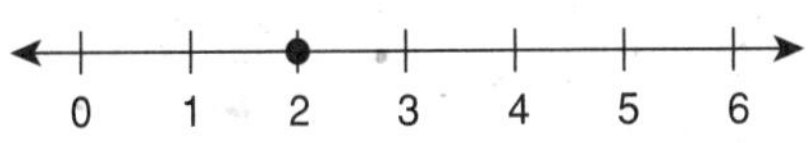

A -2 **C** 3

B 2 **D** 4

Name ______________________ Date ____________ Class ____________

COURSE 1

Diagnostic Assessment

Algebra, continued

62. Which graph is the solution to the inequality $x + 3 \geq 8$?

F

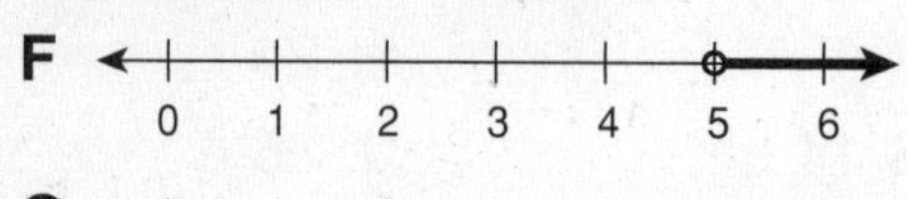

G

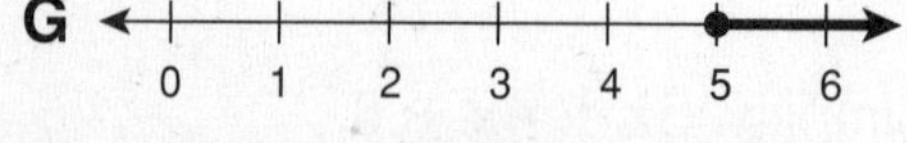

H

J

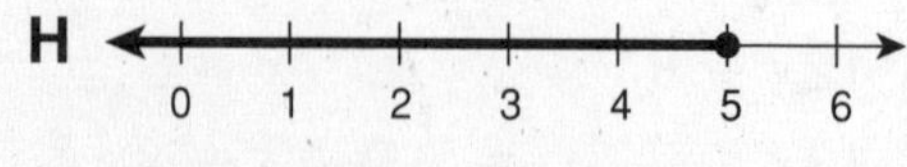

63. Which inequality represents the graph?

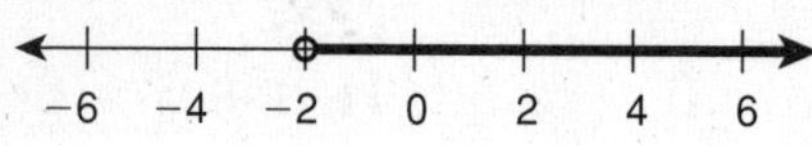

A $x > -2$ **C** $x < -2$

B $x \geq -2$ **D** $x \leq -2$

64. Which graph corresponds to the equation $y = x + 2$?

F

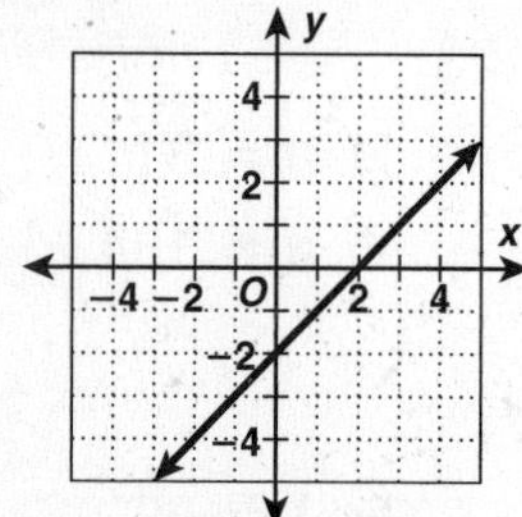

G

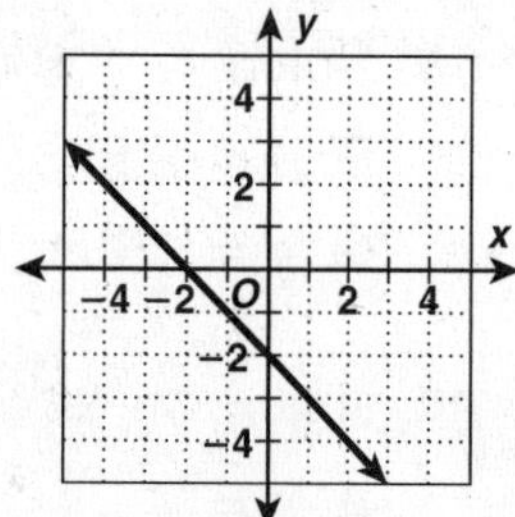

H

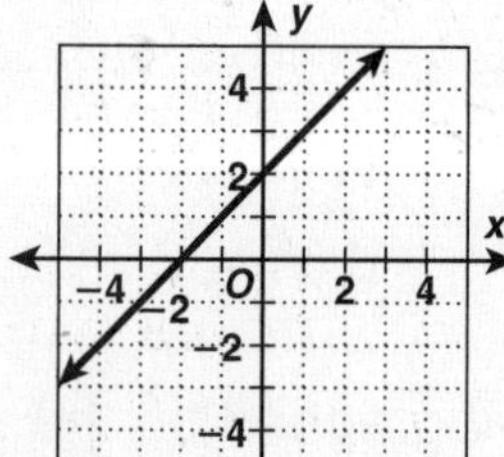

J

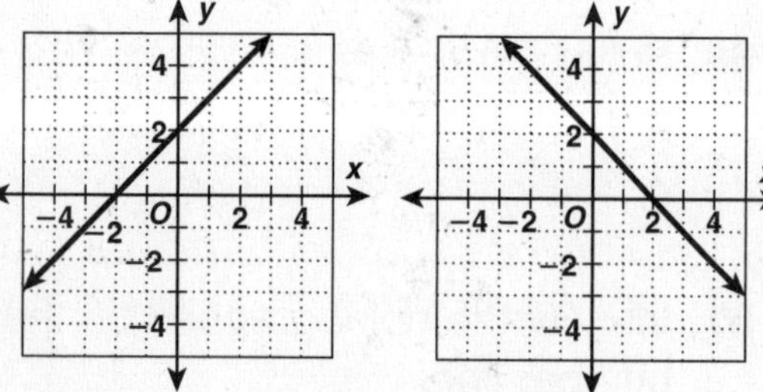

65. Solve for the value of a. $\frac{a}{10} = \frac{2}{5}$

A $a = 25$ **C** $a = 4$

B $a = 15$ **D** $a = 2$

66. 24 in. = _____ ft

F 1 **H** 3

G 2 **J** 6

67. Which term completes the function table?

Input	Algebraic Expression	Output
n	$3n$	
2		6
4		12
6		??

A 14 **C** 26

B 18 **D** 36

68. What is the ordered pair for point D?

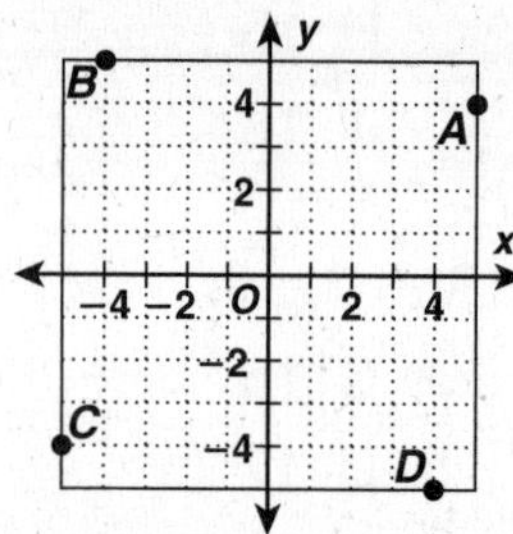

F (5, 4) **H** (−5, −4)

G (−4, 5) **J** (4, −5)

69. What is the ordered pair for point F?

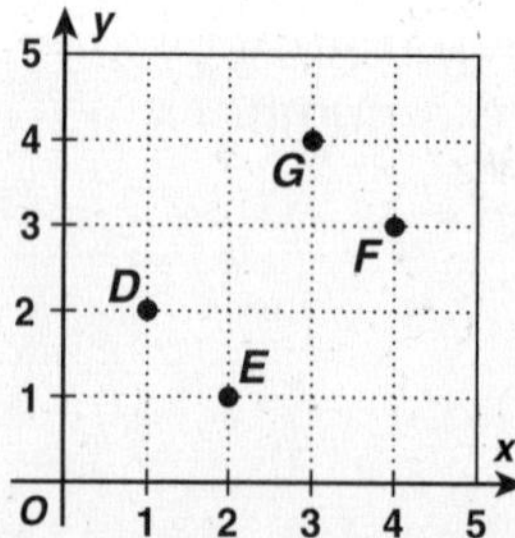

A (1, 2) **C** (4, 3)

B (2, 1) **D** (3, 4)

Name ______________________ Date ____________ Class ____________

COURSE 1

Diagnostic Assessment

Measuring

70. What temperature is shown by the letter *C*?

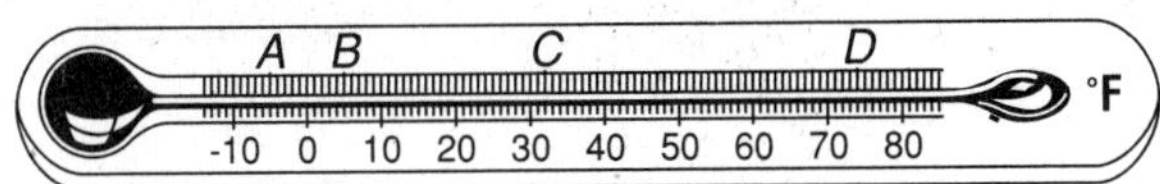

F 32° **H** 74°

G 5° **J** −5°

71. Change to the given unit.

8 c = _______ pt

A 2 **C** 16

B 4 **D** 24

72. Change to the given unit.

17,000 mg = _______ g

F 1,700 **H** 17

G 170 **J** 1.7

73. What is the length of the rabbit?

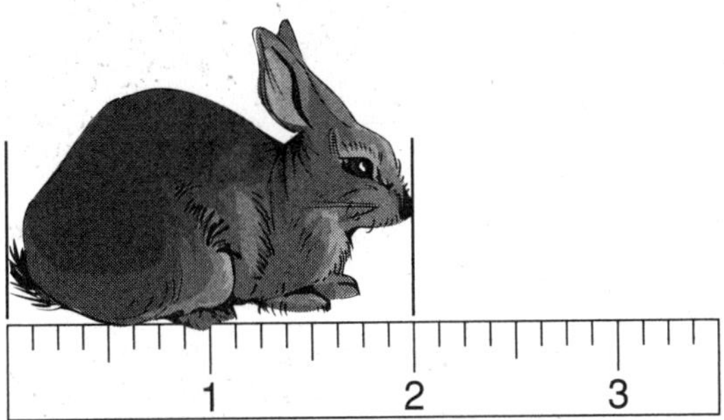

A 1 inch **C** $1\frac{3}{4}$ inches

B $1\frac{1}{4}$ inches **D** 2 inches

Name ______________________ Date __________ Class __________

COURSE 1

Diagnostic Assessment

Geometry

74. Classify the angle shown.

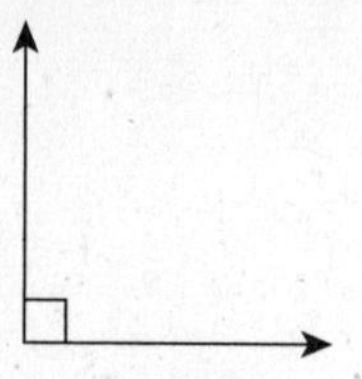

F right
G acute
H obtuse
J straight

75. Name the angle formed by the dashed rays.

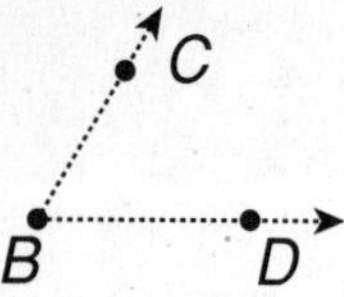

A $\angle CBD$
B $\angle BCA$
C $\angle BCD$
D $\angle DCB$

76. Identify the figure shown.

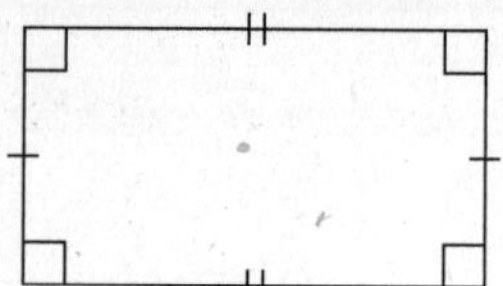

F trapezoid
G rectangle
H rhombus
J square

77. Name an acute angle in the polygon.

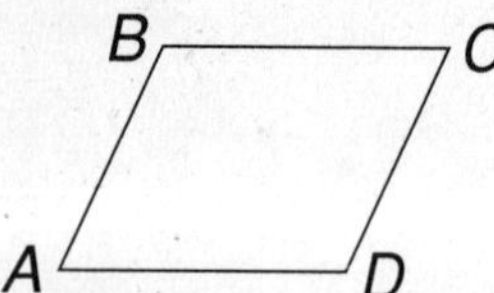

A $\angle ABC$
B $\angle CAB$
C $\angle BCD$
D $\angle ACB$

78. Identify the solid figure.

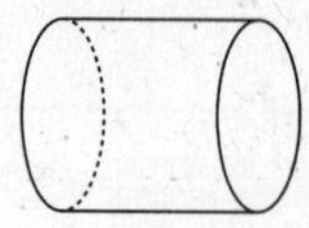

F rectangular prism
G rectangular pyramid
H cone
J cylinder

79. Identify the number of faces, edges and vertices.

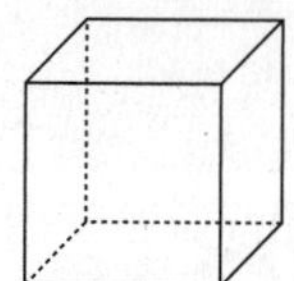

A faces = 4, edges = 8, vertices = 10
B faces = 6, edges = 10, vertices = 8
C faces = 4, edges = 8, vertices = 6
D faces = 6, edges = 12, vertices = 8

80. Which line intersects $\overleftrightarrow{AB}$?

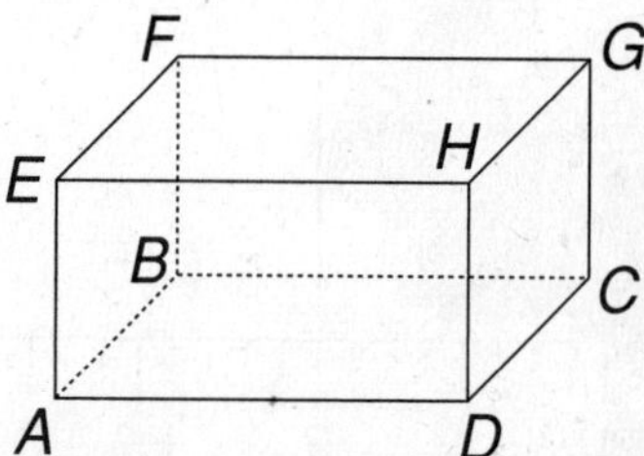

F $\overleftrightarrow{AD}$
G $\overleftrightarrow{CD}$
H $\overleftrightarrow{FG}$
J $\overleftrightarrow{HG}$

Name ______________________ Date ____________ Class ____________

COURSE 1

Diagnostic Assessment

Geometry, continued

81. Identify the set of figures that are congruent.

A

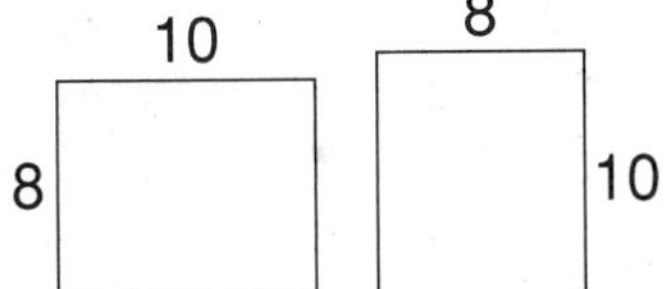

B

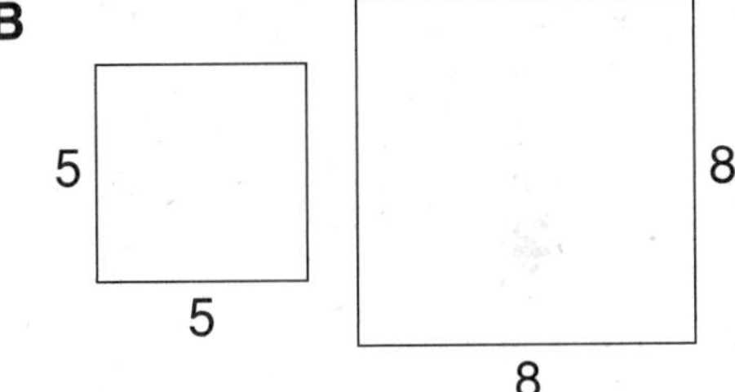

C

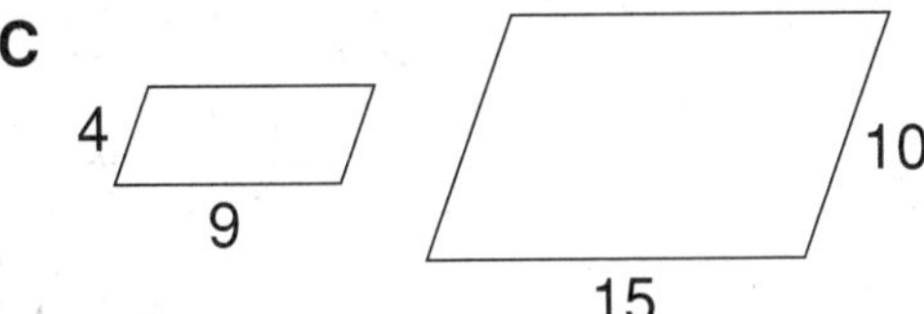

D

5 13 12

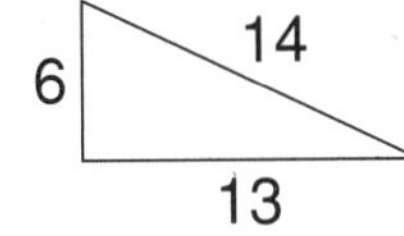

82. Identify the pair of figures that appear to be similar.

F

G

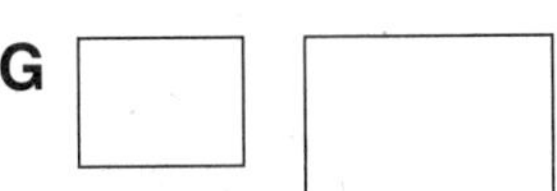

H

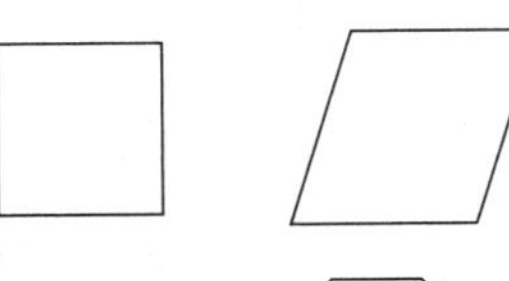

J

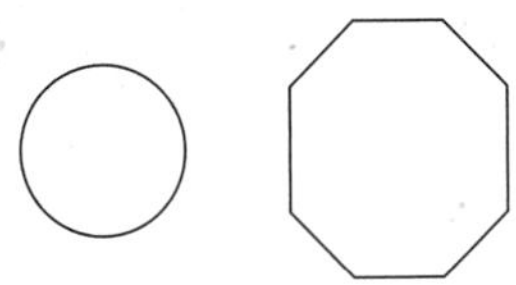

83. Find the perimeter of the figure.

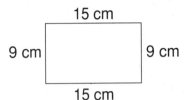

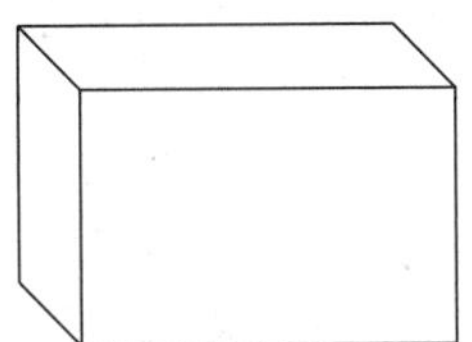

A 24 cm **C** 90 cm

B 48 cm **D** 96 cm

84. Identify the figure shown.

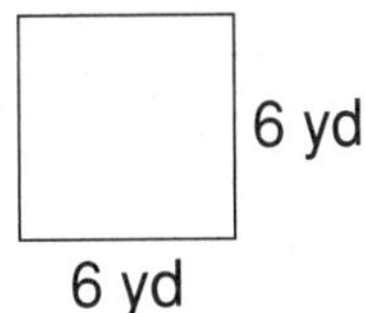

F triangular prism

G triangular pyramid

H rectangular prism

J rectangular pyramid

85. Find the area of the figure.

6 yd

6 yd

A 12 yd^2 **C** 36 yd^2

B 24 yd^2 **D** 72 yd^2

86. Find the area of the figure.

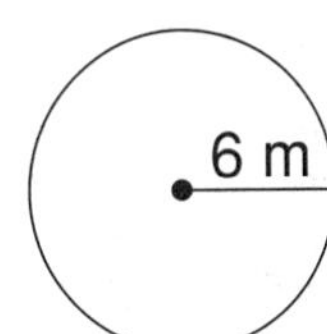

F 18.84 m^2 **H** 113.04 m^2

G 37.68 m^2 **J** 452.16 m^2

Name ______________________ Date __________ Class __________

COURSE 1

Diagnostic Assessment

Geometry, continued

87. Identify the transformation.

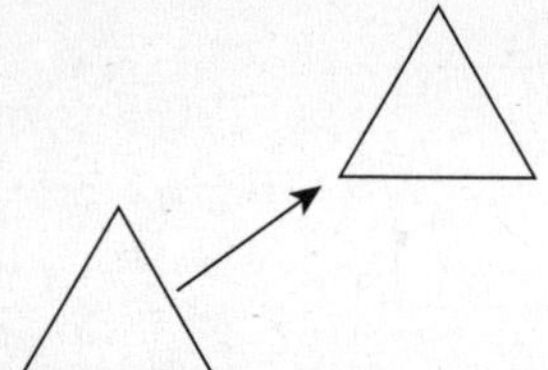

A translation

B rotation

C reflection

D transdermal

88. Identify the number of lines of symmetry in the figure.

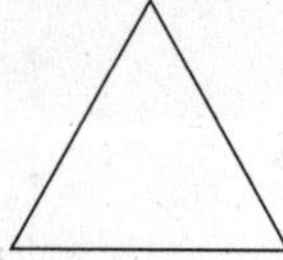

F 1

G 2

H 3

J 4

89. What is the measure of the angle?

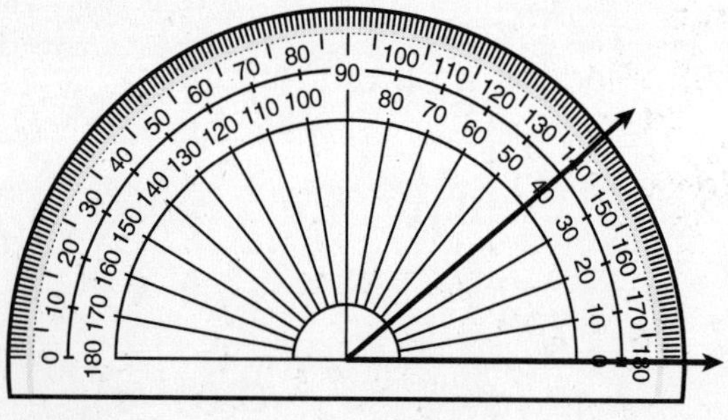

A 40°

B 50°

C 140°

D 180°

Name ________________________ Date __________ Class __________

COURSE 1

Diagnostic Assessment

Statistics and Data Analysis

90. Use the data in the table to answer the question.

	Boys	Girls
Math	7	5
English	4	8
Art	2	11
Science	13	9

Which is the favorite class among boys surveyed?

F Math **H** Art

G English **J** Science

91. What is the range of the data set?
83, 68, 87, 74, 88

A 20 **C** 80

B 68 **D** 83

92. What is the median of the data set?
8, 6, 4, 6, 8, 2

F 8 **H** 4

G 6 **J** 2

93. What is the mean of the data set?
8, 12, 7, 16, 10, 7

A 6 **C** 9

B 7 **D** 10

94. Use the bar graph to answer the question.

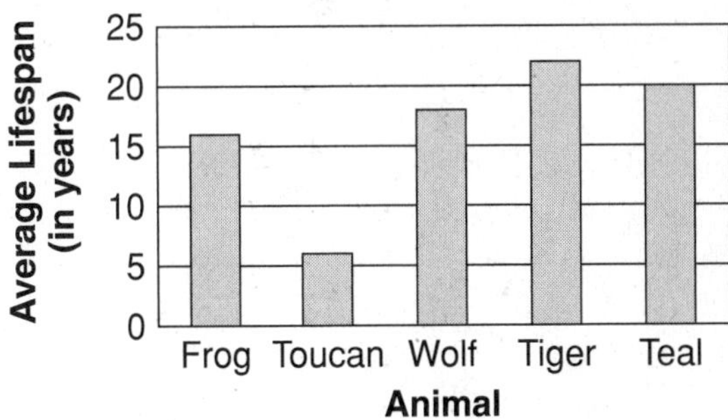

What is the average lifespan of a teal?

F 7 years **H** 20 years

G 17 years **J** 25 years

95. Use the circle graph to answer the question.

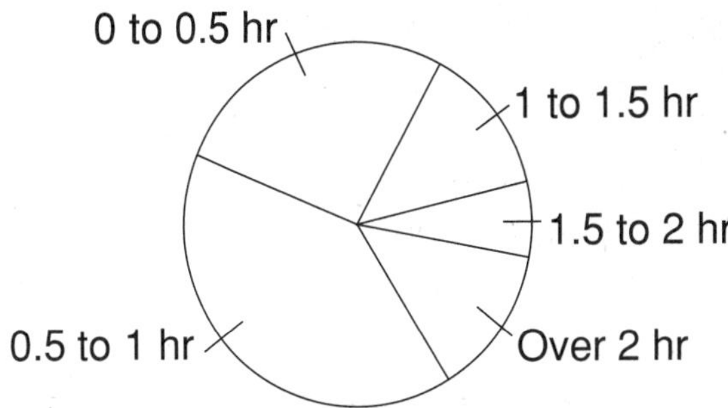

What is the most common amount of time spent on homework?

A 0 to $\frac{1}{2}$ hour **C** $1\frac{1}{2}$ to 2 hours

B $\frac{1}{2}$ to 1 hour **D** over 2 hours

Name _________________________________ Date ___________ Class ___________

Diagnostic Assessment

COURSE 1

Statistics and Data Analysis, continued

96. Use the stem-and-leaf plot to answer the question.

Test Scores

Stem	Leaves
7	0 1 3
8	2 2 3 4
9	3 3 3 7

What is the median of the test scores?

F 70 **H** 83
G 82 **J** 97

97. What is the likelihood of spinning the letter B?

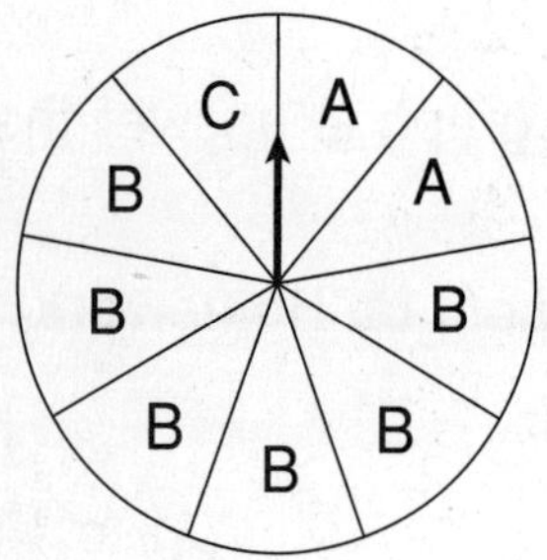

A certain **C** likely
B impossible **D** unlikely

98. How many more people attended Game 4 than Game 2?

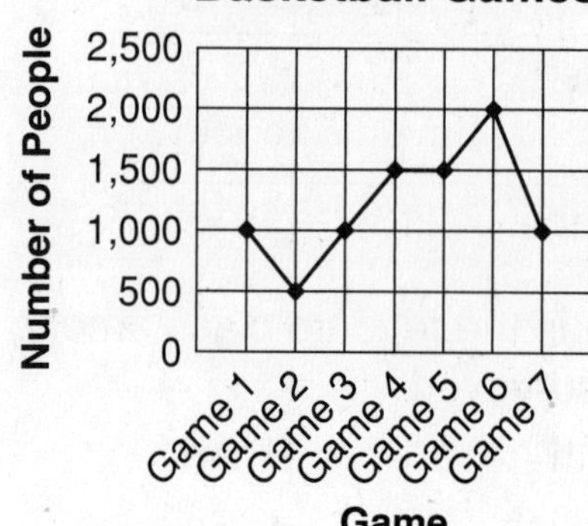

F 500 **H** 1,500
G 1,000 **J** 2,000

Place Value of Whole Numbers (billions)

15 Minutes

Using Skill 1

OBJECTIVE Identify the place value of a given digit to the billions place

Have students look at the place-value chart on Skill 1 and name the periods.

Ask: **In which period is the digit 6?** (ones period)
In which period is the digit 3? (thousands period)

Direct attention to Step 1 and have students answer the question. Continue in a similar manner with Steps 2 and 3.
You may wish to have students identify the period and value of other digits in the place-value chart.

TRY THESE In Exercises 1–3 students name the period, place, and value for the digits in a given number.

- **Exercise 1** The digit 3, in the thousands period
- **Exercise 2** The digit 2, in the millions period
- **Exercise 3** The digit 1, in the billions period

PRACTICE ON YOUR OWN Review the example at the top of the page.

Ask students to explain how they know that the value of the digit 3 is 30,000. (The digit is in the ten thousands place in the chart; 3 × 10,000 = 30,000.)

CHECK Determine if students know how to find the value of a digit. Success is indicated by 3 out of 3 correct responses.

Students who successfully complete the **Practice on Your Own** and **Check** are ready to move to the next skill.

COMMON ERRORS

- Students may confuse the period name and place name when giving the value of a digit.
- Students may not remember that any place value is 10 times as great as the place to its right, and thus may state a value as less than or greater than its actual value.

Students who made more than 3 errors in the **Practice on Your Own**, or who were not successful in the **Check** section, may benefit from the **Alternative Teaching Strategy** on the next page.

Optional

Alternative Teaching Strategy

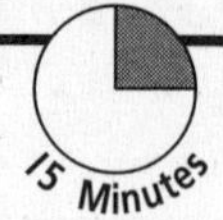

Model Place Value of Digits

OBJECTIVE Model and name the value of digits in a number

MATERIALS place-value chart to hundred thousands, number cards 0–9, with six cards for 0, place-value recording sheet

You may wish to have students work in pairs. Partners take turns. One student places number cards on the place-value chart; the other student identifies the value of the digit and records the number on the recording sheet.

Distribute a place-value chart and a set of number cards to each pair of students. Demonstrate how to use the cards to name values of digits in any place-value position.

Have students put the card for 5 in the hundreds place of the ones period. Have them fill the other places to the right with cards for 0.

Ask: **In what period is the 5?** (ones period)
In what place in the ones period is the 5? (hundreds place)
What is the value of the 5? (5 hundred)

What number do you write on the recording sheet? (500)

Have students move the card for 5 to the thousands period, and fill all places to the right with cards for 0.

Ask questions similar to the questions asked for 500.

Have students discuss how the two numbers they recorded are alike and how they are different. Point out that the value of the digit increases as it is moved to the left.

Repeat the activity several times as partners choose other cards and find the values of the numbers they form.

When students show an understanding of the naming process through the thousands period, extend the table to the millions period.

Name ______________________ Skill ______________

Place Value of Whole Numbers (billions)

Skill 1

Give the value of the digit 7 in 1,728,305,694.
Billions, Millions, Thousands, and Ones are periods. Hundreds, Tens, and Ones are places in a period.

BILLIONS			MILLIONS			THOUSANDS			ONES		
Hundreds	Tens	Ones ,	Hundreds	Tens	Ones ,	Hundreds	Tens	Ones ,	Hundreds	Tens	Ones
		1,	7	2	8,	3	0	5,	6	9	4

Step 1
Look at the periods.
In which period is the digit 7?

It is in the millions period.

Step 2
Look at the millions period.
In which place in the period is the digit 7?

It is in the hundreds place.

Step 3
Use the place and then the period to give the value.

The value of the digit 7 is **7 hundred millions** or 700,000,000.

Try These

Give the period, the place, and the value of the digit in 1,728,305,694.

1. Digit: 3

   Period ________

   Place ________

   Value ________

2. Digit: 2

   Period ________

   Place ________

   Value ________

3. Digit: 1

   Period ________

   Place ________

   Value ________

Go to the next side.

Name ____________________ Skill ____________________

Practice on Your Own

Skill 1

Give the value of the digit 3.

BILLIONS			MILLIONS			THOUSANDS			ONES		
Hundreds	Tens	Ones ,	Hundreds	Tens	Ones ,	Hundreds	Tens	Ones ,	Hundreds	Tens	Ones
		2,	9	4	0,	6	3	5,	7	1	8

The 3 is in the thousands period.
The 3 is in the tens place.
The value of the digit 3 is 3 ten thousands or 30,000.

Give the period, the place, and the value of the digit in 2,940,635,718.

1. Digit: 7
   Period ________
   Place ________
   Value ________

2. Digit: 0
   Period ________
   Place ________
   Value ________

3. Digit: 2
   Period ________
   Place ________
   Value ________

Give the value of the underlined digit.

4. 815,623,<u>4</u>97 ____________
5. 815,<u>6</u>23,497 ____________
6. <u>8</u>15,623,497 ____________
7. 1,482,700,5<u>7</u>6 ____________
8. <u>1</u>,482,700,576 ____________
9. 1,482,7<u>0</u>0,576 ____________

Check

Give the value of the underlined digit.

10. 3,175,2<u>6</u>4,358 ____________
11. 3,<u>1</u>75,264,358 ____________
12. 3,17<u>5</u>,264,358 ____________

Skill 2 Write Numbers in Standard Form

15 Minutes

Using Skill 2

OBJECTIVE Write numbers in standard form

Have the students look at the place value chart on Skill 2 and name the periods.

Ask: **In which period are there all zeros?** (millions)

Direct attention to Step 1 and have students answer the question. Continue in a similar manner with Steps 2, 3, and 4.

TRY THESE In Exercises 1–3 students name the period they start in, identify what periods will have zeros and name the number.

- **Exercise 1** Period you start billions, missing millions
- **Exercise 2** Period you start millions, missing none
- **Exercise 3** Period you start billions, missing thousands

PRACTICE ON YOUR OWN Review the example at the top of the page.

Ask students to explain how they know that there are all zeros in the millions period. (The number does not have any millions.)

CHECK Determine if students know how to write a number in standard form. Success is indicated by 2 out of 2 correct responses.

Students who successfully complete the **Practice on Your Own** and **Check** are ready to move to the next skill.

COMMON ERRORS

- Students will forget to place commas between periods. Have students use the place value chart.
- Students will omit zeros as placeholders. Have students use graph paper or a place value chart.

Students who made more than 3 errors in the **Practice on Your Own**, or who were not successful in the **Check** section, may benefit from the **Alternative Teaching Strategy** on the next page.

Optional

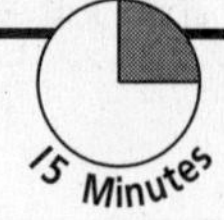

Alternative Teaching Strategy
Write Numbers in Standard Form

OBJECTIVE Write a number in standard form

MATERIALS place value chart to billions, number cards (0–9), with six cards for 0, place value recording sheet

You may wish to have students work in pairs. Partners take turns placing the numbers on the place value chart; and the other student reads the number and records the number on the recording sheet.

Distribute a place-value chart and a set of number cards to each pair of students. Demonstrate how to use the cards to place the digits in the correct locations by having the students put the number 3,256 (three thousand two hundred fifty-six) in the correct locations on the place-value chart.

Have students place the number two billion, three hundred fifty thousand, four on the place value chart.

Ask: **In what period do you start?** (billions)

Are any periods missing? (millions)

How do you fill missing periods or gaps in the chart? (use zeros)

Have students read the number aloud to see if it matches the number you stated.

Have students place the number 45 million, 2 thousand, 87 on the place value chart.

Ask similar questions to those asked before.

Repeat the activity several times as partners take turns placing the digits and recording the numbers on the recording sheet.

Name ________________ Skill ________________

Skill 2

Write Numbers in Standard Form

Write the number two billion, two hundred five thousand, three hundred twelve in standard form. Billions, Millions, Thousands, and Ones are periods. Hundreds, Tens, and Ones are places in a period.

BILLIONS			MILLIONS			THOUSANDS			ONES		
Hundreds	Tens	Ones,	Hundreds	Tens	Ones,	Hundreds	Tens	Ones,	Hundreds	Tens	Ones
		2	0	0	0	2	0	5,	3	1	2

Step 1
Read the number.
In which period do you start?

It is the billions period.

Step 2
Look at the billions period, where do you start writing a number?

The ones place.

Step 3
Write zeros in the millions period since no numbers occur.

Step 4
What is the next period mentioned? Thousands

Write 205 and finish the number.

Try These

Write the number in standard form.

1. Two billion, five hundred twenty-five thousand, four hundred fifty-two

   Period you start in. ________

   What period(s) are missing?

   ____

   Number ________________

2. 8.415 million

   Period you start in. ________

   What period(s) are missing?

   ____

   Number ________________

3. Eighteen billion, two hundred million, six hundred seventy-two

   Period you start in. ________

   What period(s) are missing?

   ____

   Number ________________

Go to the next side.

Name ______________________ Skill __________

Practice on Your Own

Skill 2

Write the number 10.25 billion in standard form.

BILLIONS			MILLIONS			THOUSANDS			ONES		
Hundreds	Tens	Ones,	Hundreds	Tens	Ones,	Hundreds	Tens	Ones,	Hundreds	Tens	Ones
	1	0,	2	5	0,	0	0	0,	0	0	0

You start in the billions period.
There are no thousands or ones so fill the spaces with zeros.

Give the period you start in and see if there are any missing periods.

1. Twelve billion, five hundred sixty-eight thousand, two hundred fifty-nine

   Period you start in: ____________

   What period(s) are missing? ______

2. Thirty-two million, nine hundred fifty thousand, one hundred twelve

   Period you start in: ____________

   What period(s) are missing? ______

3. 80.3 billion

   Period you start in: ____________

   What period(s) are missing? ______

Write the number in standard form.

4. Seven million, two hundred fifty thousand, nine hundred sixteen

   ____

5. Thirty billion, four hundred eighty-five thousand, one hundred twenty-nine

   ____

6. 216.026 billion

   ____

7. 85.76 million

   ____

Check

Write the number in standard form.

8. Two hundred sixteen million, eight hundred ninety-three thousand, twelve

   ____

9. 15.634 million

   ____

Skill 3 Round Whole Numbers

Using Skill 3

OBJECTIVE Round whole numbers

Begin by discussing what will happen in each step of Skill 3. Then point out the number 14,851 in Step 1. Explain to the students that first they will round the number to the nearest ten. Discuss the place value of each digit. Ask: **To what place are you rounding?** (tens) **What digit is in that place?** (5)

For Step 2, point out that the digit to the right of the rounding place determines whether to round up or down.

For Step 3, discuss how the rounding rule will help students decide whether to round up or round down.

Ask: **The digit 1 is to the right of the rounding place. What does the rounding rule tell you to do?** (Round down if the digit is less than 5, so round down to 0.) **So, 14,851 rounded to the nearest ten is 14,850.**

Continue with the examples for rounding to the nearest hundred, thousand, and nearest ten thousand.

Make sure students understand:

- which digit is to be rounded;
- which digit is to the right of the rounding place;
- how to apply the rounding rule.

TRY THESE In Exercises 1–4 students round numbers to the given place.

- **Exercise 1** Round to the nearest hundred.
- **Exercise 2** Round to the nearest thousand.
- **Exercise 3** Round to the nearest ten thousand.
- **Exercise 4** Round to the nearest ten.

PRACTICE ON YOUR OWN Review the example at the top of the page. Ask students to explain why the number in A is rounded down and the number in B is rounded up.

CHECK Determine if students know when to round up and when to round down. Success is indicated by 3 out of 4 correct responses.

Students who successfully complete the **Practice on Your Own** and **Check** are ready to move to the next skill.

COMMON ERRORS

- Students may use the digit in the rounding place, instead of the digit to its right, to determine how to round.
- When rounding down, students may make the digit in the rounding place one less.

Students who made more than 3 errors in the **Practice on Your Own**, or who were not successful in the **Check** section, may benefit from the **Alternative Teaching Strategy** on the next page.

Optional

Alternative Teaching Strategy
Model Rounding Whole Numbers

OBJECTIVE To round whole numbers using the number line

MATERIALS copies of number lines with 10 unlabeled intervals

Distribute number lines. Explain that sometimes numbers are rounded when an exact number is not needed. For example, to describe the number of people who attended a play an exact number may not be needed. A rounded number can be used.

Ask:
Suppose you want to round 278 to the nearest hundred. Between what two hundreds is 278? (200 and 300)

Suggest students write these numbers in the boxes on the number line.

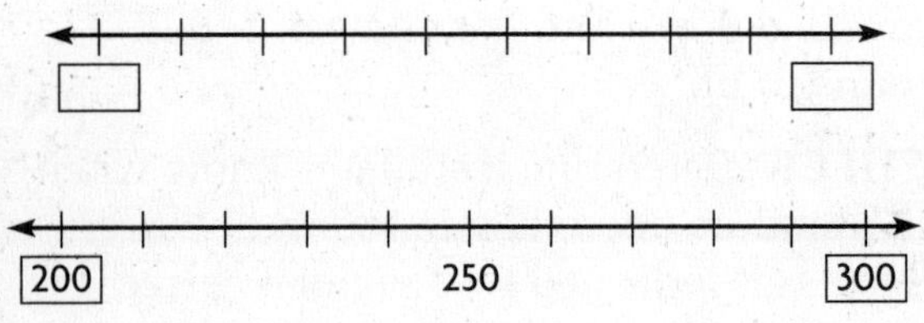

What number is halfway between 200 and 300? (250)

Have students label the point for 250.

Finally, have students determine the location of the number 278 on the number line. Ask: **Is 278 closer to 200 or to 300?** (300)
Explain that since 278 is closer to 300, 278 rounded to the nearest hundred is 300. About 300 hundred tickets were sold.

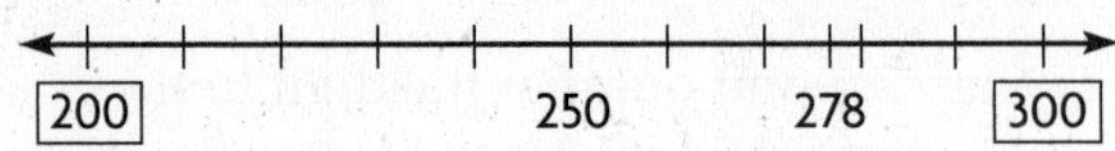

You may wish to repeat the rounding activity for these numbers:

- 25 to the nearest ten
- 89 to the nearest ten
- 451 to the nearest hundred
- 781 to the nearest hundred
- 4,350 to the nearest thousand
- 27,685 to the nearest thousand

When students round 451 using the number line, talk about the rounding rule for "5 or greater". Even though 451 is about as close to 400 as it is to 500, the halfway number determines when rounding to the next hundred must apply.

As students become comfortable with the rounding procedure, have them round numbers without the number line.

Suggest they underline the digit in the place to be rounded, and circle the number to the right, in order to focus on the correct digits.

Name ______________________ Skill ______________________

Round Whole Numbers

Skill 3

Round 14,851 to the nearest hundred, thousand, and ten thousand.

	Step 1 Underline the digit in the place to be rounded.	**Step 2** Draw an arrow above the first digit to the right.	**Step 3** If the digit to the right is 5 or greater, round up. If it is less than 5, round down.
Round to the nearest **ten.** →	$14{,}8\underline{5}1$	↓ $14{,}8\underline{5}1$	↓ $1 < 5$, so round down. $14{,}8\underline{5}1$ Answer: 14,850
Round to the nearest **hundred.** →	$14{,}\underline{8}51$	↓ $14{,}\underline{8}51$	↓ $5 = 5$, so round up. $14{,}\underline{8}51$ Answer: 14,900
Round to the nearest **thousand.** →	$1\underline{4}{,}851$	↓ $1\underline{4}{,}851$	↓ $8 > 5$, so round up. $1\underline{4}{,}851$ Answer: 15,000
Round to the nearest **ten thousand.**→	$\underline{1}4{,}851$	↓ $\underline{1}4{,}851$	↓ $4 < 5$, so round down. $\underline{1}4{,}851$ Answer: 10,000

Try These

Round the numbers.

1. Round 4,682 to the nearest hundred.
   ↓
   $4{,}\underline{6}82$
   Answer: ________

2. Round 2,359 to the nearest thousand.
   ↓
   $\underline{2}{,}359$
   Answer: ________

3. Round 18,175 to the nearest ten thousand.
   ↓
   $\underline{1}8{,}175$
   Answer: ________

4. Round 305,098 to the nearest ten.
   ↓
   $305{,}0\underline{9}8$
   Answer: ________

Go to the next side.

Name ____________________ Skill ____________________

Practice on Your Own

Skill 3

Round 438,492 to the nearest:

Think: If the digit to the right of the place to be rounded is 5 or more, round up. If it is less than 5, round down.

A. thousand
$4 < 5$, so round down.
↓
4 3 8, 4 9 2
Answer: 438,000

B. ten thousand
$8 > 5$, so round up.
↓
4 3 8,4 9 2
Answer: 440,000

Round to the nearest ten.

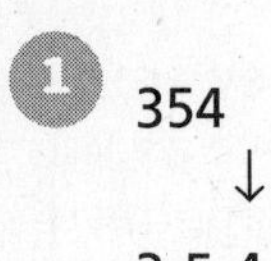

1. 354
↓
3 5 4
____

2. 2,387
↓
2, 3 8 7
____

3. 9,321
9, 3 2 1
____

4. 87,035
8 7, 0 3 5
____

Round to the nearest hundred.

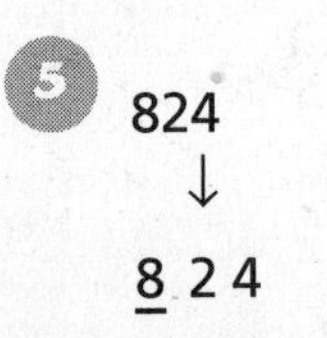

5. 824
↓
8 2 4
____

6. 1,457
↓
1, 4 5 7
____

7. 9,302
9, 3 0 2
____

8. 57,059
5 7, 0 5 9
____

Round to the nearest thousand.

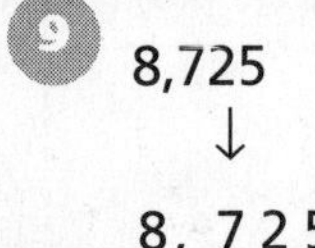

9. 8,725
↓
8, 7 2 5
____

10. 4,603
↓
4, 6 0 3
____

11. 10,516
1 0, 5 1 6
____

12. 32,498
3 2, 4 9 8
____

Round to the nearest ten thousand.

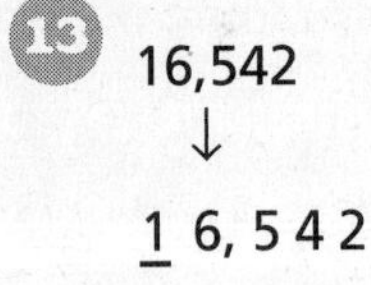

13. 16,542
↓
1 6, 5 4 2
____

14. 37,405
↓
3 7, 4 0 5
____

15. 215,430
2 1 5, 4 3 0
____

16. 424,965
4 2 4, 9 6 5
____

Check

Round the numbers.

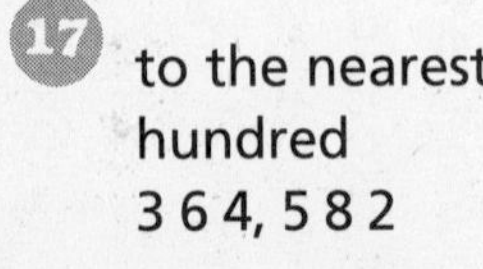

17. to the nearest hundred
3 6 4, 5 8 2
____

18. to the nearest thousand
4 3 5, 0 1 8
____

19. to the nearest ten thousand
6 7 5, 3 8 9
____

20. to the nearest ten
8 1 7, 0 2 4
____

Compare Whole Numbers

Using Skill 4

OBJECTIVE Compare whole numbers

Have the students look at the place value chart on Skill 4 and place each number to be compared in the chart.

Remind students that they always start from the left and compare digits until they are different.

Ask: **Do the two numbers hold the same place?** (yes)

Direct attention to Step 1 and have students compare the digits in the ten millions place.

Ask: **How many ten millions are in each number?** (3) **Which is larger?** (They are the same). **Which number place do you move to next?** (one millions place)

Continue in a similar manner with Steps 2 and 3.

TRY THESE In Exercises 1–3 students determine which place they need to use to compare the numbers and insert the greater than, less than, or equal to symbol.

- **Exercise 1** <, determined by the hundreds place
- **Exercise 2** >, do not hold the same place
- **Exercise 3** <, determined by the tens place

PRACTICE ON YOUR OWN Review the example at the top of the page.

Ask: **What is the furthest place to the left?** (hundred thousands)

Have students make sure that they are comparing digits in the same place by putting numbers in a chart or using lined notebook paper turned sideways.

CHECK Determine that the students can differentiate between the < and > symbols. Success is indicated by 4 out of 4 correct responses.

Students who successfully complete the **Practice on Your Own** and **Check** are ready to move on to the next skill.

COMMON ERRORS

- Students may choose the wrong number as the larger number if they do not have the same number of digits.
- Students may get confused when they put a number containing zeros in the chart.

Students who made more than 3 errors in the **Practice on Your Own**, or who were not successful in the **Check** section, may benefit from the **Alternative Teaching Strategy** on the next page.

Optional

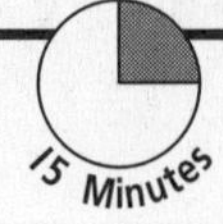

Alternative Teaching Strategy

Compare Whole Numbers

OBJECTIVE Use a number line to compare whole numbers

MATERIALS blank number line

You may wish to have students work in pairs. Give each set of students a pair of numbers such as 4,586 and 4,568. Have students label the number line according to the numbers they are given.

Partners each place a dot on the number line to show where each number is located.

Ask: **Which number is the farthest to the right?** (4,586)

4,586 is to the right of 4,568, so it is greater than 4,568.

Ask: **Which symbol would you use to compare 4,586 and 4,568?** (>)

Ask: **Which number is farthest to the left?** (4,568)

4,568 is to the left of 4,586, so it is less than 4,586.

Ask: **Which symbol would you use to compare 4,568 and 4,586?** (<)

Repeat the activity several times with different numbers including numbers that are equal. Point out that the inequality symbol always opens to the larger number.

When students show an understanding of the comparing process, give larger numbers to compare.

Name ____________________ Skill ____________________

Compare Whole Numbers

Skill 4

Use place values to compare the numbers 34,518,763 and 34,603,845.
To compare numbers, you must determine which number is greater.

MILLIONS			THOUSANDS			ONES		
Hundreds	Tens	Ones ,	Hundreds	Tens	Ones ,	Hundreds	Tens	Ones
	3	4,	5	1	8,	7	6	3
	3	4,	6	0	3,	8	4	5

Step 1
Start with the first place on the left. Compare the digits.

34,518,763
34,603,845

$3 = 3$

They are the same number.

Step 2
Compare the next place, the millions.

34,518,763
34,603,845

$4 = 4$

They are the same.

Step 3
Continue comparing digits until two are different.

34,518,763
34,603,845

$5 < 6$

Five hundred thousands are less than six hundred thousands. So, $34{,}518{,}763 < 34{,}603{,}845$.

Try These

Compare. Write <, >, or = for each.

1. 16,034 ______ 16,134

   Place value to compare: ____________________

2. 458,764 ______ 45,976

   Place value to compare: ____________________

3. 42,245,589 ______ 42,245,598

   Place value to compare: ____________________

Go to the next side.

Name ______________________________ Skill ______________________________

Practice on Your Own

Skill 4

Compare 684,582 and 648,632.

MILLIONS			THOUSANDS			ONES		
Hundreds	Tens	Ones,	Hundreds	Tens	Ones,	Hundreds	Tens	Ones
			6	8	4,	5	8	2
			6	4	8,	6	3	2

Place each number in the place value chart.
Start on the left.
Both numbers have six hundred thousands, so look to the next place to the right.
The numbers are different, so compare them.
8 > 4, so 684,582 > 648,632.

Compare. Write <, >, or = for each.

1. 6,125 ________ 6,215
   Place value to compare: ________

2. 65,851 ________ 67,264
   Place value to compare: ________

3. 5,648,602 ________ 600,687
   Place value to compare: ________

4. 725,438,900 ________ 725,428,901
   Place value to compare: ________

Find all of the digits that can replace the missing digits to make each statement true.

5. 8■4,598 < 864,689

   ____

6. 496,■56,200 > 496,745,310

   ____

Check

Compare. Write <, >, or = for each.

7. 3,548 ________ 3,548

8. 266,148 ________ 26,418

9. 6,400,512 ________ 6,401,496

10. 946,548,620 ________ 946,548,619

Order Whole Numbers

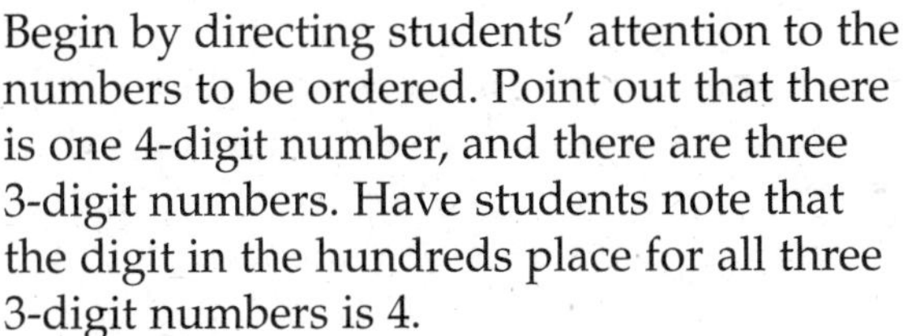

Using Skill 5

OBJECTIVE Order whole numbers

Begin by directing students' attention to the numbers to be ordered. Point out that there is one 4-digit number, and there are three 3-digit numbers. Have students note that the digit in the hundreds place for all three 3-digit numbers is 4.

For Step 1, explain how the numbers are arranged under place-value labels so that the digits in each place-value position can be easily compared. Then ask: **How many numbers have a digit in the thousands place?** (one) **Which number?** (1,650) Point out that since it is the only 4-digit number, it is the greatest.

Proceed to Step 2 and have students compare the digits in the hundreds place. Ask: **Since the digits are all the same, what digits should you compare next?** (digits in the tens place)

In Step 3, point out that because two of the numbers have a 7 in the tens place, they both are greater than 438. Ask: **Then which number is the least?** (438)

Continue to Step 4. Ask: **Which number has the greater digit in the ones place?** (476) **So, which number is greater?** (476)

Have students say the numbers in order from least to greatest and greatest to least.

TRY THESE In Exercises 1–3 students order 3-digit numbers and then 3- and 4-digit numbers.

- **Exercises 1–2** Order 3-digit numbers.
- **Exercise 3** Order 3- and 4-digit numbers.

PRACTICE ON YOUR OWN Review the example at the top of the page. Focus on the place-value labels. Ask students to explain how they use place value to order numbers.

CHECK Determine if students know how to align and compare the digits in each place to order the numbers from least to greatest. Success is indicated by 4 out of 4 correct responses.

Students who successfully complete the **Practice on Your Own** and **Check** are ready to move to the next skill.

COMMON ERRORS

- Students may compare digits from right to left instead of from left to right.

Students who made more than 2 errors in the **Practice on Your Own**, or who were not successful in the **Check** section, may benefit from the **Alternative Teaching Strategy** on the next page.

Optional

Alternative Teaching Strategy

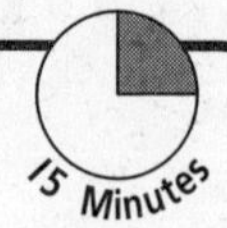

Use Models to Order Numbers

OBJECTIVE Order numbers using base-ten blocks as models

MATERIALS base-ten blocks

Have students work in pairs. Ask each partner to model one of the numbers being compared.

Display the numbers 236 and 218. Have the partners use hundreds, tens, and ones to model and order the numbers.

236

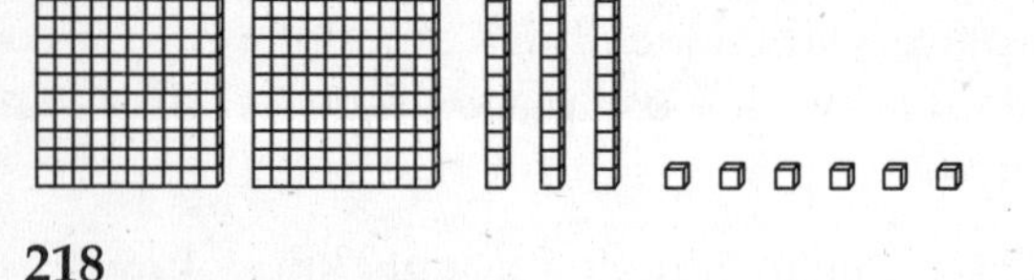

218

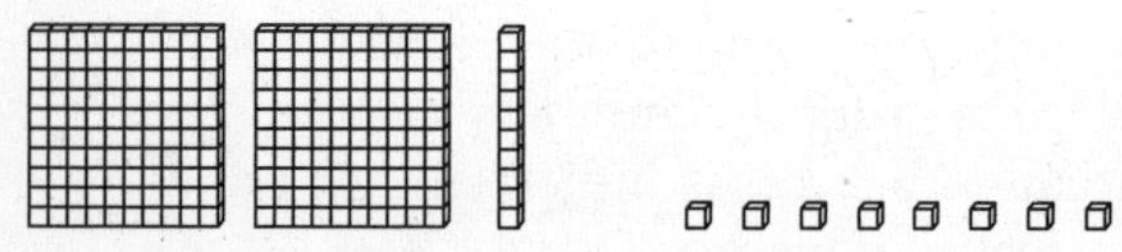

Ask: **How many hundreds did you use to show 236?** (2) **How many hundreds did you use to show 218?** (2)

Can you tell from comparing the hundreds which number is greater? (No.) **Why not?** (The hundreds are the same.)

Ask: **How many tens did you use to show 236?** (3) **How many tens did you use to show 218?** (1)

Ask: **Can you tell from the tens which number is greater?** (yes, 236.) **How do you know?** (3 tens is greater than 1 ten, so 236 is greater than 218.)

Ask: **Which number is the greatest?** (236)

Repeat the activity using the numbers, such as 423 and 427, in which the digits in both the hundreds and tens places are the same. Ask similar questions as students order the numbers.

Then present three numbers to order.
376, 374, 368

Suggest to students that they order the numbers by aligning the base-ten blocks for each number one above the other.

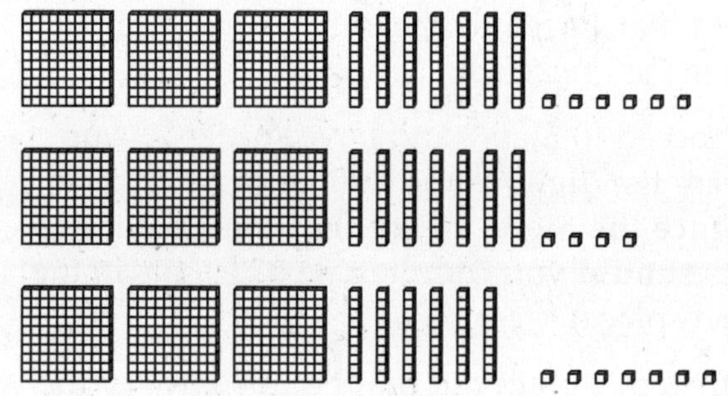

Then have students record the numbers from least to greatest (368, 374, 376) and greatest to least. (376, 374, 368)

It may help to remind students that the **least** number is the number that is *less than* all the others. The **greatest** number is the number that is *greater than* all the others.

Now include a 4-digit number and repeat the activity several times.

When students show an understanding of ordering numbers, have them order 3- and 4-digit numbers without using base-ten blocks.

Name ______________________ Skill ______________________

Skill 5

Order Whole Numbers

Order the numbers from least to greatest: 472; 1,650; 438; and 476, and from greatest to least.

Step 1 Align the digits.

Th	H	T	O
	4	7	2
1	6	5	0
	4	3	8
	4	7	6

Since 1,650 has the most places, it is the greatest number.

Step 2 Compare hundreds.

Th	H	T	O
	4	7	2
	4	3	8
	4	7	6

The digits are the same.

Step 3 Compare tens.

Th	H	T	O
	4	7	2
	4	3	8
	4	7	6

Since $3 < 7$, 438 is the least number.

Step 4 Compare ones.

Th	H	T	O
	4	7	2
	4	7	6

Since $2 < 6$, $472 < 476$.

So, the order from least to greatest is: 438, 472, 476, 1,650.

The order from greatest to least is: 1,650, 476, 472, 438.

Try These

1. Order the numbers from least to greatest. 258; 379; 251

   H T O

   2 5 8 greatest number ________

   3 7 9 ________

   2 5 1 least number ________

   Order ______________________

2. Order the numbers from greatest to least. 586; 514; 591

   H T O

   5 8 6 greatest number ________

   5 1 4 ________

   5 9 1 least number ________

   Order ______________________

3. Order the numbers from least to greatest. 635; 1,204; 499; 501

   Th H T O

   6 3 5 greatest number ________

   1 2 0 4 ________

   4 9 9 ________

   5 0 1 least number ________

   Order ______________________

Go to the next side.

Name ______________________ Skill ______________________

Practice on Your Own

Skill 5

Order the numbers from greatest to least: 436; 1,058; 375; and 497.

Think: Align the digits. Compare the numbers in each place starting with the greatest place.

Th	H	T	O
	4	3	6
1,	0	5	8
	3	7	5
	4	9	7

greatest number 1,058
497
436
least number 375

The order is 1,058, 497, 436, and 375.

Order the numbers from least to greatest.

1. 175, 182, 115

H T O
1 7 5 greatest number ________
1 8 2 ________
1 1 5 least number ________

Order ______________________

2. 867; 1,025; 876

Th H T O
8 6 7 greatest number ________
1, 0 2 5 ________
8 7 6 least number ________

Order ______________________

Order the numbers from greatest to least.

3. 279, 251, 62, 352

279 greatest number ________
251
62
352 least number ________

Order ______________________

4. 2,345; 507; 624; 2,405

2,345 greatest number ________
507
624
2,405 least number ________

Order ______________________

Check

Order the numbers from greatest to least.

5. 584; 3,896; 3,215

Order ______________________

6. 5,109; 4,116; 4,876; 823

Order ______________________

Order the numbers from least to greatest.

7. 348, 327, 316

Order ______________________

8. 835; 1,218; 1,409; 1,401

Order ______________________

Skill 6 Identify Sets of Numbers

Using Skill 6

OBJECTIVE Identify counting, whole, even, and odd numbers

Direct students' attention to the counting numbers. Have them read the numbers aloud. Ask:

What do the three dots mean? (that the set of counting numbers never ends)

Why isn't zero a counting number? (because you don't use zero when you count; you begin with 1.)

Have students look at the whole numbers. Remind students that although zero is not a counting number, zero is a whole number.

Ask: **Does the set of whole numbers ever end?** (no) **Do all whole numbers belong to the set of counting numbers?** (No, zero is not a counting number.) **Do all counting numbers belong to the set of whole numbers?** (yes)

Read about even and odd numbers. You may wish to have students divide by 2 to test for other even and odd numbers.

TRY THESE Exercises 1–4 provide practice in identifying the four sets of numbers presented in Skill 6.

- **Exercise 1** Counting number
- **Exercise 2** Whole number
- **Exercise 3** Even number
- **Exercise 4** Odd number

PRACTICE ON YOUR OWN Focus on the example at the top of the page. Ask students why a number cannot be both an even number and an odd number. Help them see that a number cannot satisfy both rules about remainders for even and odd numbers.

CHECK Determine if students can tell the difference between counting, whole, even, and odd numbers. Success is indicated by 4 out of 4 correct responses.

Students who successfully complete the **Practice On Your Own** and **Check** are ready to move to the next skill.

COMMON ERRORS

- Students may not be able to understand the difference between counting numbers and whole numbers.
- Students may include zero as a counting number.

Students who made more than 2 errors in the **Practice on Your Own**, or who were not successful in the **Check** section, may benefit from the **Alternative Teaching Strategy** on the next page.

Optional

20 Minutes

Alternative Teaching Strategy

Use Models to Identify Sets of Numbers

OBJECTIVE Identify counting, whole, even, and odd numbers

MATERIAL containers of items such as beads, counters, crayons, markers; an empty container

Make a display of containers of countable items, such as beads, counters, crayons, and markers. Each set should have a different number of items in it—include sets with odd and even numbers of items.

To introduce **counting numbers**, spill out all the beads. Ask a student to count the beads aloud. Write the numbers 1, 2, 3, 4, 5, and so forth. When the student has completed the counting, display the numbers. Explain that when the student counted, these were the numbers he or she said. They are counting numbers.

Point out that there is no end to a set of counting numbers. Three dots are used to show this. For example, 1, 2, 3, 4, 5, 6, ...

To introduce **whole numbers**, have students take turns counting the number of items in each container. Begin with the empty container, and record the numbers as an addition sentence. For example, $0 + 4 + 7 + 12 + 3 = 26$. Display the addition and point out that you recorded the numbers and added them together to find the total. Note that there are 5 addends-one addend is zero. The numbers you recorded are whole numbers. Discuss how zero is a whole number that represents an empty container. Point out that the set of whole numbers also has no end.

To illustrate **even and odd numbers**, suggest the students take a container of items each. Explain that an even number of items can be separated into groups of 2 with no leftovers. If there are any items left over, the number of items is an odd number. Have students determine which containers have an even number of items, and which have an odd number of items.

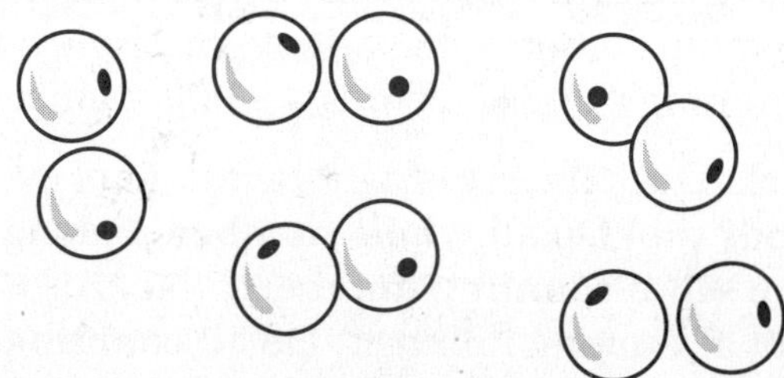

no beads left over
10 is an even number

When students understand that they can separate or divide by 2 to find even and odd numbers, have them divide given numbers to find out which are even and which are odd.

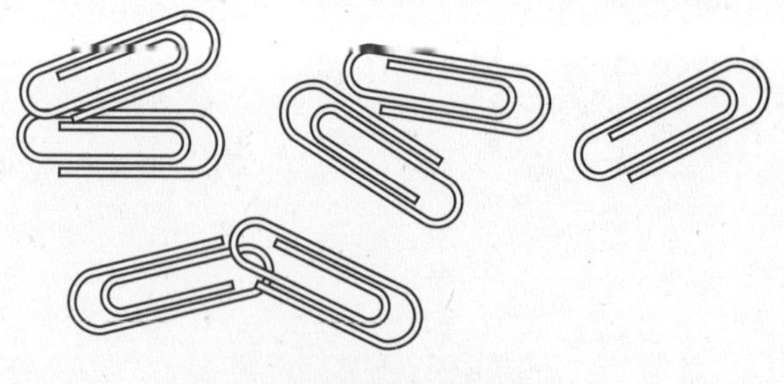

1 paper clip left over
7 is an odd number

Name ____________ Skill ____________

Skill 6

Identify Sets of Numbers

Every number belongs to one or more sets of numbers. Four of these sets are named below.

Counting Numbers	Whole Numbers	Even Numbers	Odd Numbers
Counting numbers begin with the number 1. There is no end to the set of counting numbers. 1, 2, 3, 4, 5, 6, ... 10 is a counting number.	Whole numbers begin with the number 0. There is no end to the set of whole numbers. 0, 1, 2, 3, 4, 5, ... 12 is a whole number.	There is no remainder when an even number is divided by 2. $2\overline{)14}$ = 7 ←No remainder -14 0 14 is an even number.	There is a remainder when an odd number is divided by 2. $2\overline{)17}$ = 8r1 ←A remainder -16 1 17 is an odd number.

Try These

Tell what kind of number is shown.

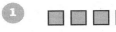

1. What counting number tells how many squares are shown? ______

2. $7 + n = 15$

   What whole number represents n in the solution for this equation? ______

3. 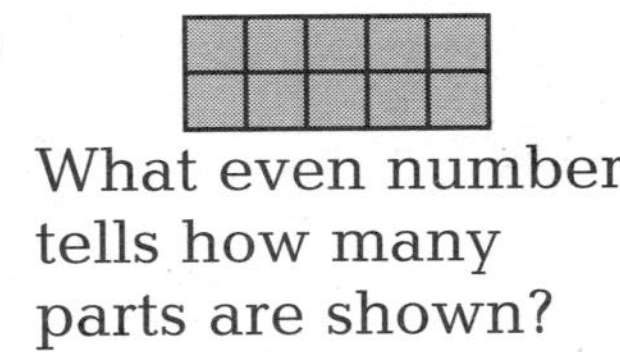

   What even number tells how many parts are shown? ______

4. 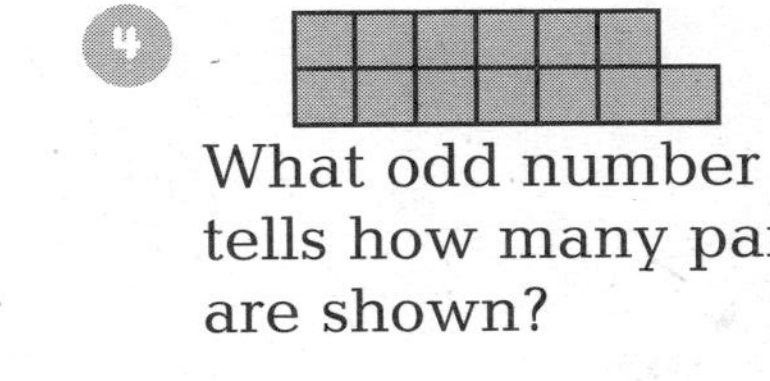

   What odd number tells how many parts are shown? ______

Name ______________________ Skill ______________________

Practice on Your Own

Skill 6

Circle the names of sets of numbers that contain the number 16.

counting numbers	You use 16 when you count. **So,** 16 is a counting number.
whole numbers	All counting numbers are whole numbers. **So,** 16 is a whole number
even numbers	$2\overline{)16}$ = 8 ← No remainder. **So,** 16 is an even number.
odd numbers	A number cannot be both an even number and an odd number. 16 is an even number. **So,** 16 is NOT an odd number.

Circle the names of sets of numbers that contain the given number.

1 2
- counting numbers
- whole numbers
- even numbers
- odd numbers

2 9
- counting numbers
- whole numbers
- even numbers
- odd numbers

3 15
- counting numbers
- whole numbers
- even numbers
- odd numbers

4 20
- counting numbers
- whole numbers
- even numbers
- odd numbers

Give four numbers less than 20 that are members of the given set.

5 counting numbers ______________

6 whole numbers ______________

7 even numbers ______________

8 odd numbers ______________

Check

Give four numbers from 40 through 50 that are members of the given set.

9 counting numbers

_____, _____, _____, _____

10 whole numbers

_____, _____, _____, _____

11 even numbers

_____, _____, _____, _____

12 odd numbers

_____, _____, _____, _____

Using Skill 7

OBJECTIVE Write the multiples of a number

Have students read the definition of a multiple given above the examples.

Ask students to count by 2s beginning with 2. Tell them that the numbers they said are multiples of 2. Have them count by 5s beginning with 5.

Ask: **The numbers you just said are multiples of what number?** (5)

Direct the students' attention to the first example.

Ask: **What is the product of 1 and 4?** (4)
2 and 4? (8) **3 and 4?** (12) **4 and 4?** (16)
What do we call these products? (multiples of 4)

Guide students to understand that they can find multiples of 4 by multiplying a whole number by 4. Proceed in a similar manner with the other two examples in the lesson. Help students understand that although they are writing the first 5 multiples for each number, they can find many more multiples.

TRY THESE In Exercises 1–3, students multiply to find the first five multiples of numbers.

- **Exercise 1** Multiples of 3
- **Exercise 2** Multiples of 2
- **Exercise 3** Multiples of 6

PRACTICE ON YOUR OWN Review the example at the top of the page. Ask students why they multiply 1, 2, 3, 4, and 5 by 5. Explain that although they can multiply any whole number except zero by 5 to get a multiple of 5, the example asks for the first five multiples only.

CHECK Determine if students know how to find the multiples of a number, and, given the first three multiples, can list the next three multiples in the sequence.

Success is indicated by 2 out of 2 correct responses.

Students who successfully complete the **Practice on Your Own** and **Check** are ready to move to the next skill.

COMMON ERRORS

- Students may list one multiple incorrectly and thus write all subsequent multiples incorrectly.
- Students may have forgotten the multiplication facts and give incorrect products.

Students who made more than 2 errors in the **Practice on Your Own**, or who were not successful in the **Check** section, may benefit from the **Alternative Teaching Strategy** on the next page.

Optional

Alternative Teaching Strategy
Use a Number Line to Find Multiples

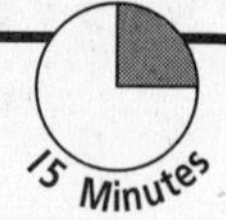

OBJECTIVE Use the number line to find multiples

MATERIALS number lines 0–25

Have students use number lines to find multiples of given numbers. Define a multiple as the product of the number and any whole number except zero.

Demonstrate how to show multiples of 3. Have students begin on the point for 0, count by threes, and draw equal jumps to the numbers as they count and name them.

Then suggest students circle all the numbers they landed on. Explain that when they count by threes, the numbers they name are the multiples of three.

Now ask students to write the multiplication expression for each multiple. Have them write 1×3 above the 3, 2×3 above the 6, and so forth.

Have students recall the definition of a multiple and determine that 0 is not a multiple and that 3 is the first multiple of the number 3. Guide them to see that the other numbers they circled are multiples also because they are the products of the whole numbers 1, 2, 3, 4, 5, 6, 7, 8, and the number 3.

Repeat the activity for multiples of 4 and 5. When you feel confident that the students understand how to find the multiples of a number, have them find the first five multiples of other numbers using multiplication only.

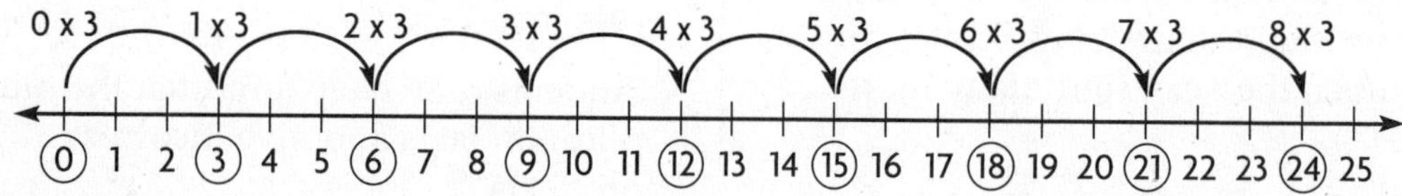

Name ______________________ Skill ______________________

Skill 7

Multiples

A multiple is the product of a number and any whole number except zero.

List the first five multiples of 4.
Multiply 4 by the numbers 1, 2, 3, 4, and 5.

0	4	8	12	16	20
0	1×4	2×4	3×4	4×4	5×4

The first five multiples of 4 are:
4, 8, 12, 16, 20.

List the first five multiples of 7.
Multiply 7 by the numbers 1, 2, 3, 4, and 5.

0	7	14	21	28	35
0	1×7	2×7	3×7	4×7	5×7

The first five multiples of 7 are:
7, 14, 21, 28, 35.

List the first five multiples of 9.
Multiply 9 by the numbers 1, 2, 3, 4, and 5.

0	9	18	27	36	45
0	1×9	2×9	3×9	4×9	5×9

The first five multiples of 9 are:
9, 18, 27, 36, 45.

Try These

List the first five multiples of the number.

1. 3

___, ___, ___, ___, ___
↑ 1×3 ↑ 2×3 ↑ 3×3 ↑ 4×3 ↑ 5×3

The first five multiples of 3 are: ______________

2. 2

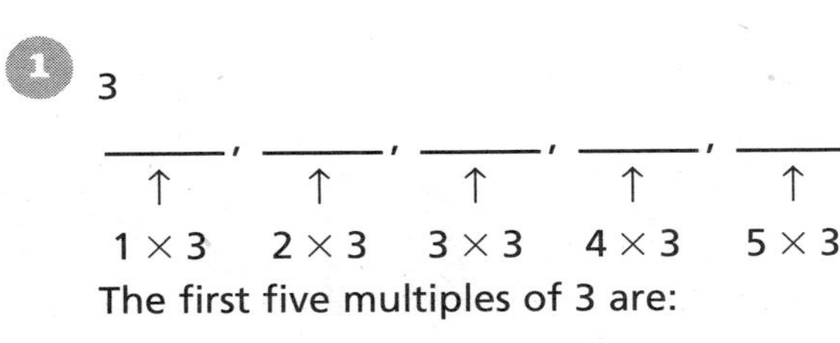

___, ___, ___, ___, ___
↑ 1×2 ↑ 2×2 ↑ 3×2 ↑ 4×2 ↑ 5×2

The first five multiples of 2 are: ______________

3. 6

___, ___, ___, ___, ___
↑ 1×6 ↑ 2×6 ↑ 3×6 ↑ 4×6 ↑ 5×6

The first five multiples of 6 are: ______________

Go to the next side.

Name ______________________ Skill ______________________

Practice on Your Own

Skill 7

Think: A multiple is the product of the number and any whole number except zero.

List the first five multiples of 5.

5, 10, 15, 20, 25

↑ ↑ ↑ ↑ ↑

1×5 2×5 3×5 4×5 5×5

The first five multiples of 5 are:

5, 10, 15, 20, 25.

List the first five multiples of the number.

1. 8

   ____, ____, ____, ____, ____

   ↑ ↑ ↑ ↑ ↑

   1×8 2×8 3×8 4×8 5×8

   The first five multiples of 8 are:

   ____

2. 10

   ____, ____, ____, ____, ____

   ↑ ↑ ↑ ↑ ↑

   1×10 2×10 3×10 4×10 5×10

   The first five multiples of 10 are:

   ____

3. 11

   The first five multiples of 11 are:

   11, ____, ____, ____, ____

   $\square \times 11$ $\square \times 11$ $\square \times 11$ $\square \times 11$ $\square \times 11$

4. 12

   The first five multiples of 12 are:

   12, ____, ____, ____, ____

   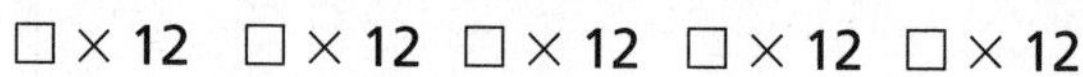

   $\square \times 12$ $\square \times 12$ $\square \times 12$ $\square \times 12$ $\square \times 12$

5. 20

   20, ____, ____, ____, ____

6. 30

   30, ____, ____, ____, ____

List the next three multiples of the number.

7. 4

   4, 8, 12, 16, 20, 24, ____, ____, ____

8. 7

   7, 14, 21, 28, 35, ____, ____, ____

Check

List the next three multiples of the number.

9. 15

   15, 30, 45, ____, ____, ____

10. 25

    25, 50, 75, ____, ____, ____

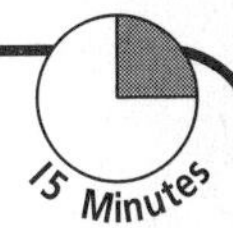

Using Skill 8

OBJECTIVE Find all the factors of a number

Begin by reviewing the meaning of factors:

Factors are two numbers that are multiplied. The result is the product. Explain that in this activity students will be asked to find all the factors of a number.

Direct students' attention to Step 1 and the statement that *every counting number* has at least two factors. (1 and itself) Provide other examples such as:

7 : 1 and 7

9 : 1 and 9

100 : 1 and 100

Point out that in this step, another important concept is introduced: A factor always divides the product without a remainder.

Direct the students' attention to Step 2. The important point in this step is that the factors of 8 are numbers from 1 to 8. Explain that the statement means that the only numbers that are reasonable to test as factors are the numbers from 1 through 8.

Direct the students' attention to Step 3.

Emphasize that when the factors repeat, then all the factors have been found. Suggest to the students that they write the factors of a number as they find them. After they have found all the factors of a number, then they can order them from least to greatest to tell if any factors repeat. Remind students that 2×4 are the same factors as 4×2. Only the order has changed.

TRY THESE Exercises 1–3 model the type of exercise students will do on the **Practice on Your Own** page.

- **Exercises 1–2** The number has 4 factors.
- **Exercise 3** The number has 5 factors.

PRACTICE ON YOUR OWN Review the example at the top of the page. Ask the students to think of the division sentence for each example shown. For $2 \times ? = 7$, think $7 \div 2 = ?$.

CHECK Determine if students can find all the factors of a number. Success is indicated by 2 out of 3 correct responses.

Students who successfully complete the **Practice on Your Own** and **Check** are ready to move to the next skill.

COMMON ERRORS

- Students may list multiples instead of factors.
- Students may omit some factors when writing the list.
- Students may lack proficiency with the basic multiplication and division facts and may write incorrect factors.

Students who made more than 3 errors in the **Practice on Your Own**, or who were not successful in the **Check** section, may benefit from the **Alternative Teaching Strategy** on the next page.

Optional

Alternative Teaching Strategy

Divide to Find Factors

OBJECTIVE Use division to find factors of a number

MATERIALS graph paper

You may wish to review division facts from 1 through 9 with the students.

Recall that one method for finding factors is to use multiplication. Another method involves division. Remind students that a factor of a number divides the number without leaving a remainder.

Start with the factors of 12. Display the following table. Explain that a table will help students keep track of the factors they test.

Possible Factor	Division	Quotient
1	12 ÷ 1 =	12
2	12 ÷ 2 =	6
3	12 ÷ 3 =	4
4	12 ÷ 4 =	3
5	12 ÷ 5 =	2 r 2

Suggest that students systematically test factors starting with 1. With each division that has no remainder, students have found 2 factors: the divisor and the quotient. You might suggest that students circle the factors in each equation if they result in a quotient without a remainder.

Ask: **For the factors of 12, what are the only possibilities that you need to test?** (the whole numbers from 1 through 12)

When students have tested factors, ask which numbers tested were not factors and why (5, 7, 8, 9, 10, and 11; the quotients all have remainders).

Continue with other examples, keeping the numbers less than 20.

If students continue to have difficulty finding factors, have them use graph paper to picture all the arrays or rectangles that are possible for a given number. When they have exhausted all possibilities, they have found the factors of the number.

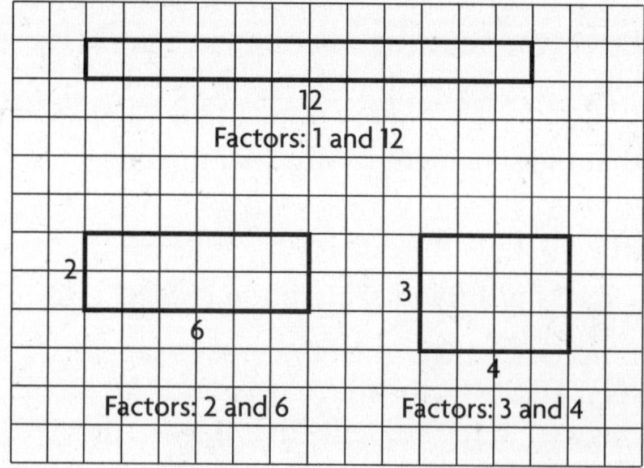

Name ____________________ Skill ____________________

Skill 8

Factors

Factors are two or more numbers that are multiplied.

Find all of the whole-number factors of 8.

Step 1 Use multiplication or division facts to find factors. Start with 1×8.

Every counting number has at least two factors, 1 and the number itself.

So, 1 and 8 are factors of 8.

$1 \times 8 = 8 \leftarrow$ product

↑

factors

A factor always divides the product without a remainder.

Step 2 Test other factor pairs.

The only possible whole-number factors of 8 are numbers from 1 to 8.

Is 2 a factor?

$1 \times 8 = 8$	1 and 8 are factors.
$2 \times 4 = 8$	2 and 4 are factors.

Step 3 Continue until the factors repeat.

$1 \times 8 = 8$	1 and 8 are factors.
$\mathbf{2} \times \mathbf{4} = 8$	2 and 4 are factors.
$3 \times ? = 8$	3 is **not** a factor, because $8 \div 3$ has a remainder.
$\mathbf{4} \times \mathbf{2} =$	When the factors repeat, you have found all the factors.

So, the factors of 8 are 1, 2, 4, and 8.

Try These

Find the whole-number factors.

1. 6

   ___ × ___ = 6

   ___ × ___ = 6

   The factors of 6 are:

   ____

2. 10

   ___ × ___ = 10

   ___ × ___ = 10

   The factors of 10 are:

   ____

3. 16

   ___ × ___ = 16

   ___ × ___ = 16

   ___ × ___ = 16

   The factors of 16 are:

   ____

Go to the next side.

Name ______________________ Skill ______________________

Practice on Your Own

Skill 8

List all of the factors of 7.

Think: Start with 1 and 7. Then try 2, then 3, then 4, and so on. If you repeat a pair of factors, you have found all the factors.

$1 \times 7 = 7 \leftarrow$ **1 and 7 are factors.**

$2 \times ? = 7 \leftarrow$ 2 is not a factor.

$3 \times ? = 7 \leftarrow$ 3 is not a factor.

$4 \times ? = 7 \leftarrow$ 4 is not a factor.

$5 \times ? = 7 \leftarrow$ 5 is not a factor.

$6 \times ? = 7 \leftarrow$ 6 is not a factor.

$7 \times 1 = 7 \leftarrow$ These repeat.

You have found all the factors.
The factors of 7 are 1 and 7.

2, 3, 4, 5, and 6 are not factors because when 7 is divided by each of these numbers, there is a remainder.

Write all the factors of the number.

1. 9

___ × ___ = 9
___ × ___ = 9
The factors of 9 are:
____

2. 14

___ × ___ = 14
___ × ___ = 14
The factors of 14 are:
____

3. 20

___ × ___ = 20
___ × ___ = 20
___ × ___ = 20
The factors of 20 are:
____

4. 12

___ × ___ = 12
___ × ___ = 12
___ × ___ = 12
The factors of 12 are:
____

5. 15

___ × ___ = 15
___ × ___ = 15
The factors of 15 are:
____

6. 11

___ × ___ = 11
The factors of 11 are:
____

7. 17

The factors of 17 are:
____

8. 24

The factors of 24 are:
____

9. 39

The factors of 39 are:
____

Check

Write all the factors of the numbers.

10. 18

The factors of 18 are:
____

11. 28

The factors of 28 are:
____

12. 13

The factors of 13 are:
____

Skill 9 Prime Numbers

Using Skill 9

OBJECTIVE Identify whether or not a whole number is prime

Begin by discussing the definition of a prime number. Emphasize that a prime number has *only* two factors: 1 and the number itself.

Provide an example: **The number 3 is prime because it has only two factors, 1 and 3. There is no other whole number that is a factor of 3. The only two whole numbers that have a product of 3 are 1 and 3.**

Ask students: **Is the number 4 a prime number?** (no) **Explain.** (It has more than two factors: $1 \times 4 = 4$ and $2 \times 2 = 4$. So, 1, 2, and 4 are factors of 4.)

Direct student's attention to Step 1. Ask: **Why do you divide 11 by 2?** (You divide to find out if 2 is a factor of 11.) **Is 2 a factor of 11? Explain.** (No; 2 does not divide 11 *evenly*; there is a remainder.)

Refer to Step 2. Ask: **Why do you stop dividing after testing 5 as a factor of 11?** (You can stop dividing when divisor and quotient repeat.)

If necessary, have students divide 11 by the remaining whole numbers—6, 7, 8, 9, 10, 11—so that they can discover for themselves that the only possible factors are 1 and 11.)

TRY THESE
Exercises 1–3 provide practice in identifying prime numbers.

- **Exercises 1, 3** prime
- **Exercise 2** not prime

PRACTICE ON YOUR OWN Review the example at the top of the page. Have students explain the testing process used to determine whether a number is prime. Ask: **Why is 2 the only number tested?** (Since 2 is a factor, then 1 and 14 are not the only factors; the test is over—14 cannot be a prime number with more than 2 factors.)

Exercises 1–6 provide the same format as was used in the **Try These** exercises.

CHECK Determine if students can identify prime numbers.

Success is indicated by 3 out of 3 correct responses.

Students who successfully complete the **Practice on Your Own** and **Check** are ready to move to the next skill.

COMMON ERRORS

- Students may reach an incorrect conclusion when dividing because they do not know their basic facts.
- Students may stop dividing too soon, before a divisor already tested is repeated as the quotient.

Students who made more than 2 errors in the **Practice on Your Own**, or who were not successful in the **Check** section, may benefit from the **Alternative Teaching Strategy** on the next page.

Optional

Alternative Teaching Strategy
Modeling Prime Numbers

OBJECTIVE Use models to determine whether or not a number is prime

MATERIALS square blocks or cubes

Tell students that they can use blocks or cubes to help them find primes.

If there is only one way to arrange a certain number of blocks or cubes as a rectangle, then that number is a prime number. If students can arrange the blocks in more than one rectangular array, then that number is not a prime number. Do not let students layer blocks. For example:

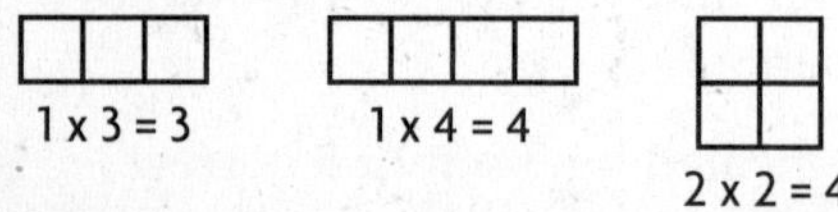

To decide if 7 is prime, have students try to arrange 7 blocks in more than one array.

They will find that the array shown below is the only array possible.

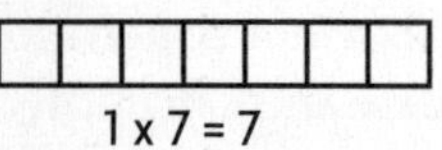

Explain that the array also models 7×1. This means 1 and 7 are the only possible factors. So, 7 is prime.

To decide if 8 is prime, have students try to arrange 8 blocks in more than one rectangular array. They will discover two different arrays are possible, $1 \times 8 = 8$ and $2 \times 4 = 8$. So, 8 is not prime.

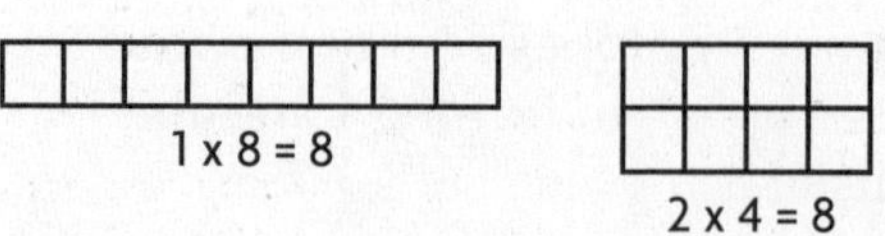

Some students will discover that it is possible to make more than two rectangular arrays for some numbers. For example, three arrays are possible for the number 12.

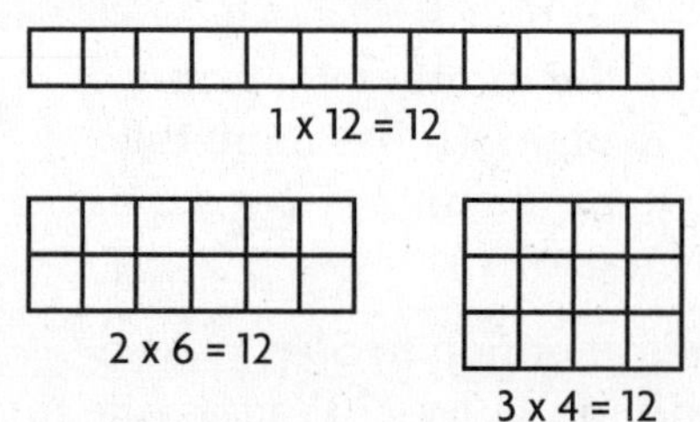

Show how each array models a set of factors for 12: 1×12, 2×6, and 3×4.

Have students repeat the activity for 5, 6, 9, 11, 13. Have them explain which numbers are prime (5, 11, 13) and how they know. (For each, there is only one possible rectangular array: 1×5, 1×11, 1×13.)

Name ______________________ Skill ______________________

Prime Numbers

Skill 9

A **prime number** is a whole number, greater than one, that has exactly two factors, 1 and the number itself. Decide if 11 is a prime number. Test numbers to determine if it has any factors other than 1 and itself. If it has no other factors, then it is a prime number.

Step 1
Divide to find possible factors. Start with 2. Test whether it is a factor.
11 ÷ 2 = 5 r 1
A factor divides a number without a remainder.
2 is **not** a factor of 11, because there is a remainder.

Step 2
Continue testing factors. Record each result in a table. Stop dividing when a divisor and quotient repeat. Remember if there is a remainder, then the number is not a factor of 11.

11 ÷ 2 = 5 r 1
11 ÷ 3 = 3 r 2
11 ÷ 4 = 2 r 3
11 ÷ 5 = 2 r 1

The divisor and quotient 2 and 5 repeat.

Stop dividing now.

Two factors of 11 are 1 and 11.

Number	Divide By	Remainder?
11	2	yes
	3	yes
	4	yes
	5	yes

The only factors of 11 are 1 and 11. So, 11 is a prime number. If you found that there were other factors of 11, then you would say that 11 is not a prime number.

Try These

Decide if each number is a prime number. Write *yes* or *no*.

1.

Number	Divide by	Remainder?
5	2	____
	____	____

Prime? ____

2.

Number	Divide by	Remainder?
6	2	____

Prime? ____

3.

Number	Divide by	Remainder?
7	2	____
	3	____

Prime? ____

Go to the next side.

Name ______________________ Skill ______________________

Practice on Your Own

Skill 9

Is 14 a prime number?

Number	Divide by	Remainder?
14	2	no

Think: You do not need to test other factors. Once you find that a number has more than 2 factors the number is not prime. So, 14 is not a prime number.

Decide if the number is a prime number. Test factors. Then write *prime* or *not prime*.

1

Number	Divide by	Remainder?
8	____	____

Think: *More than 2 factors?*

8 is ____________

2

Number	Divide by	Remainder?
17	____	____
	____	____
	____	____
	____	____

17 is ____________

3

Number	Divide by	Remainder?
12	____	____

12 is ____________

4

Number	Divide by	Remainder?
8	____	____

8 is ____________

5

Number	Divide by	Remainder?
10	____	____

10 is ____________

6

Number	Divide by	Remainder?
13	____	____

13 is ____________

7 Number: 15

15 is ____________

8 Number: 19

19 is ____________

9 Number: 20

20 is ____________

Write *prime* or *not prime*.

10 Number: 27

27 is ____________

11 Number: 23

23 is ____________

12 Number: 25

25 is ____________

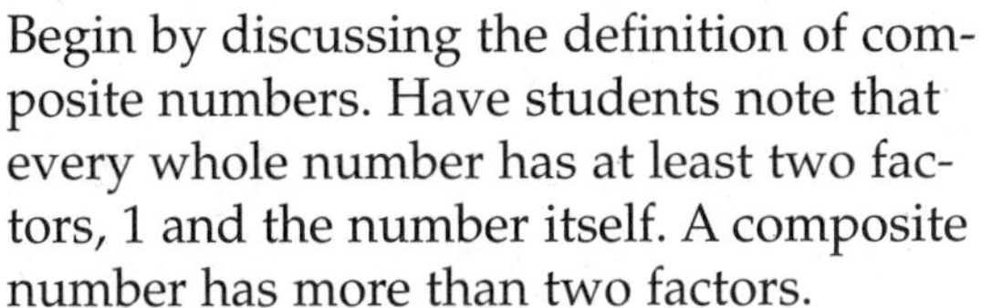

Using Skill 10

OBJECTIVE Identify composite numbers

Begin by discussing the definition of composite numbers. Have students note that every whole number has at least two factors, 1 and the number itself. A composite number has more than two factors.

Direct students' attention to Step 1. Point out that to test whether a number is a composite number they can divide. Tell students that they should test whole numbers in order beginning with 2. If there is no remainder, the whole number is a factor. Ask: **Why is it not necessary to divide by 1?** (All whole numbers have 1 and the number itself as factors.)

Begin testing by dividing by 2. Ask: **What is the remainder when you divide 35 by 2?** (1) **Is 2 a factor of 35?** (no)

Ask similar questions as students test other whole numbers in Step 2.

Why did you stop dividing after you tested 5? (5 is a factor of 35. So, I know that 35 is a composite number.)

Explain that once they find one more factor other than 1 or the number itself, there is no need to test further.

TRY THESE Exercises 1–3 guide students through the testing procedure to identify a composite number.

- **Exercises 1–2** Composite number
- **Exercise 3** Not a composite number

PRACTICE ON YOUR OWN Review the example at the top of the page. Remind students that they start testing with the number 2. Have students explain why they stop testing with the number 5.

CHECK Determine if students can identify composite numbers by using whole numbers as divisors. Success is indicated by 3 out of 3 correct responses.

Students who successfully complete the **Practice on Your Own** and **Check** are ready to move to the next skill.

COMMON ERRORS

- Students may not test whole numbers in order, resulting in missed factors.
- Students may not know basic facts, resulting in incorrect conclusions when dividing.

Students who made more than 3 errors in the **Practice on Your Own**, or who were not successful in the **Check** section, may benefit from the **Alternative Teaching Strategy** on the next page.

Optional

Alternative Teaching Strategy

15 Minutes

Use Models to Identify Composite Numbers

OBJECTIVE Use models to identify composite numbers

MATERIALS square blocks or cubes

Demonstrate how blocks can be arranged in rectangular arrays to show factors of a number. If more than one array can be shown for a number, then the number is a composite number.

Demonstrate how 1 and the number itself are always factors of whole numbers. Use 4, 7, 8, 10, 13, and 15.

Then, using 15 as an example, show how to test 2 by making an array with 2 rows of 7 blocks. Students will note that there is 1 block left over, so 2 is not a factor of 15.

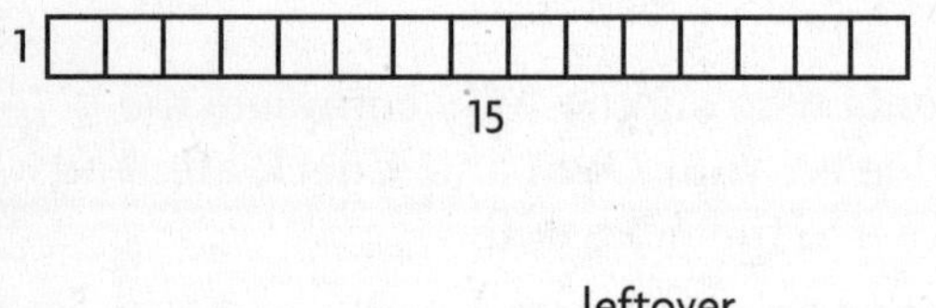

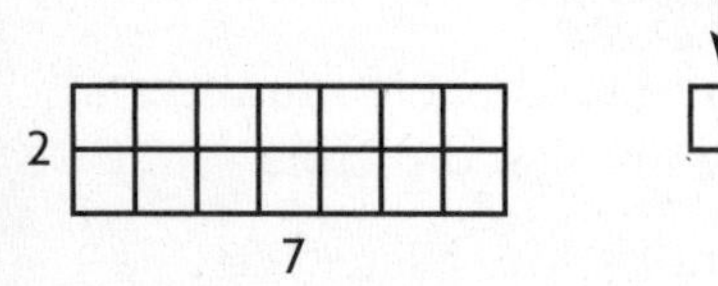

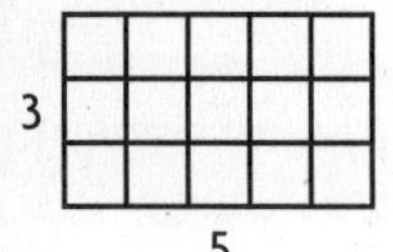

Next, test 3 by making an array with 3 rows of 5 blocks. In this case, an array can be made for 15 with no blocks leftover. So, another pair of factors, 3 and 5, has been found for 15. Thus, 15 is a composite number. There is no need to test for other factors.

Repeat the activity for 13. Make arrays using 2, 3, 4, 5, and 6 as factors. At some point, the arrays will look like another, and testing any further is unnecessary. Explain that since only one array can be made (1×13 or 13×1) without leftover blocks, 13 is not a composite number.

When students show an understanding of the testing process, have them find composite numbers without models.

Name ______________ Skill ______________

Composite Numbers

Skill 10

Decide if 35 is a composite number. Test numbers to determine if they are factors of 35. If there are more than 2 factors, then 35 is a composite number.

A **composite number** is a whole number greater than 1 that has more than two factors.

Step 1

Divide to find possible factors. If there is **no remainder**, then the number is a factor.

$35 \div 2 = 17$ r 1

2 is not a factor because it does not divide 35 without a remainder.

Step 2

Continue testing factors. Record each result in a table. Stop dividing when you find a factor other than 1 and the number itself.

$35 \div 2 = 17$ r 1

$35 \div 3 = 11$ r 2

$35 \div 4 = 8$ r 3

$35 \div 5 = 7$ ← no remainder

Stop dividing now. You have found more than two factors:

1, 35, 5, 7

So, 35 is a composite number.

Number	Divide by	Remainder?
35	2	yes
	3	yes
	4	yes
	5	**no**

Try These

Test factors to decide if each number is composite. List the factors. Write *yes* or *no* to tell whether the number is composite.

1

Number	Divide by	Remainder?
15	2	______
	______	______

Factors: 1, 15, ______

Composite? ______

2

Number	Divide by	Remainder?
10	______	______

Factors: 1, 10, ______

Composite? ______

3

Number	Divide by	Remainder?
7	______	______
	______	______

Factors: ______

Composite? ______

Go to the next side.

Name ______________________ Skill ______________________

Practice on Your Own

Skill 10

Think:

A **composite number** is a whole number greater than 1 that has more than two factors.

1 and 55 are factors.

Stop dividing. You have found more than 2 factors.

Number	Divide by	Remainder?
55	2	yes
	3	yes
	4	yes
	5	no

So, 55 is a composite number because it has more than two factors.

Test factors to decide if each number is composite.
List the factors. Write *composite* or *not composite*.

1.

Number	Divide by	Remainder?
52	____	____
	____	____

Factors: ____________

52 is ____________.

2.

Number	Divide by	Remainder?
27	____	____
	____	____

Factors: ____________

27 is ____________.

3.

Number	Divide by	Remainder?
17	____	____
	____	____
	____	____
	____	____

Factors: ____________

17 is ____________.

4.

Number	Divide by	Remainder?
21	____	____
	____	____

Factors: ____________

21 is ____________.

5. Number: 37
Factors: ____________
37 is ____________.

6. Number: 28
Factors: ____________
28 is ____________.

7. Number: 45
Factors: ____________
45 is ____________.

Check

Decide if each number is composite.

8. Number: 34
Factors: ____________
34 is ____________.

9. Number: 29
Factors: ____________
29 is ____________.

10. Number: 63
Factors: ____________
63 is ____________.

Skill 11 Find the Square of a Number

Using Skill 11

OBJECTIVE Find the square of a number

Begin by directing the students' attention to the definition at the top of the page. Explain that when you multiply a number by itself you get the square of the number. Demonstrate how an exponent is written to identify a number squared.

Explain that when you multiply a number by itself twice you get a cube of a number.

Demonstrate how an exponent is written to identify a number cubed.

TRY THESE Exercises 1–3 provide practice finding the squares and cubes of numbers.

- **Exercises 1–3** Square and cube of a number

PRACTICE ON YOUR OWN Review the examples at the top of the page. Have a student explain how to square and how to cube a number. Review the steps used to multiply whole numbers.

CHECK Determine if students can find the square and cube of a number.

Success is indicated by 5 out of 6 correct responses.

Students who successfully complete the **Practice on Your Own** and **Check** are ready to move to the next skill.

COMMON ERRORS

- Students may multiply a number by the exponent, instead of multiplying the number by itself.
- Students may not know the multiplication facts, resulting in an incorrect answer.

Students who made more than 2 errors in the **Practice on Your Own**, or who were not successful in the **Check** section, may benefit from the **Alternative Teaching Strategy** on the next page.

Optional

Alternative Teaching Strategy

10 Minutes

Model Finding the Square or Cube of a Number

OBJECTIVE Use grid paper and cubes to model squaring and cubing a number

MATERIALS grid paper, cubes

Distribute the grid paper and cubes to the students. Note that one square on the grid represents 1 square unit. Then, ask them to outline a 4×4 square on the grid paper.

Ask:
How many units are in the square? (16)
How can you find the answer without counting? (multiply 4 by 4)

Have students write the multiplication sentence that models the area of the square: $4 \times 4 = 16$.

Then have them write the exponent form: $4^2 = 16$.

Ask:
Is there another way you can show four squared? (4^2)

Point out that 4^2 does not mean 4×2. You cannot make a square array with 8 cubes.

Now have students use the cubes to build 4 layers and stack them on the square.

Ask:
How many cubes in each layer? (16)

Guide students to recognize the dimensions of the cube.

Ask: **What shape have you built?** (a cube)

Point out that the cube has 3 dimensions: width, length, and height. Ask:
How many units wide is your cube? (4 units) **How many units long?** (4) **How many units high?** (4)
How can you find the total number of cubes without counting all of them? (multiply 4 by 4 by 4)

Display: $4 \times 4 \times 4 = 4 \times 16 = 64$.

Ask: **How many cubes are in the stack?** (64)

Display $4 \times 4 \times 4 = 4^3$ and relate it to the dimensions of the cube.

Emphasize that the cube of a number has 3 factors all of the same value, just as there are 3 dimensions to a cube, all with the same value.

Display 4^3.

Ask: **What is 4 cubed?** (64)

Emphasize that 4 is a factor 3 times. Have students write $4 \times 4 \times 4$ in exponent form, 4^3. Have them point to the base, 4, and the exponent, 3.

Repeat this activity by having students model 5^2, 6^2, 7^2. When students show understanding, have them try an exercise using only paper and pencil.

square	cube
$4 \times 4 = 4^2$	$4 \times 4 \times 4 = 4^3$

Name ______________________ Skill ______________________

Find the Square of a Number

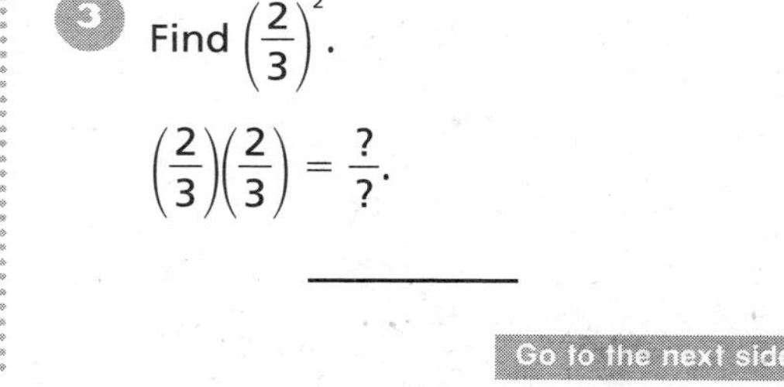

The square of a number is the product of the number and itself.
A square is expressed with the exponent 2. *Nine squared* is written as 9^2.
To find the cube of a number, use the number as a factor three times.

Example A

Find the square of 3, or 3^2.

$$\begin{array}{r} 3 \\ \times 3 \\ \hline 9 \end{array}$$

Use the number as a factor twice.

So, 3^2 is 9.

Example B

Find the cube of 4, or 4^3.

$4 \times 4 \times 4$
16×4
64

So, 4^3 is 64.

Example C

Find $\left(\frac{3}{4}\right)^2$.

$\left(\frac{3}{4}\right)\left(\frac{3}{4}\right) = \frac{9}{16}$

So, $\left(\frac{3}{4}\right)^2 = \frac{9}{16}$.

Try These

Simplify:

1. 15^2

$$\begin{array}{r} 15 \\ \times 15 \\ \hline \end{array}$$

15^3

$15 \times 15 \times 15$
225×15

So, 15^2 is ________.
So, 15^3 is ________.

2. 20^2

$$\begin{array}{r} 20 \\ \times 20 \\ \hline \end{array}$$

20^3

$20 \times 20 \times 20$
400×20

So, 20^2 is ________.
So, 20^3 is ________.

3. Find $\left(\frac{2}{3}\right)^2$.

$\left(\frac{2}{3}\right)\left(\frac{2}{3}\right) = \frac{?}{?}$.

____

Go to the next side.

Name ________________________ Skill ________________________

Practice on Your Own

Skill 11

Think: To find the square of a number, multiply the number by itself.

To find the cube of a number, multiply the number by itself 2 times.

Find the square of 7.

$$\begin{array}{r} 7 \\ \times 7 \\ \hline 49 \end{array}$$

So, 7^2 is 49.

Find the cube of 13.

$13 \times 13 \times 13$

169×13

$2{,}197$

So, 13^3 is 2,197.

Find the square of each number.

1. 18

$$\begin{array}{r} 18 \\ \times 18 \\ \hline \end{array}$$

So, 18^2 is ____.

2. 14

$$\begin{array}{r} 14 \\ \times 14 \\ \hline \end{array}$$

So, 14^2 is ____.

3. $\frac{1}{4}$

$\left(\frac{1}{4}\right)\left(\frac{1}{4}\right)$

So, $\left(\frac{1}{4}\right)^2$ is ____.

Find the cube of each number.

4. 25^3

$25 \times 25 \times 25 =$ ____

5. 12^3

$12 \times 12 \times 12 =$ ____

6. 16^3

$16 \times 16 \times 16 =$ ____

Find the square or cube of each number.

7. $48^2 =$ ____

8. $\left(\frac{5}{8}\right)^2 =$ ____

9. $40^2 =$ ____

10. $17^3 =$ ____

11. $30^3 =$ ____

12. $21^3 =$ ____

Check

Simplify.

13. $12^2 =$ ____

14. $22^2 =$ ____

15. $\left(\frac{1}{3}\right)^2 =$ ____

16. $11^3 =$ ____

17. $50^3 =$ ____

18. $40^3 =$ ____

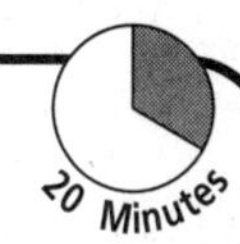

Using Skill 12

OBJECTIVE Read, write, and evaluate exponents

Direct students' attention to *Understanding Exponents*. Ask: **What are factors?** (numbers that are multiplied together) **What is the exponent in the expression 2^3?** (3) **What is the base in the expression 2^3?** (2) **How many times is 2 used as a factor in the expression 2^3?** (3) **How do you find the value of the expression 2^3?** (Find the product $2 \times 2 \times 2$.)
What is the value of the expression 2^3? (8)
How many times is 2 used as a factor in the expression 2^1? (1)

As you work through understanding and reading exponents, emphasize that any number except 0, raised to the power of zero is 1, and any number raised to a power of 1 is the number itself. You may wish to illustrate how the names *square* and *cube* are derived from their geometric interpretations.

TRY THESE In Exercises 1–3 students find the value of expressions in exponent form.

- **Exercise 1** Exponent is 2.
- **Exercise 2** Exponent is 3.
- **Exercise 3** Exponent is 4.

PRACTICE ON YOUR OWN Review the powers of 10 at the top of the page. You may wish to point out that the lead digit in a power of 10 is always 1, and the exponent tells how many zeros to write after the 1. Caution that this shortcut is used only for a power of 10.

CHECK Determine if the students know that an expression in exponent form is evaluated by using the base as a factor for the number of times indicated by the exponent.

Success is indicated by 2 out of 3 correct responses.

Students who successfully complete the **Practice on Your Own** and **Check** are ready to move to the next skill.

COMMON ERRORS

- Students may evaluate an expression by multiplying the base and the exponent; for example, $3^2 = 3 \times 2 = 6$.
- Students may multiply by an extra factor of the base when evaluating an exponent, for example: $3^2 = 3 \times 3 \times 3 = 27$.

Students who made more than 2 errors in the **Practice on Your Own**, or who were not successful in the **Check** section, may benefit from the **Alternative Teaching Strategy** on the next page.

Optional

Alternative Teaching Strategy
Modeling Exponents

OBJECTIVE Use grid paper and cubes to model expressions in exponent form

MATERIALS grid paper and cubes

First, have students model square numbers. Distribute the grid paper and ask students to outline a 1 × 1 square to show 1^2, a 2 × 2 square to show 2^2, a 3 × 3 square to show 3^2, and so forth until they have outlined ten squares up to a 10 × 10 square.

Ask: **What is the length and width of each square?** (1 by 1, 2 by 2, 3 by 3, 4 by 4, 5 by 5, 6 by 6, 7 by 7, 8 by 8, 9 by 9, and 10 by 10)
How can you find the area of each square? (Multiply the width and the length.)
What is the area of each square? (1, 4, 9, 16, 25, 36, 49, 64, 81, and 100)

Point out to the students that each square represents a number raised to the second power. Have students write the exponent form of the number for each square.

Then have the students model cubic numbers. Distribute at least 36 cubes to pairs of students. Have them build cubes for 1 × 1 × 1 to show 1^3, 2 × 2 × 2 to show 2^3, 3 × 3 × 3 to show 3^3, up to a 5 × 5 × 5 cube. (Students will need 125 cubes to model 5^3.)

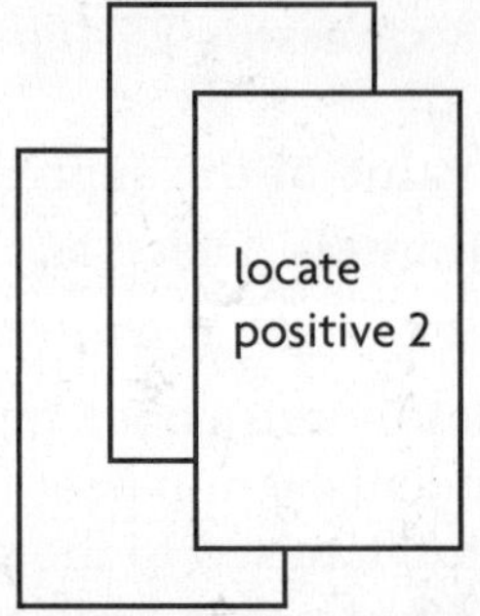

For each cube, ask: **How can you find the volume of each cube? What is the length of the cube? the width? the height?**

You may need to remind students that volume is the number of cubic units in a figure.
What is the volume of each cube?

Point out that each cube represents a number raised to the third power. Have students write the exponent form for the number for each cube.

Name ______________________ Skill ______________________

Exponents

Skill 12

An **exponent** tells how many times a number, called the **base**, is used as a factor.

2^3 ← exponent
↑ base

Understanding Exponents

Exponents show repeated factors.
$\mathbf{2}^3 = 2 \times 2 \times 2$
The base, 2, is a factor 3 times.

Find the value of an expression in exponent form by multiplying.

$2^3 = \underline{2 \times 2} \times 2$
$= \underline{4 \times 2}$
$= 8$

Any nonzero number to a power of zero is 1.
$\mathbf{2}^0 = 1$

A number to the first power is the number.
$\mathbf{2}^1 = 2$

Reading Exponents

The product of repeated factors is called a **power**.

- Read $\mathbf{2}^3$ as "the third power of 2".
- You can also say that the value, 8, is a power of 2.

Here are ways to read expressions in exponent form.

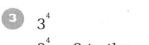

$\mathbf{2}^2 = 2 \times 2$
the second power of 2 or 2 *squared*

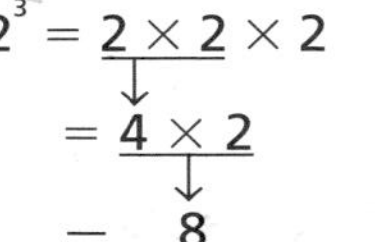

$\mathbf{2}^3 = 2 \times 2 \times 2$
the third power of 2 or 2 *cubed*

$\mathbf{2}^4 = 2 \times 2 \times 2 \times 2$
the fourth power of 2

Try These

Find the value.

1. 6^2
6^2 = 6 to the _____ power
6^2 = ___ × ___
= ___

2. 4^3
4^3 = 4 to the _____ power
4^3 = ___ × ___ × ___
= ___

3. 3^4
3^4 = 3 to the _____ power
3^4 = ___ × ___ × ___ × ___
= ___

Go to the next side.

Name ______________________ Skill ______________________

Practice on Your Own — Skill 12

Powers of Ten

10^4 ← exponent
↑
base

A **power of ten** is the product of repeated factors of 10.

$10^1 = 10$

$10^2 = 10 \times 10 = 100$

$10^3 = 10 \times 10 \times 10 = 1{,}000$

$10^4 = 10 \times 10 \times 10 \times 10 = 10{,}000$

$10^5 = 10 \times 10 \times 10 \times 10 \times 10 = 100{,}000$

$10^6 = 10 \times 10 \times 10 \times 10 \times 10 \times 10 = 1{,}000{,}000$ ←

Count the zeros after the 1. There should be 6 zeros, for 10^6.

Find the value.

1. 8^2

   8^2 = the ______ power of 8

   8^2 = ______ × ______

   = ______

2. 3^3

   3^3 = the ______ power of 3

   3^3 = ___ × ___ × ___

   = ______

3. 2^5

   2^5 = the ______ power of 2

   2^5 = _ × _ × _ × _ × _

   = ______

4. 7^2

   7^2 = ______ × ______

   = ______

5. 10^3

   10^3 = ___ × ___ × ___

   = ______

6. 2^4

   2^4 = ___ × ___ × ___ × ___

   = ______

7. 5^2 ______

8. 7^3 ______

9. 2^3 ______

10. 10^5 ______

Check

Find the value.

11. 9^2 ______

12. 10^4 ______

13. 5^3 ______

Using Skill 13

OBJECTIVE Identify and complete number patterns

Explain to students that in Skill 13 they will be identifying number patterns. Suggest to students that when they are looking for the rule to a number pattern, they first ask themselves this question: "Do the numbers increase or decrease from left to right?"

Verify that students can relate the operations of addition and multiplication to "increase", and the operations of subtraction and division to "decrease". Also confirm that the rule for a number pattern is a mathematical operation: for example, subtract 4 or multiply by 2.

Ask: **What mathematical operations do you use if the numbers increase from left to right?** (addition or multiplication) **What operations do you use if the numbers decrease?** (subtraction or division)

Direct students' attention to the example showing an addition pattern. Ask: **How do you know the numbers increase by 3 from left to right?** (Each number is 3 more than the number on its left.)
How do you find the next three numbers in the pattern? (Apply the pattern rule. Add 3 to 16 to get the fifth number: 3 + 16 = 19; add 3 to 19 to get the sixth number: 3 + 19 = 22; add 3 to 22 to get the seventh number: 3 + 22 = 25.)

Continue to ask similar questions as you work through the subtraction, multiplication, and division patterns.

TRY THESE In Exercises 1–3 students find pattern rules and the next three numbers in a pattern.

- **Exercise 1** Find and apply "add 4".
- **Exercise 2** Find and apply "multiply by 3".
- **Exercise 3** Find and apply "subtract 2".

PRACTICE ON YOUR OWN Review the two examples at the top of the page. For each, focus on the operation in the rule. Encourage students to test the rule on the first few numbers in each pattern.

CHECK Make sure that students identify and apply the rule of a number pattern. Success is indicated by 3 out of 3 correct responses.

Students who successfully complete the **Practice on Your Own** and **Check** are ready to move on to the next skill.

COMMON ERRORS

- Students may find a rule that works for one pair of numbers in the pattern and assume it will work for all numbers in the pattern.
- Students may choose the wrong operation.
- Students may make arithmetic mistakes in finding the next numbers in the pattern.

Students who made more than 2 errors in the **Practice on Your Own**, or were not successful in the **Check** section, may benefit from the **Alternative Teaching Strategy** on the next page.

Optional

Alternative Teaching Strategy

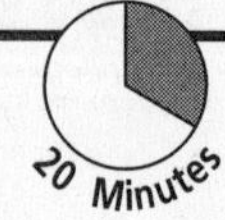

Model Number Patterns

OBJECTIVE Model number patterns

MATERIALS grid paper

Be sure that all students understand that "increase" means "get larger" and that "decrease" means "get smaller". Relate the operations of addition and multiplication to *increase;* and subtraction and division to *decrease.*

Distribute graph paper to each student.

Ask students to use the paper to model 3, 6, 9, 12, and then find the next number in the pattern.

Students begin by modeling the first number in the pattern 3. Have them shade 1 row of 3 squares across. Then have them model the next number, 6, by shading 2 rows of 3 squares. Ask: **How would you model the next number in the pattern, 9?** (Shade 3 rows of 3 squares.)

Have students model 9 on the grid paper.

Continue: **What is the next number in the pattern?** (12) **How do you model 12?** (Shade 4 rows of 3 squares.)

Now tell students to model the next number in the pattern and tell you what it is and how they know that.

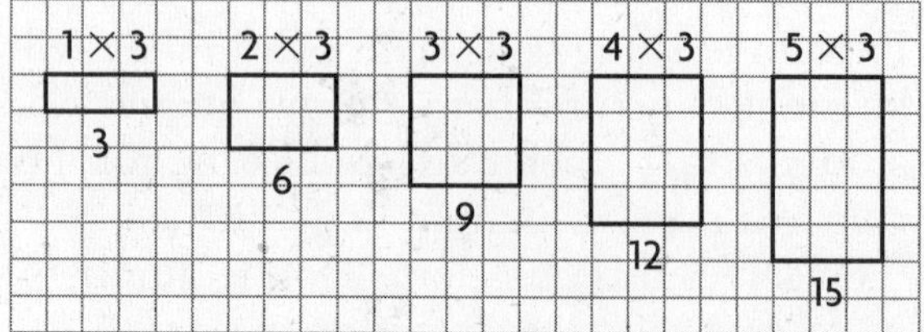

Explain to students that as they go from one model to the next, they are shading an additional three squares. Ask: **What is a rule for this number pattern?** (Add 3.)

Repeat this activity with the grid paper to model the number pattern: 16, 8, 4, 2, 1.

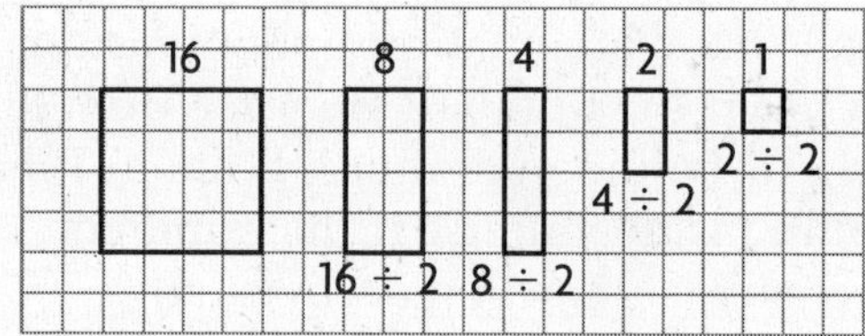

When students have finished modeling the numbers in the pattern, ask them to tell you the rule to the pattern (Divide by 2).

Name ________________ Skill ________________

Skill 13

Number Patterns

You can find some number patterns by adding, subtracting, multiplying, or dividing.

Addition

Find the next 3 numbers in this pattern.

7, 10, 13, 16, □, □, □

Think: The numbers increase by 3 from left to right.

The rule for the pattern is: *Add 3.*
So, the next three numbers are: **19, 22, 25.**

Multiplication

What are the next 3 numbers in this pattern?

1, 2, 4, 8, □, □, □

Think: Each number is twice the number to its left.

The rule for the pattern is: *Multiply by 2.*
So, the next 3 numbers are: **16, 32, 64.**

Subtraction

What are the next 3 numbers in this pattern?

24, 20, 16, 12, □, □, □

Think: The numbers decrease by 4 from left to right.

The rule for the pattern is: *Subtract 4.*
So, the next 3 numbers are: **8, 4, 0.**

Division

What are the next 3 numbers in this pattern?

4,096, 2,048, 1,024, 512, □, □, □

Think: Each number to the right is half the number to the left.

Try dividing by 2: 4,096 ÷ 2 = 2,048.
The rule for the pattern is: *Divide by 2.*
So, the next 3 numbers are: **256, 128, 64.**

Try These

Find the next three numbers in the pattern. Describe the rule for the pattern.

1. **7, 11, 15, 19, □, □, □**
   The rule for the pattern is: ______
   The next three numbers are: ______, ______, ______.

2. **1, 3, 9, 27, □, □, □**
   The rule for the pattern is: ______
   The next three numbers are: ______, ______, ______.

3. **25, 23, 21, 19, □, □, □**
   The rule for the pattern is: ______
   The next three numbers are: ______, ______, ______.

Go to the next side.

Name ______________________ Skill ______________

Practice on Your Own

Skill 13

Find the next three numbers in each pattern.

22, 28, 34, 40, □, □, □

The numbers **increase** by 6 from left to right.

The rule for the pattern is: Add 6.

$22 + 6 = 28,$

$28 + 6 = 34,$

$34 + 6 = 40$

The next three numbers in the pattern are:

46, 52, 58

729, 243, 81, 27, □, □, □

The numbers **decrease** from left to right.

Think:

What times 27 equals 81?

Try dividing by 3: **729 ÷ 3 = 243.**

The rule for the pattern is:
Divide by 3.

The next 3 numbers in the pattern are:

9, 3, 1

Describe the rule for the pattern. Find the next three numbers in the pattern.

1. 50, 46, 42, 38,

   ____, ____, ____

   The rule for the pattern is: ______.
   The next three numbers are: ____, ____, ____.

2. 8, 16, 24, 32,

   ____, ____, ____

   The rule for the pattern is: ______.
   The next three numbers are: ____, ____, ____.

3. 4,096; 1,024; 256; 64;

   ____, ____, ____

   The rule for the pattern is: ______.
   The next three numbers are: ____, ____, ____.

4. 49, 42, 35, 28,

   ____, ____, ____

   The next three numbers are: ____, ____, ____.

5. 1, 4, 16, 64,

   ____, ____, ____

   The next three numbers are: ____, ____, ____.

6. 100, 95, 90, 85,

   ____, ____, ____

   The next three numbers are: ____, ____, ____.

7. 27, 37, 47, 57,

   ____, ____, ____

8. 0, 12, 24, 36,

   ____, ____, ____

9. 1, 10, 100, 1,000,

   ____, ____, ____

Check

Find the next three numbers in the pattern.

10. 66, 55, 44, 33,

    ____, ____, ____

11. 0, 25, 50, 75,

    ____, ____, ____

12. 15,625, 3,125, 625, 125,

    ____, ____, ____

Using Skill 14

OBJECTIVE Use models to represent decimals

MATERIALS ruler, grid paper

Begin by having each student draw a 10 × 10 square on grid paper. Tell students that the square represents one whole. Have them divide the square into 10 equal parts.

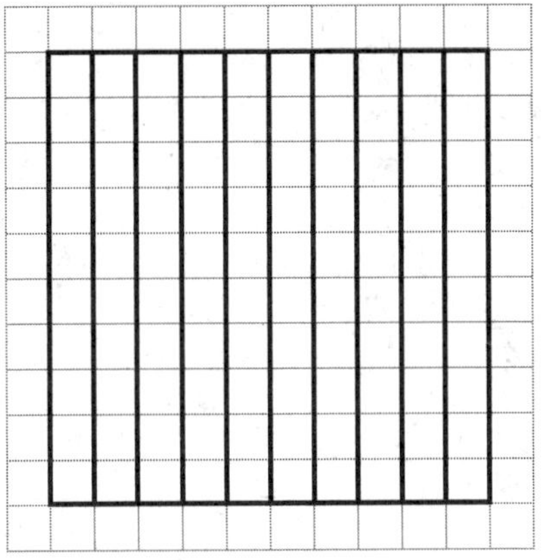

Ask: **How many equal parts are there in the whole?** (10) **What is each part called?** (one tenth)

Next, have students divide each tenth into 10 equal parts.

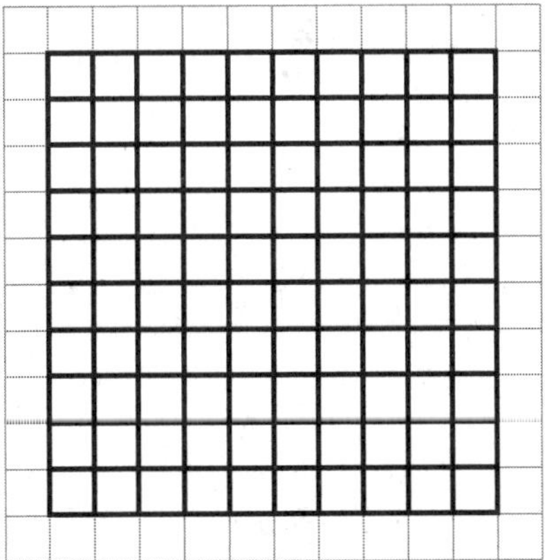

Ask: **How many equal parts are there in the whole?** (100) **What is each part called?** (one hundredth)

Direct students' attention to the examples in the lesson and discuss how tenths and hundredths can be written using words, fractions, and decimals.

TRY THESE Exercises 1–4 model the type of exercises students will find on the **Practice on Your Own** page.

- **Exercises 1–2** Fractions and decimals less than one
- **Exercises 3–4** Fractions and decimals greater than one

PRACTICE ON YOUR OWN Review the example at the top of the page. Ask questions to be sure that students understand the definitions of tenths and hundredths.

CHECK Determine if students can write a fraction or a mixed number and the equivalent decimal.

Success is indicated by 3 out of 4 correct responses.

Students who successfully complete the **Practice on Your Own** and **Check** are ready to move to the next skill.

COMMON ERRORS

- Students may confuse the decimal places and write one and six hundredths as 1.6, instead of as 1.06.
- Students may not understand decimal equivalents and write 50 hundredths as 0.050, instead of as 0.50.

Students who made more than 2 errors in the **Practice on Your Own**, or who were not successful in the **Check** section, may benefit from the **Alternative Teaching Strategy** on the next page.

Optional

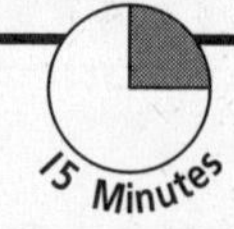

Alternative Teaching Strategy

Use Money to Model Decimals

OBJECTIVE Use paper money to model ones, tenths, and hundredths

MATERIALS play money: 1-dollar coins, bills, dimes and pennies

Ask: **How many dimes equal 1 whole dollar?** (10 dimes) **What part of a dollar is 1 dime?** (1 tenth)

Ask: **How many pennies equal 1 whole dollar?** (100 pennies) **What part of a dollar is 1 penny?** (1 hundredth)

Relate dollars, dimes, and pennies to ones, tenths, and hundredths by displaying these place-value chart headings.

dollars	.	dimes	pennies
ones	.	tenths	hundredths

Explain to the students that in this activity they will display dollars, dimes, and pennies. Then they will write the amount in words, as a fraction or mixed number, and as a decimal. Use a place-value chart to guide students to write each number three ways.

Have students display 3 dimes. As you write the dimes in the place-value chart, ask: **If 1 dime is 1 tenth of a dollar, what part of a dollar is 3 dimes?** (three tenths, $\frac{3}{10}$, 0.3)

dollars	.	dimes	pennies
ones	.	tenths	hundredths
0	.	3	

Then have students show 27 pennies. Ask: **If 1 penny is 1 hundredth of a dollar, what part of a dollar is 27 pennies?** (twenty-seven hundredths, $\frac{27}{100}$, 0.27)

dollars	.	dimes	pennies
ones	.	tenths	hundredths
0	.	2	7

Ask: **What other coins can I use to show 27 hundredths?** (2 dimes 7 pennies)

Repeat the activity for 1 dollar, 6 dimes and 2 dollars, 4 dimes, 7 pennies.

When students show understanding of the relationships among ones, tenths, and hundredths, give them decimal numbers and have them write the numbers in words or as fractions or mixed numbers.

Name ______________________ Skill ______________________

Skill 14

Represent Decimals

Use decimal squares to model decimals.

Example A

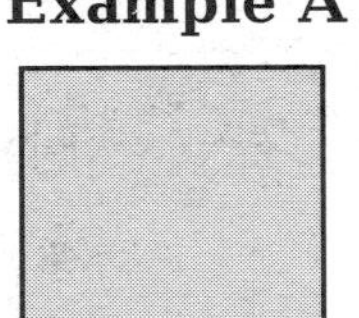

This model represents one whole, or 1.

Words: one

Fraction: $\frac{1}{1}$

Decimal: 1.0

Example B

The whole is divided into 10 equal parts.
2 out of 10 parts are shaded.
So, 2 tenths are shaded.

Words: two tenths

Fraction: $\frac{2}{10}$

Decimal: 0.2

Example C

The whole is divided into 100 equal parts.
43 out of 100 parts are shaded.
So, 43 hundredths are shaded.

Words: forty-three hundredths

Fraction: $\frac{43}{100}$

Decimal: 0.43

Example D

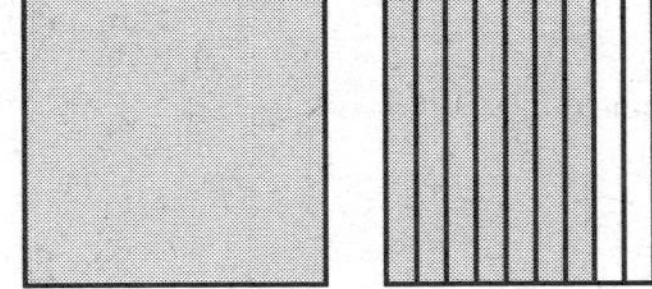

This model represents 1 whole and 7 tenths.

Words: one and seven tenths

Mixed Number: $1\frac{7}{10}$

Decimal: 1.7

Try These

Shade the squares. Write the fraction or mixed number. Write the decimal.

1. 4 tenths

fraction ______ decimal ______

2. 75 hundredths

fraction ______ decimal ______

3. 1 and 1 tenth

fraction ______ decimal ______

4. 1 and 35 hundredths

mixed number ______ decimal ______

Go to the next side.

Name ______________________ Skill ______________

Practice on Your Own

Skill 14

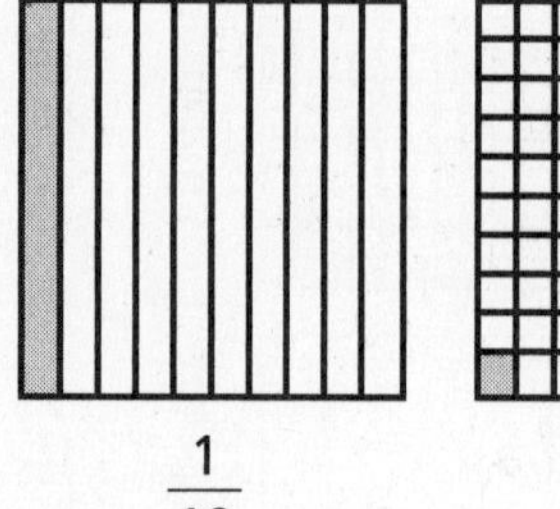
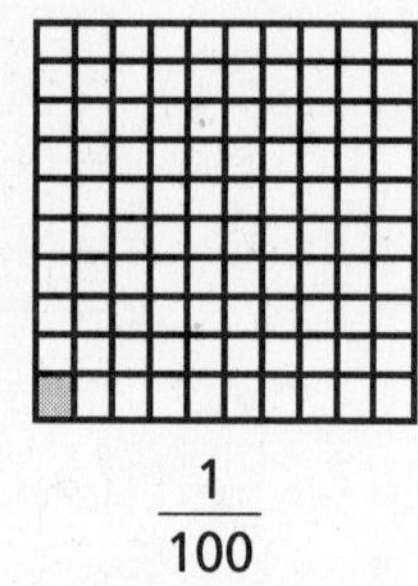

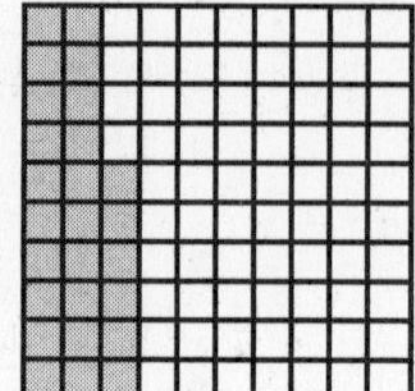

$\frac{1}{10}$ $\frac{1}{100}$

Think:
1 **tenth** is 1 of 10 equal parts
1 **hundredth** is 1 of 100 equal parts.

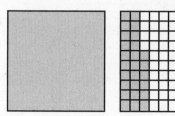

Words: one and twenty-six hundredths

Mixed Number: $1\frac{26}{100}$

Decimal: 1.26

Shade the squares. Write the fractions or mixed numbers, and decimals.

1. 3 tenths

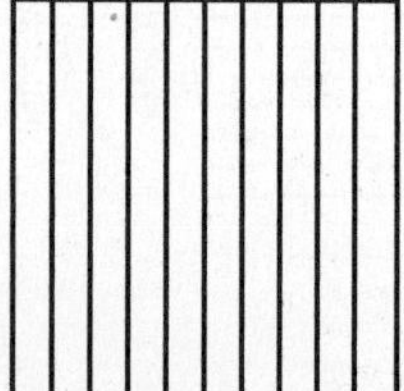

____

2. 7 tenths

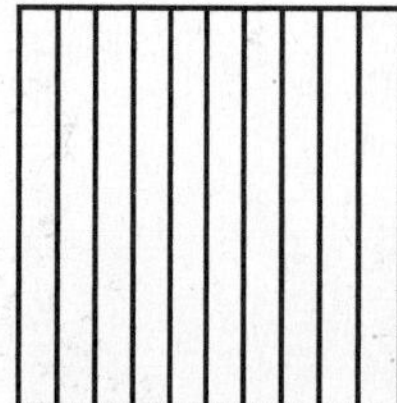

____

3. 1 tenth

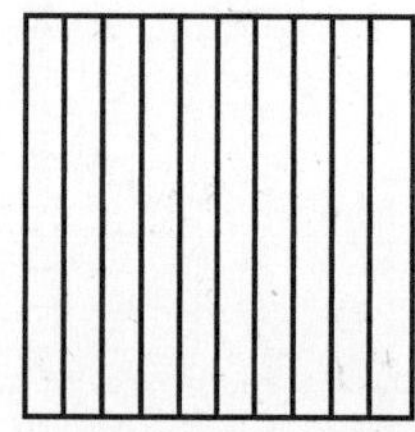

____

4. 1 and 5 tenths

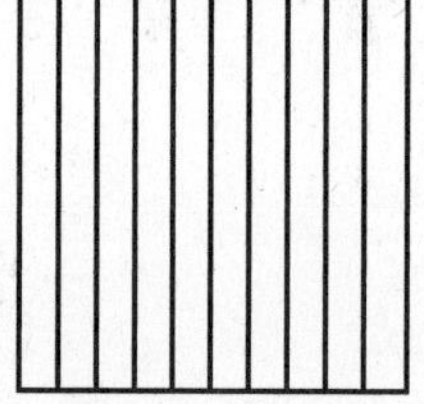

____

5. 17 hundredths

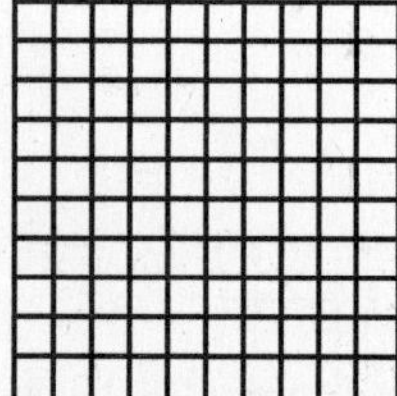

____

6. 70 hundredths

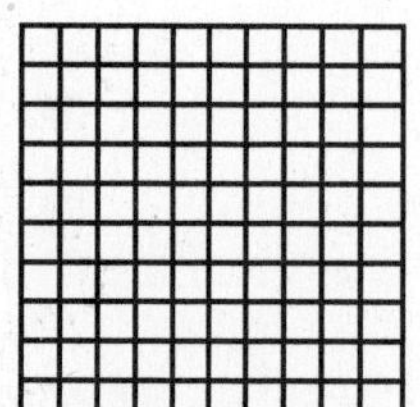

____

7. 4 hundredths

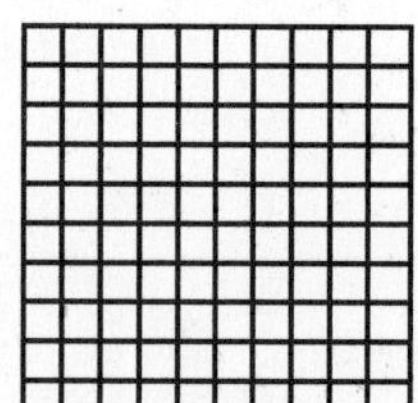

____

8. 1 and 65 hundredths

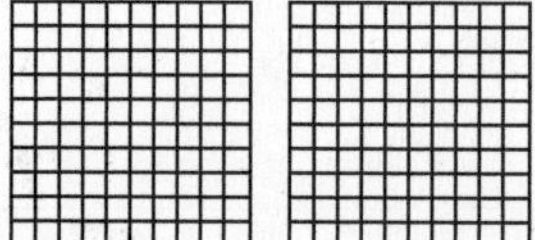

____

Check

Shade the squares. Write the fractions or mixed numbers, and decimals.

9. 9 tenths

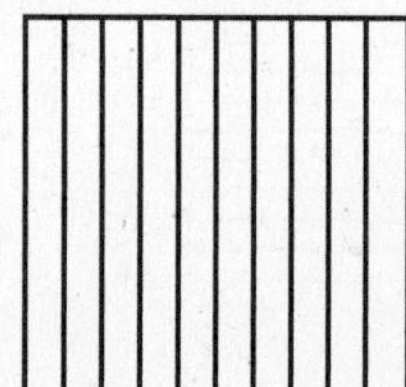

____

10. 1 and 6 tenths

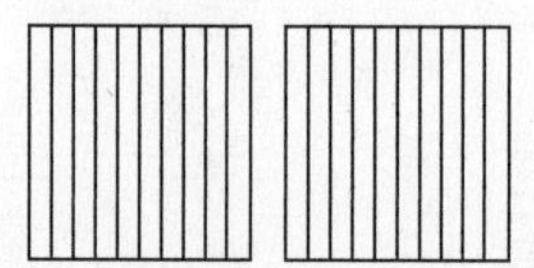

____

11. 82 hundredths

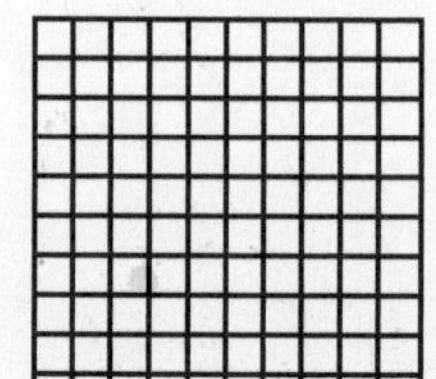

____

12. 1 and 37 hundredths

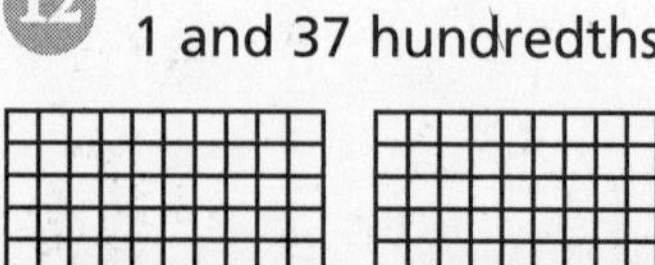
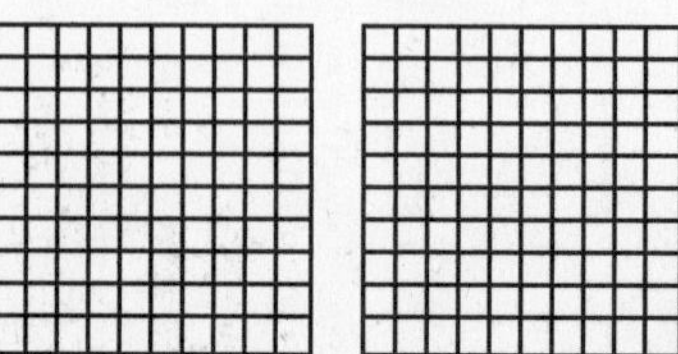

____

Using Skill 15

OBJECTIVE Write and read decimals

MATERIALS place-value chart, base-ten blocks, decimal models

Begin by displaying base-ten blocks and the following place-value chart, covering the places to the right of the decimal point.

Thousands	hundreds	tens	ones	•	tenths	hundredths
1000	100	10	1		$\frac{1}{10}$ or 0.1	$\frac{1}{100}$ or 0.01

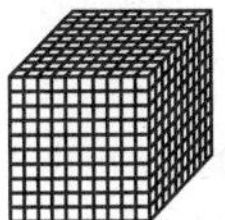 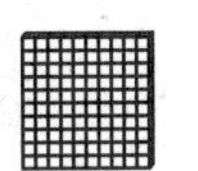   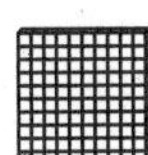

Remind students that our number system is based on 10. The value of each place is 10 times as great as the value of the place to its right. Demonstrate with the blocks. Have students state how many blocks it takes to equal the number in the next place to the left. Then discuss moving to the right on the chart. Explain that the value of each place is one-tenth of the value of the place to its left. Remove the paper from the chart and note that the place-value chart can be extended to show values less than 1. Point out that the decimal point separates ones from values less than 1.

Display the decimal models. Emphasize that the model for tenth has larger parts than the model for hundredths.

Then link the language of fractions with denominators of 10 and 100 to the decimal form of a number. Point out the tenths and hundredths in the place-value chart.

Then have students look at Skill 15. Review each example, noting the place-value position of the digits that represent decimals. Emphasize the role of the decimal point and note that the word "and" is reserved for the decimal point when reading numbers.

TRY THESE In Exercises 1 and 2 students write the standard form and word form of a number shown in a place-value chart.

- **Exercise 1** Write 826.3
- **Exercise 2** Write 4,351.22

PRACTICE ON YOUR OWN Review the example at the top of the page. Ask students to describe the value of each digit and tell you the fraction form of 8 tenths ($\frac{8}{10}$).

CHECK Determine if the students can write the word form of a number written in standard form. Success is indicated by 2 out of 2 correct responses.

Students who successfully complete the **Practice on Your Own** and **Check** are ready to move to the next skill.

COMMON ERRORS

- Students may forget to write a zero as a placeholder in a number. For example, students may write 6 and 3 thousandths as 6.3.
- Students may be unable to express the word names of numbers written in standard form. For example, they might read 5.47 as "five and 47" or "five point four seven."

Students who made more than 2 errors in the **Practice on Your Own**, or who were not successful in the **Check** section, may benefit from the **Alternative Teaching Strategy** on the next page.

Optional

Alternative Teaching Strategy

Write and Read Decimals

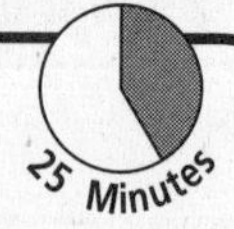

OBJECTIVE Model ones, tenths, and hundredths and write numbers in standard and word forms

MATERIALS grid paper, flip chart

In this activity, students work with only ones, tenths, and hundredths to help focus on the place value of decimals.

Review these equivalent forms and display models of each.

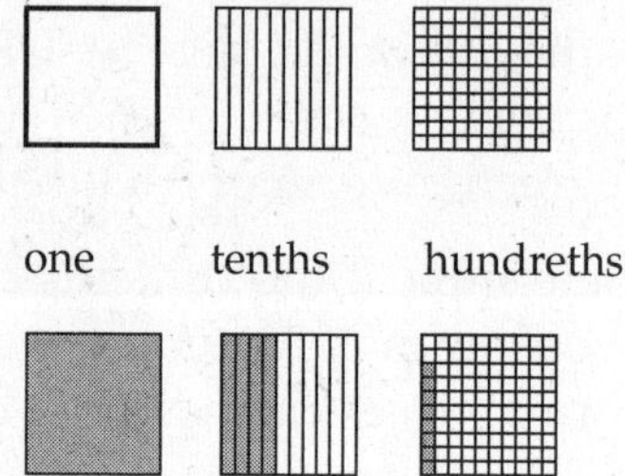

List the following on the flip chart.

1 and 5 tenths
1 and 2 hundredths
1 and 48 hundredths

Guide students to model and write the fraction form of each number.

For 1 and 5 tenths, students outline two 10×10 squares on the paper. To represent 1, they shade the entire grid; to represent 5 tenths, they outline 10 columns and shade 5. Note that they can write 1 and 5 tenths as a mixed number.

Ask: **What denominator will the fraction part of the mixed number have? Explain.** (10; the word name is 5 tenths, so the denominator is 10.)

Review decimal place-value positions and guide students to record the decimal form of the number (1.5).

Use a similar approach to help students represent 1 and 2 hundredths. Note that when recording the decimal form, students think: hundredths means two decimal places. Guide students to write the digit 2 in the hundredths place first, then record the zero in the tenths place.

1 and 2 hundredths **Think:** 1. ? ?
↓
1. ? 2
↓
1. 0 2

Then, focus on 1 and 48 hundredths. Students may write this as 1.048; it is helpful to review the expanded forms of this number:

Think: 48 hundredths =
4 tenths + 8 hundredths

So: 1 and 48 hundredths =
$1 + \frac{4}{10} + \frac{8}{100}$ or $1 + 0.4 + 0.08$

Guide students to model the number two ways:

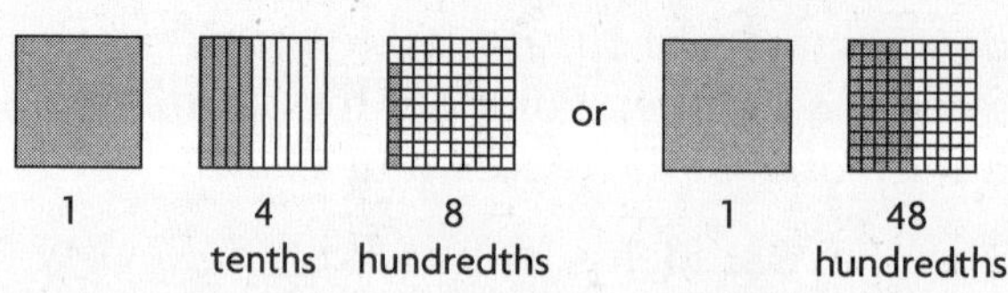

Continue building conceptual understanding using other similar examples.

Write and Read Decimals

Skill 15

You can use a place-value chart to help you read and write decimals.

Example A

tens 10	ones . 1	tenths 0.1	hundredths 0.01
6	6 .	4	3

Expanded Form: 60 + 6 + 0.4 + 0.03
Standard Form: 66.43
Word Form: 66 and 43 hundredths

Say "and" for the decimal point.

Example B

hundreds 100	tens 10	ones . 1	tenths 0.1
1	3	5 .	9

Expanded Form: 100 + 30 + 5 + 0.9
Standard Form: 135.9
Word Form: 135 and 9 tenths

Example C

thousands , 1,000	hundreds 100	tens 10	ones . 1	tenths 0.1
5 ,	3	0	1 .	8

Expanded Form: 5,000 + 300 + 0 + 1 + 0.8
Standard Form: 5,301.8
Word Form: 5 thousand, 301 and 8 tenths

use a comma to separate thousands from hundreds.

Try These

Write the decimal in standard and word form.

1. 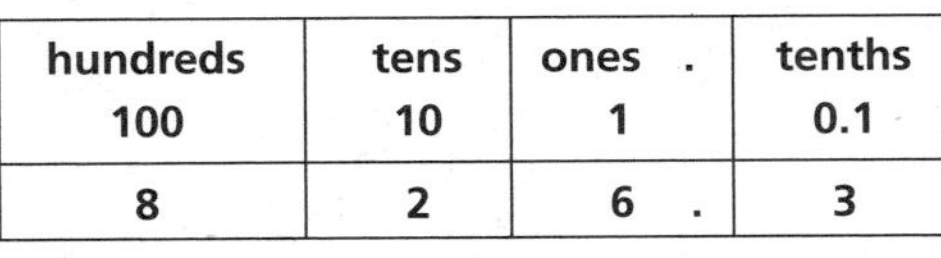

hundreds 100	tens 10	ones . 1	tenths 0.1
8	2	6 .	3

Think: 800 + 20 + 6 + 0.3
Standard Form: ________
Word Form: ________ and ________ tenths

2.

thousands , 1,000	hundreds 100	tens 10	ones . 1	tenths 0.1	hundredths 0.01
4 ,	3	5	1 .	2	2

Think: 4,000 + 300 + 50 + 1 + 0.2 + 0.02
Standard Form: ________
Word Form: ________ thousand, ________ and ________ hundredths

Go to the next side.

Name ______________________ Skill ______________________

Practice on Your Own

Think:

Use place value to help you write and read decimals.
Use a comma to separate thousands from hundreds.

hundred thousands 100,000	ten thousands 10,000	thousands , 1,000	hundreds 100	tens 10	ones . 1	tenths 0.1
6	1	1 ,	3	4	5 .	8

Expanded Form: 600,000 + 10,000 + 1,000 + 300 + 40 + 5 + 0.8

Standard Form: 611,345.8

Word Form: 611 thousand, 345 and 8 tenths

Remember to say "and" for the decimal point.

Write the decimal in standard form and word form.

1. **Think:** 20 + 3 + 0.5 + 0.07
   Standard Form: ________
   Word Form: ________ and ________ hundredths

2. **Think:** 100 + 70 + 7 + 0.6 + 0.08
   Standard Form: ________
   Word Form: ________ and ________ hundredths

3. 800 + 90 + 0 + 0.3
   Standard Form: ________
   Word Form: ________
   ____

4. 100,000 + 6,000 + 400 + 30 + 4 + 0.1 + 0.09
   Standard Form: ________
   Word Form: ________
   ____

Write the decimal in standard form.

5. 169 and 45 hundredths
   Standard Form: ________

6. 2 thousand, 165 and 5 tenths
   Standard Form: ________

Check

Write the decimal in word form.

7. 6,489.9
   Word Form: ________
   ____

8. 123,690.56
   Word Form: ________
   ____

Skill 16 Round Decimals

Using Skill 16

OBJECTIVE Round decimal numbers to the indicated place value

Refer to the numbers to be rounded at the top of the page. Have students read the three numbers, and then look at the rounding rules.

Ask: **What is the first step in rounding?** (Find the place you want to round.) Say: **If you are asked to round to the nearest whole number, to which place should you round?** (ones place) **What is the second step in rounding?** (Look at the first digit to the right.) **What is that place?** (tenths place) **Read the third and fourth steps. Explain how to round to the ones place.** (If the digit in the tenths place is less than 5, the digit in the ones places does not change; if the digit in the tenths place is 5 or greater, the digit in the ones place increases by 1.)

Focus on Example A. Make sure that the students know which place they want to round.

Ask: **What is the digit to be rounded?** (7) **What is the digit to its right?** (9) **Is this digit 5 or greater, or less than 5?** (5 or greater) **Is the digit 7 increased or does it stay the same?** (increased by 1) **What happens to the digits to the right of the ones place?** (They become zeros, so they do not have to be written.)

Lead the students through the rounding steps for Example B and Example C. Stress the steps as students work through them. Emphasize that whether they round up or down, the digits to the right of the indicated place become zeros and need not be written.

TRY THESE In Exercises 1–3, students round decimal numbers to the indicated place value.

- **Exercise 1** Round up.
- **Exercise 2** Round down.
- **Exercise 3** Round up.

PRACTICE ON YOUR OWN Review the example at the top of the page. As they work through the exercise, have the students identify the digit in the ones place.

CHECK Determine if students can round decimal numbers to the ones place.

Success is indicated by 3 out of 3 correct responses.

Students who successfully complete the **Practice on Your Own** and **Check** are ready to move to the next skill.

COMMON ERRORS

- Students may look at the last digit in a number instead of the digit to the right of the rounding place to decide how to round.
- After rounding, students may not think of digits to the right of the rounding place as zeros and may retain those digits. For example, students may round 0.65 to 0.75.

Students who made more than 2 errors in the **Practice on Your Own**, or who were not successful in the **Check** section, may benefit from the **Alternative Teaching Strategy** on the next page.

Optional

Alternative Teaching Strategy
Model Rounding Decimals

15 Minutes

OBJECTIVE Model rounding decimals to the indicated place value

MATERIALS Decimal models

Explain that you will be rounding a decimal number to the nearest whole number.

Display 2.4. Represent the number with decimal squares, using the back of the squares to represent ones.

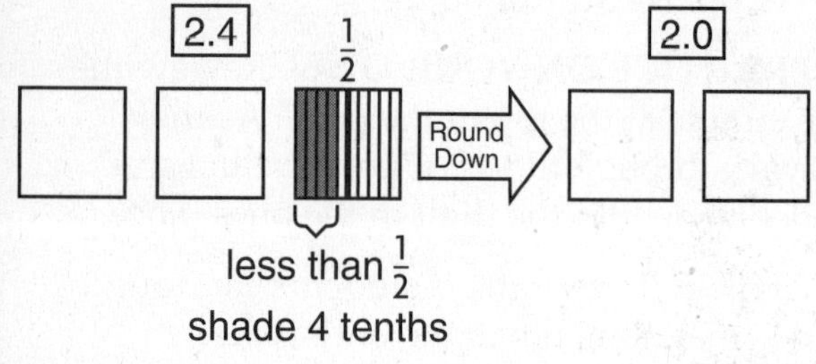

Ask: **How many ones are there?** (2) **How many tenths are there?** (4)

Show the students that 4 tenths is less than half of the tenths square.

Ask: **Are 4 tenths less than half of 1 or greater than half of 1?** (less than half of 1)

Remove the 4 tenths blocks and explain to the students that, because they represent less than half, you are removing them to model rounding down.

Work through rounding 3.5 and 1.6 using models. Stress to the students that the tenths must be equal to half or greater than half of the ones block before you round up to the next ones block.

Tell students that whether you are rounding to the tenths or thousandths position, the same rules apply.

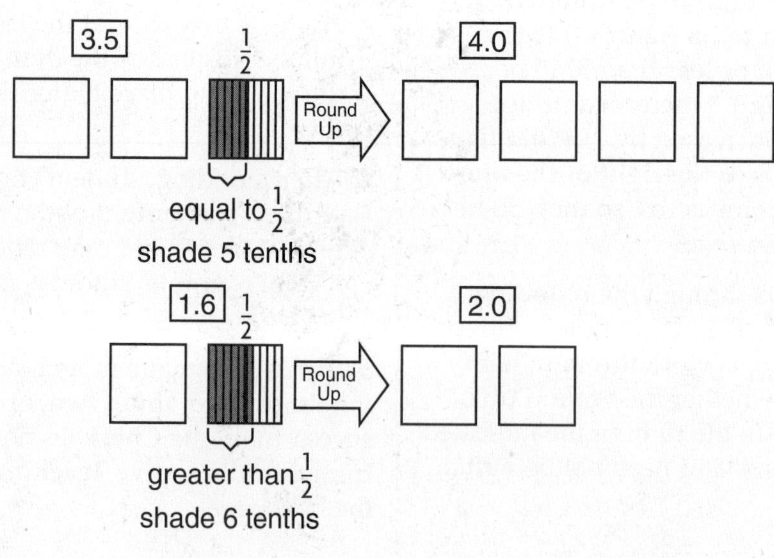

Name ______ Skill ______

Skill 16

Round Decimals

Round 37.91, 2.387 and 41.5713 to the indicated place value.

Rounding Rules

- Find the place you want to round.
- Look at the first digit to its right.
- If this digit is less than 5, the digit in the rounding place stays the same.
- If this digit is 5 or more, the digit in the rounding place increases by 1.

Example A

Round 37.91 to the nearest whole number.

Round to this place ↓ first digit to right ↓

37.91

Since $9 > 5$, the digit 7 increases by 1.

So, 37.91 rounded to the nearest whole number is 38.

Example B

Round 2.387 to the nearest tenth.

Round to this place ↓ first digit to right ↓

2.387

Since $8 > 5$, the digit 3 increases by 1.

So, 2.387 rounded to the nearest tenth is 2.4.

Example C

Round 41.5713 to the nearest thousandth.

Round to this place ↓ first digit to right ↓

41.5713

Since $3 < 5$, the digit 1 stays the same.

So, 41.5713 rounded to the nearest thousandth is 41.571.

Try These

Round the decimals to the indicated place value.

1. 7.64 whole number

   The digit to be rounded is ___.

   The digit to the right is ___.

   Is this digit 5 or more? ___.

   The rounded number is ___.

2. 13.118 tenth

   The digit to be rounded is ___.

   The digit to the right is ___.

   Is this digit 5 or more? ___.

   The rounded number is ___.

3. 28.5347 thousandth

   The digit to be rounded is ___.

   The digit to the right is ___.

   Is this digit 5 or more? ___.

   The rounded number is ___.

Go to the next side.

Name ______________________ Skill ______________________

Practice on Your Own

Skill 16

Round 7.04 to the nearest whole number.

Round to this place. digit to the right

↓ ↓
7. 0 4

Think:
The digit to be rounded is 7.
The digit to the right is 0.
The digit is less than 5.

So, 7.04 rounded to the nearest whole number is 7.

Round the decimals to the underlined place.

1. 37.49
   The digit to be rounded: _____
   The digit to the right: _____
   Is this digit 5 or more? _____
   The rounded number is _____.

2. 83.125
   The digit to be rounded: _____
   The digit to the right: _____
   Is this digit 5 or more? _____
   The rounded number is _____.

3. 62.5
   The digit to be rounded: _____
   The digit to the right: _____
   The rounded number is _____.

4. 52.4876
   The digit to be rounded: _____
   The digit to the right: _____
   The rounded number is _____.

5. 4.803
   The digit to be rounded: _____
   The rounded number is _____.

6. 27.5948
   The digit to be rounded: _____
   The rounded number is _____.

7. 1.519 _____

8. 57.098 _____

9. 0.8124 _____

Check

Round each decimal to the underlined place.

10. 62.148 _____

11. 47.50 _____

12. 35.6125 _____

20 Minutes

Using Skill 17

OBJECTIVE Compare and order decimals to hundredths

Before referring to Skill 17, review decimal place value. Recall that each place is one tenth the value of the place to its left.

Then have students look at the first example. Explain that one way to compare decimals is by finding the location of the decimals on a number line. Note that a number to the left is less than a number to the right. Review the inequality symbols and have students tell the value of the numbers being compared. Ask: **What is the value of the first number?** (7 tenths) **What is the value of the second number?** (9 tenths) **How can you tell that 7 tenths is less than 9 tenths?** (7 tenths is to the left of 9 tenths on the number line.)

Then call attention to the second example. Explain that another way to compare decimals is to compare digits in the same position in each number.

You may wish to show an example without using the place-value chart.

3.01 ◯ 3.1

Align digits. 3.01
3.10 ←

Guide students to compare ones first, then tenths. Point out that once the decimal points are aligned, it is likely that the digits will be aligned.

Then review the example for ordering decimals. Note that aligning the numbers can help students compare the digits in any place. Talk about the value of each number. For example, 1.38 is greater than 1; 0.94 is less than 1 but close to 1; 0.50 is less than 1 —it is one half; 0.98 is less than 1 but very close to 1.

PRACTICE ON YOUR OWN Review the example at the top of the page. Point out that 1.56 and 1.59 are close to $1\frac{1}{2}$, 1.23 is close to $1\frac{1}{4}$, and 1.37 is between $1\frac{1}{4}$ and $1\frac{1}{2}$. Note also that the digits in the tenths place of 1.23 and 1.37 are different, and the digits in the tenths place of 1.56 and 1.57 are the same.

CHECK Determine if students can compare and order decimals. Success is indicated by 4 out of 4 correct responses.

Students who successfully complete the **Practice on Your Own** and **Check** are ready to move to the next skill.

COMMON ERRORS

- Students may think that the number with more digits is greater, regardless of the place value of the digits. For example, they may think that 2.98 is greater than 3.1.
- Students may begin comparing digits from the right, or hundredths place.

Students who made more than 2 errors in the **Practice on Your Own**, or who were not successful in the **Check** section, may benefit from the **Alternative Teaching Strategy** on the next page.

Optional

Alternative Teaching Strategy

Model Ordering Decimals

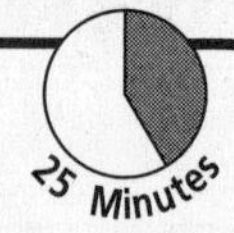

OBJECTIVE Use number cards to order decimals to hundredths

MATERIALS index cards

Have prepared sets of 10 number cards (or have students prepare the cards) such as those shown below.

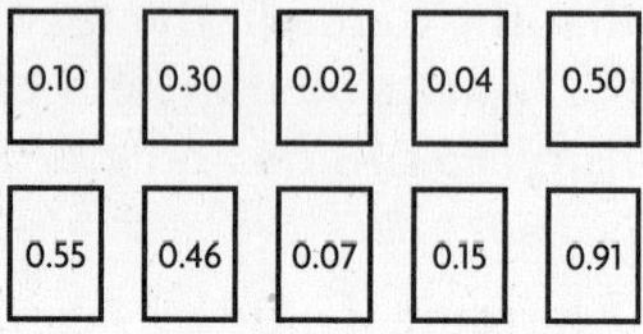

Mix up one set of 10 cards. Have partners pull two cards from the stack and set one below the other.

Have students compare the two cards, and place the cards in order from lesser to greater number. Then have students select another two cards from the stack, compare them and put them in correct order with the previous two cards.

Have students continue to compare two numbers at a time, and place them in the correct order along with the previously ordered numbers, until all 10 cards have been used.

Repeat the activity several times.

Then take 4 cards from several sets of numbers, and mix them up. Have students pull two cards, compare them and place them in order from lesser to greater number.

Have the students take one card and compare it to each card already displayed and decide how to position it with the other cards.

Have the students do the same for the fourth card, comparing it to all three numbers.

Have students try the activity one more time. Then present three decimals for students to order using only pencil and paper. When they are successful ordering three numbers, have students order four decimal numbers.

Name ______________________ Skill ______________________

Compare and Order Decimals

Skill 17

A **decimal** is a number with one or more digits to the right of the decimal point. There are different ways to compare decimals.

Use a Number Line

Compare: 0.7 ○ 0.9.

The number line is labeled in intervals of tenths from 0 to 1. Find 0.7 and 0.9 on the number line.

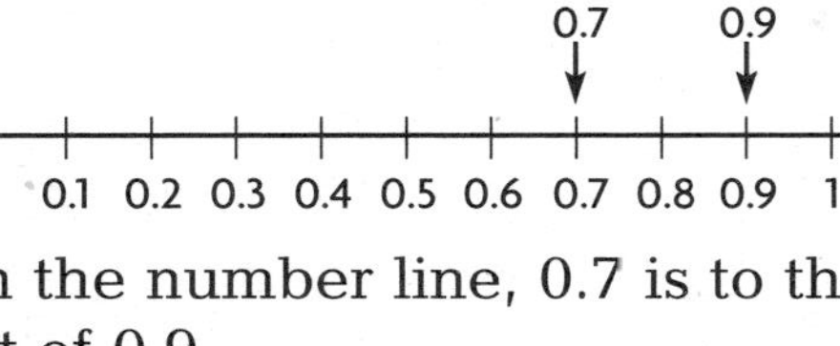

On the number line, 0.7 is to the left of 0.9.

So, $0.7 < 0.9$

Read: ***is less than.***

Use Place Value

Compare: 2.76 ○ 2.7.

Use a place value table.

- Align the digits by place values.
- Then compare digits starting with the ones place.
- Write a zero to the right of 7 in 2.7 so both numbers have the same number of places.

ones	.	tenths	hundredths
2	.	7	6
2	.	7	0

6 > 0

Ones are the same. Tenths are the same. Hundredths are different.

- Since the ones and tenths are the same, compare hundredths. 6 hundredths are greater than 0 hundredths.

So, $2.76 > 2.70$.

Read: ***is greater than.***

Order Decimals

Order from least to greatest: 1.38, 0.94, 0.5, 0.98.

- Write the numbers in a list. Align the digits. Write zeros if needed.

1.38
0.94
0.50
0.98

This number is greatest. None of the other numbers has ones.

?, ?, ?, 1.38
least ... greatest

- Compare two numbers at a time.

0.94	0.50	0.98
0.50	0.98	0.94
same 9 > 5	same 5 < 9	same 8 > 4

$0.94 > 0.5$ $0.5 < 0.98$ $0.98 > 0.94$

In order from least to greatest, the numbers are:

0.5, 0.94, 0.98, 1.38
least ... greatest

Go to the next side.

Name ______________________________ Skill ______________________

Practice on Your Own

Skill 17

Order the numbers from greatest to least: 1.37, 1.56, 1.23, 1.59.
List the numbers. Compare two numbers at a time.

1.37 ↖
1.56   **Compare these first. Their tenths digits are different.**
1.23 ←
1.59
↑
The ones digits are the same.

1.37 ○ 1.23   3 > 2   1.37 > 1.23

1.37 ○ 1.56   3 < 5   1.37 < 1.56

1.56 ○ 1.59   6 < 9   1.56 < 1.59

Ordered from greatest to least: 1.59, 1.56, 1.37, 1.23

Use the number line. Write >, <, or = for ○.

1. 0.09 ○ 0.02

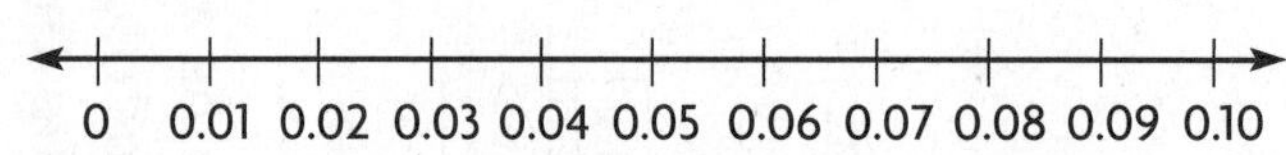

2. 0.25 ○ 0.30

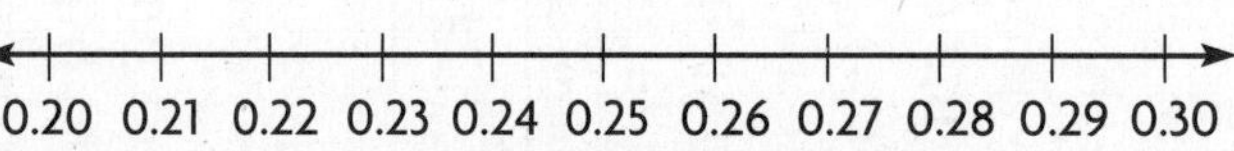

3. 0.5 ○ 0.1

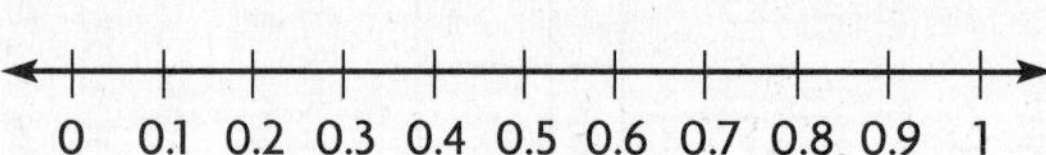

Use place value. Write >, <, or = for ○.

4. 2.06 ○ 2.10

ones	.	tenths	hundredths

5. 4.8 ○ 4.19

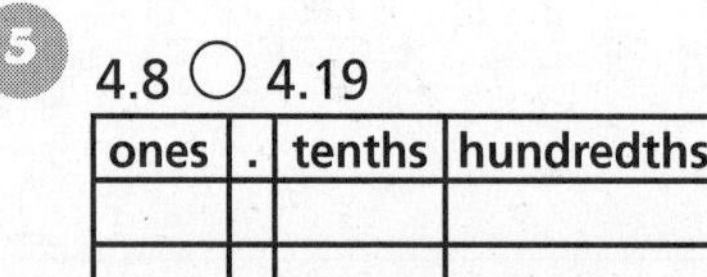

ones	.	tenths	hundredths

6. 7.36 ○ 7.36

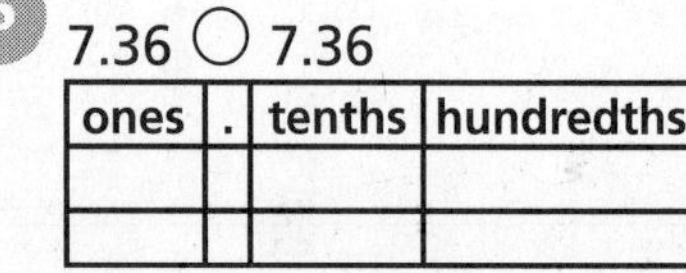

ones	.	tenths	hundredths

Order the numbers from least to greatest, or greatest to least.

7. 3.42, 0.89, 0.91

_____, _____, _____
least   greatest

8. 2.65, 0.03, 2.4, 0.5

_____, _____, _____, _____
least   greatest

9. 1.18, 1.27, 1.11, 1.3

_____, _____, _____, _____
greatest   least

Check

In Exercises 10 and 11, write >, <, or = for ○.

10. 0.72 ○ 0.7

11. 5.28 ○ 5.29

12. Order from greatest to least.
2.83, 1.7, 2.48, 2.38

____

13. Order from least to greatest.
1.38, 0.5, 1.83, 1.18

____

Skill 18 Model Fractions

Using Skill 18

OBJECTIVE Understand that a fraction names a part of a group or a part of a whole

Direct students' attention to the example for *Part of a Whole*. Ask: **What is the geometric figure?** (square) **Into how many parts is it divided?** (9) **How do the 9 parts compare to each other?** (They are all equal.) **How many parts are shaded?** (3) **What fraction of the whole is shaded?** ($\frac{3}{9}$) **Why is 9 the denominator?** (The denominator represents the total number of equal parts the whole is divided into.) **Why is 3 the numerator?** (The numerator is the number of parts that are shaded.) **What fraction of the square is not shaded?** ($\frac{6}{9}$)

As you work through the next example for *Part of a Group*, have students state that the group is the 7 circles. Point out the difference between part of a whole and part of a group using the two examples. In the final example, help students recognize the difference between the previous part-of-a-group example and this example.

TRY THESE Exercises 1–3 model the type of exercises students will find on the **Practice on Your Own** page.

- **Exercise 1** Part of a whole
- **Exercise 2** Part of a group
- **Exercise 3** Part of a group

PRACTICE ON YOUR OWN Review the example at the top of the page. As they work through the exercise, have students identify whether the fraction is a part of a whole or a part of a group.

CHECK Determine if the students know how to find a part of a whole or a part of a group.

Success is indicated by 3 out of 3 correct responses.

Students who successfully complete the **Practice on Your Own** and **Check** are ready to move to the next skill.

COMMON ERRORS

- Students may write the fraction as the number of parts not shaded.
- Students may write the number of parts shaded as the numerator and the number of parts not shaded as the denominator.

Students who made more than 2 errors in the **Practice on Your Own**, or who were not successful in the **Check** section, may benefit from the **Alternative Teaching Strategy** on the next page.

Optional

Alternative Teaching Strategy

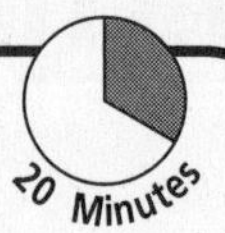

Modeling Fractions

OBJECTIVE Model parts of a whole and parts of a group

MATERIALS connecting cubes of different colors: white, blue, red, yellow, green, orange; paper

Distribute the cubes and have students connect 2 blue and 3 white cubes. Ask:
How many parts are there in the whole? (5)

How many parts out of 5 are blue? (2)

You may wish to have students draw the figure on paper. Then, help students record the 2 of 5 parts in word form as "2 fifths are blue." Ask students to write the fraction as $\frac{2}{5}$. You may also wish to have the students write the word form and fraction form for the part that is white.

5 equal parts in the whole

2 fifths are blue → $\frac{2}{5}$

3 fifths are white → $\frac{3}{5}$

Have students build other figures to represent a whole and parts of a whole.

Next, have students model parts of a group.

Ask a student to display 3 red cubes without connecting them and 1 yellow cube. Note that there are 4 cubes in the group, and each cube represents 1 fourth of the group. Ask:
How many parts of the group are red? (3)

How many fourths is that? (3 fourths)

Have students draw the group on paper. Then record "3 fourths are red" and write the fraction.

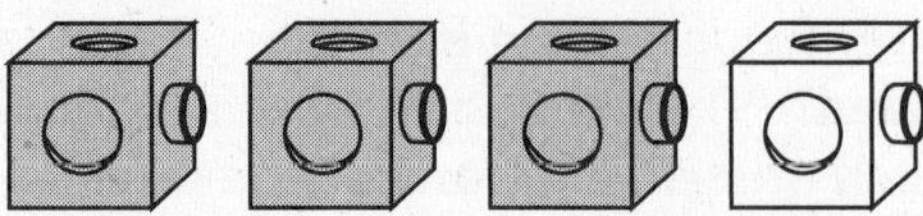

4 equal parts in the group

3 fourths are red → $\frac{3}{4}$

Continue with this example for parts of a group. Ask students to connect 2 pairs of green cubes and 1 pair of orange cubes. Observe with students that there are 3 parts in the group, each part represents 1 third, and that 2 thirds are green. Have students draw the group on paper, and record the word name and fraction for the orange part as they did in the previous two examples.

3 equal parts in the group

2 thirds are green → $\frac{2}{3}$

Summarize by having students recall that the denominator represents the number of parts in the whole or group and the numerator represents the number of parts being considered.

Name ____________________ Skill ____________________

Skill 18

Model Fractions

A **fraction** is a number that names *part of a whole or part of a group*.

Part of a Whole
The **whole** is divided into **9** equal parts. **3** out of **9** parts are shaded.

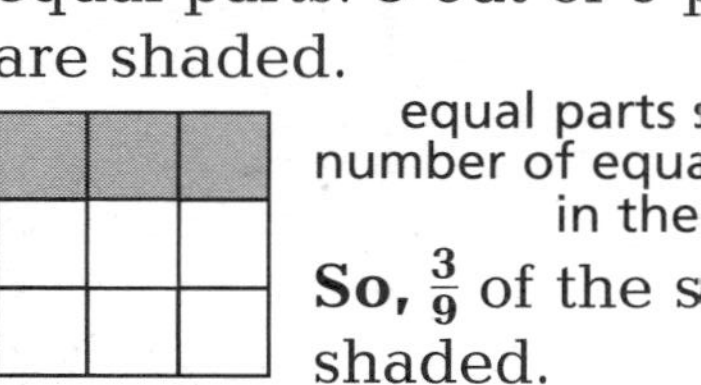

equal parts shaded → **3**
number of equal parts in the whole → **9**

So, $\frac{3}{9}$ of the square is shaded.

Part of a Group
There are **7** parts in the **group**. **3** out of **7** parts are shaded.

parts shaded → **3**
number of parts in the group → **7**

So, $\frac{3}{7}$ of the circles are shaded.

Part of a Group
There are 9 circles in this **group**. The group is divided into **3** equal parts. **1** out of **3** parts is shaded.

parts shaded → **1**
number of parts in the group → **3**

So, $\frac{1}{3}$ of the group is shaded.

Try These

Complete.

1. ___ out of ___ parts are shaded.

   equal parts shaded → □
   number of equal parts in the whole → □

2. ___ out of ___ parts are shaded.

   parts shaded → □
   number of parts in the group → □

3. 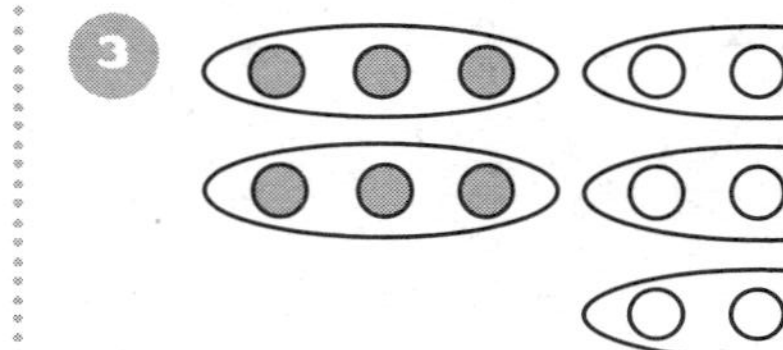

   ___ out of ___ parts are shaded.

   parts shaded → □
   number of parts in the group → □

Name ________________________ Skill ________________________

Practice on Your Own

Skill 18

There are **10** equal parts in the **whole**. **4 out of 10** equal parts are shaded.

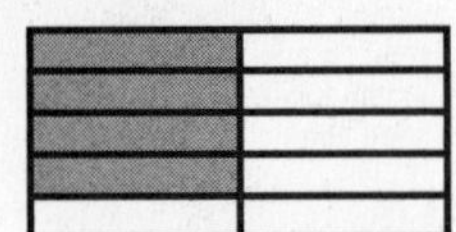

$\frac{4}{10}$ ← parts **shaded**; 10 ← number of equal parts in the **whole**

$\frac{4}{10}$ of the rectangle is shaded.

There are 10 triangles in the **group**. The group is divided into **5** parts. **3 out of 5** parts are shaded.

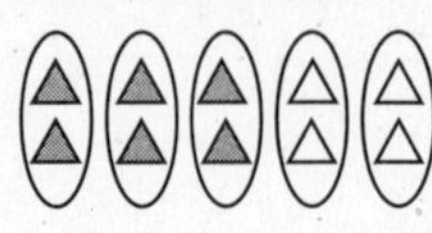

$\frac{3}{5}$ ← parts **shaded**; 5 ← number of parts in the group

$\frac{3}{5}$ of the triangles are shaded.

Complete.

1

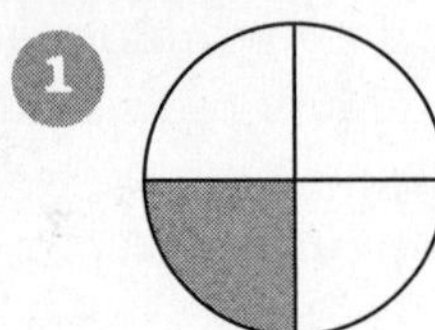

___ out of ___ parts shaded

$\frac{\square}{\square}$ ← parts shaded / ← parts in the whole

2 ● ● ● ○

___ out of ___ parts shaded

$\frac{\square}{\square}$ ← parts shaded / ← parts in the group

3

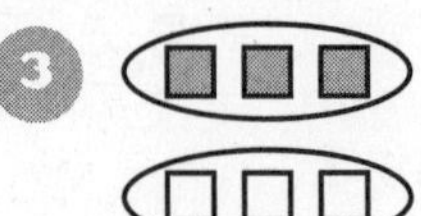

___ out of ___ parts shaded

$\frac{\square}{\square}$ ← parts shaded / ← parts in the group

4

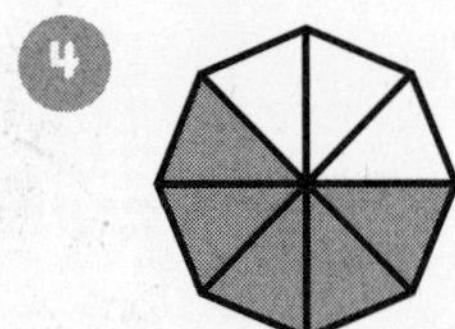

$\frac{\square}{\square}$ ← parts shaded / ← parts in the whole

5

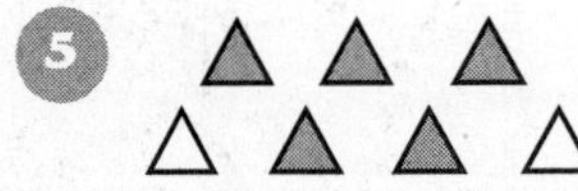

$\frac{\square}{\square}$ ← parts shaded / ← parts in the group

6

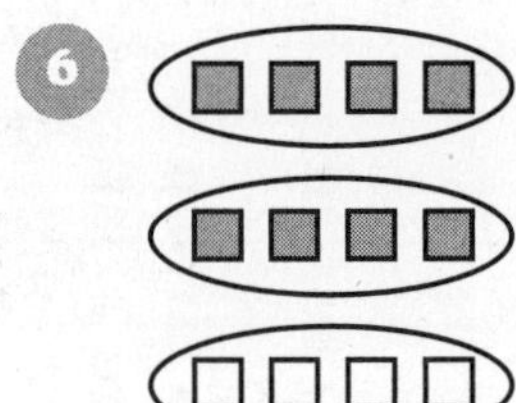

$\frac{\square}{\square}$ ← parts shaded / ← parts in the group

Write the fraction for the shaded part.

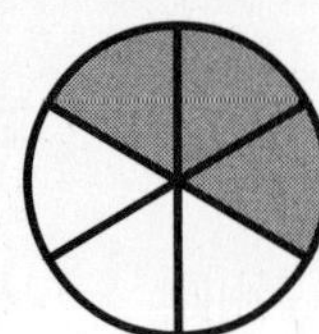

$\frac{\square}{\square}$

☆ ☆ ☆ ☆
☆ ★ ★ ★

$\frac{\square}{\square}$

Check

Write the fraction for the shaded part.

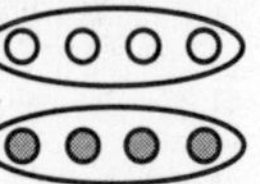

$\frac{\square}{\square}$

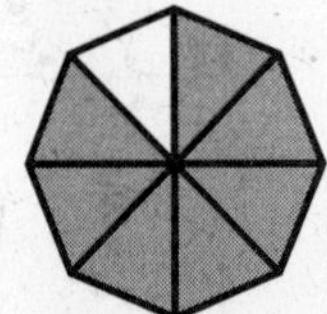

$\frac{\square}{\square}$

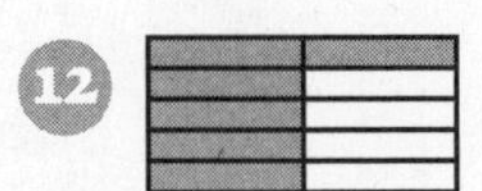

$\frac{\square}{\square}$

Skill 19 Simplify Fractions

Using Skill 19

OBJECTIVE Write a fraction in simplest form

Write $\frac{2}{3}$ on the board. Ask: **What are some factors of the numerator 2?** (1 and 2) **What are some factors of the denominator 3?** (1 and 3) **How many factors do 2 and 3 have in common?** (one) **What is it?** (1)

Direct the students' attention to the definition of *simplest form*. Ask: **Why can you say $\frac{2}{3}$ is in simplest form?** (because the only common factor of the numerator and denominator is 1)

Review the definition of *simplest form*, explaining that 1 is the *greatest* common factor of both 2 and 3.

For Step 1, have students tell you the factors of 12 and of 18. Then for Step 2, write the pairs of common factors on the board as students name them. (1, 1; 2, 2; 3, 3; 4, 4; and 6, 6) Ask: **What is the greatest common factor?** (6)

For Step 3, help students realize that $\frac{6}{6}$ is equal to 1. So, when a fraction is divided by 1, the value of the fraction does not change. Then ask: **How can you tell that is in simplest form?** (because the only common factor of the numerator and denominator is 1)

TRY THESE Exercises 1–3 model the type of exercises students will find on the **Practice on Your Own** page.

- **Exercises 1 and 3** 2 common factors
- **Exercise 2** more than 2 common factors

PRACTICE ON YOUR OWN Review the example for simplifying a fraction greater than 1 at the top of the page. Ask: **How can you tell that $\frac{28}{16}$ is greater than 1?** (The numerator is greater than the denominator.)

CHECK Determine if students know how to find factors and the greatest common factor of the numerator and denominator and use the GCF to find the simplest form. Success is indicated by 2 out of 3 correct responses.

Students who successfully complete the **Practice on Your Own** and **Check** are ready to move to the next skill.

COMMON ERRORS

- Students may divide the numerator by one factor and the denominator by a different factor.
- Students may use a common factor but not the greatest common factor.

Students who made more than 2 errors in the **Practice on Your Own**, or who were not successful in the **Check** section, may benefit from the **Alternative Teaching Strategy** on the next page.

Optional

Alternative Teaching Strategy
Modeling Simplest Forms of Fractions

OBJECTIVE Use models to find the simplest form for a fraction

MATERIALS fraction circles for halves, fourths, eighths, and sixteenths

An alternate method for finding the simplest form is to use 2, 3, or 5 as a trial divisor and keep reducing the fraction until it is in simplest form.

Have students use fraction circles. For example, write $\frac{4}{8}$ on the board. Have students find the fraction circle for eighths and shade 4 of the 8 parts.

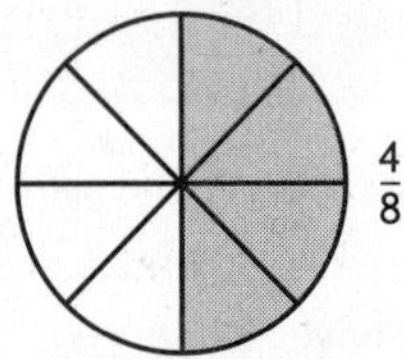

Say: **Suppose we divide the numerator and denominator by 2. What is the result?** ($\frac{2}{4}$) Have students find the fraction circle for fourths and shade 2 of them.

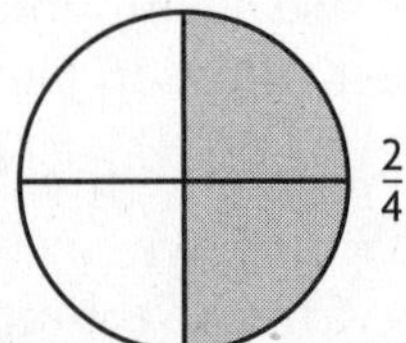

Continue: **Suppose we again divide the numerator and denominator by 2. What is the result?** ($\frac{1}{2}$) Have students find the fraction circle for halves and shade 1 of the parts.

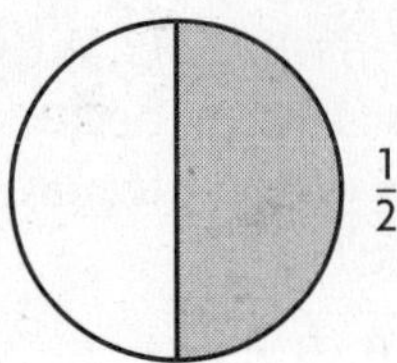

The circle models help students to visualize that any further division is not possible. At the same time they see that there can be more than one equivalent fraction for many fractions.

Repeat the activity to find the simplest form for $\frac{12}{16}$.

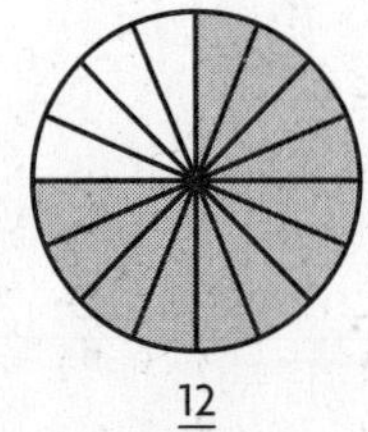

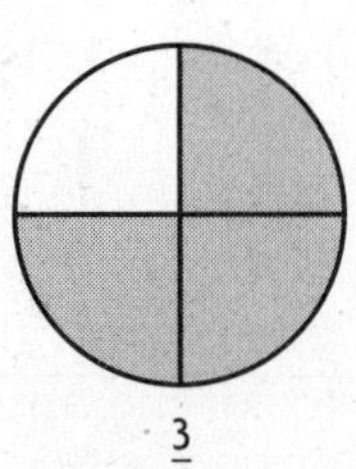

Name ______________________ Skill ______________________

Simplify Fractions

Skill 19

A fraction is in **simplest form** when the *greatest common factor*, or GCF, of the numerator and denominator is 1.

Write $\frac{12}{18}$ in simplest form.

Step 1
Write the factors of the numerator and the denominator.

numerator →	12	1, 2, 3, 4, 6, 12
denominator →	18	1, 2, 3, 6, 9, 18

Step 2
Look for common factors. Circle the greatest common factor **(GCF)**.

numerator →	12	1, 2, 3, 4, (6), 12
denominator →	18	1, 2, 3, (6), 9, 18

Step 3
Divide the numerator and the denominator by the GCF.

$\frac{12}{18} = \frac{12 \div 6}{18 \div 6} = \frac{2}{3}$

The simplest form of $\frac{12}{18}$ is $\frac{2}{3}$.

Try These

Write each fraction in simplest form.

1 $\frac{12}{15}$

Find and circle the GCF.

12	1, 2, 3, 4, 6, 12
15	1, 3, 5, 15

Divide the numerator and denominator by the GCF.

$\frac{12 \div \square}{15 \div \square} = \frac{\square}{\square}$

2 $\frac{4}{12}$

Find and circle the GCF.

4	1, 2, 4
12	1, 2, 3, 4, 6, 12

Divide the numerator and denominator by the GCF.

$\frac{4 \div \square}{12 \div \square} = \frac{\square}{\square}$

3 $\frac{8}{10}$

Find and circle the GCF.

8	1, 2, 4, 8
10	1, 2, 5, 10

Divide the numerator and denominator by the GCF.

$\frac{8 \div \square}{10 \div \square} = \frac{\square}{\square}$

Go to the next side.

Name ______________________ Skill ______________________

Practice on Your Own

Skill 19

Write $\frac{28}{16}$ in simplest form.

Step 1 List all the factors of the numerator and the denominator. Circle the GCF.	$\frac{28}{16}$ $\frac{1, 2, (4), 7, 14, 28}{1, 2, (4), 8, 16}$
Step 2 Divide the numerator and the denominator by the GCF.	$\frac{28}{16} = \frac{28 \div 4}{16 \div 4} = \frac{7}{4}$, or $1\frac{3}{4}$

Write each fraction in simplest form.

1. $\frac{9}{12}$

Circle the GCF.

$\frac{9}{12}$ $\frac{1, 3, 9}{1, 2, 3, 4, 6, 12}$

Divide numerator and denominator by the GCF.

$\frac{9 \div \square}{12 \div \square} = \frac{\square}{\square}$

2. $\frac{6}{15}$

Circle the GCF.

$\frac{6}{15}$ $\frac{1, 2, 3, 6}{1, 3, 5, 15}$

Divide numerator and denominator by the GCF.

$\frac{6 \div \square}{15 \div \square} = \frac{\square}{\square}$

3. $\frac{3}{18}$

Circle the GCF.

$\frac{3}{18}$ $\frac{1, 3}{1, 2, 3, 6, 9, 18}$

Divide numerator and denominator by the GCF.

$\frac{3 \div \square}{18 \div \square} = \frac{\square}{\square}$

Write the factors. Find the GCF. Then write the fraction in simplest form.

4. $\frac{12}{14}$

12 ____________

14 ____________

GCF ______

simplest form ______

5. $\frac{30}{40}$

30 ____________

40 ____________

GCF ______

simplest form ______

6. $\frac{18}{15}$

18 ____________

15 ____________

GCF ______

simplest form ______

Write the fraction in simplest form.

7. $\frac{8}{12}$ ____________

8. $\frac{27}{9}$ ____________

9. $\frac{15}{25}$ ____________

Check

Write the fraction in simplest form.

10. $\frac{10}{25}$ ____________

11. $\frac{9}{18}$ ____________

12. $\frac{24}{16}$ ____________

Using Skill 20

OBJECTIVE Round fractions on a number line

MATERIALS number lines or lined paper turned sideways

20 Minutes

Begin by explaining to students that they can think of the part of the number line between 0 and 1 as a whole divided into parts. The number line is labeled from zero to one with fractions. Tell the students that the benchmark numbers 0, $\frac{1}{2}$, and 1 are used to round fractions.

Then direct students' attention to the first example, observing that the number line is labeled in sixths. Point out the benchmarks 0, $\frac{1}{2}$, and 1 labeled above the number line.

Ask: **What fraction is shown below zero on the number line?** ($\frac{0}{6}$)

What fraction is shown below $\frac{1}{2}$? ($\frac{3}{6}$) Note that $\frac{3}{6}$ and $\frac{1}{2}$ are equivalent fractions.

What fraction is shown below 1? ($\frac{6}{6}$) Note that $\frac{6}{6}$ is another name for 1.

Continue with the example. Ask: **Is $\frac{2}{6}$ between 0 and $\frac{1}{2}$ or between $\frac{1}{2}$ and 1?** (0 and $\frac{1}{2}$)

How far from 0 is $\frac{2}{6}$? (2 spaces)

How far from $\frac{1}{2}$ is $\frac{2}{6}$? (1 space)

Is $\frac{2}{6}$ closer to 0 or $\frac{1}{2}$? ($\frac{1}{2}$)

Continue to ask similar questions as you work through the next two examples.

TRY THESE Exercises 1–3 model the type of exercises students will find on the **Practice on Your Own** page.

- **Exercise 1** Round to 0
- **Exercise 2** Round to 1
- **Exercise 3** Round to $\frac{1}{2}$

PRACTICE ON YOUR OWN
Review the example at the top of the page. Ask students to explain how they can tell that $\frac{6}{15}$ is closer to $\frac{1}{2}$ than it is to 0.

CHECK Determine if students can round fractions. Success is indicated by 4 out of 4 correct responses.

Students who successfully complete the **Practice on Your Own** and **Check** are ready to move to the next skill.

COMMON ERRORS

- Students may place $\frac{1}{2}$ in the wrong place on a number line that shows denominators that are odd numbers.
- Students may round all fractions greater than $\frac{1}{2}$ to 1.

Students who made more than 3 errors in the **Practice on Your Own**, or who were not successful in the **Check** section, may benefit from the **Alternative Teaching Strategy** on the next page.

Optional

Alternate Teaching Strategy
Modeling Rounding Fractions

OBJECTIVE Use fraction strips to model rounding fractions on a number line

MATERIALS inch grid paper, scissors

Distribute the grid paper and demonstrate how to draw the number line below. Ask students to draw a number line on the graph paper and label it with the fractions $\frac{0}{5}$, $\frac{1}{5}$, $\frac{2}{5}$, $\frac{3}{5}$, $\frac{4}{5}$, and $\frac{5}{5}$.

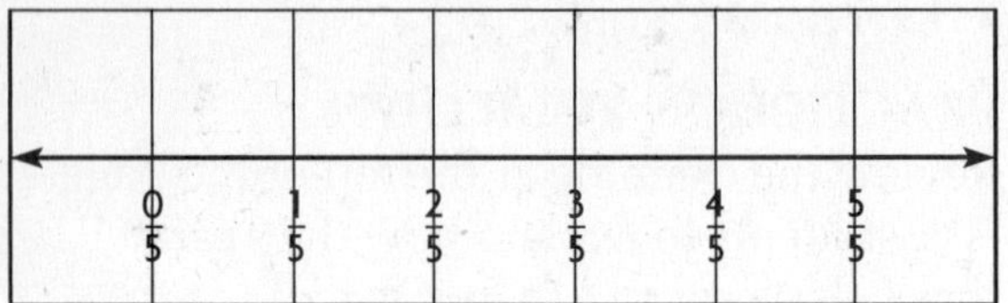

Make sure that each student uses the lines on the graph paper to evenly divide a number line into fifths.

Then have students cut out the number line and fold it into four equal sections. When they unfold it, the number line will have three creases in it.

Ask: **Which crease represents the fraction $\frac{1}{2}$?** (the second one)

Between which two fractions is $\frac{1}{2}$ located? (between $\frac{2}{5}$ and $\frac{3}{5}$)

If you were rounding $\frac{2}{5}$, would you round it to 0, $\frac{1}{2}$, or 1? ($\frac{1}{2}$)

Have the students round the other fractions on the number line.

Repeat this activity for sevenths, ninths, and fifteenths.

Name ______________________ Skill ______________________

Round Fractions

Skill 20

Use a number line to round fractions.

Is $\frac{2}{6}$ closest to 0, $\frac{1}{2}$, or 1?
The number line shows that $\frac{2}{6}$ is closer to $\frac{1}{2}$ than to 0.

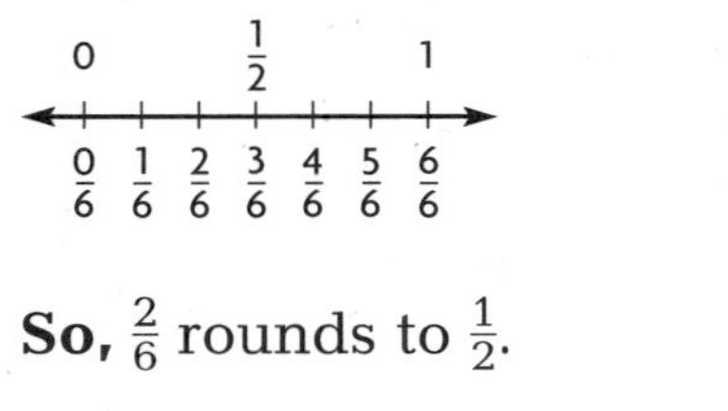

So, $\frac{2}{6}$ rounds to $\frac{1}{2}$.

Is $\frac{9}{11}$ closest to 0, $\frac{1}{2}$, or 1?
The number line shows that $\frac{9}{11}$ is closer to 1 than to $\frac{1}{2}$.

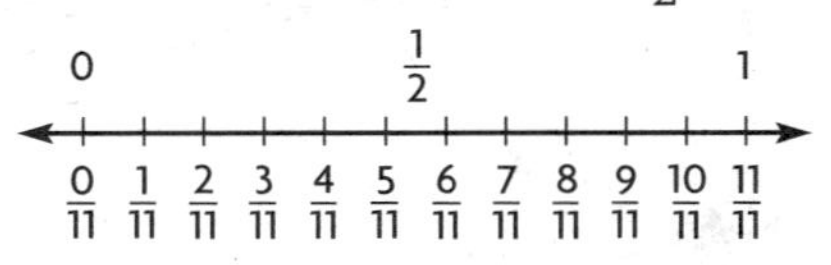

So, $\frac{9}{11}$ rounds to 1.

Model C
Is $\frac{2}{15}$ closest to 0, $\frac{1}{2}$, or 1?
The number line shows that $\frac{2}{15}$ is closer to 0 than to $\frac{1}{2}$.

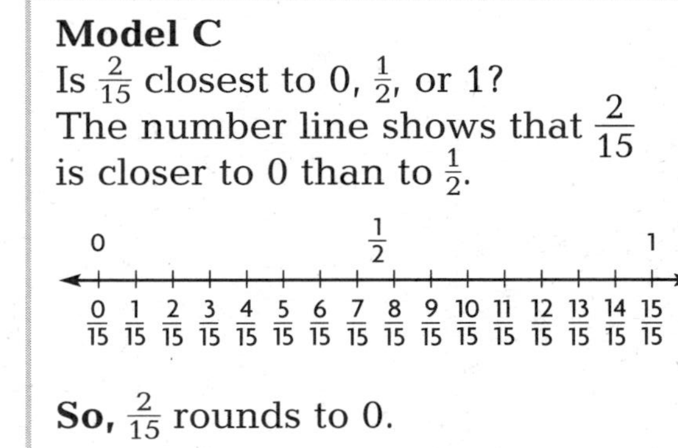

So, $\frac{2}{15}$ rounds to 0.

Try These

Use a number line. Round each fraction to 0, $\frac{1}{2}$, or 1.

1. $\frac{1}{7}$

0 $\frac{1}{2}$ 1

$\frac{0}{7}$ $\frac{1}{7}$ $\frac{2}{7}$ $\frac{3}{7}$ $\frac{4}{7}$ $\frac{5}{7}$ $\frac{6}{7}$ $\frac{7}{7}$

Closer to 0 or $\frac{1}{2}$?

$\frac{1}{7}$ rounds to ____.

2. $\frac{7}{9}$

0 $\frac{1}{2}$ 1

$\frac{0}{9}$ $\frac{1}{9}$ $\frac{2}{9}$ $\frac{3}{9}$ $\frac{4}{9}$ $\frac{5}{9}$ $\frac{6}{9}$ $\frac{7}{9}$ $\frac{8}{9}$ $\frac{9}{9}$

Closer to $\frac{1}{2}$ or 1?

$\frac{7}{9}$ rounds to ____.

3. $\frac{4}{12}$

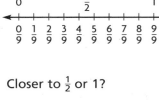

0 $\frac{1}{2}$ 1

$\frac{0}{12}$ $\frac{1}{12}$ $\frac{2}{12}$ $\frac{3}{12}$ $\frac{4}{12}$ $\frac{5}{12}$ $\frac{6}{12}$ $\frac{7}{12}$ $\frac{8}{12}$ $\frac{9}{12}$ $\frac{10}{12}$ $\frac{11}{12}$ $\frac{12}{12}$

Closer to 0 or $\frac{1}{2}$?

$\frac{4}{12}$ rounds to ____.

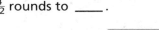

Go to the next side.

Name ______________________ Skill ______________________

Practice on Your Own

Skill 20

Use a number line to round fractions.

Round $\frac{6}{15}$.

Think:

Is $\frac{6}{15}$ closer to $0, \frac{1}{2}$, or 1?

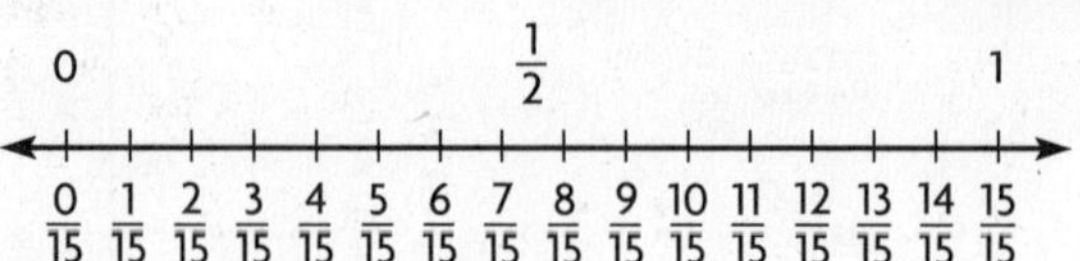

$\frac{6}{15}$ rounds to $\frac{1}{2}$.

Use a number line. Round each fraction to $0, \frac{1}{2}$, or 1.

1. $\frac{4}{7}$

0/7 1/7 2/7 3/7 4/7 5/7 6/7 7/7

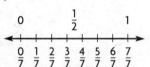

$\frac{4}{7}$ rounds to ___.

2. $\frac{3}{9}$

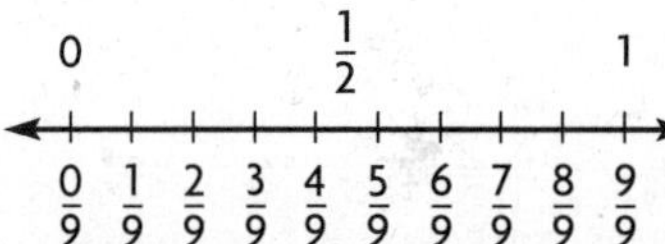

$\frac{3}{9}$ rounds to ___.

3. $\frac{10}{12}$

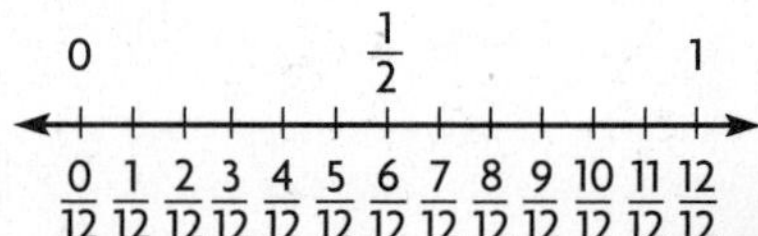

$\frac{10}{12}$ rounds to ___.

4. $\frac{5}{8}$

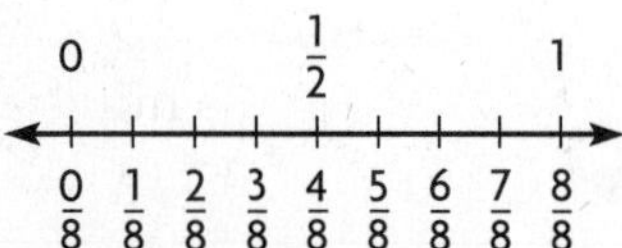

$\frac{5}{8}$ rounds to ___.

5. $\frac{1}{5}$

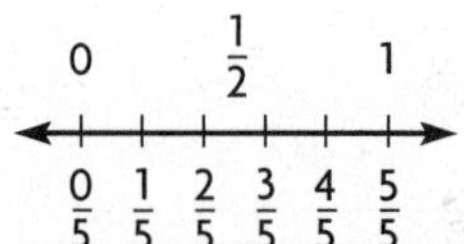

$\frac{1}{5}$ rounds to ___.

6. $\frac{8}{10}$

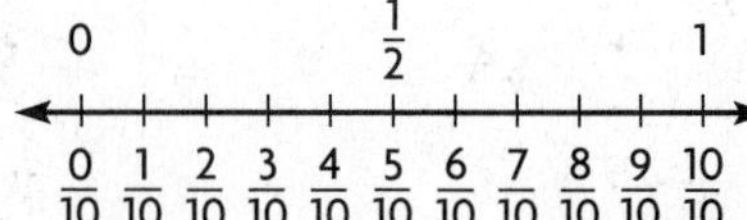

$\frac{8}{10}$ rounds to ___.

Round each fraction to $0, \frac{1}{2}$, or 1.

7. $\frac{13}{15}$ ___
8. $\frac{3}{20}$ ___
9. $\frac{4}{5}$ ___
10. $\frac{6}{10}$ ___

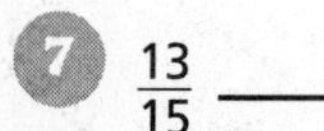

Check

Round each fraction to $0, \frac{1}{2}$, or 1.

11. $\frac{13}{16}$ ___
12. $\frac{4}{25}$ ___
13. $\frac{3}{6}$ ___
14. $\frac{17}{20}$ ___

Skill 21 Write an Improper Fraction as a Mixed Number

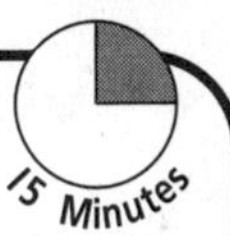

Using Skill 21

OBJECTIVE Write a mixed number for an improper fraction

Begin by asking: **How can you tell when a fraction is equal to 1?** (when the numerator and denominator are equal)

How can you tell when a fraction is an improper fraction? (when the numerator is greater than the denominator)

Have students discuss the steps on Skill 21, focusing on how 9 fourths are regrouped. Ask: **How many fourths equal 1 whole? (4 fourths)**

How many groups of 4 fourths can you make with 9 fourths? (2 groups)

So, how many wholes are in 9 fourths? (2 wholes) **What is left over?** (1 fourth) Note that $\frac{9}{4} = 2\frac{1}{4}$.

TRY THESE Exercises 1–3 model the type of exercises students will find on the **Practice on Your Own** page.

- **Exercise 1** Write $\frac{3}{2}$ as $1\frac{1}{2}$.
- **Exercise 2** Write $\frac{5}{3}$ as $1\frac{2}{3}$.
- **Exercise 3** Write $\frac{11}{4}$ as $2\frac{3}{4}$.

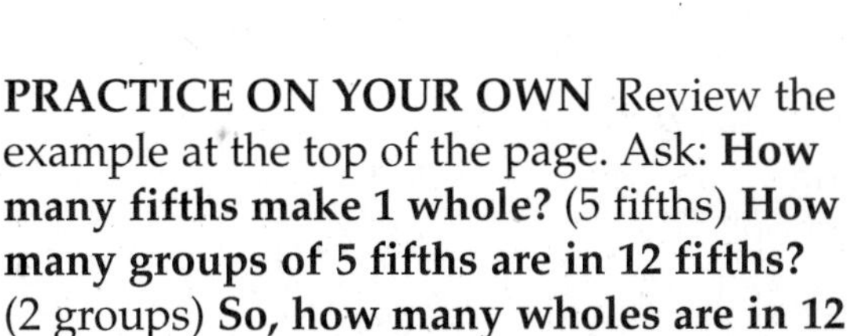

PRACTICE ON YOUR OWN Review the example at the top of the page. Ask: **How many fifths make 1 whole?** (5 fifths) **How many groups of 5 fifths are in 12 fifths?** (2 groups) **So, how many wholes are in 12 fifths?** (2 wholes) **What is left over?** (2 fifths)

CHECK Determine if students know how to tell the number of fractional parts that make 1 whole and how to find the number of these wholes in the given fraction. Success is indicated by 2 out of 3 correct responses.

Students who successfully complete the **Practice on Your Own** and **Check** are ready to move on to the next skill.

COMMON ERRORS

- Students may think they can simply subtract the denominator from the numerator to find the whole number part of the mixed number.
- Students may miscount the number of wholes in an improper fraction.

Students who made more than 2 errors in the **Practice on Your Own**, or who were not successful in the **Check** section, may benefit from the **Alternative Teaching Strategy** on the next page.

Optional

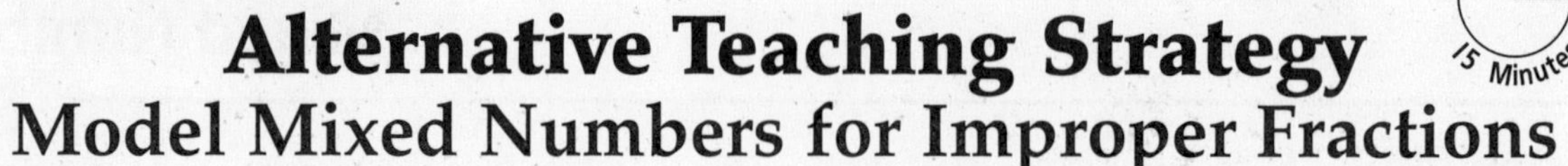

Alternative Teaching Strategy

Model Mixed Numbers for Improper Fractions

OBJECTIVE Use models to find mixed numbers for improper fractions

MATERIALS fraction circles for fourths and for fifths

Have students use fraction circles as models to find mixed numbers for improper fractions.

To find the mixed number for $\frac{11}{4}$, have students use or make fraction circles divided into fourths. Taking the circles one at a time, they shade fourths, counting as they go. They stop shading when they reach $\frac{11}{4}$.

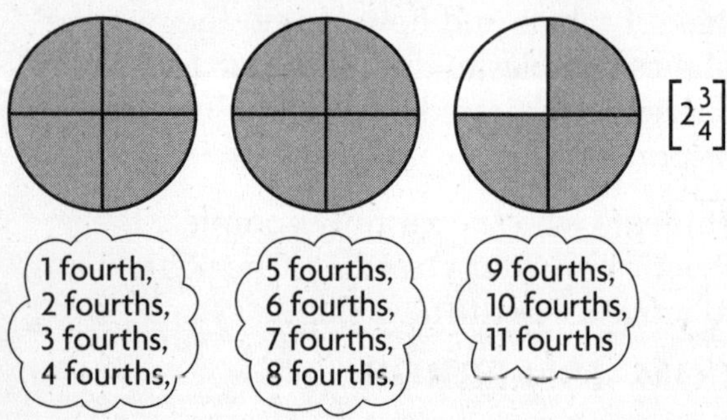

Then they count the number of wholes they have shaded, 2 wholes, and add the parts, 3 fourths.

$$\frac{11}{4} = 2\frac{3}{4}$$

To find the mixed number for $\frac{12}{5}$, have students take or make fraction circles divided into fifths. Taking the circles one at a time, they shade fifths, counting as they go. They stop shading when they reach $\frac{12}{5}$.

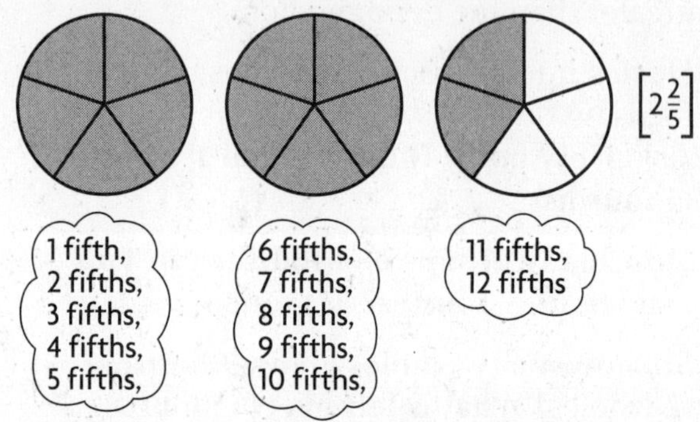

Then they count the number of wholes they have shaded, 2 wholes, and add the parts, 2 fifths.

$$\frac{12}{5} = 2\frac{2}{5}$$

Repeat as necessary for other fractions, such as $\frac{5}{4}$ ($1\frac{1}{4}$), $\frac{15}{4}$ ($3\frac{3}{4}$), $\frac{9}{5}$ ($1\frac{4}{5}$), $\frac{11}{5}$ ($2\frac{1}{5}$), and $\frac{17}{5}$ ($3\frac{2}{5}$).

Name ____________________ Skill ____________________

Write an Improper Fraction as a Mixed Number

Skill 21

You can write an improper fraction as a mixed number. Write the fraction $\frac{9}{4}$ as a mixed number.

These are some different names for 1: $\frac{2}{2}$ $\frac{3}{3}$ $\frac{4}{4}$ $\frac{5}{5}$ $\frac{6}{6}$ $\frac{7}{7}$ $\frac{8}{8}$

Step 1
Model $\frac{9}{4}$ with circles for $\frac{1}{4}$.

$\frac{9}{4} = \frac{4}{4} + \frac{4}{4} + \frac{1}{4}$

Step 2
Group the $\frac{1}{4}$ parts as wholes and parts.

$\frac{9}{4} = \frac{4}{4} + \frac{4}{4} + \frac{1}{4}$

$= 1 + 1 + \frac{1}{4}$

Step 3
Write the sum as a mixed number.

$\frac{9}{4} = 1 + 1 + \frac{1}{4}$

$= 2 + \frac{1}{4}$

$= 2\frac{1}{4}$

So, $\frac{9}{4}$ written as a mixed number is $2\frac{1}{4}$.

Try These

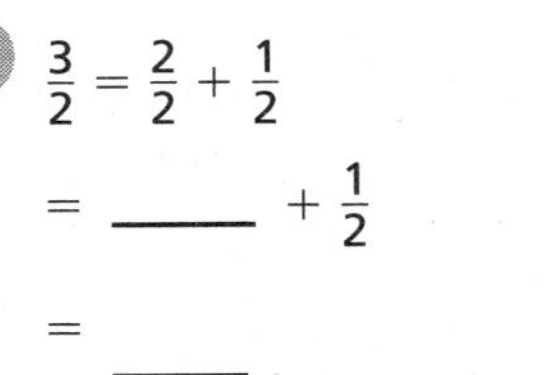

Write each improper fraction as a mixed number.

1. $\frac{3}{2} = \frac{2}{2} + \frac{1}{2}$

$=$ ______ $+ \frac{1}{2}$

$=$ ______

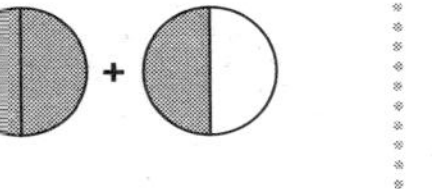

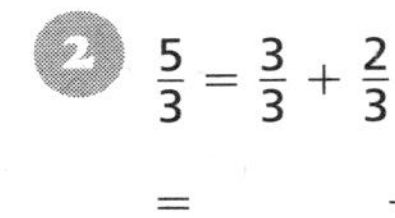

2. $\frac{5}{3} = \frac{3}{3} + \frac{2}{3}$

$=$ ______ $+ \frac{2}{3}$

$=$ ______

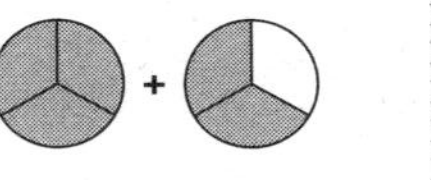

3. $\frac{11}{4} = \frac{4}{4} + \frac{4}{4} + \frac{3}{4}$

$=$ ______ $+$ ______ $+ \frac{3}{4}$

$=$ ______

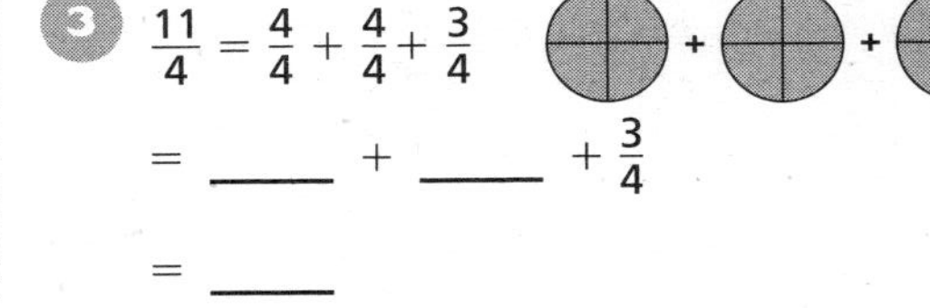

Go to the next side.

Name ______________________________ Skill ______________________________

Practice on Your Own

Skill 21

Think:
Find the names for 1 in fraction form.
Then add the names for 1 and the fraction.
Write the sum as a mixed number.

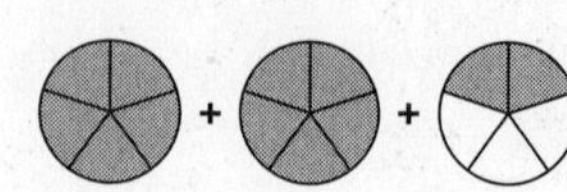

$$\frac{12}{5} = \frac{5}{5} + \frac{5}{5} + \frac{2}{5}$$
$$= 1 + 1 + \frac{2}{5}$$
$$= 2 + \frac{2}{5}$$
$$= 2\frac{2}{5}$$

Write each improper fraction as a mixed number.

1. $\frac{9}{2} = \frac{\square}{2} + \frac{\square}{2} + \frac{\square}{2} + \frac{\square}{2} + \frac{\square}{2}$
   = ___ + ___ + ___ + ___ + ___
   = ___ + ___
   = ______

2. $\frac{8}{3} = \frac{\square}{3} + \frac{\square}{3} + \frac{\square}{3}$
   = ___ + ___ + ___
   = ___ + ___
   = ______

3. $\frac{15}{4} = \frac{\square}{4} + \frac{\square}{4} + \frac{\square}{4} + \frac{\square}{4}$
   = ___ + ___ + ___ + ___
   = ___ + ___
   = ______

4. $\frac{13}{5} = \frac{\square}{\square} + \frac{\square}{\square} + \frac{\square}{\square}$
   = ___ + ___ + ___
   = ___ + ___
   = ______

5. $\frac{7}{2} = \frac{\square}{\square} + \frac{\square}{\square} + \frac{\square}{\square} + \frac{\square}{\square}$
   = ___ + ___ + ___ + ___
   = ___ + ___
   = ______

6. $\frac{11}{3} = \frac{\square}{\square} + \frac{\square}{\square} + \frac{\square}{\square} + \frac{\square}{\square}$
   = ___ + ___ + ___ + ___
   = ___ + ___
   = ______

7. $\frac{15}{8} =$ ______

8. $\frac{24}{5} =$ ______

9. $\frac{19}{6} =$ ______

Check

Write each improper fraction as a mixed number.

10. $\frac{25}{8} =$ ______

11. $\frac{27}{10} =$ ______

12. $\frac{17}{4} =$ ______

Skill 22 Write a Mixed Number as an Improper Fraction

Using Skill 22

OBJECTIVE Write an improper fraction for a mixed number

Begin by asking: **How many halves equal 1 whole?** (2 halves)

How many thirds equal 1 whole? (3 thirds)

How many fourths equal 1 whole? (4 fourths)

Help students recall that when the numerator and the denominator of a fraction are the same, the fraction is equal to 1. Have students discuss the steps on Skill 22, focusing on how to rename the whole-number part as an equivalent number of 1s and then how to rename each 1 as an equivalent number of halves.

For Step 1, ask: **How many ones equal 3?** (3 ones)

For Step 2, ask: **How many halves equal each whole?** (2 halves)

For Step 3, ask: **How do you find the number of halves there are in all?** (Add the numerators of the fractions.) Note that the fraction for $3\frac{1}{2}$ is $\frac{7}{2}$.

TRY THESE Exercises 1–3 model the type of exercises students will find on the **Practice on Your Own** page.

- **Exercise 1** Write $2\frac{1}{3}$ as $\frac{7}{3}$.
- **Exercise 2** Write $3\frac{3}{4}$ as $\frac{15}{4}$.
- **Exercise 3** Write $1\frac{4}{5}$ as $\frac{9}{5}$.

PRACTICE ON YOUR OWN Review the example at the top of the page. Ask: **How many ones make 2 wholes?** (2 ones) **How many fifths make each whole?** (5 fifths) **So, how many fifths are there in all?** (12 fifths)

CHECK Determine if students know how to rename the whole-number part of a mixed number as an equivalent number of 1s and then how to rename each 1 as an equivalent number of parts indicated by the denominator of the fraction part. Success is indicated by 2 out of 3 correct responses.

Students who successfully complete the **Practice on Your Own** and **Check** are ready to move to the next skill.

COMMON ERRORS

- Students may add the denominator, the whole number, and the numerator to get the numerator for the improper fraction.
- Students may miscount the number of wholes when renaming them as fractions.

Students who made more than 2 errors in the **Practice on Your Own**, or who were not successful in the **Check** section, may benefit from the **Alternative Teaching Strategy** on the next page.

Optional

Alternative Teaching Strategy

15 Minutes

Model Improper Fractions for Mixed Numbers

OBJECTIVE Make models of improper fractions for mixed numbers

MATERIALS fraction circles for halves and fourths

Have students use fraction circles as models to show fractions for whole numbers and mixed numbers.

Begin by asking students to show how many halves are in 1 whole. Students shade 2 halves of 1 whole circle.

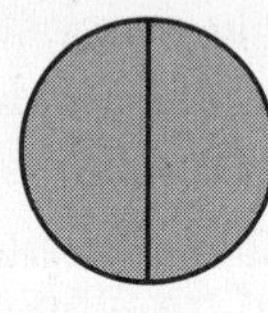

1 whole = $\frac{2}{2}$

Than ask them to show how many halves are in 2 wholes. Students shade 4 halves using 2 whole circles.

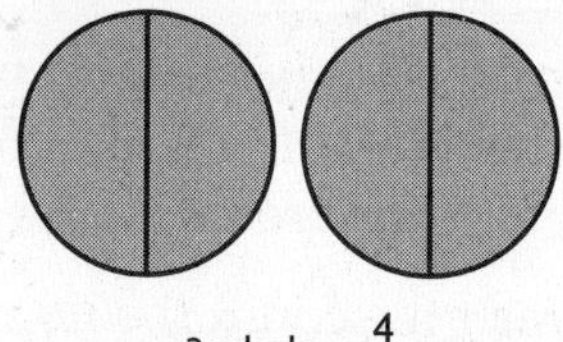

2 wholes = $\frac{4}{2}$

Then ask them to show how many halves are in 2 wholes and 1 half. Students shade 5 halves using 3 whole circles.

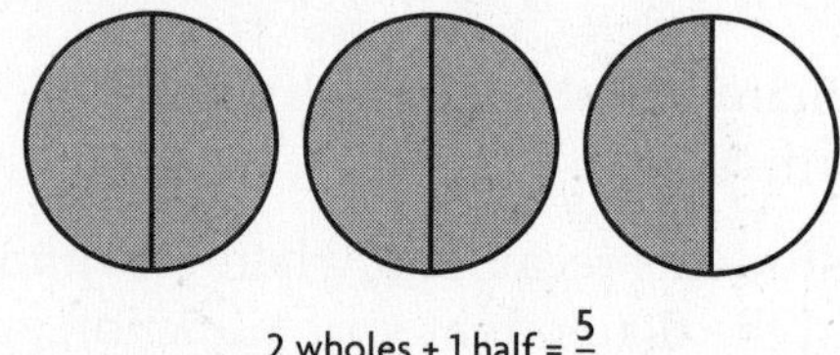

2 wholes + 1 half = $\frac{5}{2}$

Next, have students discuss how they might show an improper fraction for $3\frac{3}{4}$. Ask: **How many whole circles will you need to show the whole-number part?** (3 whole circles)

How will you show the fraction part? (Shade 3 of the 4 parts of another whole circle.)

Have the students make the model.

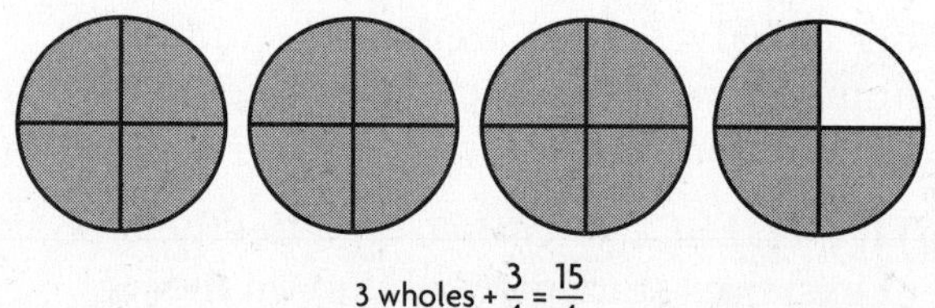

3 wholes + $\frac{3}{4} = \frac{15}{4}$

Name ______________________ Skill ______________________

Write a Mixed Number as a Fraction

Skill 22

Write the mixed number $3\frac{1}{2}$ as an improper fraction.

Step 1
Write the whole number as a sum of ones.

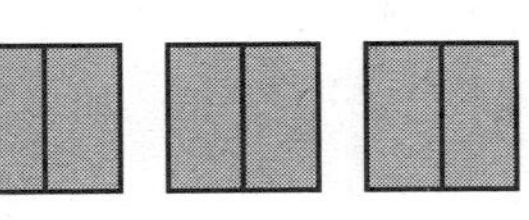

$3\frac{1}{2} = 1 + 1 + 1 + \frac{1}{2}$

Step 2
Use the denominator of the fraction to write equivalent fractions for the ones.

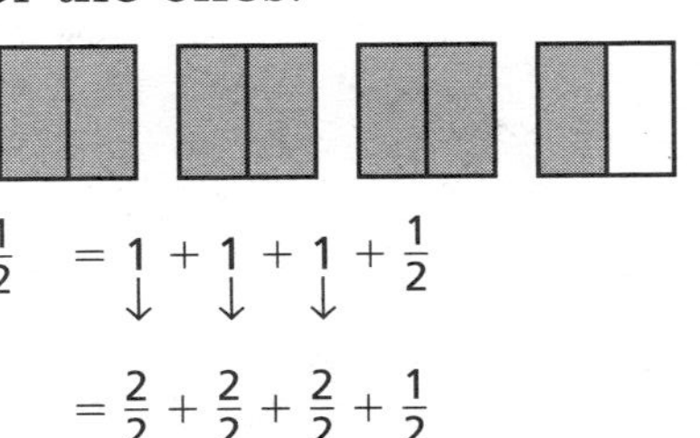

$3\frac{1}{2} = 1 + 1 + 1 + \frac{1}{2}$

$\;\;\;\;\downarrow\;\;\;\downarrow\;\;\;\downarrow$

$= \frac{2}{2} + \frac{2}{2} + \frac{2}{2} + \frac{1}{2}$

Step 3
Add the numerators to find the improper fraction.

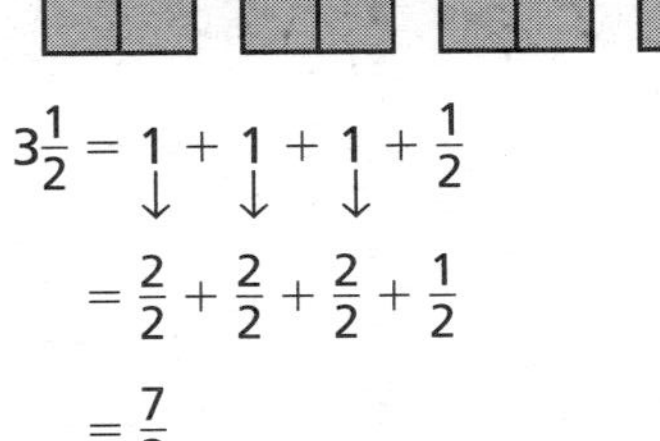

$3\frac{1}{2} = 1 + 1 + 1 + \frac{1}{2}$

$\;\;\;\;\downarrow\;\;\;\downarrow\;\;\;\downarrow$

$= \frac{2}{2} + \frac{2}{2} + \frac{2}{2} + \frac{1}{2}$

$= \frac{7}{2}$

So, the fraction for $3\frac{1}{2}$ is $\frac{7}{2}$.

Try These

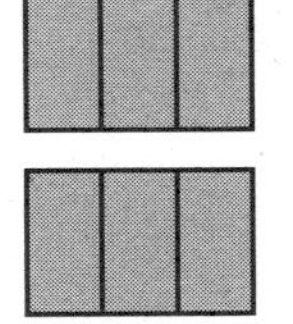

Write each mixed number as an improper fraction.

1 $2\frac{1}{3}$

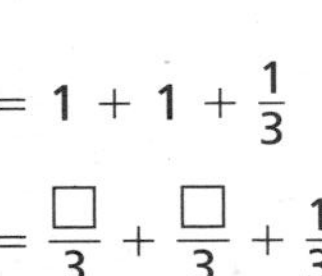

$2\frac{1}{3} = 1 + 1 + \frac{1}{3}$

$= \frac{\square}{3} + \frac{\square}{3} + \frac{1}{3}$

$= \frac{\square}{3}$

2 $3\frac{3}{4}$

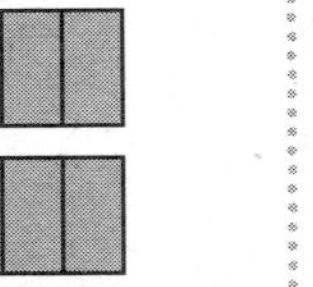

$3\frac{3}{4} = 1 + 1 + 1 + \frac{3}{4}$

$= \frac{\square}{4} + \frac{\square}{4} + \frac{\square}{4} + \frac{3}{4}$

$= \frac{\square}{\square}$

3 $1\frac{4}{5}$

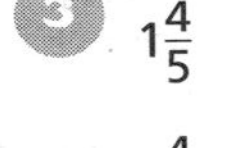
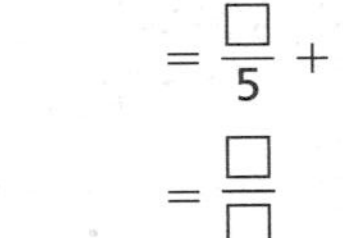
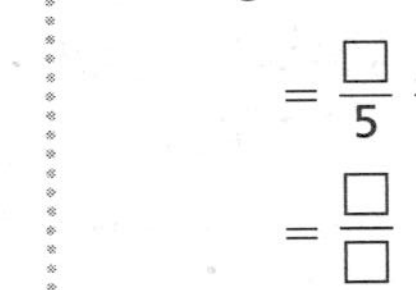

$1\frac{4}{5} = 1 + \frac{4}{5}$

$= \frac{\square}{5} + \frac{4}{5}$

$= \frac{\square}{\square}$

Name ______________________ Skill ______________________

Practice on Your Own

Skill 22

Think:
Write the whole number as a sum of ones.
Write equivalent fractions for the ones.
Add the numerators to find the fraction.

$$2\tfrac{2}{5} = 1 + 1 + \tfrac{2}{5}$$
$$= \tfrac{5}{5} + \tfrac{5}{5} + \tfrac{2}{5}$$
$$= \tfrac{12}{5}$$

Write each mixed number as an improper fraction.

1. $4\tfrac{1}{2}$

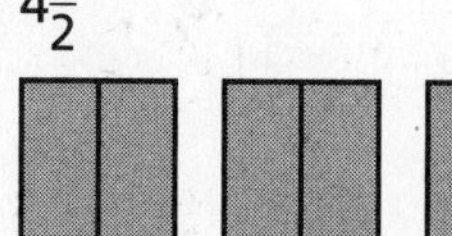
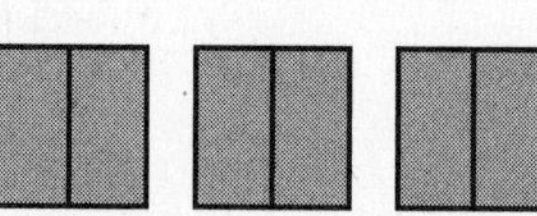
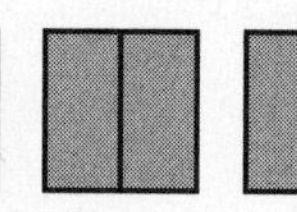

$$4\tfrac{1}{2} = 1 + 1 + 1 + 1 + \tfrac{1}{2}$$
$$= \tfrac{\square}{2} + \tfrac{\square}{2} + \tfrac{\square}{2} + \tfrac{\square}{2} + \tfrac{1}{2}$$
$$= \tfrac{\square}{\square}$$

2. $2\tfrac{3}{4}$

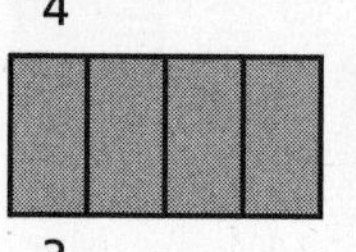
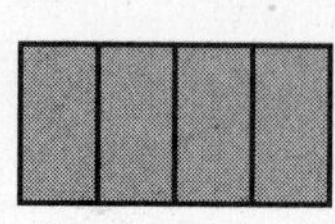
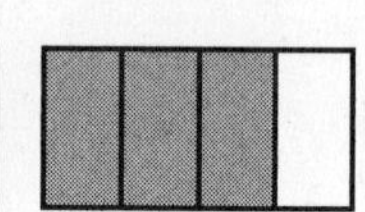

$$2\tfrac{3}{4} = 1 + 1 + \tfrac{3}{4}$$
$$= \tfrac{\square}{4} + \tfrac{\square}{4} + \tfrac{3}{4}$$
$$= \tfrac{\square}{\square}$$

3. $3\tfrac{2}{3}$

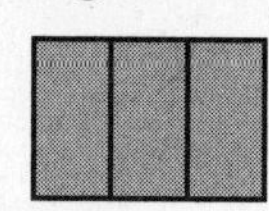
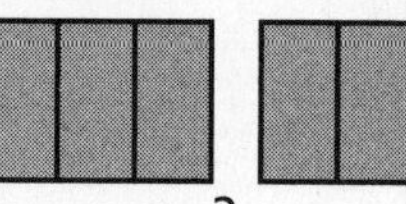
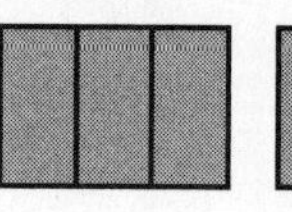
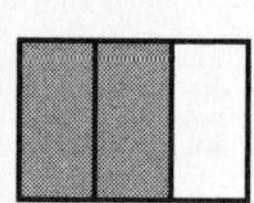

$$3\tfrac{2}{3} = 1 + 1 + 1 + \tfrac{2}{3}$$
$$= \tfrac{\square}{3} + \tfrac{\square}{3} + \tfrac{\square}{3} + \tfrac{2}{3}$$
$$= \tfrac{\square}{\square}$$

4. $3\tfrac{2}{5}$

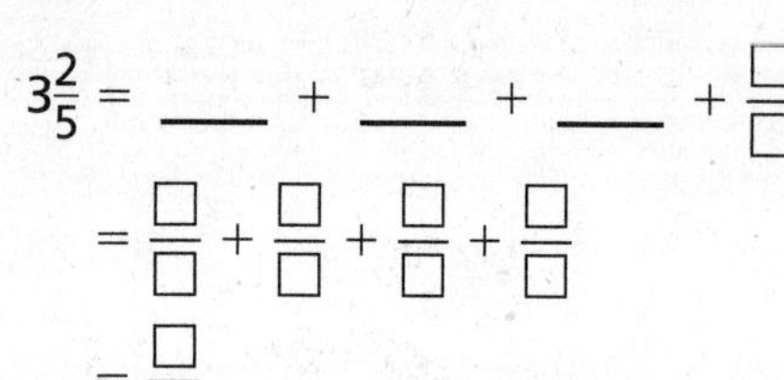

$$3\tfrac{2}{5} = \_\_\_ + \_\_\_ + \_\_\_ + \tfrac{\square}{\square}$$
$$= \tfrac{\square}{\square} + \tfrac{\square}{\square} + \tfrac{\square}{\square} + \tfrac{\square}{\square}$$
$$= \tfrac{\square}{\square}$$

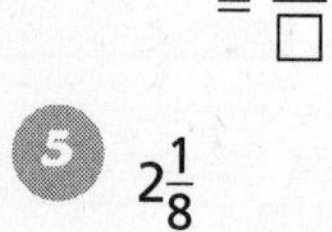
5. $2\tfrac{1}{8}$

$$2\tfrac{1}{8} = \_\_\_ + \_\_\_ + \tfrac{\square}{\square}$$
$$= \tfrac{\square}{\square} + \tfrac{\square}{\square} + \tfrac{\square}{\square}$$
$$= \tfrac{\square}{\square}$$

6. $3\tfrac{5}{6}$

$$3\tfrac{5}{6} = \_\_\_ + \_\_\_ + \_\_\_ + \tfrac{\square}{\square}$$
$$= \tfrac{\square}{\square} + \tfrac{\square}{\square} + \tfrac{\square}{\square} + \tfrac{\square}{\square}$$
$$= \tfrac{\square}{\square}$$

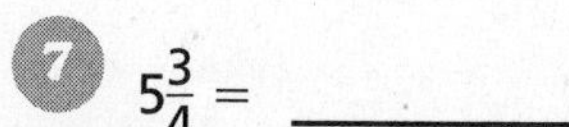
7. $5\tfrac{3}{4} =$ ________

8. $8\tfrac{4}{5} =$ ________

9. $6\tfrac{2}{3} =$ ________

Check

Write each mixed number as an improper fraction.

10. $5\tfrac{3}{4} =$ ________

11. $6\tfrac{1}{8} =$ ________

12. $4\tfrac{3}{5} =$ ________

Find Common Denominators

15 Minutes

Using Skill 23

OBJECTIVE Find a common denominator

Have students look at the problem on Skill 23.

Ask: **What is the denominator of each number?** (8 and 6)

Are the denominators the same? (no)

Direct students' attention to Step 1 and have students list the multiples of each number.
Direct students to complete Steps 2 and 3.

TRY THESE In Exercises 1–3 students list the multiples of each number, and circle the lowest common multiple to find the common denominator.

- **Exercise 1** The multiples of 10 are: 10, 20, 30, 40, 50, 60, 70, 80, 90, ...
The multiples of 8 are: 8, 16, 24, 32, 40, 48, 56, 64, 72, 80, ...
The LCM is 80.
- **Exercise 2** The multiples of 4 are: 4, 8, 12, 16, 20, ...
The multiples of 16 are: 16, 32, 48, ...
The LCM is 16.
- **Exercise 3** The multiples of 4 are: 4, 8, 12, 16, 20, 24, 28, ...
The multiples of 5 are: 5, 10, 15, 20, 25, ...
The LCM is 20.

PRACTICE ON YOUR OWN Review the example at the top of the page.

Ask students to explain how they know if they have listed enough numbers? (When a number from the first list repeats in the second list they have listed enough numbers.)

CHECK Determine if students know how to find a common denominator. Success is indicated by 3 out of 3 correct responses.

Students who successfully complete the **Practice on Your Own** and **Check** are ready to move to the next skill.

COMMON ERRORS

- Students will add the two denominators together rather than determine the LCD. Stress listing the multiples of each number.
- Students will multiply the two denominators together rather than determining the lowest common denominator.

Students who made more than 3 errors in the **Practice on Your Own**, or who were not successful in the **Check** section, may benefit from the **Alternative Teaching Strategy** on the next page.

Optional

Alternative Teaching Strategy

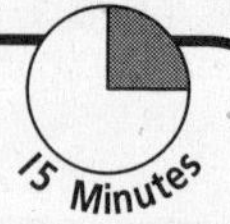

Find Common Denominators

OBJECTIVE Find a common denominator

You may wish to have students work in pairs. Partners take turns finding the prime factorization of each number.

Find the common denominator for $\frac{1}{15} + \frac{1}{18}$.

Have students find the prime factorization of 15 and 18.

$15 = 3 \times 5$

$18 = 2 \times 3 \times 3$

Ask: **What are the different factors?** (2, 3 and 5)

What is the greatest number of times 2 occurs? (once)

What is the greatest number of times 3 occurs? (twice)

What is the greatest number of times 5 occurs? (once)

Have students circle the different factors where they appear the greatest number of times.

Have students write the different factors out and multiply. ($2 \times 3 \times 3 \times 5 = 90$)
The common denominator is 90.

Have students work another example.
$\frac{1}{12} + \frac{1}{16}$ (The common denominator is 48.)

Ask questions similar to the questions asked before.

Repeat the activity several times.

When students show an understanding of the process of finding a common denominator using prime factorization, extend the process to actually finding equivalent fractions.

Name ________________ Skill ________________

Find a Common Denominator

Find a common denominator for $\frac{1}{8} + \frac{1}{6}$.

Remember that the least common denominator (LCD) of two fractions is the least common multiple (LCM) of the denominators.

Step 1
List the multiples of each number.

8: 8, 16, 24, 32, 40, ...
6: 6, 12, 18, 24, 30, ...

Step 2
Circle the lowest multiple the numbers have in common.

8: 8, 16, (24) 32, 40, ...
6: 6, 12, 18, (24) 30, ...

Step 3
What is the lowest multiple the numbers have in common? This is the common denominator.

24

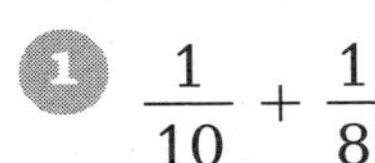

Find the common denominator.

1. $\frac{1}{10} + \frac{1}{8}$
List the multiples of each number.
10: ________
8: ________
What is the lowest multiple the numbers have in common?
____

2. $\frac{1}{4} + \frac{1}{16}$
List the multiples of each number.
4: ________
16: ________
What is the lowest multiple the numbers have in common?
____

3. $\frac{3}{4} + \frac{4}{5}$
List the multiples of each number.
4: ________
5: ________
What is the lowest multiple the numbers have in common?
____

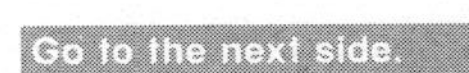

Name ______________________________ Skill ____________________

Practice on Your Own

Skill 23

Find the common denominator for $\frac{1}{15} + \frac{1}{12}$.

List the multiples of each number.
15: 15, 30, 45, 60, 75, 90, ...
12: 12, 24, 36, 48, 60, 72, ...

Circle the lowest multiple the two lists have in common.
The common denominator is 60.

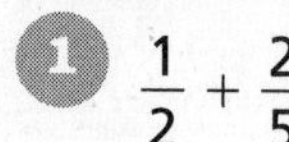

Find the common denominator.

1. $\frac{1}{2} + \frac{2}{5}$
List the multiples of each number.
2: ________
5: ________
What is the lowest multiple the numbers have in common? ________

2. $\frac{2}{3} + \frac{5}{6}$
List the multiples of each number.
3: ________
6: ________
What is the lowest multiple the numbers have in common? ________

3. $\frac{3}{7} + \frac{5}{14}$
List the multiples of each number.
7: ________
14: ________
What is the lowest multiple the numbers have in common? ________

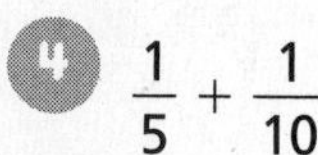

Find the common denominator.

4. $\frac{1}{5} + \frac{1}{10}$

5. $\frac{7}{8} + \frac{5}{12}$

6. $\frac{1}{3} + \frac{3}{5}$

7. $\frac{7}{12} + \frac{9}{16}$

8. $\frac{4}{15} + \frac{1}{30}$

9. $\frac{5}{24} + \frac{1}{18}$

Check

Find the common denominator.

10. $\frac{4}{5} + \frac{5}{6}$

11. $\frac{1}{8} + \frac{9}{32}$

12. $\frac{1}{8} + \frac{1}{14}$

Skill 24 Write Equivalent Fractions

Using Skill 24

OBJECTIVE Use different methods to write equivalent fractions

MATERIALS fraction models

Discuss with your students the meaning of *equivalent*. (equal in value, same amount)

Direct students' attention to Model A. Ask: **To find equivalent fractions, do the fraction models have to be the same length?** (yes) **How many parts is the first fraction model divided into?** (3) **How many parts is the second fraction model divided into?** (6)

How many parts in the second model are equal to 1 part in the first model? (2)

Direct students' attention to Model B. Ask: **What is the factor that both the numerator and the denominator are multiplied by?** (2)

Emphasize that both the numerator and denominator are multiplied by the same number. Ask: **What is the value of $\frac{2}{2}$?** (1) Then recall that any number multiplied by 1 is that number. So, when the fraction $\frac{2}{6}$ is multiplied by $\frac{2}{2}$, the result is an equivalent fraction, $\frac{4}{12}$.

Continue to ask similar questions as you work through Model C.

TRY THESE Exercises 1–4 model the type of exercises students will find in the **Practice on Your Own** page.

- **Exercises 1–2** Equivalent fractions using models
- **Exercises 3–4** Equivalent fractions using multiplication and division; mathematical cues provided

PRACTICE ON YOUR OWN Review the example at the top of the page. Ask students to explain how they know that the models are equivalent and why the numerators and denominators are multiplied or divided by the same number.

CHECK Make sure that the students multiply or divide the numerator and denominator by the same number. Success is indicated by 3 out of 4 correct responses.

Students who successfully complete the **Practice on Your Own** and **Check** are ready to move to the next skill.

COMMON ERRORS

- Students may forget to multiply or divide both the numerator and the denominator by the same number.

Students who made more than 3 errors in the **Practice on Your Own**, or who were not successful in the **Check** section, may benefit from the **Alternative Teaching Strategy** on the next page.

Optional

Alternate Teaching Strategy

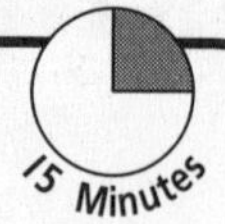

Modeling Equivalent Fractions

OBJECTIVE Use fraction models to model equivalent fractions

MATERIALS models in halves, thirds, fourths, fifths, sixths, eighths, and tenths

You may wish to have the students work in pairs. Have partners take turns. One student models the fraction with the fraction models while the other student records the results on paper.

Write $\frac{1}{2} = \frac{?}{4}$ on the board.

Distribute the fraction models. Direct students to select the fraction model that shows $\frac{1}{2}$.

Ask: **How many equal parts is the fraction model divided into?** (2) **How many parts are shaded?** (1)

Explain that this fraction model is called the **halves** fraction model.

Now point to the fraction $\frac{?}{4}$. Ask: **Which fraction model should you choose next?** (One that is divided into 4 equal parts.)

Which fraction model showing 4 equal parts is equivalent to $\frac{1}{2}$? (The one with 2 of the 4 equal parts shaded.)

Explain that this fraction model is called the **fourths** fraction model because it represents four equal parts.

Have students compare the shaded parts of the two fraction models. Ask: **How many shaded parts in the fourths fraction model are equal to the shaded part in the halves fraction model?** (2)

Have students record the answer on their papers.

Then demonstrate how they can find the same answer by multiplying both the numerator and denominator by 2.

Repeat this activity using fraction models with fractions such as $\frac{1}{4}$ and $\frac{2}{8}$; $\frac{3}{5}$ and $\frac{6}{10}$. For each model, demonstrate how to use multiplication to find the equivalent fraction.

When the students show that they understand how to find equivalent fractions, remove the fraction models and have them use multiplication.

$\frac{1}{2}$	$\frac{1}{2}$	$\frac{1}{2}$

$\frac{1}{4}$	$\frac{1}{4}$	$\frac{1}{4}$	$\frac{1}{4}$	$\frac{2}{4}$

Name ______________________ Skill ______________________

Write Equivalent Fractions

Skill 24

Equivalent fractions represent the same amount. You can use different methods to find equivalent fractions.

Model A
Make a model to show thirds.
Shade $\frac{1}{3}$.
Make another model to show sixths.

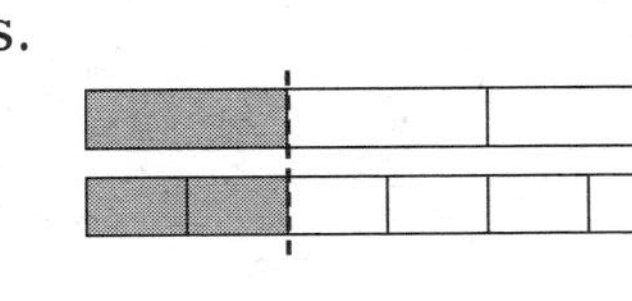

$\frac{1}{3} = \frac{2}{6}$

$\frac{1}{3}$ and $\frac{2}{6}$ represent the same size part.

So, $\frac{1}{3} = \frac{2}{6}$.

Model B
Multiply the numerator and the denominator by the same number to find an equivalent fraction.

$\frac{2 \times 2}{6 \times 2} = \frac{4}{12}$

So, $\frac{2}{6} = \frac{4}{12}$.

Model C
Divide the numerator and the denominator by the same number to find an equivalent fraction.

$\frac{2 \div 2}{6 \div 2} = \frac{1}{3}$

So, $\frac{2}{6} = \frac{1}{3}$.

Try These

Write the equivalent fraction.

1. 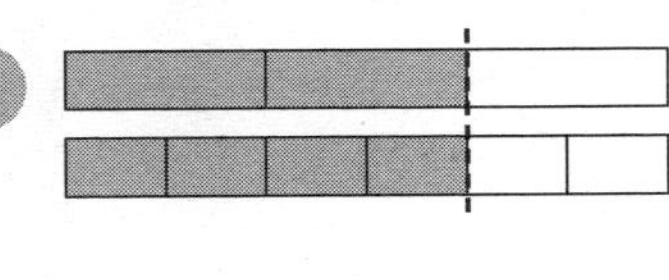

$\frac{2}{3} = \frac{\square}{6}$

2.  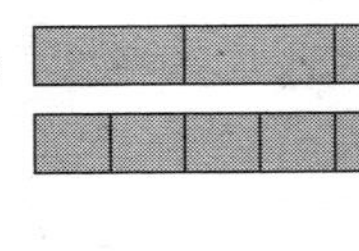 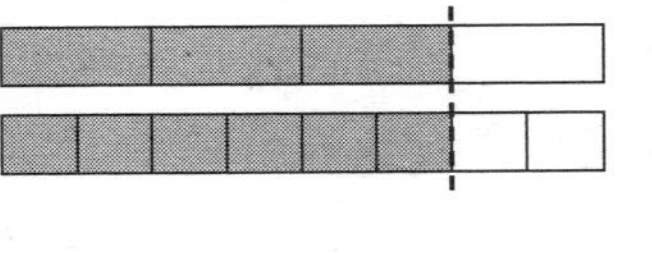

$\frac{3}{4} = \frac{\square}{8}$

3. $\frac{3}{5} = \frac{3 \times 2}{5 \times 2} = \frac{\square}{10}$

4. $\frac{3}{12} = \frac{3 \div 3}{12 \div 3} = \frac{\square}{4}$

Go to the next side.

Name ______________________ Skill ______________________

Practice on Your Own

Skill 24

Think: Multiply or **divide** to find an equivalent fraction.

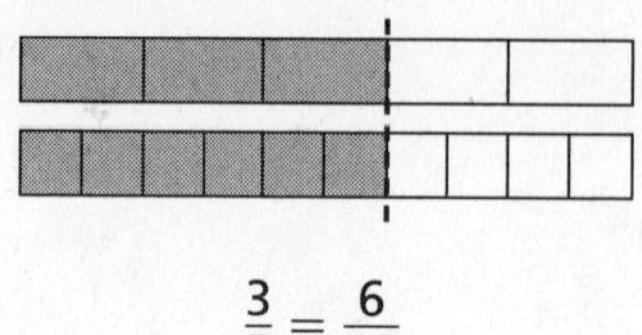

$\frac{3}{5} = \frac{6}{10}$

Multiply

$\frac{3}{5} = \frac{3 \times 2}{5 \times 2} = \frac{6}{10}$

$\frac{3}{5} = \frac{6}{10}$

Divide

$\frac{6}{10} = \frac{6 \div 2}{10 \div 2} = \frac{3}{5}$

$\frac{6}{10} = \frac{3}{5}$

Write the equivalent fraction.

1. $\frac{1}{5} = \frac{?}{10}$

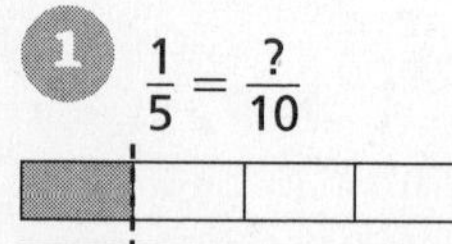

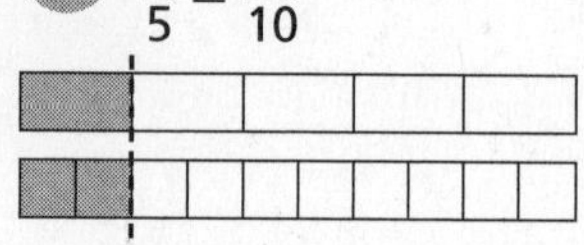

$\frac{1}{5} = \frac{\square}{10}$

2. $\frac{1}{4} = \frac{?}{8}$

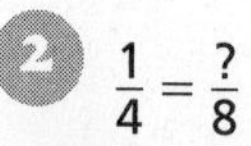

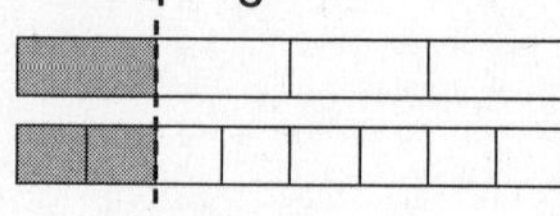

$\frac{1}{4} = \frac{\square}{8}$

3. $\frac{5}{8} = \frac{?}{16}$

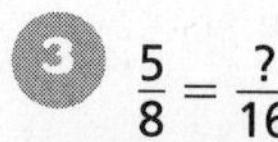

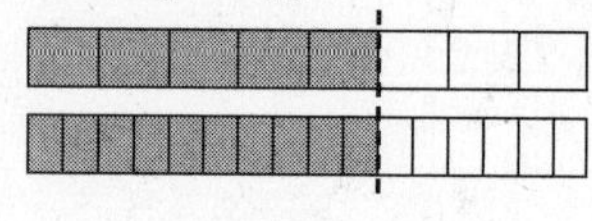

$\frac{5}{8} = \frac{\square}{16}$

4. $\frac{2}{3} = \frac{?}{9}$

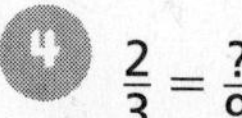

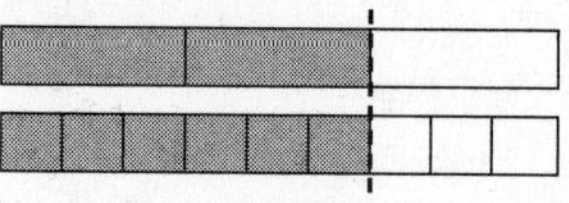

$\frac{2}{3} = \frac{\square}{9}$

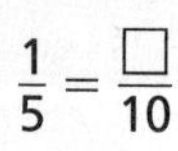

5. $\frac{1}{2} = \frac{?}{6}$

$\frac{\square}{\square} = \frac{\square \times 3}{\square \times 3} = \frac{\square}{6}$

$\frac{1}{2} = \frac{\square}{6}$

6. $\frac{3}{4} = \frac{?}{12}$

$\frac{\square}{\square} = \frac{\square \times 3}{\square \times 3} = \frac{\square}{12}$

$\frac{3}{4} = \frac{\square}{12}$

7. $\frac{1}{6} = \frac{?}{12}$

$\frac{1}{6} = \frac{1 \times \square}{6 \times \square} = \frac{\square}{12}$

$\frac{1}{6} = \frac{\square}{12}$

8. $\frac{2}{5} = \frac{?}{15}$

$\frac{2}{5} = \frac{2 \times \square}{5 \times \square} = \frac{\square}{15}$

$\frac{2}{5} = \frac{\square}{15}$

9. $\frac{6}{16} = \frac{?}{8}$

$\frac{6}{16} = \frac{6 \div 2}{16 \div 2} = \frac{\square}{8}$

$\frac{6}{16} = \frac{\square}{8}$

10. $\frac{12}{12} = \frac{?}{4}$

$\frac{12}{12} = \frac{12 \div 3}{12 \div 3} = \frac{\square}{4}$

$\frac{12}{12} = \frac{\square}{4}$

11. $\frac{2}{18} = \frac{?}{9}$

$\frac{2}{18} = \frac{2 \div \square}{18 \div \square} = \frac{\square}{9}$

$\frac{2}{18} = \frac{\square}{9}$

12. $\frac{4}{20} = \frac{?}{5}$

$\frac{4}{20} = \frac{4 \div \square}{20 \div \square} = \frac{\square}{5}$

13. $\frac{4}{4} = \frac{\square}{8}$

14. $\frac{7}{14} = \frac{\square}{2}$

15. $\frac{15}{25} = \frac{\square}{5}$

16. $\frac{1}{3} = \frac{\square}{21}$

Check

Write the equivalent fraction.

17. $\frac{1}{2} = \frac{\square}{10}$

18. $\frac{8}{12} = \frac{\square}{6}$

19. $\frac{7}{21} = \frac{\square}{3}$

20. $\frac{7}{8} = \frac{\square}{16}$

Skill 25 Compare Fractions

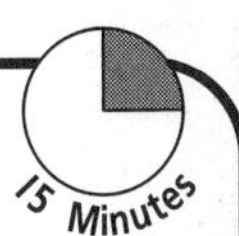

Using Skill 25

OBJECTIVE Compare fractions

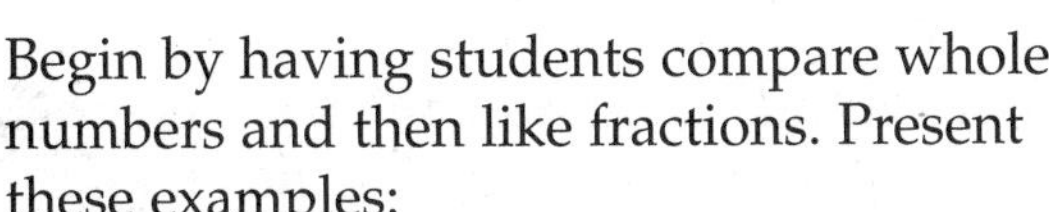

Begin by having students compare whole numbers and then like fractions. Present these examples:

3 ○ 5 $\frac{3}{8}$ ○ $\frac{5}{8}$

Ask: **Is 3 less than, equal to, or greater than 5?** (less than)

Display these symbols: < = >.

Ask: **Which of these symbols do you use to show that 3 is less than 5?** (<)

Display 3 < 5. Point out that the fractions $\frac{3}{8}$ and $\frac{5}{8}$ have like denominators.

Ask: **When you compare two fractions, and the denominators of the fractions are the same, what part of each fraction do you look at?** (the numerator) **Why?** (The numerator tells how many equal parts are being considered. When the denominators are equal, then the size of the equal parts are the same. So, compare the number of parts considered in each fraction.)

Continue: **Is $\frac{3}{8}$ less than, equal to, or greater than $\frac{5}{8}$?** (less than) **How do you know?** (3 is less than 5) **Which symbol do you write to show this?** (<) Display $\frac{3}{8} < \frac{5}{8}$.

For the first example, recall how to write equivalent fractions.

For *Comparing Mixed Numbers,* ask: **What if you are comparing $3\frac{3}{4}$ and $2\frac{5}{6}$, which mixed number do you think is greater?** ($3\frac{3}{4}$) **How can you tell?** (Because you can compare the whole numbers: 3 and 2; since 3 is greater than 2, then $3\frac{3}{4} > 2\frac{5}{6}$.)

For *Comparing Fractions Greater* than 1, ask: **How can you tell that a fraction is greater than 1?** (The numerator is greater than the denominator.)

TRY THESE Exercises 1–4 model the type of exercises students will find on the **Practice on Your Own** page.

- **Exercise 1** Fractions less than 1
- **Exercise 2** Mixed numbers
- **Exercise 3** A fraction less than 1 and a fraction greater than 1
- **Exercise 4** Fractions greater than 1

PRACTICE ON YOUR OWN Review the example at the top of the page. Have students explain why they should change $\frac{10}{5}$ to a whole number.

CHECK Determine if students can compare fractions less than or greater than one.

Success is indicated by 3 out of 3 correct responses.

Students who successfully complete the **Practice on Your Own** and **Check** are ready to move to the next skill.

COMMON ERRORS

- Students may compare numerators without first checking to make sure the denominators are the same.
- Students may compare the fraction parts of two mixed numbers when it is only necessary to compare the whole-number parts.
- Students may not know how to find equivalent fractions.

Students who made more than 3 errors in the **Practice on Your Own**, or who were not successful in the **Check** section, may benefit from the **Alternative Teaching Strategy** on the next page.

Optional

Alternative Teaching Strategy

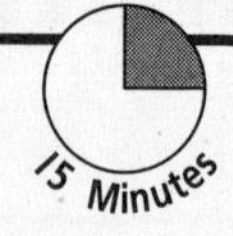

Compare Fractions on a Ruler

OBJECTIVE Use a ruler to compare fractions

MATERIALS inch ruler showing halves, fourths, eighths, and sixteenths

Provide students with rulers or number lines labeled in intervals of halves, fourths, eighths, and sixteenths. If you wish, students can use customary rulers to make their own number lines.

Present like fractions to compare: $\frac{3}{4}$ ○ $\frac{1}{4}$. Students find the point for $\frac{3}{4}$. Then they find the point for $\frac{1}{4}$.

Remind the students that as they move from left to right on the number line, the numbers are greater.

Ask: **Which fraction is greater?** ($\frac{3}{4}$)

Next, show a pair of unlike fractions less than one: $\frac{3}{8}$ ○ $\frac{3}{4}$. Some students may believe that $\frac{3}{8}$ is greater than $\frac{3}{4}$, because the numeral 8 is greater than 4. Use the ruler as a model to help students recognize that the intervals for fourths are greater than the intervals for eighths.

Ask: **Are these fractions, $\frac{3}{8}$ and $\frac{3}{4}$, *equivalent fractions*?** (no) **How do you know?** (They have the same numerator, but different denominators.)

First have students locate $\frac{3}{8}$ and $\frac{3}{4}$ on the ruler. Guide students as they determine that $\frac{3}{8}$ is less than $\frac{3}{4}$.

Ask: **How do you compare these fractions when you do not have a ruler?** (Find equivalent fractions with a common denominator)

Then have students find how many eighths are in $\frac{3}{4}$ by counting the eighth-inch marks on the ruler.

Display $\frac{3}{4} = \frac{6}{8}$ and $\frac{3}{8} = \frac{3}{8}$.

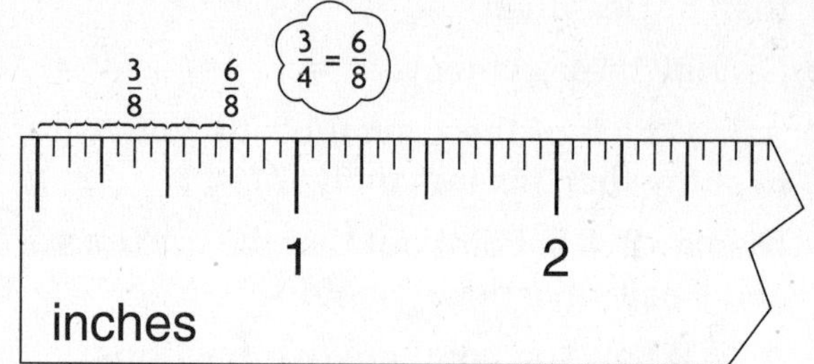

Continue in a similar manner to compare other fractions. Point out that sometimes students only have to compare the whole number parts of mixed numbers to determine the greater number.

$\frac{3}{16}$ ○ $\frac{5}{16}$ (<)

$\frac{5}{8}$ ○ $\frac{3}{4}$ (<)

$\frac{7}{4}$ ○ $\frac{9}{16}$ (>)

$\frac{9}{8}$ ○ $\frac{13}{4}$ (<)

$1\frac{1}{8}$ ○ $1\frac{5}{8}$ (<)

$3\frac{3}{4}$ ○ $4\frac{1}{4}$ (<)

As students demonstrate facility with comparing fractions on the ruler, provide some examples to be completed without the ruler.

Name ______________________ Skill ______________

Compare Fractions

Skill 25

Compare Fractions

Compare $\frac{2}{3}$ and $\frac{5}{9}$.

Since the denominators are different, write equivalent fractions with the same denominator.

$\frac{2}{3} = \frac{2 \times 3}{3 \times 3} = \frac{6}{9}$

$\frac{6}{9} \bigcirc \frac{5}{9}$

Think: 9 is a multiple of 3, so rewrite $\frac{2}{3}$ as an equivalent fraction with a denominator of 9.

Compare numerators.

Since $6 > 5$, then $\frac{6}{9} > \frac{5}{9}$.

So, $\frac{2}{3} > \frac{5}{9}$.

Compare Mixed Numbers

Compare $1\frac{3}{4}$ and $1\frac{5}{6}$.

Compare the whole numbers first. They are the same.

$\frac{3}{4} = \frac{3 \times 3}{4 \times 3} = \frac{9}{12}$

$\frac{5}{6} = \frac{5 \times 2}{6 \times 2} = \frac{10}{12}$

$\frac{9}{12} \bigcirc \frac{10}{12}$

Since denominators are different, rewrite each fraction as an equivalent fraction with the same denominator. Compare numerators.

Since $9 < 10$, then $\frac{9}{12} < \frac{10}{12}$.

So, $1\frac{3}{4} < 1\frac{5}{6}$.

Compare Fractions Greater than 1

Compare $\frac{3}{5}$ and $\frac{5}{3}$.

$\frac{3}{5} \bigcirc \frac{5}{3}$

Since $\frac{5}{5} = 1$, then $\frac{3}{5} < 1$.

If $\frac{3}{3} = 1$, then $\frac{5}{3} > 1$.

So, $\frac{3}{5} < \frac{5}{3}$.

Compare $\frac{18}{9}$ and $\frac{15}{3}$.

$\frac{18}{9} \bigcirc \frac{15}{3}$

Each fraction is greater than 1. Divide the numerator by the denominator.

$18 \div 9 = 2$ $\quad$ $15 \div 3 = 5$

$2 < 5$

Compare whole numbers.

Since $2 < 5$, then $\frac{18}{9} < \frac{15}{3}$.

So, $\frac{18}{9} < \frac{15}{3}$.

Try These

Compare. Write >, <, or =.

1. $\frac{1}{2} \bigcirc \frac{3}{4}$

   Same denominator? ____

   $\frac{2}{4} \bigcirc \frac{3}{4}$

   $\frac{1}{2} \bigcirc \frac{3}{4}$

2. $2\frac{1}{3} \bigcirc 2\frac{1}{4}$

   Whole numbers same? ____

   Same denominator? ____

   $2\frac{\square}{12} \bigcirc 2\frac{\square}{12}$

   $2\frac{1}{3} \bigcirc 2\frac{1}{4}$

3. $\frac{3}{4} \bigcirc \frac{5}{3}$

   Less than 1 or greater than 1?

   $\frac{3}{4} \bigcirc \frac{5}{3}$

4. $\frac{14}{7} \bigcirc \frac{10}{5}$

   ↓ $\quad$ ↓

   $14 \div 7$ $\quad$ $10 \div 5$

   ↓ $\quad$ ↓

   ____ $\bigcirc$ ____

Go to the next side.

Name ______________________ Skill ______________________

Practice on Your Own

Skill 25

Compare $5\frac{1}{10}$ and $\frac{10}{5}$.

$5\frac{1}{10} \bigcirc \frac{10}{5}$	The fraction is greater than 1.
$10 \div 5 = 2$	Divide the numerator by the denominator.
$5\frac{1}{10} > 2$	Compare whole numbers. Since $5 > 2$, then $5\frac{1}{10} > \frac{10}{5}$.

So, $5\frac{1}{10} > \frac{10}{5}$.

Compare. Write >, <, or =.

1. $\frac{5}{6} \bigcirc \frac{4}{12}$
   Same denominator? $\underline{\ ?\ }$
   $\frac{\square}{12} \bigcirc \frac{4}{12}$
   $\frac{5}{6} \bigcirc \frac{4}{12}$

2. $4\frac{3}{5} \bigcirc 4\frac{7}{10}$
   Whole numbers same? ____
   Same denominator? ____
   $4\frac{\square}{10} \bigcirc 4\frac{7}{10}$
   $4\frac{3}{5} \bigcirc 4\frac{7}{10}$

3. $2\frac{1}{3} \bigcirc \frac{6}{2}$
   ↓
   $6 \div 2$
   $2\frac{1}{3} \bigcirc 3$

4. $\frac{3}{6} \bigcirc \frac{5}{12}$
   Same denominator? ____
   $\frac{\square}{12} \bigcirc \frac{5}{12}$
   $\frac{3}{6} \bigcirc \frac{5}{12}$

5. $\frac{4}{5} \bigcirc \frac{5}{4}$ Less than 1 or greater than 1?

6. $2\frac{1}{3} \bigcirc \frac{10}{5}$
   $10 \div 5$
   ↓ ↓
   $2\frac{1}{3}$ $\bigcirc$ ____

7. $3\frac{3}{5} \bigcirc 3\frac{3}{4}$
   Whole numbers same? ____
   Same denominator? ____
   $3\frac{\square}{20} \bigcirc 3\frac{\square}{20}$
   $3\frac{3}{5} \bigcirc 3\frac{3}{4}$

8. $\frac{5}{7} \bigcirc \frac{7}{4}$ Less than 1 or greater than 1?

9. $4\frac{1}{3} \bigcirc \frac{9}{3}$
   ↓
   $9 \div 3$
   $4\frac{1}{3} \bigcirc$ ____

10. $\frac{2}{5} \bigcirc \frac{3}{4}$

11. $\frac{8}{3} \bigcirc \frac{3}{8}$

12. $2\frac{1}{8} \bigcirc \frac{8}{2}$

Check

Compare. Write >, <, or =.

13. $\frac{1}{3} \bigcirc \frac{1}{4}$

14. $2\frac{5}{6} \bigcirc 2\frac{1}{4}$

15. $\frac{8}{4} \bigcirc \frac{9}{3}$

Skill 26 Write Fractions as Decimals

Using Skill 26

OBJECTIVE Write a decimal for a fraction

You may wish to begin by reviewing the different ways to show division.

$1 \div 2 \qquad 2\overline{)1} \qquad \frac{1}{2}$

Explain to students that to write a fraction as a decimal, divide.

Direct students' attention to Step 1. Ask: **Which number is the divisor in the fraction $\frac{1}{2}$?** (2) **Which number is the dividend?** (1) **Which number is the divisor in the fraction $\frac{3}{4}$?** (4) **Which number is the dividend?** (3)

Direct students' attention to Step 2. Show how to place the decimal point and a zero in the dividend. Ask: **Where do you place the decimal point in the quotient?** (above the decimal point in the dividend)

Direct students' attention to Step 3. Point out that they divide decimals as they would whole numbers. Then work through the division steps with students. Emphasize how to write zeros in the dividend until the remainder equals zero or until they have the number of decimal places in the quotient that they need.

TRY THESE In Exercises 1–3 students divide to write a fraction as a decimal.

- **Exercise 1** Write $\frac{2}{5}$ as 0.4.
- **Exercise 2** Write $\frac{3}{20}$ as 0.15.
- **Exercise 3** Write $\frac{3}{50}$ as 0.06.

PRACTICE ON YOUR OWN Review the example at the top of the page. Ask: **Which number in the fraction $\frac{5}{8}$ is the divisor?** (8) **Which number is the dividend?** (5) Discuss how to place the decimal point in the quotient and then divide as if dividing whole numbers.

CHECK Determine if students know how to divide the numerator of a fraction by the denominator to find an equivalent decimal. Success is indicated by 3 out of 3 correct responses.

Students who successfully complete the **Practice on Your Own** and **Check** are ready to move to the next skill.

COMMON ERRORS

- Students may misplace the decimal point or not write it at all in the quotient.
- Students may make errors in dividing because they have not yet mastered their division facts.
- Students may forget to write a zero in the quotient and may write the quotient 2.01 as 2.1.

Students who made more than 1 error in the **Practice on Your Own**, or who were not successful in the **Check** section, may benefit from the **Alternative Teaching Strategy** on the next page.

Optional

Alternative Teaching Strategy

15 Minutes

Use Questioning Strategies to Understand Equivalent Fractions and Decimals

OBJECTIVE Find equivalent fractions with denominators of 10, 100, or 1,000 to write equivalent decimals

Recall with students that a fraction can be written as an equivalent decimal. Remind students that all decimals can be written as fractions with denominators of 10, 100, 1,000, and so on. Guide students to understand that if they write a fraction as an equivalent fraction with a denominator of 10, 100, or 1,000, then they can write the equivalent decimal.

Display $\frac{1}{2} = \frac{?}{10}$. Mention that one way to write equivalent fractions is to multiply the numerator and denominator by the same number. Ask: **What number times 2 equals 10?** (5) **Say: If we multiply the denominator by 5, what must we do to the numerator?** (Multiply it by 5.) Display $\frac{1}{2} = \frac{5}{10}$. Ask: **Is 10 a multiple of 2?** (yes) **How many tenths equal $\frac{1}{2}$?** (5) **How do you write 5 tenths as a decimal?** (0.5)

Point out that the fraction $\frac{1}{2}$ is equivalent to the decimal 0.5.

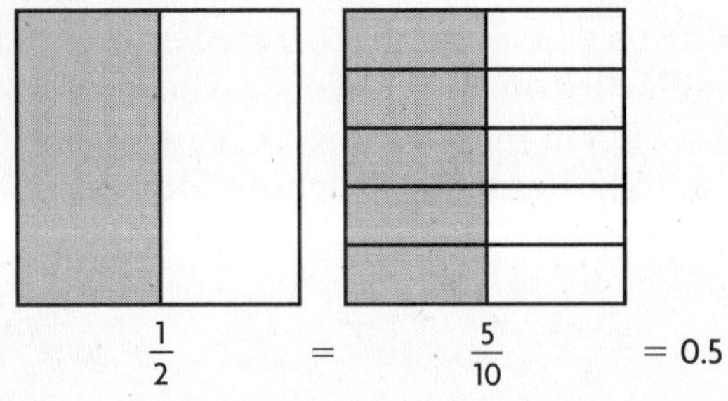

$\frac{1}{2} = \frac{5}{10} = 0.5$

Next, display $\frac{3}{4} = \frac{?}{100}$.

Ask: **What number times 4 equals 100?** (25) **If we multiply the denominator by 25, what must we do to the numerator?** (Multiply it by 25.)

Display: $\frac{3}{4} = \frac{75}{100}$. Ask: **How do you write 75 hundredths as a decimal?** (0.75)

Point out that the fraction $\frac{3}{4}$ is equivalent to the decimal 0.75.

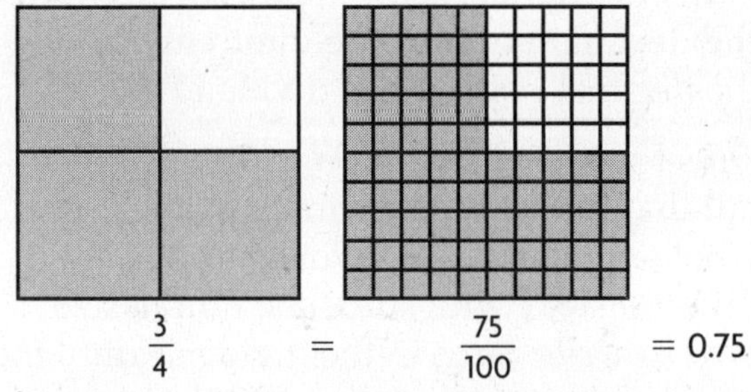

$\frac{3}{4} = \frac{75}{100} = 0.75$

Display $\frac{13}{20} = \frac{?}{100}$. Use the same questioning as in the previous two examples.

Point out that the fraction $\frac{13}{20}$ is equivalent to the decimal 0.65.

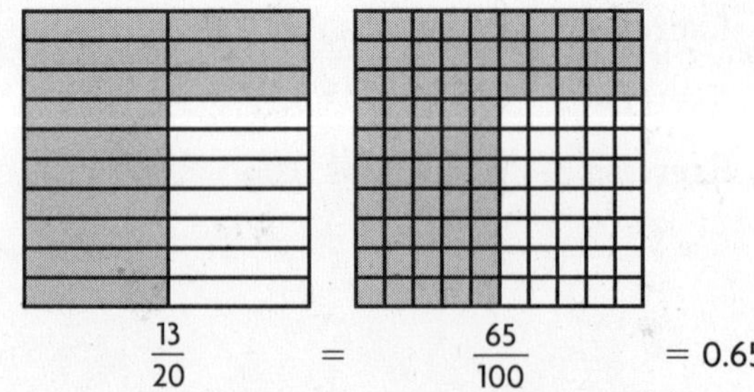

$\frac{13}{20} = \frac{65}{100} = 0.65$

Repeat the activity using the fractions

$\frac{1}{4}$ ($\frac{25}{100}$, 0.25), $\frac{3}{5}$ ($\frac{6}{10}$, 0.6), $\frac{7}{20}$ ($\frac{35}{100}$, 0.35), $\frac{19}{25}$ ($\frac{76}{100}$, 0.76), and $\frac{7}{8}$ ($\frac{875}{1,000}$, 0.875).

Name ____________________ Skill ____________________

Write Fractions as Decimals

Skill 26

Divide to write a fraction as a decimal.
Write $\frac{1}{2}$ and $\frac{3}{4}$ as decimals.

Step 1
Divide the numerator by the denominator.

$\frac{1}{2} \rightarrow 2\overline{)1}$ $\qquad \frac{3}{4} \rightarrow 4\overline{)3}$

Remember you can think of a fraction $\frac{a}{b}$ as $a \div b$.

Step 2
Write a decimal point followed by a 0 in the dividend. Then place a decimal point in the quotient.

$2\overline{)1.0}$ $\qquad 4\overline{)3.0}$

Step 3
Divide as you would with whole numbers, until the remainder is 0 or until you have the number of decimal places you need.

$$\begin{array}{r} 0.5 \\ 2\overline{)1.0} \\ -1\,0 \\ \hline 0 \end{array} \qquad \begin{array}{rl} 0.75 & \\ 4\overline{)3.00} & \\ -2\,8 & \leftarrow 7 \times 4 = 28 \\ \hline 20 & \\ -20 & \leftarrow 5 \times 4 = 20 \\ \hline 0 & \end{array}$$

So, $\frac{1}{2} = 0.5$ and $\frac{3}{4} = 0.75$.

Try These

Write each fraction as a decimal.

1. $\frac{2}{5} \rightarrow$ $\begin{array}{r} 0.\square \\ 5\overline{)2.0} \\ -\square\square \\ \hline \square \end{array}$

2. $\frac{3}{20} \rightarrow$ $\begin{array}{r} 0.1\square \\ 20\overline{)3.00} \\ -\square\square \\ \hline \square\square\square \\ -\square\square\square \\ \hline \square \end{array}$

3. $\frac{3}{50} \rightarrow$ $\begin{array}{r} 0.0\square \\ 50\overline{)3.0\,0} \\ -\square\square\square \\ \hline \square \end{array}$

Go to the next side.

Name ______________________ Skill ______________________

Practice on Your Own

Skill 26

Think:

First, write the fraction as a division problem. Then write a decimal point and a zero in the dividend. Place a decimal point in the quotient. Write more zeros in the dividend, if necessary.

$\frac{5}{8} \rightarrow$ $8\overline{)5.000}$ = 0.625

-48 $6 \times 8 = 48$

20

-16 $2 \times 8 = 16$

40

-40 $5 \times 8 = 40$

0

Write each fraction as a decimal.

1. $\frac{4}{5} \rightarrow$ $5\overline{)4.0}$ = 0.□; −□□; □

   $\frac{4}{5}$ = ______

2. $\frac{1}{4} \rightarrow$ $4\overline{)1.0\,0}$ = 0.□□; −□; □□; −□□; □

   $\frac{1}{4}$ = ______

3. $\frac{13}{20} \rightarrow$ $20\overline{)13.0\,0}$ = 0.□□; −□□□; □□□; −□□□; □

   $\frac{13}{20}$ = ______

4. $\frac{7}{10} \rightarrow$ $10\overline{)7.0}$ = 0.

   $\frac{7}{10}$ = ______

5. $\frac{1}{5} \rightarrow$ $5\overline{)1.0}$ = 0.

   $\frac{1}{5}$ = ______

6. $\frac{5}{8} \rightarrow$ $8\overline{)5.000}$ = 0.

   $\frac{5}{8}$ = ______

7. $\frac{1}{2}$ = ______

8. $\frac{12}{25}$ = ______

9. $\frac{7}{8}$ = ______

Check

Write each fraction as a decimal.

10. $\frac{9}{20}$ = ______

11. $\frac{3}{8}$ = ______

12. $\frac{2}{25}$ = ______

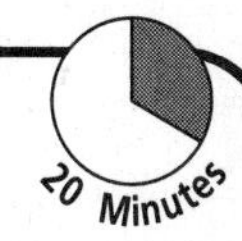

Using Skill 27

OBJECTIVE Write ratios

Have students look at the problem and remind them that the terms of a ratio are the numbers or items that they are comparing.

Direct students' attention to Step 1 and have students answer the questions. How many hearts (3) and squares (5) are there?

Ask: **How do you know in what order to write the numbers?** (By the order the words are given.)

What would the ratio represent if it was written 5:3? (The number of squares to the number of hearts.)

Direct students to look at Step 2 and teach the three ways ratios can be written.

TRY THESE In Exercises 1–3 students answer the questions and write the appropriate ratio in three different ways.

- **Exercise 1** 4 to 3; 4:3; or $\frac{4}{3}$
- **Exercise 2** 6 to 5: 6:5; or $\frac{6}{5}$
- **Exercise 3** 6 to 11; 6:11 or $\frac{6}{11}$

PRACTICE ON YOUR OWN Review the example at the top of the page.

Make sure students understand that the 9 is listed first in the ratio because you are comparing squares to triangles.

CHECK Determine if students know how to write a ratio. Success is indicated by 3 out of 3 correct responses.

Students who successfully complete the **Practice on Your Own** and **Check** are ready to move to the next skill.

COMMON ERRORS

- Students will write the terms in the incorrect order. Have students write the words and then the number that corresponds to each word.

Students who made more than 3 errors in the **Practice on Your Own**, or who were not successful in the **Check** section, may benefit from the **Alternative Teaching Strategy** on the next page.

Optional

Alternative Teaching Strategy

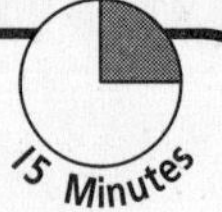

Using Manipulatives to Write Ratios

OBJECTIVE Write a ratio

MATERIALS one package or container containing 20 colored candies for each student or pair of students

You may wish to have students work in pairs. One student counts the candy and the other student records the results.

Create a vertical chart on the chalkboard with the different colors of candy as the headings (red, brown, orange, yellow, green, blue).

Remind students that a ratio is a comparison of two numbers and that they can be written 3 different ways.

Have students copy the chart from the chalkboard onto a sheet of paper.

Have students count the number of each color of candy from their bags and record the results in the chart.

Ask: **What is the ratio of red to the total number of candy?** (Answers will vary but the denominator will be 20)

What is the ratio of red to brown?

Have students write the ratio they have for each color to the total.

Have the students eat half (10) of the candy (any color they wish) and then make a new chart with the new ratios.

If students are still having difficulty writing ratios repeat the activity one more time by having them eat half (5) more of the candy and completing the chart with the new ratios.

Candy Chart

Red	Brown	Orange	Yellow	Green	Blue
~~||||~~	|||	|	||	||||	~~||||~~

Name ______________________ Skill ______________________

Writing Ratios

Skill 27

Write the ratio of hearts to squares.

Remember that the terms of a ratio are the numbers you are comparing.

Step 1	**Step 2**
Identify the terms of the ratio.	Write the ratio of hearts to squares.
How many hearts are there?	A ratio can be written 3 different ways:
How many squares are there?	Word form: 3 to 5
	Ratio form: 3:5
	Fraction form: $\frac{3}{5}$

Try These

Write each ratio three different ways.

1. 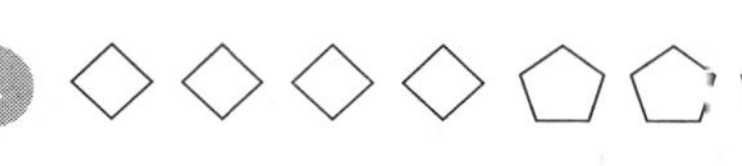

Diamonds to pentagons
How many diamonds are there? ____
How many pentagons are there? ____
Ratios: ______________________

2. 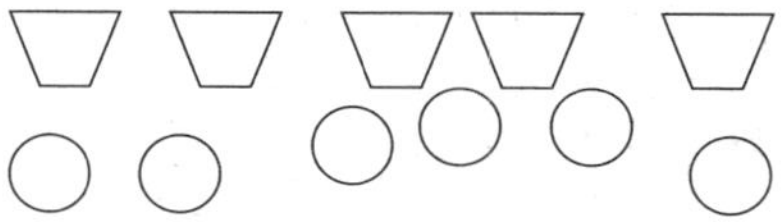 Circles to trapezoids
How many circles are there? ____
How many trapezoids are there? ____
Ratios: ______________________

3. 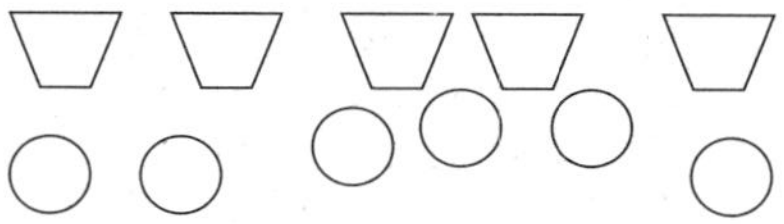 Circles to total figures
How many circles are there? ____
What is the total number of figures? ____
Ratios: ______________________

Go to the next side.

Practice on Your Own

Skill 27

Write the ratio of squares to triangles.

Count the number of squares.
Count the number of triangles
Write the ratio 3 different ways.

Word Form	Ratio Form	Fraction form
9 to 7	9:7	$\frac{9}{7}$

Write each ratio three different ways.
Use the figure for Exercises 1 to 3.

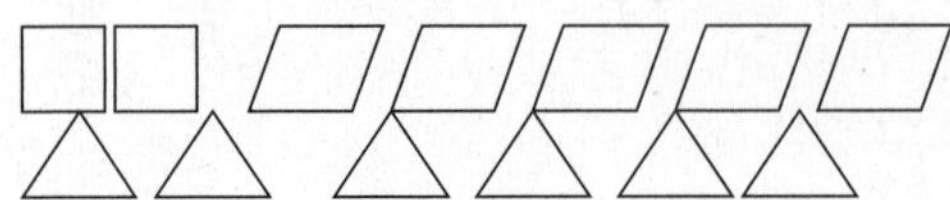

1. squares to triangles
   How many squares? ____
   How many triangles? ____
   Ratios: ______________

2. parallelograms to squares. How many parallelograms? ____
   How many squares? ____
   Ratios: ______________

3. triangles to all shapes
   How many triangles? ____
   How many shapes? ____
   Ratios: ______________

Write each ratio three different ways.

4. 25 girls to 15 boys ______________
5. 13 apples to 12 plums ______________
6. 24 pencils to 11 pens ______________
7. 9 forks to 13 spoons ______________
8. 15 chairs to 7 desks ______________
9. 12 cups to 7 plates ______________

Check

Write each ratio three different ways.

10. 
    smiley faces to hearts ______________

11. 15 cars to 21 tires ______________

12. 9 gloves to 2 balls ______________

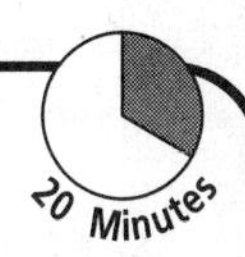

Using Skill 28

OBJECTIVE Simplify ratios

Have students look at the example at the top of the page.
Ask: **Is the ratio in simplest form?** (no)
How do you know? (The numerator and denominator are both even numbers and contain a common factor)

Direct students' attention to Step 1 and have students work through the process to simplify the ratio.

TRY THESE In Exercises 1–3 students find the GCF and then divide to simplify the ratio.

- **Exercise 1** $\frac{2}{5}$
- **Exercise 2** GCF $= 6$; $\frac{3}{2}$
- **Exercise 3** GCF $= 2$; $\frac{16}{45}$

PRACTICE ON YOUR OWN Review the example at the top of the page.

Ask students to explain how they know whether a ratio is in simplified form. (The numerator and denominator do not have any factors in common other than 1.)

CHECK Determine if students know how to simplify a ratio. Success is indicated by 3 out of 3 correct responses.

Students who successfully complete the **Practice On Your Own** and **Check** are ready to move to the next skill.

COMMON ERRORS

- Students reduce the ratio incorrectly. Stress that they need to divide the numerator and denominator by the same number.

Students who made more than 3 errors in the **Practice On Your Own**, or who were not successful in the **Check** section, may benefit from the **Alternative Teaching Strategy** on the next page.

Optional

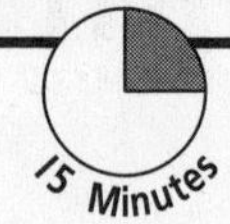

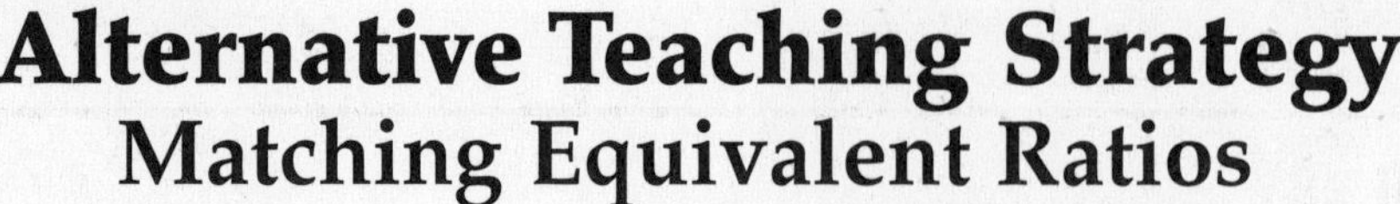

Alternative Teaching Strategy

Matching Equivalent Ratios

OBJECTIVE Simplify a ratio

MATERIALS set of cards with equivalent ratios

Place students in groups of 2, 3 or 4.

Prepare a set of cards for each group of students. For each pair of cards, one card should contain a simplified ratio and the other should have a ratio equivalent to the simplified ratio. For example:

$\frac{2}{3}$ $\frac{6}{9}$  $\frac{3}{4}$

Have students shuffle the cards and place them face down. One student turns over two cards. If they are a set of equivalent ratios, they keep the cards and take another turn. If the cards do not "match", they turn the cards over and play passes to the next player.

If students are still having difficulty identifying simplified ratios, have them repeat the activity with another set of cards.

Name ______________________ Skill ______________________

Simplify Ratios

Skill 28

A ratio is in simplest form when the *greatest common factor*, or GCF of the numerator and denominator is 1.
Simplify: 24 girls to 12 boys.

Step 1
Write the ratio as a simplified fraction.

$\frac{24}{12}$

Write the factors of the numerator and denominator.

$\frac{\text{numerator} \rightarrow \ 24}{\text{denominator} \rightarrow \ 12} \quad \frac{1, 2, 3, 4, 6, 8, 12, 24}{1, 2, 3, 4, 6, 12}$

Step 2
Look for the common factors. Circle the greatest common factor. (*GCF*)

$\frac{\text{numerator} \rightarrow \ 24}{\text{denominator} \rightarrow \ 12} \quad \frac{1, 2, 3, 4, 6, 8, (12), 24}{1, 2, 3, 4, 6, (12)}$

Step 3
Divide the numerator and the denominator by the GCF.

$\frac{24}{12} = \frac{24 \div 12}{12 \div 12} = \frac{2}{1}$

The simplest form of 24:12 is 2:1.

Try These

Simplify each ratio.

1. 6:15

   Find and circle the GCF.

   $\frac{6}{15} \quad \frac{1, 2, 3, 6}{1, 3, 5, 15}$

   Divide the numerator and denominator by the GCF.

   $\frac{6 \div 3}{15 \div 3} = \frac{\square}{\square}$

2. 18 to 12

   Find and circle the GCF.

   $\frac{18}{12} \quad \frac{1, 2, 3, 6, 9, 18}{1, 2, 3, 4, 6, 12}$

   Divide the numerator and denominator by the GCF.

   $\frac{18 \div \square}{12 \div \square} = \frac{\square}{\square}$

3. 32 plates to 90 cups

   Find and circle the GCF.

   $\frac{32}{90} \quad \frac{1, 2, 4, 8, 16, 32}{1, 2, 3, 5, 6, 9, 10, 15, 18, 30, 45, 90}$

   Divide the numerator and denominator by the GCF.

   $\frac{32 \div \square}{90 \div \square} = \frac{\square}{\square}$

Go to the next side.

Name ______________________ Skill ______________

Practice on Your Own — Skill 28

Write the ratio 45 stars to 25 moons in simplest form.

Step 1 List all the factors of the numerator and the denominator. Circle the GCF.	$\frac{45}{25}$ $\frac{1, 3, (5), 9, 15, 45}{1, (5), 25}$
Step 2 Divide the numerator and denominator by the GCF.	$\frac{45}{25} = \frac{45 \div 5}{25 \div 5} = \frac{9}{5}$

Write each ratio in simplest form.

1. $\frac{10}{5}$

   Circle the GCF.

   $\frac{10}{5}$ $\frac{1, 2, 5, 10}{1, 5}$

   Divide the numerator and denominator by the GCF.

   $\frac{10 \div \square}{5 \div \square} = \frac{\square}{\square}$

2. $\frac{21}{27}$

   Circle the GCF.

   $\frac{21}{27}$ $\frac{1, 3, 7, 21}{1, 3, 9, 27}$

   Divide the numerator and denominator by the GCF.

   $\frac{21 \div \square}{27 \div \square} = \frac{\square}{\square}$

3. 30 to 20

   Circle the GCF.

   $\frac{30}{20}$ $\frac{1, 2, 3, 5, 6, 10, 15, 30}{1, 2, 4, 5, 10, 20}$

   Divide the numerator and denominator by the GCF.

   $\frac{30 \div \square}{20 \div \square} = \frac{\square}{\square}$

Write the factors. Find the GCF. Then write the ratio in simplest form.

4. 8:10

   8 ________

   10 ________

   GCF ____

   simplest form ____

5. $\frac{12}{8}$

   12 ________

   8 ________

   GCF ____

   simplest form ____

6. 24 bats to 30 balls

   24 ________

   30 ________

   GCF ____

   simplest form ____

Write each ratio in simplest form.

7. 40 to 35

   ____

8. $\frac{30}{18}$

   ____

9. 85 spoons to 15 forks

   ____

Check

Write each ratio in simplest form.

10. 5 to 20

    ____

11. 15 hearts to 5 stars

    ____

12. $\frac{16}{12}$

    ____

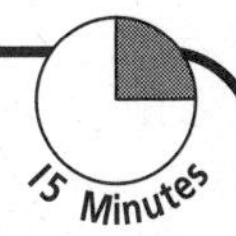

Using Skill 29

OBJECTIVE Understand that a percent is a ratio of a number to 100

Before beginning the skill, recall that a *ratio* is a comparison between two numbers. Then review the meaning of *percent:* the ratio of a number to 100. Point out that students can use a 10 × 10 grid to represent percents.

Direct student's attention to the first example. Ask: **How many squares in all are in the grid?** (100) **How many squares are shaded?** (100)

Discuss with students how to write a ratio to represent the number of shaded squares to the total number of squares. Ask: **What is the ratio of shaded squares to total number of squares in the grid?** ($\frac{100}{100}$)

Explain that students can look at the numerator to determine how to write a fraction as a percent. Since percent means per hundred, the numerator represents the number to the left of the percent sign.

What percent of the grid is shaded? (100%)

Continue in a similar way for the remaining three examples.

TRY THESE Exercises 1–4 model the type of exercises students will find on the **Practice on Your Own** page.

- **Exercise 1** Percent for 24 of 100 squares
- **Exercise 2** Percent for 35 of 100 squares
- **Exercise 3** Percent for 68 of 100 squares
- **Exercise 4** Percent for 81 of 100 squares

PRACTICE ON YOUR OWN Review the example at the top of the page. In Exercises 1–3, students write the ratio and percent for the number of shaded squares in a 10 × 10 grid. In Exercises 4–6, students write only the percent for the number of shaded squares in a 10 × 10 grid.

CHECK Determine if students can write the percent for the number of shaded squares in a 10 × 10 grid. Success is indicated by 2 out of 3 correct responses.

Students who successfully complete the **Practice on Your Own** and **Check** are ready to move to the next skill.

COMMON ERRORS

- Students may make an error in counting the number of shaded squares in a 10 × 10 grid.
- Students may write the number of unshaded squares as the percent.

Students who made more than 2 errors in the **Practice on Your Own**, or who were not successful in the **Check** section, may benefit from the **Alternative Teaching Strategy** on the next page.

Optional

Alternative Teaching Strategy

Modeling Percents

OBJECTIVE Understand percent as a ratio of a number to 100

MATERIALS graph paper, pencil

Distribute graph paper to students. Have students outline a 10×10 grid. Ask:

How many squares are there in the grid? (100)

Ask students to shade 25 squares in the grid.

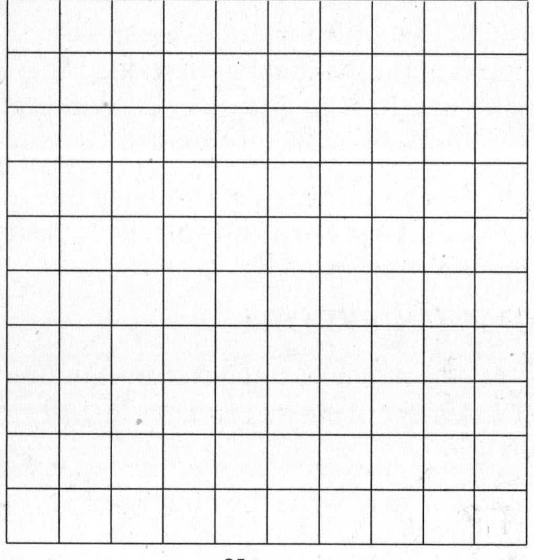

$\frac{25}{100} = 25\%$

Discuss with students the fact that of the 100 total squares 25 are shaded. Tell students that comparing the number of shaded squares to the total number of squares is called a ratio. Ask:

What is the ratio of shaded squares to total squares in this grid? ($\frac{25}{100}$)

Remind students that a *percent* is a ratio of a number to 100. Guide students to understand that if a denominator is 100, then the numerator is the percent. Ask:

What percent of the grid is shaded? (25%)

Have students record the ratio and the equivalent percent below the grid.

Repeat this activity with similar examples. When students show understanding, have them try an exercise using only paper and pencil.

Name ______________________ Skill ______________________

Skill 29

Model Percents

Percent means "per hundred".
Percent is a ratio of a number to 100. Use a 10 x 10 grid to represent percents.

There are 100 squares in the grid.

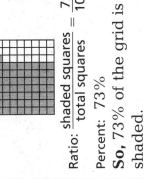

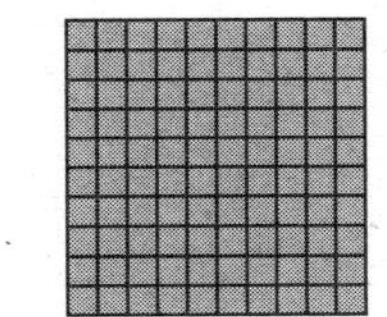

Ratio: $\frac{\text{shaded squares}}{\text{total squares}} = \frac{100}{100}$

So, 100% of the grid is shaded.

In this grid, 1 out of 100 squares is shaded.

Ratio: $\frac{\text{shaded squares}}{\text{total squares}} = \frac{1}{100}$

Percent: 1%

So, 1% of the grid is shaded.

In this grid, 20 out of 100 squares are shaded.

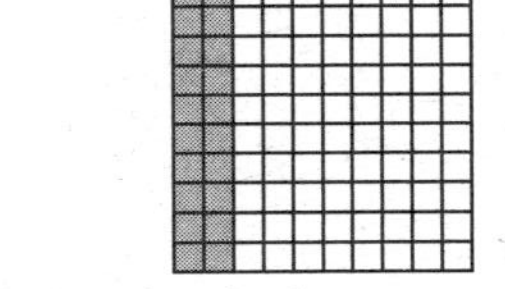

Ratio: $\frac{\text{shaded squares}}{\text{total squares}} = \frac{20}{100}$

Percent: 20%

So, 20% of the grid is shaded.

In this grid, 73 out of 100 squares are shaded.

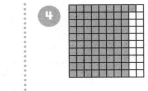

Ratio: $\frac{\text{shaded squares}}{\text{total squares}} = \frac{73}{100}$

Percent: 73%

So, 73% of the grid is shaded.

Try These

Write the ratio of shaded squares to total squares. Write the percent that tells what part is shaded.

1. 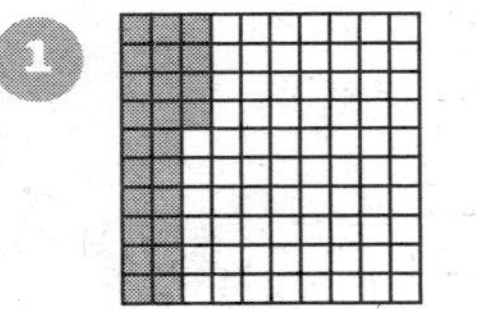

   Ratio: $\frac{\text{shaded}}{\text{total}} = \frac{\square}{100}$

   Percent: ____ %

2. 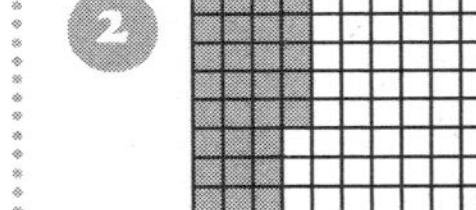

   Ratio: $\frac{\text{shaded}}{\text{total}} = \frac{\square}{100}$

   Percent: ____ %

3. 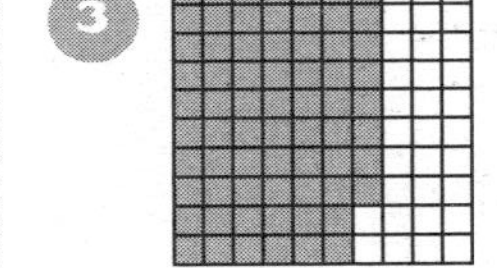

   Ratio: $\frac{\text{shaded}}{\text{total}} = \frac{\square}{100}$

   Percent: ____ %

4. 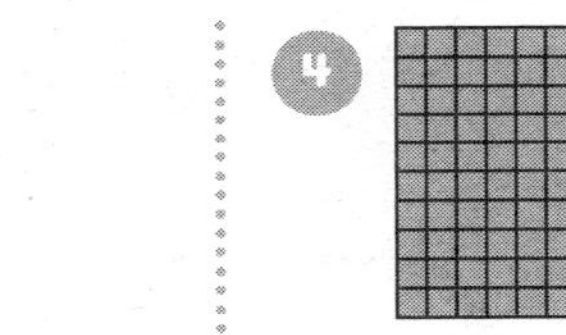

   Ratio: $\frac{\text{shaded}}{\text{total}} = \frac{\square}{100}$

   Percent: ____ %

Go to the next side.

Name ______________________ Skill ______________________

Practice on Your Own

Skill 29

A percent is a ratio of a number to 100.

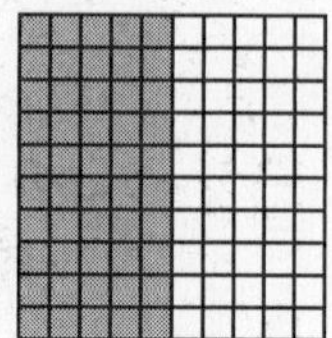

50 out of 100 squares are shaded.
So, 50% of the squares are shaded.

Ratio: $\frac{\text{shaded squares}}{\text{total squares}} = \frac{50}{100} = 50\%$

Write the ratio of shaded squares to total squares.
Write the percent that tells what part is shaded.

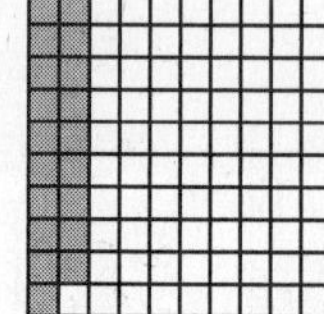

Ratio: $\frac{\text{shaded}}{\text{total}} = \frac{\square}{100}$

Percent: _____ %

2 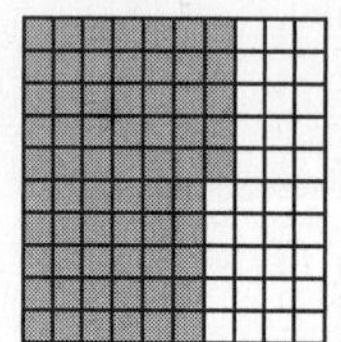

Ratio: $\frac{\text{shaded}}{\text{total}} = \frac{\square}{100}$

Percent: _____ %

3 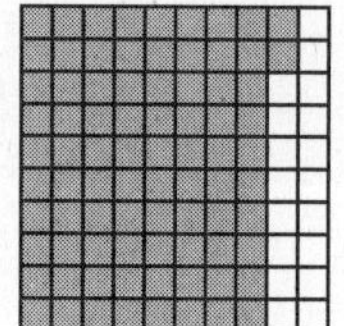

Ratio: $\frac{\text{shaded}}{\text{total}} = \frac{\square}{100}$

Percent: _____ %

Write the percent for the shaded part.

4 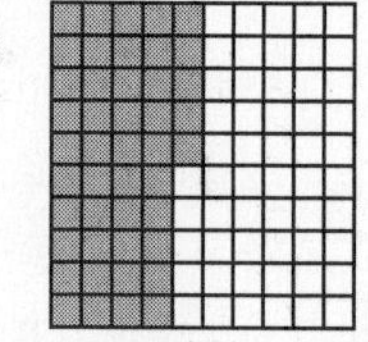

Ratio: $\frac{\text{shaded}}{\text{total}} = \frac{\square}{100}$

Percent: _____ %

5 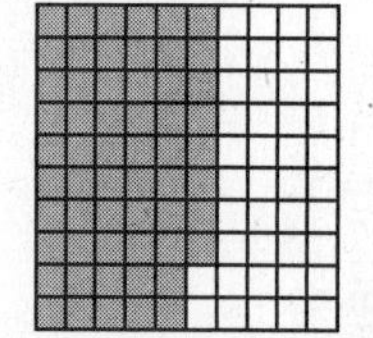

Ratio: $\frac{\text{shaded}}{\text{total}} = \frac{\square}{100}$

Percent: _____ %

6 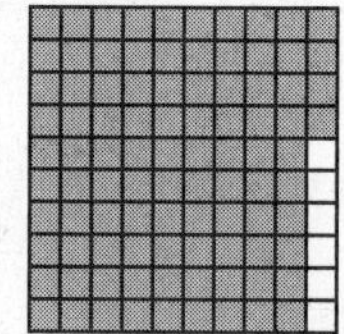

Ratio: $\frac{\text{shaded}}{\text{total}} = \frac{\square}{100}$

Percent: _____ %

Check

Write the percent for the shaded part.

7 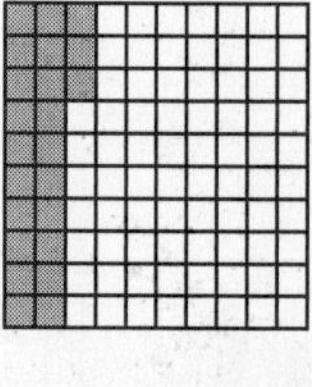

_____ %

8 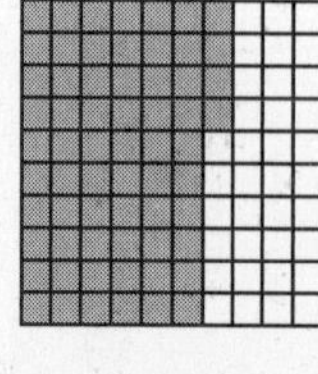

_____ %

9 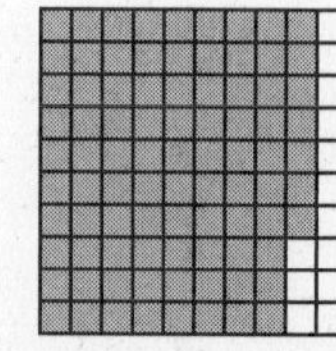

_____ %

Skill 30 Percents and Decimals

Using Skill 30

OBJECTIVE Write percents as decimals and decimals as percents

Have students read about percent at the top of the page. Explain to students that, just as they modeled percents and fractions, they can model percents and decimals. Look at Example A.

Ask: **How can you write 15% as a fraction?** (The percent is a ratio of a number to 100, so the ratio 15 to 100 can be written in fractional form as $\frac{15}{100}$.)

Ask: **Where is the hundredths place?** (two places to the right of the decimal point) **How do you write 15% as a decimal?** (0.15)

Have students compare the percent, fraction, and decimal notation to the pictorial representation. Point out that the picture is a representation of all three forms of the number. Examine the second set of decimal squares.

Ask: **How many squares are shaded?** (103) **What percent of 100 would this be?** (103%) **What is the percent written as a fraction?** ($\frac{103}{100}$) **How is the fraction $\frac{103}{100}$ special?** (It is greater than 1.) **How can you write a fraction greater than 1 as a mixed number?** (You divide the numerator by the denominator to get the whole number part; write the remainder over the denominator to get the fraction part; $\frac{103}{100} = 1\frac{3}{100}$.) **What is 103% written in decimal form?** (1.03)

Lead students through Example B by having them focus on reading the decimal to get the fraction and then the percent.

TRY THESE Exercises 1 and 2 require the students to write percents as decimals. Exercises 3 and 4 require students to write decimals as percents.

- **Exercises 1–2** Write a percent as a decimal.
- **Exercises 3–4** Write a decimal as a percent.

PRACTICE ON YOUR OWN Review the example at the top of the page. As they work through the exercise, have students explain how they know that 125% is greater than 1. Ask them why, when writing a decimal as a percent, you move the decimal point two places to the right.

CHECK Determine if the students know how to convert a percent to a decimal and a decimal to a percent. Success is indicated by 4 out of 4 correct responses.

Students who successfully complete the **Practice on Your Own** and **Check** are ready to move to the next skill.

COMMON ERRORS

- Students may not write the zeros needed to allow the decimal point to move 2 places.
- Students may move the decimal to the right when writing a percent as a decimal.

Students who made more than 4 errors in the **Practice on Your Own**, or who were not successful in the **Check** section, may benefit from the **Alternative Teaching Strategy** on the next page.

Optional

Alternative Teaching Strategy
Modeling Percents and Decimals

OBJECTIVE Using money to model percents and decimals

MATERIALS play money

Distribute play money to students. Say: **Get 4 dimes and a nickel.**

Ask: **How much money is that?** ($0.45)

How do you write that as a decimal? ($0.45)

What fraction of a dollar is that? ($\frac{45}{100}$)

What is a percent? (A ratio of a number to 100.)

Is $\frac{45}{100}$ a ratio of a number to 100? (yes)

What is the number? (45)

What percent is that? (45%)

So, $0.45 is 45% of a dollar.

Repeat this activity with similar examples.

Say: **Use the coins to show 22% of a dollar.**

Ask: **How do you write 22% as a fraction?** ($\frac{22}{100}$)

How many cents is $\frac{22}{100}$? (22 cents)

How is this written as a decimal? ($0.22)

Repeat this activity with similar examples.

When students show understanding, have them try an exercise without using play money models.

Skill 30

Percents and Decimals

Percent means "per hundred."

Percent is a ratio of a number to 100. When you write a percent as a ratio in fraction form, you use a denominator of 100. You can use this fact to write a percent as a decimal.

Example A Percent as a Decimal

- Write 15% as a decimal.
  15% written as a ratio is 15 out of 100 or $\frac{15}{100}$.
  Fifteen hundredths written as a decimal is 0.15.

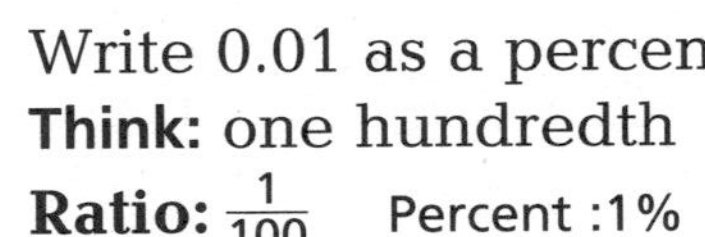

- Write 103% as a decimal.
  Think: $103\% = 100\% + 3\%$

$$\downarrow \qquad \downarrow$$
$$\frac{100}{100} + \frac{3}{100}$$
$$\downarrow \qquad \downarrow$$
$$1 + \frac{3}{100}$$

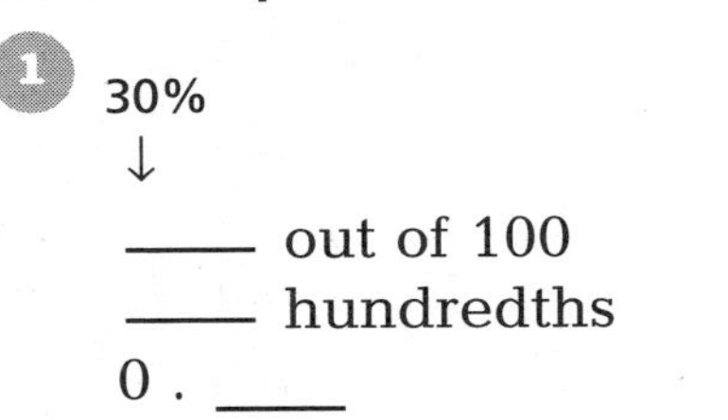

One and three hundredths written as a decimal is 1.03.

Example B Decimal as a Percent

- Write 0.38 as a percent.
  Think: thirty-eight hundredths
  Ratio: $\frac{38}{100}$ Percent: 38%
- Write 0.01 as a percent.
  Think: one hundredth
  Ratio: $\frac{1}{100}$ Percent :1%
- Write 1.5 as a percent.
  Think: one and five tenths or one and fifty hundredths
  Ratio: $\frac{150}{100}$ Percent: 150%

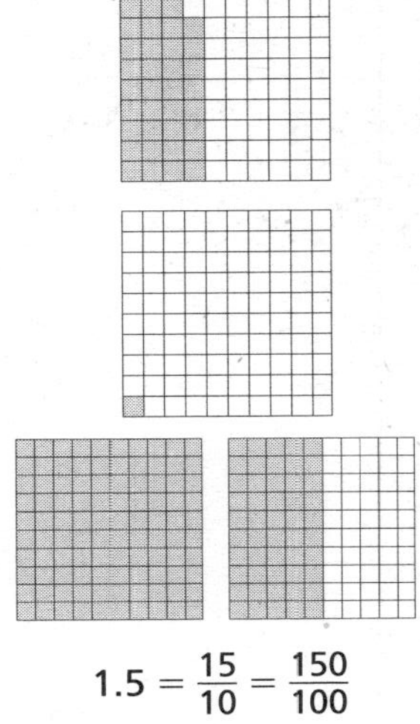

$1.5 = \frac{15}{10} = \frac{150}{100}$

Try These

Write the percent as a decimal.

1. 30%
   ↓
   ____ out of 100
   ____ hundredths
   0 . ____

2. 9%
   ↓
   ____ out of 100
   ____ hundredths
   0.0 ____

Write the decimal as a percent.

3. 0.4
   ↓
   ____ hundredths
   $\frac{\square}{100}$ or ____ %

4. 1.25
   ↓
   __ and __ hundredths
   $\frac{\square}{100}$ or ____ %

Go to the next side.

Name ______________________ Skill ______________________

Practice on Your Own

Skill 30

Write 125% as a decimal.

$$125\% = 100\% + 25\%$$

$$\downarrow \qquad \downarrow$$

$$\frac{100}{100} + \frac{25}{100}$$

$$\downarrow \qquad \downarrow$$

$$1 + \frac{25}{100}$$

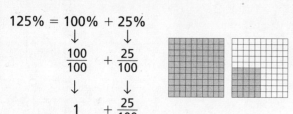

One and twenty-five hundredths written as a decimal is **1.25.**

Write 0.06 as a percent.

6 hundredths

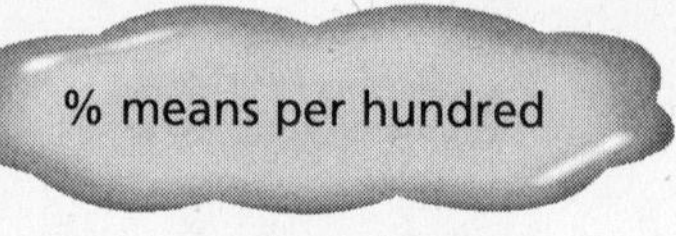

Ratio: $\frac{6}{100}$

Percent: 6%

Write the percent as a decimal.

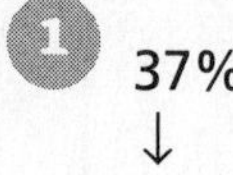

1. 37% ↓ ___ out of 100 ___ hundredths 0 . ___ ___
2. 60% ↓ ___ out of 100 ___ hundredths 0 . ___

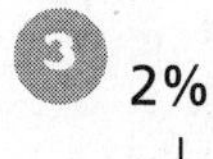

3. 2% ↓ ___ out of 100 ___ hundredths 0.0 ___

4. 75% ↓ ___ out of 100 ___ hundredths ___ . ___ ___

Write the decimal as a percent.

5. 0.55 ↓ ___ hundredths $\frac{\square}{100}$ or ___ %
6. 0.08 ↓ ___ hundredths $\frac{\square}{100}$ or ___ %

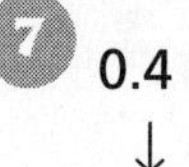

7. 0.4 ↓ ___ hundredths $\frac{\square}{100}$ or ___ %

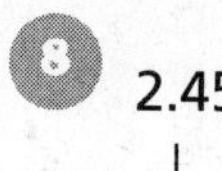

8. 2.45 ↓ ___ and ___ hundredths $\frac{\square}{100}$ or ___ %

Write the percent as a decimal.

9. 99% ________
10. 20% ________

11. 5% ________

12. 100% ________

Write the decimal as a percent.

13. 0.86 ________

14. 0.01 ________

15. 0.3 ________

16. 2.1 ________

Check

Write the percent as a decimal or the decimal as a percent

17. 3% ________

18. 42% ________

19. 0.7 ________
20. 1.5 ________

Fractions, Decimals, Percents

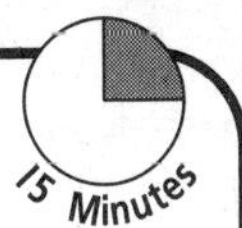

Using Skill 31

OBJECTIVE Find equivalent fractions, decimals, and percents

Begin the lesson by defining percents as ratios with a denominator of 100. Explain that any fraction with a denominator of 100, and any decimal written as hundredths, can be easily expressed as a percent. Suggest that students look at the first model and then ask: **How do you find an equivalent fraction for $\frac{2}{5}$ that has a denominator of 100?** (Multiply the numerator and denominator of $\frac{2}{5}$ by 20.) **What is the decimal equivalent to $\frac{40}{100}$?** (0.40) **What is the percent equivalent to $\frac{40}{100}$?** (40%)

Tell students that another way to find an equivalent decimal for a fraction is to divide the numerator by the denominator. Direct their attention to the second model. Ask: **After you divide the numerator by the denominator, what is the first thing you do?** (Place the decimal point in the quotient.) **Why do you carry the quotient out to hundredths?** (A quotient in hundredths can be written as a percent) **What percent is equivalent to 0.60?** (60%)

TRY THESE Exercises 1–4 model both methods of writing fractions as percents.

- **Exercises 1–2** Find an equivalent fraction.
- **Exercises 3–4** Divide the numerator by the denominator.

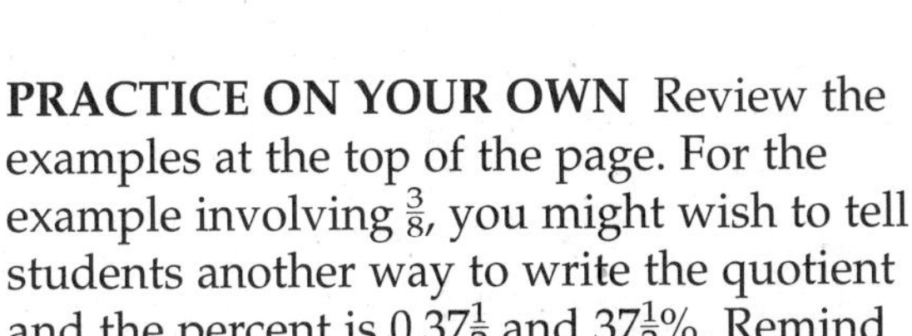

PRACTICE ON YOUR OWN Review the examples at the top of the page. For the example involving $\frac{3}{8}$, you might wish to tell students another way to write the quotient and the percent is $0.37\frac{1}{2}$ and $37\frac{1}{2}\%$. Remind students to place the decimal point in the quotient.

CHECK Determine if students know how to find equivalent fractions and decimals with denominators of 100, and how to write the equivalent percents.

Success is indicated by 3 out of 3 correct responses.

Students who successfully complete **Practice on Your Own** and **Check** are ready to move to the next skill.

COMMON ERRORS

- Students may not understand how fractions, decimals, and percents relate.
- Students may place the decimal point in the quotient incorrectly, or divide incorrectly when finding an equivalent decimal.
- Students may use the wrong factor or multiply incorrectly when finding an equivalent fraction.

Students who made more than 2 errors in the **Practice on Your Own**, or who were not successful in the **Check** section, may benefit from the **Alternative Teaching Strategy** on the next page.

Optional

Alternative Teaching Strategy

15 Minutes

Use Models for Equivalent Fractions, Decimals, and Percents

OBJECTIVE Make models to show equivalent fractions, decimals, and percents

MATERIALS grid paper, blank paper

Prepare 10 by 10 squares with grid paper. Then divide blank squares of the same size into fourths, fifths, tenths, and twenty-fifths.

Begin the activity by explaining to the students that they can use models to find equivalent fractions, decimals, and percents.

Have students find the equivalent decimal and percent for the fraction $\frac{3}{4}$. Have them take a square showing fourths and shade $\frac{3}{4}$. Then have them divide the hundredths square into fourths. Suggest they compare both squares. Ask: **Three-fourths of the square you shaded is equal to how many hundredths?** (75 hundredths)

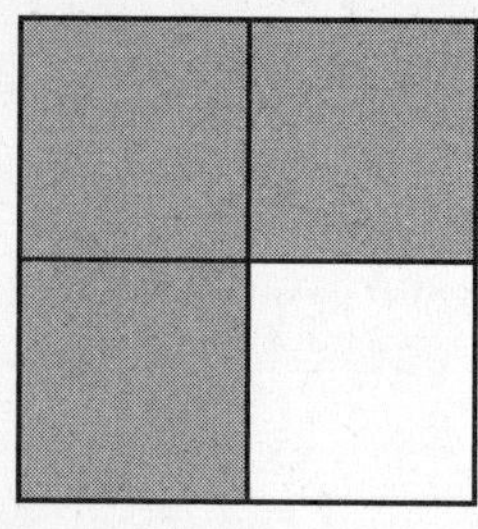

$\frac{3}{4}$

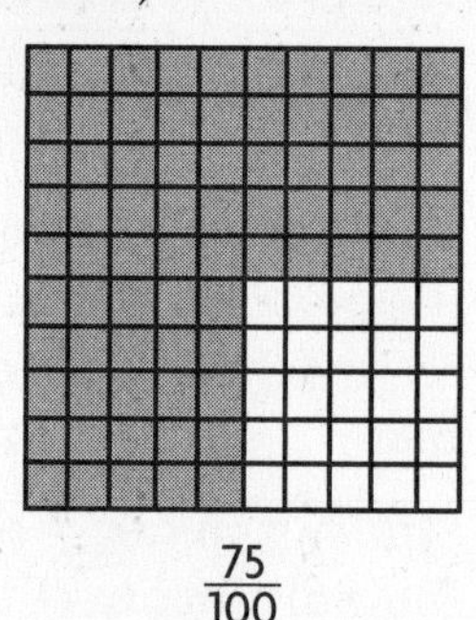

$\frac{75}{100}$

Guide students to see $\frac{3}{4} = \frac{75}{100}$. Recall that $\frac{75}{100}$ means 75 per hundred. Then explain how a fraction with a denominator of 100 can easily be written as a decimal and as a percent.

$$\frac{3}{4} = \frac{75}{100} = 0.75 = 75\%$$

Repeat the activity by finding the equivalent decimal and percent for these fractions.

$$\frac{1}{5} = \frac{20}{100} = 0.20 = 20\%$$

$$\frac{7}{10} = \frac{70}{100} = 0.70 = 70\%$$

$$\frac{13}{25} = \frac{52}{100} = 0.52 = 52\%$$

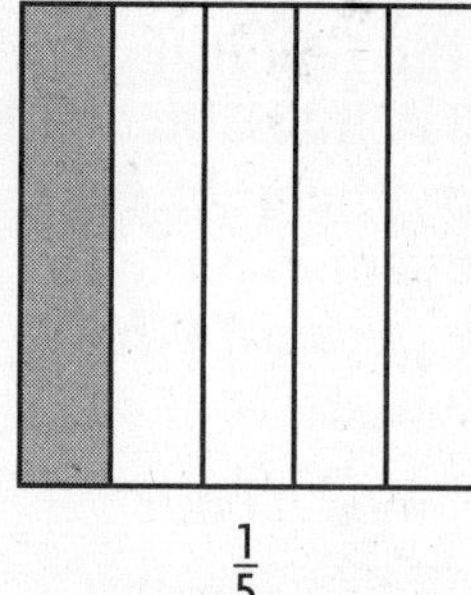

$\frac{1}{5}$

$\frac{20}{100}$

When students understand the concept of using models to find equivalent fractions, decimals, and percents, review how to find them by multiplying both the numerator and denominator by the same factor, or by dividing the numerator by the denominator.

Name ______________________ Skill ______________________

Skill 31

Fractions, Decimals, Percents

25 out of 100 squares shaded
25% shaded

Percent means *per hundred.* Percent is a ratio of a number to 100.
Write fractions as equivalent decimals and percents.

Model A

Write $\frac{2}{5}$ as a decimal and a percent.

Step 1

Find an equivalent decimal by first writing an equivalent fraction with a denominator of 100.

Think:

What number times 5 equals 100?
Since $5 \times 20 = 100$, multiply the numerator and denominator by 20.

$\frac{2}{5} = \frac{2 \times 20}{5 \times 20} = \frac{40}{100}$

Step 2

Write the decimal for *40 hundredths.* Then write the decimal as a percent.

$\mathbf{\frac{40}{100} = 0.40}$

0.40 = 40%

Think: $\frac{40}{100}$ means 40 per 100.

Model B

Write $\frac{15}{25}$ as a decimal and a percent.

Divide the numerator by the denominator.

- Write a decimal point followed by 2 zeros in the dividend.
- Then write a decimal point in the quotient.
- Write the decimal as a percent.

$\frac{15}{25} = 15 \div 25$

$$\begin{array}{r} 0.60 \\ 25\overline{)15.00} \\ -150 \\ \hline 0 \end{array}$$

0.60 = 60%

Think: 60 hundredths means 60 per 100.

Try These

Write the fraction as a decimal and a percent.

1. $\frac{3}{4}$

   $\frac{3}{4} = \frac{3 \times \square}{4 \times \square} = \frac{\square}{100}$

   $\frac{3}{4} = \frac{\square}{100} =$ ___ . ___ ___

   $=$ ___ %

2. $\frac{1}{5}$

   $\frac{1}{5} = \frac{1 \times \square}{5 \times \square} = \frac{\square}{100}$

   $\frac{1}{5} = \frac{\square}{100} =$ ___ . ___ ___

   $=$ ___ %

3. $\frac{9}{10}$

   $\frac{9}{10} = 10\overline{)9.\square\square}$ (quotient $0.\square\square$; $-\square\square$; remainder $\square$)

   $\frac{9}{10} =$ ___ . ___ ___ $=$ ___ %

4. $\frac{3}{25}$

   $\frac{3}{25} = 25\overline{)3.\square\square}$ (quotient $0.\square\square$; $-\square\square$; $\square\square$; $-\square\square$; remainder $\square$)

   $\frac{3}{25} =$ ___ . ___ ___ $=$ ___ %

Go to the next side.

Name ______________________ Skill ______________________

Practice on Your Own

Skill 31

Write the fraction as a decimal and a percent.

$\frac{7}{20}$

$\frac{7}{20} = \frac{7 \times 5}{20 \times 5} = \frac{35}{100}$

$\frac{7}{20} = \frac{35}{100} = 0.35 = 35\%$

Think: What number times 20 equals 100?

$\frac{3}{8} = 8\overline{)3.000}$ with quotient 0.375 ← Write zeros after the decimal point.

$$\begin{array}{r} 0.375 \\ 8\overline{)3.000} \\ -\underline{24} \\ 60 \\ -\underline{56} \\ 40 \\ -\underline{40} \\ 0 \end{array}$$

0.375 = 37.5% ← Move decimal point 2 places to the right.

Write the fraction as a decimal and a percent.

1. $\frac{1}{2}$

$\frac{1}{2} = \frac{1 \times \square}{2 \times \square} = \frac{\square}{100}$

$\frac{1}{2} = \frac{\square}{100} = $ _._ _

= __%

2. $\frac{3}{5}$

$\frac{3}{5} = \frac{3 \times \square}{5 \times \square} = \frac{\square}{100}$

$\frac{3}{5} = \frac{\square}{100} = $ _._ _

= __%

3. $\frac{6}{20}$

$\frac{6}{20} = \frac{6 \times \square}{20 \times \square} = \frac{\square}{100}$

$\frac{6}{20} = \frac{\square}{100} = $ _._ _

= __%

4. $\frac{22}{40}$

$\frac{22}{40} =$

$$\begin{array}{r} 0.\square\square \\ 40\overline{)22.\square\square} \\ -\underline{\square\square\square} \\ \square\square\square \\ -\underline{\square\square\square} \\ \square \end{array}$$

$\frac{22}{40} = $ _._ _ = __%

5. $\frac{2}{3}$

$\frac{2}{3} =$

$$\begin{array}{r} 0.\square\square \\ 3\overline{)2.\square\square} \\ -\underline{\square\square} \\ \square\square \\ -\underline{\square\square} \\ \square \end{array}$$

$\frac{2}{3} = $ _._ _ = __%

6. $\frac{5}{8}$

$\frac{5}{8} =$

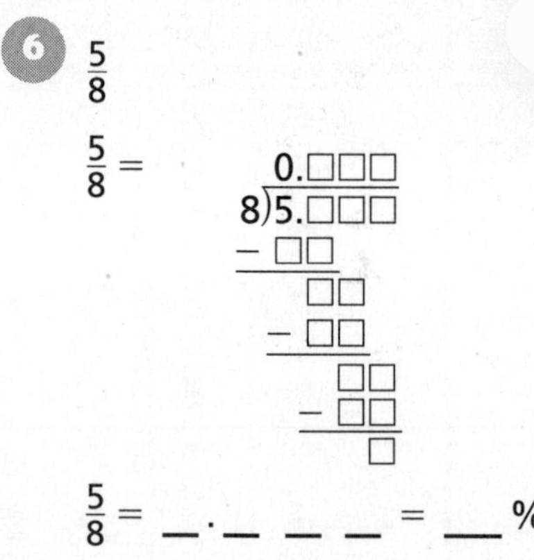

$$\begin{array}{r} 0.\square\square\square \\ 8\overline{)5.\square\square\square} \\ -\underline{\square\square} \\ \square\square \\ -\underline{\square\square} \\ \square\square \\ -\underline{\square\square} \\ \square \end{array}$$

$\frac{5}{8} = $ _._ _ _ = __%

7. $\frac{4}{5}$

_._ _ = __%

8. $\frac{21}{25}$

_._ _ = __%

9. $\frac{1}{8}$

_._ _ _ = __%

Check

Write the fraction as a decimal and as a percent.

10. $\frac{5}{10}$

_._ _ = __%

11. $\frac{33}{50}$

_._ _ = __%

12. $\frac{11}{25}$

_._ _ = __%

Skill 32 Compare Fractions, Decimals, and Percents

Using Skill 32

OBJECTIVE Compare fractions, decimals and percents

Have the students change all fractions and percents to decimals before trying to compare.

When comparing a fraction to a decimal direct students to the first box.

Ask: **What is the decimal equivalent of $\frac{3}{5}$?** (0.60)

Remind students that they always start from the left and compare digits to the right until they are different.

Ask: **What digits do you need to compare?** (0 and 5) **Which is larger?** (5).

Ask: **Which is larger $\frac{3}{5}$ or 0.65?** (0.65)

Continue in a similar manner with the other examples, reminding students to convert all fractions and percents to decimals before comparing.

TRY THESE In Exercises 1–3, students determine which number is larger by converting the fractions and percents to decimals. They compare the numbers and insert the appropriate symbol <, > or =.

- **Exercise 1** <, $\frac{3}{10} = \frac{30}{100} = 0.30$
- **Exercise 2** <, 87% = 0.87
- **Exercise 3** >, $\frac{3}{4} = \frac{75}{100} = 0.75$
  71% = 0.71

PRACTICE ON YOUR OWN Review the examples at the top of the page.

Be sure students are converting to decimals before comparing.

Ask: **Which place do you look at first when comparing decimals?** (tenths)

CHECK Be sure that students can change fractions and percents to decimals. Determine that the students can differentiate between the < and > symbols. Success is indicated by 5 out of 6 correct responses.

Students who successfully complete the **Practice on Your Own** and **Check** are ready to move on to the next skill.

COMMON ERRORS

- Students may make an error when converting to decimals.
- Students may choose the wrong number as the larger number if they do not have the same number of decimal places. (Ex: 0.375 and 0.42, thinking 375 is larger than 42)

Students who made more than 3 errors in the **Practice on Your Own**, or who were not successful in the **Check** section, may benefit from the **Alternative Teaching Strategy** on the next page.

Optional

Alternative Teaching Strategy

15 Minutes

Compare Fractions, Decimals, and Percents

OBJECTIVE Compare fractions, decimals, and percents in a card game

MATERIALS index cards with fractions, percents, and decimals written on them

Have students select a partner. Give each set of students 24 cards. Eight cards should have a fraction, eight should have a decimal and the remaining eight should have a percent written on them.

The game will be played like the traditional "WAR" card game.

Students shuffle the cards and distribute them evenly between players. Each player should have 12 cards stacked face down in front of them.

Each player, at the same time, turns the top card of his or her pile over. The player with the card with the largest value gets both cards. If the values are equivalent, then each player will place one card face down and another card face up. The player with the card with the largest value wins the "WAR."

Note: Players may need a piece of paper and pencil to do conversions.

The game continues until one player is able to win all of the other players' cards.

The students will be comparing a variety of combinations of fractions, decimals and percents.

Have students switch sets of cards with another group to get new values and have them play again.

Name ______________________ Skill ______________________

Compare Fractions, Decimals, and Percents

Skill 32

To compare numbers you must determine which number is greater. Change fractions and percents to decimals, to make it easier to compare.

Compare a fraction and a decimal.

Compare $\frac{3}{5}$ and 0.65.

Change $\frac{3}{5}$ to a decimal.

Compare 0.60 ____ 0.65.

Compare the digits starting at the farthest place to the left, the tenths place. Since 6 = 6, look to the next place to the right, the hundredths place. Since 0 is less than 5, 0.60 < 0.65.

$\frac{3}{5} < 0.65$

Compare a decimal and a percent.

Compare 0.45 and 32%.

Change 32% to a decimal. Compare the decimals.
0.45 ____ 0.32.

Compare the digits in the farthest place to the left, the tenths place. Since 4 is greater than 3, 0.45 > 0.32.

0.45 > 32%

Compare a fraction and a percent.

Compare $\frac{5}{8}$ and 64%.

Change both the fraction and the percent to a decimal.

$\frac{5}{8} = 0.625$ 64% = 0.64

Compare the digits in the farthest place to the left, the tenths place. Since 6 = 6, look to the next place to the right. Since 2 is less than 4, 0.625 < 0.64.

$\frac{5}{8} < 0.64$

Try These

Compare. Use <, >, or =.

1. $\frac{3}{10}$ ____ 0.36

   $\frac{3}{10} = \frac{\square}{100} = 0.$__ __

2. 0.83 ____ 87%

   87% = 0.__ __

3. $\frac{3}{4}$ ____ 71%

   $\frac{3}{4} = \frac{\square}{100} = 0.$__ __ | 71% = 0.__ __

Go to the next side.

Name ______________________ Skill ______________________

Skill 32

Practice on Your Own

Think: Compare numbers written in the same form. Convert fractions and percents to decimals, then compare.

Compare $\frac{12}{25}$ and 0.51.	Compare 0.74 and 78%.	Compare $\frac{9}{10}$ and 86%.
$\frac{12}{25} = \frac{48}{100} = 0.48$	$78\% = 0.78$	$\frac{9}{10} = \frac{90}{100} = 0.90$ | $86\% = 0.86$
$0.48 < 0.51$, so $\frac{12}{25} < 0.51$	$0.74 < 0.78$, so $0.74 < 78\%$	$0.90 > 0.86$, so $\frac{9}{10} > 86\%$

Compare. Use <, >, or =.

1. $\frac{4}{5}$ ___ 77%

   $\frac{4}{5} = \frac{\square}{100} = 0.\_\_$ | $77\% = 0.\_\_$

2. 0.23 ___ 32%

   $32\% = 0.\_\_$

3. $\frac{7}{25}$ ___ 28%

   $\frac{7}{25} = \frac{\square}{100} = 0.\_\_$ | $28\% = 0.\_\_$

4. 0.625 ___ $\frac{3}{5}$

   $\frac{3}{5} = \frac{\square}{100} = 0.\_\_$

Check

Compare. Use <, >, or =.

5. $\frac{9}{20}$ ___ 45%
6. 62% ___ 0.266
7. 13% ___ 0.31
8. $\frac{3}{50}$ ___ 60%
9. 0.57 ___ $\frac{1}{2}$
10. $\frac{3}{4}$ ___ 72.5%

Understand Integers

Using Skill 33

OBJECTIVE Use integers to represent a situation

Begin the lesson by reviewing the meaning of *opposites*. Generate a list of examples such as *hot/cold, up/down, on/off* and so on.

Direct students' attention to the first example. Ask: **What temperature separates the positive temperatures from the negative temperatures?** (0°) **The negative temperatures are located in what direction from 0°?** (down) **How far from zero is negative 4°?** (4 units) **How far from zero is positive 4°?** (4 units) **What can you say about opposite temperatures on the thermometer?** (They are each an equal distance from 0°, but in opposite directions.)

Direct students' attention to the number line that models football yardage. Guide students to recognize that 0 separates the positive yardage from the negative yardage. Ask: **Where is the positive yardage located on the number line?** (right of 0) **What integer represents a gain of 5 yards?** ($^+5$) **What integer represents a loss of 3 yards?** ($^-3$) **Are $^+5$ and $^-3$ the same distance from zero?** (no) **Are $^+5$ and $^-3$ opposite integers?** (no)

Point out to students that opposite integers on a number line must represent the same distance from zero in opposite directions.

Continue to ask similar questions as you discuss the model of a checkbook register. Help students realize that deposits and withdrawals represent opposite situations and can be represented with integers.

TRY THESE In Exercises 1–3 students name integers.

- **Exercise 1** Identify a positive integer; name the integer
- **Exercises 2–3** Identify a negative integer; name the integer

PRACTICE ON YOUR OWN Review the example at the top of the page. Ask students to identify other situations that can be represented by an integer and its opposite.

CHECK Make sure students can distinguish between situations represented by a positive integer and situations represented by a negative integer.

Success is indicated by 3 out of 4 correct responses.

Students who successfully complete the **Practice on Your Own** and **Check** are ready to move to the next skill.

COMMON ERRORS

- Students may be unable to distinguish between a positive and negative situation and thus may use the wrong sign to represent a situation.
- Students may move in the wrong direction from 0.

Students who made more than 3 errors in the **Practice on Your Own**, or who were not successful in the **Check** section, may benefit from the **Alternative Teaching Strategy** on the next page.

Optional

Alternative Teaching Strategy

Model Understanding Integers

OBJECTIVE Use opposite situations to illustrate concept of integers

MATERIALS index cards; flip chart

Prepare index cards with situations that can be represented by an integer. For example:

A gain of
3 points

On the flip chart draw the number line shown below.

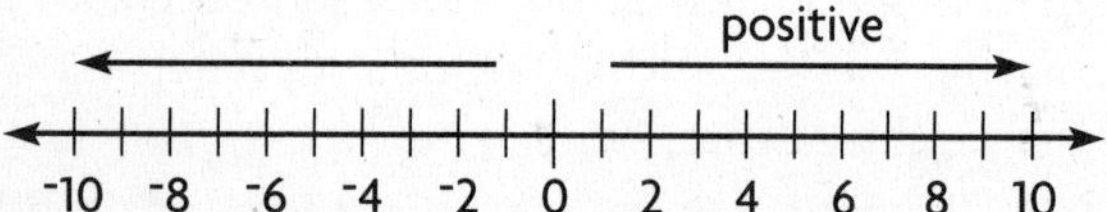

Read the situation described on the first index card. Ask a student to name the integer that describes the situation. ($^+3$) Ask another student to locate the integer on the number line. Then have the first student describe the opposite situation. (a loss of 3 points) Have the second student find its opposite on the number line. ($^-3$)

Some students may benefit from pointing to zero on the number line, and moving with the direction arrows to locate the numbers.

Guide students to see that for every nonzero integer there is an opposite integer. Use the number line on the flip chart to show that the integer and its opposite are an equal distance from zero.

Remind students that zero does not have an opposite.

Name ____________________ Skill ____________________

Understand Integers

Skill 33

Integers include all positive and negative whole numbers and zero. Zero is neither positive nor negative. You can use integers to represent a situation and its opposite.

Temperature

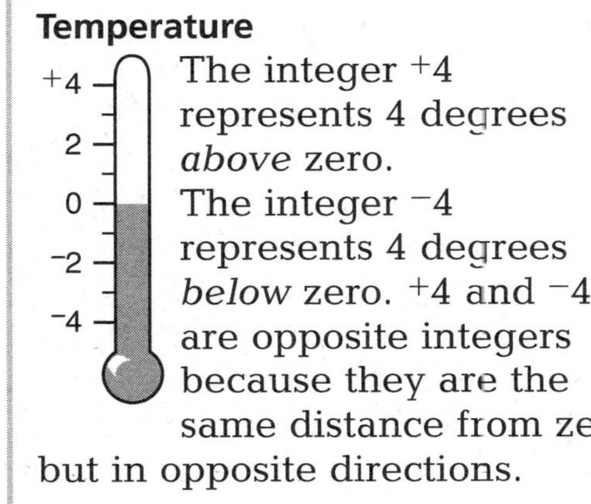

The integer $^{+}4$ represents 4 degrees *above* zero. The integer $^{-}4$ represents 4 degrees *below* zero. $^{+}4$ and $^{-}4$ are opposite integers because they are the same distance from zero, but in opposite directions.

Football Yardage

-3
27
+5
35
20 30 40

The integer $^{+}5$ represents a 5-yard gain. The integer $^{-}3$ represents a 3-yard loss.

Money

Check #	To	-	+	Balance
	Deposit		5.00	5.00
101	Leon	5.00		0

The checkbook shows deposits and withdrawals.
$^{+}5$ represents a \$5 deposit.
$^{-}5$ represents a \$5 withdrawal.
$^{+}5$ and $^{-}5$ are opposite integers.
The increase and decrease are the same amounts. The integer 0 has neither the $^{+}$ symbol nor the $^{-}$ symbol.

Try These

Name each integer.

1. 20°F above 0°

   This integer is:

   Positive ___ Negative ___

   The integer is: ________

2. 15 feet below sea level

   This integer is:

   Positive ___ Negative ___

   The integer is: ________

3. loss of \$12

   This integer is:

   Positive ___ Negative ___

   The integer is: ________

Go to the next side.

Name ____________________ Skill ____________________

Practice on Your Own

Skill 33

Integers can be used to show opposite situations.
Sometimes positive integers do not use the $^{+}$ symbol.
Zero has neither a $^{-}$ symbol nor a $^{+}$ symbol.

Write an integer for each situation.
A baby gains 3 pounds.
gain of 3 pounds → $^{+}3$

The price drops 10 cents.
drop of 10 cents → $^{-}10$

Tell whether the integer is positive or negative.

1. temperature above zero
   positive ___
   negative ___
2. opposite of a negative number
   positive ___
   negative ___
3. loss of money
   positive ___
   negative ___
4. submarine dive
   positive ___
   negative ___

Write the opposite of each integer.

5. $^{+}12$ ___
6. $^{-}125$ ___
7. 4 ___
8. $^{+}25$ ___
9. 17 ___
10. 0 ___
11. $^{-}45$ ___
12. $^{+}33$ ___

Write a positive or negative integer to represent each situation.

13. 110 ft below sea level ______
14. $35 prize-money ______
15. 12 floors above the lobby ______
16. 40 lb weight loss ______
17. $10 allowance ______
18. 6 point score ______
19. $5 debt ______
20. 13 votes ______

Check

Write a positive or negative integer to represent each situation.

21. 9 point gain ______
22. $36 loss ______
23. 2-foot drop ______

24. 6 floors below ______

Skill 34 Whole Number Operations

Using Skill 34

OBJECTIVE Add, subtract, multiply, and divide whole numbers

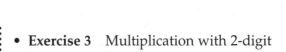

Begin by reviewing with students the term that describes the answer for each operation:

addition → sum

subtraction → difference

multiplication → product

division → quotient

Direct students' attention to the addition example. Ask: **Why do you regroup when adding the ones?** (There are more than 9 ones.) Say: **There are 12 ones, so regroup 10 of those ones as 1 ten.**

Continue to focus on regrouping in the subtraction example. Ask: **Can you subtract the ones without regrouping?** (No; 6 > 2.) **What do you do?** (Regroup 1 ten as 10 ones.)

For the multiplication example, ask: **After multiplying 42 by 4, why do you multiply 42 by 50?** (The digit 5 is in the tens place and represents 5 tens or 50.)

As you work through the division example, ask: **Why do you place the 7 in the ones place of the quotient?** (The estimate for the quotient is less than 10.)

TRY THESE
Exercises provide practice with whole-number operations.

- **Exercise 1** Addition with regrouping
- **Exercise 2** Subtraction with regrouping
- **Exercise 3** Multiplication with 2-digit factors
- **Exercise 4** Division with a 2-digit divisor

PRACTICE ON YOUR OWN For each example at the top of the page, have students explain the step-by-step process used to find the answer. Each row of exercises in the **Practice on Your Own** section focuses on one of the whole-number operations.

CHECK Determine if students can use regrouping and basic facts to add, subtract, multiply, and divide. Success is indicated by 4 out of 4 correct responses.

Students who successfully complete the **Practice on Your Own** and **Check** are ready to move to the next skill.

COMMON ERRORS

- When subtracting, students may subtract the top digit from the bottom digit instead of regrouping.
- When multiplying by tens, students may not use 0 as a placeholder, causing them to align the partial products incorrectly.

Students who made more than 1 error in each operation in the **Practice on Your Own**, or who were not successful in the **Check** section, may benefit from the **Alternative Teaching Strategy** on the next page.

Optional

Alternative Teaching Strategy

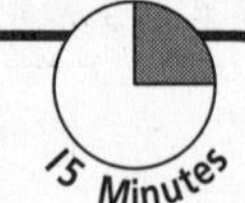

Model Addition, Subtraction, Multiplication, and Division

OBJECTIVE Use models to show addition, subtraction, multiplication, and division

MATERIALS base-ten block models, place-value grids

As students model each operation, ask questions that guide students through the thinking process.

Have them record each exercise in a place-value grid to reinforce the value of each digit.

For addition, emphasize the regrouping step. Model 158 +126.

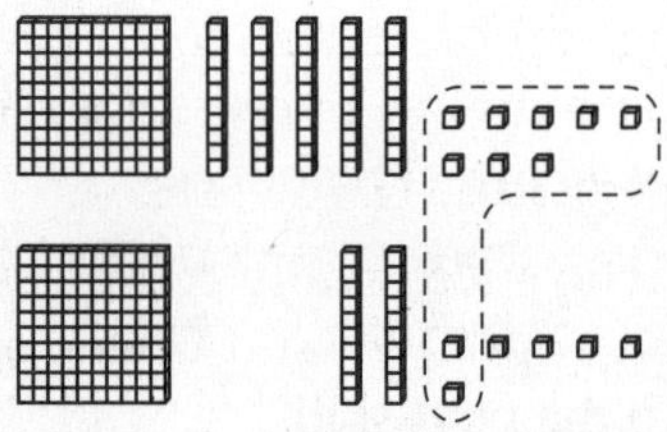

Do you need to regroup ones? (Yes) **Why?** (There are more than 9 ones; 8 + 6 = 14.) **How do you regroup the ones?** (Regroup 10 ones as 1 ten. 14 = 1 ten and 4 ones.) **Add the tens and hundreds. What is the sum?** (284)

Subtract: 433 − 128. Be aware that some students may subtract the top digit from the bottom digit instead of regrouping. Ask questions similar to those for addition as students model the regrouping step. (305)

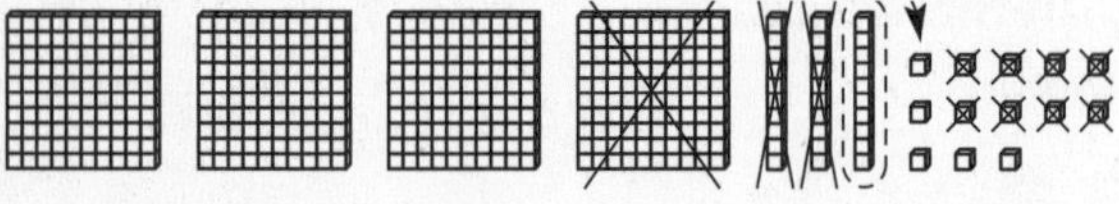

Multiply: 12 × 14. Explain to students that they are modeling 12 groups of 14. As students record the multiplication by a 2-digit number, remind them to think of 12 as 10 + 2. The first step is to multiply 14 by 2. Then, they multiply 14 by 10.

$$\begin{array}{r} 14 \\ \times\ 12 \\ \hline 28 \\ +\ 140 \\ \hline 168 \end{array} \qquad \begin{array}{l} \text{Think: } 10 + 2 \\ 2 \times 14 \\ 10 \times 14 \end{array}$$

Monitor students as they work to make sure that they record the digits of each partial product in the correct place.

Use models to divide 118 ÷ 5.

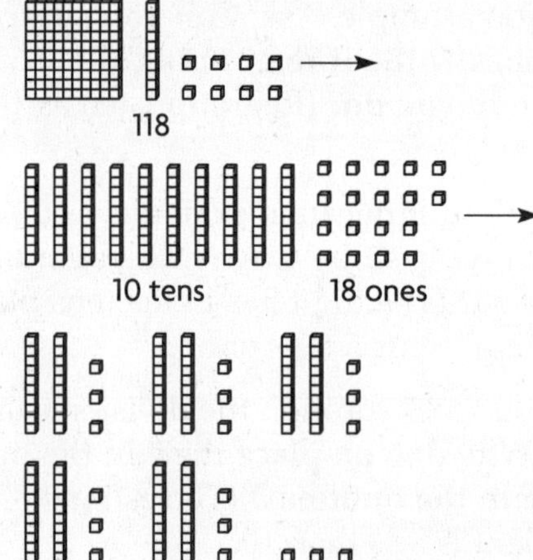

Suggest that one way to model 118 ÷ 5 is to regroup the 1 hundred as 10 tens and regroup the 1 ten as 10 ones. Thus students divide both 10 tens (100) and 18 ones (1 ten and 8 ones) into 5 equal groups. The results will be 5 equal groups of 2 tens and 3 ones, with 3 ones remaining. (23 r 3)

As students show understanding have them work without models and use greater numbers.

Name ______________________ Skill ______________________

Skill 34

Whole Number Operations

Add, subtract, multiply, or divide.

Find the sum.	**Find the difference.**	**Find the product.**	**Find the quotient.**
235 + 47	382 − 56	42 × 54	363 ÷ 48
$\begin{array}{r} \overset{1}{2}35 \\ +\ 47 \\ \hline 282 \end{array}$ **Think:** 7 ones + 5 ones = 12 ones Regroup 10 ones as 1 ten.	$\begin{array}{r} 3\overset{7}{8}\overset{12}{2} \\ -56 \\ \hline 326 \end{array}$ **Think:** 6 > 2 Regroup 1 ten as 10 ones. 1 ten + 2 ones = 12 ones Subtract: 12 − 6	$\begin{array}{r} 42 \\ \times 54 \\ \hline 168 \\ 2{,}100 \\ \hline 2{,}268 \end{array}$ **Think:** 4 × 42 50 × 42 Add the partial products.	$\begin{array}{r} 7 \text{ r } 27 \\ 48\overline{)363} \\ -336 \\ \hline 27 \end{array}$ **Estimate the quotient.** basic fact: $5\overline{)35}$ = 7 compatible numbers: 50 and 350

Try These

1. Find the sum.
   418 + 37
   $\begin{array}{r} \square\ \ \\ 4\ 1\ 8 \\ +\ \ \ 3\ 7 \\ \hline \square\square\square \end{array}$

2. Find the difference.
   375 − 126
   $\begin{array}{r} \square\square\ \\ 3\ \not{7}\ \not{5} \\ -\ 1\ 2\ 6 \\ \hline \square\square\square \end{array}$

3. Find the product.
   93 × 72
   $\begin{array}{r} 9\ 3 \\ \times\ 7\ 2 \\ \hline \square\square\square \\ \square,\square\square\square \\ \hline \square,\square\square\square \end{array}$

4. Find the quotient.
   $\begin{array}{r} \square \text{r} \square\square \\ 58\overline{)4\ 9\ 8} \\ -\square\square\square \\ \hline \square\square \end{array}$

Go to the next side.

Name ______________________ Skill ______________________

Practice on Your Own

Skill 34

Find the difference.
Think:
Do you need to regroup?

$$\begin{array}{r} 400 \\ -\ 52 \\ \hline 348 \end{array}$$

Find the product.

$$\begin{array}{r} 310 \\ \times\ 62 \\ \hline 620 \\ +18{,}600 \\ \hline 19{,}220 \end{array}$$

2×310

60×310

Estimate the quotient and then divide.
Look for a basic fact.

$48 \div 6 = 8$
and
$480 \div 60 = 8$

$$\begin{array}{r} 8 \text{ r } 6 \\ 57\overline{)462} \\ -456 \\ \hline 6 \end{array}$$

Add, subtract, multiply, or divide.

1. □
 4 8
 +2 7
 □□

2. □□
 2 6 5
 + 4 8
 □□□

3. 427
 +139

4. 164
 24
 + 87

5. □□
 7̸ 3
 −4 5

6. □□□
 4̸ 3̸ 8
 − 6 9

7. 613
 −125

8. 800
 −247

9. 7 2
 ×4 5
 □□□
 +□□□□

10. 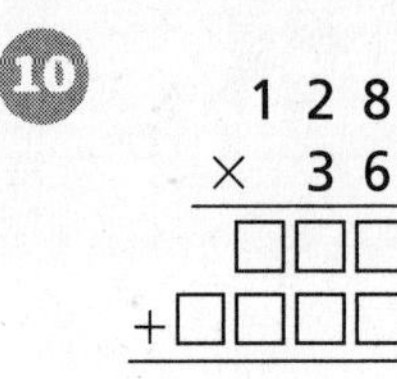
1 2 8
 × 3 6
 □□□
 +□□□□

11. 409
 × 87

12. 684
 × 20

13. 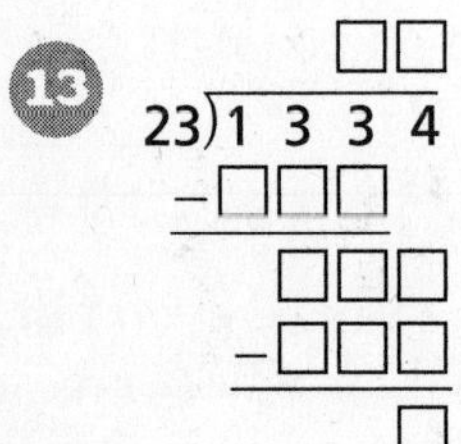
□□
 $23\overline{)1\ 3\ 3\ 4}$
 −□□□
 □□□
 −□□□
 □

14. 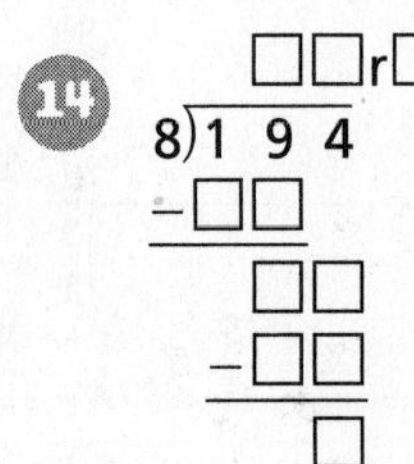
□□r□
 $8\overline{)1\ 9\ 4}$
 −□□
 □□
 −□□
 □

15. $48\overline{)1{,}584}$

16. $7\overline{)2{,}272}$

Check

Add, subtract, multiply, or divide.

17. 357
 + 64

18. 835
 − 96

19. 207
 × 35

20. $5\overline{)375}$

Using Skill 35

OBJECTIVE Understand repeated multiplication

Begin by recalling that numbers that are multiplied are called factors; the result is the product.

Direct students' attention to the multiplication at the top of the page. Have students identify the factor, 3.

Ask: **How many times is 3 used as a factor?** (4 times)

Tell students that repeated multiplication means the same factor is multiplied.

Focus on the steps that show how to multiply. Ask: **What do you multiply first?** (the first two factors, 3×3) **Then what do you do?** (Multiply the result, 9, and the next factor, 3.) **Then what?** (Multiply that result, 27, and the next factor, 3.)

What is the final product? (81)

How do you know when you can stop multiplying? (You stop when there are no more factors left to multiply.)

Suggest to students that they use arrows or cross out factors as a way of keeping track of the factors as they multiply.

TRY THESE Exercises 1–4 provide practice with repeated multiplication.

- **Exercise 1** Factor is used twice.
- **Exercise 2** Factor is used three times.
- **Exercise 3** Factor is used four times.
- **Exercise 4** Factor is used five times.

PRACTICE ON YOUR OWN Review the example at the top of the page. Have a student explain the procedure they would use to multiply the four factors.

CHECK Determine if students account for all the factors when multiplying. Success is indicated by 3 out of 3 correct responses.

Students who successfully complete the **Practice on Your Own** and **Check** are ready to move to the next skill.

COMMON ERRORS

- Students may multiply too many or too few factors.
- Students may understand the multiplication process but may not know basic multiplication facts.

Students who made more than 2 errors in the **Practice on Your Own**, or who were not successful in the **Check** section, may benefit from the **Alternative Teaching Strategy** on the next page.

Optional

Alternative Teaching Strategy
Model Repeated Multiplication

20 Minutes

OBJECTIVE Use counters to model repeated multiplication

MATERIALS counters or cubes

Review with students the meaning of the words *factor* and *product* by writing this on the board.

factors ↓ ↓ product ↓

$2 \times 2 = 4$

Ask: **What are factors?** (numbers that are multiplied)

In this expression, what is the factor that is repeated? (2)

How many times is it used as a factor? (2 times)

Then display the following expression: $2 \times 2 \times 2 \times 2 \times 2$. Use counters to model the repeated multiplication.

Show 2 rows of 2 counters. Have students count 4 counters.

Write $2 \times 2 = 4$.

Then show 4 rows of 2 counters. Have students count 8 counters.

Write $4 \times 2 = 8$.

Next show 8 rows of 2 counters. Have students count 16 counters.

Write $8 \times 2 = 16$.

Finally, show 16 rows of 2 counters. Have students count 32 counters.

Write $16 \times 2 = 32$.

Ask: **How many times is 2 used as a factor?** (5 times)

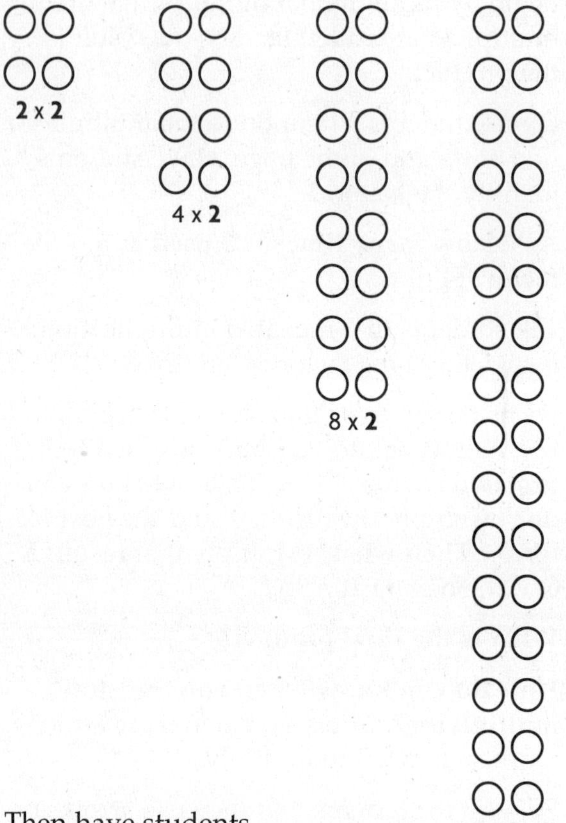

Then have students use counters to model the repeated multiplication for the following expression: $4 \times 4 \times 4 \times 4$.

Have them write the multiplication for each of the steps:

$4 \times 4 \times 4 \times 4$

↓ ↓ ↓

16×4

↓

64×4

↓

256

When students are able to multiply without counters, have them complete exercises with pencil and paper.

Name ______________________ Skill ______________________

Use Repeated Multiplication — Skill 35

Find 3 × 3 × 3 × 3.

Multiply the first two factors.	Multiply the result by the third factor.	Multiply the next result by the the fourth factor.
3 × **3** × 3 × 3 → **9**	3 × 3 × 3 × **3** → 9 × **3** → **27**	3 × 3 × 3 × **3** → 27 × **3** → **81**
		So, 3 × 3 × 3 × 3 = 81.

Try These

Find the product.

1. 2 × 2 → 4 ______

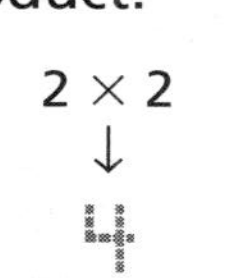

2. 2 × 2 × 2 → ______ × ______ → ______

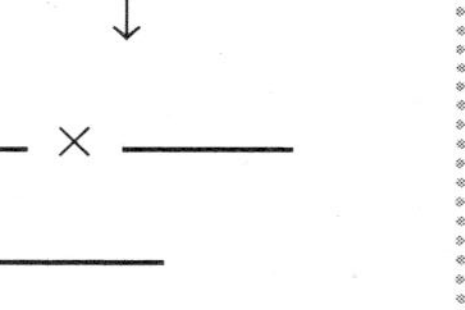

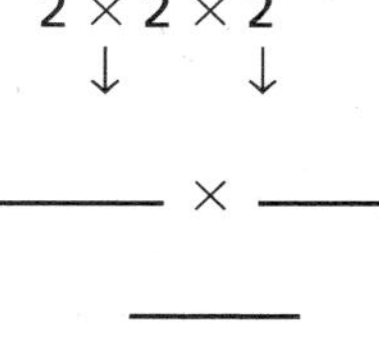

3. 2 × 2 × 2 × 2 → ______ × 2 → ______ × 2 → ______

4. 2 × 2 × 2 × 2 × 2 → ______ × 2 → ______ × 2 → ______ × 2 → ______

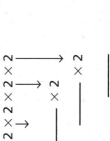

Go to the next side.

Name ______________________ Skill ______________________

Practice on Your Own

Skill 35

Think: Multiply the first two factors. Then multiply the result by the next factor.
Now multiply that result by the next factor. Keep multiplying until there are no more factors to multiply.

$4 \times 4 \times 4 \times 4$

16×4

64×4

256

Find the product.

1. $4 \times 4 \times 4$
   ____ $\times 4$
   ____

2. $5 \times 5 \times 5 \times 5$
   ____ $\times 5$
   ____ $\times 5$
   ____

3. $3 \times 3 \times 3 \times 3 \times 3$
   ____ $\times 3$
   ____ $\times 3$
   ____ $\times 3$
   ____

4. $10 \times 10 \times 10 \times 10$
   ____ $\times 10$
   ____ $\times 10$
   ____

5. $9 \times 9 \times 9$
   ____ $\times 9$
   ____

6. $6 \times 6 \times 6$
   ____ $\times 6$
   ____

7. $5 \times 5 \times 5$ ____

8. $7 \times 7 \times 7$ ____

9. $4 \times 4 \times 4 \times 4 \times 4$ ____

10. $8 \times 8 \times 8$ ____

11. $9 \times 9 \times 9 \times 9$ ____

12. $11 \times 11 \times 11$ ____

Check

Find the product.

13. $8 \times 8 \times 8 \times 8$ ____

14. $10 \times 10 \times 10$ ____

15. $2 \times 2 \times 2 \times 2 \times 2 \times 2$ ____

Using Skill 36

OBJECTIVE Use strategies to recall multiplication facts

MATERIALS multiplication table

Begin the lesson by reminding students that, just as they can use strategies to help them recall addition facts, they can use strategies to help recall multiplication facts.

Direct students' attention to the skill. Be sure they are familiar with the words used in multiplication. Ask: **What do you call the numbers you multiply?** (factors) **What do you call the result?** (product)

Focus on each strategy. For Use Facts You Know, ask: **Why do you add 7 in 7 × 6 = 35 + 7?** (There is 1 *more* group of 7 in 7 × 6 than in 7 × 5, so we *add* 7.)

For Use Patterns, assist students in using the table, showing them how to very carefully read across and down the rows. Help them identify patterns for 10 × 1 to 10 × 9 and 11 × 1 to 11 × 9.

TRY THESE Exercises 1–3 model using strategies.

- **Exercise 1** Use facts you know and add to get "next" fact
- **Exercise 2** Use patterns of 10 to multiply

PRACTICE ON YOUR OWN Focus on the examples at the top of the page. Be sure students understand when the various strategies can be helpful. Ask: **If you know 5 × 5, why add 5 when multiplying 6 × 5?** (There is 1 more group of 5.) Finally, review the patterns for products of 9, 10, 11, and 12.

CHECK Make sure students understand that multiple strategies are possible and that there is no one correct strategy.

Success is indicated by 6 out of 8 correct responses. Students who successfully complete the **Practice on Your Own** and **Check** are ready to move to the next skill.

COMMON ERRORS

- When using facts they know, students may forget what to add. For example, when using 8 × 5 to find 9 × 5, they need to think 40 + 5 = 45.

Students who made more than 3 errors in the **Practice on Your Own** or were not successful in the **Check** section, may benefit from the **Alternative Teaching Strategy** on the next page.

Optional

Alternative Teaching Strategy
Arrays for Multiplication Facts

OBJECTIVE Use arrays to model strategies for recalling multiplication facts

MATERIALS tiles, chart of multiplication facts

Have students use tiles to model a strategy for recalling multiplication facts.

Have students use tiles to model a fact they know. Then have them lay out addition tiles to show the "next fact." For example: $4 \times 3 = 12$. Then, add 4 tiles to make 16, so, $4 \times 4 = 16$.

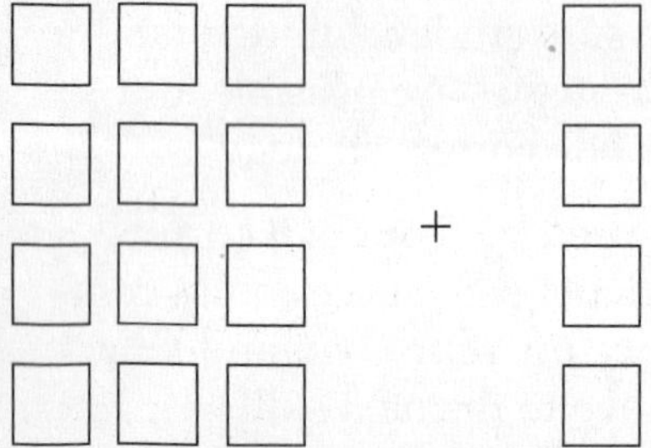

Repeat with several different facts.

Have students use a multiplication table to find patterns.

What patterns can be found in the table? For facts of 2, the ones digits repeat: 0, 2, 4, 6, 8, …

What other patterns can be found?

Name ______________________ Skill ______________________

Skill 36

Multiplication Facts

Use strategies to recall multiplication facts.

Use Facts You Know
Use a fact you already know to find a fact you do not know.

If you know: $3 \times 8 = 24$

Then you also know: $8 \times 3 = 24$

If you know: $7 \times 5 = 35$

Then you can find: $7 \times 6 = \square$

Think: 7×6 is $(7 \times 5) + 7$, or $35 + 7$, or 42.

So, $7 \times 6 = 42$.

Use Patterns
If you use a multiplication table, you can look for patterns in products.

Multiply by 9, 10, 11, 12

Facts for 9 × 1 to 9 × 10: Ones digits decrease by 1. Tens digits increase by 1. The sum of the digits in the product is 9.

Facts for 12 × 0 to 12 × 9: Ones digits repeat: 0, 2, 4, 6, 8, ...

What other patterns can you find?

Try These

Use strategies to multiply.

1. Use facts you know.

$2 \times 8 =$ _____ So, $8 \times 2 =$ _____

$3 \times 8 =$ _____ So, $3 \times 9 =$ _____

2. Use patterns.

$10 \times 1 =$ _____ $10 \times 2 =$ _____

$10 \times 3 =$ _____ $10 \times 4 =$ _____

$10 \times 5 =$ _____ $10 \times 6 =$ _____

Go to the next side.

Name ______________________ Skill ______________________

Practice on Your Own

Skill 36

Use Facts You Know

$6 \times 5 = \square$

If you know:

$5 \times 5 = 25$

Then think:

$6 \times 5 = (5 \times 5) + 5$, or 30

So, $6 \times 5 = 30$.

Use Patterns

Look for patterns to help you remember multiplication facts.

For products of 9 and 1 through 9, the digits of all multiples of 9 add up to 9.

Products of 10 end in 0.

For products of 11 and 1 through 9, you see the same digit in the tens and ones place.

Products of 12 end in 0, 2, 4, 6, or 8.

Use facts you know.

1. $4 \times 8 =$ _____
   So, $4 \times 9 =$ _____
2. $5 \times 8 =$ _____
   So, $5 \times 9 =$ _____
3. $6 \times 8 =$ _____
   So, $6 \times 9 =$ _____
4. $3 \times 5 =$ _____
   So, $3 \times 6 =$ _____
5. $2 \times 5 =$ _____
   So, $2 \times 6 =$ _____
6. $4 \times 3 =$ _____
   So, $4 \times 4 =$ _____

Use patterns.

7. $10 \times 5 =$ ___ $10 \times 6 =$ ___
   $10 \times 7 =$ ___ $10 \times 8 =$ ___
8. $11 \times 3 =$ ___ $11 \times 4 =$ ___
   $11 \times 5 =$ ___ $11 \times 6 =$ ___
9. $12 \times 4 =$ ___ $12 \times 5 =$ ___
   $12 \times 6 =$ ___ $12 \times 7 =$ ___

Multiply.

10. $8 \times 7 =$ _____
11. $10 \times 9 =$ _____
12. $9 \times 11 =$ _____
13. 12×8 _____

Check

Multiply.

14. $4 \times 7 =$ _____
15. $6 \times 6 =$ _____
16. $10 \times 3 =$ _____
17. $11 \times 7 =$ _____
18. $10 \times 5 =$ _____
19. $7 \times 9 =$ _____
20. $5 \times 11 =$ _____
21. $12 \times 11 =$ _____

Skill 37

Multiply and Divide by Powers of 10

20 Minutes

Using Skill 37

OBJECTIVE Multiply and divide by powers of 10

Direct student attention to Example A.

Ask: **Where is the decimal point?** (At the end of the 3; it is understood to be at the end of the number and does not have to be written.)

What is the pattern? (Move the decimal point the same number of places as the number of zeros.)

Direct students to look at Example B.

Ask: **What is the pattern?** (Move the decimal point the same number of places as the number of zeros.)

How do you know what direction to move the decimal point? (When you multiply the number gets larger; move the decimal to the right. When you divide the number gets smaller; move the decimal to the left.)

TRY THESE In Exercises 1–2 students find the product and quotient.

- **Exercise 1** 70, 700, 7,000, 70,000
- **Exercise 2** 9.2, 0.92, 0.092, 0.0092

PRACTICE ON YOUR OWN Review the summary at the top of the page.

Ask students to explain how they know how many places to move the decimal point. (The same number of places as the number of zeros.)

CHECK Determine if students know how to multiply or divide by a power of 10. Success is indicated by 3 out of 3 correct responses when multiplying and 3 out of 3 correct when dividing.

Students who successfully complete the **Practice on Your Own** and **Check** are ready to move to the next skill.

COMMON ERRORS

- The students will have the incorrect number of zeros in the product.
- The students will forget to add zeros as placeholders when dividing.

Students who made more than 3 errors in the **Practice on Your Own**, or who were not successful in the **Check** section, may benefit from the **Alternative Teaching Strategy** on the next page.

Optional

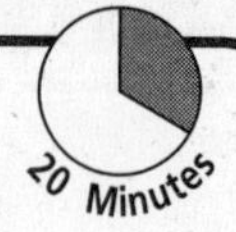

Alternative Teaching Strategy

Multiply and Divide by Powers of 10

OBJECTIVE Multiply or divide by a power of 10

MATERIAL number cards 0–9, with six cards for 0

You may wish to have students work in pairs. Partners take turns placing the number cards on the table.

Distribute a set of number cards to each pair of students.

Have students select any card and place it on the table. Have them multiply by a power of 10, i.e. 100.
Ask: **How many places should you move the decimal point?** (2)

How many zeros are there? (2)

In which direction will you move the decimal point? (right)

Have students add two zeros to the end of the number.

Repeat the activity several times as partners choose other cards and multiply by different powers of 10.

Ask questions similar to those asked before.

When students show an understanding of multiplying by powers of 10, switch to dividing by powers of ten.

Have students select any card and place it on the table. Have them divide by a power of 10, i.e. 100.

Ask: **How many places should you move the decimal point?** (2)

In which direction will you move the decimal point? (left)

Have students place their finger at the end of the number and move 2 places left. If they need to add zeros for placeholders remind them to do so.

Repeat the activity several times as the partners choose other cards and divide by different powers of 10.

Ask questions similar to those asked before.

Name ______________________ Skill ______________________

Skill 37

Multiply and Divide by Powers of 10

Use a pattern to multiply or divide by a power of 10.

Example A:
Multiply by powers of 10.

$3 \times 10 = 30$	Multiply by 10. Decimal point moves 1 place to the right.
$3 \times 100 = 300$	Multiply by 100. Decimal point moves 2 places to the right.
$3 \times 1{,}000 = 3{,}000$	Multiply by 1,000. Decimal point moves 3 places to the right.
$3 \times 10{,}000 = 30{,}000$	Multiply by 10,000. Decimal point moves 4 places to the right.

Example B:
Divide by powers of 10.

$54 \div 10 = 5.4$	Divide by 10. Decimal point moves 1 place to the left.
$54 \div 100 = 0.54$	Divide by 100. Decimal point moves 2 places to the left.
$54 \div 1{,}000 = 0.054$	Divide by 1,000. Decimal point moves 3 places to the left.
$54 \div 10{,}000 = 0.0054$	Divide by 10,000. Decimal point moves 4 places to the left.

Try These

Find the product.

1. $7 \times 10 =$ ________

   $7 \times 100 =$ ________

   $7 \times 1{,}000 =$ ________

   $7 \times 10{,}000 =$ ________

Find the quotient.

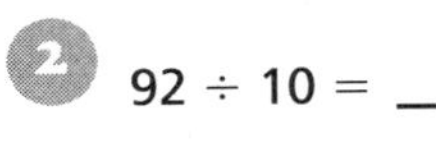

2. $92 \div 10 =$ ________

   $92 \div 100 =$ ________

   $92 \div 1{,}000 =$ ________

   $92 \div 10{,}000 =$ ________

Go to the next side.

Name ______________________ Skill ______________________

Practice on Your Own

Skill 37

Use a pattern to multiply or divide by a power of 10.
Ask yourself: Am I multiplying or dividing?
If you are multiplying move the decimal to the right.
If you are dividing move the decimal to the left.

Find the product.

1. $5 \times 10 =$ ______
   $5 \times 100 =$ ______
   $5 \times 1{,}000 =$ ______

2. $12 \times 10 =$ ______
   $12 \times 100 =$ ______
   $12 \times 1{,}000 =$ ______

3. $152 \times 10 =$ ______
   $152 \times 100 =$ ______
   $152 \times 1{,}000 =$ ______

Find the quotient.

4. $3 \div 10 =$ ______
   $3 \div 100 =$ ______
   $3 \div 1{,}000 =$ ______

5. $24 \div 10 =$ ______
   $24 \div 100 =$ ______
   $24 \div 1{,}000 =$ ______

6. $574 \div 10 =$ ______
   $574 \div 1{,}000 =$ ______
   $574 \div 10{,}000 =$ ______

Find the product or quotient. Tell how many places you move the decimal point and in which direction.

7. $17 \times 10{,}000 =$ ______
   move ______ place(s)
   left or right

8. $17 \div 10{,}000 =$ ______
   move ______ place(s)
   left or right

9. $7 \times 100 =$ ______
   move ______ place(s)
   left or right

10. $68 \div 1{,}000 =$ ______
    move ______ place(s)
    left or right

11. $9 \times 10 =$ ______
    move ______ place(s)
    left or right

12. $118 \div 100 =$ ______
    move ______ place(s)
    left or right

Find the product or quotient.

13. $98 \times 1{,}000 =$ ______

14. $34 \div 10{,}000 =$ ______

15. $124 \times 100 =$ ______

Check

Find the product or quotient.

16. $28 \times 1{,}000 =$ ______

17. $25 \times 100 =$ ______

18. $136 \times 10 =$ ______

19. $18 \div 1{,}000 =$ ______

20. $197 \div 100 =$ ______

21. $14 \div 100 =$ ______

Using Skill 38

OBJECTIVE Use multiplication facts to find quotients for division facts

MATERIALS multiplication table

Begin by having students examine the multiplication table. Review with them how to use the table to find products.

Direct students' attention to the first example. Ask: **What does 63 ÷ 7 mean?** (63 objects are separated into 7 equal groups.)
If you made 3 groups of 7, how could you find the total number of objects? (Multiply 3 by 7.)

Explain to students that multiplication is the inverse of division.
What number times 7 equals 63? (9)

Use the multiplication table to show how to find 63 ÷ 7 = 9.

TRY THESE Exercises provide students with practice recalling quotients for division facts.

- **Exercises 1–4** Provide prompts for students to find missing factors and quotients.

PRACTICE ON YOUR OWN Review the examples at the top of the page. Ask students to explain how division and multiplication are related. Reconfirm that division is the *inverse*, or opposite, of multiplication.

CHECK Determine if students can recall multiplication facts to help them divide. Success is indicated by 4 out of 4 correct responses.

Students who successfully complete the **Practice on Your Own** and **Check** are ready to move to the next skill.

COMMON ERRORS

- Students may use the wrong multiplication fact.
- Students may give the wrong factor.

Students who made more than 4 errors in the **Practice on Your Own**, or who were not successful in the **Check** section, may benefit from the **Alternative Teaching Strategy** on the next page.

Optional

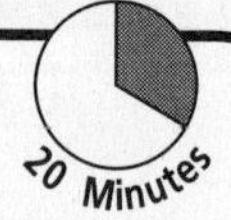

Alternative Teaching Strategy

Model Division

OBJECTIVE Use counters to model the relationship between division and multiplication

MATERIAL counters

Have students work with a partner. One student models division sentences with counters while the other student records the results.

Distribute the counters.

Ask: **How could you use the counters to model the division sentence 12 ÷ 3?** (Separate 12 counters into 3 equal groups.)

Direct students to separate the 12 counters into 3 equal groups. You might even have 1 student "deal" 12 counters to 3 other students.

Ask: **How many counters are there in each group now?** (4)

Have students look at their groups of counters. Ask: **What multiplication sentence describes how these 12 counters are grouped?** (3 × 4 and 4 × 3)

Repeat this activity with similar division sentences that use basic facts, such as 9 ÷ 3 or 18 ÷ 6. When students start to see the connection between division and multiplication, remove the counters and have them try some exercises using only paper and pencil.

Name ____________ Skill ____________

Skill 38

Division Facts

Division is the opposite or **inverse** of multiplication. Use this idea to help recall division facts.

63 ÷ 7 = □
Think of a related multiplication fact to find the quotient.

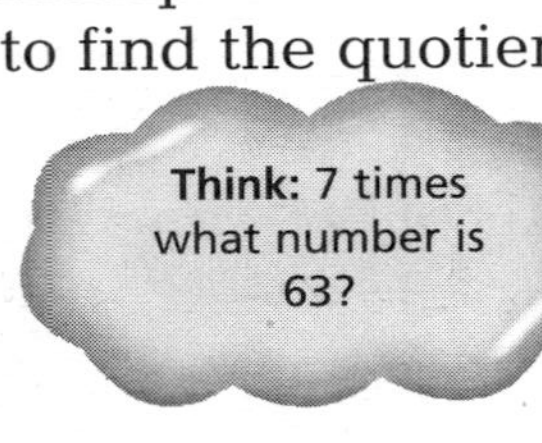
Think: 7 times what number is 63?

63 ÷ 7 = □
7 × 9 = 63
So, 63 ÷ 7 = 9.

Since multiplication is the inverse of division, you can use a multiplication table to find quotients for division facts.
To find 108 ÷ 12:

1. Look down the factor column. Find 12.
2. Then look across the 12-row. Find 108.
3. Trace up from 108. Find the factor in the factor-row at the top. It is 9.

So, 12 × 9 = 108 and 108 ÷ 12 = 9.

x	0	1	2	3	4	5	6	7	8	9	10	11	12
0	0	0	0	0	0	0	0	0	0	0	0	0	0
1	0	1	2	3	4	5	6	7	8	9	10	11	12
2	0	2	4	6	8	10	12	14	16	18	20	22	24
3	0	3	6	9	12	15	18	21	24	27	30	33	36
4	0	4	8	12	16	20	24	28	32	36	40	44	48
5	0	5	10	15	20	25	30	35	40	45	50	55	60
6	0	6	12	18	24	30	36	42	48	54	60	66	72
7	0	7	14	21	28	35	42	49	56	63	70	77	84
8	0	8	16	24	32	40	48	56	64	72	80	88	96
9	0	9	18	27	36	45	54	63	72	81	90	99	108
10	0	10	20	30	40	50	60	70	80	90	100	110	120
11	0	11	22	33	44	55	66	77	88	99	110	121	132
12	0	12	24	36	48	60	72	84	96	108	120	132	144

Try These

Use multiplication to divide.

1. 48 ÷ 6 = ___

   Think: 6 × ___ is 48.

   So, 48 ÷ 6 = ___.

2. 81 ÷ 9 = ___

   Think: 9 × ___ is 81.

   So, 81 ÷ 9 = ___.

3. 55 ÷ 5 = ___

   Think: 5 × ___ is 55.

   So, 55 ÷ 5 = ___.

4. 84 ÷ 12 = ___

   Think: 12 × ___ is 84.

   So, 84 ÷ 12 = ___.

Go to the next side.

Name ______________________ Skill ______________________

Practice on Your Own

Skill 38

Find: 27 ÷ 3 = □

Think: 3 times what number is 27?

3 × 9 = 27
So, 27 ÷ 3 = 9.

Find: 48 ÷ 6 = □
Use the multiplication table.

- Look across the top row to 6.
- Then look down to 48.
- Trace back from 48 to find the factor at the far left. It is 8.

So, 6 × 8 = 48
and 48 ÷ 6 = 8.

x	0	1	2	3	4	5	6
0	0	0	0	0	0	0	0
1	0	1	2	3	4	5	6
2	0	2	4	6	8	10	12
3	0	3	6	9	12	15	18
4	0	4	8	12	16	20	24
5	0	5	10	15	20	25	30
6	0	6	12	18	24	30	36
7	0	7	14	21	28	35	42
8	0	8	16	24	32	40	48

Use multiplication to divide.

1. **Think:** 7 × 4 = ___ So, 28 ÷ 7 = ___
2. **Think:** 9 × 7 = ___ So, 63 ÷ 9 = ___
3. **Think:** 4 × 10 = ___ So, 40 ÷ 4 = ___
4. **Think:** 12 × 4 = ___ So, 48 ÷ 12 = ___
5. **Think:** 5 × 6 = ___ So, 30 ÷ 5 = ___.
6. **Think:** 7 × 7 = ___ So, 49 ÷ 7 = ___.
7. **Think:** 3 × 12 = ___ So, 36 ÷ 3 = ___.
8. **Think:** 9 × 10 = ___ So, 90 ÷ 9 = ___.

Divide.

9. 56 ÷ 8 = ___
10. 33 ÷ 3 = ___
11. 42 ÷ 7 = ___
12. 54 ÷ 9 = ___
13. 32 ÷ 8 = ___
14. 28 ÷ 7 = ___
15. 44 ÷ 4 = ___
16. 84 ÷ 7 = ___
17. 36 ÷ 9 = ___
18. 24 ÷ 3 = ___
19. 81 ÷ 9 = ___
20. 56 ÷ 7 = ___
21. 49 ÷ 7 = ___
22. 108 ÷ 12 = ___
23. 72 ÷ 12 = ___
24. 48 ÷ 12 = ___

Check

Divide.

25. 35 ÷ 5 = ___
26. 22 ÷ 11 = ___
27. 99 ÷ 9 = ___
28. 60 ÷ 12 = ___

15 Minutes

Using Skill 39

OBJECTIVE Express a remainder as a whole number, fraction, or decimal

You may wish to start by reviewing simple division with no remainders. Then tell students that the examples show division with a remainder written in 3 ways—as a whole number, a fraction, or a decimal.

Direct students' attention to the first division. Point out that the remainder is shown as a whole number. Ask: **How is the remainder written in the quotient?** (r 7)

Draw attention to the second division. Point out that the remainder is shown as a fraction. Say: **To write the remainder as a fraction, use the remainder as the numerator and the divisor as the denominator.** Ask: **What number will be the numerator?** (7) **What number will be the denominator?** (14) **Can $\frac{7}{14}$ be written in simpler form?** (yes) **What is the simplest form of $\frac{7}{14}$?** ($\frac{1}{2}$) Say: **The remainder is written as $\frac{1}{2}$.**

Draw attention to the third division. Point out that the remainder is written as a decimal. Locate the decimal point in the quotient and in the dividend. Ask: **How many zeros are written after the decimal point in the dividend?** (1) Work through the division to show that you stop writing zeros in the dividend when the remainder is 0.

Say: **What is the quotient?** (12.5) **How is the remainder written?** (as 0.5)

TRY THESE Exercises 1–3 model the three different ways to write the remainder.

- **Exercise 1** Write remainder as a whole number.
- **Exercise 2** Write remainder as a fraction.
- **Exercise 3** Write remainder as a decimal.

PRACTICE ON YOUR OWN Review the example at the top of the page. Explain how to write zeros in order to express a remainder as a decimal.

CHECK Make sure students can correctly write the remainder in 3 different forms.

Success is indicated by 3 out of 3 correct responses.

Students who successfully complete the **Practice on Your Own** and **Check** are ready to move to the next skill.

COMMON ERRORS

- Students may not write enough zeros to find a decimal remainder.
- Students may confuse the numerator and denominator when writing the remainder as a fraction.
- Students may multiply and subtract incorrectly.

Students who made more than 1 error in each row of Exercises 1–9 of **Practice on Your Own**, or who were not successful in the **Check** section, may benefit from the **Alternative Teaching Strategy** on the next page.

Optional

Alternative Teaching Strategy

Model Remainders

OBJECTIVE Express a remainder as a whole number, a fraction, or a decimal

MATERIALS counters, paper, pencil

Provide students with an odd number of counters, for example, 7. Direct students to divide the counters into two equal groups. Have students write the division sentence on their paper.

Have students verbalize the result. That is, there are 2 equal groups with 1 counter left over, or 1 remainder.

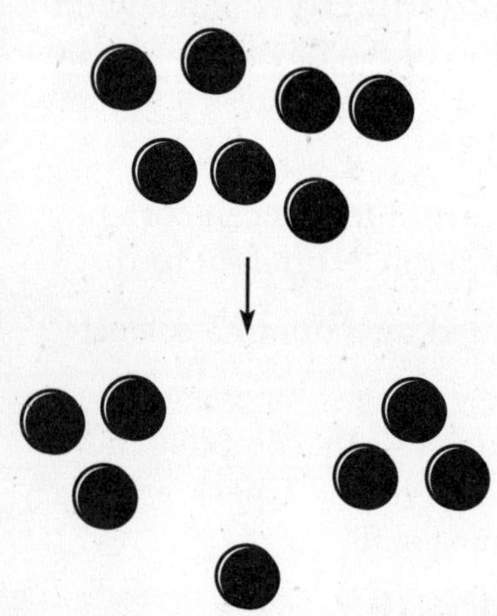

Point out to students that there are 3 different ways to express the remainder. Have the students record the division on their paper, showing the remainder in three different ways.

As a whole number

r1 The letter r stands for remainder.

As a fraction

$\frac{1}{2}$ ← remainder / ← divisor

Help students recognize that the remainder is the numerator, and the divisor is the denominator.

As a decimal

```
   3.5
2 )7.0
 - 6↓
   1 0
 - 1 0
     0
```

Continue with other examples.

10 ÷ 4	11 ÷ 5	17 ÷ 2
(2r2 2.5; $2\frac{1}{2}$)	(2r1, 2.2; $2\frac{1}{5}$)	(8r1, 8.5; $8\frac{1}{2}$)

Name ______________________ Skill ______________________

Skill 39

Remainders

You can express a remainder as a whole number, fraction, or decimal.
Find 175 ÷ 14 = □. Show three ways to write the remainder.

Write the remainder as a whole number.

```
                 12 r 7
Divisor →    14)175
                - 14
                  35
                - 28
Remainder →        7
```

So, 175 ÷ 14 = 12 r 7.

Write the remainder as a fraction.

```
   12 1/2
14)175
  -14
    35
  - 28
     7
```

Write the remainder over the divisor: $\frac{7}{14}$ Simplify the fraction: $\frac{7}{14} = \frac{1}{2}$

So, $175 \div 14 = 12\frac{1}{2}$

Write the remainder as a decimal.

```
    12.5
14)175.0
  -14
    35
  - 28
     70
   - 70
      0
```

Write a *decimal point* in the dividend and the quotient. Write enough zeros to divide until the remainder equals zero.

So, 175 ÷ 14 = 12.5

Try These

1. Divide. Write the remainder as a whole number.

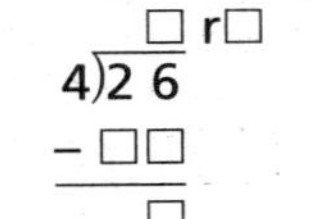

2. Divide. Write the remainder as a fraction.

3. Divide. Write the remainder as a decimal.

```
    □□.□□
12)2 6 7.□□
  -□□
    □□
   -□□
     □□
    -□□
      □□
     -□□
```

Go to the next side.

Name ______________________ Skill ______________________

Practice on Your Own

Skill 39

You can write a remainder as a:
- whole number
- fraction
- decimal

Find 54 ÷ 8 = □. Write the remainder as a decimal.

```
   6.75
8)54.00
 -48
   6 0
  -5 6
    40
  - 40
     0
```

Remember:
- Write a decimal point in the quotient.
- Write enough zeros to divide until the remainder equals zero.

Divide. Write the remainder as a whole number.

1. 5)47 = □r□

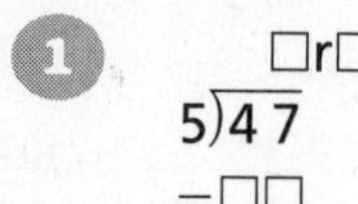

2. 11)190 = □□r□

3. 16)1,941 = □□□r□

Divide. Write the remainder as a fraction.

4. 4)34 = $□\frac{□}{□}$

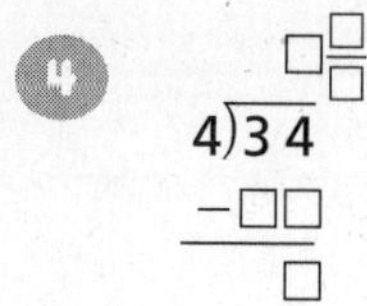

5. 16)404 = $□□\frac{□}{□}$

6. 37)1,299 = $□□\frac{□}{□}$

Divide. Write the remainder as a decimal.

7. 4)27.□□ = □.□□

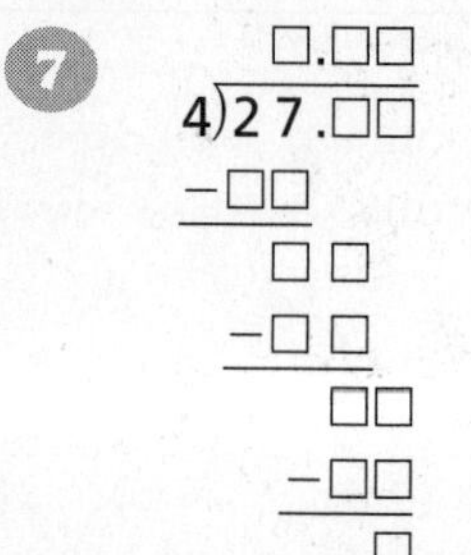

8. 15)783.□ = □□.□

9. 36)5,490.□ = □□□.□

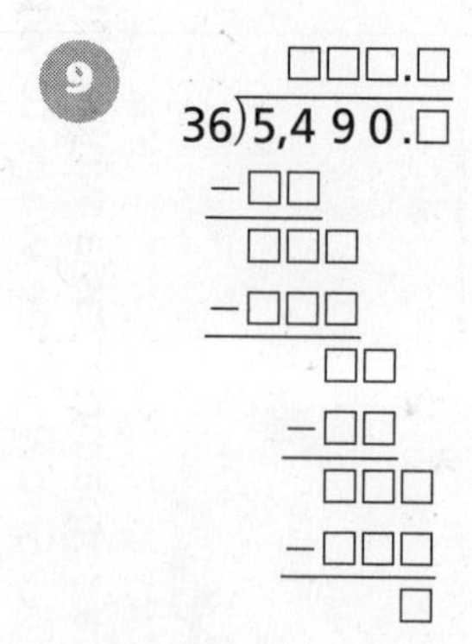

Check

Show your work on a separate piece of paper.

10. Divide. Write the remainder as a whole number.

6)77

11. Divide. Write the remainder as a fraction.

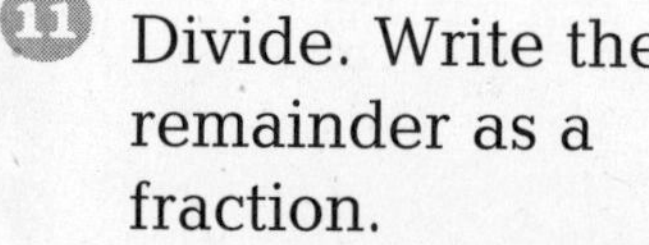

12)184

12. Divide. Write the remainder as a decimal.

18)369

Skill 40

Decimal Operations

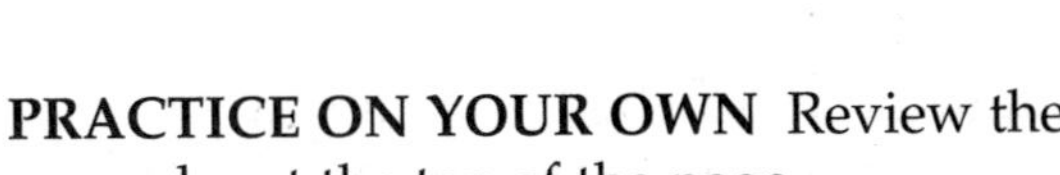

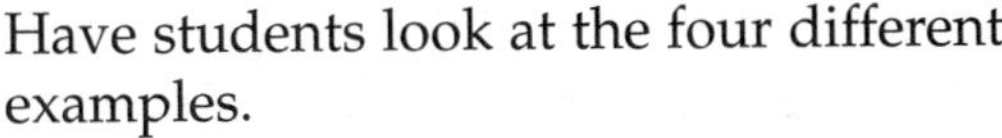

Using Skill 40

OBJECTIVE Perform operations with decimals

Have students look at the four different examples.

Ask: **What is important to remember when adding or subtracting decimals?** (Align the decimal points.)

Ask: **When multiplying decimals, how do you determine where the decimal point goes in the product?** (Count the total number of decimal places in the factors and then move the decimal point that many positions to the left in the product.)

What do you have to remember to do when dividing a decimal by a decimal? (Change the divisor to a whole number by moving the decimal point in the dividend and divisor.)

TRY THESE In Exercises 1–4 students add, subtract, multiply and divide using decimals.

- **Exercise 1** 71.62
- **Exercise 2** 20.7
- **Exercise 3** 5.076
- **Exercise 4** 9.4

PRACTICE ON YOUR OWN Review the examples at the top of the page.

CHECK Determine if students know how to perform operations with decimals. Success is indicated by 5 out of 6 correct responses.

Students who successfully complete the **Practice on Your Own** and **Check** are ready to move to the next skill.

COMMON ERRORS

- Misalignment of decimal points. Encourage students to use lined paper or graph paper to keep decimal aligned.
- Mistaking place values. When adding or subtracting numbers with a different number of place values (0.6 + 4.56), encourage students to add zeros or use a place value chart to align the places correctly.
- Misplaced decimal point in the product. Have students count the number of decimal points in each factor and then place the decimal point in the product.
- Missing the decimal point in the quotient. Have students immediately place the decimal point in the quotient.

Students who made more than 3 errors in the **Practice on Your Own**, or who were not successful in the **Check** section, may benefit from the **Alternative Teaching Strategy** on the next page.

Optional

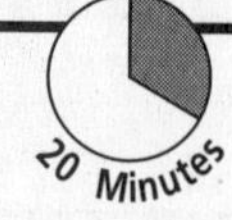

Alternative Teaching Strategy
Perform Operations with Decimals

OBJECTIVE Perform operations with decimals

MATERIALS index cards with problems written on them

If students are having difficulty with adding, subtracting, multiplying, or dividing decimals, you may need to provide four separate instructional periods to review each skill.

Students might recognize that the processes for adding and subtracting decimals are similar but that different procedures are needed to multiply and divide decimals.

To help develop number sense, prepare a set of cards with exercises similar to these:

A. 17.26 + 18.543
B. 23.54 − 9.547
C. 9.82 × 2.14
D. 8.85 ÷ 3.54

Without computing, have students identify either orally or in writing, what is necessary to carry out each operation.

For A, students should realize the need to rewrite the problem and align the decimal points. They should recognize the value of adding a zero to 17.26 so that both numbers have the same number of decimal places.

For B, students should realize the need to rewrite the problem and align the decimal points. Students should recognize the value of adding a zero to 23.54 so that each number has the same number of decimal places. You might ask students if regrouping will be necessary when they subtract.

For C, students should recognize the need to rewrite the problem vertically. Students should recognize that multiplying decimals is very similar to multiplying whole numbers. Ask students how many decimal places the answer will have (4).

For D, students should recognize the need to rewrite the problem. They should know it is necessary to move the decimal point two places in both the dividend and divisor.

Name ______________________ Skill ______________________

Skill 40

Decimal Operations

Adding Decimals
Find 8.93 + 2.46.

Rewrite the problem so the decimal points are aligned.

```
  8.93
+2.46   add
 11.39
```

Subtracting Decimals
Find 34.5 − 17.32.

Rewrite the problem so the decimal points are aligned.

```
  34.5
−17.32

  34.50   If necessary, add
−17.32   zeros as
  17.18   placeholders and
          regroup when
          subtracting.
```

Multiplying Decimals
Find 3.24 × 0.3.

Rewrite the problem.

Determine the number of decimal places in the product.

```
 3.24   ←   2 decimal places
× 0.3   ←  +1 decimal place
0.972   ←   3 decimal places
```

Dividing Decimals
Find 1.75 ÷ 3.5.

Rewrite the problem.

$3.5\overline{)1.75}$ Change the divisor to a whole number and move the decimal point in the dividend.

$3.5\overline{)1.75}$

```
    0.5    Divided as you
35)17.5    would for whole
   175     numbers.
     0
```

Try These

Solve.

1. 17.23 + 54.39

```
  17.23
+54.39    Align decimals.
```

2. 45.6 − 24.9

```
  45.6
−24.9    Align decimals.
```

3. 4.23 × 1.2

```
 4.23   ←   □ decimal places
× 1.2   ←  +□ decimal place
        ←   □ decimal places
```

4. 6.11 ÷ 0.65

$0.65\overline{)6.11}$ Move the decimal point.

Go to the next side.

Name ______________________ Skill ______________________

Practice on Your Own

Skill 40

Think: To add and subtract decimals, align the decimal points.

Think: When multiplying decimals, determine the number of place values the product will have.

Think: When dividing decimals, remember to move the decimal point so you are dividing by a whole number.

Solve.

1. 74.25 + 21.38

   74.25
   +21.38 ← align

2. 2.17 × 0.4

   2.17 ← □ decimal place
   × 0.4 ← +□ decimal place
   ← □ decimal places

3. 7.77 ÷ 2.1

   2.1)7.77 move decimal

Solve.

4. 9.73 + 3.688 ________

5. 80.2 − 4.57 ________

6. 6.45 ÷ 1.2 ________

7. 3.69 ÷ 0.4 ________

8. 6.1 × 3.7 ________

9. 0.5 × 0.85 ________

Check

Solve.

10. 23.81 − 5.4 ________

11. 11.52 ÷ 3.2 ________

12. 37.4 + 8.01 ________

13. 9.71 − 3.226 ________

14. 0.75 × 4.1 ________

15. 9.51 × 0.7 ________

Skill 

Multiply Decimals by Powers of 10

Using Skill 41

OBJECTIVE Use a pattern to multiply a decimal by 10, 100, or 1,000

Begin by explaining to students that they can use a pattern that will help them multiply decimals by 10, 100, and 1,000.

Direct students' attention to the first example. Explain that the multiplication sentences show the results of multiplying 10 × 0.3, 100 × 0.3, and 1,000 × 0.3. Emphasize that the placement of the decimal point shows a pattern that is helpful when multiplying any decimal by 10 and powers of 10. Ask: **When you multiply 0.3 by 10, what is the product?** (3) **What happens to the decimal point?** (The decimal point moves 1 place to the right, since 3 is the same as 3.0) **When you multiply 0.3 by 100, what is the product?** (30) **What happens to the decimal point?** (It moves 2 places to the right.)

Prompt students with similar questions for multiplying by 1,000.

Guide students to understand the pattern: the decimal point moves the same number of places as there are zeros in the factors 10, 100, 1,000.

Continue in a similar way for the remaining two examples. Lead students to understand that the pattern also applies when multiplying hundredths and when multiplying ones and tenths.

TRY THESE In Exercises 1–3 students use a pattern to multiply decimals by powers of 10.

- **Exercise 1** Multiply tenths by 10, 100, 1,000
- **Exercise 2** Multiply hundredths by 10, 100, 1,000
- **Exercise 3** Multiply ones and tenths by 10, 100, 1,000

PRACTICE ON YOUR OWN Review the examples at the top of the page. Explain that although the factors are reversed, the pattern can still be used. In Exercises 1–3, students multiply decimals by powers of 10. In Exercises 4–9, students multiply decimals by powers by 10 and write how many places to move the decimal point. In Exercises 10–12, students multiply decimals by powers of 10.

CHECK Determine if students can use a pattern to multiply decimals by 10, 100, and 1,000. Success is indicated by 5 out of 6 correct responses.

Students who successfully complete the **Practice on Your Own** and **Check** are ready to move to the next skill.

COMMON ERRORS

- Students may move the decimal point an incorrect number of places.
- Students may move the decimal point to the left.

Students who made more than 3 errors in the **Practice on Your Own**, or who were not successful in the **Check** section, may benefit from the **Alternative Teaching Strategy** on the next page.

Optional

Alternative Teaching Strategy

15 Minutes

Use Money to Model a Multiplication Pattern

OBJECTIVE Use money amounts and a pattern to multiply by 10, 100, and 1,000

MATERIALS flip chart, paper and pencil

Explain to students that they can use a pattern to multiply money amounts by 10, 100 and 1000. Recall that a dime is **one tenth** of a dollar. Ask: **How do you write one tenth as a decimal?** (0.1)

Display this pattern on the flip chart.

$$10 \times \$0.1 = 1 \text{ dollar}$$
$$100 \times \$0.1 = 10 \text{ dollars}$$
$$1{,}000 \times \$0.1 = 100 \text{ dollars}$$

Ask: **How do you write 1 dollar using a decimal?** ($1.00) **How do you write 10 dollars?** ($10.00) **How do you write 100 dollars?** ($100.00)

Rewrite the pattern using decimals in the products.

$$10 \times \$0.1 = \$1.00$$
$$100 \times \$0.1 = \$10.00$$
$$1{,}000 \times \$0.1 = \$100.00$$

Have students look at the multiplication sentences and examine what happens to the placement of the decimal point.

Demonstrate the pattern. Show how the decimal point moves one place to the right when you multiply by 10, two places to the right when you multiply by 100, and three places to the right when you multiply by 1,000. Explain that this pattern can be used when any money amount or decimal is multiplied by 10, 100, or 1,000.

Repeat the activity for pennies, quarters, and half dollars, using the decimals 0.01, 0.25, 0.50.

When students show an understanding of the pattern with amounts less than one dollar, have them use the pattern to multiply amounts greater than one dollar.

$$10 \times \$1.20 = \$12.00$$
$$100 \times \$1.20 = \$120.00$$
$$1{,}000 \times \$1.20 = \$1{,}200.00$$

Name ______________________ Skill ______________________

Multiply Decimals by Powers of 10

Skill 41

Use a pattern to multiply a decimal by 10, 100, or 1,000.

Example A
Multiply tenths.

$10 \times 0.3 = 3$ ← Multiply by 10. Decimal point moves **1** place to the right.

$100 \times 0.3\mathbf{0} = 30$ ← Multiply by 100. Decimal point moves **2** places to the right.

$1{,}000 \times 0.3\mathbf{00} = 300$ ← Multiply by 1,000. Decimal point moves **3** places to the right.

Example B
Multiply hundredths.

$10 \times 0.05 = 0.5$ ←1 place to the right

$100 \times 0.05 = 5$ ←2 places to the right

$1{,}000 \times 0.050 = 50$ ←3 places to the right

Example C
Multiply ones and tenths.

$10 \times 1.2 = 12$

$100 \times 1.20 = 120$

$1{,}000 \times 1.200 = 1{,}200$

Try These

Find the product.

1. $10 \times 0.4 =$ ________

   $100 \times 0.4\mathbf{0} =$ ________

   $1{,}000 \times 0.4\mathbf{00} =$ ________

2. $10 \times 0.06 =$ ________

   $100 \times 0.06 =$ ________

   $1{,}000 \times 0.06\mathbf{0} =$ ________

3. $10 \times 1.5 =$ ________

   $100 \times 1.5\mathbf{0} =$ ________

   $1{,}000 \times 1.5\mathbf{00} =$ ________

Go to the next side.

Name ______________________ Skill ______________________

Practice on Your Own

Skill 41

Use a pattern to multiply by 10, 100, and 1,000.

0.8 × 10 = 8	0.09 × 10 = 0.9	Multiply by 10. Decimal point moves 1 place to the right.
0.8**0** × 100 = 80	0.09 × 100 = 9	Multiply by 100. Decimal point moves 2 places to the right.
0.8**00** × 1,000 = 800	0.09**0** × 1,000 = 90	Multiply by 1,000. Decimal point moves 3 places to the right.

Find the product.

1. 10 × 0.5 = ______
   100 × 0.5**0** = ______
   1,000 × 0.5**00** = ______

2. 10 × 0.18 = ______
   100 × 0.18 = ______
   1,000 × 0.18**0** = ______

3. 7.6 × 10 = ______
   7.6**0** × 100 = ______
   7.6**00** × 1,000 = ______

Find the product. Tell how many places you moved the decimal to the right.

4. 10 × 0.9 = ______
   Move ______ place(s).

5. 0.2 × 100 = ______
   Move ______ place(s).

6. 1,000 × 1.9 = ______
   Move ______ place(s).

7. 100 × 2.4 = ______
   Move ______ place(s).

8. 1,000 × 5.08 = ______
   Move ______ place(s).

9. 0.61 × 10 = ______
   Move ______ place(s).

Find the product.

10. 5.7 × 1,000 = ______

11. 1.23 × 10 = ______

12. 0.07 × 100 = ______

Check

Find the product.

13. 10 × 8.9 = ______

14. 1,000 × 0.04 = ______

15. 100 × 5.38 = ______

16. 1.6 × 10 = ______

17. 8.39 × 1,000 = ______

18. 2.7 × 100 = ______

Skill 42 Operations with Fractions

Using Skill 42

OBJECTIVE Adding, subtracting, multiplying, and dividing fractions

Read about the least common denominator (LCD) of two fractions. Tell students that they will need to use the LCD when they are adding or subtracting fractions with unlike denominators.

Look at Example A. Ask: **What are the denominators of the fractions?** (4 and 5) **When you add fractions with different denominators, what is the first step?** (Find the least common denominator.) **What do you do after you find the LCD, but before you add?** (Use the same factor that changed the denominator to multiply the numerator.)

Each fraction is written as an equivalent fraction with 20 as the denominator because 20 is the least common multiple of 4 and 5. This means that 20 is the least common denominator. For $\frac{3}{4}$, you multiplied 4 by 5 to get 20, so multiply the numerator, 3, by 5 to get your new numerator.

Look at Example B. Stress the need to find the least common denominator before you subtract. Subtract the numerators and use the common denominator in the difference.

Look at Example C. Ask: **How is the process of multiplying fractions different from the process of adding like fractions?** (To add like fractions, you add numerators and keep the denominator the same; to multiply fractions, you multiply numerators and multiply denominators.)

Look at Example D. Ask: **How is dividing fractions different from multiplying fractions?** (When you multiply, you multiply numerators and denominators; when you divide, you find the reciprocal of the divisor, then multiply that by the dividend.)

TRY THESE Exercises 1–4 require students to determine the appropriate algorithm for computing with fractions, decide whether and how to find common denominators, and decide whether and how to simplify answers.

- **Exercise 1:** add fractions
- **Exercise 2:** subtract fractions
- **Exercise 3:** multiply fractions
- **Exercise 4:** divide fractions

PRACTICE ON YOUR OWN Review the example at the top of the page. As students work through the exercise, make sure that they find the LCD to subtract and find the reciprocal of the divisor to divide.

CHECK Determine if the students know how to add, subtract, multiply, and divide fractions. Success is indicated by 4 out of 4 correct responses.

Students who successfully complete the **Practice on Your Own** and **Check** are ready to move to the next skill.

COMMON ERRORS

- Students may not find a common denominator before they add or subtract.
- Students may find the reciprocal of the dividend instead of the divisor when dividing fractions.
- Students may not recognize a fraction that can be simplified.

Students who made more than 2 errors in the **Practice on Your Own**, or who were not successful in the **Check** section, may benefit from the **Alternative Teaching Strategy** on the next page.

Optional

Alternative Teaching Strategy
Modeling Operations with Fractions

OBJECTIVE Use rectangles to model operations with fractions

MATERIALS graph paper, colored pencils

Identify the operations that are difficult for students and focus on helping students see the connection between a visual model and an algorithm. Encourage students to use the visual model until they are comfortable (and accurate) without it. This may take several sessions.

Adding fractions with like denominators

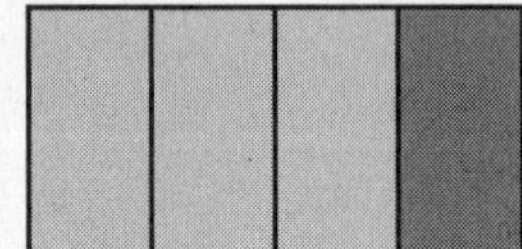

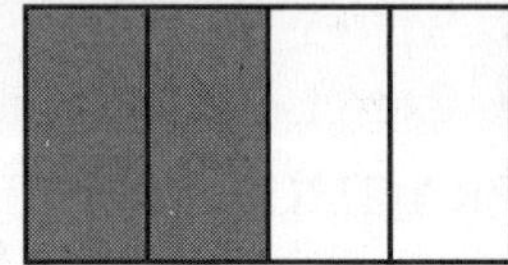

$\frac{3}{4} + \frac{3}{4}$

Draw a rectangle. Show fourths. Shade 3 of the fourths. There are not enough fourths to shade 3 more, so draw another rectangle and show fourths. Now shade 3 more fourths. Count the fourths. There are $\frac{6}{4}$. This is the same as one whole and 2 more fourths. $1\frac{2}{4} = 1\frac{1}{2}$.

Adding fractions with unlike denominators

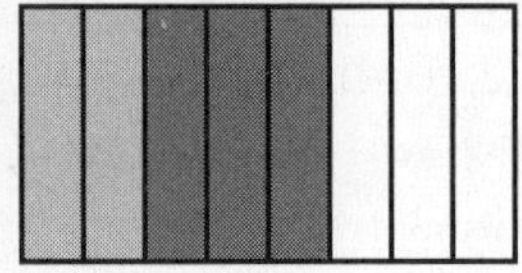

$\frac{1}{4} + \frac{3}{8}$

Draw a rectangle. Show fourths <u>and</u> eighths. Shade 1 fourth. Shade 3 eighths. Count the parts of the rectangle. There are 8 parts. This is the denominator. Count the shaded eighths. There are 5 shaded parts. The sum is $\frac{5}{8}$.

Subtracting fractions

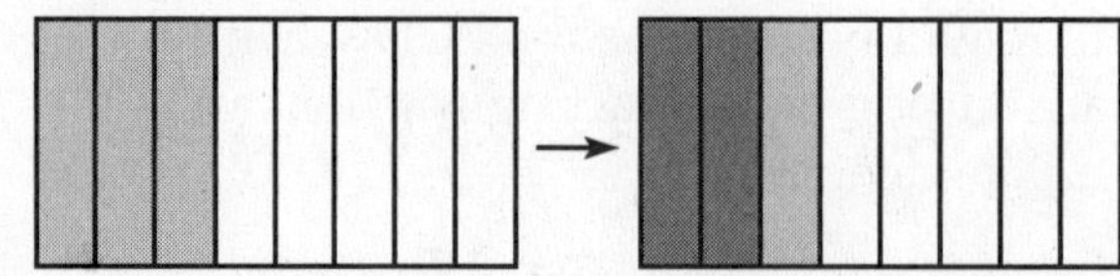

$\frac{3}{8} - \frac{1}{4}$

Draw a rectangle. Show fourths <u>and</u> eighths. Shade 3 eighths. Shade again the 1 fourth you are going to take away from $\frac{3}{8}$. Ask: **What part is left from the original $\frac{3}{8}$?** ($\frac{1}{8}$ is the difference.)

Multiplying fractions

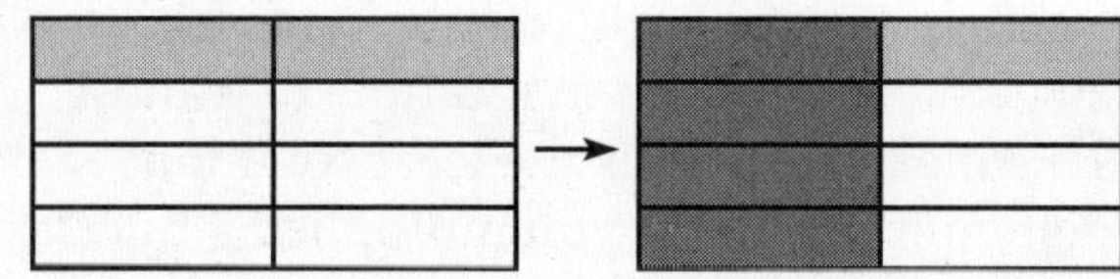

$\frac{1}{2} \times \frac{1}{4}$

Draw a rectangle. Show fourths in one direction. Shade $\frac{1}{4}$. Show halves in the other direction. Shade $\frac{1}{2}$. Ask: **How many equal parts are in the rectangle?** (8) **How many parts are shaded twice?** (1) $\frac{1}{2}$ of $\frac{1}{4}$ is $\frac{1}{8}$. When you multiply fractions less than 1, the product is less than the factors.

Dividing fractions

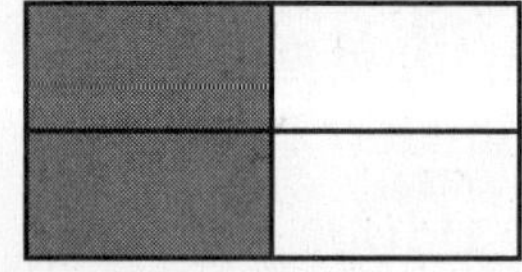

$\frac{1}{2} \div \frac{1}{4}$

Draw a rectangle. Show halves <u>and</u> fourths. Count the number of fourths in one of the halves. There are 2 fourths in $\frac{1}{2}$. $\frac{1}{2} \div \frac{1}{4}$ can be interpreted as *how many fourths are in one half*. The quotient is 2.

Name ______________________ Skill ______________________

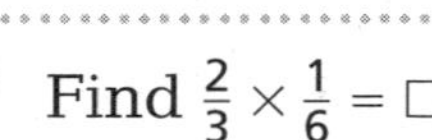

Skill 42

Operations with Fractions

Remember: The **least common denominator** (LCD) of two fractions is the least common multiple (LCM) of the denominators. The **greatest common factor** (GCF) is the largest number that is a factor of two or more numbers.

You can add, subtract, multiply, and divide with fractions.

Example A Add. $\frac{3}{4} + \frac{2}{5} = \square$

The denominators are different.
So, use the LCD to write equivalent fractions.

$$\frac{3}{4} = \frac{3 \times 5}{4 \times 5} = \frac{15}{20} \quad \text{LCD is 20.}$$
$$+\frac{2}{5} = +\frac{2 \times 4}{5 \times 4} = +\frac{8}{20} \quad \text{Add the numerators.}$$

Simplify the answer. $\frac{23}{20} = \frac{20}{20} + \frac{3}{20} = 1\frac{3}{20}$

So, $\frac{3}{4} + \frac{2}{5} = 1\frac{3}{20}$.

Example B Subtract. $\frac{13}{15} - \frac{2}{3} = \square$

The denominators are different.
So, use the LCD to write equivalent fractions.

$$\frac{13}{15} = \rightarrow = \frac{13}{15} \quad \text{LCD is 15.}$$
$$-\frac{2}{3} = -\frac{2 \times 5}{3 \times 5} = -\frac{10}{15} \quad \text{Subtract the numerators.}$$

Simplify the answer. $\frac{3}{15} = \frac{1}{5}$

So, $\frac{13}{15} - \frac{2}{3} = \frac{1}{5}$.

Example C Multiply. $\frac{3}{6} \times \frac{4}{12} = \square$

Multiply the numerators.
Then multiply the denominators.

Divide by GCF, 12.

$$\frac{3}{6} \times \frac{4}{12} = \frac{3 \times 4}{6 \times 12} = \frac{12}{72} = \frac{12 \div 12}{72 \div 12} = \frac{1}{6}$$

So, $\frac{3}{6} \times \frac{4}{12} = \frac{1}{6}$.

Example D Divide. $\frac{5}{7} \div \frac{1}{2} = \square$

To divide with fractions, first write
the reciprocal of the divisor. Then multiply.

reciprocal of $\frac{1}{2}$ Simplify

$$\frac{5}{7} \div \frac{1}{2} = \frac{5}{7} \times \frac{2}{1} = \frac{10}{7}, \text{ or } 1\frac{3}{7}$$

So, $\frac{5}{7} \div \frac{1}{2} = 1\frac{3}{7}$.

Try These

1. Find $\frac{1}{2} + \frac{2}{5} = \square$.
2. Find $\frac{5}{6} - \frac{1}{3} = \square$.
3. Find $\frac{2}{3} \times \frac{1}{6} = \square$.
4. Find $\frac{4}{7} \div \frac{2}{14} = \square$.

Go to the next side.

Name ______________________ Skill ______________________

Practice on Your Own

Skill 42

Find $\frac{6}{7} - \frac{2}{3}$.

Use the LCD to write equivalent fractions.

LCD is 21.

$$\frac{6}{7} = \frac{6 \times 3}{7 \times 3} = \frac{18}{21}$$

$$-\frac{2}{3} = -\frac{2 \times 7}{3 \times 7} = -\frac{14}{21}$$

Subtract the numerators. $\frac{4}{21}$

So, $\frac{6}{7} - \frac{2}{3} = \frac{4}{21}$.

Find $\frac{3}{8} \div \frac{1}{6}$.

Write the reciprocal of the divisor. Multiply.

$$\frac{3}{8} \div \frac{1}{6} = \frac{3}{8} \times \frac{6}{1}$$

$$= \frac{18}{8} \qquad 3 \times 6 = 18, \quad 8 \times 1 = 8$$

$$= \frac{9}{4}, \text{ or } 2\frac{1}{4} \qquad \text{Simplify.}$$

So, $\frac{3}{8} \div \frac{1}{6} = 2\frac{1}{4}$.

Add.

1. Rewrite with the LCD.

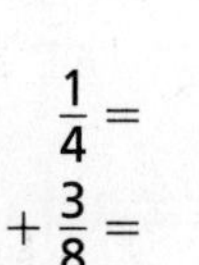

$$\frac{1}{4} =$$
$$+\frac{3}{8} =$$

2.

$$\frac{5}{12} =$$
$$+\frac{7}{9} =$$

Subtract.

3. Rewrite with the LCD.

$$\frac{4}{5} =$$
$$-\frac{2}{3} =$$

4.

$$\frac{11}{15} =$$
$$-\frac{6}{10} =$$

Multiply.

5. $\frac{3}{5} \times \frac{1}{6} = \frac{\square \times \square}{\square \times \square} =$ ________

Simplest form: ________

6. $\frac{5}{8} \times \frac{3}{10} = \frac{\square \times \square}{\square \times \square} =$ ________

Simplest form: ________

Divide.

7. $\frac{4}{9} \div \frac{1}{3} = \frac{4 \times \square}{9 \times \square} =$ ________

Simplest form: ________

8. $\frac{9}{10} \div \frac{3}{6} = \frac{\square \times \square}{\square \times \square} =$ ________

Simplest form: ________

Check

Add, subtract, multiply, or divide. Write the answer in simplest form.

9.

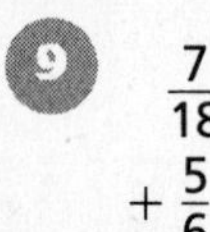

$$\frac{7}{18}$$
$$+\frac{5}{6}$$

10.

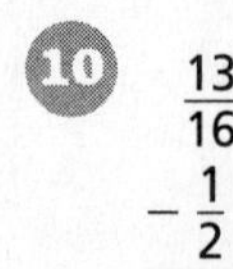

$$\frac{13}{16}$$
$$-\frac{1}{2}$$

11. $\frac{4}{7} \times \frac{3}{12} =$ ____

12. $\frac{6}{15} \div \frac{8}{9} =$ ____

Skill 43 Add and Subtract Like Fractions

Using Skills 43

OBJECTIVE Add and subtract like fractions

Mention to students that Skill 43 reviews addition and subtraction of fractions with like denominators. Determine if they recall that with like fractions, students need only add or subtract numerators.

Draw attention to Step 1.

Ask: **To add fractions, what has to be true about the fractions?** (The denominators must be the same.)

What is the denominator in the fraction $\frac{2}{7}$? $\frac{3}{7}$? (7, 7)

Are the denominators the same? (Yes)

When adding fractions, do you add the numerators or the denominators? (numerators)

Explain to the students that a fraction is in simplest form if the greatest common factor of the numerator and denominator is 1.

Do 5 and 7 have any factors in common other than 1? (no)

Continue to ask similar questions as you work through the steps of the other examples for addition and subtraction.

TRY THESE Exercises 1–3 model the type of exercises students will find on the **Practice on Your Own** page.

- **Exercise 1** Add like fractions
- **Exercise 2** Subtract like fractions
- **Exercise 3** Subtract like fractions and simplify the result

PRACTICE ON YOUR OWN Review the example at the top of the page. Ask students to explain why they can add or subtract each fraction and explain how they know if the answer is in simplest form.

CHECK Determine if the students can add or subtract fractions and can recognize whether a fraction is in simplest form. Success is indicated by 3 out of 4 correct responses.

Students who successfully complete the **Practice on Your Own** and **Check** are ready to move to the next skill.

COMMON ERRORS

- Students add the denominators of the fractions.
- Students simplify fractions by dividing the numerator and denominator by different factors.

Students who made more than 3 errors in the **Practice on Your Own**, or who were not successful in the **Check** section, may benefit from the **Alternative Teaching Strategy** on the next page.

Optional

Alternative Teaching Strategy

10 Minutes

Model Adding and Subtracting Like Fractions

OBJECTIVE Use fraction strips to add and subtract like fractions

MATERIALS fraction strips in halves, fourths, and eighths

You may wish to have the students work in pairs. One student can model the steps for adding or subtracting using the fraction strips and the other student can record the steps on paper.

Distribute the fraction strips and have the students model $\frac{1}{8} + \frac{3}{8}$.

Ask: **Do both of the fraction strips have the same size parts?** (yes)

When you combine the two fraction strips how many parts in all are shaded? (4)

Have the students record the sum.

Determine if students recognize that the sum is not in simplest form.

Say: **Try to find other fraction strips that have the same area shaded as the one you have.**

Ask: **What other fraction strips equal $\frac{4}{8}$?** ($\frac{1}{2}$, $\frac{2}{4}$)

Which is the simplest form of $\frac{4}{8}$? ($\frac{1}{2}$)

When students show an understanding of adding or subtracting fractions with like denominators, have them summarize by stating a rule for adding or subtracting like fractions.

When students use the strips to model subtraction, they will be modeling comparison subtraction. Parts on the two strips are matched, and the part(s) left over is the difference.

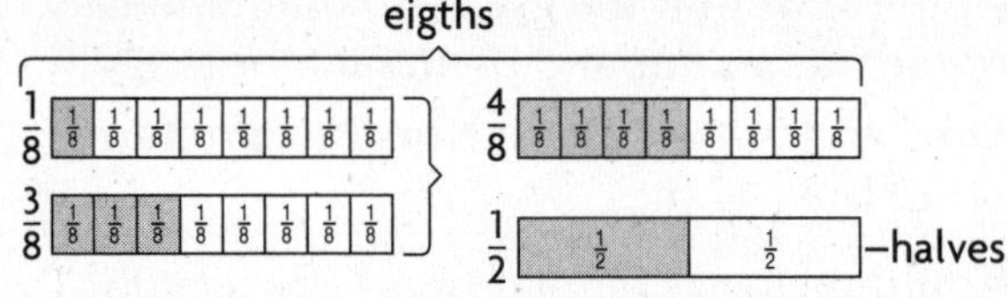

Name ______________________ Skill ______________________

Skill 43

Add and Subtract Like Fractions

Before you add or subtract fractions, compare the denominators to be sure they are the same.

Add Like Fractions

Find $\frac{2}{7} + \frac{3}{7}$.

Step 1 The denominators are the same. Add the numerators.

$\frac{2}{7} + \frac{3}{7} = \frac{\square}{7}$ $\qquad 2 + 3 = 5$

same denominator

Step 2 Write the sum over the denominator.

$\frac{2}{7} + \frac{3}{7} = \frac{5}{7}$

Subtract Like Fractions

Find $\frac{7}{8} - \frac{4}{8}$.

Step 1 The denominators are the same. Subtract the numerators.

$\frac{7}{8} - \frac{4}{8} = \frac{\square}{8}$ $\qquad 7 - 4 = 3$

same denominator

Step 2 Write the difference over the denominator.

$\frac{7}{8} - \frac{4}{8} = \frac{3}{8}$

Try These

Add or subtract. Write each answer in simplest form.

1. $\frac{3}{5} + \frac{1}{5}$

   Denominators the same? ____

   Add: $\frac{3}{5} + \frac{1}{5} = \frac{\quad}{\quad}$

   Simplest form? ____

2. $\frac{6}{7} - \frac{4}{7}$

   Denominators the same? ____

   Subtract numerators:

   $\frac{6}{7} - \frac{4}{7} =$ ____

   Simplest form? ____

3. $\frac{7}{8} - \frac{3}{8}$

   Denominators the same? ____

   Subtract numerators: $\frac{7}{8} - \frac{3}{8} =$ ____

   Simplest form? ____

   $\frac{\square \div \square}{\square \div \square} = \frac{\square}{\square}$

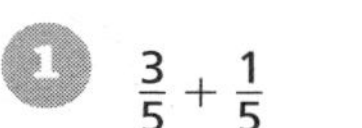

Name ______________________ Skill ______________________

Practice on Your Own

Skill 43

Add like fractions. $\frac{3}{8} + \frac{1}{8} =$

$\frac{3}{8} + \frac{1}{8}$ The denominators are the same.

$\frac{3}{8} + \frac{1}{8} = \frac{4}{8}$ **So,** add the numerators.

Answer is **not** in simplest form.

$\frac{4}{8} \div \frac{4}{4} = \frac{1}{2}$ **So,** divide by the greatest common factor.

$\frac{3}{8} + \frac{1}{8} = \frac{1}{2}$

Subtract like fractions. $\frac{8}{9} - \frac{2}{9} =$

$\frac{8}{9} - \frac{2}{9}$ The denominators are the same.

$\frac{8}{9} - \frac{2}{9} = \frac{6}{9}$ **So,** subtract the numerators.

Answer is **not** in simplest form.

$\frac{6}{9} \div \frac{3}{3} = \frac{2}{3}$ **So,** divide by the greatest common factor.

$\frac{8}{9} - \frac{2}{9} = \frac{2}{3}$

Add or subtract. Write each answer in simplest form.

1. $\frac{2}{6} + \frac{3}{6}$
   Denominators the same? ___
   Add:
   ___ + ___ = ___
   Simplest form? ___

2. $\frac{4}{5} - \frac{3}{5}$
   Denominators the same? ___
   Subtract:
   ___ − ___ = ___
   Simplest form? ___

3. $\frac{7}{10} + \frac{1}{10}$
   Denominators the same? ___
   Add:
   ___ + ___ = ___
   Simplest form? ___

4. $\frac{2}{5} + \frac{1}{5} =$ ___
   Simplest form? ___

5. $\frac{7}{8} - \frac{3}{8} =$ ___
   Simplest form? ___

6. $\frac{10}{10} - \frac{8}{10} =$ ___
   Simplest form? ___

7. $\frac{4}{7} - \frac{2}{7}$ ______

8. $\frac{1}{9} + \frac{3}{9}$ ______

9. $\frac{5}{8} - \frac{1}{8}$ ______

10. $\frac{5}{6} + \frac{1}{6}$ ______

Check

Add or Subtract. Write each answer in simplest form.

11. $\frac{3}{3} - \frac{2}{3}$ ______

12. $\frac{6}{8} + \frac{1}{8}$ ______

13. $\frac{8}{9} - \frac{5}{9}$ ______

14. $\frac{4}{10} + \frac{4}{10}$ ______

Skill 44 Multiply Fractions

Using Skill 44

OBJECTIVE Find the product of two fractions

Direct students' attention to the first example. Explain that they can use models to find the product of two fractions. Review how a model can be used to represent fractions. Ask: **Into how many equal parts would you divide a model to show thirds?** (3) **How many of these parts would you shade to show $\frac{2}{3}$?** (2)

Then ask: **Into how many equal parts would you divide the model to show eighths?** (8) **How many of these parts would you shade to show $\frac{3}{8}$?** (3)

Have students relate these models to the model of the product of $\frac{2}{3}$ and $\frac{3}{8}$, focusing on the intersection of the two shaded parts. Ask: **Into how many equal parts is the whole model divided?** (24) **How many of these equal parts are shaded twice?** (6) **So, 6 out of 24, or $\frac{6}{24}$ is the product of two-thirds and three-eighths.**

Direct students' attention to the second example. Refer to the model to help students understand the definition of multiplication of fractions: the product is equal to the product of the numerators over the product of the denominators. Remind students that the product should be written in simplest form.

TRY THESE Exercises 1–3 model the type of exercises students will find on the **Practice on Your Own** page.

- **Exercises 1–2** Product is in simplest form.
- **Exercise 3** Product must be written in simplest form.

PRACTICE ON YOUR OWN Review the example at the top of the page. Ask: **What is the product of the numerators?** (12) **What is the product of the denominators?** (20) **So, what is the product of $\frac{3}{4}$ and $\frac{4}{5}$?** ($\frac{12}{20}$, or $\frac{3}{5}$)

CHECK Determine if students can find the product of two fractions by finding the product of the numerators and writing it over the product of the denominators. Success is indicated by 3 out of 3 correct responses.

Students who successfully complete the **Practice on Your Own** and **Check** are ready to move to the next skill.

COMMON ERRORS

- Students may multiply the numerators and write the product over one of the denominators, confusing fraction multiplication with fraction addition.
- Students may incorrectly multiply numerators or denominators.

Students who made more than 2 errors in the **Practice on Your Own**, or who were not successful in the **Check** section, may benefit from the **Alternative Teaching Strategy** on the next page.

Optional

Alternative Teaching Strategy

Use Counters to Model Multiplying Fractions

15 Minutes

OBJECTIVE Use counters to model the product of two fractions

MATERIALS counters, lengths of yarn

To find the product of $\frac{1}{3}$ and $\frac{4}{5}$, have students make an array to show the product of the denominators.

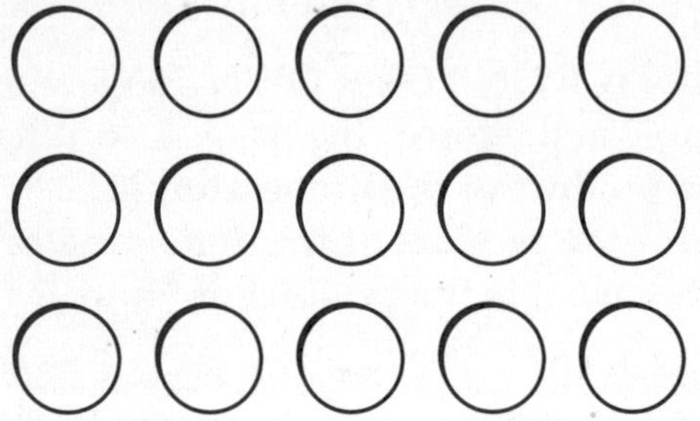

Have them use a piece of yarn to loop $\frac{1}{3}$ of the counters.

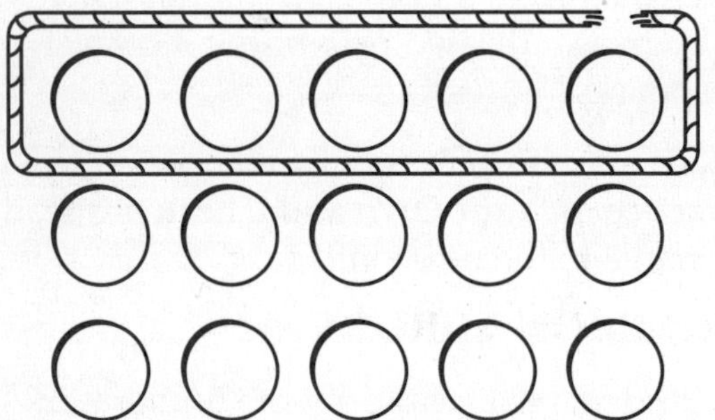

Have them use another piece of yarn to loop $\frac{4}{5}$ of the counters.

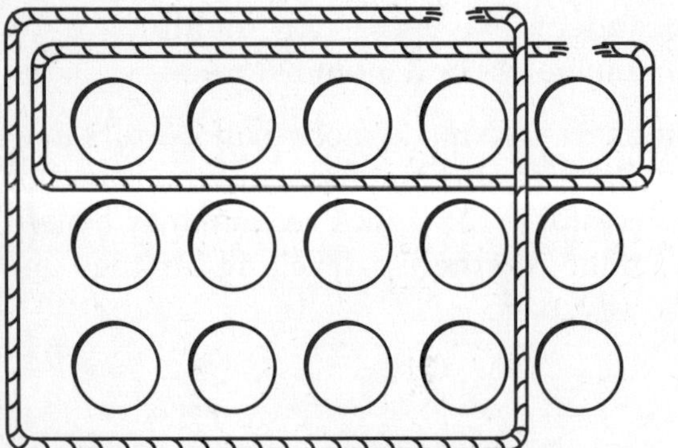

Ask: **How many parts are there in all?** (15) **How many parts have been looped twice?** (4)

Explain that 4 out of 15 parts looped means that $\frac{1}{3} \times \frac{4}{5} = \frac{4}{15}$.

Display $\frac{2}{3} \times \frac{5}{8}$. Have students make an array to show the product of the denominators.

Have them use a piece of yarn to loop $\frac{2}{3}$ of the counters.

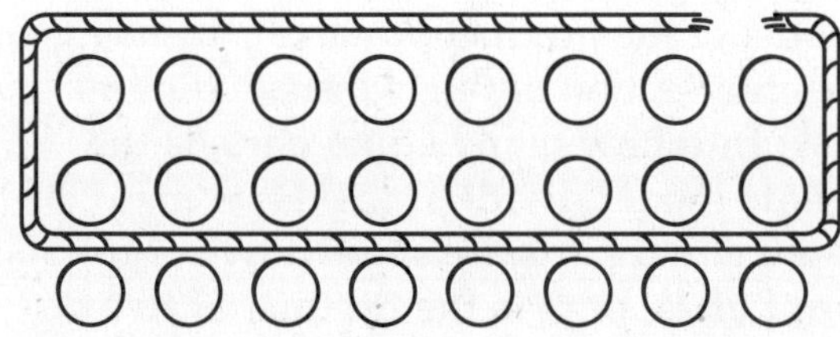

Have them use another piece of yarn to loop $\frac{5}{8}$ of the counters.

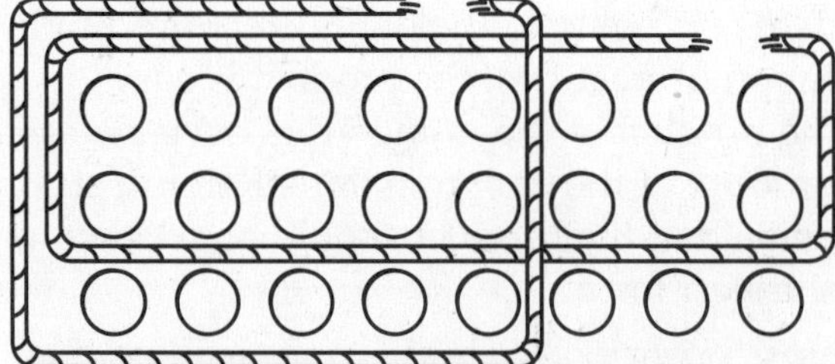

Ask: **How many part are there in all?** (24) **How many parts out of 24 have you looped twice?** (10) **So, what is the product of $\frac{2}{3}$ and $\frac{5}{8}$?** ($\frac{10}{24}$)

Review with students how to write $\frac{10}{24}$ in simplest form. ($\frac{5}{12}$)

You may wish to repeat the activity using additional exercises from the **Practice on Your Own.**

Multiply Fractions

Skill 44

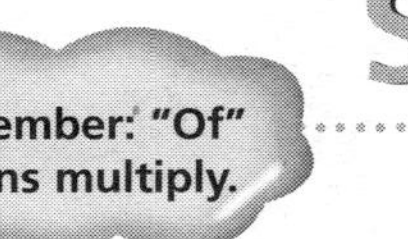
Remember: "Of" means multiply.

When you multiply two fractions less than one, the product is less than each of the factors. Find $\frac{2}{3}$ of $\frac{3}{8}$.

Use models to find the product.

Step 1 Divide the model into 3 equal rows. Shade two rows to show $\frac{2}{3}$.

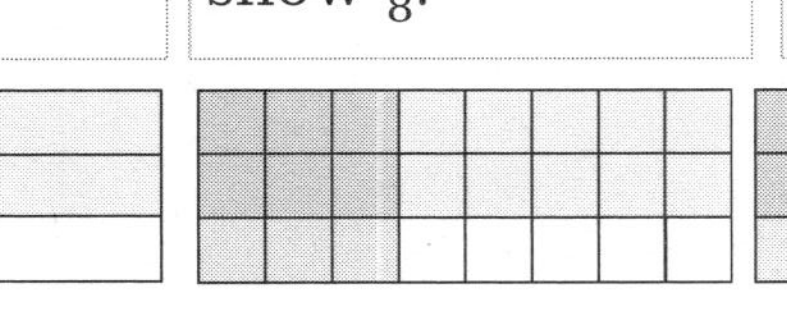

Step 2 Now divide the model into 8 equal columns. Shade 3 columns to show $\frac{3}{8}$.

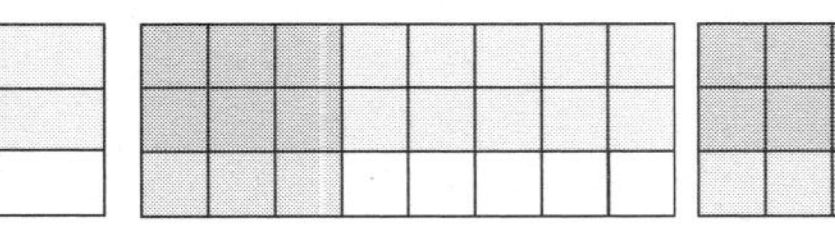

Step 3 The section where the shading overlaps is the product.

The model is now divided into 24 equal parts. The shading overlaps in 6 of 24 parts

$$\frac{2}{3} \times \frac{3}{8} = \frac{6}{24}$$

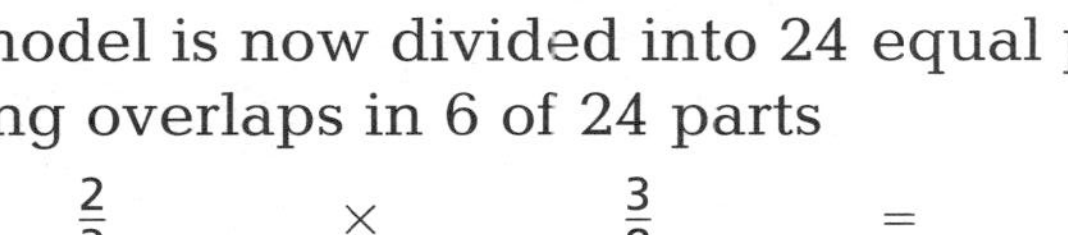

Multiply to find the product.

Step 1 Multiply the numerators. Multiply the denominators.

$$\frac{2}{3} \times \frac{3}{8} = \frac{2 \times 3}{3 \times 8} = \frac{6}{24}$$

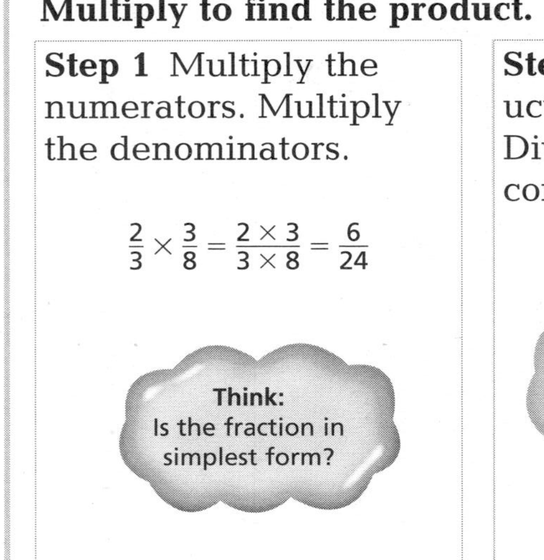
Think:
Is the fraction in simplest form?

Step 2 Write the product in simplest form. Divide by the greatest common factor.

$$\frac{6}{24}$$

Factors of 6: 1, 2, 3, 6

Factors of 24: 1, 2, 3, 4, 6, 8, 12, 24

GCF = 6

$$\frac{6}{24} = \frac{1}{4}$$

Think:
$6 \div 6 = 1$
$24 \div 6 = 4$

So, $\frac{2}{3} \times \frac{3}{8} = \frac{1}{4}$.

Try These

Multiply. Write the answer in simplest form.

1. $\frac{1}{3} \times \frac{1}{4}$

   $\frac{1}{3} \times \frac{1}{4} = \frac{1 \times 1}{3 \times 4} = \frac{\square}{\square}$

2. $\frac{1}{2} \times \frac{3}{4}$

   $\frac{1}{2} \times \frac{3}{4} = \frac{1 \times 3}{2 \times 4} = \frac{\square}{\square}$

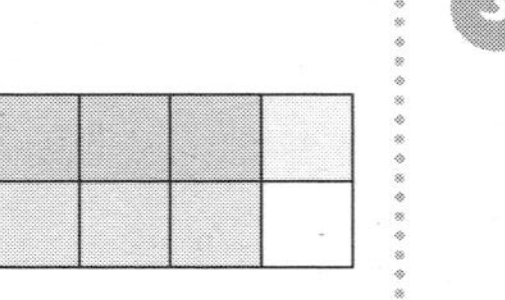
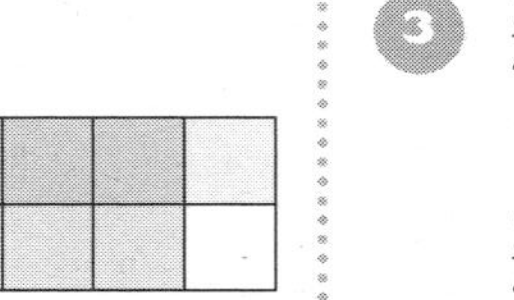
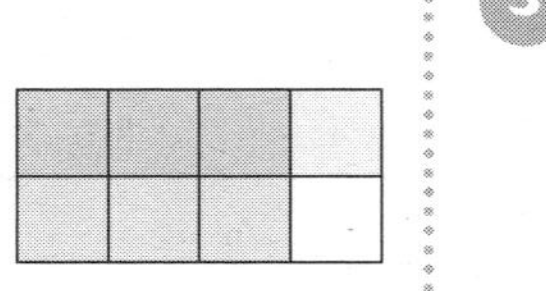
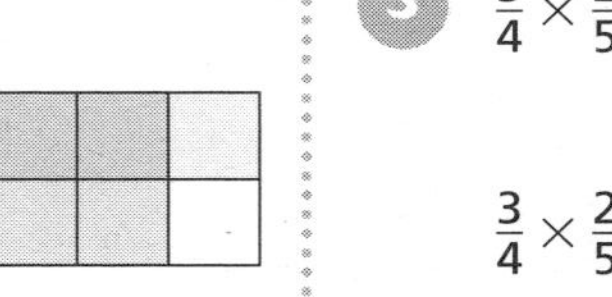

3. $\frac{3}{4} \times \frac{2}{5}$

   $\frac{3}{4} \times \frac{2}{5} = \frac{3 \times 2}{4 \times 5} = \frac{\square}{\square} = \frac{\square}{\square}$

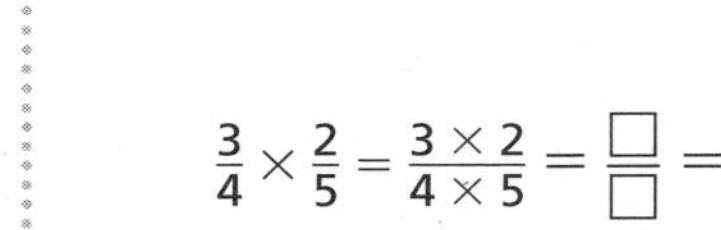
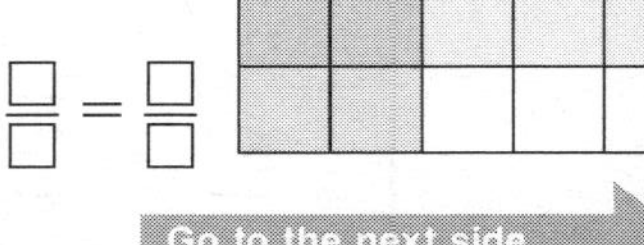

Go to the next side.

Name ______________________ Skill ______________________

Practice on Your Own

Skill 44

Find $\frac{3}{4}$ of $\frac{4}{5}$.

Think:

To find the product $\frac{3}{4} \times \frac{4}{5}$:

- multiply the numerators
- multiply the denominators
- simplify the answer.

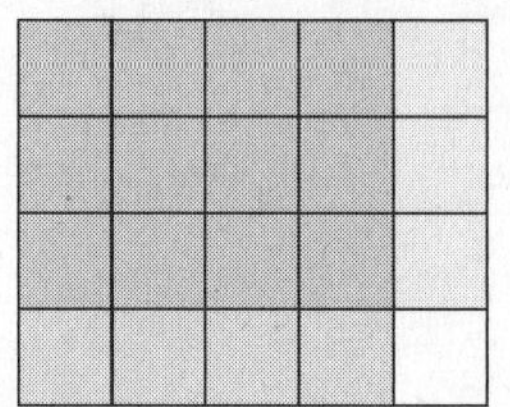

$$\frac{3}{4} \times \frac{4}{5} = \frac{3 \times 4}{4 \times 5} = \frac{12}{20} = \frac{3}{5}$$

The shading overlaps in 12 of the 20 squares.

Multiply. Write the answer in simplest form.

1 $\frac{1}{2} \times \frac{1}{2}$

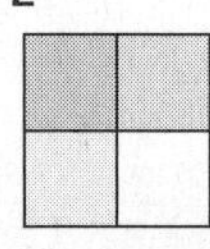

$\frac{1}{2} \times \frac{1}{2} = \frac{1 \times 1}{2 \times 2}$

$= \frac{\square}{\square}$

2 $\frac{1}{4} \times \frac{3}{4}$

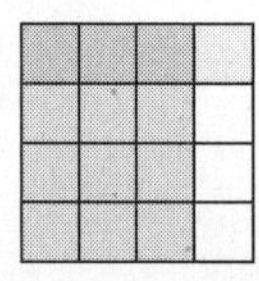

$\frac{1}{4} \times \frac{3}{4} = \frac{1 \times 3}{4 \times 4}$

$= \frac{\square}{\square}$

3 $\frac{2}{3} \times \frac{3}{5}$

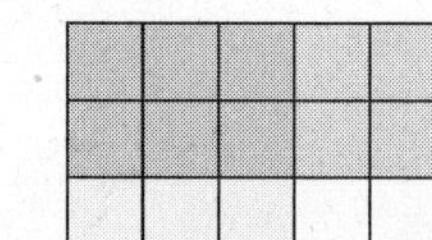

$\frac{2}{3} \times \frac{3}{5} = \frac{2 \times 3}{3 \times 5} = \frac{\square}{\square}$

$= \frac{\square}{\square}$

4 $\frac{1}{4} \times \frac{1}{5}$

$\frac{1}{4} \times \frac{1}{5} = \frac{\square \times \square}{\square \times \square}$

$= \frac{\square}{\square}$

5 $\frac{2}{3} \times \frac{1}{6}$

$\frac{2}{3} \times \frac{1}{6} = \frac{\square \times \square}{\square \times \square}$

$= \frac{\square}{\square}$

6 $\frac{4}{5} \times \frac{5}{6}$

$\frac{4}{5} \times \frac{5}{6} = \frac{\square \times \square}{\square \times \square} = \frac{\square}{\square}$

$= \frac{\square}{\square}$

7 $\frac{1}{5} \times \frac{1}{7} =$ __________

8 $\frac{3}{8} \times \frac{1}{6} =$ __________

9 $\frac{5}{9} \times \frac{3}{5} =$ __________

Check

Multiply. Write the answer in simplest form.

10 $\frac{1}{3} \times \frac{1}{9} =$ __________

11 $\frac{3}{4} \times \frac{1}{6} =$ __________

12 $\frac{2}{3} \times \frac{3}{8} =$ __________

Skill 45 Multiply with Fractions and Decimals

Using Skill 45

OBJECTIVE Multiply whole numbers by fractions and decimals

Direct students' attention to the question at the top of the page. Explain that they can first write 25 hundredths as a decimal or a fraction and then find the product. Ask: **How do you write 25 hundredths as a decimal?** (0.25) **How do you write 25 hundredths as a fraction?** ($\frac{25}{100}$)

Direct students' attention to the first frame. Explain that you multiply by a decimal as you would by a whole number. Point out the placement of the decimal point in the product. Ask: **How many decimal places are in twenty-five hundredths?** (2) **How many decimal places are in the product?** (2)

Point out to students that 15.00 can be written as 15. Ask: **What is twenty-five hundredths of 60?** (15)

Next, direct students' attention to the second frame. Explain that you can also multiply 60 by the fraction 25 hundredths. Ask: **How do you write $\frac{25}{100}$ in simplest form?** ($\frac{1}{4}$)

Explain that you can write the whole number 60 as a fraction and then multiply fractions to find the product. Ask: **How do you write 60 as a fraction?** ($\frac{60}{1}$)

Work through multiplying numerators and denominators to find the product. Ask: **What is the product of $\frac{1}{4}$ and $\frac{60}{1}$?** ($\frac{60}{4}$) **How do you write $\frac{60}{4}$ in simplest form?** (15)

Point out to students that the product, 15, is the same in both frames. Guide students to see that you can use either a decimal or a fraction to find the product. Discuss why it might be easier to multiply with one or the other.

TRY THESE Exercises 1–2 provide practice multiplying a whole number by a decimal and by a fraction.

- **Exercise 1** Multiply a whole number by a decimal
- **Exercise 2** Multiply a whole number by a fraction

PRACTICE ON YOUR OWN Review the example at the top of the page.

CHECK Determine if students can multiply whole numbers by a fraction, a decimal, and a mixed number. Success is indicated by 3 out of 3 correct responses. Students who successfully complete **Practice on Your Own** and **Check** are ready to move to the next skill.

COMMON ERRORS

- Students may not recall basic multiplication facts.
- When multiplying by a fraction, students may multiply the whole number by the denominator rather than the numerator of the fraction.

Students who made more than 2 errors in the **Practice on Your Own**, or who were not successful in the **Check** section, may benefit from the **Alternative Teaching Strategy** on the next page.

Optional

Alternative Teaching Strategy

15 Minutes

Model Multiplying Whole Numbers by Fractions and Decimals

OBJECTIVE Model multiplication of whole numbers by fractions and decimals

MATERIALS number lines labeled in tenths to show decimals and in halves, fourths, fifths, and tenths to show fractions

Explain to students that they can use a number line to show the product of a whole number and a fraction or decimal.

Display the following:

Find 4 tenths of 3.

Remind students that 4 tenths can be written as a fraction or a decimal. Tell students that first, they will multiply by the fraction, $\frac{4}{10}$. Have students use the fraction number line. Ask: **How do you write $\frac{4}{10}$ in simplest form?** ($\frac{2}{5}$)

Explain that $\frac{2}{5} \times 3$ equals $3 \times \frac{2}{5}$.

Have students make three jumps of $\frac{2}{5}$ on the number line. Ask: **What number did you end on?** ($1\frac{1}{5}$)

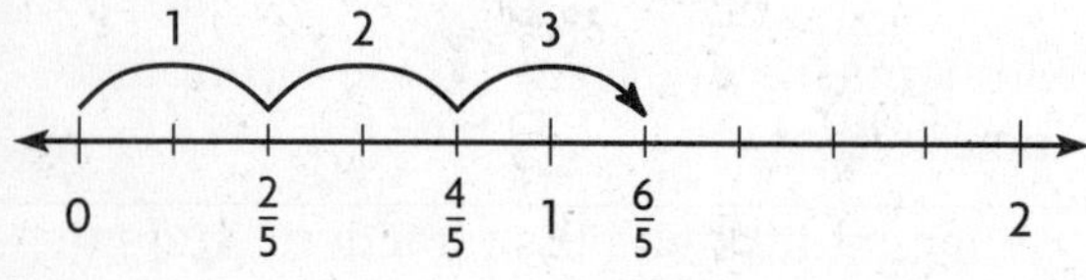

Next, tell students that they will multiply by the decimal, 0.4. Have them use the decimal number line. Ask: **How do you write 4 tenths as a decimal?** (0.4)

Explain that 0.4×3 equals 3×0.4. Have students make three jumps of 0.4 on the number line. Ask:
What number did you end on? (1.2)

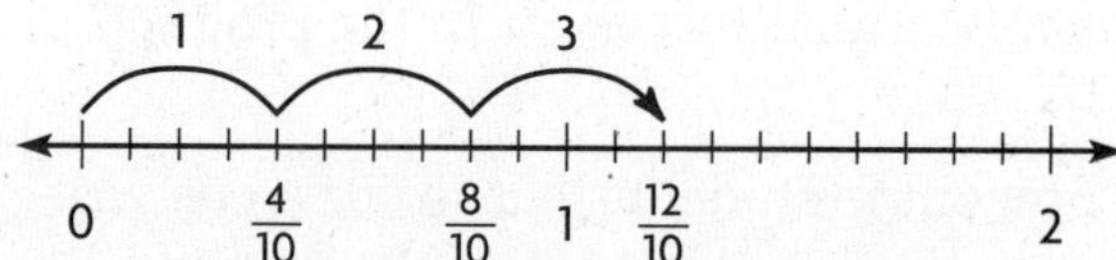

Make sure students understand that $1\frac{1}{5}$ is equal to 1.2.

Repeat the activity using the following exercises: 1 half of 4, 3 tenths of 5, 3 fourths of 2, 2 fifths of 3. (2, 1.5, 1.5, 1.2)

Name ____________________ Skill ____________________

Skill 45 Multiply with Fractions and Decimals

You can multiply a whole number by a decimal or a fraction.
What is 25 hundredths of 60?

Multiply by a decimal.

0.25 of 60

Step 1
Multiply as you would with whole numbers.

$$\begin{array}{r} 60 \\ \times 0.25 \\ \hline 300 \\ +\,1{,}200 \\ \hline 1{,}500 \end{array}$$

300 ←5 × 60
1,200 ←20 × 60

Step 2
Place the decimal point in the answer.

$$\begin{array}{r} 60 \\ \times 0.25 \\ \hline 300 \\ +\,1{,}200 \\ \hline 15.00 \end{array}$$

0.25 ←2 decimal places
15.00 ←2 decimal places

Multiply by a fraction.

$\frac{25}{100}$ of 60

Step 1 $\frac{1}{4} \times 60$ ←Write an equivalent fraction in simplest form. $\frac{25}{100} = \frac{1}{4}$

Step 2 $\frac{1}{4} \times \frac{60}{1}$ ←Write the whole number in fraction form.

Step 3 $\frac{1 \times 60}{4 \times 1} = \frac{60}{4}$ ←Multiply numerators. Multiply denominators.

Step 4 $\frac{60 \div 4}{4 \div 4} = \frac{15}{1} = 15$ ←Simplify the fraction.

So, 25 hundredths of 60 is 15.

Try These

Multiply.

1. $\begin{array}{r} 75 \\ \times 0.20 \\ \hline \end{array}$ Number of decimal places in the product: ___

2. $\frac{20}{100} \times 75$
   $\frac{20}{100} = \frac{1}{\square}$ ←Write an equivalent fraction in simplest form.
   $\frac{1 \times 75}{\square \times \square} = \frac{\square}{\square}$ ←Multiply the numerators. ←Multiply the denominators.
   = ___ Express the product in simplest form.

Go to the next side.

Name ________________________ Skill ________________________

Practice on Your Own

Find 2.5 × 80.

Multiply as you would with whole numbers. Then place the decimal point in the answer.

$$\begin{array}{r} 80 \\ \times 2.5 \\ \hline 400 \\ +1600 \\ \hline 200.0 \end{array}$$

1 decimal place

Find $2\frac{1}{2} \times 80$.

$2\frac{1}{2} \times 80$ ←Write both numbers as fractions.

$\frac{5}{2} \times \frac{80}{1}$

$\frac{5 \times 80}{2 \times 1} = \frac{400}{2}$ ←Multiply.

$= 200$ ←Write the product in simplest form.

Multiply.

1. $\begin{array}{r} 70 \\ \times 0.6 \\ \hline \end{array}$ number of decimal places ___

2. $\begin{array}{r} 40 \\ \times 0.75 \\ \hline \end{array}$ number of decimal places ___

3. $\begin{array}{r} 80 \\ \times 1.25 \\ \hline \end{array}$ number of decimal places ___

Multiply. Write the product in simplest form.

4. $\frac{6}{10} \times 7$

5. $\frac{75}{100} \times 40$

6. $\frac{25}{100} \times 80$

7. $\begin{array}{r} 2.4 \\ \times 52 \\ \hline \end{array}$

8. $4\frac{1}{3} \times 297$

9. $\begin{array}{r} 1.16 \\ \times 26 \\ \hline \end{array}$

Check

Multiply.

10. $\frac{3}{5} \times 95$

11. $\begin{array}{r} 4.15 \\ \times 78 \\ \hline \end{array}$

12. $1\frac{1}{8} \times 64$

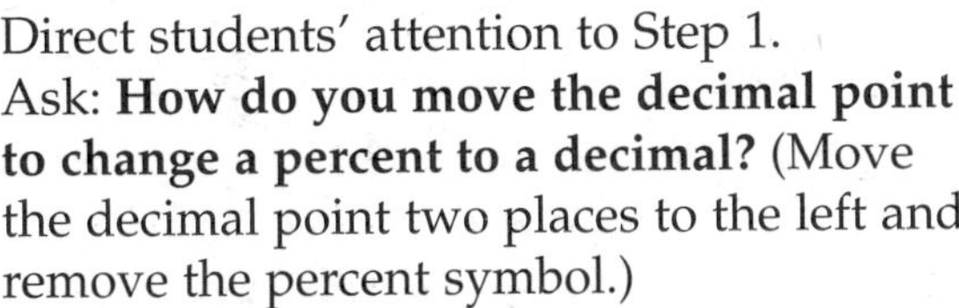

Find the Percent of a Number

Using Skill 46

OBJECTIVE Find the percent of a number

Direct students' attention to Step 1.
Ask: **How do you move the decimal point to change a percent to a decimal?** (Move the decimal point two places to the left and remove the percent symbol.)

What do you have to remember about the product when multiplying by a decimal? (The number of decimal places in the product must equal the number of decimal places in the factors.)

TRY THESE In Exercises 1–3 students find the percent of a number.

- **Exercise 1** 0.15; 9
- **Exercise 2** 0.65; 26
- **Exercise 3** 0.75; 3

PRACTICE ON YOUR OWN Review the steps at the top of the page. Remind students to change the percent to a decimal.

CHECK Determine if students know how to find the percent of a number.

Success is indicated by 3 out of 3 correct responses.

Students who successfully complete the **Practice on Your Own** and **Check** are ready to move to the next skill.

COMMON ERRORS

- Students may forget to change the percent to a decimal.
- Students may misplace the decimal point. Have students estimate the product before multiplying.

Students who made more than 3 errors in the **Practice on Your Own**, or who were not successful in the **Check** section, may benefit from the **Alternative Teaching Strategy** on the next page.

Optional

Alternative Teaching Strategy

20 Minutes

Using Proportions to Find the Percent of a Number

OBJECTIVE Find the percent of a number **MATERIALS** none

Explain that students will be finding the percent of a number using a proportion.

For example: What is 35% of 20?

Ask: **What does percent mean?** (out of 100)

Have students write the percent as a ratio. $\left(\frac{35}{100}\right)$

Then have students choose a variable to represent the unknown number. (x)

Set up a proportion that can be solved for the variable. ($\frac{35}{100} = \frac{x}{20}$)

Ask: **What are the cross products?** ($35 \bullet 20$ and $x \bullet 100$)

How do you solve for the variable? (Use inverse operations, divide both sides by 100.)

What is the unknown? (7)

Say: So 7 is 35% of 20.

Repeat the activity several times by finding percents of different numbers.

When students understand the concept of finding the percent of a number have them try several problems on their own.

Name ______________________ Skill ______________

Skill 46

Find the Percent of a Number

Forty model cars are on display in a hobby store and 25% of the cars are black. How many cars are black?

What is 25% of 40?

Step 1
Write the percent as a decimal.

$25\% = 0.25$

Step 2
Multiply. 40×0.25

$$\begin{array}{r} 40 \\ \underline{\times 0.25} \\ 200 \\ \underline{800} \\ 10.00 \end{array}$$

$\times 0.25$ ← 2 decimal places in the factors

10.00 ← 2 decimal places in the product.

So 10 is 25% of 40.

Try These

Solve.

1. What is 15% of 60?
   Write the percent as a decimal.
   ____
   Multiply 60×0.15. ________

2. What is 65% of 40?
   Write the percent as a decimal.
   ____
   Multiply 40×0.65. ________

3. What is 75% of 4?
   Write the percent as a decimal.
   ____
   Multiply 4×0.75. ________

Go to the next side.

Name ________________________ Skill ________________________

Practice on Your Own

Skill 46

To find the percent of a number use these steps.

Step 1 Change the percent to a decimal.

Step 2 Multiply. (Remember to place the decimal point correctly in the product.)

Solve.

1. What is 10% of 80?
   Write the percent as a decimal. ________
   Multiply 80 × 0.10.
   ____

2. What is 45% of 60?
   Write the percent as a decimal. ________
   Multiply 60 × 0.45.
   ____

3. What is 90% of 50?
   Write the percent as a decimal. ________
   Multiply 50 × 0.90.
   ____

Solve.

4. What is 20% of 20? ________

5. What is 75% of 8? ________

6. What is 50% of 48? ________

7. What is 8% of 500? ________

8. What is 35% of 400? ________

9. What is 15% of 90? ________

Check

Solve each problem.

10. What is 16% of 25? ________

11. What is 7% of 60? ________

12. What is 18% of 250? ________

Using Skill 47

OBJECTIVE Add, subtract, multiply, and divide integers

Begin with adding integers. Direct students to Example 1.

Ask: **Do the addends have the same sign?** (yes)
When addends have the same sign, add the absolute values and use the sign of the addends for the answer. Recall the meaning of absolute value.

Direct students to the second problem in Example 1.
Ask: **Do the addends have the same sign?** (no)
When addends have different signs, subtract the lesser absolute value, the 3, and use the sign of the addend with the greater absolute value, the −9.

Direct students to Example 2. When subtracting integers, add the opposite of the integer and then follow the rules for adding.

Example 3 shows the rules for multiplying and dividing integers. When signs of integers are alike, then the product is positive. When the signs are different, then the product is negative. Have students look at each problem shown in the example.

TRY THESE

- **Exercise 1** Add with different signs.
- **Exercise 2** Subtract with different signs.
- **Exercise 3** Multiply with the same signs.
- **Exercise 4** Divide with different signs.

PRACTICE ON YOUR OWN Review the examples at the top of the page.
In Exercises 1–4, students add or subtract, noting if the signs are the same or different.
In Exercises 5–8, students multiply or divide, deciding if the signs are the same or different.

CHECK Determine whether students can identify the sign of each integer. Make sure students remember how to find the absolute value of a number. Success is indicated by 4 out of 4 correct responses.

Students who successfully complete the **Practice on Your Own** and **Check** are ready to move to the next skill.

COMMON ERRORS

- Students may forget how to find the absolute value of a number.
- Students may forget to *add* the *opposite* when subtracting.
- Students may confuse a subtraction sign with a negative sign.

Students who made more than 3 errors in the **Practice on Your Own**, or who were not successful in the **Check** section, may benefit from the **Alternative Teaching Strategy** on the next page.

Optional

Alternative Teaching Strategy

20 Minutes

Using Number Lines in Integer Operations

OBJECTIVE Use operation sense to understand adding, subtracting, multiplying and dividing integers

MATERIALS index cards and a blank number line

Note: You may need to provide two separate instruction periods to review adding and subtracting, and then multiplying and dividing integers.

For adding and subtracting integers it may be helpful for the students to have a number line. Have students label the number line according to the numbers they are given.

Have students place the first integer on the number line.

Ask: **Which direction do you move if adding a positive number?** (right)
Ask: **Which direction do you move if adding a negative number?** (left)

After the students have a good understanding of adding integers on a number line, show students how to use a number line to subtract integers. Have students once again place the first number on the number line.

Ask: **Which direction do you move if subtracting a positive number?** (left)
Ask: **Which direction do you move if subtracting a negative number?** (right)
Why? (You add the opposite.)

For multiplying and dividing integers, prepare a set of cards with multiplication and division facts on them making sure they include a variety of sign combinations.

Have students draw a card one at a time and state the rule such as "positive times negative is negative". By concentrating only on the signs, students will learn the rules. Then, have students give their product or quotient with the correct sign.

Repeat the activities several times with different combinations of numbers.
When students show an understanding give larger numbers to compute.

Name ______________________ Skill ______________________

Skill 47

Integer Operations

When you add, subtract, multiply, and divide integers, remember to follow the rules. It is important to look at the sign of each integer.

Example 1

Adding Integers: Same Sign

Add the absolute values. Use the sign of the addends for the sum.

$-4 + -6 = \square$

$|-4| + |-6| = 10$, so $-4 + -6 = -10$

Adding Integers: Different Signs

Subtract the lesser absolute value. Use the sign of the addend with the greater absolute value.

$-9 + 3 = \square$

$|-9| - |3| = 9 - 3 = 6$

Since $|-9| > |3|$, use the sign on -9.

$-9 + 3 = -6$

Example 2

Subtracting Integers.

When subtracting integers, add the opposite and then use the rules for adding integers.

$5 - 8 = \square$

$5 + (-8) =$

$|-8| - |5| = 3$

Since $|-8| > |5|$, use the sign on -8.

$5 - 8 = -3$

Example 3

Multiplying and Dividing Integers.

Like Signs = Positive

$(+) \times (+) = (+)$ $\quad (-) \times (-) = (+)$

$(+) \div (+) = (+)$ $\quad (-) \div (-) = (+)$

Unlike Signs = Negative

$(+) \times (-) = (-)$ $\quad (-) \times (+) = (-)$

$(+) \div (-) = (-)$ $\quad (-) \div (+) = (-)$

$-6 \times (-8) = \square$

The signs are the same so the answer is +48.

$64 \div (-8) = \square$

The signs are different so the answer is −8.

Try These

Complete. State whether the signs of the integers are the same or different.

1. $-142 + 249 = \square$
   Same or different? ________

2. $-79 - 147 = \square$
   Same or different? ________

3. $-14 \times (-7) = \square$
   Same or different? ________

4. $104 \div (-4) = \square$
   Same or different? ________

Go to the next side.

Name ______________________ Skill ______________________

Practice on Your Own

Skill 47

Find $-8 + 3$. **Think:** Different signs, subtract the lesser absolute value from the greater absolute value. Use the sign of the addend with the greater absolute value. $-8 + 3$ $\lvert -8 \rvert - \lvert 3 \rvert = 5$ So, $-8 + 3 = -5$.	Find $-7 - (-8)$. **Think:** To subtract, add the opposite, then follow the rules of addition. Use the sign of the number with the greater absolute value. $-7 - (-8)$ $-7 + 8$ $\lvert 8 \rvert - \lvert -7 \rvert = 1$ So, $-7 - (-8) = 1$.
Find -5×9. **Think:** Signs are different, so the answer is negative. $-5 \times 9 = -45$	Find $-128 \div (-8)$. **Think:** Signs are alike, so the answer is positive. $-128 \div (-8) = 16$

Add or subtract. State if the signs are the same or different.

1. $-14 + 9 =$ ___ signs are ______
2. $23 - (-4) =$ ___ signs are ______
3. $-7 + (-18) =$ ___ signs are ______
4. $-11 - 7 =$ ___ signs are ______

Multiply or divide. State if the signs are the same or different.

5. $16 \times (-5) =$ ___ signs are ______
6. $-72 \div (-6) =$ ___ signs are ______
7. $-7 \times (-12) =$ ___ signs are ______
8. $-45 \div 3 =$ ___ signs are ______

Check

Perform the given operation.

9. $31 + (-7) =$ ________
10. $17 \times (-4) =$ ________
11. $-19 - 4 =$ ________
12. $-136 \div (-8) =$ ________

Skill 48 Multiplication Properties (Associative, Zero, and Commutative)

20 Minutes

Using Skill 48

OBJECTIVE Use the properties of multiplication to simplify expressions and solve equations

Before students turn their attention to Skill 48, have them look up the definitions of *commute* and *associate* in a dictionary.

After reading about the commutative and associative properties of multiplication, guide students to distinguish between the two properties.

***Commute* means to *change* or *exchange*.** Ask: **How can this meaning help you remember the *Commutative* Property?** (The commutative property is about changing the order of two factors.)

Emphasize that they can change the order of factors but the product is the same—it does not change.

Continue: ***Associate* means to join or connect together. How does this meaning relate to the *Associative Property*?** (The Associative Property is about the way factors are connected or joined together in order to compute.)

Emphasize that factors can be joined or grouped in any way without changing the product. You might want to extend the analogy, by pointing out that when the only operation in an expression is multiplication, the parentheses really do not matter.

When reviewing the *Property of One* and the *Property of Zero* for Multiplication, ask: **Do you think these properties are commutative?** (yes) **Why?** (All multiplication is commutative.)

Conclude that the multiplication properties can help students remember basic facts and, therefore, multiply more easily.

TRY THESE Students complete Exercises 1–4 to show each of the properties.

- **Exercise 1** Commutative Property
- **Exercise 2** Associative Property
- **Exercise 3** Property of One
- **Exercise 4** Property of Zero

PRACTICE ON YOUR OWN Have students answer each of the *Ask yourself* questions for every example and exercise. Note that if students answer *yes* to the first question, then they are using the Commutative Property; if *yes* to the second question, then they are using the Associate Property.

CHECK Determine if students can identify and apply the four properties of multiplication. Success is indicated by 4 out of 4 correct responses.

Students who successfully complete the **Practice on Your Own** and **Check** are ready to move to the next skill.

COMMON ERRORS

- Students may forget or confuse the names of the properties.
- Students may make computational errors because they have not mastered basic facts.

Students who made more than 3 errors in the **Practice on Your Own**, or who were not successful in the **Check** section, may benefit from the **Alternative Teaching Strategy** on the next page.

Optional

Alternative Teaching Strategy

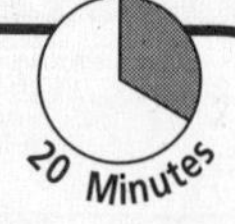

Model the Multiplication Properties

OBJECTIVE Use models to show the properties of multiplication

MATERIALS centimeter grid paper, scissors

Explain to the students that they can use models to demonstrate the Commutative and Associative properties, and the Property of One. Have students cut out and use pieces of grid paper to model the equations.

For the Commutative Property of Multiplication, present this example:

$$2 \times 3 = 3 \times 2$$

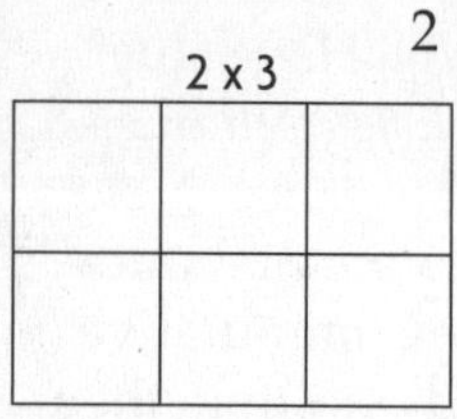

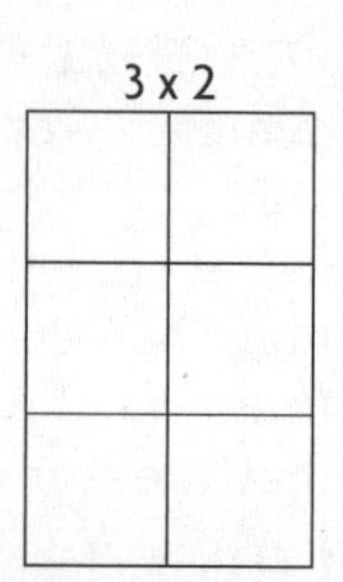

Ask: **Is the grid for 2 × 3 the same as the grid for 3 × 2?** (yes)

How do you know? (There are six centimeter squares in each model.)

Continue: **This model shows that the factors can be multiplied in any order without changing the product.**

Next, for the Associative Property of Multiplication, present this example. Recall the rules for order of operations with parentheses.

$$(2 \times 3) \times 4 = 2 \times (3 \times 4)$$

Ask: **Do 4 groups of 2 × 3 have the same number of squares as 2 groups of 3 × 4?** (yes) **How do you know?** (I counted to find the total number of squares in each; I used multiplication and found the products were the same.)

Continue: **This model for the Associative Property shows that factors can be grouped in any way without changing the product.**

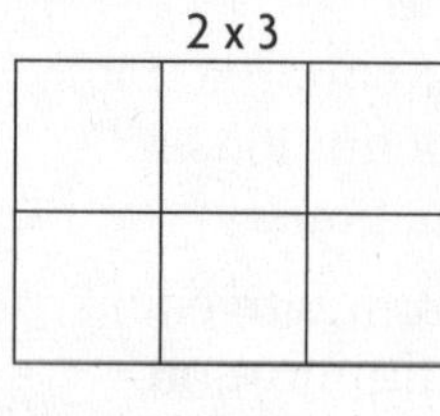

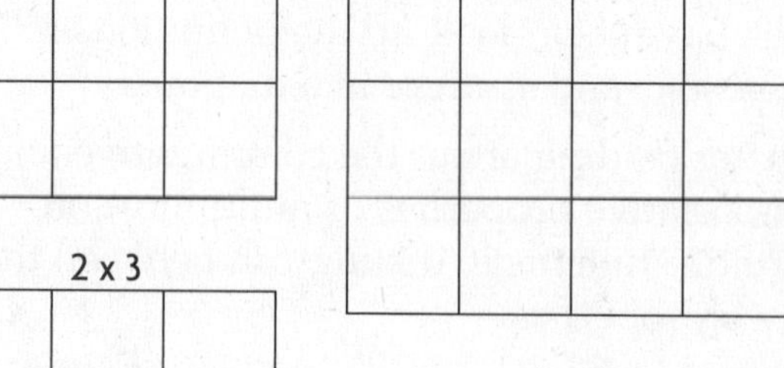

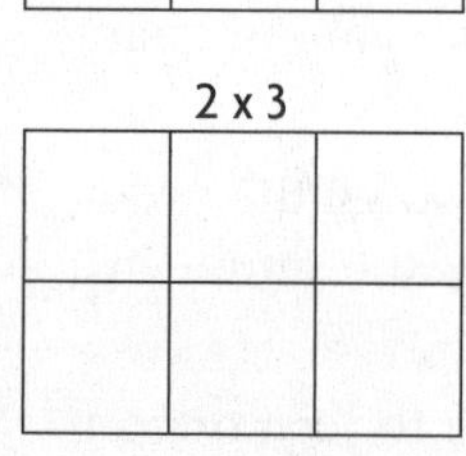

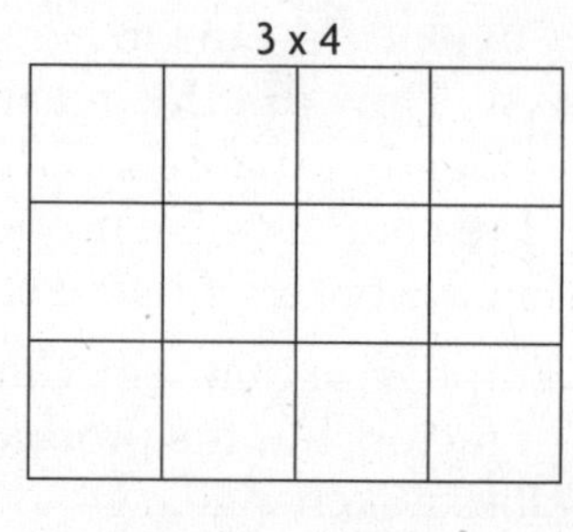

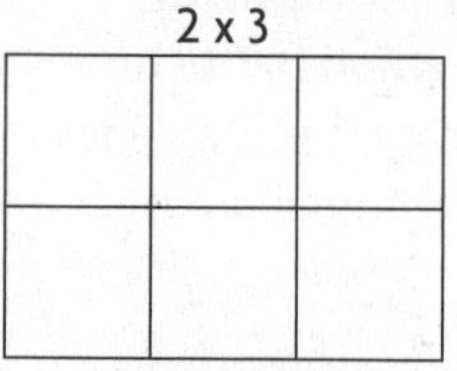

2 x 3

For the Property of One, present these examples: $1 \times 4 = 4$ $1 \times 5 = 5$

$1 \times 2 = 2$ $1 \times 7 = 7$

Guide students to conclude that *the product of any factor and 1 is the factor.* You may wish to repeat some examples more than once.

Name ____________________ Skill ____________________

Multiplication Properties (Associative, Zero, and Commutative)

Skill 48

You can use properties of multiplication to help simplify expressions and solve equations.

Commutative Property of Multiplication
Factors can be multiplied in any order without changing the product.

$$a \times b = b \times a$$
$$3 \times 7 = 7 \times 3$$
$$21 = 21$$

Associative Property of Multiplication
Factors can be grouped in any way without changing the product.

$$(a \times b) \times c = a \times (b \times c)$$
$$(3 \times 4) \times 5 = 3 \times (4 \times 5)$$
$$12 \times 5 = 3 \times 20$$
$$60 = 60$$

Property of One for Multiplication
The product of any factor and 1 is the factor.

$$1 \times a = a$$
$$1 \times 3 = 3$$
$$9 \times 1 = 9$$

Property of Zero for Multiplication
The product of any factor and zero is zero.

$$0 \times a = 0$$
$$0 \times 7 = 0$$
$$10 \times 0 = 0$$

Try These

Complete to show the property.

1. Commutative Property of Multiplication

   $7 \times 6 =$ _____ $\times$ _____

2. Associative Property of Multiplication

   $(2 \times 8) \times 5 =$ _____ $\times$ (_____ $\times$ _____)

3. Property of One for Multiplication

   $12 \times$ _____ $= 12$

4. Property of Zero for Multiplication

   _____ $\times 9 = 0$

Go to the next side.

Name ______________________ Skill ______________________

Practice on Your Own

Skill 48

Write the name of the multiplication property used in the equation.

Ask yourself: Is the order of the factors changed?
Are the factors grouped differently?
Is one of the factors zero or one?

$5 \times (8 \times 3) = (5 \times 8) \times 3$

Think: the factors are grouped differently.

Associative Property of Multiplication

$37 \times 6 = 6 \times 37$

Think: the order is changed.

Commutative Property of Multiplication

Write the name of the multiplication property shown.

1. $68 \times 5 = 5 \times 68$ ______________________
2. $35 \times 0 = 0$ ______________________
3. $1 \times 456 = 456$ ______________________
4. $(2 \times 7) \times 10 = 2 \times (7 \times 10)$ ______________________

Complete the equation. Write the name of the property you used.

5. $27 \times$ ____ $= 0$ ______________________
6. ____ $\times 58 = 58$ ______________________
7. $9 \times 32 =$ ____ $\times 9$ ______________________
8. $(5 \times 8) \times 4 =$ ____ $\times (8 \times 4)$ ______________________
9. $17 \times ($ ____ $\times 10) = (17 \times 2) \times 10$ ______________________
10. ____ $\times 15 = 15 \times 4$ ______________________

Check

Complete the equation. Write the name of the property you used.

11. ____ $\times 48 = 0$ ______________________
12. $10 \times (5 \times 2) = (10 \times$ ____ $) \times 2$ ______________________
13. $7 \times$ ____ $= 15 \times 7$ ______________________
14. ____ $\times 1 = 52$ ______________________

Skill 

Multiplication Properties (Distributive)

Using Skill 49

OBJECTIVE Use the distributive property to multiply tens and ones

Begin by giving the students the following exercises. Remind them to do the operations within parentheses first.

$6 \times 5 =$ ___

$6 \times (3 + 2) =$ ___

$(6 \times 3) + (6 \times 2) =$ ___

Compare and discuss the results. Then review the definition of the Distributive Property of Multiplication.
As students review Step 1, ask: **How many squares high is the array?** (6)

How many squares long is it? (17)

How can you use the array to find the product of 6 and 17? (Count the number of squares; multiply 6×17.)

For Step 2, ask: **How does breaking apart the array change the total number of squares?** (It doesn't.)

Continue: **So what can you say about the relationship between (6 × 10) + (6 × 7) and 6 × 17?** (They are equal; they have the same product.)

Have students explain how breaking apart the factor 17 makes it easier to find the product 6×17.

TRY THESE Exercises 1–3 model the type of exercise students will find on the Practice on Your Own page.

- **Exercise 1** Break apart 12: 10 and 2
- **Exercise 2** Break apart 15: 10 and 5
- **Exercise 3** Break apart 19: 10 and 9

PRACTICE ON YOUR OWN Review the example at the top of the page. Discuss why 23 was broken apart as 20 and 3, rather than 17 and 6, or 18 and 5. Encourage students to note that it is easier to multiply by multiples of 10.

CHECK Determine if students can use the Distributive Property to break apart a factor into tens and ones, and then find the product.

Success is indicated by 2 out of 2 correct responses.

Students who successfully complete the **Practice on Your Own** and **Check** are ready to move to the next skill.

COMMON ERRORS

- Students may rewrite an expression using all multiplication, $a \times (b \times c)$, or using only addition, $(a + b) + (a + c)$.
- Students may rewrite the expression correctly but compute incorrectly.

Students who made more than 1 error in the **Practice on Your Own**, or who were not successful in the **Check** section, may benefit from the **Alternative Teaching Strategy** on the next page.

Optional

Alternative Teaching Strategy

15 Minutes

Make and Use Models of the Distributive Property

OBJECTIVE Use models of the Distributive Property to find products

MATERIALS centimeter grid paper, scissors

Begin by explaining to the students that they can use models to demonstrate the Distributive Property of Multiplication. Present these expressions.

4×12 $\quad$ 3×18

5×24 $\quad$ 7×46

Guide students as they make an array to show each expression. For 4×12 ask: **How many squares high should the array be?** (4 squares) Have students mark the graph paper to show this.

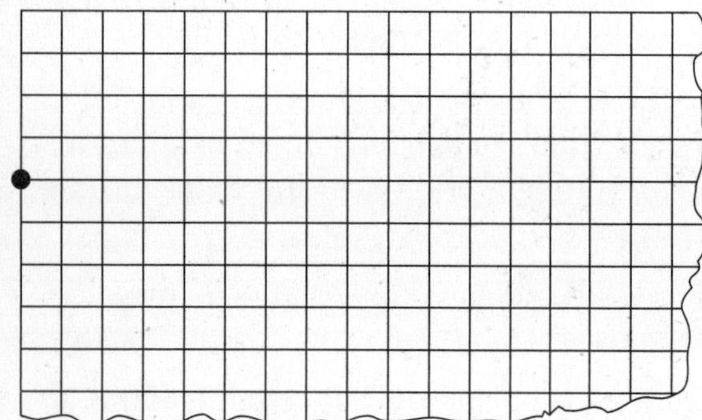

How many squares long should the array be? (12) Have them make another pencil mark to show this.

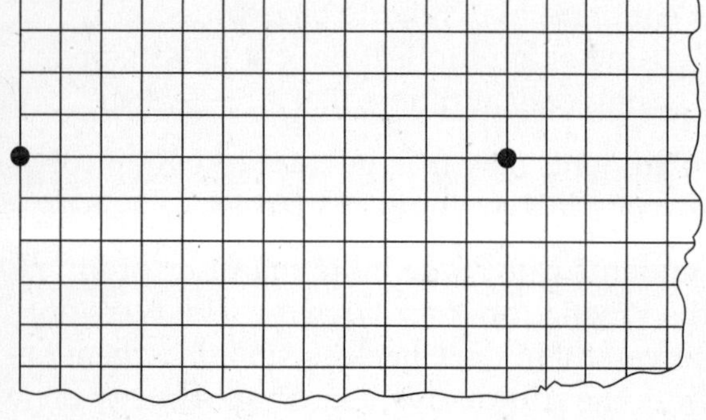

Have students outline the array and cut it out.

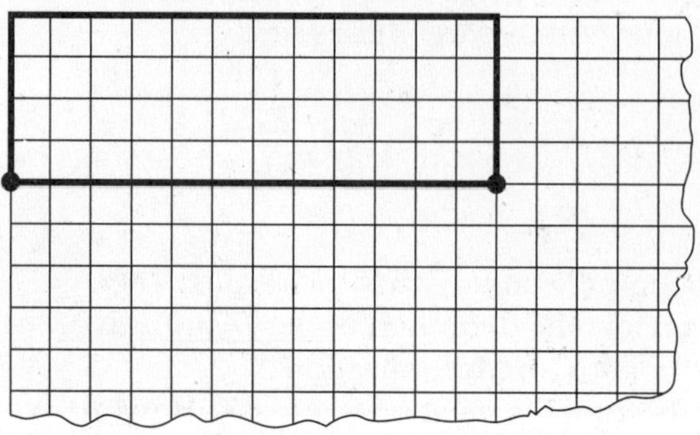

Demonstrate how to fold the array to break apart the rows of 12 columns into rows of 10 columns and 2 columns.

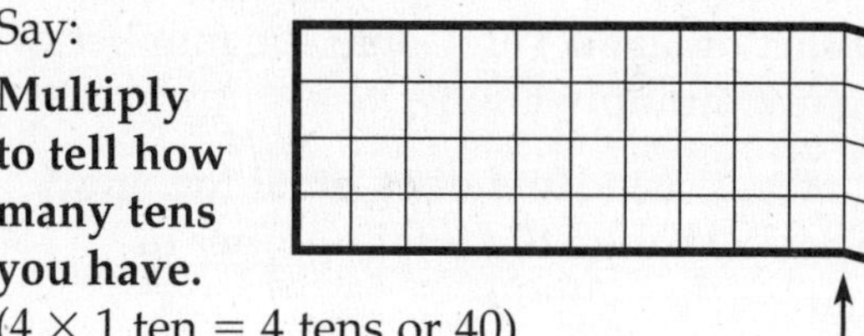

Say:
Multiply to tell how many tens you have.
(4×1 ten = 4 tens or 40)
Multiply to tell how many ones you have. (4×2 ones = 8 ones or 8)
How many do you have in all?
(4 tens, 8 ones; $40 + 8 = 48$)

Display: $4 \times 12 = (4 \times 10) + (4 \times 2) = 48$
Work through the math with students. Emphasize when to multiply and when to add.

Guide students to recognize that multiplying a sum (in this case, 12) by a certain factor (in this case, 4) is the same as multiplying each addend (in this case, 10 and 2) by that factor and then adding their products ($40 + 8$).

Proceed in a similar manner with the remaining expressions. When students are able to work without models, give them additional opportunities to use the Distributive Property to find a product.

Name ______________________ Skill ______________________

Multiplication Properties (Distributive) — Skill 49

Use the distributive property to find 6×17.

The Distributive Property of Multiplication
Multiplying a sum by a number is the same as multiplying each addend by the number and then adding the products.

$a \times (b + c) = (a \times b) + (a \times c)$

Step 1
Use grid paper.
Draw an array that shows 6×17.

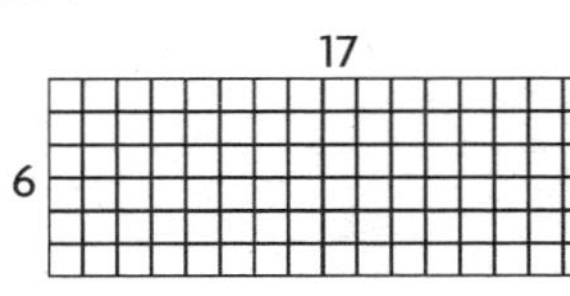

Step 2
Break apart the grid to show the factor 17 as the addends 10 + 7.

$6 \times (10 + 7) = (6 \times 10) + (6 \times 7)$

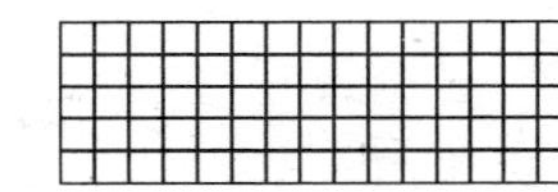

$(6 \times 10) + (6 \times 7)$ ← Multiply.
$60 + 42$ ← Add.
102

So, $6 \times 17 = (6 \times 10) + (6 \times 7) = 102$.

Try These

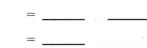

Use the Distributive Property to find the products.

1

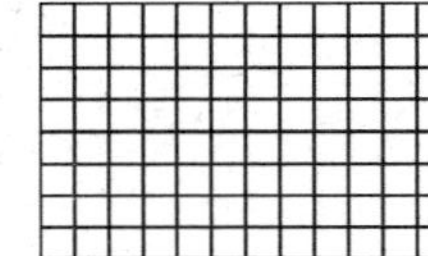

8×12
$8 \times 12 = (8 \times 10) + (8 \times 2)$
= ______ ______
= ______

2

7×15
$7 \times 15 = (7 \times 10) + (7 \times 5)$
= ______ ______
= ______

3

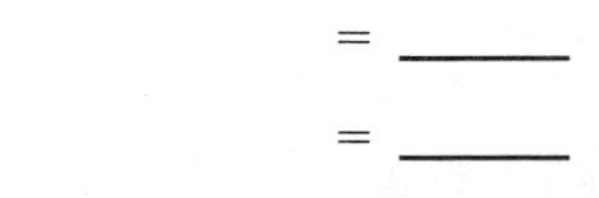

5×19
$5 \times 19 = (5 \times 10) + (5 \times 9)$
= ______ ______
= ______

Go to the next side.

Name ______________________ Skill ______________________

Practice on Your Own

Skill 49

Use the Distributive Property. Find 5 × 23.

1. Draw a 5 by 23 grid.
2. Break apart 23 as 20 and 3.
3. Find 5 × 20 and 5 × 3.
4. Add the products.

$$5 \times 23 = (5 \times 20) + (5 \times 3)$$
$$= 100 + 15$$
$$= 115$$

Use the Distributive Property to find the product.

1. 4 × 16

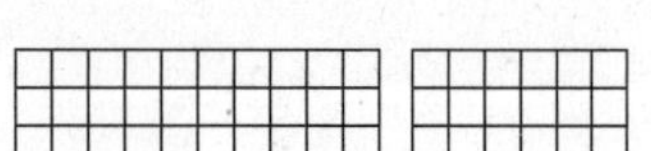

4 × 16 = (4 × ____) + (4 × ____)
= ____ + ____
= ____

2. 6 × 22

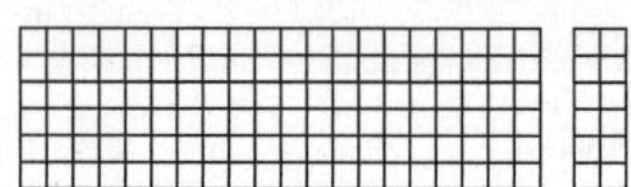

6 × 22 = (6 × ____) + (6 × ____)
= ____ + ____
= ____

3. 5 × 15

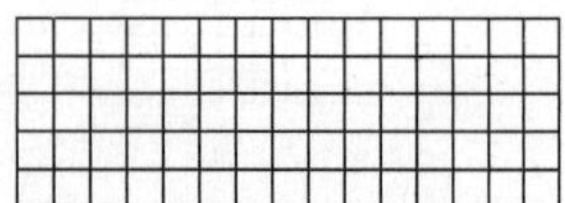

5 × 15 = (____ × ____)
+ (____ × ____)
= ____ + ____
= ____

4. 5 × 21

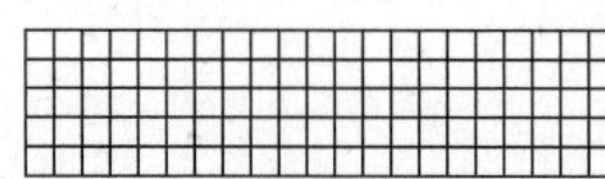

5 × 21 = (____ × ____)
+ (____ × ____)
= ____ + ____
= ____

Check

Use the Distributive Property to find the product.

5. 8 × 16

8 × 16 = (____ × ____)
+ (____ × ____)
= ____ + ____
= ____

6. 7 × 24

7 × 24 = (____ × ____)
+ (____ × ____)
= ____ + ____
= ____

Skill 50 Use of Parentheses

Using Skill 50

OBJECTIVE Use parentheses in expressions or equations

Direct students to the example for *Expressions*. Explain that parentheses are used to show which operation should be performed first. Point out that the order in which the operations are done affects the value of the expression.

Ask: **What three numbers are used in each expression?** (3, 8, 6)

In the expression on the left, what numbers do you work with first? (3 and 8) **Why?** (They are inside parentheses.)

In the expression on the right, what numbers do you work with first? (8 and 6) **Why?** (They are inside parentheses.)

Guide the students as they evaluate each expression. Then ask: **Do you get the same result for each expression?** (no)

What causes the different results? (working inside the parentheses first)

In the examples for *Equations*, discuss the properties shown. Emphasize that parentheses are important grouping symbols when demonstrating the properties of addition and multiplication.

TRY THESE In Exercises 1–3 students use parentheses in both expressions and equations.

- **Exercises 1–2** Evaluate expressions with parentheses
- **Exercise 3** Use the Distributive Property to solve for *a*

PRACTICE ON YOUR OWN Review the examples at the top of the page. Ask students to tell what operation they should do first. Then ask what the equal signs in the equations mean.

CHECK Determine if students can use parentheses correctly when evaluating expressions and solving equations.

Success is indicated by 3 out of 3 correct responses.

Students who successfully complete the **Practice on Your Own** and **Check** are ready to move to the next skill.

COMMON ERRORS

- Students may not do what is inside the parentheses first, but rather perform the operations from left to right or randomly.
- Students may work inside the parentheses first, but may not be able to find the correct value of a variable.

Students who made more than 3 errors in the **Practice on Your Own**, or who were not successful in the **Check** section, may benefit from the **Alternative Teaching Strategy** on the next page.

Optional

Alternative Teaching Strategy
Using Parentheses

OBJECTIVE Use parentheses to evaluate expressions

MATERIALS paper and pencil

Explain to students the order of operations.

Explain the rule for any number sentence or expression containing only numbers and signs of operation: **Multiply and divide before you add and subtract.**

Demonstrate with two examples.

DO NOT USE RULE	USE RULE
A. $3 + 2 \times 5$	**B.** $3 + 2 \times 5$
5×5	$3 + 10$
25	13

Explain that if students want the answer in A to be correct, then they must use parentheses to indicate that 3 and 2 are added first.

A. $(3 + 2) \times 5$
5×5
25

When students understand the significance of parentheses, provide them with some of the following exercises to confirm their understanding.

Simplify each expression.

1. $5 + 8 - 4$ (9)
2. $10 - 4 + 3$ (9)
3. $3 + 4 \times 5$ (23)
4. $3 \times 1 + 6$ (9)
5. $9 - 6 \div 3$ (7)
6. $12 \div 4 - 1$ (2)
7. $5 + (7 - 6)$ (6)
8. $9 - (8 - 7)$ (8)
9. $(6 + 8) \div 7$ (2)
10. $20 - (15 - 12)$ (17)
11. $4 + (6 - 5) \times 2$ (6)
12. $8 - 8 \div (4 + 4)$ (7)

After the correct answers are verified, have students find what the results would be if all parentheses were removed.

Name ______________________ Skill ______________________

Use of Parentheses

Skill 50

Parentheses in an expression or in an equation means do the operation inside the parentheses first.

Expressions

Find the value of, or **evaluate**, the expressions. Compare the results. Are they the same?

	$(3 \times 8) - 6$	$3 \times (8 - 6)$
Step 1	$(3 \times 8) - 6$	$3 \times (8 - 6)$
Do the operation inside parentheses	↓ $24 - 6$	↓ 3×2
Step 2 Do all other operations.	↓ **18**	↓ **6**

You can see that the results are different.

So, where parentheses are placed affects the value of some expressions.

Equations

You can solve some equations that contain parentheses by using properties.

Distributive Property

Find the value of a.

$(5 \times 2) + (5 \times 6) = 5 \times (a + 6)$

$(5 \times 2) + (5 \times 6) = 5 \times (\mathbf{2} + 6)$

So, $a = 2$.

Associative Property

Find the value of c.

$c \times (5 \times 9) = (3 \times 5) \times 9$

$\mathbf{3} \times (5 \times 9) = (3 \times 5) \times 9$

So, $c = 3$.

Commutative Property

Find the value of p.

$6 + (5 + 9) = (5 + 9) + p$

$6 + (5 + 9) = (5 + 9) + \mathbf{6}$

So, $p = 6$.

Try These

Evaluate the expression

1. $(5 + 3) + 9$
   ↓
   ___ $+ 9$
   ↓
   ___

2. $4 \times (8 - 2)$
   ↓
   $4 \times$ ___
   ↓
   ___

Find the value of a.

3. $(3 \times 2) + (3 \times 4) = 3 \times (a + 4)$

   $(3 \times 2) + (3 \times 4) = 3 \times (2 + 4)$

   So, $a =$ ___

Use the Distributive Property of Multiplication to help you solve.

Go to the next side.

Name ______________________ Skill ______________________

Practice on Your Own

Skill 50

Do the operation inside the parentheses first.

Evaluate.	Associative Property of Multiplication	Distributive Property of Multiplication
$4 \times (2 + 6 + 1)$	$6 \times (4 \times 5) = (6 \times 4) \times 5$	$(5 \times 3) + (5 \times 2) = b \times (3 + 2)$
↓	↓	↓
$4 \times \mathbf{9}$	$6 \times (4 \times 5) = (a \times 4) \times 5$	$(5 \times 3) + (5 \times 2) = 5 \times (3 + 2)$
36	**So,** $a = 6$	**So,** $b = 5$

Evaluate the expression.

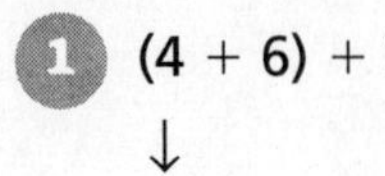

1. $(4 + 6) + 3$
   ↓
   ___ + 3
   ↓
   ___

2. $(10 - 4) + 6$
   ↓
   ___ + 6
   ↓
   ___

3. $7 \times (3 \times 2)$
   ↓
   $7 \times$ ___
   ↓
   ___

4. $3 \times (9 - 6)$
   ↓
   $3 \times$ ___
   ↓
   ___

5. $(15 - 6) + 8$ ___

6. $15 - (6 + 8)$ ___

7. $(5 \times 3) \times 10$ ___

8. $4 \times (5 \times 2)$ ___

Solve the equation

9. $(4 \times 6) + (4 \times 1) = c \times (6 + 1)$
   $(4 \times 6) + (4 \times 1) = 4 \times (6 + 1)$
   $c =$ ___

10. $a + (3 + 5) = (2 + 3) + 5$
    $2 + (3 + 5) = (2 + 3) + 5$
    $a =$ ___

11. $8 \times 6 \times 4 = p \times 8 \times 4$
    $8 \times 6 \times 4 = 6 \times 8 \times 4$
    $p =$ ___

12. $7 \times (6 + 2) = (b \times 6) + (b \times 2)$
    $b =$ ___

13. $y + 6 + 9 = 9 + 6 + 1$
    $y =$ ___

14. $(9 \times 5) \times 11 = 9 \times (5 \times c)$
    $c =$ ___

Check

Evaluate.

15. $27 + (30 - 7)$ ______

16. $35 - (24 + 11)$ ______

Find the value of *y*.

17. $7 \times (6 + 2) = (y \times 6) + (y \times 2)$
    $y =$ ______

Skill 51 Order of Operations

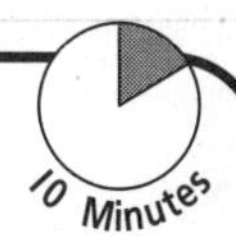

Using Skill 51

OBJECTIVE Evaluate expressions using the order of operations

Read the order of operations at the top of the page. Discuss why it is important to have a set of rules for deciding the order of computation. Demonstrate by doing the first example left to right instead of with order of operations.

Refer to the first problem.

Ask: **What operations are in the problem?** (addition and multiplication) **Which operation do you perform first?** (multiplication) **Which operation do you perform second?** (addition)

Focus on the second problem. Have students state the order in which they will do the operations. Make sure that they see the exponent. (Help students to understand that the parentheses do not affect the answer because even without parentheses they would divide before adding.)

Ask: **What is the first thing you do in this problem?** (divide) **What is the second thing you do?** (simplify the exponent) **What is 3^2?** (9) **What is the last thing you do?** (add) **What is the value of the expression?** (11)

Lead students through the third problem. Stress that the fraction bar is actually a grouping symbol that requires them to simplify the numerator, then simplify the denominator before dividing the numerator by the denominator.

TRY THESE In Exercises 1–4 students use the order of operations to evaluate expressions.

- **Exercise 1** Divide then add
- **Exercise 2** Simplify within parentheses, then multiply
- **Exercise 3** Subtract, divide, then multiply
- **Exercise 4** Simplify within parentheses, simplify exponent, then subtract

PRACTICE ON YOUR OWN Review the example at the top of the page. As they work through the exercise, have the students focus on the fraction bar as a division symbol.

CHECK Determine if the students know the order of operations.

Success is indicated by 3 out of 3 correct responses.

Students who successfully complete the **Practice on Your Own** and **Check** are ready to move to the next skill.

COMMON ERRORS

- Students may not recall how to compute with exponents.
- Students may always work from left to right and forget to consider parentheses.

Students who made more than 1 error in the **Practice on Your Own**, or who were not successful in the **Check** section, may benefit from the **Alternative Teaching Strategy** on the next page.

Optional

Alternative Teaching Strategy

Model Order of Operations

OBJECTIVE Model evaluating an expression using the order of operations

Say: **We're going to solve this problem. If I have 5 cubes and then John, Maria, and Remy each give me 2 cubes, how many cubes will I have?** (11)

Ask: **What is an expression that describes this problem?** ($5 + 3 \times 2$) **If we work this problem left to right, what value do we get?** (16)

Now, demonstrate with cubes. Ask students to take on the roles from the problem and follow it exactly. Discuss why you only have 11 cubes. Lead students to conclude that multiplication must come before addition, unless parentheses tell you otherwise.

Act out and solve the following problems. In each case, discuss whether parentheses are needed.

- I have 2 cubes. Pedro has 25 cubes that he will share equally with Anne, Tara, Kim, and me. When I get my share, how many cubes will I have? ($2 + 25 \div 5 = 7$; note that if Pedro is sharing, he gets a share too; parentheses are not needed.)
- I had 25 cubes, but I gave 9 of them to Junior before I shared the ones I had left with Jan, Rita, and Omar. How many do I have now? ($(25 - 9) \div 4 = 4$; Parentheses are necessary.)
- I had 25 cubes and I gave 3 of them to each of 4 students. How many do I have now? ($25 - 3 \times 4 = 13$; Parentheses are not needed.)

Name ____________________ Skill ____________________

Skill 51

Order of Operations

Evaluate an expression by using the order of operations.

Order of Operations

1. Do the operation in parentheses.
2. Simplify exponents.
3. Multiply and divide from left to right.
4. Add and subtract from left to right.

Evaluate $7 + 2 \times 3$.

$2 \times 3 = 6$

$7 + 2 \times 3$	Multiply first.
$7 + 6$	Then add.
13	

The value of the expression is 13.

Evaluate $3^2 + (4 \div 2)$.

$2\overline{)4}$ = 2

$3^2 + (4 \div 2)$	Operate within parentheses.
$3^2 + 2$	Simplify the exponent.
$3 \times 3 = 9$	
$9 + 2$	Add.
11	

The value of the expression is 11.

Evaluate $\frac{(4 + 2)}{3} + 4^2$.

$\frac{(4+2)}{3} + 4^2$	$4 + 2 = 6$
$\frac{6}{3} + 4^2$	Operate within parentheses.
$\frac{6}{3} + 16$	Simplify the exponent.
$2 + 16$	Divide.
18	Add.

The value of the expression is 18.

Try These

Evaluate each expression. Write what you do.

1. $3 + 8 \div 2$
   First do: __________
   Then do: __________
   The value is ________.

2. $(5 + 3) \times 7$
   First do: __________
   Then do: __________
   The value is ________.

3. $\frac{(12 - 3)}{3} \times 8$
   First do: __________
   Next do: __________
   Then do: __________
   The value is ________.

4. $5^2 - (10 - 6)$
   First do: __________
   Next do: __________
   Then do: __________
   The value is ________.

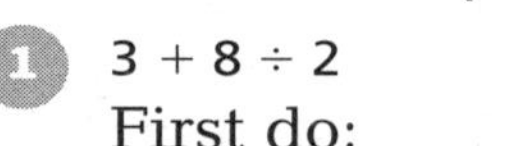

Practice on Your Own

Skill 51

Think:
Order of operations:
1. Operate within parentheses.
2. Simplify exponents.
3. Multiply and divide from left to right.
4. Add and subtract from left to right.

Evaluate $\frac{(29 - 5)}{4} + 2^3$.

$\frac{(29-5)}{4} + 2^3$	Operate within parentheses. $29 - 5 = 24$
$\frac{24}{4} + 2^3$	Simplify the exponent. $2 \times 2 \times 2 = 8$
$\frac{24}{4} + 8$	Divide. $24 \div 4 = 6$
$6 + 8$	Add.
14	

The value of the expression is 14.

Evaluate each expression.

1 $7 + 10 \div 5$

First do: ________

Then do: ________

The value is ________.

2 $\frac{(18 - 6)}{4} \times 2$

First do: ________

Next do: ________

Then do: ________

The value is ________.

3 $\frac{(15 - 6)}{3} + 4^2$

First do: ________

Next do: ________

Then do: ________

Then do: ________

The value is ________.

Evaluate each expression. Write the steps you use to evaluate.

4 $5^2 \div (8 - 3)$

____

____

____

 **5** $(18 + 18) \div 3^2$

____

____

____

 **6** $\frac{(12 - 3)}{3} \times 8$

____

____

____

Check

Evaluate each expression. Write the steps you use to evaluate.

7 $(5 \times 2) + (8 - 3)$

____

____

8 $4^2 - (13 - 5)$

____

____

____

 **9** $\frac{(16 - 7)}{9} + 6^2$

____

____

____

____

Skill 52 Simplify Numeric Expressions

10 Minutes

Using Skill 52

OBJECTIVE Simplify numeric expressions

A numeric expression has numbers and operation signs. It does not have an equal sign.

Ask: **What do the parentheses indicate?** (They tell what to do first.)

Direct students to Example 1.
Ask: **What operation do you do first?** (Add the 3 and the 2.)

Ask: **Then what do you do?** (Multiply $\frac{1}{2}$ by 8 then multiply the result by 5.)

Continue in a similar manner with Example 2, simplifying the exponent first.

TRY THESE In Exercises 1–3 students determine what to do first, and then second, to simplify the expression.

- **Exercise 1** Multiply $\frac{1}{2}$ by 6 then multiply the result by 3.
- **Exercise 2** Multiply 2 by 3.14, then multiply the result by 14.
- **Exercise 3** Add the 4 and the 7, then multiply from left to right.

PRACTICE ON YOUR OWN Review the examples at the top of the page.
Remind students of the order of operations.
1. Perform operations inside parentheses.
2. Simplify exponents.
3. Multiply or divide from left to right.
4. Add or subtract from left to right.

Explain that it may be easier to multiply if you can cancel the fraction. Always check for ways to simplify.

CHECK Determine whether students are simplifying according to the order of operations. Success is indicated by 3 out of 3 correct responses.

Students who successfully complete the **Practice on Your Own** and **Check** are ready to move on to the next skill.

COMMON ERRORS

- Students may perform the operations from left to right, regardless of the parentheses.
- Students may forget to simplify an exponent or simplify incorrectly.

Optional

Alternative Teaching Strategy
Simplify Numeric Expressions

OBJECTIVE Simplify numeric expressions

MATERIALS index cards

On each index card write either a whole number, a number with an exponent, a fraction, and π (as a decimal 3.14 or a fraction $\frac{22}{7}$). Create a pile of each type of number. (Whole numbers in one pile, numbers with exponents in a second pile, fractions in a third pile, etc.)

Have students draw 3 cards from different piles. Students should then multiply the numbers together following the order of operations.

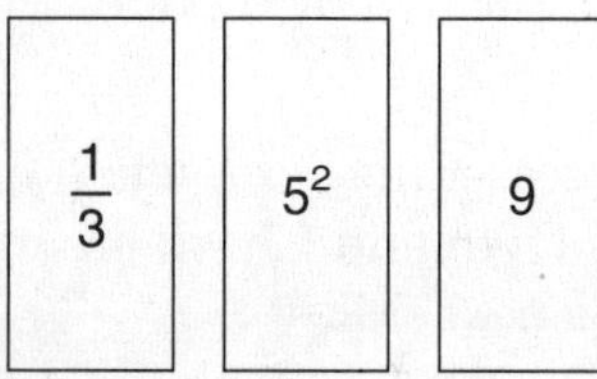

Ask: **What will you do first?** (Simplify the exponent.)

Ask: **What will you do next?** (Multiply from left to right.)

Students may arrange cards to make the simplifying easier

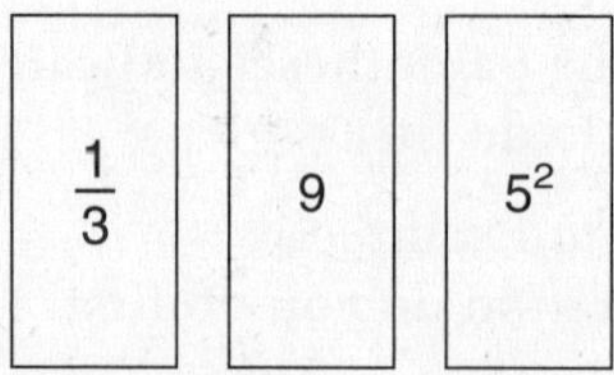

Repeat the activity several times with different expressions.

When students show an understanding of the simplifying process with three cards, give four cards to each student.

Name ____________ Skill ____________

Skill 52

Simplifying Numeric Expressions

Simplify each numeric expression. Remember order of operations.

Example 1 Simplify $\frac{1}{2}(8)(3 + 2)$.

$\frac{1}{2}(8)(3 + 2)$ First, add 3 + 2.

↓

$\frac{1}{2}(8)(5)$ Then, multiply $\frac{1}{2}$ by 8.

↓

$4(5)$ Then multiply by 5.

So, $\frac{1}{2}(8)(3 + 2) = 20$.

Example 2 Simplify $\frac{1}{2}(4)^2(8)$.

$\frac{1}{2}(4)^2(8)$ Simplify the exponent.

↓

$\frac{1}{2}(16)(8)$ Multiply $\frac{1}{2}$ by 16.

↓

$(8)(8)$ Multiply 8 by 8.

So, $\frac{1}{2}(4)^2(8) = 64$.

Try These

Simplify each expression by following the steps.

1. $\frac{1}{2}(6)(3)$
   First do: ________
   Then do: ________
   The value is ________.

2. $2(3.14)(14)$
   First do: ________
   Then do: ________
   The value is ________.

3. $\frac{1}{2}(8)(4 + 7)$
   First do: ________
   Then do: ________
   The value is ________.

Go to the next side.

Name ______________________ Skill ______________________

Practice on Your Own

Skill 52

Simplify 2(3.14)(6).	Simplify $\frac{1}{2}(6.5)^2(4)$.
Think: Multiply from left to right.	**Think:** Simplify the exponent first.
$2(3.14)(6)$	$\frac{1}{2}(6.5)^2(4)$
↓	↓
$6.28(6)$	$\frac{1}{2}(42.25)(4)$ Multiply from left to right.
↓	↓
37.68	84.5

Tell what you would do first, and then simplify the expression.

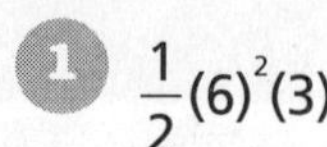

1. $\frac{1}{2}(6)^2(3)$

   First do: ________

   The value is ________.

2. $\frac{1}{2}(10)(2 + 6)$

   First do: ________

   The value is ________.

3. $\frac{1}{3}(3.14)(4)^2(9)$

   First do: ________

   The value is ________.

4. $3.14(5)^2(3)$

   First do: ________

   The value is ________.

5. $\frac{1}{2}(6)(5.75)$

   First do: ________

   The value is ________.

6. $\frac{1}{2}(16)(3 + 7)$

   First do: ________

   The value is ________.

Check

Simplify each expression.

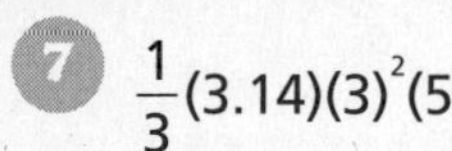

7. $\frac{1}{3}(3.14)(3)^2(5)$ ________

8. $\frac{1}{2}(18)(12 + 16)$ ________

9. $\frac{1}{3}\left(\frac{22}{7}\right)(3)^2(7)$ ________

Skill 53 Words for Operations

Using Skill 53

OBJECTIVE Write an algebraic expression for a word expression

Direct students' attention to the first example. Ask: **What is an algebraic expression?** (an expression containing numbers, operations and variables) **What are the four operations?** (addition, subtraction, multiplication, division) **In the word expression "the sum of 6 and *n*," which word refers to the operation?** (sum) **To which operation does the word *sum* refer?** (addition) **In the word expression, "the sum of 6 and *n*," what are the addends?** (6 and n) **What is the algebraic expression?** ($6 + n$) **What other way could you write the expression?** ($n + 6$)

As you work through each word expression, have the students identify the word(s) that signify the operation used. Remind students of the importance of keeping the numbers and variables in the correct order when using subtraction or division.

In the section *Writing a Word Expression for an Algebraic Expression*, point out to students that each algebraic expression can be written as different word expressions. Guide students to understand that each of the word expressions represents the same algebraic expression.

TRY THESE Exercises 1–2 provide practice identifying operations in word expressions, writing algebraic expressions, and connecting algebraic expressions to word expressions.

- **Exercises 1–2** Write the operation and algebraic expression.

PRACTICE ON YOUR OWN Review the example at the top of the page. Have a student tell which words indicate the operation used.

CHECK Determine if students know the operation used in word expressions and can write the algebraic expression. Success is indicated by 4 out of 4 correct responses.

Students who successfully complete the **Practice on Your Own** and **Check** are ready to move to the next skill.

COMMON ERRORS

- Students may incorrectly write $a - b$ for *a less than b*, or $a \div 45$ for *the quotient of 45 and a*.
- For expressions that contain more than one operation, students may show only one of the operations.

Students who made more than 3 errors in the **Practice on Your Own**, or who were not successful in the **Check** section, may benefit from the **Alternative Teaching Strategy** on the next page.

Optional

Alternative Teaching Strategy

Words for Operations

OBJECTIVE Use index cards to write algebraic expressions for a word expression

MATERIALS index cards

Write on each index card a numeric expression such as:

$6 + 4 \qquad 7 - 3 \qquad 4 \times 2 \qquad 18 \div 9$

Divide students into groups of four. Have one student hold up an index card. Have each student in the group read aloud the expression. Try to get students to use as many different phrases as possible. Ask students to record each phrase on an index card.

Then, for each expression, have students replace one of the numbers with a variable. For example:

$a + 4 \qquad 7 - b \qquad 4 \times t \qquad m \div 9$

Again, have each student in the group read the expression aloud using as many different phrases as they can. Record each phrase on an index card.

Next, remove the symbolic expressions. Distribute the index cards with the algebraic expressions in word form and have students write the symbolic form.

Repeat the activity in another session for expressions with more than one operation. Again, start with numeric expressions, then replace some of the numbers with variables. Repeat the steps described for expressions with one operation.

Name ____________________ Skill ____________________

Skill 53

Words for Operations

Write an algebraic expression for a word expression.

Write an Algebraic Expression for a Word Expression

Read the word expression.
Decide what operation to use.
Then write the algebraic expression.

- the sum of 6 and n
  addition
  $6 + n$
- the product of 8 and n
  multiplication
  $8n$

Remember there are different forms for multiplication:

$8 \times n$, $8n$

- the difference of 15 and b
  subtraction
  $15 - b$
- the quotient of 36 and n
  division
  $\frac{36}{n}$

Remember there are different forms for division:

$2\overline{)4}$, $4 \div 2$, $\frac{4}{2}$

Think: An algebraic expression can contain one or more numbers, operations, and variables.

Write a Word Expression for an Algebraic Expression

There are different phrases that you can use to represent algebraic expressions.

Algebraic Expression	Word Expression
$2 + n$	the sum of 2 and n 2 increased by n 2 plus n 2 more than n a number n plus 2
$n - 6$	the difference of n and 6 n decreased by 6 n minus 6 6 less than a number n
xyz	the product of x, y, and z x times y times z
$\frac{45}{a}$	the quotient of 45 and a 45 divided by a

Try These

Write the operation and algebraic expression for each word expression.

1. 5 **increased** by t

   Operation: __________

   Algebraic expression: ____________________

2. The **difference** of 12 and p.

   Operation: __________

   Algebraic expression: ____________________

Go to the next side.

Name ______________________ Skill ______________________

Practice on Your Own

Skill 53

Sometimes there is more than one operation in an expression.

Word Expression	Algebraic Expression
the difference of the product of *a* and *b* and 7 subtraction multiplication	$ab - 7$
y less than the quotient of 64 and 8 division subtraction	$\frac{64}{8} - y$

Write the operation and algebraic expression for each word expression.

1. the **product** of *m* and 2
Operation: __________
Algebraic expression: __________

2. 8 **less than** x
Operation: __________
Algebraic expression: __________

3. the **quotient** of 24 and *c*
Operation: __________
Algebraic expression: __________

4. the sum of 4 and *s*
Operation: __________
Algebraic expression: __________

5. 5 times *b*
Operation: __________
Algebraic expression: __________

6. *r* decreased by 11
Operation: __________
Algebraic expression: __________

Write the letter of the word expression for the algebraic expression.

7. $\frac{t}{5}$ ______
8. $5t$ ______
9. $t + 5$ ______
10. $t - 5$ ______

a. the product of 5 and *t*
b. a number *t* plus 5
c. *t* decreased by 5
d. the quotient of *t* and 5

Write the operation(s) and algebraic expression.

11. the sum of 3 and the quantity 8 times *p*
____
____

12. the difference of the product of 7 and *n* and 4
____
____

13. 6 less than the quotient of *a* and 4
____
____

Check

Write the operation(s) and algebraic expression.

14. the sum of 17 and x
____
____

15. 8 less than the product of 29 and y
____

Write the letter of the word expression for the algebraic expression.

16. $10m$ ______
17. $10 + m$ ______

a. 10 increased by *m*
b. 10 times *m*

Skill 54 Evaluate Expressions

Using Skill 54

OBJECTIVE Find the value of an expression using the order of operations

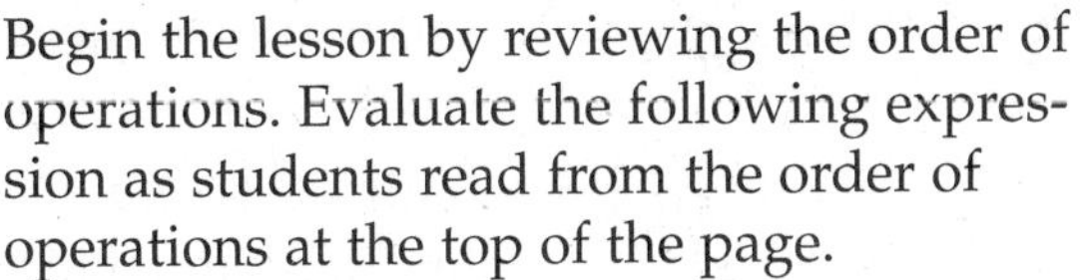

Begin the lesson by reviewing the order of operations. Evaluate the following expression as students read from the order of operations at the top of the page.

	$2^2 + (3 \times 4) \div 6$
1. Operate inside parentheses.	$2^2 + 12 \div 6$
2. Evaluate terms with exponents.	$4 + 12 \div 6$
3. Multiply and divide from left to right.	$4 + 2$
4. Add and subtract from left to right.	6

You may wish to review rules for operations with integers. Then, have students look at the first example. Ask:
What operations will you use to evaluate the expression? (multiplication, addition)
Using the order of operations which operation will you do first? (Multiply 2 times b)
What do you do before you multiply? (Replace the variable b with $^-4$.) **After you multiply what numbers do you add?** ($^-8 + 3$) **What is the sum?** ($^-5$)

Why is the sum a negative integer? (With addends of different signs, subtract the lesser absolute value from the greater absolute value and use the sign of the addend with the greater absolute value, in this case, a negative sign.)

Use similar questions to evaluate the expressions in the last two examples. Caution students that, to have an accurate answer, they must use the order of operations.

TRY THESE In Exercises 1–3 students use the order of operations to evaluate expressions.

- **Exercise 1** Multiply, subtract
- **Exercise 2** Multiply, divide, add
- **Exercise 3** Operate inside parentheses, evaluate terms with exponents, multiply

PRACTICE ON YOUR OWN Review the example at the top of the page. Have students note that they are replacing more than one variable with given values. Have students work through the example step-by-step.

CHECK Determine if the students can evaluate expressions using the order of operations, and perform the operations with integers correctly.

Success is indicated by 2 out of 3 correct responses.

Students who successfully complete the **Practice on Your Own** and **Check** are ready to move to the next skill.

COMMON ERRORS

- Students may not use the order of operations correctly.
- Students may not know the rules for signs when using operations with integers.
- Students may calculate the results incorrectly.

Students who made more than 3 errors in the **Practice on Your Own**, or who were not successful in the **Check** section, may benefit from the **Alternative Teaching Strategy** on the next page.

Optional

Alternative Teaching Strategy

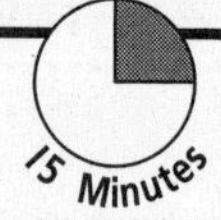

Evaluate Expressions

OBJECTIVE Evaluate expressions using the order of operations

MATERIALS index cards, paper

Prepare sets of cards ahead of time. On each index card show one of the following: 2 sets of digits 0–9; symbols ×, ÷, +, −, (,), •; the variable *a*, the exponents 2 and 3.

As you begin the lesson, recall that when evaluating expressions students must use the order of operations. The order of operations ensures that everyone will get the same answer. Display the following.

Order of Operations

1. Operate inside the parentheses.
2. Evaluate terms with exponents.
3. Multiply and divide from left to right.
4. Add and subtract from left to right.

Present $2^2 \times (19 - 9)$ and have students represent it with cards. Ask:
What operations do you see in the expression? (find the square of 2, multiply, subtract)
According to the order of operations what do you do first? (I operate inside the parentheses first.) **What is the difference?** (10)

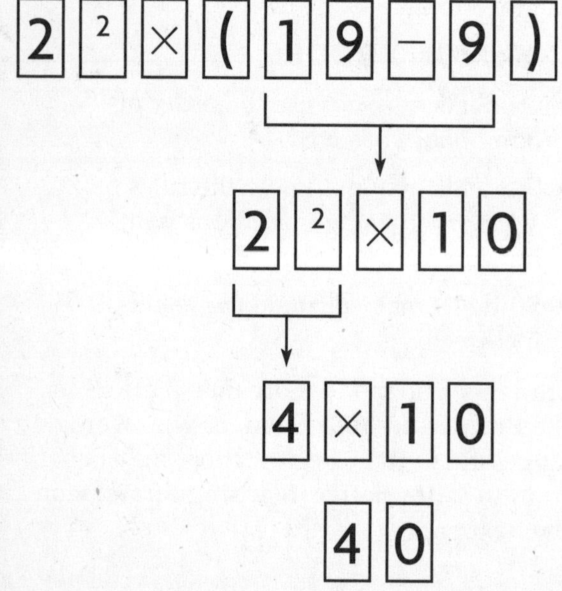

Have students replace "19 − 9" with 10. Say: **According to the order of operations, what do you do next?** (Find the square of 2; it is 4.)

Have students replace 2^2 with a 4. Guide students as they find 4 × 10 and determine that the value of $2^2 \times (19 - 9)$ is 40.

Now present this expression: $5a + (7 - 5)$ Explain that $a = 5$. Then point out that before students use the order of operations, they replace *a* with 5. Have students replace the variable card with a card for 5. Then work through the evaluation procedure as before.

5 • 5 = 25 and 25 + 2 = 27. The value of the expression is 27.

Repeat the activity with expressions such as these:

$(2 + 4) \times 4^2$		(96)
$3^3 \div (14 - 5)$		(3)
$(a \div 2) + (15 \times 2)$	$a = 18$	(39)
$(-9 + 3) + a^2$	$a = 5$	(19)

When students understand how to evaluate expressions using the order of operations, have them evaluate expressions with paper and pencil.

Name ______________________ Skill ______________

Skill 54

Evaluate Expressions

You can **evaluate**, or find the value of, an expression by using the order of operations.

Order of Operations

1. Operate inside parentheses.
2. Evaluate terms with exponents.
3. Multiply and divide from left to right.
4. Add and subtract from left to right.

Evaluate $2b + 3$ for $b = {}^{-}4$.

$2b + 3$ Replace b with $^{-}4$.

↓

$2 \bullet {}^{-}4 + 3$ Multiply first.
Think: $2 \bullet {}^{-}4 = {}^{-}8$

$^{-}8 + 3$ Then add.
Think: $^{-}8 + 3 = {}^{-}5$

$^{-}5$

So, when $b = {}^{-}4$, the value of $2b + 3$ is $^{-}5$.

Evaluate $\frac{2a}{3} - 4$ for $a = 9$.

$\frac{2a}{3} - 4$ Replace a with 9.

↓

$\frac{2 \bullet 9}{3} - 4$ Multiply first.
Think: $2 \bullet 9 = 18$

$\frac{18}{3} - 4$ Then divide.
Think: $18 \div 3 = 6$

$6 - 4$ Finally, subtract.
Think: $6 - 4 = 2$

2

So, when $a = 9$, the value of $\frac{2a}{3} - 4$ is 2.

Evaluate $5(s + 3)^2$ for $s = 2$.

$5(s + 3)^2$ Replace s with 2.

↓

$5(2 + 3)^2$ Operate inside parentheses.
Think: $2 + 3 = 5$

$5 \bullet 5^2$ Evaluate 5^2.
Think: $5^2 = 5 \times 5$, or 25

$5 \bullet 25$ Multiply.

125 **Think:** $5 \bullet 25 = 125$

So, when $s = 2$, the value of $5(s + 3)^2$ is 125.

Try These

Evaluate the expression for the given value of the variable. Write each step.

1 $a = 5$

$4a - 6$ Replace a with 5.

↓

$4 \bullet \square - 6$ Multiply.

_____ Subtract.

_____

The value of $4a - 6$ is _____.

2 $b = 4$

$\frac{1 \bullet b}{2} + 1$ Replace b with 4.

↓

$\frac{1 \bullet \square}{2} + 1$ Multiply first.

$\frac{\square}{2} + 1$ Divide.

_____ Add.

_____

The value of $\frac{1 \bullet b}{2} + 1$ is _____.

3 $c = 3$

$2(10 - c)^2$ Replace c with 3.

$2(10 - \square)^2$ Operate inside parentheses.

_____ Evaluate term with exponent.

_____ Multiply.

_____

The value of $2(10 - c)^2$ is _____.

Go to the next side.

Name ______________________ Skill ______________________

Practice on Your Own

Skill 54

Remember:

When you multiply a negative number by a positive number, the product is a negative number.

Evaluate $(x + 3)^2 + 4xy$, for $x = 7$ and $y = {}^-2$.

$(x + 3)^2 + 4xy$ ↓ ↓	Replace x with 7 and y with $^-2$.
$(7 + 3)^2 + 4 \bullet 7 \bullet {}^-2$	Operate inside parentheses.
$10^2 + 4 \bullet 7 \bullet {}^-2$	Evaluate 10^2.
$100 + 4 \bullet 7 \bullet {}^-2$	Multiply.
$100 + 28 \bullet {}^-2$	Multiply.
$100 + {}^-56$	Add.
44	

The value of $(x + 3)^2 + 4xy$ is 44.

Evaluate the expression for the given value of the variable. Write each step.

1 $m = 5$

$n = 2$

$7mn - 3$ — Replace m with 5 and n with 2.

$7 \bullet \square \bullet \square - 3$

______ Multiply.

______ Subtract.

The value of $7mn - 3$ is ______.

2 $p = {}^-8$

$5(p + 10)^2$

$5(\square + 10)^2$ — Replace p with $^-8$.

______ Parentheses

______ Exponents

______ Multiply.

The value $5(p + 10)^2$ is ______.

3 $t = 24$

$\frac{3t}{4} + 8$ — **Think:**

______ Multiply.

______ Divide.

______ Add.

Value: ______

4 $z = {}^-4$

$3\,(z + 8)^2$ — **Think:**

______ Parentheses

______ then

______ exponents

Value: ______

5 $p = 7, g = {}^-3$

$pg + 12$

______

______

______

Value: ______

Evaluate the expression for the given value of the variable.

6 $5c^2$ for $c = 3$

Value: ______

7 $^-2ab + 3$ for $a = {}^-1$ and $b = {}^-6$

Value: ______

8 $3(n + 5)^2$ for $n = 4$

Value: ______

Check

Evaluate the expression for the given value of the variable.

9 $20 + 5d$ for $d = {}^-2$

Value: ______

10 $\frac{1}{2}xy + 7$ for $x = 2$ and $y = 8$

Value: ______

11 $4\,(t - 1)^2$ for $t = 7$

Value: ______

Skill 55 Simplify Algebraic Expressions

Using Skill 55

OBJECTIVE Simplify algebraic expressions.

Discuss with students that to simplify algebraic expressions, you combine like terms.

Remind students that a term is a number, a variable, or the product of numbers and variables. Recall that if a term has a variable, the number with the variable is called the coefficient. A constant term does not contain a variable.

Guide students to see that terms are like terms if they have exactly the same variable factors. You can combine like terms by adding coefficients.

Focus on Example 1.

Ask: **What is the coefficient of $3x$?** (3)
Grouping terms can help students to see what can be combined.
Ask: **In the example, what terms have the variable?** ($3x$)
Ask: **What are the constant terms?** (5, 1)
Group the terms in the expression and simplify.
Ask: **Why can you not combine the $3x$ and the 4?** (They do not have the same variable. They are not like terms.)
Work through Examples 2 and 3 in a similar manner.

TRY THESE

- **Exercise 1** terms with x and constant
- **Exercise 2** terms with a and constant
- **Exercise 3** terms with x, y, and constant

PRACTICE ON YOUR OWN Review the example at the top of the page.
In Exercises 1–6, students group the terms to simplify the algebraic expression.

CHECK Determine if the students can group like terms correctly, then combine them. Success is indicated by 3 out of 3 correct responses.

Students who successfully complete the **Practice on Your Own** and **Check** are ready to move on to the next skill.

COMMON ERRORS

- Students may forget that a variable by itself has a coefficient of 1.
- Students may drop the sign of the coefficient when combining like terms.

Students who made 3 or more errors in the **Practice on Your Own** may benefit from the **Alternative Teaching Strategy**.

Optional

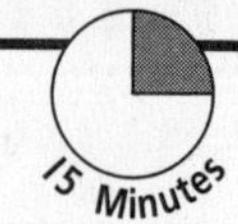

Alternative Teaching Strategy

Use Algebra Tiles to Simplify Algebraic Expressions

OBJECTIVE Simplify algebraic expressions with algebra tiles

MATERIALS algebra tiles

Write the algebraic expression on the board.

$5a - 6 - 2a + 8$

Have students model the equation with algebra tiles.

Key:

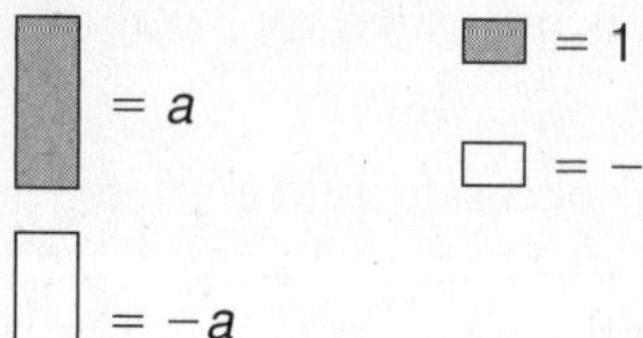

Ask: **Which type of tiles do you need to represent 5*a*? How many tiles do you need?**
(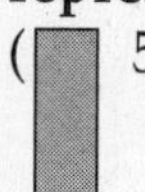 5)

Draw the following on the board.

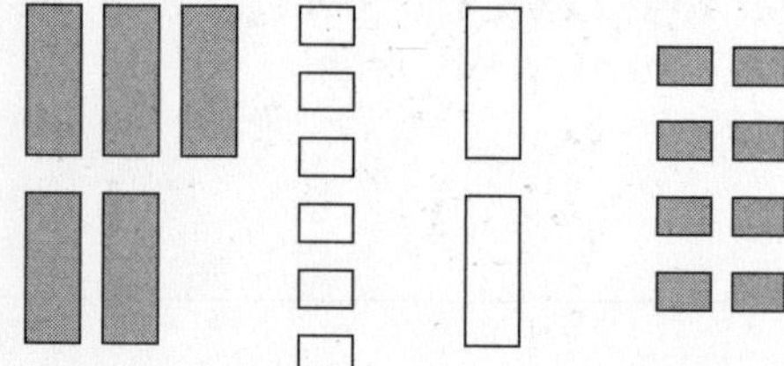

Have students model and combine tiles by removing zero pairs.

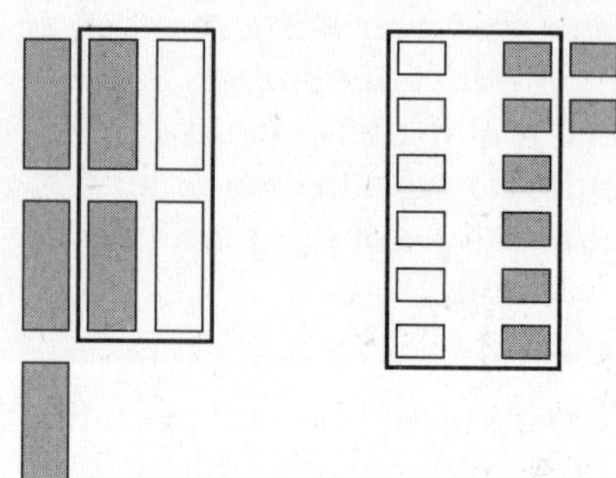

Ask: **What remains?** ( )

Ask: **What does this represent?** (3a + 2)

Repeat the activity several times with different combinations of numbers and variables. When students show understanding, give larger numbers or terms with 2 variables to simplify.

Name ______________________ Skill ______________________

Simplifying Algebraic Expressions

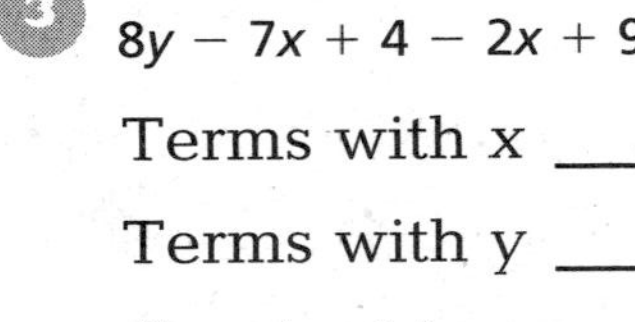

Skill 55

To simplify algebraic expressions, combine like terms.

Example 1

$5 + 3x - 1$

Put a square around the terms with the variable x and a circle around the constant terms.

(5) [+ 3x] (−1)

Combine the terms in each shape.

[+ 3x] (5 − 1)

$3x + 4$

Example 2

$b + 7 + 6b + 5$

Put a square around the terms with a variable *b* and a circle around the constant terms.

[b] (+ 7) [+ 6b] (+ 5)

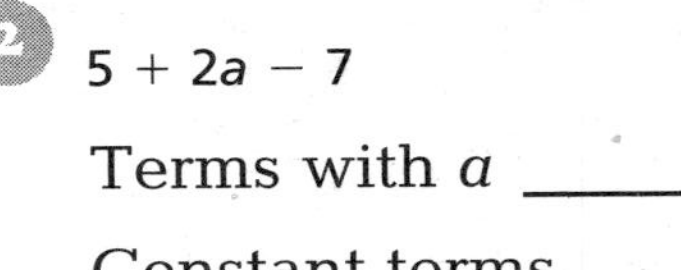

Combine the terms in each shape. **Think:** The coefficient of the first *b* is 1.

[b + 6b] (7 + 5)

$7b + 12$

Example 3

$3a + 7b - 4 + 9a - 2b$

Put a square around the terms with a variable *a*, a circle around terms with a variable *b*, and a triangle around the constant terms.

[3a] (+7b) △−4 [+9a] (−2b)

Combine the terms in each shape.

[3a + 9a] (7b − 2b) △−4

$12a + 5b - 4$

Try These

Simplify each algebraic expression.

1. $7 + 3x - x - 4$

Terms with x __________

Constant terms __________

2. $5 + 2a - 7$

Terms with *a* __________

Constant terms __________

3. $8y - 7x + 4 - 2x + 9$

Terms with x __________

Terms with y __________

Constant terms __________

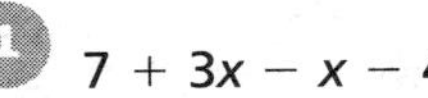

Go to the next side.

Name ______________________ Skill ______________________

Practice on Your Own

Skill 55

Simplify. $9x - 4y + 5x - 8 + y$

Think: Group like terms by drawing circles, squares and triangles around the like terms.

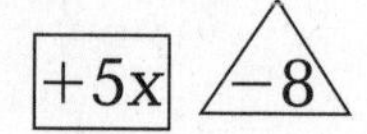 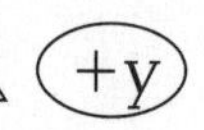 Combine the terms in the same shape.

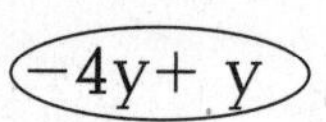 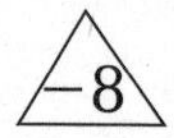 **Think:** The coefficient of y is 1.

$14x - 3y - 8$ Simplify.

Simplify each algebraic expression by combining like terms.

1. $6n - 3n + 2$

terms with n ________

constant terms ________

____

2. $4 + 5y + y - 6$

terms with y ________

constant terms ________

____

3. $2a - 5b - b - a$

terms with a ________

terms with b ________

____

4. $26 - y + 4y + 4$

terms with y ________

constant terms ________

____

5. $-x + 7y - 4x + 6$

terms with x ________

terms with y ________

constant terms ________

____

6. $3a + 6 - 4b + 7 - b$

terms with a ________

terms with b ________

constant terms ________

____

Check

Simplify each algebraic expression.

7. $9y + 5 + 2y - 4y$

____

8. $6b + 4a + 9 - 2a - 7$

____

9. $2n + 6m - 9n + 8 - 6m - 3$

____

Skill 56 Connect Words and Equations

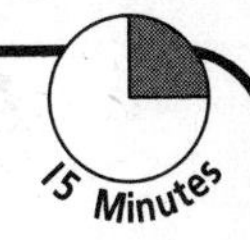

Using Skill 56

OBJECTIVE Write an algebraic equation for a word sentence

Begin the lesson by recalling for students that equations are sentences that show that two quantities are equal. Remind students that equations always contain an equal sign. Ask: **What is the difference between an algebraic expression and an algebraic equation?** (An algebraic equation has an equal sign and an algebraic expression does not have an equal sign.)

Tell students that they can follow steps to write an algebraic equation for a word sentence. Direct students' attention to Example 1. Have a student read the first word sentence. Now direct students' attention to Example 2. Tell them that they can identify the operation, the unknown quantity, and the placement of the equal sign. Ask: **Which words in the sentence refer to the operation?** (increased by) **What is the operation?** (addition) **Which words in the sentence refer to the unknown quantity?** (a number)

Which word in the sentence refers to the equal sign? (is) **Which two amounts are added together?** (a number and 4) **Where should you place the equal sign in the equation?** (between the 4 and the 12)

Refer students to Example 1. Tell them that they can choose a variable to represent the unknown quantity. Ask: **What letter was chosen for the variable in Example 1?** (n)

Tell students that they can now write the equation. Ask:
What is the equation in Example 1?
($n + 4 = 12$)

Continue using similar questioning for the other word sentences. Have the students state the steps as they perform them.

TRY THESE Exercises 1–4 provide practice identifying operations and writing algebraic equations for word sentences.

- **Exercise 1** Addition
- **Exercise 2** Subtraction
- **Exercise 3** Multiplication
- **Exercise 4** Division

PRACTICE ON YOUR OWN Review the example at the top of the page. Have a student identify the word(s) indicating the operation used and the placement of the equal sign.

CHECK Determine if students can write an algebraic equation for a word sentence and correctly place the equal sign.

Success is indicated by 5 out of 6 correct responses.

Students who successfully complete the **Practice on Your Own** and **Check** are ready to move to the next skill.

COMMON ERRORS

- Students may not know the terms associated with operations, and thus may use the wrong operation.
- Students may incorrectly place the equal sign in the equation.

Students who made more than 4 errors in the **Practice on Your Own**, or who were not successful in the **Check** section, may benefit from the **Alternative Teaching Strategy** on the next page.

Optional

Alternative Teaching Strategy

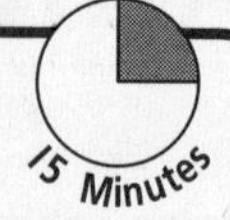

Model Connecting Words and Equations

OBJECTIVE Use counters and cups to model word sentences and write algebraic equations

MATERIALS counters, cups, slips of paper labeled +, −, ×, ÷, and =

Distribute cups and counters to students. Explain to the students that the cups will represent the unknown quantity in a word sentence. Have the students copy this word sentence: A number increased by 5 is 12.

Ask:

What can you use to represent the phrase "a number" in the word sentence? (a cup)

Which operation does "increased by" indicate? (addition)

What symbol can you use for the word "is"? (equal sign)

Say:

Use the cup and counters to model the word sentence.

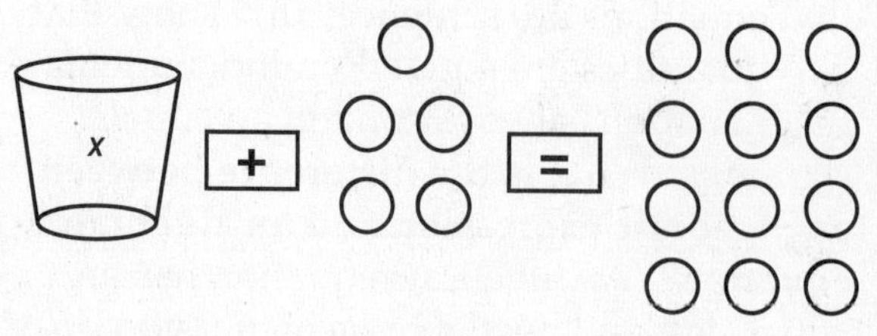

Check students' models to see that they are correct.

Continue:

What algebraic sentence can you write that matches the model of the cups and counters? ($x + 5 = 12$)

Point out to students that they can also write $a + 5 = 12$ or $m + 5 = 12$. Guide students to understand that any letter may be used to represent the unknown quantity.

Have the students use the cups and counters to model other word sentences.

When students show understanding, remove the cups and counters and have them try an exercise using only paper and pencil.

Name ______________________ Skill ______________________

Skill 56

Connect Words and Equations

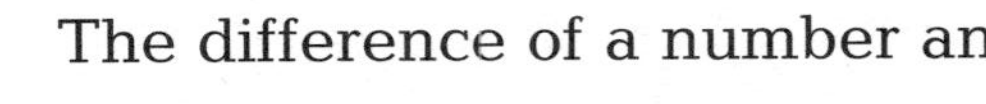

Remember: An equation is an algebraic or numerical sentence that shows two quantities are equal.

You can write an algebraic equation for a word sentence. An algebraic equation is an equation that contains a variable.

Follow these steps to write an algebraic equation for a word sentence.

Step 1 Read the sentence.

Step 2 Identify operations, the unknown quantity, and the placement of the equal sign.

Step 3 Choose a variable.

Step 4 Write the equation.

Example 1 A number increased by 4 is 12. unknown addition equals $n + 4 = 12$	**Example 2** The difference of a number and 15 is 7. subtraction unknown equals $a - 15 = 7$
Example 3 The product of 2 and a number is 10. multiplication unknown equals $2b = 12$	**Example 4** A number divided by 6 is 3. unknown division equals $\frac{c}{6} = 3$

Try These

Write the operation. Then write an algebraic equation for the word sentence.

1. Twelve plus a number is 17.
Operation: ______________________
Equation: ______________________

2. The difference of a number and 1 is 2.
Operation: ______________________
Equation: ______________________

3. A number times 3 is 15.
Operation: ______________________
Equation: ______________________

4. The quotient of 24 and a number is 6.
Operation: ______________________
Equation: ______________________

Go to the next side.

Name ______________________ Skill ______________________

Practice on Your Own

Skill 56

Think:
Use the word sentence to determine the operation, the unknown value, or variable, and the placement of the equal sign. Then write the equation.

Word Sentence	Algebraic Equation
10 is 3 more than a number. equals addition unknown	$10 = x + 3$
4.5 less than a number is 3.2. subtraction unknown equals	$x - 4.5 = 3.2$
Twice a number is $^-56$. multiplication unknown equals	$2x = {}^-56$
A number divided by 6 is $\frac{1}{2}$. unknown division equals	$\frac{x}{6} = \frac{1}{2}$

Write the operation. Then write an algebraic equation for the word sentence.

1. A number plus 8 is 19.
Operation: ______
Equation: ______

2. The difference of a number and 6.8 is 1.1.
Operation: ______
Equation: ______

3. The quotient of a number and 3 is 9.
Operation: ______
Equation: ______

4. Twice a number is 30.
Operation: ______
Equation: ______

5. 31 is 8 more than a number.
Operation: ______
Equation: ______

6. A number divided by 16 is $\frac{3}{8}$.
Operation: ______
Equation: ______

Write an algebraic equation for the word sentence.

7. A number increased by 12 is 45.
______

8. 16 less than a number is 5.
______

9. 7 times a number is $^-35$.
______

10. 28.9 is 7.2 more than a number.
______

11. The product of a number and 3 is 33.
______

12. The quotient of 8 and a number is $^-2$.
______

Check

Write an algebraic equation for the word sentence.

13. 7 times a number is 84.
______

14. 19.2 decreased by a number is 6.7.
______

15. A number divided by 6 is $\frac{2}{3}$.
______

16. A number increased by 12 is 67.
______

17. 15 less than a number is 82.
______

18. 3 times a number is $^-36$.
______

Skill 57 Inverse Operations

Using Skill 57

OBJECTIVE Understand that addition and subtraction are inverse operations and that multiplication and division are inverse operations

Begin by defining *inverse* operations as operations that undo each other.

Direct students' attention to the *Addition* and *Subtraction* example. Have a student read the subtraction equation $n - 15 = 8$. Ask: **What mathematical operation is used in this equation?** (subtraction)

What does the n represent? (the number that 15 is subtracted from to get a difference of 8.)

How does using addition help you find out what n is? (If I know that $8 + 15 = 23$, then I know that $23 - 15 = 8$.)

What is the value of n in $n - 15 = 8$? (23)

Emphasize that subtraction and addition are inverse operations.

Ask similar questions as you work through the examples for subtraction, multiplication, and division. Guide students to identify the inverse operation for each equation and state the value of n. Have them check by substituting the value of n in the equation.

TRY THESE In Exercises 1–4 students use inverse operations to solve equations.

- **Exercise 1** Inverse of subtraction
- **Exercise 2** Inverse of addition
- **Exercise 3** Inverse of division
- **Exercise 4** Inverse of multiplication

PRACTICE ON YOUR OWN Review the examples at the top of the page. Focus on the inverse operation of each equation by having students explain how one operation undoes another and how to find and check the value of n.

CHECK Determine if the students know that addition and subtraction are inverse operations and that multiplication and division are inverse operations.

Success is indicated by 6 out of 8 correct responses.

Students who successfully complete the **Practice on Your Own** and **Check** are ready to move to the next skill.

COMMON ERRORS

- Students may not know their facts well enough to use inverse operations correctly.
- Students may not understand the role of the variable in the equation.
- Students may add instead of subtract; for example, $n + 3 = 7$, $n = 7 + 3$, $n = 10$.
- Students may multiply instead of divide; for example, $n \times 3 = 12$, $n = 12 \times 3$, $n = 36$.

Students who made more than 5 errors in the **Practice on Your Own**, or who were not successful in the **Check** section, may benefit from the **Alternative Teaching Strategy** on the next page.

Optional

Alternative Teaching Strategy

Modeling Inverse Operations

OBJECTIVE Use cups and cubes to model inverse operations

MATERIALS paper cups, cubes, index cards labeled +, −, ×, ÷, and =

Begin by reviewing the names of mathematical *operations*: addition, subtraction, multiplication, division. Then define *inverse operation* as a mathematical operation that undoes another. It may also help students to think of *opposite* operations. Say:
For example, subtraction and addition are called *inverse operations* because subtracting undoes adding, and adding undoes subtracting. Addition and subtraction are opposite operations.

If necessary, make sure that students understand the meaning of *equation*: a number sentence with an equal sign showing that two quantities are equal.

Display this equation: $n + 3 = 7$. Point out that it is an addition sentence. Distribute 1 cup and 14 cubes to each student. Demonstrate how to model the equation with the cubes, symbols, and cup. First turn the cup upside down and place four cubes underneath it without showing the 4 cubes to the students. Put down the addition symbol, followed by 3 cubes to the right of the symbol. Then place the equal sign and to the right of that, a set 7 cubes.

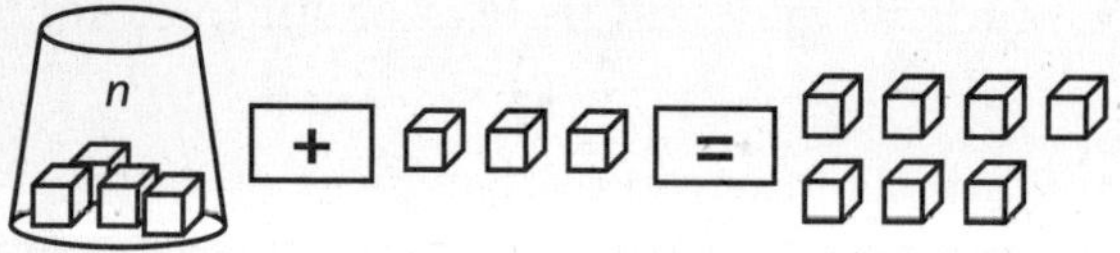

Tell students that the cup represents n in the equation $n + 3 = 7$.

Recall that the equal sign means that the amounts on both sides are equal quantities.

Suggest *subtracting* 3 from both sides of the equation.

Have students remove 3 cubes from the group of 7 and the 3 cubes representing the addend 3.

Guide students to see that $n = 4$. Ask:
Without lifting the cup, tell me how many cubes are underneath it? (4 cubes) **How do you know?** (There has to be the same number on both sides of the equal sign.)

To model multiplication and division as inverse operations, use a simple equation such as $2 \times n = 6$.

Label 2 cups n and place 3 cubes under each cup without letting students see the cubes. Place the equal sign and then 6 cubes to its right. Note that there are 2 groups of n (or $2n$). Then to determine how many are in each group of n, the cubes to the right can be divided into 2 groups. The result is the value of n. Have students separate the cubes into 2 groups to find that $n = 3$. Have them check under the cups to verify the result.

Emphasize that multiplication and division are inverse operations. If students know that $2 \times 3 = 6$, then they know that $6 \div 3 = 2$, and that $6 \div 2 = 3$.

Name ____________________ Skill ____________________

Skill 57

Inverse Operations

Inverse operations are operations that undo each other.

Addition and Subtraction

- You can use addition to solve a subtraction equation.

  $n - 15 = 8$

  Think: 8 plus 15 is what number?

  $8 + 15 = \mathbf{23}$ Then: $n - 15 = 8$

  $\mathbf{23} - 15 = 8$

- You can use subtraction to solve an addition equation.

  $n + 6 = 11$

  Think: 11 minus 6 is what number?

  $11 - 6 = \mathbf{5}$ Then: $n + 6 = 11$

  $\mathbf{5} + 6 = 11$

- You can use addition to check subtraction and subtraction to check addition.

$68 - 35 = 33 \rightarrow 33 + 35 = 68$

$49 + 27 = 76 \rightarrow 76 - 27 = 49$

Multiplication and Division

- You can use multiplication to solve a division equation.

  $36 \div n = 9$

  Think: What number times 9 is 36?

  $\mathbf{4} \times 9 = 36$ Then: $36 \div n = 9$

  $36 \div \mathbf{4} = 9$

- You can use division to solve a multiplication equation.

  $n \times 5 = 35$

  Think: 35 divided by 5 is what number?

  $35 \div 5 = \mathbf{7}$ Then: $n \times 5 = 35$

  $\mathbf{7} \times 5 = 35$

- You can use multiplication to check division and division to check mulitplication.

$72 \div 6 = 12 \rightarrow 12 \times 6 = 72$

$12 \times 9 = 108 \rightarrow 108 \div 9 = 12$

Try These

Choose addition, subtraction, multiplication or division for the inverse operation. Write and solve the equation.

1. $n - 7 = 2$
   Inverse operation: __________
   Equation: __________
   Solution: $n =$ __________

2. $n + 3 = 7$
   Inverse operation: __________
   Equation: __________
   Solution: $n =$ __________

3. $24 \div n = 4$
   Inverse operation: __________
   Equation: __________
   Solution: $n =$ __________

4. $6 \times n = 12$
   Inverse operation: __________
   Equation: __________
   Solution: $n =$ __________

Go to the next side.

Name ______________________ Skill ______________________

Practice on Your Own

Skill 57

Think:
Addition is the inverse of subtraction.
Multiplication is the inverse of division.

Remember: You can check the solution to an equation using the inverse operation.

Equation	Inverse
$n - 12 = 5$	$5 + 12 = n$
$n + 4 = 10$	$10 - 4 = n$
$48 \div n = 12$	$12 \times n = 48$
$n \times 3 = 18$	$18 \div 3 = n$

Use the inverse operation to write an equation. Solve.

1. $n - 7 = 2$
   Equation: ____________
   $n =$ ______
2. $n + 12 = 25$
   Equation: ____________
   $n =$ ______
3. $32 \div n = 8$
   Equation: ____________
   $n =$ ______
4. $5 \times n = 30$
   Equation: ____________
   $n =$ ______
5. $18 - n = 11$
   ____
   $n =$ ______
6. $n + 12 = 27$
   ____
   $n =$ ______
7. $63 \div n = 9$
   ____
   $n =$ ______
8. $9 \times n = 81$
   ____
   $n =$ ______

Use the inverse operation to write an equation. Solve.

9. $39 - 24 = 15$
   $15 + 24 =$
   ____
10. $43 + 52 = 95$
    $95 - 52 =$
    ____
11. $45 \div 9 = 5$
    $5 \times 9 =$
    ____
12. $6 \times 22 = 132$
    $132 \div 22 =$
    ____
13. $220 \div 11 = 20$
    ____
14. $135 + 253 = 388$
    ____
15. $15 \times 32 = 480$
    ____
16. $348 - 172 = 176$
    ____

Check

Use the inverse operation to solve or check the equation.

17. $7 \times n = 105$
    $n =$ ______
18. $38 - n = 25$
    $n =$ ______
19. $99 \div n = 11$
    $n =$ ______
20. $n + 43 = 69$
    $n =$ ______
21. $229 - 78 = 151$
    ____
22. $14 \times 9 = 126$
    ____
23. $178 + 109 = 287$
    ____
24. $216 \div 12 = 18$
    ____

Skill 58 Solve One-Step Equations

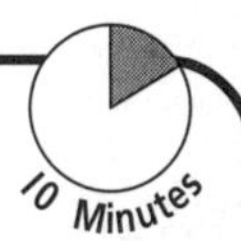

Using Skill 58

OBJECTIVE Solving equations using mental math

Read about equations at the top of the page. Explain to students how an equation is like a balance scale. To be in balance, both trays of the scale must hold the same weight.

Refer to Example A.

Ask: **What is the equation?** ($3 + x = 7$) **What operation is on the left?** (addition) **What do you think the solution is? Explain.** (4, because the addition fact is $3 + 4 = 7$) **How can you check to see if you have the correct solution?** (Substitute 4 for x and see whether it makes a true statement.)

Have students look at Example B. Make sure that they note that the equation uses subtraction.

Ask: **What is the equation that you must solve?** ($10 - t = 2$) **What operation is on the left?** (subtraction) **What do you think the solution is? Explain.** (8, because the subtraction fact is $10 - 8 = 2$) **How can you check to see if you have the correct solution?** (Substitute 8 for t and see whether it makes a true statement.)

Have students work through Example C and Example D. Point out that Example C uses multiplication and Example D uses division. Help students check their work by substituting.

TRY THESE In Exercises 1–4 students use mental math to solve equations.

- **Exercise 1** Addition
- **Exercise 2** Subtraction
- **Exercise 3** Multiplication
- **Exercise 4** Division

PRACTICE ON YOUR OWN Review the example at the top of the page. As they work through the exercise, have students state which operation is being used in each equation.

CHECK Determine if the students can use mental math to solve an equation. Success is indicated by 3 out of 3 correct responses.

Students who successfully complete the **Practice on Your Own** and **Check** are ready to move to the next skill.

COMMON ERRORS

- Students may use the wrong operation to solve the equation.
- Students may not know basic facts.

Students who made more than 2 errors in the **Practice on Your Own**, or who were not successful in the **Check** section, may benefit from the **Alternative Teaching Strategy** on the next page.

Optional

Alternative Teaching Strategy

Model Equations

OBJECTIVE Model solving equations using mental math

MATERIALS cups, cubes, an index card with a large equals symbol written on it

Write the example $x + 3 = 6$.

Ask: **What is the variable?** (x)

Model the equation using a cup and cubes. Tell the students that the cubes hidden in the cup are represented by the variable x. Place an addition symbol and 3 cubes beside the cup, put the equals symbol to the right, and 6 cubes to the right of the equals symbol. Without the students seeing, put 3 cubes in the cup.

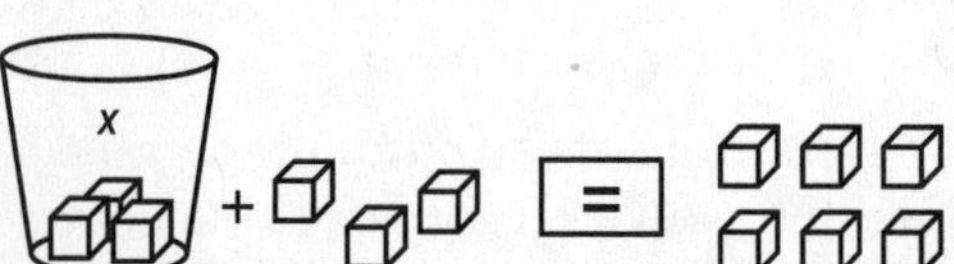

Ask: **If this is a true equation, how many cubes must be to the left of the equals symbol?** (6) **How many can you see there?** (3) **How many cubes must be in the cup?** (3)

To model subtraction, put 8 cubes in the cup. Let students watch you removing 6 cubes from the cup. Write the equation, $x - 6 = 2$ and discuss how to determine a value for x.

To model multiplication, put 2 cubes in each of 6 cups. Write and discuss the equation, $6x = 12$.

To model division, show 16 cubes and 4 empty cups. Write and discuss the equation $16 \div x = 4$.

Name ______________ Skill ______________

Equations

Skill 58

An **equation** is a statement showing that two quantities are equal. When there is a **variable,** a letter that stands for a number, find the value of the variable that makes the equation true. The value is called the **solution**.

Example A

$3 + x = 7$

Think: What number added to 3 equals 7?

$3 + \mathbf{4} = 7$

$x = 4$

Check.
Replace x with 4.

$3 + 4 = 7$

$7 = 7$ 3 + 4 is equal to 7.

Example B

$10 - t = 2$

Think: What number subtracted from 10 equals 2?

$10 - \mathbf{8} = 2$

$t = 8$

Check.
Replace *t* with 8.

$10 - 8 = 2$

$2 = 2$ 10 − 8 is equal to 2.

Example C

$5d = 20$

Think: 5 times what number equals 20?

$5 \cdot \mathbf{4} = 20$

$d = 4$

Check.
Replace *d* with 4.

$5 \cdot 4 = 20$

$20 = 20$ 5 · 4 is equal to 20.

Example D

$\frac{x}{3} = 6$

Think: What number divided by 3 equals 6?

$\frac{\mathbf{18}}{3} = 6$

$x = 18$

Check.
Replace x with 18.

$\frac{18}{3} = 6$

$6 = 6$ 18 ÷ 3 is equal to 6.

Try These

Use mental math to solve each equation. Use the inverse operation to check.

1. $9 + x = 16$

   Think: What number added to 9 equals 16?

   9 + ____ = 16

   x = ____

   Check:

   9 + ____ = 16

   ____ = ____

2. $25 - s = 15$

   Think: What number subtracted from 25 equals 15?

   25 − ____ = 15

   s = ____

   Check:

   25 − ____ = 15

   ____ = ____

3. $7r = 28$

   Think: 7 times what number equals 28?

   7 · ____ = 28

   r = ____

   Check:

   7 · ____ = 28

   ____ = ____

4. $\frac{x}{8} = 10$

   Think: What number divided by 8 equals 10?

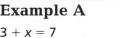

   ____ ÷ 8 = 10

   x = ____

   Check:

   $\frac{\square}{8} = 10$

   ____ = ____

Go to the next side.

Practice on Your Own

Skill 58

$1.2 + x = 2.4$

What number added to 1.2 equals 2.4?

$1.2 + \mathbf{1.2} = 2.4$

$x = 1.2$

Check:

$1.2 + 1.2 = 2.4$

$2.4 = 2.4$

$2.5 - y = 1.0$

2.5 less what number equals 1.0?

$2.5 - \mathbf{1.5} = 1.0$

$y = 1.5$

Check:

$2.5 - 1.5 = 1.0$

$1.0 = 1.0$

$3c = 1.5$

What number times 3 equals 1.5?

$3 \cdot \mathbf{0.5} = 1.5$

$c = 0.5$

Check:

$3 \cdot 0.5 = 1.5$

$1.5 = 1.5$

$\frac{a}{4} = 12$

What number divided by 4 equals 12?

$\mathbf{48} \div 4 = 12$

$a = 48$

Check:

$\frac{48}{4} = 12$

$12 = 12$

Use mental math to solve each equation.

1 $4y = 16$

$4 \cdot$ ____ $= 16$

$y =$ ____

4 times what number is 16?

Check:

$4 \cdot$ ____ $= 16$

____ = ____

2 $\frac{z}{3} = 12$

____ $\div 3 = 12$

$z =$ ____

What number divided by 3 is 12?

Check:

$\frac{\square}{3} = 12$

____ = ____

3 $x - 8 = 10$

____ $- 8 = 10$

$x =$ ____

What number less 8 is 10?

Check:

____ $- 8 = 10$

____ = ____

4 $a + 12 = 14$

____ $+ 12 = 14$

$a =$ ____

Check:

____ $+ 12 = 14$

____ = ____

5 $3b = 1.2$

$3 \cdot$ ____ $= 1.2$

$b =$ ____

Check:

$3 \cdot$ ____ $= 1.2$

____ = ____

6 $9 - x = 1.5$

$9 -$ ____ $= 1.5$

$x =$ ____

Check:

$9 -$ ____ $= 1.5$

____ = ____

7 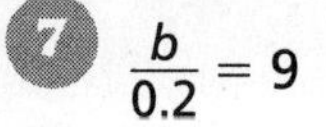

$\frac{b}{0.2} = 9$

$b =$ ____

8 $x + 5.4 = 6.0$

$x =$ ____

9 $y - 6.3 = 6.3$

$y =$ ____

Check

Use mental math to solve each equation.

10 $x + 1.5 = 16$

$x =$ ____

11 $8y = 64$

$y =$ ____

12 $\frac{a}{9} = 7$

$a =$ ____

Skill 59 Solve Multiplication Equations

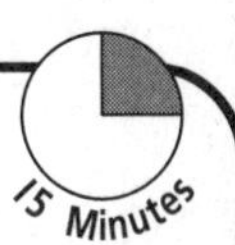

Using Skill 59

OBJECTIVE Solve multiplication equations by using the inverse operation of division

Begin by reviewing the Division Property of Equality and the Identity Property of One. Recall for students that they can solve multiplication equations by using the inverse operation, division.

Direct students' attention to Example A. Ask: **Why can you divide both sides of an equation by the same non-zero number?** (The Division Property of Equality states that both sides will remain equal.) **What is the equation in Example A that you are asked to solve?** ($48 = 3n$) **To which operation does $3n$ refer?** (multiplication) **What is the inverse operation of multiplication?** (division) **By what number should you divide both sides of the equation?** (3) **Why?** (to have n alone on one side of the equation) **What is $48 \div 3$?** (16) **What is $3n \div 3$?** ($1n$)

Say: **Now you have $16 = 1n$.**

Ask: **What is another way you can write $1n$?** (n) **How do you justify that step?** (Identity Property of One)

Say: **So, $n = 16$.**

Now tell students they can check this answer by substituting 16 for n in the original equation. Review the check with the students.

As you work through the next example, have students identify which number they will divide by and the properties they use. Remind students of the importance of checking their solution.

TRY THESE Exercises 1–2 model the type of exercises students will find on the **Practice on Your Own** page.

- **Exercise 1** Solve whole number multiplication equation
- **Exercise 2** Solve decimal multiplication equation

PRACTICE ON YOUR OWN Review the example at the top of the page. Remind students that when they divide by a fraction, they use the reciprocal of the fraction and multiply.

CHECK Determine if the students can use the inverse operation of division to solve multiplication equations. Success is indicated by 4 out of 4 correct responses.

Students who successfully complete the **Practice on Your Own** and **Check** are ready to move to the next skill.

COMMON ERRORS

- Students may multiply, instead of divide, by the coefficient of the variable.
- Students may divide both sides of the equation by the constant instead of the coefficient of the variable.

Students who made more than 3 errors in the **Practice on Your Own**, or who were not successful in the **Check** section, may benefit from the **Alternative Teaching Strategy** on the next page.

Optional

Alternative Teaching Strategy

10 Minutes

Model Solving Multiplication Equations

OBJECTIVE Use counters to model solving multiplication equations

MATERIALS counters

Display $3x = 12$.

Distribute counters to each student. Explain to students they will use the counters to model the multiplication equation $3x = 12$. **What letter represents the unknown quantity in this equation?** (x)

Ask: **To which operation does $3x$ refer?** (multiplication)

Say: **So, 3 times an unknown quantity equals 12.**

Have the students display 12 counters. Tell the students to move the counters one at a time into three groups.

Ask: **How many counters are in each group?** (4)

Do three groups of 4 counters equal 12? (yes)

Point out to students that 4 represents the unknown quantity.

Lead students to understand that separating counters into groups represents division and that they used division to solve the multiplication equation.

Repeat this activity with similar examples. When students show understanding, have them try an exercise using only paper and pencil.

Name ______________________ Skill ______________

Skill 59

Solve Multiplication Equations

To solve an algebraic equation, get the variable alone on one side of the equation.
You can solve a multiplication equation using the inverse operation, division. You justify that step, using the Division Property of Equality.

Division Property of Equality
If you divide both sides of an equation by the same non–zero number, the sides remain equal.

$4 = 4$

$\frac{4}{2} = \frac{4}{2}$ Divide both sides by 2. The results are equal.

$2 = 2$

Identity Property of One
The product of any factor and 1 is the factor.

$4 \cdot 1 = 4$

$n \cdot 1 = n$

Example A Solve: $48 = 3n$

$48 = 3n$	Write the equation.
$\frac{48}{3} = \frac{3n}{3}$	Use Division Property of Equality.
	Think: Divide both sides by 3 to get n alone.
$16 = 1n$	**Think:** $48 \div 3 = 16$ and $3 \div 3 = 1$.
$16 = n$	Use the Identity Property of One.
$48 = 3n$	Check your solution.
$48 = 3 \cdot 16$	Replace n with 16.
	Think: $3 \cdot 16 = 48$
$48 = 48\surd$	The solution checks.
So, $n = 16$	

Example B Solve: $0.4w = 1.2$

$0.4w = 1.2$	Write the equation.
$\frac{0.4w}{0.4} = \frac{1.2}{0.4}$	Use Division Property of Equality.
	Think: Divide both sides by 0.4
$1w = 3$	**Think:** $0.4\overline{)1.2}$ = 3.
$w = 3$	Use the Identity Property of One.
$0.4w = 1.2$	Check your solution.
$0.4 \cdot 3 = 1.2$	Replace w with 3. **Think:** $0.4 \cdot 3 = 1.2$
$1.2 = 1.2\surd$	The solution checks
So, $w = 3$	

Try These

Complete the solution and the check for each equation.

1 $2n = 14$

$\frac{2n}{2} = \frac{14}{2}$

____ = ____

____ = ____

Check

$2n = 14$

$2 \cdot$ ____ $= 14$

____ $= 14$

2 $0.05t = 3.5$

$\frac{0.05t}{0.05} = \frac{3.5}{0.05}$

____ = ____

____ = ____

Check

$0.05t = 3.5$

$0.05 \cdot$ ____ $= 3.5$

____ $= 3.5$

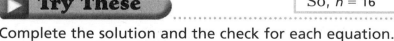

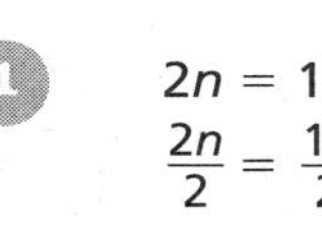

Name ______________________ Skill ______________________

Practice on Your Own

Skill 59

Think:
The reciprocal of $\frac{1}{2}$ is $\frac{2}{1}$, or 2.

Solve. $24 = \frac{1}{2}a$

Think: $\frac{24}{\frac{1}{2}} = \frac{\frac{1}{2}a}{\frac{1}{2}}$ — Write the equation. Use the Division Property of Equality. **Think:** $\frac{1}{2} \div \frac{1}{2} = 1$

$24 \div \frac{1}{2} = 1a$ — Use the Identity Property of 1.

$24 \bullet \frac{2}{1} = a$ — Multiply by the reciprocal. **Think:** $2 \times 24 = 48$

$48 = a$ — **So,** $a = 48$.

Check:
$24 = \frac{1}{2}a$
$24 = \frac{1}{2} \cdot 48$
$24 = 24\surd$
The solution checks.

Complete the solution and check.

1 $6 = \frac{2}{3}c$

$\frac{6}{\frac{2}{3}} = \frac{\frac{2}{3}c}{\frac{2}{3}}$

___ $\div \frac{\square}{\square} =$ ___

___ $\cdot \frac{\square}{\square} =$ ___

___ $=$ ___

Check $6 = \frac{2}{3}c$
$6 = \frac{2}{3}$ ___
$6 =$ ___

2 $15 = \frac{3}{4}y$

$\frac{15}{\frac{3}{4}} = \frac{\frac{3}{4}y}{\frac{3}{4}}$

___ $\div \frac{\square}{\square} =$ ___

___ $\cdot \frac{\square}{\square} =$ ___

___ $=$ ___

Check $15 = \frac{3}{4}y$
$15 = \frac{3}{4} \cdot$ ___
$15 =$ ___

3 $4n = 16$
Divide both sides by ___ .
___ = ___

4 $72 = 12h$
Divide both sides by ___ .
___ = ___

5 $0.2x = 5$
Divide both sides by ___ .
___ = ___

6 $0.3b = 21$
Divide both sides by ___ .
___ = ___

7 $45 = 9n$
$n =$ ___

8 $\frac{1}{2}t = 15$
$t =$ ___

9 $0.7r = 5.6$
$r =$ ___

10 $156 = 12p$
$p =$ ___

Check

Solve.

11 $0.02h = 0.4$
$h =$ ___

12 $\frac{2}{3}n = 36$
$n =$ ___

13 $84 = 7a$
$a =$ ___

14 $15k = 195$
$k =$ ___

Solve Two-Step Equations

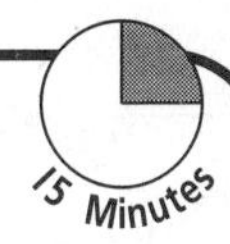

Using Skill 60

OBJECTIVE Solve two-step equations

Have students recall that an equation is a number sentence with an equals sign. A variable is used to represent the value of a number. The value of the variable that makes the solution true is called the solution.

A two-step equation is an equation that has two operations.

Discuss with students that order of operations is not necessary in solving two-step equations, but the process is made easier when you add or subtract before you multiply or divide.

Recall that inverse operations are operations that undo one another.
Ask: **What is the inverse operation of addition?** (subtraction)
Ask: **What is the inverse operation of division?** (multiplication)

Direct students to Example 1.
Ask: **What operation do you do first?** (Subtract 3 from each side.)

Ask: **What do you next?** (Divide each side by 2)

Continue in a similar manner with Example 2.

Explain that solving an equation that contains all variables is similar to solving an equation and getting a solution.

TRY THESE In Exercises 1–3 students determine what to do first, and then second to solve the equation.

- **Exercise 1** Subtract and divide.
- **Exercise 2** Subtract and multiply.
- **Exercise 3** Solve for a variable, add and divide.

PRACTICE ON YOUR OWN Review the examples at the top of the page.
Ask: **What do you always do first?** (Add or subtract.)
Ask: **How do you check your answer?** (By substituting your answer into the original equation and simplifying.)

CHECK Determine that the students are isolating the variable to solve each equation. Success is indicated by 3 out of 3 correct responses.

Students who successfully complete the **Practice on Your Own** and **Check** are ready to move on to the next skill.

COMMON ERRORS

- Students may multiply or divide before adding and subtracting. Although the solution is still correct, the process is easier when you add or subtract first.
- Students may perform an operation on only one side of the equation.

Optional

Alternative Teaching Strategy

Use Algebra Tiles to Solve Two-Step Equations

OBJECTIVE Solve two-step equations with algebra tiles

MATERIALS Algebra tiles

Write the equation on the board.

$3a - 1 = 8$

Have students model the equation with algebraic tiles.

Key:

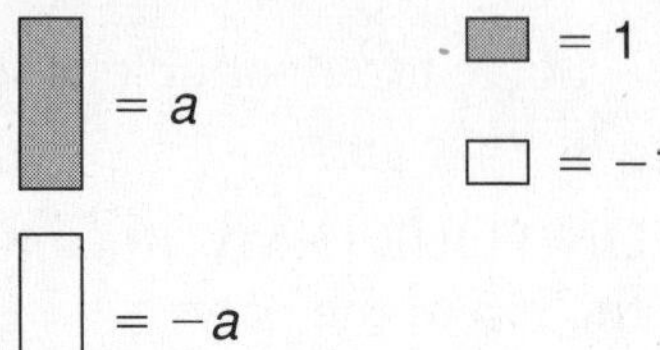

Ask: **Which type of tiles do you need to represent 3*a*? How many tiles do you need?** (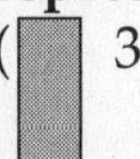 3)

Remind students that the vertical line represents the equals sign.

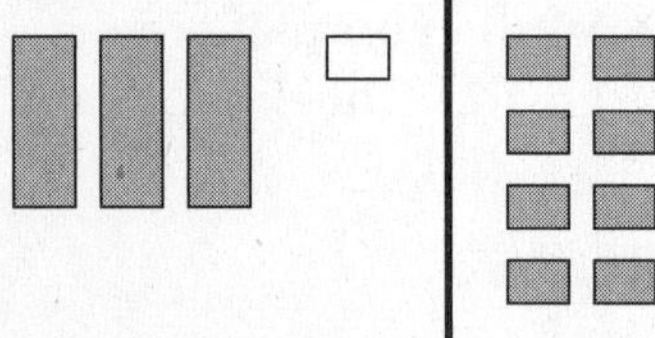

Ask: **What do you do first?** (Add 1 to each side.)
Have students add one tile to each side of the equation and remove the zero pairs.

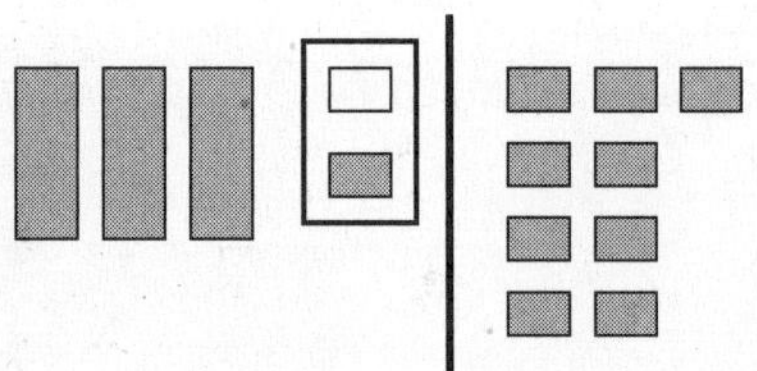

Ask: **What is left?**

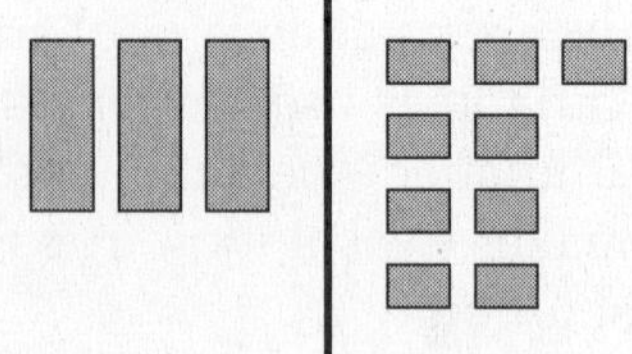

Ask: **What does this represent?** ($3a = 9$)

Ask: **What do you do next?** (Divide each side by 3.)

Have students divide each side into 3 groups of equal size.

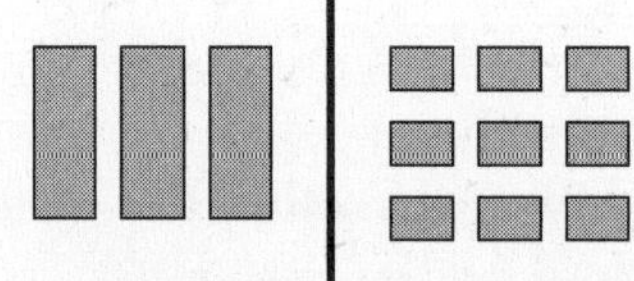

Remove one group from each side.

Ask: **For every ▮ tile, how many ▪ tiles are there?** (3)

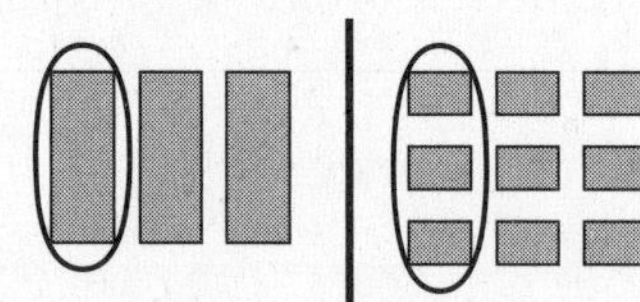

The solution is $a = 3$. Have students check their answer by substituting 3 in the original equation for *a* and solve.

Repeat the activity several times with different equations. When students show understanding let the variables represent larger or negative numbers.

Name ______________________ Skill ______________

Skill 60

Solve Two-Step Equations

Solve each equation by isolating the variable on one side of the equals sign. Add or subtract before you multiply or divide.

Example 1 $2y + 3 = -11$ **Think:** What number times 2 added to 3 equals −11?

$2y + 3 - 3 = -11 - 3$ Subtract 3 from each side.

$2y = -14$

$\frac{2y}{2} = \frac{-14}{2}$ Divide each side by 2.

$y = -7$

Check: Replace y with −7.

$2(-7) + 3 \stackrel{?}{=} -11$

$-14 + 3 \stackrel{?}{=} -11$

$-11 = -11\checkmark$

Example 2 $\frac{x}{3} - 5 = 2$ **Think:** What number divided by 3 minus 5 equals 2?

$\frac{x}{3} - 5 + 5 = 2 + 5$ Add 5 to both sides.

$\frac{x}{3} = 7$

$\frac{x}{3} \cdot \frac{3}{1} = 7 \cdot 3$ Multiply each side by 3.

$x = 21$

Check: Replace the x with 21.

$\frac{21}{3} - 5 \stackrel{?}{=} 2$

$2 = 2\checkmark$

Try These

Solve each equation by following the steps.

1. $4a + 3 = -5$

$4a + 3 - 3 = -5 - 3$

$4a =$ ____

$\frac{4a}{4} = \frac{?}{4}$

$a =$ ____

Check: $4(?) + 3 = -5$

$4($____$) + 3 \stackrel{?}{=} -5$

____ = ____

2. $\frac{y}{3} + 4 = 7$

$\frac{y}{3} + 4 - 4 = 7 - 4$

$\frac{y}{3} =$ ____

$y = ?\,(3)$

$y =$ ____

3. Solve $3x - y = 7$ for x.

$3x - y + y = 7 + y$

$3x =$ ____

$\frac{3x}{3} = \frac{?}{3}$

$x =$ ____

Go to the next side.

Name ______________________ Skill ______________________

Practice on Your Own

Skill 60

Solve each equation for the variable.

Solve $2a + 3.5 = 7.5$. $2a + 3.5 - 3.5 = 7.5 - 3.5$ $2a = 4$ $a = 2$ **Check:** $2(2) + 3.5 \stackrel{?}{=} 7.5$ $4 + 3.5 \stackrel{?}{=} 7.5$ $7.5 = 7.5$ √	**Think:** What number times 2 plus 3.5 equals 7.5?	Solve $4y + w = 9$ for y. $4y + w - w = 9 - w$ $4y = 9 - w$ $\frac{4y}{4} = \frac{9-w}{4}$ $y = \frac{9-w}{4}$

Solve and check each equation.

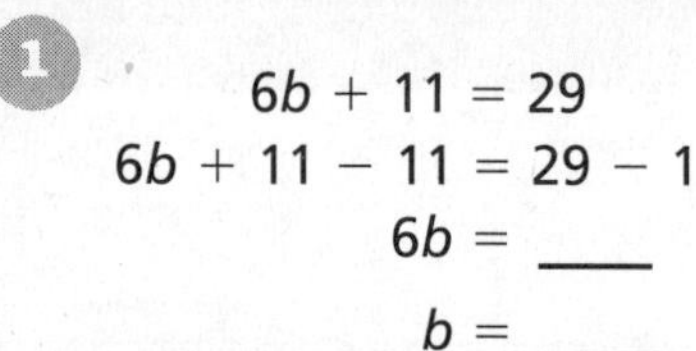

1
$6b + 11 = 29$
$6b + 11 - 11 = 29 - 11$
$6b =$ ____
$b =$ ____
Check: 6(?) + 11 = 29
____ = 29

2
$4a + 8 = 20$
$4a + 8 - 8 = 20 - 8$
$4a =$ ____
$a =$ ____
Check: 4(?) + 8 = 20
____ = 20

3
$3m + 2 = 5x$ for m
$3m + 2 - 2 = 5x - 2$
$3m =$ ____
$m =$ ____

4
$\frac{x}{6} + 7 = 9$
$\frac{x}{6} + 7 - 7 = 9 - 7$
$\frac{x}{6} =$ ____
$x =$ ____
Check: $\frac{?}{6} + 7 = 9$
____ = 9

5
$\frac{n}{0.4} - 3.5 = 11.5$
$\frac{n}{0.4} - 3.5 + 3.5 = 11.5 + 3.5$
$\frac{n}{0.4} =$ ____
$n =$ ____
Check: $\frac{?}{0.4} - 3.5 = 11.5$
____ = 11.5

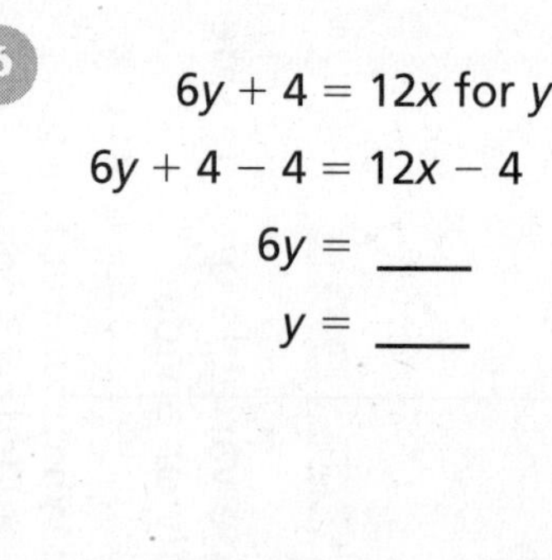

6
$6y + 4 = 12x$ for y
$6y + 4 - 4 = 12x - 4$
$6y =$ ____
$y =$ ____

Check

Solve each equation.

7 $4x + 7 = -1$
$x =$ ____

8 $\frac{a}{7} - 4 = 0$
$a =$ ____

9 $5c + a = 8$ for c
$c =$ ____

Skill 61 Locate Points on a Number Line

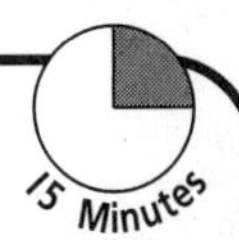

Using Skill 61

OBJECTIVE Graph numbers on a number line

On Skill 61, draw students' attention to the different number lines. Be sure students know how to read a number line. Direct students' attention to both number lines. Ask: **What number is in the middle of both number lines?** (0)

Guide students to move their fingers to the right of zero. Ask: **What type of numbers are located to the right of zero?** (positive)

Repeat the experience for numbers to the left of zero. Ask: **What type of numbers do you see to the left of zero?** (negative)

Help students realize that the graph of a number is the point associated with that number on a number line.

Ask: **How are the two number lines different from each other?** (One number line has an interval of one and the other number line has an interval of two.) **How are the number lines alike?** (Both have intervals, and zero is in the middle.)

Guide students to recognize that the sign of any number determines the direction from zero.

PRACTICE ON YOUR OWN Review the example at the top of the page. Ask students to state the direction from zero for the graph of a given number.

CHECK Determine if students can graph a number correctly on a number line.

Success is indicated by 3 out of 4 correct responses.

Students who successfully complete the **Practice on Your Own** and **Check** are ready to move on to the next skill.

COMMON ERRORS

- Students might graph numbers on the incorrect side of zero.
- Students might count units from zero incorrectly.

Students who made more than 4 errors in the **Practice on Your Own**, or who were not successful in the **Check** section, may benefit from the **Alternative Teaching Strategy** on the next page.

Optional

Alternative Teaching Strategy

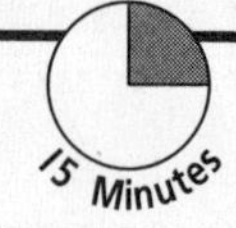

Plotting on a Number Line

OBJECTIVE Locate points on a number line **MATERIALS** index cards, number line

Prepare on index cards instructions for students to locate points on a number line. For example,

- *locate –3 on the number line*
- *locate the opposite of 4 on the number line,*
- *name the point that is 5 units to the left of zero*
- *locate positive 2*

Present students with a number line such as the one below.

Remind students that all numbers to the left of zero name negative numbers and include negative signs (–). All numbers to the right of zero name positive numbers and may or may not include positive signs (+).

Remind students that the number zero has no sign, because it is neither positive nor negative.

It may help some students to put their fingers on the number line, and actually move their fingers to the left or right of zero to locate points. Encourage students to say "positive" as they move to the right of zero, and "negative" as they move to the left of zero.

Next, ask volunteers to draw from the stack of prepared index cards. After reading aloud, encourage students to verbalize or explain the movement on the number line.

As students become more comfortable with locating numbers on a number line, the number line can be extended to include a wider range of numbers and the difficulty level of the instructions on the index cards can be increased.

Name ______________________ Skill ______________________

Skill 61

Locate Points on a Number Line

Graph numbers on a number line.

Graph $^{-}2$ and $^{+}3$ on the number line.

Step 1
$^{-}2$ is a *negative* number.
So start at 0. Count 2 units to the *left*.
Mark the point on the number line.

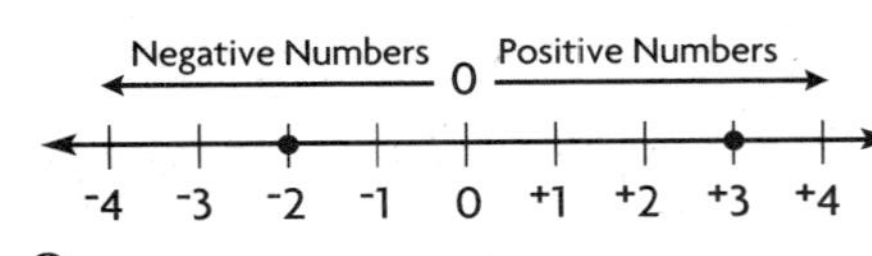

Step 2
3 is a *positive* number.
So start at 0. Count 3 units to the *right*.
Mark the point on the number line.

Graph $^{-}4$, 2, $^{-}12$ and 10 on the number line.

Step 1
−4 is a *negative* number.
So start at 0. Each mark on the number line represents 2 so move 2 spaces to the left.
Mark the point on the number line.

Step 2
2 is a *positive* number.
So start at 0. Count 1 space to the right.
Mark the point on the number line.

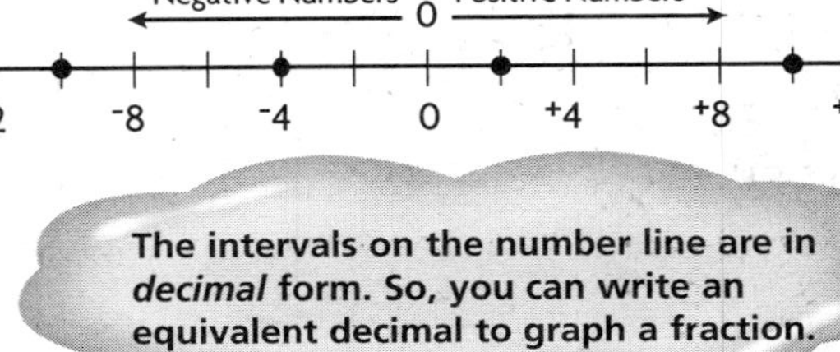

Step 3
$^{-}10$ is a *negative* number
So start at 0. Count 5 spaces to the *left*.
Mark the point on the number line.

Step 4
10 is a *positive* number.
So start at 0. Count 5 spaces to the *right*.
Mark the point on the number line.

Go to the next side.

Name ________________________ Skill ________________________

Practice on Your Own

Skill 61

Think:
The sign in front of a number tells you the direction from zero on the number line.

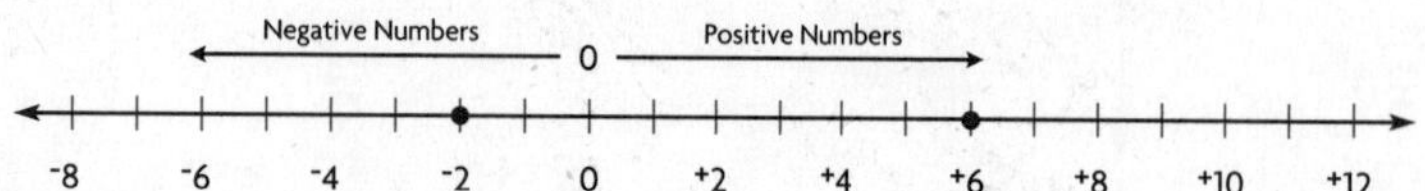

Graph ⁻2 and 6 on the number line.
⁻2 is a *negative* number.
Start at 0, count 2 spaces to the *left*.

6 is a *positive* number.
Start at 0, count 6 spaces to the *right*.

Graph each number on the number line. Complete each statement.

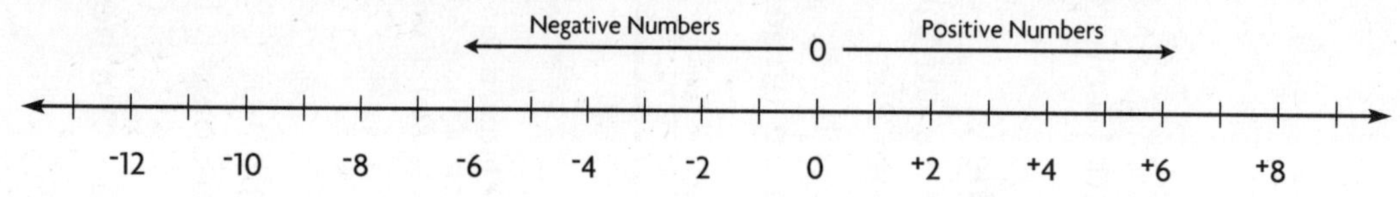

1 ⁻7

⁻7 is a <u>*negative*</u> number.
Start at 0. Move to the ______.

Mark the point.

2 1

1 is a ________ number.
Start at ___. Move to the ______.

Mark the point.

3 ⁻10

⁻10 is a ________ number.
Start at ___. Move to the ______.

Mark the point.

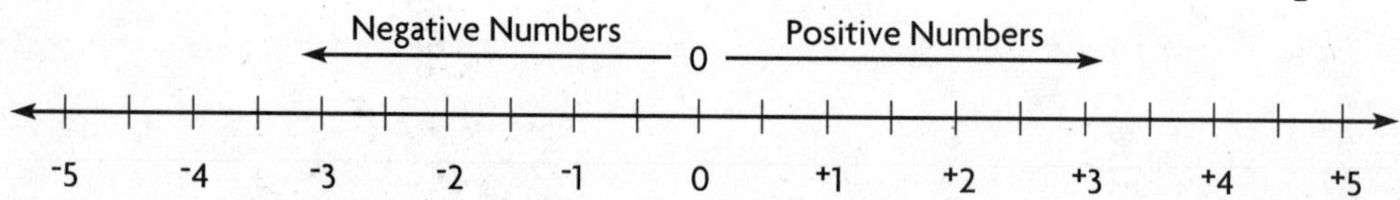

4 4

<u>*positive*</u> number.
Move to the ________.

5 ⁻1

________ number.
Move to the ________.

6 2

________ number.
Move to the ________.

7 ⁻5

________ number.
Move to the ________.

Check

Graph each number on the number line.

-4 -3 -2 -1 0 +1 +2 +3

8 2

9 ⁻3

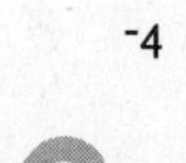

10 0.5

11 ⁻2

Skill 62 Solve and Graph Inequalities

Using Skill 62

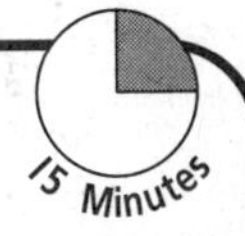

OBJECTIVE Solve and graph inequalities

Have students look at Step 1 on Skill 62.
Ask: **How do you solve the inequality?** (Add 1 to both sides.)

Is 4 a solution to the inequality? (No, 4 is not greater than 5 or equal to 5)

Is 6 a solution? (Yes, 6 is greater than or equal to 5.)

Is 5 a solution? (Yes, since it is greater than or equal to 5.)

Direct students' attention to Step 2, review the symbols and their meanings.

Go to Step 3:
Ask: **Will an open or closed circle be used when graphing the solution set?** (Closed circle since 5 is included in the solution set.)

TRY THESE In Exercises 1–3 students solve and graph inequalities.

- **Exercise 1** open; right
- **Exercise 2** closed; left
- **Exercise 3** open; left

PRACTICE ON YOUR OWN Review the example at the top of the page.
In Exercises 1–4, students solve and graph an inequality.

CHECK Determine that the students can solve and graph an inequality. Success is indicated by 4 out of 4 correct responses.

Students who successfully complete the **Practice on Your Own** and **Check** are ready to move on to the next skill.

COMMON ERRORS

- Students may confuse the symbols $<$ and $\leq$ with their respective meanings: less than and less than or equal to. Explain that the line under the symbol is considered half an equal sign.
- Students may confuse the open dot and closed dot when graphing. Have students remember that when the dot is open, the number is not contained in the solution set. When the dot is closed, the number is contained in the solution set.

Students who made more than 3 errors in the **Practice on Your Own**, or who were not successful in the **Check** section, may benefit from the **Alternative Teaching Strategy** on the next page.

Optional

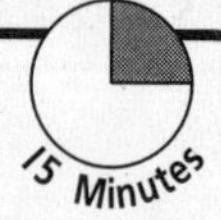

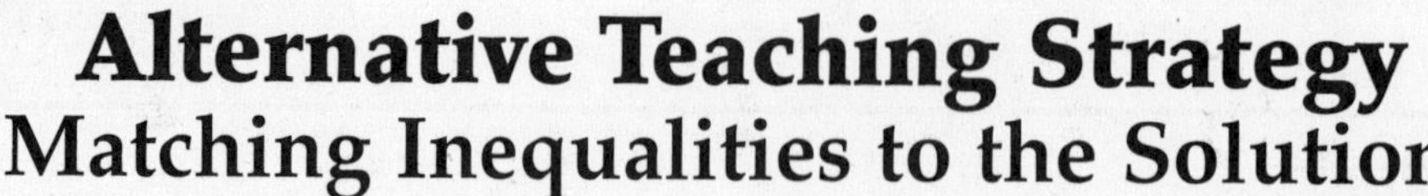

Alternative Teaching Strategy

Matching Inequalities to the Solution

OBJECTIVE Solve and graph inequalities

MATERIALS index cards with inequalities written on them

Prepare a set of index cards with exercises and graphs similar to these.

A	B
$a + 9 \leq 12$	$a + 4 \geq 12$

C	D
$a - 7 < 1$	$3a - 9 > 12$

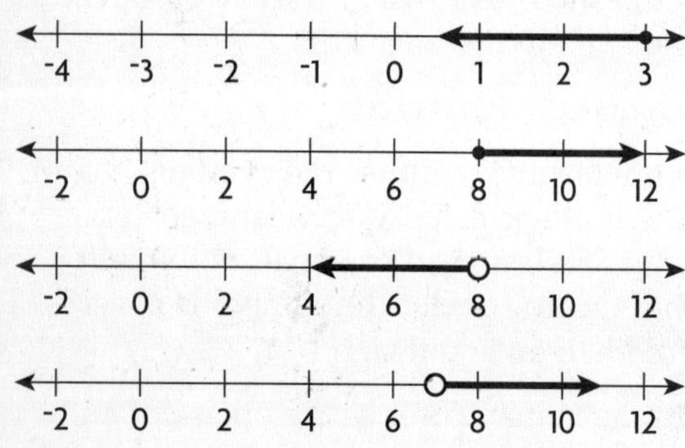

Without computing, have students match up the inequality with its solution.

For **A**, students should recognize the need to subtract 9 from each side. They should be able to describe that the graph will be a closed circle and extend to the left.

For **B**, students should recognize the need to subtract 4 from each side. They should be able to describe that the graph will be a closed circle and extend to the right.

For **C**, students should recognize the need to add 7 to each side. They should be able to describe that the graph will be an open circle and extend to the left.

For **D**, students should recognize the need to add 9 to each side and then divide by 3. They should be able to describe that the graph will be an open circle and extend to the right.

Solve and Graph Inequalities

Skill 62

You can use a number line to show the solutions to an inequality.

Step 1: Solve the inequality.

$$a - 1 \geq 4$$
$$a - 1 + 1 \geq 4 + 1$$
$$a \geq 5$$

Step 2: Review symbols.

Think: Symbols and their meanings:

$<$ means *less than*, open circle
$\leq$ means *less than or equal to*, closed circle
$>$ means *greater than*, open circle
$\geq$ means *greater than or equal to*, closed circle

Step 3: Graph

Think: What type of circle will be used to graph $a \geq 5$?

Which direction will the line go?

⁻6 ⁻4 ⁻2 0 2 4 6

Try These

Solve and graph the inequalities.

1. $a + 5 > 9$

What type of circle will be used?

____

Which direction will the line go?

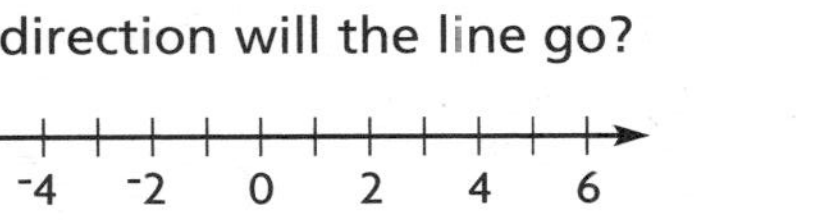

2. $w - 3 \leq 2$

What type of circle will be used?

____

Which direction will the line go?

⁻6 ⁻4 ⁻2 0 2 4 6

3. $2y + 5 < 9$

What type of circle will be used?

____

Which direction will the line go?

⁻6 ⁻4 ⁻2 0 2 4 6

Go to the next side.

Name ______________________ Skill ______________________

Practice on Your Own

Skill 62

Step 1 Solve the inequality.

$w - 8 < -4$
$w < -4 + 8$
$w < 4$

Step 2 Decide on the appropriate circle.

$<$ means *less than*, open circle
$\leq$ means *less than or equal to*, closed circle
$>$ means *greater than*, open circle
$\geq$ means *greater than or equal to*, closed circle

Step 3 Graph the solution.

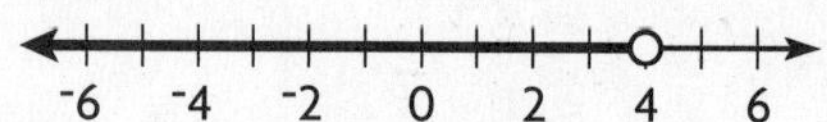

Solve and graph each inequality.

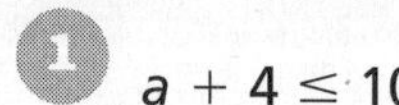

1. $a + 4 \leq 10$

What type of circle will be used? ______

Which direction will the line go? ______

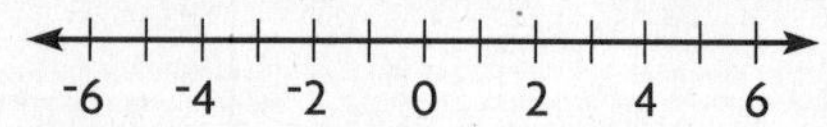

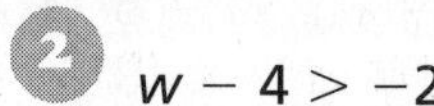

2. $w - 4 > -2$

What type of circle will be used? ______

Which direction will the line go? ______

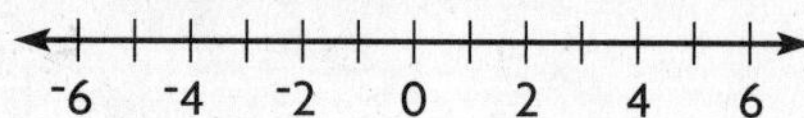

Solve and graph each inequality.

3. $y + 8 < 12$

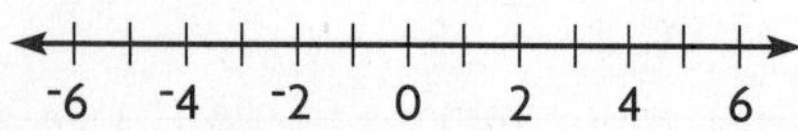

4. $z - 8 \geq -3$

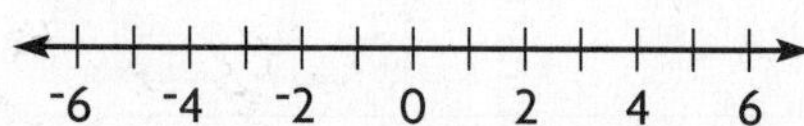

Check

Solve and graph each inequality.

5. $w + 4 < 5$

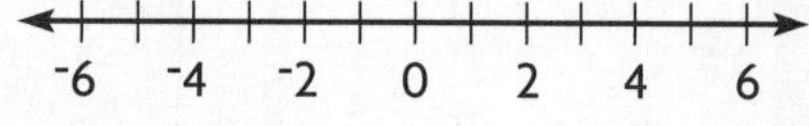

6. $y - 3 \geq 2$

⁻6 ⁻4 ⁻2 0 2 4 6

7. $b - 4 > -3$

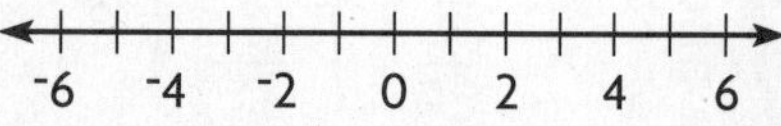

8. $a + 3 \leq 2$

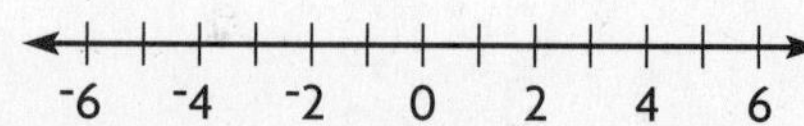

Skill 63 Write an Inequality for a Graph

Using Skill 63

OBJECTIVE Write an inequality for a graph

Review the symbols and their meanings in the first box.

Direct students' attention to the example.

Ask: **Which number is the circle on?** (5)

Should the circle be open or closed? (Closed since 5 is included in the solution set.)

How do you know which direction to draw the arrow? (The arrow points in the direction of the numbers included in the solution set.)

TRY THESE In Exercises 1–3 students write the inequality for a graph.

- **Exercise 1** -4, open, left, $a < -4$
- **Exercise 2** -2, closed, right, $a \geq -2$
- **Exercise 3** 3, closed, left, $a \leq 3$

PRACTICE ON YOUR OWN Review the example at the top of the page.
In Exercises 1–4, students write the inequality from the given graph.

CHECK Determine that the students can write an inequality from a graph. Success is indicated by 4 out of 4 correct responses.

Students who successfully complete the **Practice on Your Own** and **Check** are ready to move on to the next skill.

COMMON ERRORS

- Students may confuse the symbols $<$ and $\leq$ with their respective meanings: less than and less than or equal to. Explain that the line under the symbol is considered half an equal sign.
- Students may write the inequality in the incorrect order. Have students read what they have written to see if it matches the graph.

Students who made more than 3 errors in the **Practice on Your Own**, or who were not successful in the **Check** section, may benefit from the **Alternative Teaching Strategy** on the next page.

Optional

Alternative Teaching Strategy

15 Minutes

Matching Inequalities and Their Graphs

OBJECTIVE Write an inequality from a graph

MATERIALS Set of index cards with inequalities and their matching graphs

Place students in groups of 2, 3 or 4.

Have a set of cards for each group of students. The prepared cards should have an inequality on one card and its matching graph on another card. It is preferable to have a different sets of cards for each group so that additional practice can take place for those students having difficulty.

Students shuffle the cards and place them face down. One student turns over two cards. If the cards show an inequality and its matching graph, they keep the cards and take another turn. If the cards do not match, the student turns the cards over and play passes to the next player.

If students are still having difficulty identifying inequalities and their graphs, have them repeat the activity with another set of cards.

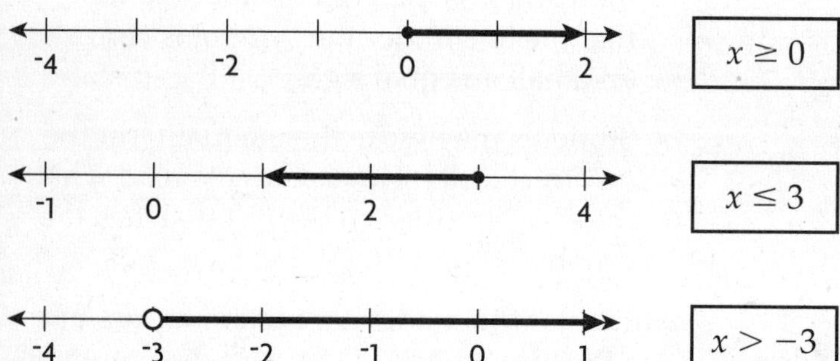

Name ____________________ Skill ____________________

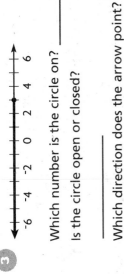

Skill 63

Write an Inequality for a Graph

You can use a number line to show the solutions to an inequality.

Think: Symbols and their meanings:

$<$ means *less than*, open circle

$\leq$ means *less than or equal to*, closed circle

$>$ means *greater than*, open circle

$\geq$ means *greater than or equal to*, closed circle

Example:
Write the inequality for the graph.

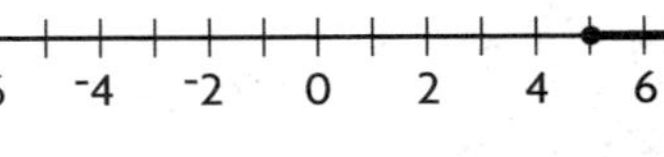

Think: Which number is the circle on? 5

Think: Is the answer included in the solution set?
yes; which means a closed circle

Which direction does the arrow point? right

Write the inequality. $a \geq 5$

Try These

Write the inequality for each graph.

1

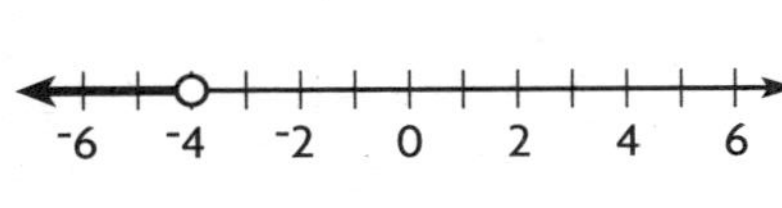

Which number is the circle on? ________

Is the circle open or closed?

____

Which direction does the arrow point?

____

Write the inequality. ________

2

⁻6 ⁻4 ⁻2 0 2 4 6

Which number is the circle on? ________

Is the circle open or closed?

____

Which direction does the arrow point?

____

Write the inequality. ________

3

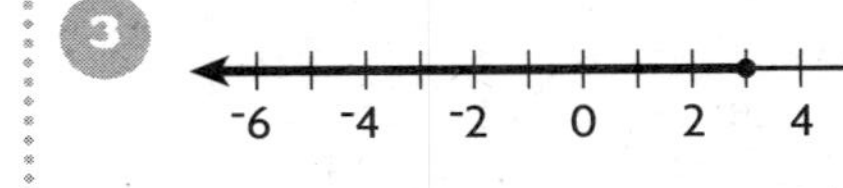

Which number is the circle on? ________

Is the circle open or closed?

____

Which direction does the arrow point?

____

Write the inequality. ________

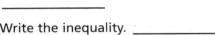

Go to the next side.

Name ______________________ Skill ______________________

Practice on Your Own

Skill 63

Write an inequality for the graph. 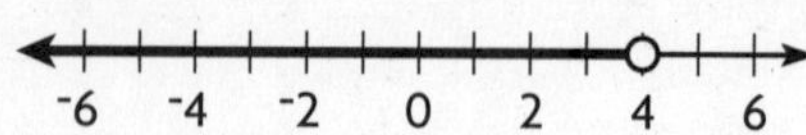

Step 1 Decide on the appropriate circle.

$<$ means *less than*, open circle

$\leq$ means *less than or equal to*, closed circle

$>$ means *greater than*, open circle

$\geq$ means *greater than or equal to*, closed circle

Step 2 Write the inequality: $a < 4$

Write the inequality for each graph.

1. 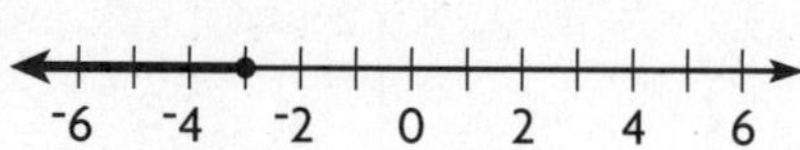

Which number is the circle on? ________

Is the circle open or closed?

____

Which direction does the arrow point?

____

Write the inequality. ________

2. 

Which number is the circle on? ________

Is the circle open or closed?

____

Which direction does the arrow point?

____

Write the inequality. ________

Write the inequality for each graph.

3. 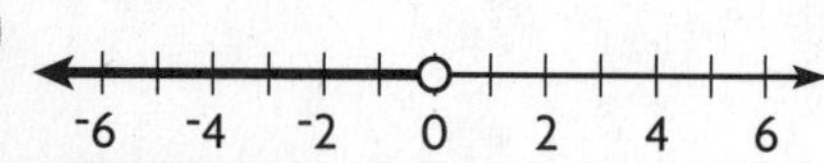

____

4. 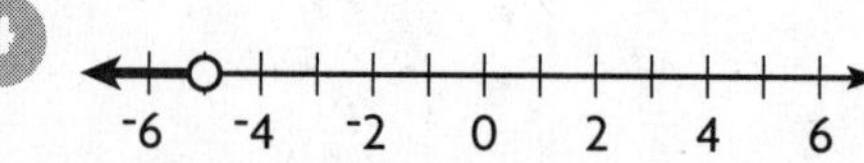

____

Check

Write the inequality for each graph.

5. 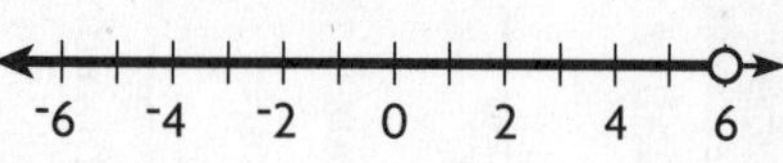

____

6. 

____

7. 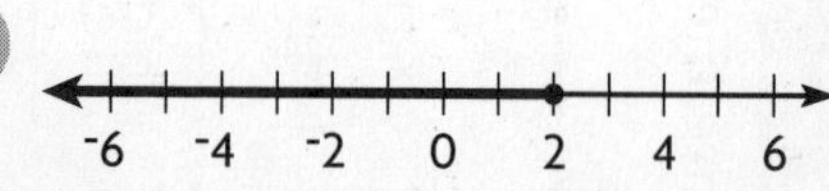

____

8. 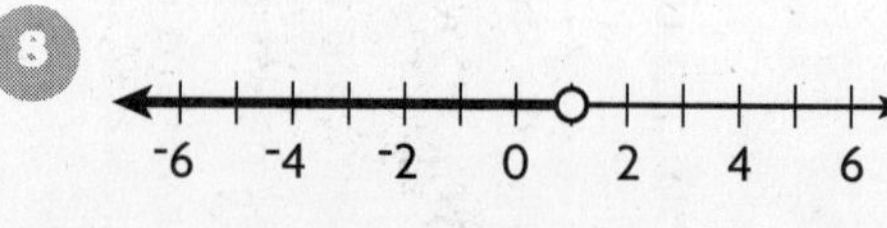

____

Skill 64 Graph Linear Equations

Using Skill 64

OBJECTIVE Graph linear equations

Direct students to Step 1. Ask: **Does it matter what values you choose for x?** (No, any number will work, smaller numbers are easier to work with and graph.)

For Step 2: **Which value comes first in an ordered pair?** (x)

How do you plot an ordered pair? (The x-coordinate indicates how many units to move left or right and the y-coordinate indicates how many units to move up or down.)

For Step 3: **Why is the line extended past the plotted points?** (The line represents all coordinates that are solutions to the equation and not just those points that can be plotted on the graph.)

TRY THESE In Exercise 1 students create a table of values, plot the ordered pairs, and draw the line for an equation.

- **Exercise 1**

x	$x + 2$	y	(x, y)
−2	−2 + 2	0	(−2, 0)
−1	−1 + 2	1	(−1, 1)
0	0 + 2	2	(0, 2)
1	1 + 2	3	(1, 3)

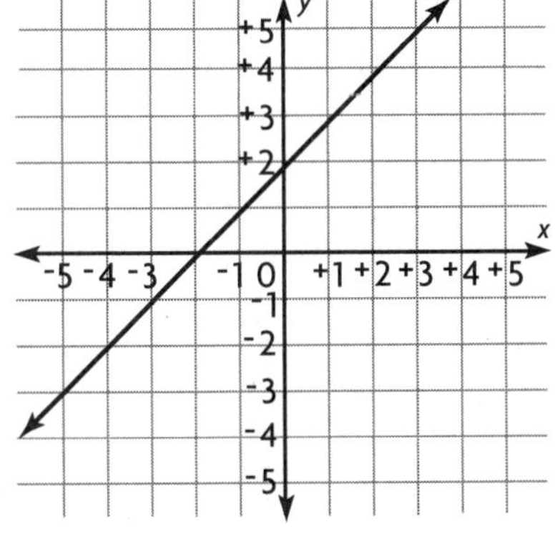

PRACTICE ON YOUR OWN Review the steps at the top of the page.
In Exercises 1–3, students graph a linear equation.

CHECK Determine that students know how to graph a linear equation. Success is indicated by 1 out of 1 correct responses.

Students who successfully complete the **Practice on Your Own** and **Check** are ready to move on to the next skill.

COMMON ERRORS

- Students may switch the x- and y-coordinates. Stress that the x-coordinate moves left or right and the y-coordinate moves up or down.
- Students may not plot enough ordered pairs to ensure that their line is straight.

Students who made more than 3 errors in the **Practice on Your Own**, or who were not successful in the **Check** section, may benefit from the **Alternative Teaching Strategy** on the next page.

Optional

Alternative Teaching Strategy

Graphing Linear Equations Using Intercepts

15 Minutes

OBJECTIVE Graph a linear equation

MATERIALS graph paper, ruler

Distribute graph paper and rulers to students. Write the equation $x + y = 1$ on the board.

Ask: **How many points determine a line?** (2)

Have students determine the x- and y- intercepts of the equation.

Ask: **When the graph crosses the y-axis, what is the value of x?** (0)

To find the y-intercept, have students substitute 0 in for x and solve.

$y + 0 = 1$; $y = 1$. The ordered pair is written as (0, 1).

Ask: **When the graph crosses the x-axis, what is the value of y?** (0)
To find the x-intercept, have students substitute 0 in for y and solve.
$x + 0 = 1$; $x = 1$. The ordered pair is written as (1, 0).

Have students create a coordinate grid on their graph paper. Then have students plot the two ordered pairs on their grid: (0, 1) and (1, 0).

Ask: **How do you plot the coordinates?** (The x-coordinate tells you how many units to move left or right, the y-coordinate tells you how many units to move up or down.)

Point out that the order of the coordinates is important. Have students draw a line through the two points.

Repeat the activity several times with different equations.

When students show an understanding of the graphing process using whole numbers, change the equations to include fractions.

Name ______________________ Skill ______________

Skill 64

Graph Linear Equations

The graph of an equation is the graph of all the points whose coordinates are solutions of the equation. Graph the equation $y = x + 3$.

Step 1: Choose values for x and create a table of values.

x	$x + 3$	y	(x, y)
0	$0 + 3$	3	(0, 3)
1	$1 + 3$	4	(1, 4)
−3	$-3 + 3$	0	(−3, 0)
−2	$-2 + 3$	1	(−2, 1)

Step 2: Graph the ordered pairs.

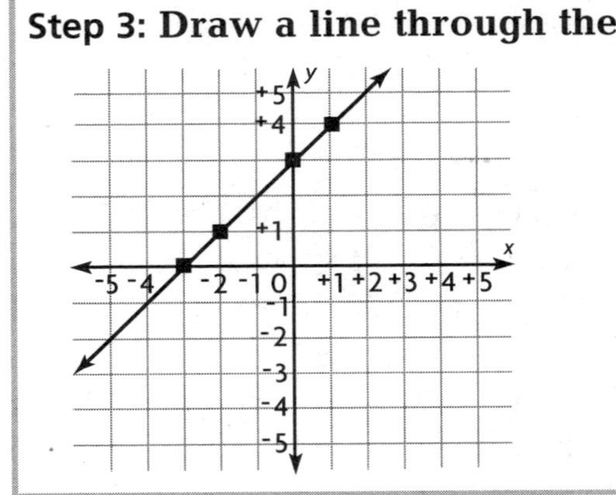

Step 3: Draw a line through the points.

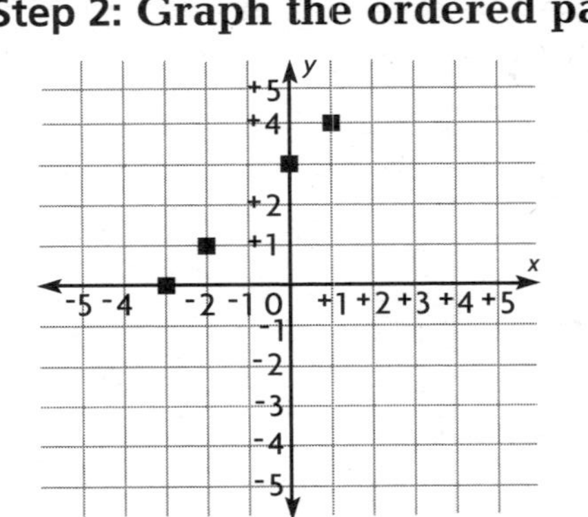

Try These

Graph the equation on a coordinate plane.

1. $y = x + 2$

Create a table of values:

x	$x + 2$	y	(x, y)
−2			(__, __)
−1			(__, __)
0			(__, __)
1			(__, __)

Plot the points and draw the line.

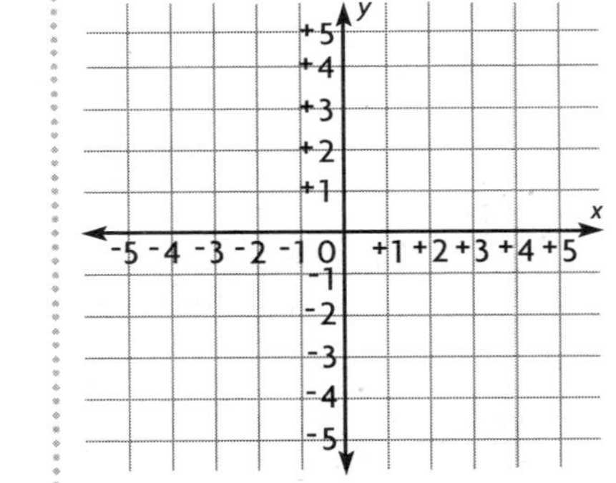

Go to the next side.

Name ______________________ Skill ______________________

Practice on Your Own

Skill 64

To graph a linear equation follow these steps.

Step 1: Make a table of values.
Step 2: Plot the ordered pairs.
Step 3: Draw a line through the points.

Graph each equation on a coordinate plane.

1. $y = x - 1$

Create a table of values:

x	$x - 1$	y	(x, y)
−2			(__, __)
−1			(__, __)
0			(__, __)
1			(__, __)

Plot the points and draw the line.

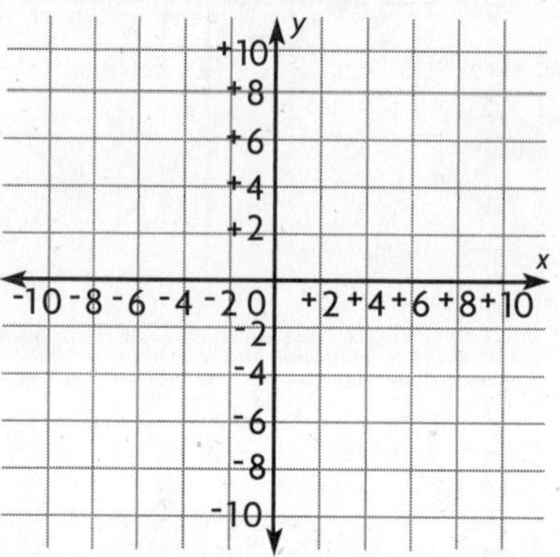

2. $y = x + 5$

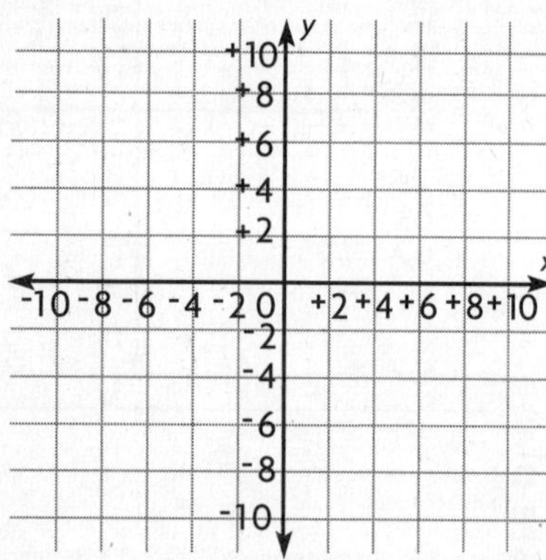

3. $y = 2x + 1$

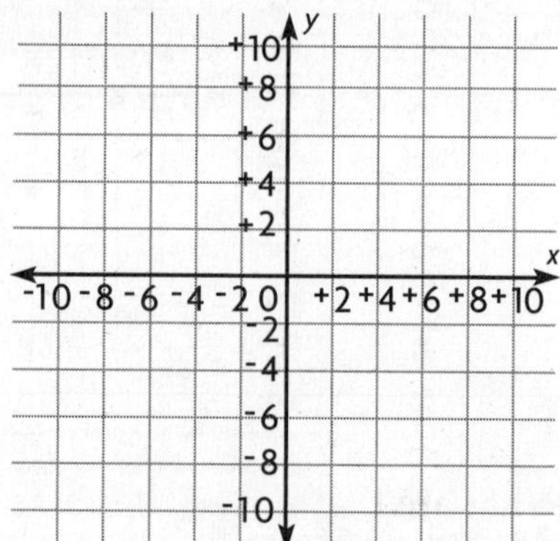

Check

Graph the equation on a coordinate plane.

4. $y = 2x - 1$

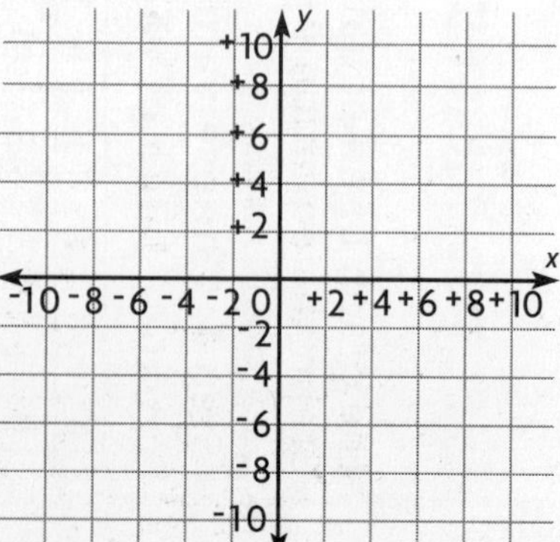

Skill 65 Solve Proportions

Using Skill 65

OBJECTIVE Solve proportions using cross products

Read about proportions at the top of the page. Tell students that they can think of proportions as two equivalent fractions. Discuss cross products of familiar equivalent fractions so students will understand that cross products of equivalent fractions are equal. Try $\frac{1}{2} = \frac{2}{4}$; $\frac{3}{8} = \frac{6}{16}$; and $\frac{3}{4} = \frac{75}{100}$.

Refer to Step 1.

Ask: **What are the two ratios?** ($\frac{3}{8}$ and $\frac{n}{24}$) **What are the two cross products?** (3×24 and $8 \times n$) **What is another way to write $8 \times n$?** ($8n$)

In Step 2, have the students make note of each step in the process for solving the equation that arises from the cross products of the proportion.

Ask: **What does $8n$ stand for?** (8 multiplied by n) **What is the inverse operation of multiplication?** (division) **Why do we divide both sides of the equation by 8?** (We want to know the value of $1n$; $\frac{8}{8} = 1$; if we divide both sides of an equation by the same number, the equation is still true.)

Stress the importance of checking the answer.

Ask: **What are the ratios when $n = 9$?** ($\frac{3}{8}$ and $\frac{9}{24}$) **What are the cross products?** (3×24 and 8×9) **What is the value of each cross product?** (72, 72)

Lead students to conclude that, since the cross products are equal, the ratios are equivalent.

TRY THESE Exercises 1–3 provide a framework for solving proportions.

- **Exercises 1–2** Missing denominator
- **Exercise 3** Missing numerator

PRACTICE ON YOUR OWN Review the example at the top of the page. Focus on finding the cross products. Encourage students to check their work by substituting their solutions into the original proportion and finding the cross products again.

CHECK Determine if the students know how to solve a proportion.

Success is indicated by 3 out of 3 correct responses.

Students who successfully complete the **Practice on Your Own** and **Check** are ready to move to the next skill.

COMMON ERRORS

- Students may multiply the numerators together and the denominators together, instead of finding the cross products.

Students who made more than 2 errors in the **Practice on Your Own**, or who were not successful in the **Check** section, may benefit from the **Alternative Teaching Strategy** on the next page.

Optional

Alternative Teaching Strategy

Model Solving Proportions

OBJECTIVE Model solving proportions

MATERIALS cubes, dry tempera (red and yellow), clear cups, teaspoon measure

Say: **I am going to show you the lemonade recipe I use.**

Place 2 white cubes (sugar), 2 yellow cubes (lemon juice), and 8 blue cubes (water) in a cup and explain that this cup of lemonade tastes perfect.

Ask and demonstrate:
What would happen if I made a new batch with 4 white cubes, 2 yellow cubes, and 8 blue cubes? (It would be too sweet.) **What if I used 2 white cubes, 2 yellow cubes, and 10 blue cubes?** (too weak) **What if I used 2 white cubes, 4 yellow cubes, and 8 blue cubes?** (too sour)

Discuss the way that those changes in the recipe put it out of proportion. Ask: **How would you make 2 cups of perfect lemonade?** (Use exactly twice the amount of each ingredient required for 1 cup of perfect lemonade.) **What if you wanted to make 4 cups of perfect lemonade?** (Use exactly 4 times the amount of each ingredient required for 1 cup of perfect lemonade.)

Now use dry tempera to mix up various shades of orange. Mix 3 teaspoons of red tempera and 2 teaspoons of yellow tempera in a cup. Write the ratio $\frac{3 \text{ red}}{2 \text{ yellow}}$.

Ask: **How much yellow would be required to turn 6 teaspoons of red into the same orange color?**

Set up the proportion:

$\frac{3}{2} = \frac{6}{y}$

Help students realize that, since there is twice as much red, there must be twice as much yellow, just as if they were looking for equivalent fractions.

$$\frac{3 \times 2}{2 \times 2} = \frac{6}{4}$$

Now use this newly solved proportion to show that cross products are equal. You may not need to use cross products to solve a proportion when you are doubling the numerator and the denominator, but it will help immensely when solving this proportion.

$$\frac{3 \text{ red}}{2 \text{ yellow}} = \frac{8 \text{ red}}{y}$$

$y = 5\frac{1}{3}$ teaspoons.

Continue with other quantities of tempera to make other shades of orange.

Skill 65

Solve Proportions

A **proportion** is an equation that shows two equivalent ratios.

Solve for n. $\frac{3}{8} = \frac{n}{24}$.

Step 1

Equal ratios have equal cross products. Find the cross products.

$\frac{3}{8} = \frac{n}{24}$ $\quad 8 \times n$

$\quad 3 \times 24$

Remember $8 \times n$ can be written as $8n$. $\quad 8 \times n = 3 \times 24$

$8n = 3 \times 24$

Step 2

Solve the equation for n.

$\frac{3}{8} = \frac{n}{24}$

$8n = 3 \times 24$

$8n = 72$ Mulitply 3×24 to simplify.

$\frac{8n}{8} = \frac{72}{8}$ Divide both sides by 8.

$n = 9$

Step 3

Check the solution. Replace n with 9 to tell if the cross products are equal.

$\frac{3}{8} = \frac{9}{24}$

$8 \times 9 = 3 \times 24$

$72 = 72$

So, $\frac{3}{8} = \frac{9}{24}$.

Try These

Solve for n.

1. $\frac{2}{12} = \frac{9}{n}$ $\qquad \frac{2}{12} = \frac{9}{n}$

Write the cross products. $\quad 2 \times n = 12 \times \square$

$2n = \square$

Simplify. $\quad \frac{2n}{2} = \frac{\square}{2}$

Solve for n. $\quad n =$ ____

2. $\frac{8}{12} = \frac{6}{n}$ $\qquad \frac{8}{12} = \frac{6}{n}$

Write the cross products. $\quad 8 \times n = 12 \times \square$

$8n = \square$

Simplify. $\quad \frac{8n}{8} = \frac{\square}{8}$

Solve for n. $\quad n =$ ____

3. $\frac{5}{9} = \frac{n}{27}$ $\qquad \frac{5}{9} = \frac{n}{27}$

Write the cross products. $\quad 9 \times n = 5 \times \square$

$9n = \square$

Simplify. $\quad \frac{9n}{9} = \frac{\square}{9}$

Solve for n. $\quad n =$ ____

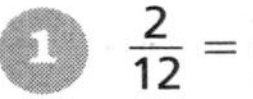

Go to the next side.

Name ______________________ Skill ______________________

Practice on Your Own

Skill 65

Think:

To solve for n in a proportion:

1. Write the cross products.
2. Simplify, if necessary.
3. Solve for n.
4. Check the answer.

	$\frac{2}{n} = \frac{16}{48}$	$\frac{3}{5} = \frac{21}{n}$
1. Write the cross products.	$n \times 16 = 2 \times 48$	$3n = 5 \times 21$
2. Simplify, if necessary.	$16n = 96$	$3n = 105$
3. Solve for n.	$\frac{16n}{16} = \frac{96}{16}$, $n = 6$	$\frac{3n}{3} = \frac{105}{3}$, $n = 35$
4. Check the answer.	$6 \times 16 = 2 \times 48$, $96 = 96$	$3 \times 35 = 5 \times 21$, $105 = 105$

Solve for n. Check that the cross products are equal.

1. $\frac{4}{5} = \frac{n}{20}$ $5 \times n = \square \times 20$

   Write the cross products. $5n = \square$

   Simplify. $\frac{5n}{\square} = \frac{\square}{\square}$

   Solve. $n =$ ___

   Check. ___ = ___

2. $\frac{6}{8} = \frac{9}{n}$ $6 \times n = \square \times 9$

   Write the cross products. $6n = \square$

   Simplify. $\frac{6n}{\square} = \frac{\square}{\square}$

   Solve. $n =$ ___

   Check. ___ = ___

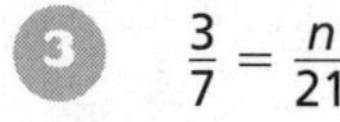

3. $\frac{3}{7} = \frac{n}{21}$

   $7n = \square \times 21$

   $7n = \square$

   $\frac{7n}{\square} = \frac{\square}{\square}$

   $n =$ ___

4. $\frac{9}{15} = \frac{3}{n}$

   $15 \times \square = 9 \times n$

   $\square = 9n$

   $\frac{\square}{\square} = \frac{9n}{\square}$

   $n =$ ___

5. $\frac{7}{10} = \frac{n}{90}$

   $n =$ ___

6. $\frac{14}{n} = \frac{42}{12}$

   $n =$ ___

Check

7. $\frac{3}{n} = \frac{9}{24}$

   $n =$ ___

8. $\frac{8}{12} = \frac{4}{n}$

   $n =$ ___

9. $\frac{n}{4} = \frac{18}{24}$

   $n =$ ___

Skill 66 Change Units

Using Skill 66

OBJECTIVE Change between units of the same measurement system by multiplying or dividing

Before beginning the skill, review customary units of measure with students and recall the abbreviations used for each unit of measure.

Draw students' attention to the example for customary units. Ask: **How many feet equal 1 yard?** (3 feet) **When you change yards to feet, are you changing from a larger unit to a smaller unit or from a smaller unit to a larger unit?** (larger unit to a smaller unit)

To change from a larger unit to a smaller unit, do you multiply or divide? (multiply)

Ask similar questions as you work through the example for finding how many yards are in 108 inches.

Continue with the example for metric units. Explain to students that the meter is the basic unit of length in the metric system. All other units have the word "meter" as the root. The prefixes tell how many or what part of a meter each unit is.

milli - thousandth
centi - hundredth
deci - tenth
kilo - thousand

Note the patterns of powers of 10 that make the metric system easier to use than the customary system. You may also wish to review the metric prefixes that help to identify each unit.

TRY THESE In Exercises 1–4 students change from one unit to another in the same measurement system.

- **Exercises 1–2** Change customary units
- **Exercises 3–4** Change metric units

PRACTICE ON YOUR OWN Review the example at the top of the page. In Exercises 1–6, students identify whether they multiply or divide and change customary or metric units of measure. In Exercises 7–16, students change customary or metric units of measure.

CHECK Determine if students can change between units of the same measurement system by multiplying or dividing. Success is indicated by 3 out of 4 correct responses.

Students who successfully complete the **Practice on Your Own** and **Check** are ready to move to the next skill.

COMMON ERRORS

- Students may multiply when they should divide, or divide when they should multiply.
- Students may multiply or divide by the wrong multiple of ten when changing metric units.

Students who made more than 3 errors in the **Practice on Your Own**, or who were not successful in the **Check** section, may benefit from the **Alternative Teaching Strategy** on the next page.

Optional

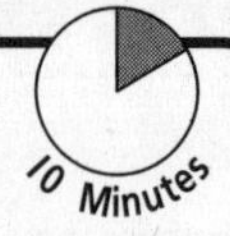

Alternative Teaching Strategy
Modeling Changing Units

OBJECTIVE Understand the basic unit of measure in the customary and metric systems

MATERIALS inch cubes, customary rulers, yardsticks, centimeter cubes, metric rulers, meter sticks

You may wish to have two sessions for this activity, treating the customary and metric systems separately.

Have the students gather around a table to examine the inch-cubes, inch-ruler, and yardstick.

Display 12 inch cubes. Have students verify that 1 cube is 1 inch long. Display the inch ruler. Note that it takes 12 cubes or 12 inches to equal 1 ruler or 1 foot. Help students understand the relative size of each unit. Ask: **How many groups of 12 inches make 1 foot?** (1)

Note that when changing from a smaller to a larger unit the result is fewer units, so the operation used is division.

Model the same process for changing from feet to yards, once again emphasizing the relative size of each unit. You may wish to point out that the foot is 12 times as long as an inch and a yard is 36 times as long as an inch.

Then reverse the process, changing yards to feet, noting that when changing from a larger to a smaller unit, the result will be more units. So, the operation used is multiplication.

As you model the same process for the metric system, emphasize powers of ten. Help students understand that the same operations—multiplication and division—that were used to change units in the customary system are also used with the metric system.

Name ________________ Skill ________________

Skill 66

Change Units

Use multiplication or division to change from one unit of measure to another.

Multiply to change a larger unit to a smaller unit.
Divide to change a smaller unit to a larger unit.

Customary Units

- **5 yd = □ ft**

  ↑ larger unit ↑ smaller unit

  To change yards to feet, **multiply** by 3.

  5 × 3 = 15

  So, 5 yd = 15ft.

- **108 in. = □ yd**

  ↑ smaller unit ↑ larger unit

  To change inches to yards, **divide** by 36.

  108 ÷ 36 = 3

1 ft = 12 in.
1 yd = 3 ft
1 yd = 36 in.
1 mi = 5,280 ft
1 mi = 1,760 yd

Remember:
inch→in.
feet→ft
yard→yd
mile→mi

Metric Units

- **3 km = □ m**

  ↑ larger unit ↑ smaller unit

  To change kilometers to meters, **multiply** by 1,000.

  So, 3 km = 3,000 m.

- **50 mm = □ cm**

  ↑ smaller unit ↑ larger unit

  To change millimeters to centimeters, **divide** by 10.

  50 ÷ 10 = 5

  So, 50 mm = 5 cm

1 cm = 10 mm
1 m = 100 cm
1 m = 1,000 mm
1 km = 1,000 m

Remember:
millimeter→mm
centimeter→cm
meter→m
kilometer→km

Try These

Complete. Change to the given unit.

1. 6 yd = □ ft
   To change ______ to feet, multiply by ______.
   6 yd = ______ ft

2. 72 in. = □ ft
   To change ______ to feet, divide by ______.
   72 in. = ______ ft

3. 4 m = □ cm
   To change ______ to centimeters, multiply by ______.
   4 m = ______ cm

4. 700 cm = □ m
   To change ______ to meters, divide by ______.
   700 cm = ______ m

Go to the next side.

Name ______________________ Skill ______________

Practice on Your Own

Skill 66

Multiply to change larger units to smaller units.

2 mi = □ yd
2 × 1,760 = 3,520
So, 2 mi = 3,520 yd

Miles to yards: Multiply by 1,760

Divide to change smaller units to larger units.

5 m = □ km
5 ÷ 1,000 = 0.005
So, 5 m = 0.005 km

Complete. Write *multiply* or *divide*. Then change to the given unit.

1. 4 mi = □ yd
   ________ by 1,760.
   4 mi = ________ yd

2. 8 cm = □ mm
   ________ by 10.
   8 cm = ________ mm

3. 7 yd = □ ft
   ________ by 3.
   7 yd = ________ ft

4. 144 in. = □ yd
   ________ by 36.
   144 in. = ________ yd

5. 7 m = □ km
   ________ by 1,000.
   7 m = ________ km

6. 36 in. = □ ft
   ________ by 12.
   36 in. = ________ ft

Change to the given unit.

7. 2 ft = ________ in.
8. 6 m = ________ mm
9. 4 km = ________ m
10. 60 in. = ________ ft
11. 30 mm = ________ cm
12. 900 cm = ________ m
13. 15 yd = ________ ft
14. 3 m = ________ cm
15. 180 in. = ________ yd
16. 90 mm = ________ cm

Check

Change to the given unit.

17. 5 mi = ________ yd
18. 83 cm = ________ mm
19. 48 in. = ________ ft
20. 4 m = ________ km

Skill 67 Function Tables

15 Minutes

Using Skill 67

OBJECTIVE Determine the output for a function table given the input and a rule written as an algebraic expression

Direct students' attention to the first function table. Review the meaning of each column to be sure students understand how to read a function table. Ask: **What is the title of the first column?** (Input)

Say: **In the column for input, the variable x represents the input number. What are the values for x?** (1, 2, 3, 4, 5)

Focus on the second column. Say: **The title of this column is Algebraic Expression. What is the algebraic expression, or rule, this column shows?** ($x + 3$)

Guide students to understand that this algebraic expression means add 3 to the input number to get the output number. Then tell students that the third column, Output, shows the result of adding 3 to the input number. Ask: **What is the value of $x + 3$ when you substitute 1 for x?** (4) **Where does the value of 4 go in the table?** (in the output column, in the same row as the input of 1)

As you work through the other input values in the function table, have students explain how each output value was determined.

In the next example, have students state the rule in words. Then guide them through each input value to determine each corresponding output value.

TRY THESE In Exercises 1–2 students write the outputs in function tables.

- **Exercise 1** Function table with addition rule
- **Exercise 2** Function table with subtraction rule

PRACTICE ON YOUR OWN Review the example at the top of the page. In Exercises 1–2, students complete function tables with algebraic expressions provided as cues. In Exercises 3–6, students complete function tables with operation signs provided as clues.

CHECK Determine if students can complete function tables given the input and a rule written as an algebraic expression. Success is indicated by 2 out of 2 correct responses.

Students who successfully complete the **Practice on Your Own** and **Check** are ready to move to the next skill.

COMMON ERRORS

- Students may perform the wrong operation for a given rule.
- Students may write input in the Output column without performing the operation.

Students who made more than 2 errors in the **Practice on Your Own**, or who were not successful in the **Check** section, may benefit from the **Alternative Teaching Strategy** on the next page.

Optional

Alternative Teaching Strategy

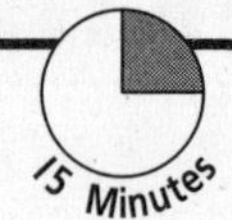

Modeling Function Tables

OBJECTIVE Determine the output for a function table given the input and the rule written as an algebraic expression

MATERIALS flip chart, counters, box, paper, pencil, small plastic bags

Prepare a function table prior to beginning the activity.

Distribute counters to students. Put bags of 2 counters in the box. On the box write the rule "$x + 2$." Have one student put 4 counters into the box.

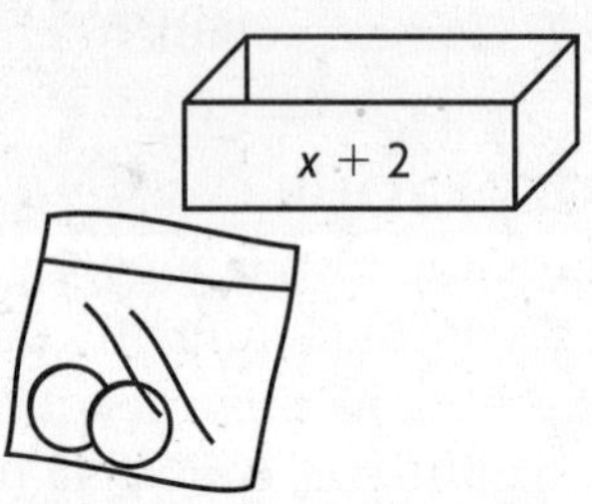

Ask: **The rule reads "$x + 2$." How many counters will you take out based on the rule?** (6) **Why?** (because you substitute 4 for x in the algebraic expression, then simplify)

Have the student remove the 4 counters and a bag of 2 counters. Record the steps in the function table on the flip chart.

Continue to have students put a given number of counters into the box and take out the number based on the rule. Have students record the results of each input in the function table.

Repeat the activity with rules for other operations.

When students show understanding, have them try the exercise using only paper and pencil.

Name ______________________ Skill ______________________

Skill 67

Function Tables

A **function table** uses input numbers and a rule to find output numbers. Sometimes the rule is written as an algebraic expression. The rule tells you what to do with the input numbers.

Understand Function Tables

- In this function table, the input number is represented by x. The column for input numbers shows different values for x.
- The column for the rule or algebraic expression shows that you add 3 to the input number to get the output number.
- The column for output shows the result of adding 3 to the input number.

Values of x Input	Rule Algebraic Expression	Result Output
x	$x + 3$	
1	1 + 3	4
2	2 + 3	5
3	3 + 3	6
4	4 + 3	7
5	5 + 3	8

So, when x = 1, the value of x + 3 is 1 + 3, or 4.

Use a Function Table

The rule for this table is $n - 4.1$.

Find the missing values in the table.

Input	Algebraic Expression	Output
n	$n - 4.1$	
10.7	□	□
15.4	□	□

Step 1 Substitute each value for n in the input column for n in the algebraic expression.

Step 2 Use the rule.

Step 3 Write the output.

Input	Algebraic Expression	Output
n	$n - 4.1$	
10.7	10.7 − 4.1	6.6
15.4	15.4 − 4.1	11.3

So, when $n = 10.7$, the value of $n - 4.1$ is 10.7 − 4.1, or 6.6.

Try These

Write the output.

1.

Input	Algebraic Expression	Output
x	$x + 6$	
4	4 + 6	______
5	5 + 6	______

2.

Input	Algebraic Expression	Output
n	$n - 2.1$	
3.2	3.2 − 2.1	______
5.4	5.4 − 2.1	______

Go to the next side.

Name ______________________ Skill ______________________

Practice on Your Own

Skill 67

Think:
The rule is to divide the input number by 3. The result is the output number.

When $b = 15$, the value of $b \div 3$ is $15 \div 3$, or 5.

Input	Algebraic Expression	Output
b	$b \div 3$	
15	$15 \div 3$	5
27	$27 \div 3$	9
36	$36 \div 3$	12

Complete each function table.

1.

Input	Algebraic Expression	Output
c	$c \cdot 7$	
3	$3 \cdot 7$	____
6	$6 \cdot 7$	____

2.

Input	Algebraic Expression	Output
x	$x \div 4$	
16	$16 \div 4$	____
24	$24 \div 4$	____

3.

Input	Algebraic Expression	Output
w	$w + 11.8$	
10.1	____ + ____	____
12.3	____ + ____	____
14.1	____ + ____	____

4.

Input	Algebraic Expression	Output
r	$r - 3.5$	
5.9	____ − ____	____
13.1	____ − ____	____
15.6	____ − ____	____

5.

Input	Algebraic Expression	Output
p	$p \cdot 5$	
15	____ · ____	____
24	____ · ____	____
37	____ · ____	____

6.

Input	Algebraic Expression	Output
j	$j \div 12$	
84	____ ÷ ____	____
108	____ ÷ ____	____
132	____ ÷ ____	____

Check

Complete each function table.

7.

Input	Algebraic Expression	Output
x	$x - 6.7$	
29.8	____ − ____	____
42.9	____ − ____	____
58.3	____ − ____	____

8.

Input	Algebraic Expression	Output
n	$n \cdot 14$	
3	____ · ____	____
7	____ · ____	____
11	____ · ____	____

Using Skill 68

OBJECTIVE Find a point for an ordered pair and find an ordered pair for a point on a coordinate plane

Begin by directing students' attention to the coordinate grid. Make sure students can identify and distinguish each axis. Ask: **In what direction does the *x*-axis extend?** (left and right) **In what direction does the *y*-axis extend?** (up and down) **What is the name of the point where the two axes cross?** (origin) **On the *x*-axis, which direction is positive?** (right) **Which direction is negative?** (left) **On the *y*-axis, which direction is positive?** (up) **Which direction is negative?** (down)

Ask: **Which letter comes first in the alphabet, *x* or *y*?** (*x*)

Say: **The first number in the ordered pair tells you how to move along the *x*-axis.**

Continue: **To get to point *A*, you start at the origin. Then, do you move left or right?** (right) **How do you know?** (The first number in the ordered pair is positive.) **How many units do you move to the right?** (2) **From there, do you move up or down, to get to point *A*?** (up) **Is up the positive or negative direction for the *y*-axis?** (positive) **How many units *up* do you move?** (3) **How do you know to move up 3 units?** (The second number in the ordered pair is 3.)

As you work through locating the other points on the coordinate plane, have students identify and explain the direction they move for each number in the ordered pair.

TRY THESE Exercises 1–3 model the type of exercises students will find on the **Practice on Your Own** page.

- **Exercises 1 and 2** Find the point given the ordered pair.
- **Exercise 3** Find the ordered pair given the point.

PRACTICE ON YOUR OWN As students work through the example at the top of the page, have them recall and explain the direction they move for each number in the ordered pair.

CHECK Determine if the students can write the ordered pair for a point given on a coordinate plane.

Success is indicated by 4 out of 4 correct responses.

Students who successfully complete the **Practice on Your Own** and **Check** are ready to move to the next skill.

COMMON ERRORS

- Students may reverse the order of the numbers in the ordered pair.
- Students may confuse directions when given negative integers in an ordered pair.

Students who made more than 3 errors in the **Practice on Your Own**, or who were not successful in the **Check** section, may benefit from the **Alternative Teaching Strategy** on the next page.

Optional

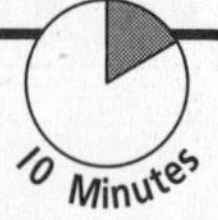

Alternative Teaching Strategy

Plot Ordered Pairs on a Coordinate Grid

OBJECTIVE Graph ordered pairs on a coordinate plane

MATERIALS overhead projector, two different colored erasable markers, prepared transparency of coordinate plane

Begin by displaying the table below. Show students how to write ordered pairs for the numbers in the table, for example (6,4).

x	y
6	4
5	$^{-}4$
2	3
0	$^{-}1$
$^{-}4$	5

Use the overhead projector and the transparency of the coordinate plane to show students how to find the point for each ordered pair in the table.

Model plotting the point for the ordered pair (6, 4). Remind students the table makes it clear how many places to move on each axis.

Ask: **Where do you start?** (at the origin, where the x-axis and y-axis cross.)

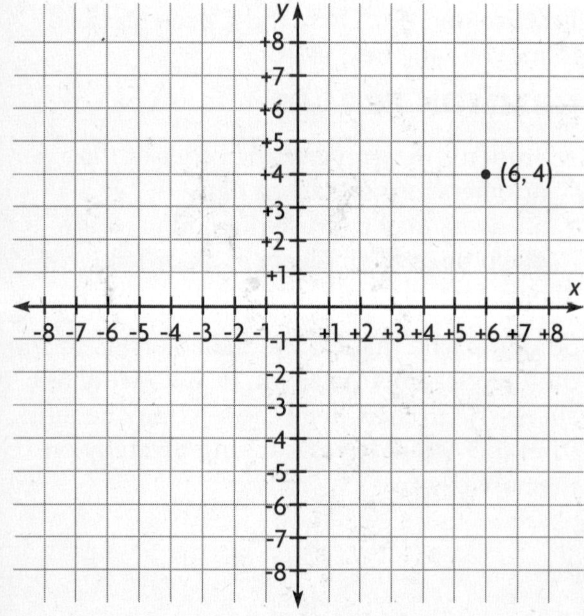

Assign one color of erasable marker to indicate a positive integer, and another to indicate a negative integer. You might also color-coordinate the integers in the column you display.

For example, you could use blue to indicate positive integers, and red to indicate negative.

To model finding point (6, 4) draw a blue arrow along the x-axis from 0 to 6. Then, from 6 on the x-axis, draw a blue arrow up 4 places. Point out to students how you stop drawing as soon as you reach the line that crosses the y-axis at 4.

Now invite a student to come to the overhead projector to find the point for the next ordered pair, (5, $^{-}4$).

Work through the process with the student. Ask: **Where do you start?** (origin) **Do you move along the x-axis or the y-axis first?** (the x-axis) **Do you move to the left or to the right?** (to the right) **Where do you stop?** (at the 5 on the x-axis) **Then do you move up or down?** (down)

At this point, hand the student the color marker indicating negative direction. Remind students to use this color whenever drawing *down* or to the *left*.

Continue: **How many units down do you draw the arrow?** (4)

Relate the $^{-}4$ to moving down the y-axis.

Continue guiding students to find a point on the coordinate plane for each ordered pair.

Name ______________ Skill ______________

Ordered Pairs

Skill 68

An **ordered pair** is a pair of numbers used to locate a point on a coordinate plane. It is called an ordered pair because the order in which you move on the coordinate plane is important.

Example

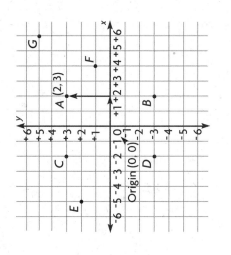

- The first number in the pair represents the x-coordinate. It tells you how many units to move right or left on the x-axis.

x-coordinate ↘ ↙ y-coordinate
(2, 3)
ordered pair

- The second number represents the y-coordinate. It tells you how many units to move **up** or **down** on the y-axis.Find the points named by each ordered pair. For each x-coordinate, start at the **origin,** the point where the x-axis and y-axis intersect (0, 0).

Ordered Pair	x-axis	y-axis	point
(2, 3)	move 2 units right	move 3 units up	*A*
$(2, ^-3)$	move 2 units right	move 3 units down	*B*
$(^-2, 3)$	move 2 units left	move 3 units up	*C*
$(^-2, ^-3)$	move 2 units left	move 3 units down	*D*

Try These

Use the coordinate plane above. Complete each statement.

1. Find the point for (4, 1).
x-axis: move ____ units to the right
y-axis: move ____ units up
(4, 1) names point ____.

2. Find the point for $(^-5, 2)$.
x-axis: move ____ units to the left
y-axis: move ____ units up
$(^-5, 2)$ names point ____.

3. Write the ordered pair for point *G*.
x-axis: move ____ units to the right
y-axis: move ____ units up
The ordered pair for point *G* is ____.

Name ______________________ Skill ______________________

Practice on Your Own

Skill 68

Think:

To find the ordered pair for point *B*, start at the origin. Move 5 units to the left, then move 2 units down.

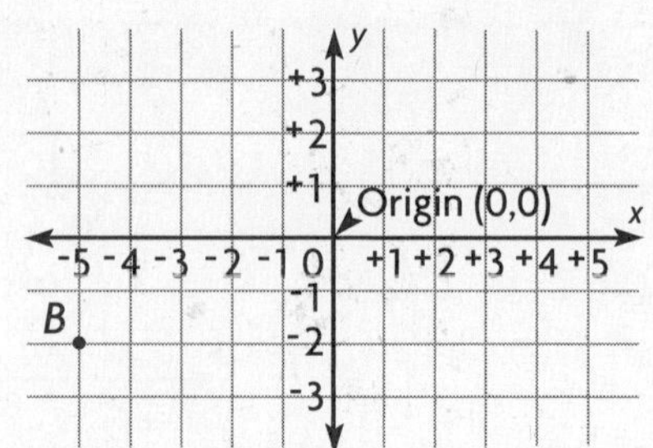

The ordered pair for point B is (⁻5, ⁻2)

Use the coordinate plane at the right.
Complete. Write the ordered pair for each point.

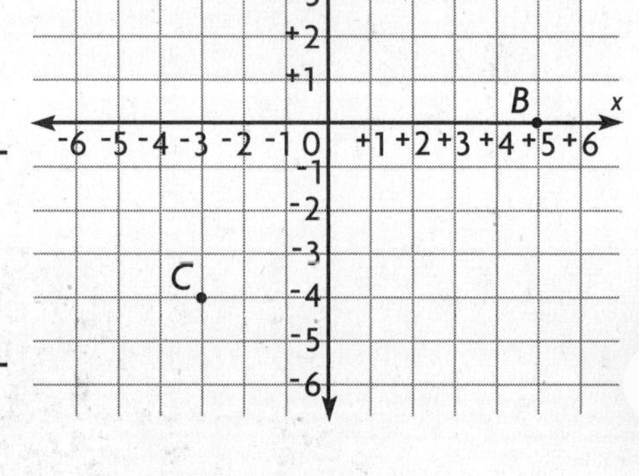

1. point *A* x-axis: move ___ units to the ___
   y-axis: move ___ units ___
   ordered pair: _____

2. point *B* x-axis: move ___ units to the ___
   y-axis: move ___ units ___
   ordered pair: _____

3. point *C* x-axis: move ___ units to the ___
   y-axis: move ___ units ___
   ordered pair: _____

Use the coordinate plane below. Write the ordered pair for each point.

4. point *M*
   ordered pair: _____

5. point *N*
   ordered pair: _____

6. point *P*
   ordered pair: _____

7. point *Q*
   ordered pair: _____

8. point *R*
   ordered pair: _____

9. point *S*
   ordered pair: _____

Check

Use the coordinate plane below. Write the ordered pair for each point.

10. point *T*
    ordered pair: _____

11. point *U*
    ordered pair: _____

12. point *V*
    ordered pair: _____

13. point *W*
    ordered pair: _____

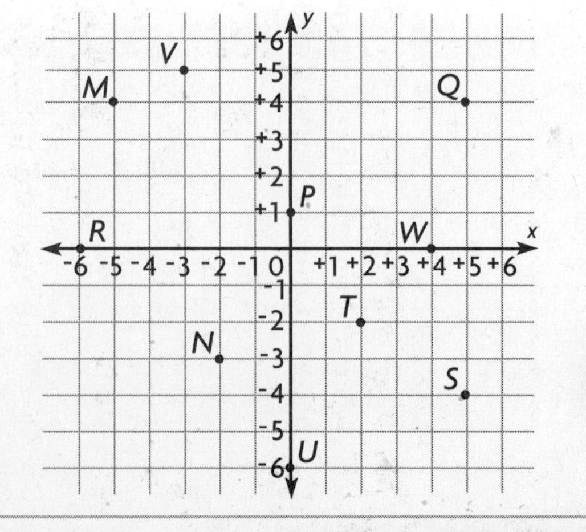

Skill 69 Graph Ordered Pairs (First Quadrant)

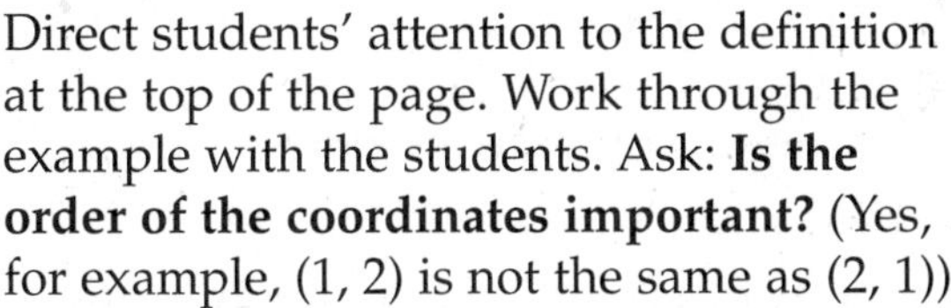

Using Skill 69

OBJECTIVE Graph ordered pairs (first quadrant)

Direct students' attention to the definition at the top of the page. Work through the example with the students. Ask: **Is the order of the coordinates important?** (Yes, for example, (1, 2) is not the same as (2, 1))

Emphasize the need to be careful writing the ordered pairs. The x-coordinate is first, then the y-coordinate. For students having difficulty remembering the order, point out that the variables in the ordered pair (x, y) are in alphabetical order.

TRY THESE In Exercises 1–3, students determine where certain stores are located by moving right and up in a coordinate plane.

- **Exercise 1** 1, 4, (1, 4)
- **Exercise 2** 6, 5, (6, 5)
- **Exercise 3** Video Store

PRACTICE ON YOUR OWN Review the example at the top of the page.

In Exercises 1–3, students are guided to find the ordered pair for a point. In Exercises 4–10, students have to determine the coordinates of a particular point.

CHECK Determine that the students can graph an ordered pair. Success is indicated by 4 out of 4 correct responses.

Students who successfully complete the **Practice on Your Own** and **Check** are ready to move on to the next skill.

COMMON ERRORS

- Students may transpose the coordinates. Stress that the x-coordinate is first and the y-coordinate is second.
- Students may count incorrectly. Have students count the lines and not the spaces between numbers.

Students who made more than 3 errors in the **Practice on Your Own**, or who were not successful in the **Check** section, may benefit from the **Alternative Teaching Strategy** on the next page.

Optional

Alternative Teaching Strategy

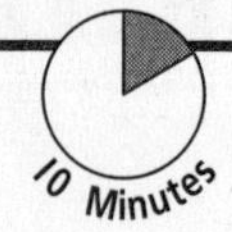

Graphing Ordered Pairs

OBJECTIVE Graph ordered pairs

MATERIALS index cards with ordered pairs, graph paper

Prepare a set of cards with ordered pairs. The ordered pairs should match the number of rows and columns in the classroom. For example, if there are 5 rows and 5 columns the ordered pairs should not be larger than (5, 5).

Arrange the classroom desks into rows and columns. As shown below.

☐	☐	☐	☐	☐
☐	☐	☐	☐	☐
☐	☐	☐	☐	☐
☐	☐	☐	☐	☐

Shuffle the cards and distribute one per student.

Tell the students that the classroom is a coordinate plane.
Ask: **Where is the starting point?** (zero, origin)

Where is the starting point on our coordinate plane? (Have a student stand at the (origin) zero point.)

Have the student standing at the (origin) zero point read the ordered pair on the card and move to the location on their card. Stress the need to move right and up.

Repeat this activity several times. When students show an understanding of moving to their location switch the activity around. Place a student somewhere on the "grid" and have another student describe how to get to them.

When students show an understanding, have them try the exercise using graph paper and a pencil.

Name ______________________ Skill ______________________

Skill 69

Graph Ordered Pairs (First Quadrant)

An **ordered pair** is a pair of numbers used to locate a point on a coordinate plane.

Example

The first number in the pair represents the x-coordinate. It tells you how many units to move **right** on the x-axis.

The second number represents the y-coordinate. It tells you how many units to move **up** on the y-axis.

x-coordinate ↘ (4, 1) ↙ y-coordinate

Always start at 0.
Find the Post Office on the coordinate plane shown.
Always start at 0.
First, move 4 spaces to the right.
Then, move 3 spaces up.
Ordered pair (4, 3)

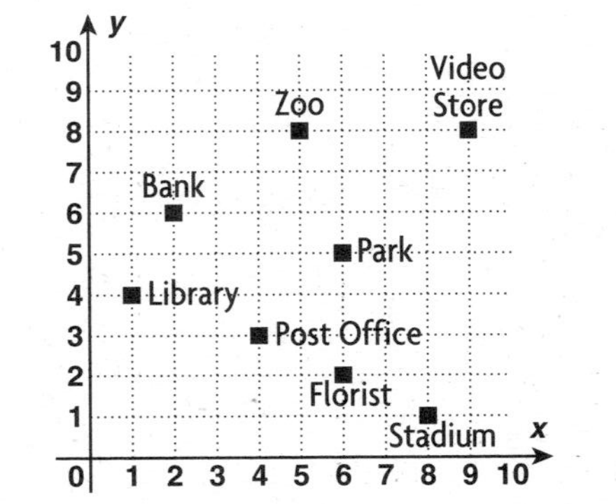

Try These

Use the coordinate plane shown above to complete each statement.

1. What are the coordinates for the Library.
First move ____ spaces right.
Next, move ____ spaces up.
Ordered pair (_,_)

2. What are the coordinates for the Park?
First move ____ spaces right.
Next, move ____ spaces up.
Ordered pair (_,_)

3. What store is located at (9, 8).
First move 9 spaces right.
Next, move 8 spaces up.
____

Go to the next side.

Name ____________________ Skill ____________________

Practice on Your Own

Skill 69

Think:

To find the ordered pair for point A, start at 0. Move 5 units to the right, then move 3 units up.

The ordered pair for point A is (5, 3).

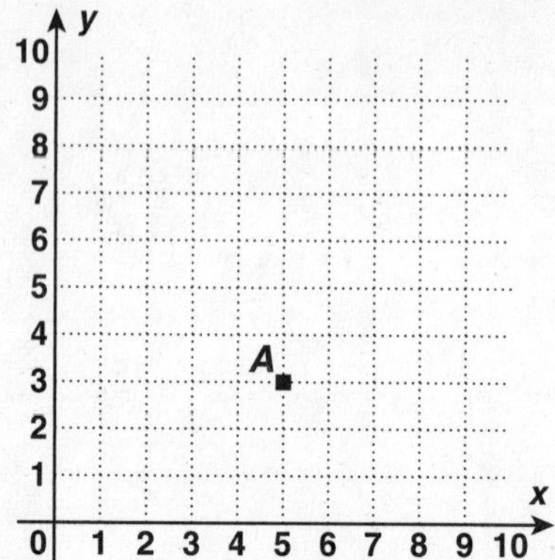

Use the coordinate plane at the right. Complete. Write the ordered pair for each point.

1. point A Move ___ units to the right.
Move ___ units up.
ordered pair: (__,__)

2. point B Move ___ units to the right.
Move ___ units up.
ordered pair: (__,__)

3. point C Move ___ units to the right.
Move ___ units up.
ordered pair: (__,__)

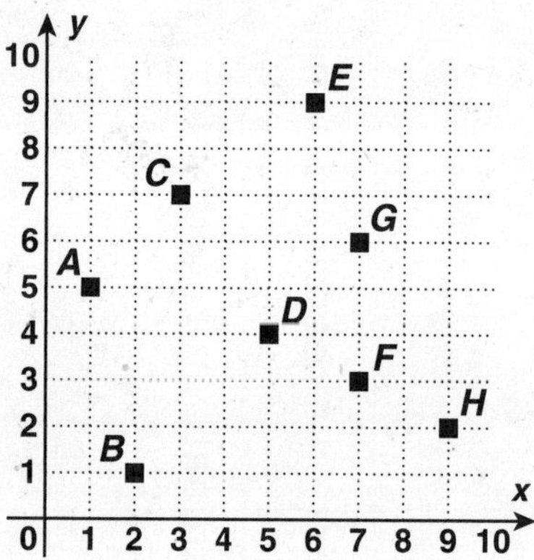

Use the coordinate plane above. Write the ordered pair for each point.

4. point D
ordered pair: (__,__)

5. point E
ordered pair: (__,__)

6. point F
ordered pair: (__,__)

Check

Use the coordinate plane below. Write the ordered pair for each point.

7. point A
ordered pair: (__,__)

8. point B
ordered pair: (__,__)

9. point C
ordered pair: (__,__)

10. point D
ordered pair: (__,__)

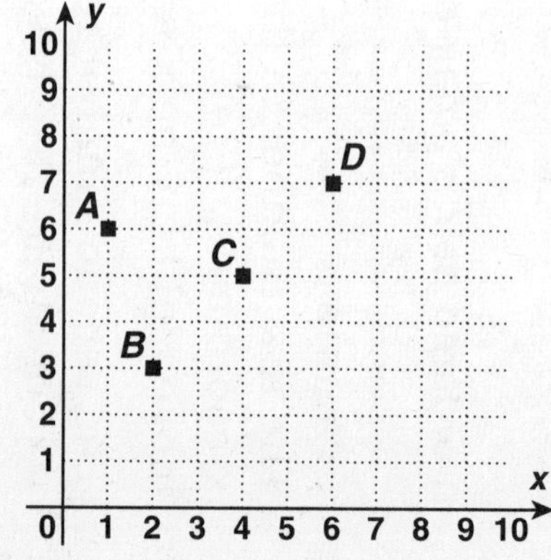

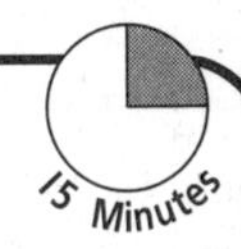

15 Minutes

Using Skill 70

OBJECTIVE Read a thermometer

Relate a horizontal number line to the vertical number line in a thermometer. Ask: **How is the number line positioned in the thermometer?** (vertically) **What number separates the positive and negative temperatures?** (0°) **In which direction are the positive temperatures?** (up, or above 0°) **In which direction are negative temperatures?** (down, or below 0°)

Guide students to see that every interval of 10° is labeled on both thermometers. Between these major intervals are smaller ones. Make sure students know the value of each interval. Ask: **How many degrees does each of the smaller intervals represent?** (2°)

Focus on Point *A*. Ask: **Between which two temperatures is Point *A*?** (40°F and 50°F)

Help students recognize that they can either count up from 40°F or count down from 50°F to read Point *A*. Ask: **Since each interval is 2°, what is the temperature at Point A?** (46°F)

Draw attention to Point *B*. Help students recognize the position of the temperature reading. Ask: **Is Point *B* above or below zero?** (below) **Are points below zero positive or negative?** (negative)

Help students recognize that they can either count up from ⁻20°F or count down from ⁻10°F to read Point *B*. Ask: **What is the temperature at Point *B*?** (⁻14°F)

TRY THESE In Exercises 1–4 students name temperature for a thermometer with 2°F intervals.

- **Exercises 1, 2, 4** Name a positive temperature.
- **Exercise 3** Name a negative temperature.

PRACTICE ON YOUR OWN Review the example at the top of the page. Have students name the two numbers between which Point *M* lies. Ask if the temperature is positive or negative. Then ask students to verbalize how to name the temperature.

CHECK Determine if students can read the points above zero as positive temperatures and the points below zero as negative temperatures.

Success is indicated by 6 out of 8 correct responses.

Students who successfully complete **Practice on Your Own** and **Check** are ready to move to the next skill.

COMMON ERRORS

- Students may not know the value of each interval, especially the smaller intervals between labeled temperatures.
- Students may confuse the direction of the positive and negative temperatures.
- Students may read negative temperatures incorrectly. For example, students may think that ⁻14°F increased by 2° is 16°F, instead of ⁻12°F.

Students who made more than 2 errors in the **Practice on Your Own**, or who were not successful in the **Check** section, may benefit from the **Alternative Teaching Strategy** on the next page.

Optional

Alternative Teaching Strategy

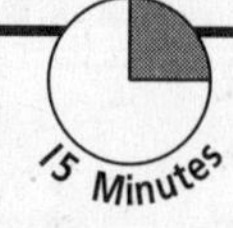

Counting Intervals

OBJECTIVE Count intervals on a number line

MATERIALS flip chart, number lines

Draw these number lines on a flip chart.

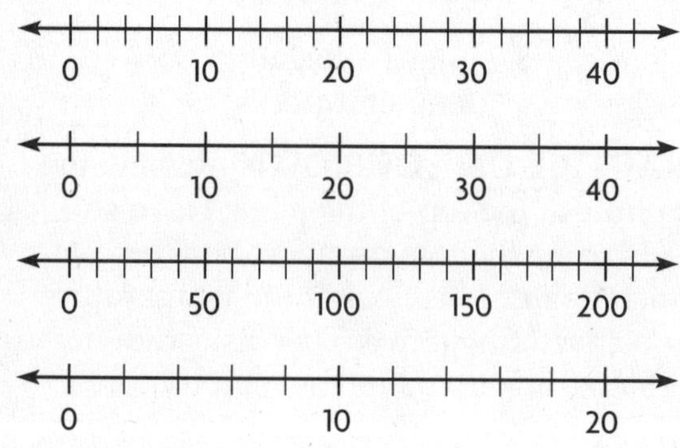

Review skip counting by 2s, 5s, and 10s.

Ask a volunteer to skip count by 2s. Direct students to match each number counted with a tick mark on one of the number lines. Help students recognize that the labels on the correct number line will match the skip counting.

Repeat the count and match process with skip counting by 5s and by 10s. After students are comfortable with counting positive numbers, extend the number lines to include negative numbers.

For some students, it might help to point to each interval as they skip count. Especially emphasize the tick marks when the counting and the label match.

Once students have mastered counting on the horizontal number line, present the same number lines in vertical position.

Repeat the count and match process. Help students recognize that the method for identifying the value of the intervals is the same as it was for the horizontal number line.

Name ______________________ Skill ______________________

Skill 70

Temperature

Think of a thermometer as a vertical number line.

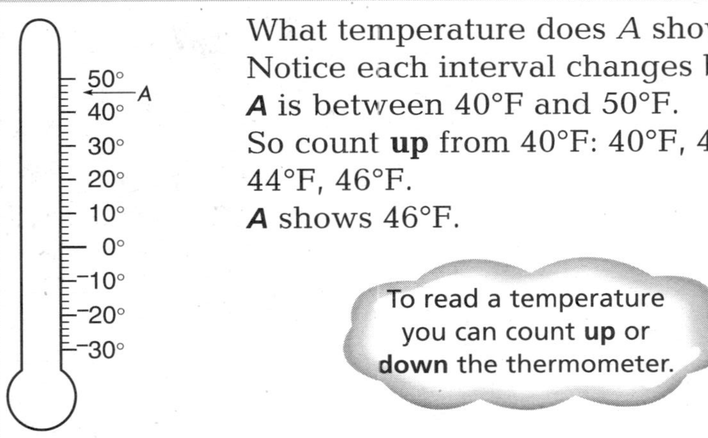

What temperature does *A* show?
Notice each interval changes by 2°F.
A is between 40°F and 50°F.
So count **up** from 40°F: 40°F, 42°F, 44°F, 46°F.
A shows 46°F.

To read a temperature you can count **up** or **down** the thermometer.

What temperature does *B* show?
REMEMBER: Each interval changes by 2°F.
B is between ⁻10°F and ⁻20°F.
So count **down** from ⁻10°F: ⁻10°F, ⁻12°F, ⁻14°F.
B shows ⁻14°F.

The temperatures above zero are **positive**. The ones below zero are **negative**.

Try These

Name the temperature shown by the letters. Remember to show temperatures below zero as negative numbers.

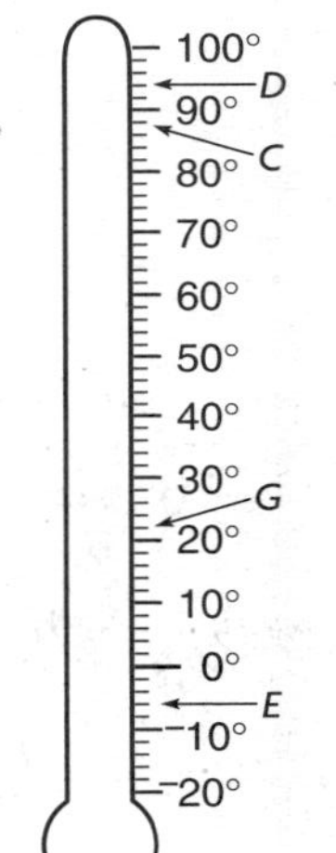

1. ***C*** is between ____ °F and ____ °F.
   Count ____ from ____ °F.
   C shows ____ °F.
2. ***D*** is between ____ °F and ____ °F.
   Count ____ from ____ °F.
   D shows ____ °F.
3. ***E*** is between ____ °F and ____ °F.
   Count ____ from ____ °F.
   E shows ____ °F.
4. ***G*** is between ____ °F and ____ °F.
   Count ____ from ____ °F.
   G shows ____ °F.

Go to the next side.

Name ______________________ Skill ______________________

Skill 70

Practice on Your Own

Think:
You can count **up** or **down** a thermometer. Think of it as a vertical number line.

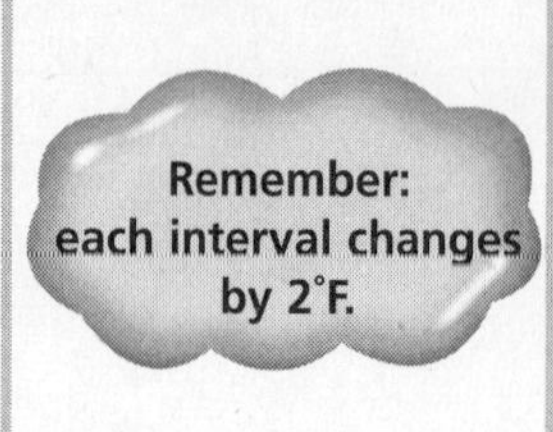

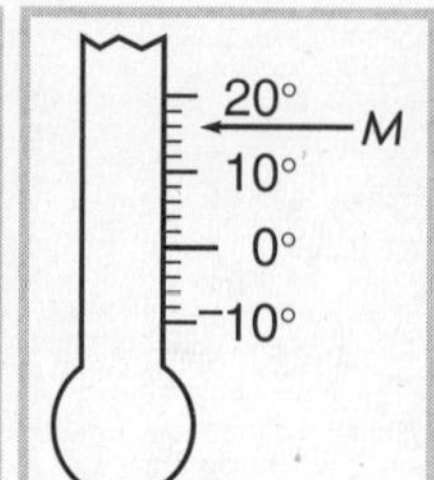

Name the temperature shown.
M is between 10°F and 20°F. So count **up** from 10°F: 10°F, 12°F, 14°F, 16°F. ***M*** shows 16°F.

Name the temperature. Remember to show temperatures below zero as a negative number.

1. *Q* shows ____ °F.
2. *R* is between ____ °F and ____ °F.
   Count ____ from ____ °F.
   R shows ____ °F.
3. *T* is between ____ °F and ____ °F.
   Count ____ from ____ °F.
   T shows ____ °F.
4. *S* is between ____ °F and ____ °F.
   Count ____ from ____ °F.
   S shows ____ °F.
5. What temperature does *Z* show?
   Count from ____ °F.
   Z shows ____ °F.
6. What temperature does *G* show?
   Count from ____ °F.
   G shows ____ °F.
7. What temperature does *H* show?
   Count from ____ °F.
   H shows ____ °F.
8. What temperature does *J* show?
   Count from ____ °F.
   J shows ____ °F.
9. *K* shows ____ °F.
10. *L* shows ____ °F.
11. *M* shows ____ °F.
12. *N* shows ____ °F.
13. *O* shows ____ °F.
14. *P* shows ____ °F.
15. *Q* shows ____ °F.
16. *R* shows ____ °F.

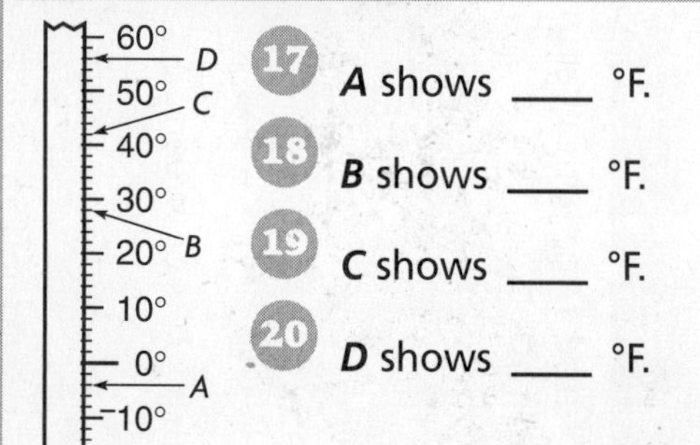

17. *A* shows ____ °F.
18. *B* shows ____ °F.
19. *C* shows ____ °F.
20. *D* shows ____ °F.

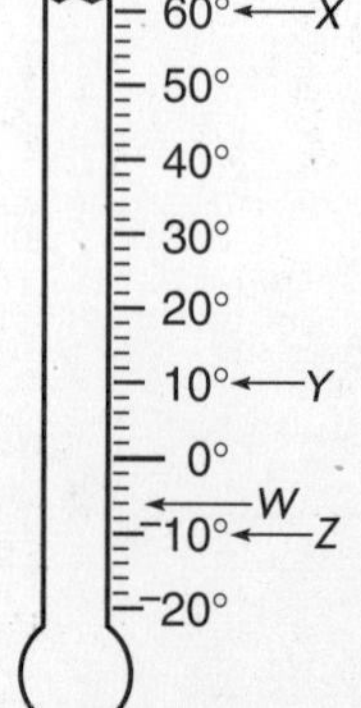

21. *W* shows ____ °F.
22. *X* shows ____ °F.
23. *Y* shows ____ °F.
24. *Z* shows ____ °F.

Skill 71 Customary Units

Using Skill 71

OBJECTIVE Use multiplication or division to change customary units of measure

MATERIALS yardstick, three 12-inch rulers

You may wish to review basic multiplication facts as well as division by a 2-digit number.

Begin by making sure students have a good understanding of the relative size of the different customary units of measure. Focus on the units of length. Ask: **When changing from yards to feet, is the result a larger or a smaller unit of measure?** (smaller)

It is important for students to realize that a smaller unit of measure will result in a greater number of units. Ask: **When changing from yards to feet is the result a larger or smaller unit of measure?** (smaller)
Use the yardstick and rulers to illustrate the conversion. Explain to students that this is the reason multiplication is used to change from a larger unit to a smaller unit of measure and division is used to change from a smaller unit to a larger unit of measure.

For units of capacity, explain to students that capacity refers to liquid or dry measures. Help students name some things, such as milk, water, or rice, that they might measure in units of capacity. Again, make sure students understand the relative size of the different units of measure.

Ask: **Compared to quarts, is a gallon a larger unit or a smaller unit of capacity?** (larger) **To change from quarts to gallons, do you multiply or divide?** (divide)

Direct students' attention to the units of weight. Continue with the focus on multiplying to change from a larger unit to a smaller unit, and dividing to change from a smaller unit to a larger unit.

TRY THESE Exercises 1–3 model using multiplication to change from a larger unit to a smaller unit of measure.

- **Exercise 1** Change yards to feet.
- **Exercise 2** Change gallons to quarts.
- **Exercise 3** Change pounds to ounces.

PRACTICE ON YOUR OWN Review the examples at the top of the page. Have students explain how to use multiplication or division to change from one unit of measure to another.

CHECK Determine if students can use multiplication or division to change units of length, capacity, and weight.

Success is indicated by 4 out of 6 correct responses.

Students who successfully complete the **Practice on Your Own** and **Check** are ready to move to the next skill.

COMMON ERRORS

- Students may not be familiar with the names or relative sizes of different units of measure, and thus may be unable to change between units.
- Students may not know multiplication or division facts.
- Students may confuse the equivalencies used to change from one unit of measure to another.

Students who made more than 4 errors in the **Practice on Your Own**, or who were not successful in the **Check** section, may benefit from the **Alternative Teaching Strategy** on the next page.

Optional

Alternative Teaching Strategy

Adding and Subtracting to Change Units of Measure

OBJECTIVE Use repeated addition and repeated subtraction to change customary units of measure

MATERIALS yarn, 12-inch rulers, flip chart

Prepare ahead of time two strips of yarn: 36 inches and 48 inches long.

Show students the 36-inch yarn. Stretch it from end to end. Tell students that the yarn is 1-yard long. Using the 12-inch rulers, guide students to recognize that the length of the yarn is equal to 3 rulers lined end-to-end, or 3 feet.

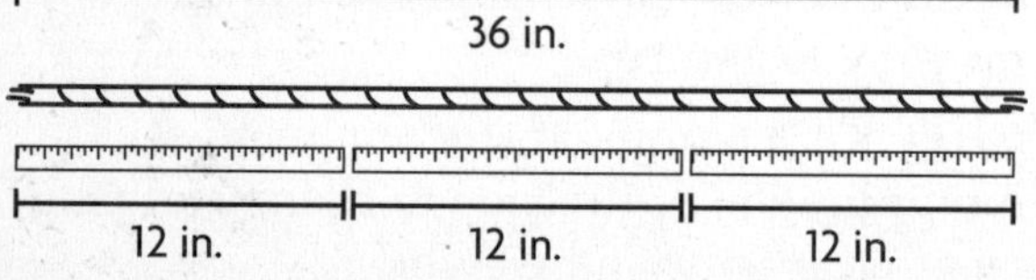

On a flip chart, help students write an equation to show the equivalency.

1 yard = 3 feet

Guide students to understand that a yard represents a larger unit of measure than a foot. It takes 3 feet to equal 1 yard.

Next, help students verbalize a method for finding the number of inches in one yard. Direct students to use their rulers to measure the length of the yarn.

Students should record their findings on the flip chart.

$$12 + 12 + 12 = 36$$

Help students see that 3×12 is a shorter and more efficient way to express the repeated addition.

Explain to students that they have just changed from larger units of measure to smaller units of measure (yards to feet and feet to inches).

Now show students the 48-inch length of yarn. Guide students to change 48 inches to feet. Help students recognize that they are changing from a smaller unit to a larger unit of measure.

Some students might subtract groups of 12 inches from 48 inches as shown.

$$\begin{array}{r} 48 \\ \underline{-12} \\ 36 \\ \underline{-12} \\ 24 \\ \underline{-12} \\ 12 \\ \underline{-12} \\ 0 \end{array}$$

Help students recognize that a more efficient method is to divide 48 by 12.

After a few more examples with units of length, guide students to convert other units of measure.

Customary Units

Skill 71

Use multiplication or division to change from one customary unit of measure to another.

Multiply to change a larger unit to smaller unit.
Divide to change a smaller unit to larger unit.

Units of Length	Units of Capacity	Units of Weight
1 yd = 3 ft 12 in. = 1 ft	1 gal = 4 qt 2 c = 1 pt	1 lb = 16 oz
4 yd = □ ft ↑ larger unit ↑ smaller unit	**5 gal = □ qt** ↑ larger unit ↑ smaller unit	**8 lb = □ oz** ↑ larger unit ↑ smaller unit
To change yards to feet, **multiply** by 3. 4 × 3 = 12 **So,** 4 yd = 12 ft.	To change gallons to quarts, **multiply** by 4. 5 × 4 = 20 **So,** 5 gal = 20 qt.	To change pounds to ounces, **multiply** by 16. 8 × 16 = 128 **So,** 8 lb = 128 oz.
84 in. = □ ft ↑ smaller unit ↑ larger unit	**6 c = □ pt** ↑ smaller unit ↑ larger unit	**64 oz = □ lb** ↑ smaller unit ↑ larger unit
To change inches to feet, **divide** by 12. 84 ÷ 12 = 7 **So,** 84 in. = 7 ft.	To change cups to pints, **divide** by 2. 6 ÷ 2 = 3 **So,** 6 c = 3 pt.	To change ounces to pounds, **divide** by 16. 64 ÷ 16 = 4 **So,** 64 oz = 4 lb.

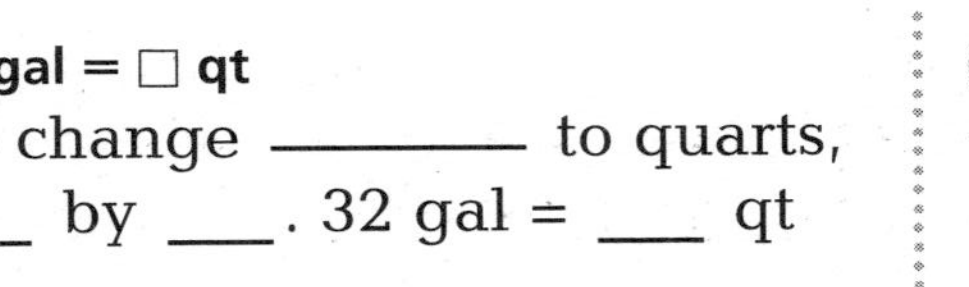

Try These

Complete. Change to the given unit.

1. **12 yd = □ ft**
   To change yards to feet, ___ by ___. 12 yd = ___ ft

2. **32 gal = □ qt**
   To change ________ to quarts, ___ by ___. 32 gal = ___ qt

3. **25 lb = □ oz**
   To change pounds to ______, ___ by ___. 25 lb = ___ oz

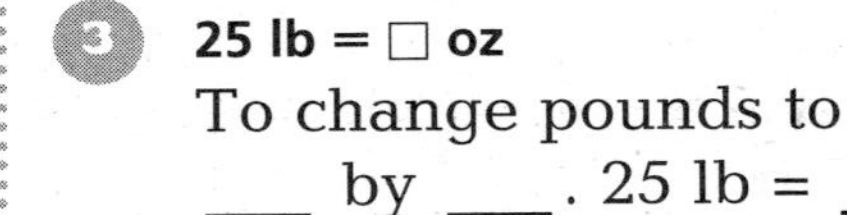

Name ______________________ Skill ______________________

Practice on Your Own

Skill 71

Multiply to change larger units to smaller units.

Divide to change smaller units to larger units.

Change to the given unit.

48 yd = □ ft

$48 \times 3 = 144$

So, 48 yd = 144 ft.

To change yards to feet, multiply by 3.

64 oz = □ lb

$64 \div 16 = 4$

So, 64 oz = 4 lb.

To change ounces to pounds, divide by 16.

Complete. Change to the given unit.

1. 9 yd = □ ft
To change _____ to feet, _____ by 3.
9 yd = _____ ft

2. 25 gal = □ qt
To change _____ to quarts, _____ by 4.
25 gal = _____ qt

3. 40 lb = □ oz
To change _____ to ounces, _____ by 16.
40 lb = _____ oz

4. 108 in. = □ ft
To change _____ to feet, _____ by 12.
108 in. = _____ ft

5. 30 c = □ pt
To change _____ to pints, _____ by 2.
30 c = _____ pt

6. 192 oz = □ lb
To change _____ to pounds, _____ by 16
192 oz = _____ lb

Change to the given unit. Write multiply or divide.

7. 27 yd = □ ft
_____

8. 75 gal = □ qt
_____

9. 480 gal = □ qt
_____

10. 240 in. = □ ft
_____

11. 90 c = □ pt
_____

12. 576 oz = □ lb
_____

Change to the given unit.

13. 18 yd = _____ ft

14. 60 gal = _____ qt

15. 72 lb = _____ oz

16. 144 in. = _____ ft

17. 56 c = _____ pt

18. 112 oz = _____ lb

Check

Change to the given unit.

19. 54 yd = _____ ft

20. 36 gal = _____ qt

21. 27 lb = _____ oz

22. 120 in. = _____ ft

23. 26 c = _____ pt

24. 128 oz = _____ lb

TABLE OF MEASURES

METRIC	CUSTOMARY
Length	
1 millimeter (mm) = 0.001 meter (m)	1 foot (ft) = 12 inches (in.)
1 centimeter (cm) = 0.01 meter	1 yard (yd) = 36 inches
1 decimeter (dm) = 0.1 meter	1 yard = 3 feet
1 kilometer (km) = 1,000 meters	1 mile (mi) = 5,280 feet
	1 mile = 1,760 yards
	1 nautical mile = 6,076.115 feet
Capacity	
1 milliliter (mL) = 0.001 liter (L)	1 teaspoon (tsp) = $\frac{1}{5}$ fluid ounce (fl oz)
1 centiliter (cL) = 0.01 liter	1 tablespoon (tbsp) = $\frac{1}{2}$ fluid ounce
1 deciliter (dL) = 0.1 liter	1 cup (c) = 8 fluid ounces
1 kiloliter (kL) = 1,000 liters	1 pint (pt) = 2 cups
	1 quart (qt) = 2 pints
	1 quart (qt) = 4 cups
	1 gallon (gal) = 4 quarts
Mass/Weight	
1 milligram (mg) = 0.001 gram (g)	1 pound (lb) = 16 ounces (oz)
1 centigram (cg) = 0.01 gram	1 ton (T) = 2,000 pounds
1 decigram (dg) = 0.1 gram	
1 kilogram (kg) = 1,000 grams	
1 metric ton (t) = 1,000 kilograms	

Volume/Capacity/Mass for Water

1 cubic centimeter (cm^3) → 1 milliliter → 1 gram

1,000 cubic centimeters → 1 liter → 1 kilogram

TIME

1 minute (min) = 60 seconds (sec)	1 year (yr) = 12 months (mo), or about 52 weeks
1 hour (hr) = 60 minutes	1 year = 365 days
1 day = 24 hours	1 leap year = 366 days
1 week (wk) = 7 days	

Skill 72

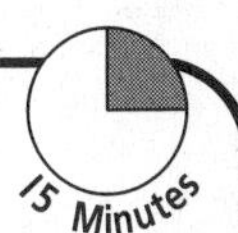

Using Skill 72

OBJECTIVE Use multiplication or division to change metric units

MATERIALS meterstick

Begin the lesson with a review of metric measure names and abbreviations: *kilometer (km), meter (m), centimeter (cm), decimeter (dm), millimeter (mm); liter (L), milliliter (mL); kilogram (kg), gram (g), milligram (mg).* You may also wish to review the strategies for multiplying and dividing by 10, 100, and 1,000.

Draw attention to the *Units of Length* section. Be sure students understand the relative size of each unit. For example, a kilometer may be used to measure the distance between cities. A millimeter may be used to measure the diameter of lead in a pencil.

Ask: **What is the order of the metric units of length from least to greatest?** (millimeter, centimeter, decimeter, meter, kilometer) **Why do you multiply to change from a larger unit to a smaller unit?** (It takes more of a smaller unit to measure the same length.)

Show students a meterstick. Point out the different unit intervals on the ruler. Explain that the meterstick is divided into 100 equal intervals. Each interval is called a *centimeter.* The meterstick can also be divided into 1,000 equal intervals. Each of those intervals is called a *millimeter.* When a meterstick is divided into 10 equal intervals, each is called a *decimeter.*

Continue with similar examples to illustrate the *Units of Capacity* and *Units of Mass* sections. Students should understand the reason for multiplying when changing from a larger unit to a smaller unit, and for dividing when changing from a smaller unit to a larger unit.

TRY THESE Exercises 1–3 model changing from a larger unit to a smaller unit of measure.

- **Exercise 1** Meters to centimeters
- **Exercise 2** Liters to milliliters
- **Exercise 3** Grams to milligrams

PRACTICE ON YOUR OWN Review the examples at the top of the page. Have students notice that the first example requires multiplication and the second example requires division. Point out that the metric system is based on powers of ten, so they can use their mental math skills to change units.

CHECK Determine if students can recognize when to multiply and when to divide when changing units of measure.

Success is indicated by 4 out of 6 correct responses.

Students who successfully complete **Practice on Your Own** and **Check** are ready to move to the next skill.

COMMON ERRORS

- Students might confuse the word *smaller* as used in this context. They may think of dividing to get a "smaller" number. They may not understand that they should multiply when changing from a larger unit to a smaller unit and divide when changing from a smaller unit to a larger unit.

Students who made more than 6 errors in the **Practice on Your Own**, or who were not successful in the **Check** section, may benefit from the **Alternative Teaching Strategy** on the next page.

Optional

Alternative Teaching Strategy

Model Changing Metric Units of Measure

OBJECTIVE Use repeated addition and multiplication to change metric units of measure

MATERIALS yarn, scissors, centimeter rulers

On a large sheet of paper, draw a line segment 1 m long. Cut about 20 pieces of yarn, each 10 cm long.

Provide students with a piece of the pre-cut yarn and a centimeter ruler. Direct them to find the length of the yarn in centimeters.

Next, direct students' attention to the meter-long line segment. Place a piece of yarn at one end of the line segment. Ask students to predict how many pieces of yarn will be needed to equal the entire length of the line segment.

Ask students to place the pieces of pre-cut yarn alongside the line segment.

When students have covered the segment with lengths of yarn, ask them to express the number of centimeters as repeated addition.

$10 + 10 + 10 + 10 + 10 + 10 + 10 + 10 + 10 + 10 = 100$

Help students notice that the addend is repeated 10 times. Note that a shorter, more efficient way to express this repeated addition is by multiplying 10 by 10.

$$10 \times 10 = 100$$

Help students reason through the equivalence: 10 pieces of yarn equals 1 meter-long line segment. Since each piece measures 10 cm, that means 1 m is equal to 100 cm.

Explain to students that they have just changed from a longer unit of measure (meter) to a shorter unit of measure (centimeter).

Ask:

If 1 centimeter is 1 hundredth of a meter, what do you think a decimeter is? (1 tenth of a meter). **How many decimeters are there in a meter?** (10)

Help students to conclude that, when one unit is smaller than another, it takes more of the smaller units to measure the same distance.

You can do a similar modeling exercise for units of capacity by filling a liter container with deciliters. For units of mass, balance a kilogram with 1000 grams.

Name ______________________ Skill ______________________

Metric Units

Skill 72

Use multiplication or division to change one metric unit of measure to another.

Units of Length

- 2 m = □ cm (larger unit ↑, smaller unit ↑)

1 m = 100 cm
10 mm = 1 cm

To change meters to centimeters, multiply by 100.

2 × 100 = 200
So, 2 m = 200 cm.

- 30 mm = □ cm (smaller unit ↑, larger unit ↗)

To change millimeters to centimeters, **divide** by 10.

30 ÷ 10 = 3
So, 30 mm = 3 cm.

Remember:
kilometer = km
meter = m
centimeter = cm
millimeter = mm

Units of Capacity

- 5 L = □ mL (larger unit ↑, smaller unit ↑)

1 L = 1,000 mL
1,000 mL = 1 L

To change liters to milliliters, multiply by 1,000.

5 × 1,000 = 5,000
So, 5 L = 5,000 mL.

- 6,000 mL = □ L (smaller unit ↑, larger unit ↗)

To change milliliters to liters, **divide** by 1,000.

6,000 ÷ 1,000 = 6
So, 6,000 mL = 6 L.

Remember:
kiloliter = kL
liter = L
milliliter = mL

Units of Mass

- 8 g = □ mg (larger unit ↑, smaller unit ↑)

1 g = 1,000 mg
1,000 g = 1 kg

To change grams to milligrams, multiply by 1,000.

8 × 1,000 = 8,000
So, 8 g = 8,000 mg.

- 2,000 g = □ kg (smaller unit ↑, larger unit ↗)

To change grams to kilograms, **divide** by 1,000.

2,000 ÷ 1,000 = 2
So, 2,000 g = 2 kg.

Remember:
kilogram = kg
gram = g
milligram = mg

Try These

Complete.

1. 400 m = □ cm
   To change *meters* to centimeters, ____ by ____.
   400 m = ____ cm

2. 7 L = □ mL
   To change ____ to milliliters, ____ by ____.
   7 L = ____ mL

3. 25 g = □ mg
   To change grams to ____, ____ by ____.
   25 g = ____ milligrams

Go to the next side.

Name ______________________________ Skill ______________________

Practice on Your Own

Skill 72

Think:

Multiply to change larger units to smaller units.

Divide to change smaller units to larger units.

Complete.

5 km = ☐ m

5 × 1,000 = 5,000

So, 5 km = 5,000 m.

700 cm = ☐ m

700 ÷ 100 = 7

So, 700 cm = 7 m.

To change kilometers to meters, multiply by 1,000.

To change centimeters to meters, divide by 100.

Complete.

1. 3 km = ☐ m
   To change kilometers to meters, multiply by 1,000.
   3 km = ______ m

2. 200 L = ☐ mL
   To change liters to milliliters, ______ by 1,000.
   200 L = ______ mL

3. 6 kg = ☐ g
   To change kilograms to grams, ______ by 1,000.
   6 kg = ______ g

4. 70 mm = ☐ cm
   To change, millimeters to centi meters, *divide* by 10.

5. 4,000 mL = ☐ L
   To change milliliters to liters, ______ by 1,000.
   4,000 mL = ______ L

6. 25,000 mg = ☐ g
   To change milligrams to grams, ______ by 1,000.
   25,000 mg = ______ g

7. 27 m = ______ cm

8. 75 L = ______ mL

9. 12 g = ______ mg

10. 2,400 cm = ______ m

11. 1,000 mL = ______ L

12. 1,000 g = ______ kg

Check

Change to the given unit.

13. 18 m = ______ cm

14. 71 L = ______ mL

15. 72 g = ______ mg

16. 270 mm = ______ cm

17. 54,000 mL = ______ L

18. 18,000 g = ______ kg

Skill 73

Measure with Customary and Metric Units

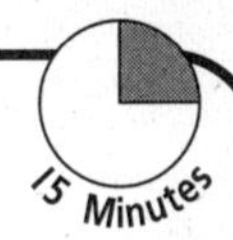

Using Skill 73

OBJECTIVE Measure with customary and metric units

Standard units are most often used to measure length.

Have students recall that customary units of length are inch, foot, yard, and mile. They are also called American Standard units. Metric units are used in most countries of the world. The common metric units of length are centimeter, decimeter, meter, and kilometer. Remind students that the inch unit is abbreviated in. and the centimeter is abbreviated cm.

Discuss with students that an inch is about the length of a paper clip or from the knuckle to the tip of the thumb. A centimeter is about the width of a paper clip or the width of a fingernail.

Start with an inch. Have each student look at their ruler. Make sure that all students have a ruler with one-eighth inch markings. Explain that each mark on the ruler represents $\frac{1}{8}$ of an inch. Make sure that each student can locate $\frac{1}{8}, \frac{1}{4}, \frac{3}{8}, \frac{1}{2}, \frac{5}{8}, \frac{3}{4}, \frac{7}{8}$ inch marks on the ruler.

Ask : **What mark is after the $\frac{1}{2}$ inch mark?** ($\frac{5}{8}$ inch)

Ask: **What mark is before the $\frac{7}{8}$ inch mark?** ($\frac{3}{4}$ inch)

Direct students to Example 1. Have students look at the fly.

Ask: **How long is the fly?** ($1\frac{1}{4}$ inches)

Direct students to Example 2. Help students to measure the beetle to the nearest half-centimeter. Remind students that 1 inch is equal to 2.54 centimeters.

TRY THESE In Exercises 1–3 students measure the object according to the ruler given.

- **Exercise 1** inches
- **Exercise 2** centimeters
- **Exercise 3** inches

PRACTICE ON YOUR OWN Review the examples at the top of the page.

CHECK Verify that the students are measuring correctly in inches and centimeters. Success is indicated by 3 out of 3 correct responses.

Students who successfully complete the **Practice on Your Own** and **Check** are ready to move on to the next skill.

COMMON ERRORS

- Students may confuse the fractional units on the inch ruler.

Optional

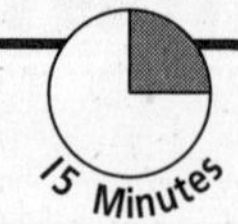

Alternative Teaching Strategy
Measuring with Nonstandard Units

OBJECTIVE Measure with students' own units

MATERIALS index cards

Have students work in pairs. Have each student create his or her own nonstandard unit of measure and label it on an index card. Let each student teach their unit of measure to their partner.

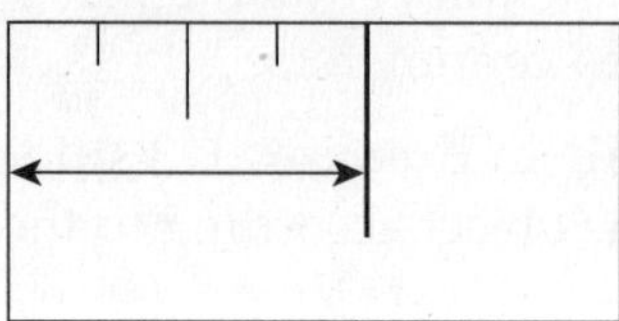

Ask: **Is your unit of measure longer or shorter than an inch? A centimeter?** (Answers will vary.)

Have each student measure the same 3 objects with their unit of measure and write down their answer to the nearest unit of their measure (or $\frac{1}{4}$, $\frac{1}{2}$, $\frac{3}{4}$ for more advanced students) Then, have students trade units of measure and measure the objects again. After the partner has measured the objects have the other partner check their work. Discuss how the number of the unit increases or decreases the length of the object.

Repeat the activities several times with different partners. When students show an understanding have them compare their measurements to inches and centimeters.

Name ____________________ Skill ____________________

Measure with Customary and Metric Units

Skill 73

The inch is the customary unit of measure and the centimeter is a common metric unit.

Example 1

Measure the fly in inches. The fly measures $1\frac{1}{4}$ inch.

Think: Each mark is equal to $\frac{1}{8}$ inch.

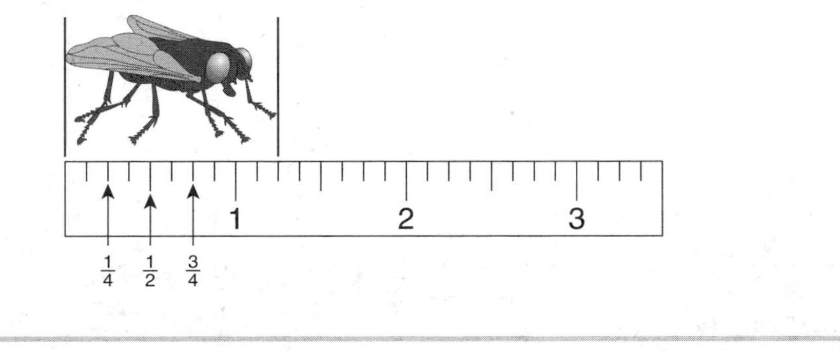

Example 2

Measure the beetle in centimeters. The beetle is 4 cm.

Think: Each dark line represents $\frac{1}{2}$ cm.

0 1 2 3 4 5 6
centimeters
$\frac{1}{2}$

Try These

Measure each object with the given ruler.

1. **Think:** Ruler is in eighths.

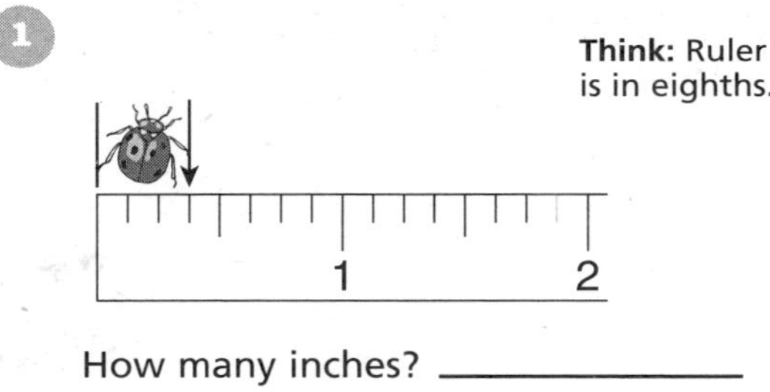

How many inches? ________

2. 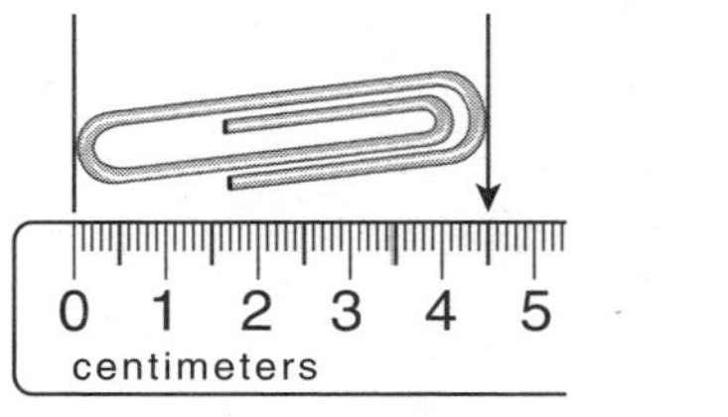

How many centimeters? ________

3. **Think:** Ruler is in eighths.

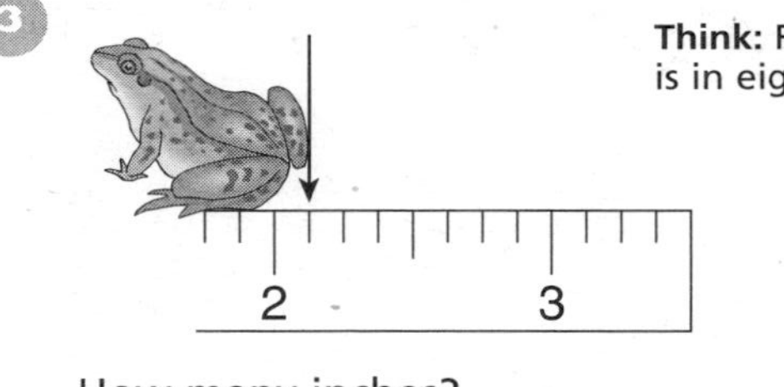

How many inches? ________

Go to the next side.

Name ______________________ Skill ______________________

Practice on Your Own

Skill 73

Measure each object with the given ruler.

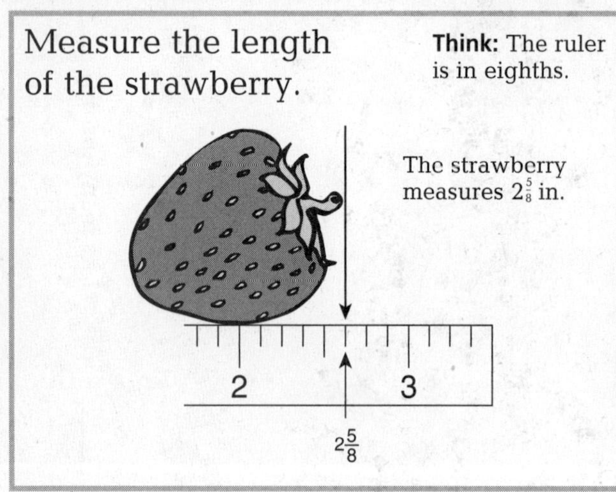

Measure the length of the strawberry.

Think: The ruler is in eighths.

The strawberry measures $2\frac{5}{8}$ in.

Measure the wingspan of the butterfly.

The arrow points to the mark half way between the 12 and the 13 so the wingspan is $12\frac{1}{2}$ cm or 12.5 cm.

Measure each object and decide which is the better measurement.

1. an unsharpened pencil

   $7\frac{1}{2}$ in. or $9\frac{3}{4}$ in.

   ____

2. the diameter of a quarter

   1 cm or $2\frac{1}{2}$ cm

   ____

3. the length of a piece of notebook paper

   10 in. or 12 in.

   ____

Measure the following items with the given standard unit.

4. the height of a desk in inches (nearest $\frac{1}{8}$ in.)

   ____

5. the length of an eraser in centimeters (nearest $\frac{1}{2}$ cm)

   ____

6. the length of your shoe in inches (nearest $\frac{1}{8}$ in.)

   ____

Check

Measure each to the nearest $\frac{1}{8}$ inch and nearest $\frac{1}{2}$ centimeter.

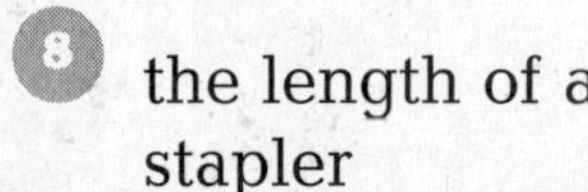

7. the length of a new piece of chalk

   ____

8. the length of a stapler

   ____

9. the height of a chair

   ____

Skill 74 Classify Angles (Acute, Obtuse, Right, Straight)

15 Minutes

Using Skill 74

OBJECTIVE Identify acute, right, obtuse, and straight angles

MATERIALS large clock model, index card

You can use the hands on a clock to model angles.

Discuss the definitions for *angle, point,* and *ray* at the top of the page. Point out that it is the space between the rays, and not the length of the rays that determines the size of the angle.

Explain that the hands of a clock can help demonstrate the four types of angles. Begin by setting the hands of the clock at 12 and 3. Say: **The hands of the clock point to 12 and 3. The angle formed by the hands looks like a square corner. It is called a right angle.**

Verify that the angle is a right angle by placing the corners of an index card at the intersection of the hour hand and minute hand.

Discuss items that have square corners. Then explain that students can use a right angle as a guide to find angles whose measures are greater than or less than a right angle.

Continue using the clock to demonstrate an acute angle, an obtuse angle, and a straight angle. Ask: **What objects in the classroom model the angles we have discussed?**

TRY THESE In Exercises 1–4 students classify angles.

- **Exercise 1** Right angle
- **Exercise 2** Acute angle
- **Exercise 3** Obtuse angle
- **Exercise 4** Straight angle

PRACTICE ON YOUR OWN Review the example at the top of the page. Remind students that the way an angle is positioned does not affect the measure of the angle.

CHECK Determine if students can compare an angle with a right angle to identify whether the angle is right, acute, obtuse, or straight.

Success is indicated by 3 out of 3 correct responses.

Students who successfully complete the **Practice on Your Own** and **Check** are ready to move to the next skill.

COMMON ERRORS

- Students may confuse the names of the angles when identifying them as obtuse or acute.
- Students may not recognize that two angles in different positions can have the same measure.

Students who made more than 2 errors in the **Practice on Your Own**, or who were not successful in the **Check** section, may benefit from the **Alternative Teaching Strategy** on the next page.

Optional

15 Minutes

Alternative Teaching Strategy
Make and Use a Model to Classify Angles

OBJECTIVE Use a square corner to classify angles

MATERIALS index card, right angles, acute angles, obtuse angles, and straight angles drawn on paper

Distribute the papers with the angles and the index cards to the students. Explain that once they can identify a right angle, students can use the right angle as a guide to name or classify other angles.

Suggest that students use the index card as a right-angle tester.

Have students use their right-angle testers to identify angles larger than or smaller than a right angle.

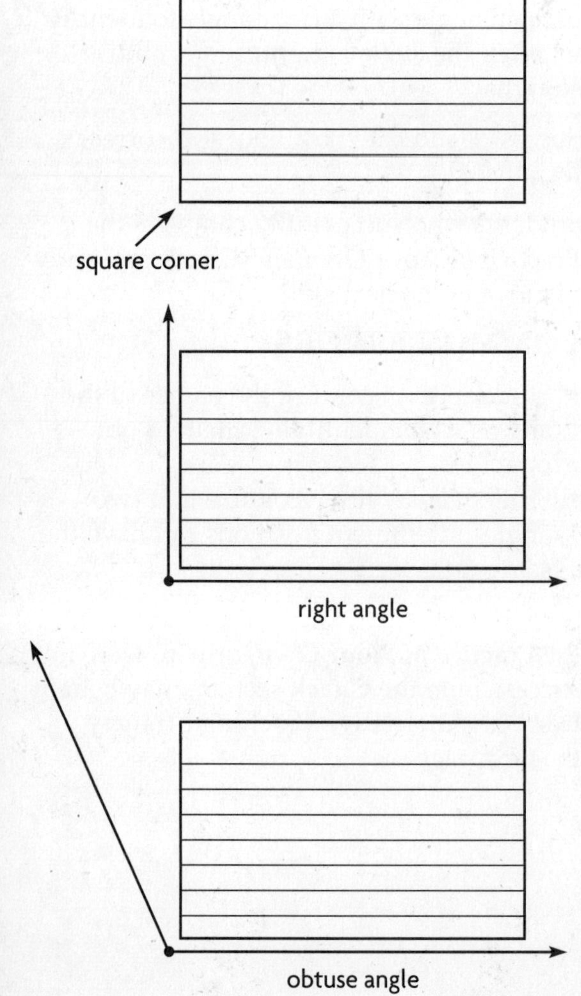

For a right angle, demonstrate how the edges of the tester will align with the two rays.

Because an acute angle is smaller than a right angle, one of the rays will be hidden by the tester.

For an obtuse angle, the space between the rays will be greater than the square corner on the tester.

A straight angle will align only along the bottom of the tester.

Change the position of the angles and test them again.

As students become more comfortable classifying angles, ask them to draw an example of each kind of angle.

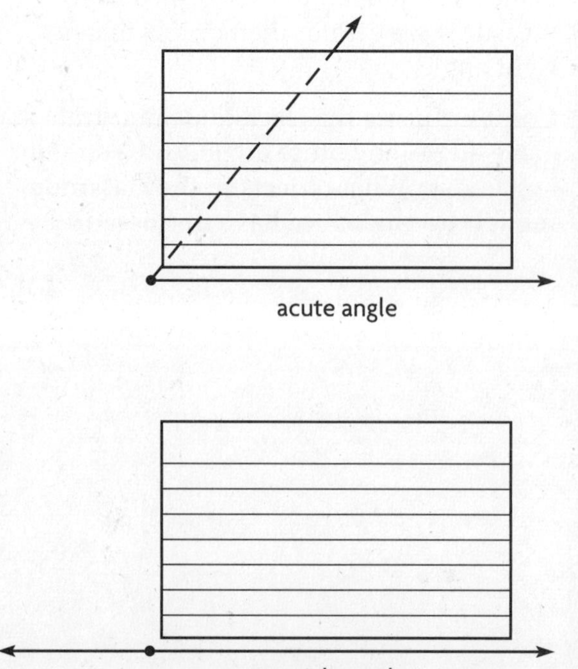

Name ______________________ Skill ______________________

Classify Angles (Acute, Obtuse, Right, Straight)

Skill 74

An **angle** is formed by two rays that have the same endpoint.
You classify angles by their measure.
Angles are measured in degrees. (°)

Remember:
A **point** marks an exact location in space.
A **ray** is part of a line that has one endpoint.
A ray extends without end in one direction.

point M

$\overrightarrow{NP}$
ray NP

Right Angle

A right angle forms a square corner.
The corner of an envelope or a piece of notebook paper forms a right angle.

Acute Angle

An acute angle is smaller than a right angle.

Obtuse Angle

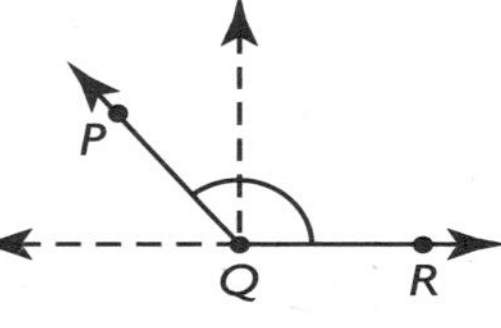

An obtuse angle is larger than a right angle.

Straight Angle

A straight angle forms a line.

Try These

Classify each angle. Choose *right, acute, obtuse,* or *straight angle.*

1
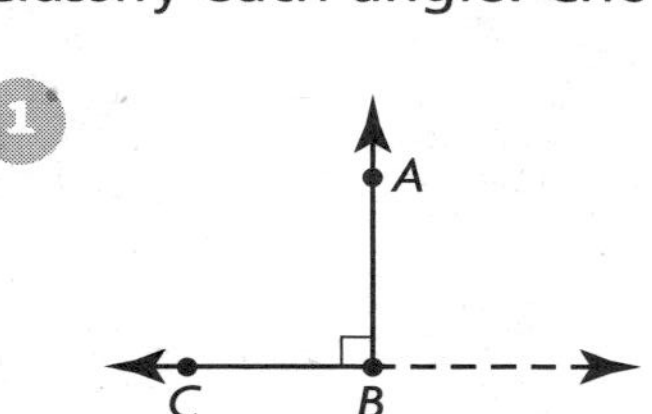

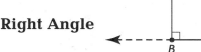

2
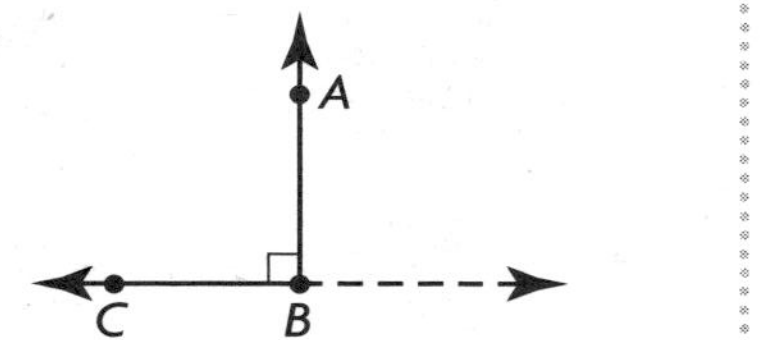

3

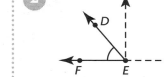

4
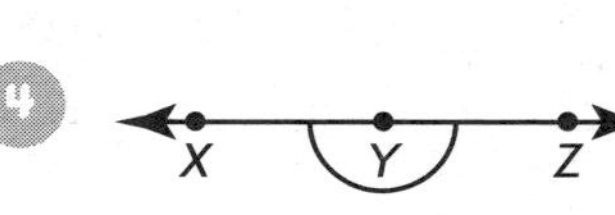

Go to the next side.

Name ______________________ Skill ______________________

Practice on Your Own

Skill 74

Think:
Classify an angle by comparing it to a right angle.

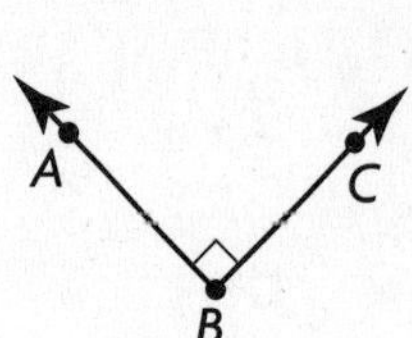

right angle

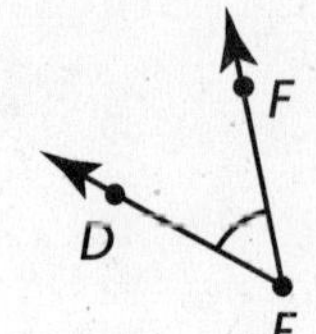

acute angle

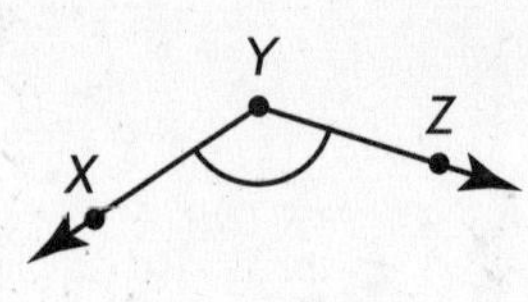

obtuse angle

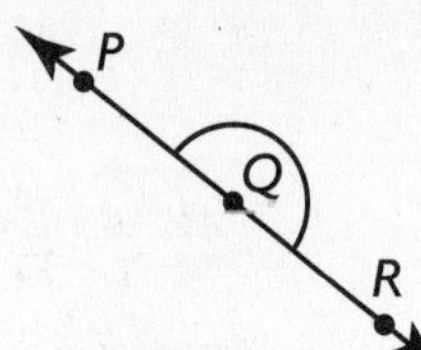

straight angle

Classify each angle. Choose *right, acute, obtuse, or straight angle.*

1. 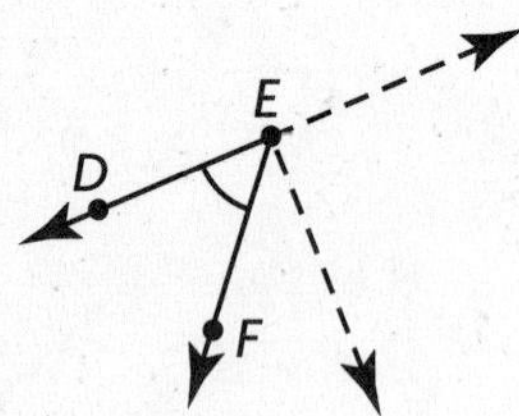

____

2. 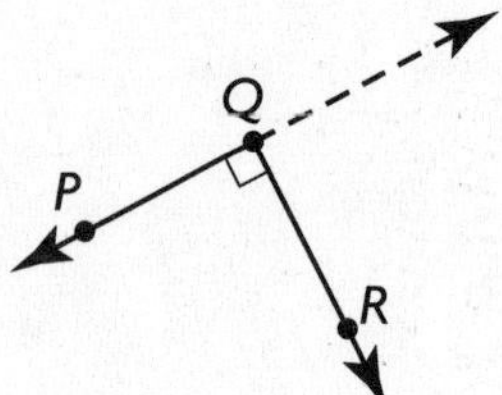

____

3. 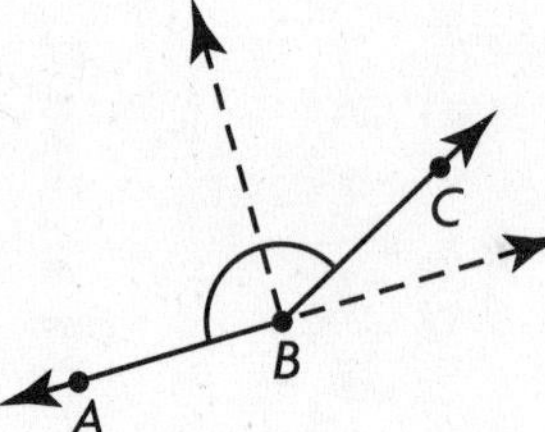

____

4. 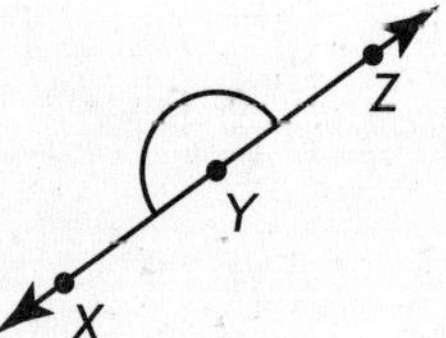

____

5. 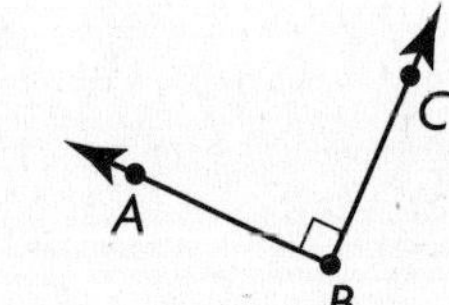

____

6. 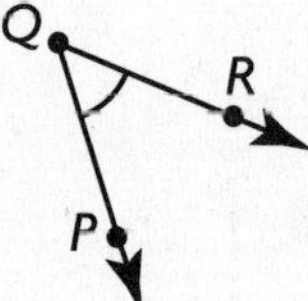

____

7. 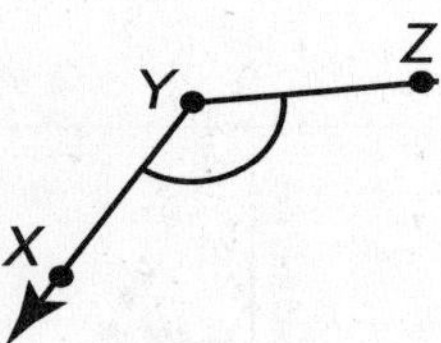

____

8. 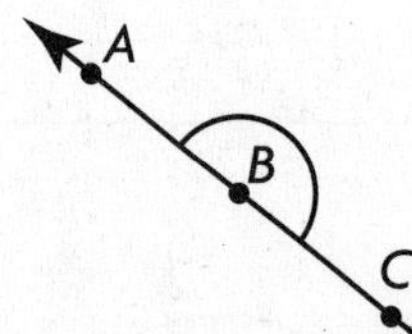

____

9. 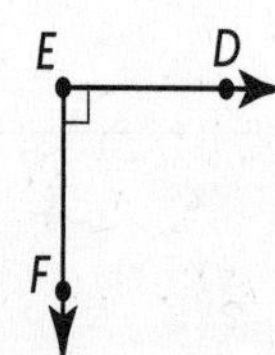

____

Check

Classify each angle. Choose *right, acute, obtuse, or straight angle.*

10. 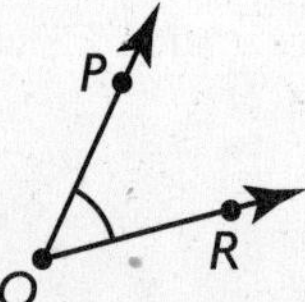

____

11. 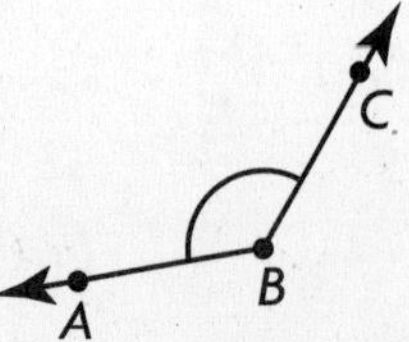

____

12. 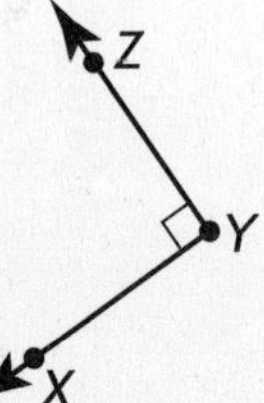

____

Name Angles

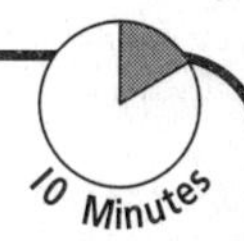

Using Skill 75

OBJECTIVE Name angles using letters and numbers

Begin by equating the *vertex* with the *endpoint* shared by two rays forming an angle. Have students read through the introduction to Skill 75. Then direct their attention to the angle shown in Example A. Ask: **How is this angle different from ∠*PNM*?** (The angle opens down; the angle is labeled with different letters.) **How many points do you see labeled on the angle?** (3) **How are these points labeled?** (Possible response: with the letters *A*, *B*, *C*)

Point out that the angle is formed by 2 rays, $\overrightarrow{BA}$ and $\overrightarrow{BC}$. Ask: **Where do the rays meet?** (at point *B*)

Emphasize that this endpoint is called the **vertex.**

Review two possible names for this angle, using all labeled points: ∠*ABC* or ∠*CBA*. Ask: **Why is Point *B* in the middle?** (*B* is the common endpoint; you have to list the points in order.) **If you name this angle using only one point, which point do you use, and why?** (Point *B* because that is the vertex.)

In Example B, point out that the angle is labeled on the inside.

In Example C, have students explain why *F* is not included in the name of ∠*EDG*. Ask: **Is ray *DF* a part of ∠*EDG*?** (no)

TRY THESE In Exercises 1–3 students name angles.

- **Exercise 1** Use 3 points to name an angle.
- **Exercise 2** Use one letter to name an angle.
- **Exercise 3** Use 3 points to isolate and name an angle.

PRACTICE ON YOUR OWN Review the example at the top of the page. Have students identify the vertex of the first and third angles. Have them explain why they cannot name the vertex of the angle in the last example.

CHECK Determine if students can distinguish and name an angle according to the points labeled.

Success is indicated by 3 out of 3 correct responses.

Students who successfully complete the **Practice on Your Own** and **Check** are ready to move to the next skill.

COMMON ERRORS

- Students may list the points of the angle with the vertex first.
- Students may try to name an angle by its vertex when there are multiple angles sharing that vertex.
- Students may become confused by certain orientations of an angle.

Students who made more than 2 errors in the **Practice on Your Own**, or who were not successful in the **Check** section, may benefit from the **Alternative Teaching Strategy** on the next page.

Optional

Alternative Teaching Strategy
Modeling Naming Angles

OBJECTIVE Use a model to make and name angles

MATERIALS 2 pieces of rope or string

Select three students to become "points" on an angle. Give two students each a long piece of string. Then have another student take hold of the two strings to form a vertex. Have the student in the middle stand still, while the other two hold onto their ends and walk away to stretch out the string and create an angle.

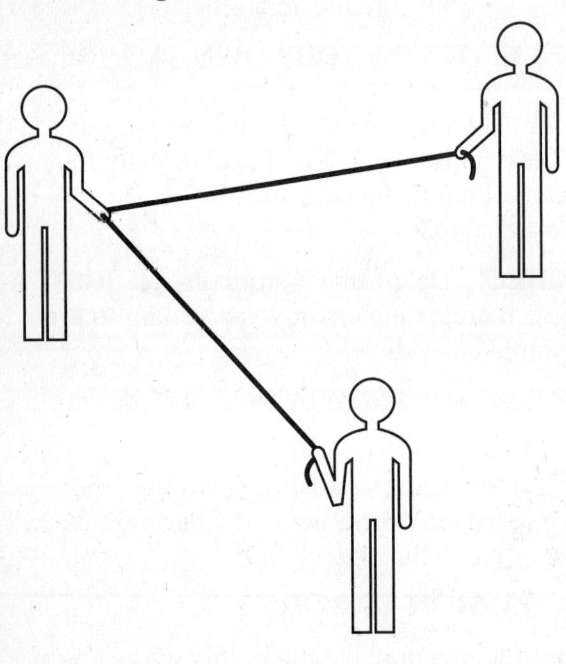

Ask:
What part of the angle does the person in the middle represent? (the vertex)
What does the string between the middle person and one person on the end represent? (a ray)

How many rays does an angle have? (2)

How many ways can we name the angle? (3)

Use the students' names to name the angle. For example, if Pat, Al, and Joel are the three students holding the string, the names for the angle would be Pat-Al-Joel, Joel-Al-Pat, and Al.

Select four students to form two adjacent angles. Have the students identify who is the vertex and distinguish the three different angles they have formed.

Repeat this activity with similar examples. When students show understanding, have them try an exercise using paper and pencil.

Name Angles

Skill 75

Angles are named by three letters:

- In the angle at the right, the vertex is N.
- On one side is a point labeled M.
  On the other side, a point is labeled P.

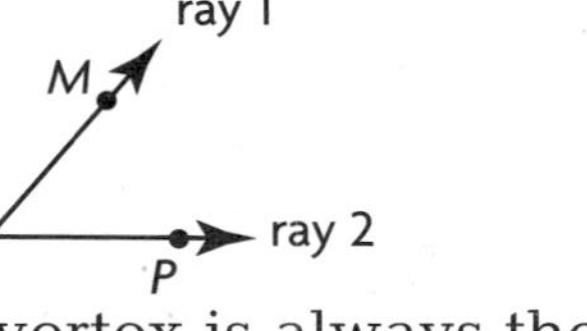

So, the angle can be named $\angle MNP$ or $\angle PNM$. The vertex is always the middle letter.
The symbol for angle is $\angle$. The angle can also be named using only the vertex. **So,** the angle can be named $\angle N$.

Example A

Name the angle three ways.

$\angle ABC$, $\angle CBA$, or $\angle B$

Example B

Name the angle formed by the dashed rays.

The dashed rays form $\angle a$.

Example C

Name the angle formed by the dashed rays two ways.

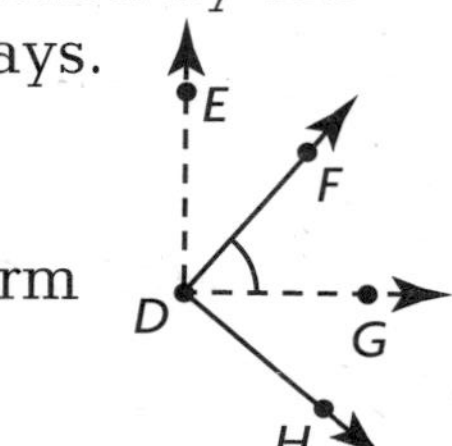

The dashed rays form $\angle EDG$ or $\angle GDE$.

Try These

Name the angle formed by dashed rays.

1. 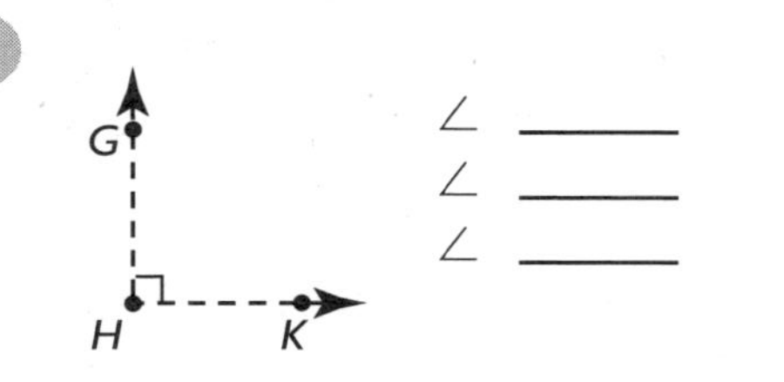

$\angle$ ______
$\angle$ ______
$\angle$ ______

2. 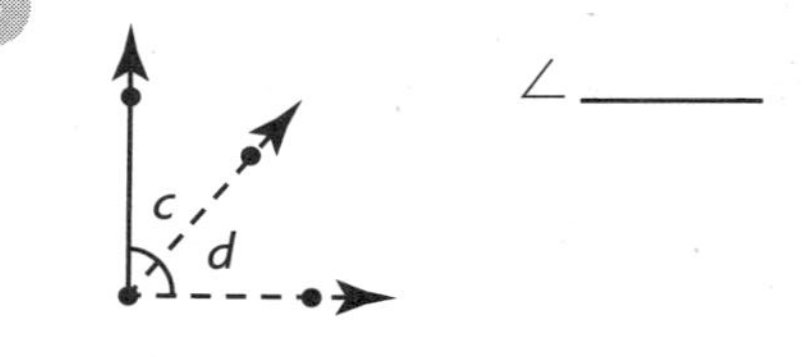

$\angle$ ______

3. 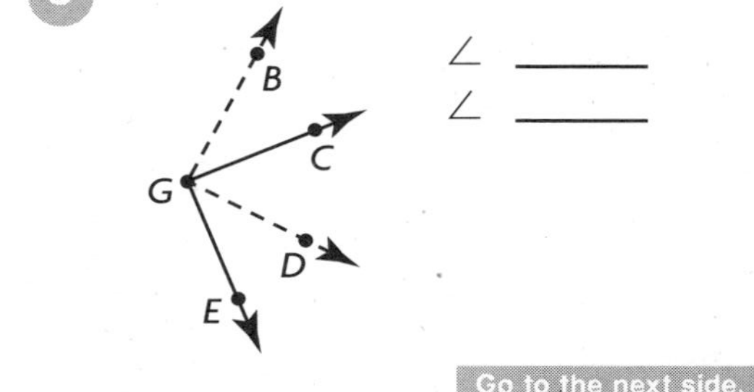

$\angle$ ______
$\angle$ ______

Go to the next side.

Name ______________________ Skill ______________________

Practice on Your Own

Skill 75

Think:

Use the vertex to name the angle.

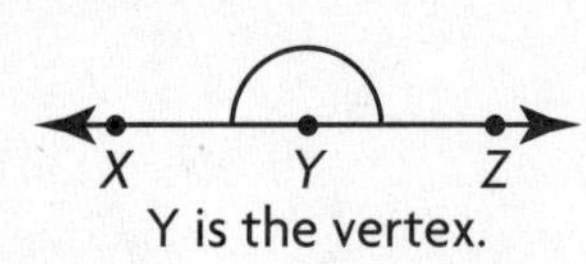

Name the angle formed by dashed rays.

∠ means angle

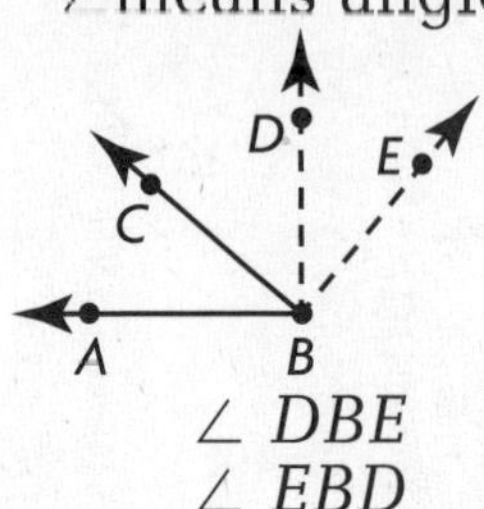

There are no points on the rays.
The angles are named by number.

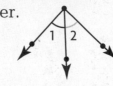

∠ 2

Name the angle formed by the dashed rays.

1. 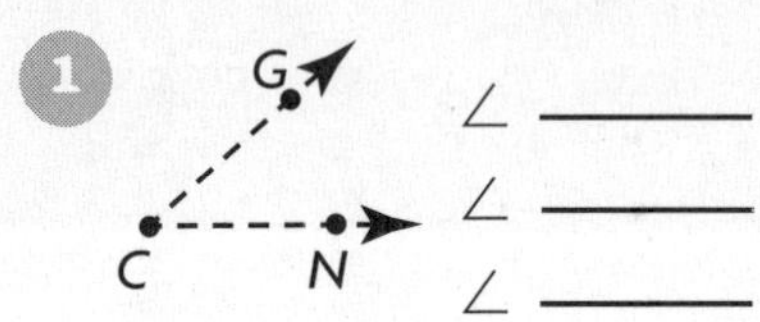

∠ ______
∠ ______
∠ ______

2. 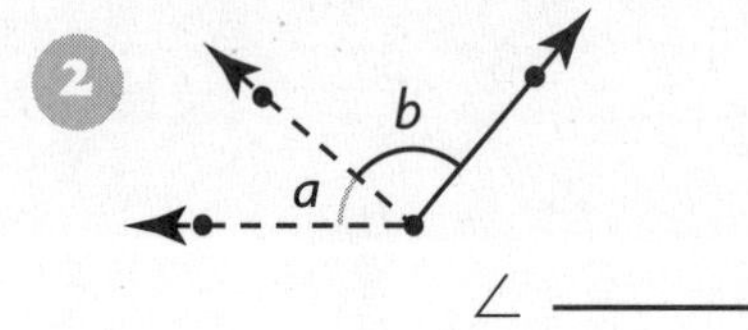

∠ ______

3. 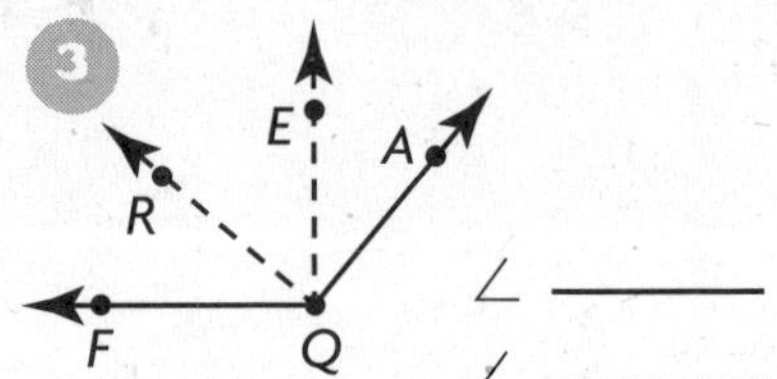

∠ ______
∠ ______

4. 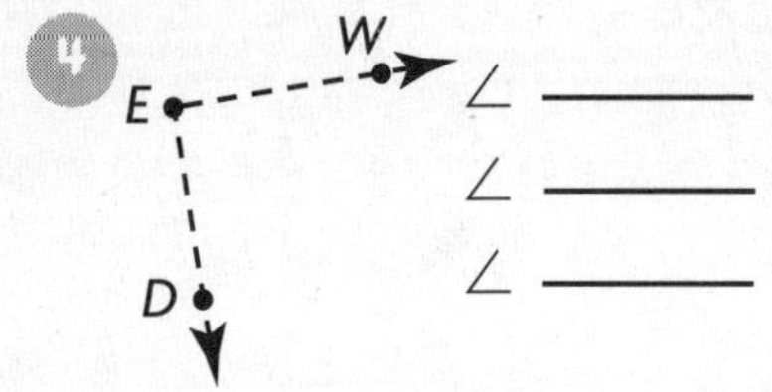

∠ ______
∠ ______
∠ ______

5. 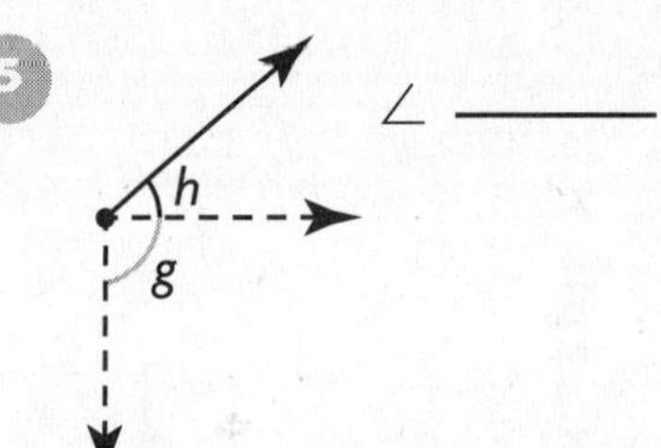

∠ ______

6. 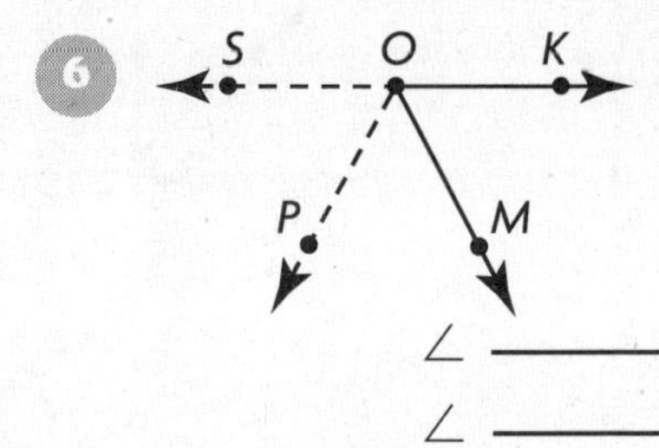

∠ ______
∠ ______

7. 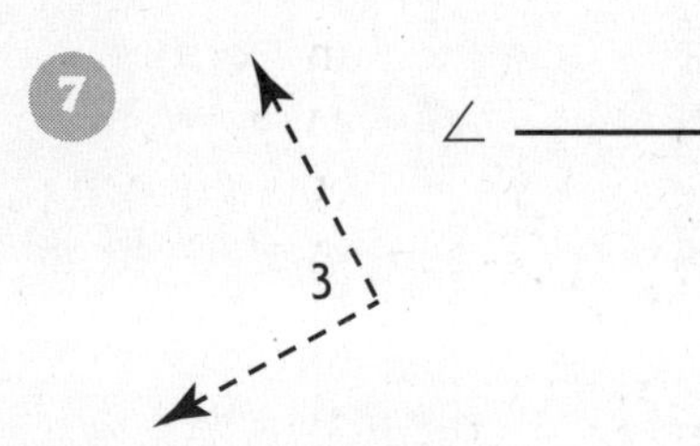

∠ ______

8. 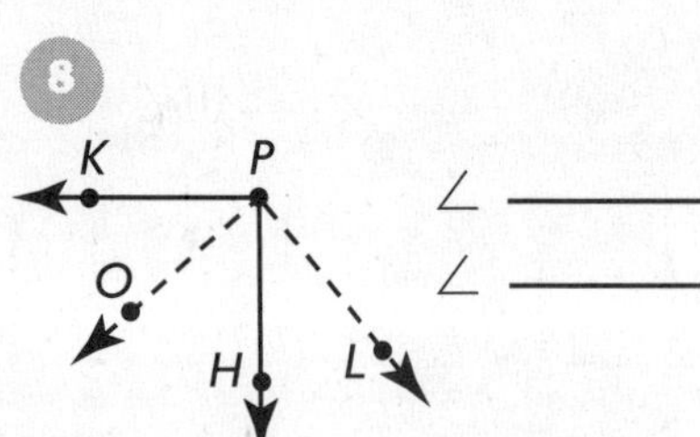

∠ ______
∠ ______

9. 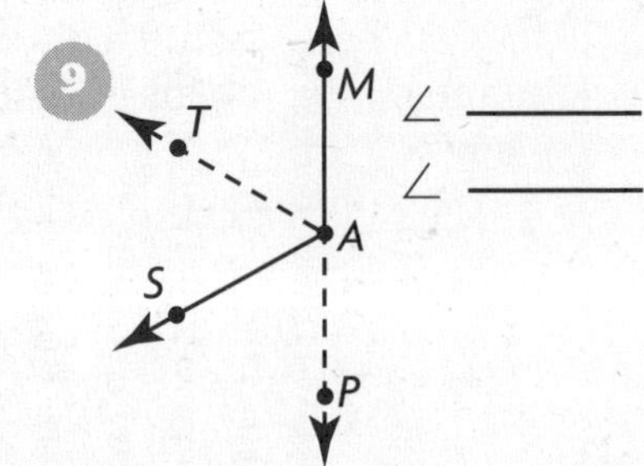

∠ ______
∠ ______

Check

Name the angle formed by the dashed rays.

10. 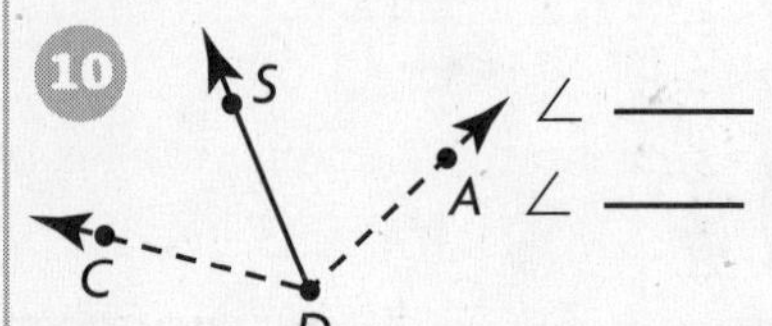

∠ ______
∠ ______

11. 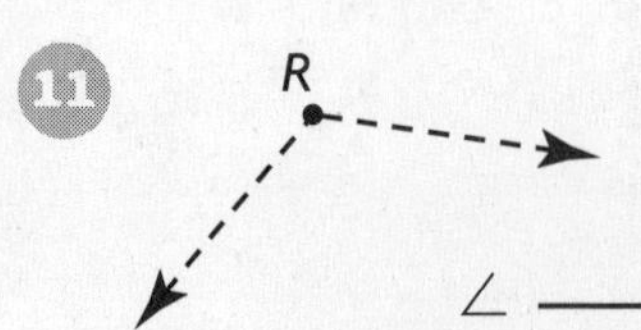

∠ ______

12. 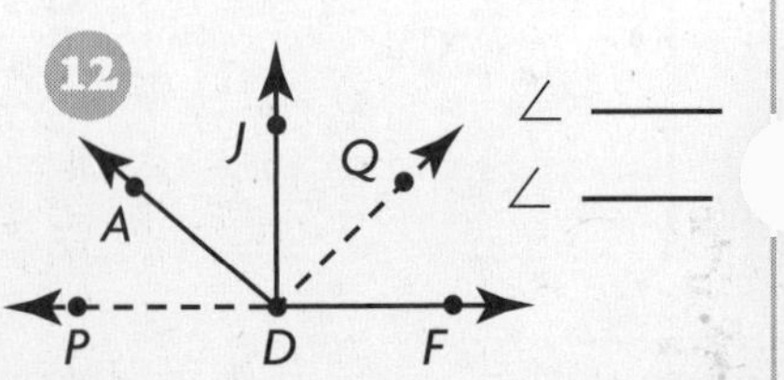

∠ ______
∠ ______

Skill 76 Identify Polygons

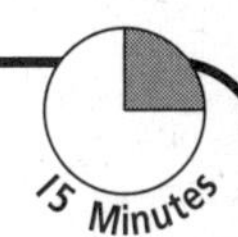

Using Skill 76

OBJECTIVE Name a polygon by the number of its sides and angles

Review the definition of a *polygon* and then direct students' attention to the example for *Triangles*. Ask: **How many sides do all of the triangles have?** (3) **How many angles do all of the triangles have?** (3)

Have students contrast the isosceles, scalene, and equilateral triangles and tell the lengths of the sides of each triangle. Ask: **What do you call a triangle that has all three sides the same length?** (an *equilateral* triangle) **What do you call a triangle that has just two sides the same length?** (an *isosceles* triangle) **How is a scalene triangle different from an equilateral or isosceles triangle?** (A *scalene* triangle has *no* sides of equal length.)

As you work through the descriptions of the other triangles, have students identify each type of angle in the triangles.

In *Quadrilaterals,* point out the right angles and the congruent sides.

When reviewing the last three polygons, students should make note of the number of sides. Emphasize the meaning of root words to help students remember the names: *gon,* means angle; *penta-* means 5, *hexa*-6, and *octa*-8. Have students count the number of angles in each polygon and compare it to the number of sides. Ask: **Does each polygon have the same number of angles as it does sides?** (yes)

PRACTICE ON YOUR OWN As students review the example at the top of the page, have them identify the properties that give each polygon its name.

CHECK Determine if the students can identify a square or rhombus, an isosceles triangle, a rectangle, and a parallelogram.

Success is indicated by 4 out of 4 correct responses.

Students who successfully complete the **Practice on Your Own** and **Check** are ready to move to the next skill.

COMMON ERRORS

- Students may label a parallelogram without right angles as a rectangle.
- Students may label a right triangle as an acute triangle.
- Students may label a rhombus as a square or trapezoid, or a trapezoid as a parallelogram.
- Students may not recognize non-regular polygons.

Students who made more than 3 errors in the **Practice on Your Own**, or who were not successful in the **Check** section, may benefit from the **Alternative Teaching Strategy** on the next page.

Optional

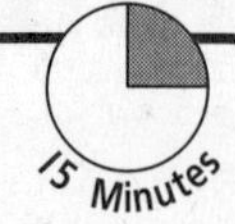

Alternative Teaching Strategy
Use Models to Identify Polygons

OBJECTIVE Use models to distinguish and name each polygon by its properties

MATERIALS index card, models of polygons: triangles, quadrilaterals, pentagons, hexagons, and octagons

Distribute models to students and have them sort the polygons by the number of sides. Ask:

How many groups do you have? (5)

How many sides do the figures in each group have? (3, 4, 5, 6, 8)

Have students point to the group of triangles. Ask them to sort the triangles by the lengths of the sides. If necessary have students use a ruler to measure the sides. Ask:

How many triangles have three congruent sides? (Answers will vary.)

Say:
This is an *equilateral* triangle. How many triangles have two congruent sides? (Answers will vary.)

Say:
This is an *isosceles* triangle. How many triangles have a different length on each side? (Answers will vary.)

Say:
This is a *scalene* triangle.

Emphasize that a triangle can be classified by its sides. A triangle with three congruent sides is equilateral. A triangle with two congruent sides is isosceles. A triangle with no congruent sides is scalene.

Next, have the students use the corner of an index card to classify the angles in some of the triangles.

Have them show you an example of a right angle, an obtuse angle, and an acute angle. Recall that the measure of an *acute* angle is less than the measure of a right angle, and the measure of an *obtuse* angle is greater than the measure of a right angle.

Repeat this activity using the other polygon models.

Have students state the name of each type of polygon.

Name ______________________ Skill ______________________

Skill 76

Identify Polygons

A **polygon** is a closed plane figure formed by three or more line segments. Polygons are named by the number of their sides and angles.

Remember:
A line segment is part of a line between two endpoints.

Triangles

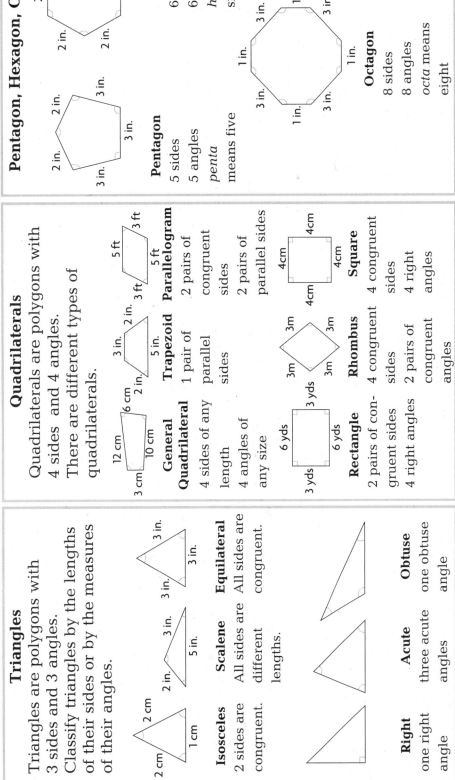

Triangles are polygons with 3 sides and 3 angles.
Classify triangles by the lengths of their sides or by the measures of their angles.

2 cm, 2 cm, 1 cm — 2 in., 3 in., 5 in. — 3 in., 3 in., 3 in.

Isosceles	**Scalene**	**Equilateral**
2 sides are congruent.	All sides are different lengths.	All sides are congruent.

Right	**Acute**	**Obtuse**
one right angle	three acute angles	one obtuse angle

Quadrilaterals

Quadrilaterals are polygons with 4 sides and 4 angles.
There are different types of quadrilaterals.

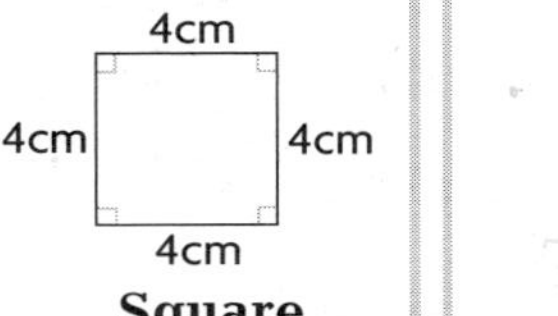
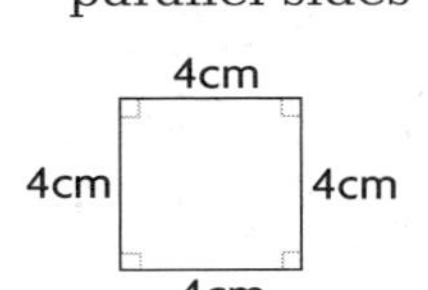
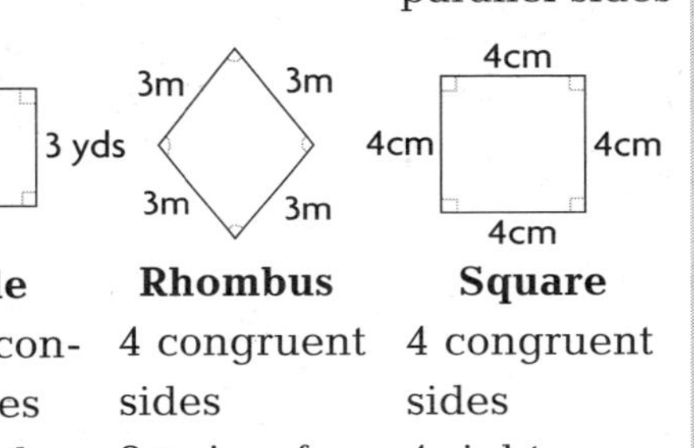
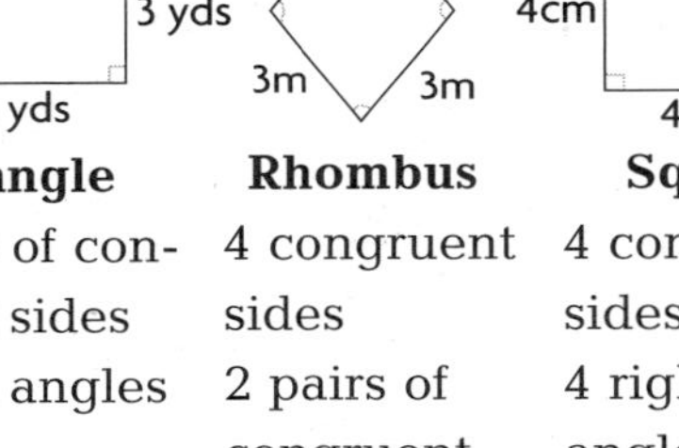

General Quadrilateral	**Trapezoid**	**Parallelogram**
4 sides of any length 4 angles of any size	1 pair of parallel sides	2 pairs of congruent sides 2 pairs of parallel sides

Rectangle	**Rhombus**	**Square**
2 pairs of congruent sides 4 right angles	4 congruent sides 2 pairs of congruent angles	4 congruent sides 4 right angles

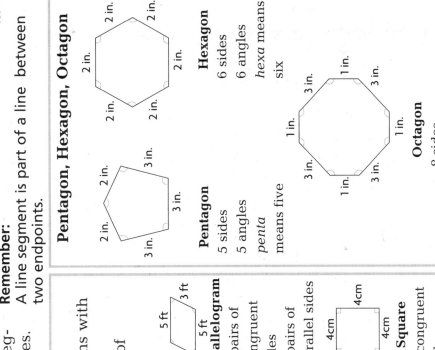

Pentagon, Hexagon, Octagon

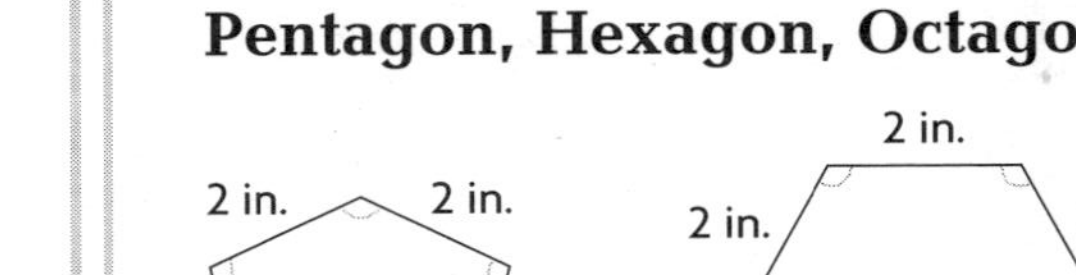

Pentagon
5 sides
5 angles
penta means five

Hexagon
6 sides
6 angles
hexa means six

Octagon
8 sides
8 angles
octa means eight

Go to the next side.

Name ______________________ Skill ______________________

Practice on Your Own

Skill 76

TRIANGLES			QUADRILATERALS				
isosceles	scalene	equilateral	general	trapezoid	parallelogram	pentagon	hexagon
right	acute	obtuse	rectangle	rhombus	square	octagon	

Name each triangle. Choose isosceles, equilateral, right, or obtuse triangle.

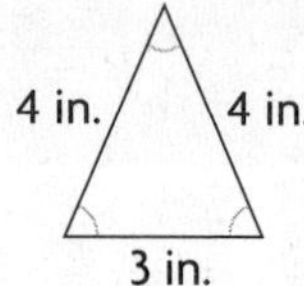

______

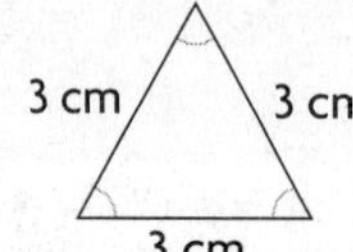

______

3
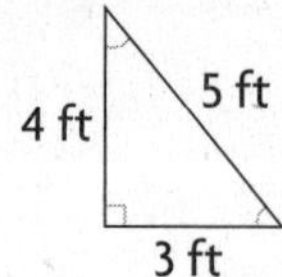

______

4
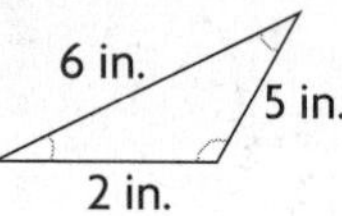

______

Name each quadrilateral. Choose parallelogram, rectangle, rhombus, or trapezoid.

5
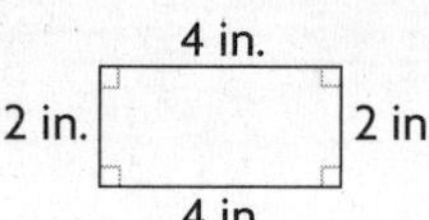

______

6
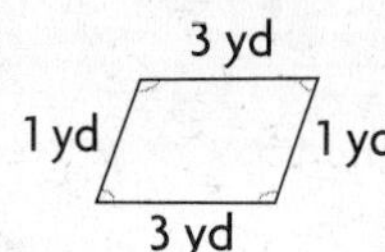

______

7
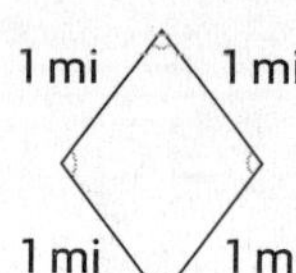

______

8 1 in. 3 in. 5 in. 1 in.

______

Name each figure.

9 5 in. 3 in. 3 in. 4 in. 4 in.

______

10 2 in. 3 in. 3 in. 3 in. 3 in. 2 in.

______

11 1 in. 1 in. 1 in. 1 in. 1 in. 1 in. 1 in. 1 in.

______

12
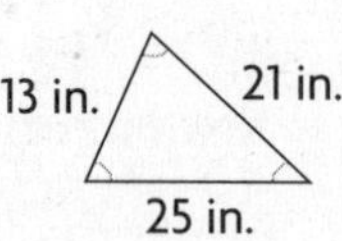

______

Check

Name each figure.

13
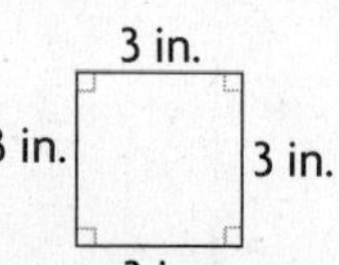

______

14 5 in. 5 in. 8 in.

______

15
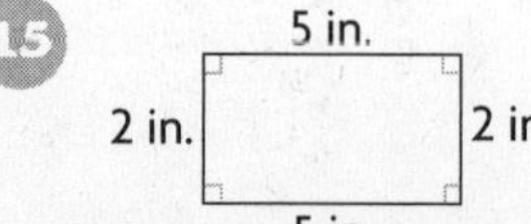

______

16 5 in. 2 in. 2 in. 5 in.

______

Skill 77 Angles in Polygons

Using Skill 77

OBJECTIVE Name and classify angles in polygons as right, acute, or obtuse

Discuss the meanings of *line, line segment,* and *ray.* Remind students that a line goes on forever in both directions; it has no endpoints. A line segment is part of a line; it has two endpoints. A ray is also part of a line; but, it has one endpoint.

Read the material about angles and polygons at the top of the page. Ask: **How is an angle formed?** (by two rays that have the same endpoint) **What is a polygon?** (a closed plane figure formed by three or more line segments) Define a plane as a flat surface that has no end. Look at one of the angles of the polygon. **What do you call the point at which two sides of a polygon meet?** (vertex)

Have students name the rays that make up angle *E*. Then review the three names for the angle.

Direct students' attention to the rectangle. Have them name the line segments that form it. Then have them name the right angles. Ask: **How many sides does a rectangle have?** (4) **How many vertices does it have?** (4) **Does it have the same number of sides and angles?** (yes)

Read about triangles, pentagons, and trapezoids. In each example, relate the number of sides to the number of angles in the polygon. Ask: **What do you call an angle whose measure is less than a right angle?** (acute angle) **What do you call an angle whose measure is greater than a right angle?** (obtuse angle)

TRY THESE Exercises 1–3 provide practice in naming and classifying angles in polygons.

- **Exercises 1 and 2** Name angles
- **Exercise 3** Classify angles

PRACTICE ON YOUR OWN Focus on the trapezoid at the top of the page. Be sure students are aware that the middle letter in the name of an angle names the vertex.

CHECK Determine that students understand the differences among right, acute, and obtuse angles. Success is indicated by 3 out of 3 correct responses.

Students who successfully complete the **Practice on Your Own** and **Check** are ready to move to the next skill.

COMMON ERRORS

- Students may confuse obtuse and acute angles.
- When naming an angle, students may not write the letter of the vertex in the middle.

Students who made more than 2 errors in the **Practice on Your Own**, or who were not successful in the **Check** section, may benefit from the **Alternative Teaching Strategy** on the next page.

Optional

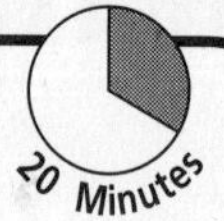

Alternative Teaching Strategy
Angles in Polygons

OBJECTIVE Name and classify angles in polygons as right, acute, or obtuse

MATERIALS index cards

Ask: **Does a line end?** (No. It goes on forever in both directions.) Draw a representation of a line, with arrowheads on the ends. Label points *A* and *B*. Use dashes to mark ray *AB*. Ask: **How many endpoints does ray *AB* have?** (one) Draw another ray, $\overrightarrow{AC}$. Point to the angle formed. Help students name the angle three ways, as angle *A*, angle *CAB*, and angle *BAC*.

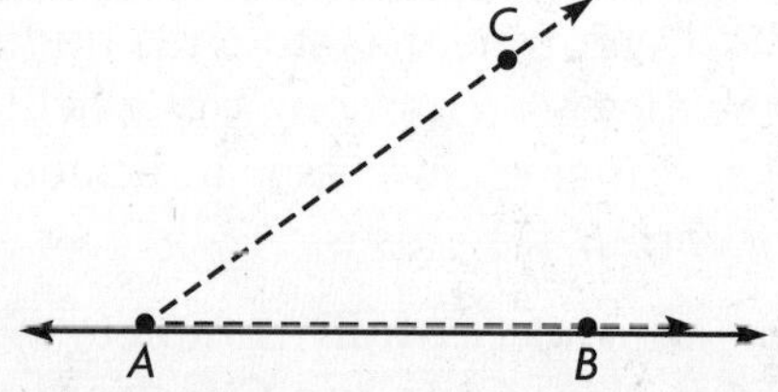

Draw line segment *DE*. Ask: **How many endpoints does line segment *DE* have?** (two) Draw two more line segments so that they form triangle *DEF*. Ask: **How many sides does this figure have?** (3) Have students name the line segments that form the triangle. (line segments *DE*, *EF*, and *FD*)

Ask: **How many angles does this figure have?** (3) **What do you think *tri-* means?** (3)

Have students use three letters to name each angle. (angles *FDE*, *DEF*, *EFD*) Ask: **What does the middle letter of each angle name?** (vertex) Relate the number of sides to the number of angles in the triangle.

Show students how use an index card to determine whether an angle is right, acute, or obtuse.

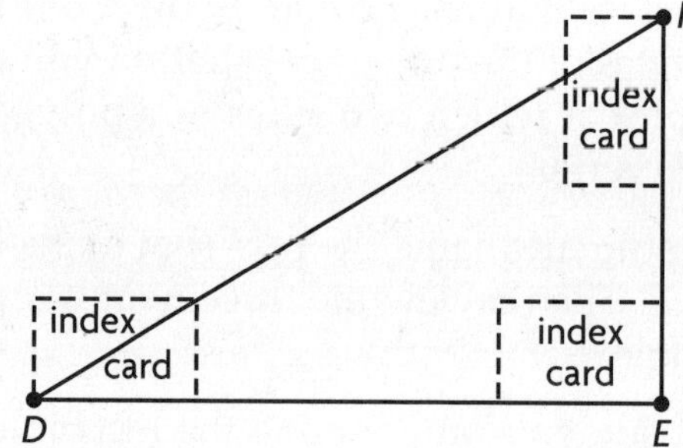

Finally, have students describe the angles in this triangle. (one right angle, two acute angles)

Repeat this activity with an obtuse triangle, a square, and a parallelogram.

Name ______________________ Skill ______________________

Skill 77

Angles in Polygons

Remember: An angle is formed by two rays that have the same endpoint. A polygon is a closed plane figure formed by three or more line segments. Angles are formed at the point where the line segments meet. This point is called the vertex.

Write: $\angle FED$ $\angle DEF$ $\angle E$
Read: angle *FED* angle *DEF* angle *E*

Example A
The rectangle has four angles:
$\angle ABC$, $\angle BCD$, $\angle CDA$, and $\angle DAB$.
All the angles are *right* angles.

Example B
The triangle has three angles:
$\angle JKL$, $\angle KLJ$, $\angle LJK$.
$\angle JKL$ is a right angle.
$\angle KLJ$ and $\angle LJK$ are both smaller than a right angle.
So, they are both *acute* angles.

Example C
The pentagon has five angles:
$\angle RMN$, $\angle MNP$, $\angle NPQ$,
$\angle PQR$, $\angle QRM$.
All the angles are **greater than** a right angle.
So, all the angles are *obtuse* angles.

Example D
The trapezoid has four angles.
$\angle VST$, $\angle STU$, $\angle TUV$, $\angle UVS$.
$\angle VST$ and $\angle STU$ are both larger than a right angle. Both are obtuse angles.
$\angle TUV$ and $\angle UVS$ are both smaller than a right angle. Both are acute angles.

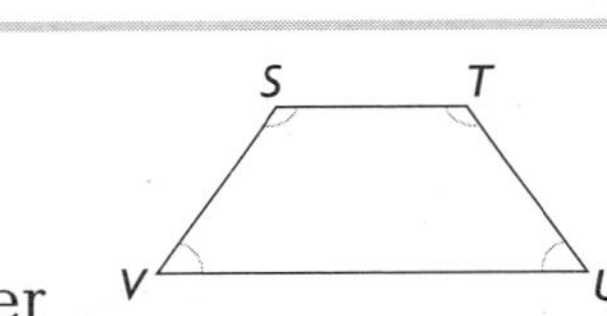

Try These

Name all the angles in each figure. Classify each angle as *right*, *acute*, or *obtuse*.

1. $\angle$ ______
$\angle$ ______
$\angle$ ______
$\angle$ ______

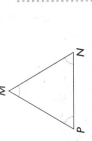

2. $\angle$ ______
$\angle$ ______
$\angle$ ______

3. $\angle WXY$ ______
$\angle XYZ$ ______
$\angle YZW$ ______
$\angle ZWX$ ______

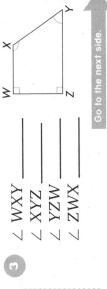

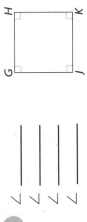

Go to the next side.

Name ______________________ Skill ______________________

Practice on Your Own

Skill 77

Think:
Use three letters to name an angle. The middle letter names the vertex.

There are four angles in the trapezoid. $\angle NPL$ and $\angle PLM$ are obtuse angles. $\angle LMN$ and $\angle MNP$ are acute angles.

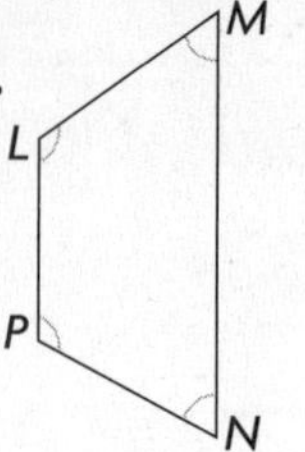

Name all the angles in each figure.

1. 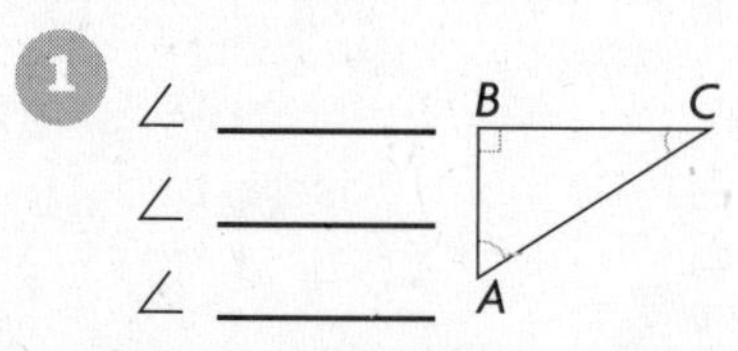

$\angle$ ______
$\angle$ ______
$\angle$ ______

2. 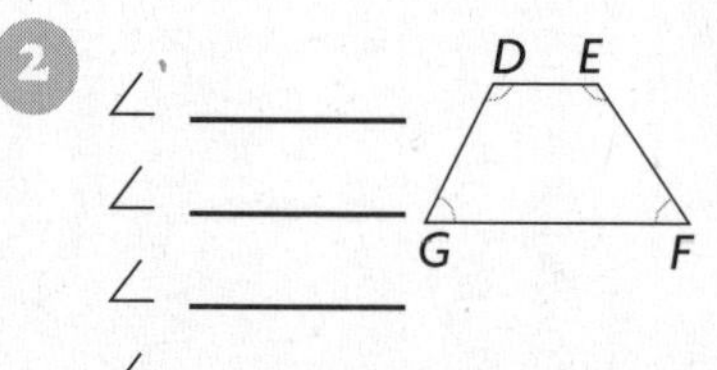

$\angle$ ______
$\angle$ ______
$\angle$ ______
$\angle$ ______

3. 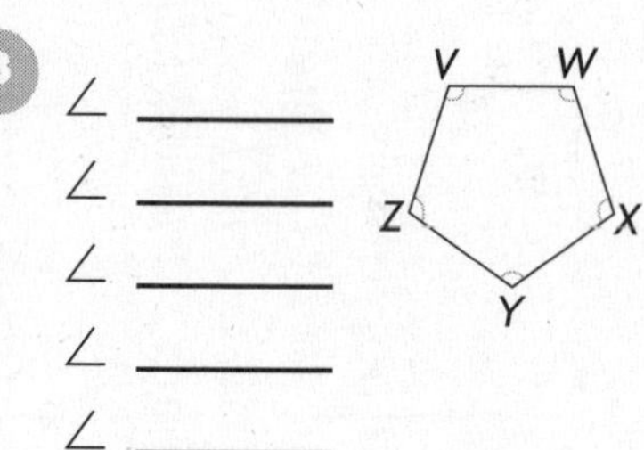

$\angle$ ______
$\angle$ ______
$\angle$ ______
$\angle$ ______
$\angle$ ______

Classify each angle as *right*, *acute*, or *obtuse*.

4. 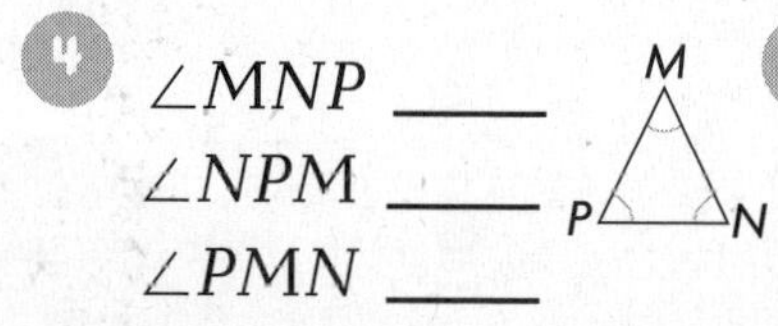

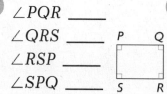

$\angle MNP$ ______
$\angle NPM$ ______
$\angle PMN$ ______

5. $\angle PQR$ ______
$\angle QRS$ ______
$\angle RSP$ ______
$\angle SPQ$ ______

6. 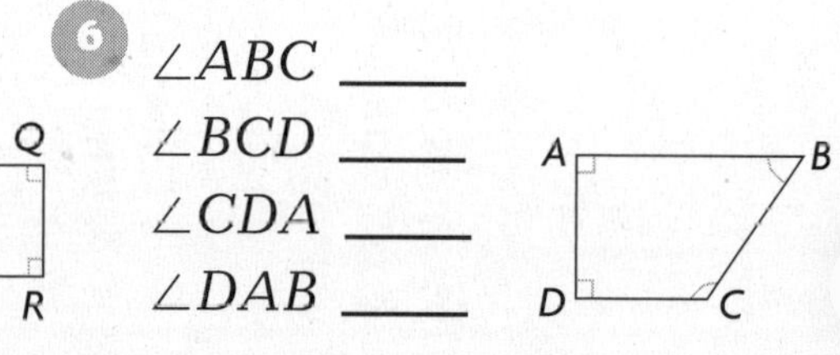

$\angle ABC$ ______
$\angle BCD$ ______
$\angle CDA$ ______
$\angle DAB$ ______

Name each angle in the polygon. Tell whether it is *right*, *acute*, or *obtuse*.

7. 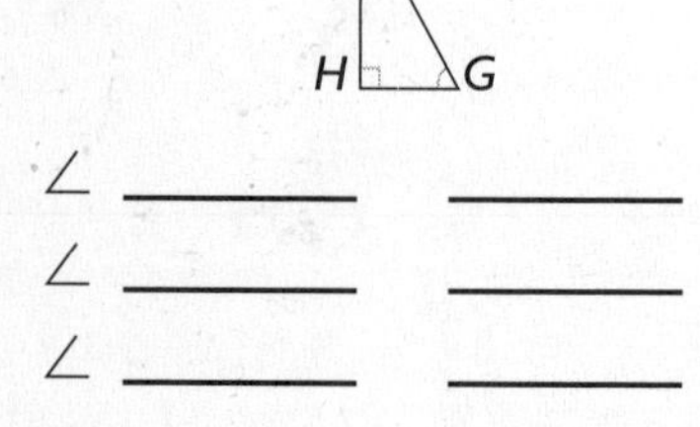

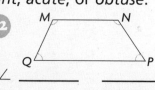

$\angle$ ______ ______
$\angle$ ______ ______
$\angle$ ______ ______

8. 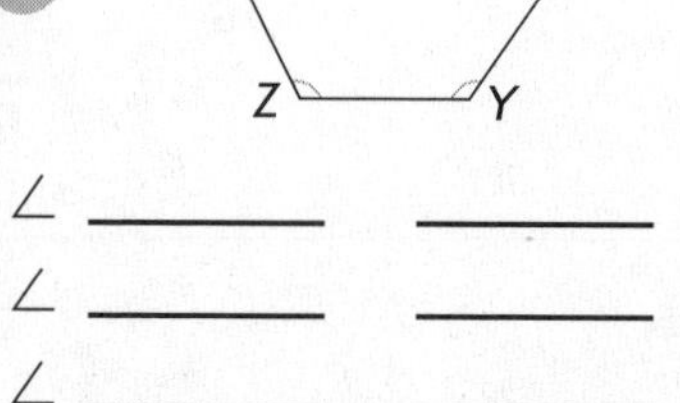

$\angle$ ______ ______
$\angle$ ______ ______
$\angle$ ______ ______
$\angle$ ______ ______

9. 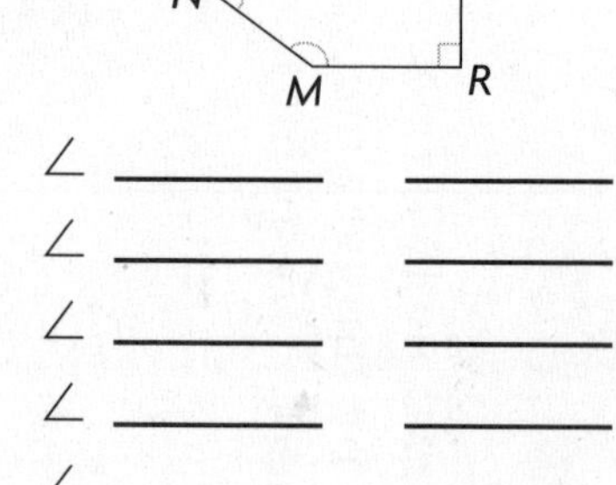

$\angle$ ______ ______
$\angle$ ______ ______
$\angle$ ______ ______
$\angle$ ______ ______
$\angle$ ______ ______

Name each angle in the polygon. Tell whether it is *right*, *acute*, or *obtuse*.

10. 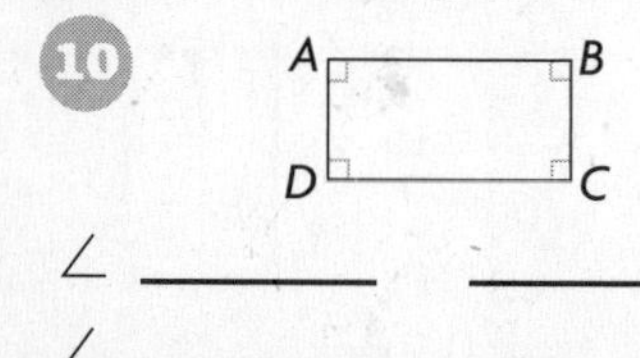

$\angle$ ______ ______
$\angle$ ______ ______
$\angle$ ______ ______
$\angle$ ______ ______

11. 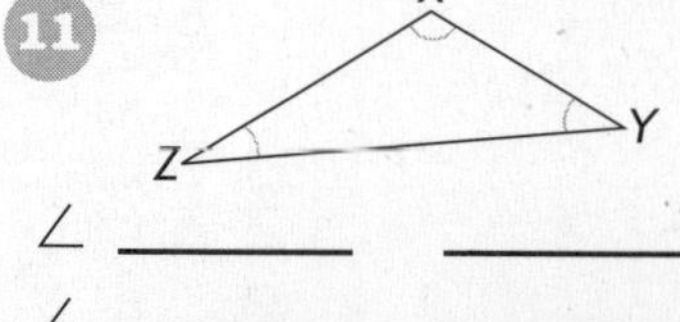

$\angle$ ______ ______
$\angle$ ______ ______
$\angle$ ______ ______

12. $\angle$ ______ ______
$\angle$ ______ ______
$\angle$ ______ ______
$\angle$ ______ ______

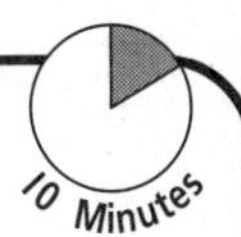

Using Skill 78

OBJECTIVE Identify solid figures: prisms, pyramids, and solid figures with curved surfaces

Begin by reading the definition of *polyhedron* at the top of Skill 78. Have students recall the definition of a *polygon.* Then have students look at the *prisms,* and point to and name the polygon–shaped faces.

Help students recognized key attributes of *prisms.* Ask: **What do all of the prisms have in common?** (All of the faces are polygons and the two bases are parallel to each other.)

Stress that the name for a prism is taken from the shape of its bases and that all of the other faces are rectangles.

Now have students look at the *pyramids.* Ask: **What do all of the pyramids have in common?** (All of the faces are polygons and there is one base. The other faces are triangles.)

Stress that the name for a pyramid is taken from the shape of its base and that the triangular faces of a pyramid always meet at a common vertex.

In the example of *Curved Surfaces,* have students point out the curved surface for each figure and ask: **Why are the solid figures with curved surfaces not polyhedrons?** (A polyhedron has faces that are polygons and the curved shape is not a polygon.) **Is a cylinder a prism? Why or why not?** (No; a cylinder has 2 parallel, congruent bases, but those bases are not polygons.)

PRACTICE ON YOUR OWN Review the example at the top of the page. Have students distinguish polyhedrons from figures with curved surfaces, and then point to and name the polygon-shaped base(s) of each polyhedron.

CHECK Determine if the students can identify solid figures. Success is indicated by 4 out of 4 correct responses.

Students who successfully complete the **Practice on Your Own** and **Check** are ready to move to the next skill.

COMMON ERRORS

- Students may not be able to distinguish between prisms and pyramids.

Students who made more than 3 errors in the **Practice on Your Own**, or who were not successful in the **Check** section, may benefit from the **Alternative Teaching Strategy** on the next page.

Optional

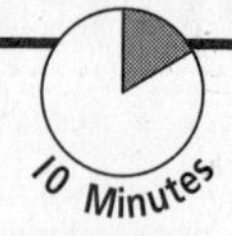

Alternative Teaching Strategy
Model Identifying Solid Figures

OBJECTIVE Use models to identify prisms and pyramids

MATERIALS solid figures

Students who have difficulty distinguishing between prisms and pyramids will benefit by closely examining the solid figures and comparing their attributes. As you begin the lesson, list the following:

Prism

1. There are **two** congruent bases.
2. The bases are polygons.
3. Other faces are **rectangles.**

Review the list with the students, and then hold up a triangular prism. Point to the congruent bases, and ask:

How many bases does this solid figure have? (two)

Are the bases polygons? (yes) **What are the bases?** (triangles)

What are the other faces in the figure? (rectangles) **Is it a prism?** (yes)

Guide students as they recognize that it is a triangular prism because its bases are triangles.

Have students examine and name other prisms, using the list as a guide.

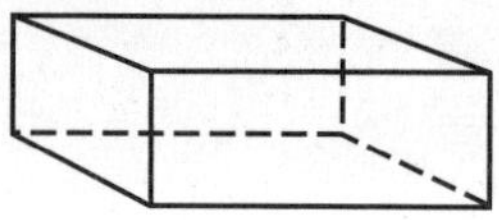

Then display this list:

Pyramid

1. There is **one** base.
2. The base is a polygon.
3. Other faces are **triangles.**
4. The other faces meet at a common vertex.

Hold up a square pyramid, and examine it as students check the statements on the list. Ask:

How many bases does the solid figure have? (one)

Is the base a polygon? (yes) **What is the base?** (square)

Continue to rotate the square pyramid and pause to have students identify each face.

What are all the other faces? (triangles) **Do they meet at a common vertex?** (yes)

Is it a prism or a pyramid? (pyramid)

If the base is square, what is its name? (square pyramid)

Repeat the questions as students examine other pyramids. When students are able to identify prisms and pyramids easily, put the figures into a bag. Have them choose a solid figure and name it, telling why they named it as they did.

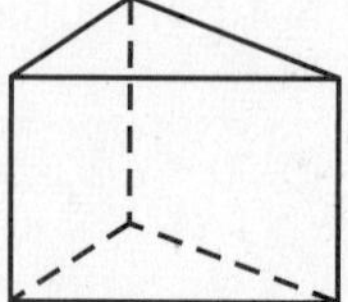

Skill 78

Identify Solid Figures

A **polyhedron** is a solid figure with faces that are polygons. Below are three types of solid figures: *prisms, pyramids*, and solids with *curved surfaces*.

Prism

A **prism** is a solid figure that has *two* congruent, polygon-shaped faces called **bases**.
All other faces of a prism are rectangles.

Base

Base

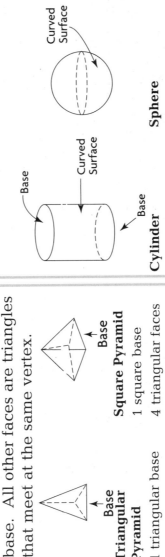

Triangular Prism
2 triangular bases
3 rectangular faces

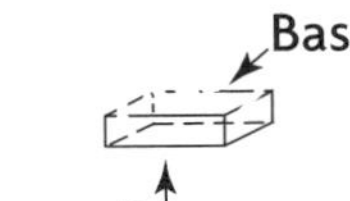
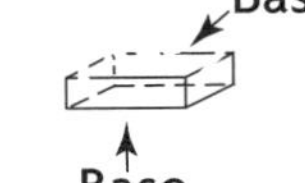

Rectangular Prism
2 rectangular bases
4 rectangular faces

Base

Base

Pentagonal Prism
2 pentagonal bases
5 rectangular faces

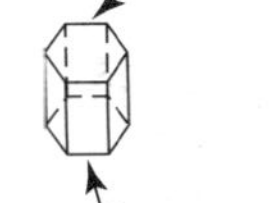

Hexagonal Prism
2 hexagonal bases
6 rectangular faces

Pyramid

A **pyramid** is a solid figure that has only *one* polygon-shaped base. All other faces are triangles that meet at the same vertex.

Base

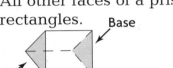

Triangular Pyramid
1 triangular base
3 triangular faces

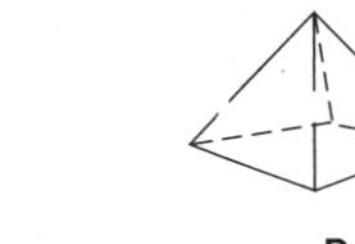

Square Pyramid
1 square base
4 triangular faces

Vertex

Base

Pentagonal Pyramid
1 pentagonal base
5 triangular faces

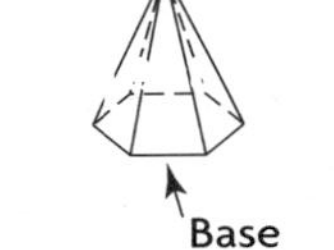

Hexagonal Pyramid
1 hexagonal base
6 triangular faces

Curved Surfaces

Solids with **curved surfaces** are **not** polyhedrons.

Base

Curved Surface

Base

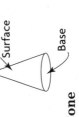

Cylinder
2 flat circular bases
1 curved surface

Curved Surface

Sphere
no flat bases
1 curved surface

Curved Surface

Base

Cone
1 flat circular base
1 curved surface

Go to the next side.

Name ______________________________ Skill ______________________

Practice on Your Own

Skill 78

Prisms

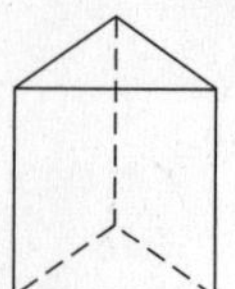
Triangular Prism

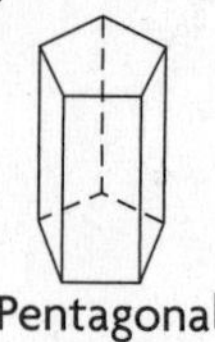
Pentagonal Prism

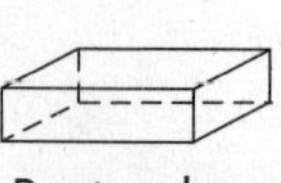
Rectagular Prism

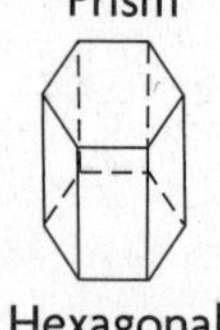
Hexagonal Prism

Pyramids

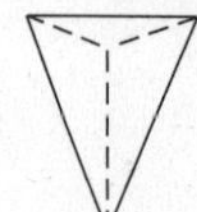
Triangular Pyramid

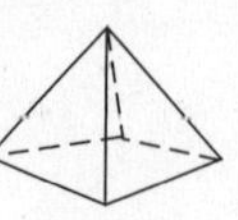
Square Pyramid

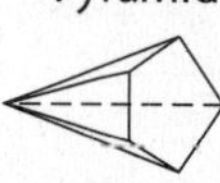
Pentagonal Pyramid

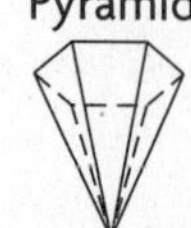
Hexagonal Pyramid

Curved Surfaces

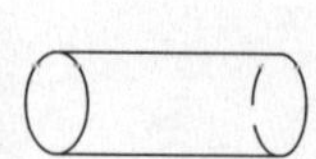
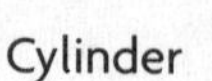
Cylinder

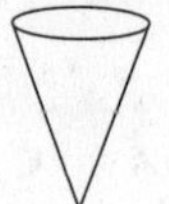
Cone

Sphere

Complete. Name each solid figure.

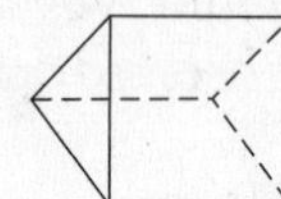

Number of bases ____
Shape of bases ______
Name of figure ______

2 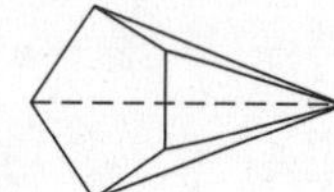

Number of bases ____
Shape of base ______
Name of figure ______

3 

Number of bases ____
Shape of bases ______
Name of figure ______

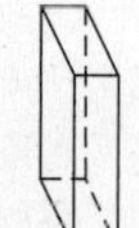

Number of bases ____
Shape of bases ______
Name of figure ______

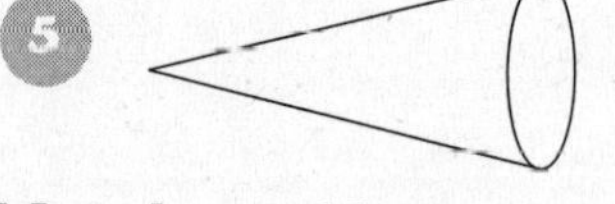

Number of bases ____
Shape of base ______
Name of figure ______

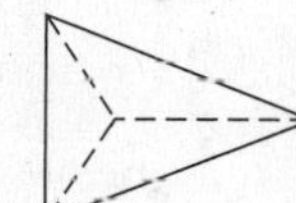

Number of bases ____
Shape of base ______
Name of figure ______

Name each solid figure.

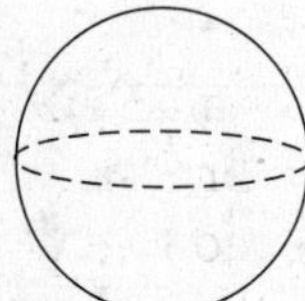
______

8 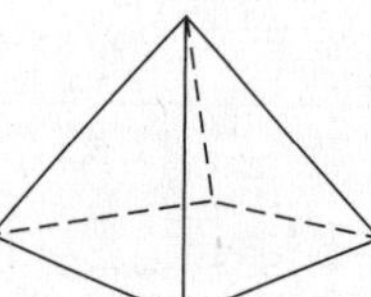
______

9 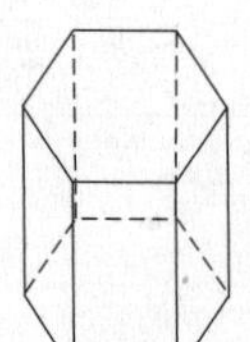
______

10 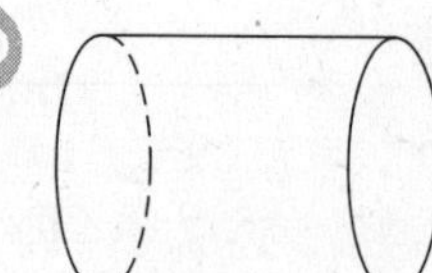
______

Check

Name each solid figure.

______

12 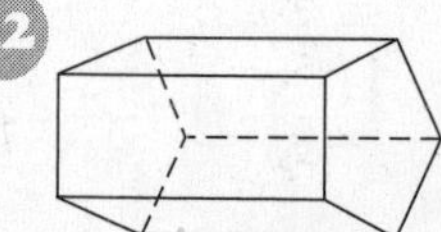
______

13 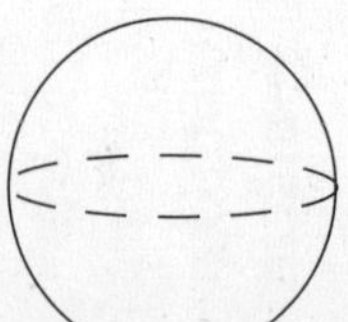
______

14 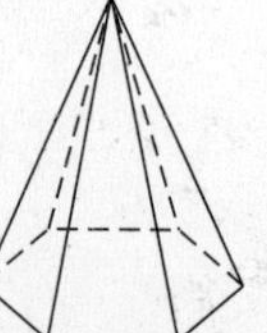
______

Skill 79 Faces, Edges, Vertices

Using Skill 79

OBJECTIVE Identify the faces, edges, and vertices on polyhedrons

MATERIALS triangular pyramid, rectangular prism

Have students read about faces, edges, and vertices at the top of Skill 79. Explain that they can find the number of faces, edges, and vertices on the rectangular prism and the triangular pyramid by counting them, or by using a formula. Ask: **How is a pyramid different from a prism?** (A prism has two congruent, parallel bases, and all its faces are rectangles; a pyramid has just one base and all the other faces are triangles.)

You may wish to demonstrate counting using the model or have students count using the picture. Have them count the faces, edges, and vertices for the rectangular prism and the triangular pyramid. Suggest they mark each part as they count it.

Direct the students' attention to the example for formulas. As students analyze the formulas for a prism, use the model to demonstrate that n is the number of sides of one base only. Then show how the formulas relate to the other parts of the prism.

Suggest that students compare the number of faces, edges, and vertices they found by counting to the number they found by using the formulas.

After students have examined the formulas for a pyramid and worked through the example, have them note that the formulas for prisms and pyramids are different. Suggest that first they identify whether the solid figure is a prism or pyramid, and then they can use the appropriate formulas.

PRACTICE ON YOUR OWN Review the examples at the top of the page. As students work through the two examples, have them identify each figure's base and the number of edges on that base. Relate that number to the value of n in the formula.

CHECK Determine if the students can find the number of faces, edges, and vertices on a polyhedron. Success is indicated by 3 out of 3 correct responses.

Students who successfully complete the **Practice on Your Own** and **Check** are ready to move to the next skill.

COMMON ERRORS

- Students may not identify the base correctly and thus use the wrong value for n in the formula.
- Students may use the wrong formula for a prism or pyramid.
- Students may not be able to visualize the parts of a 3-dimensional figure from a picture, and thus be unable to count the faces, edges, and vertices.

Students who made more than 2 errors in the **Practice on Your Own**, or who were not successful in the **Check** section, may benefit from the **Alternative Teaching Strategy** on the next page.

Optional

Alternative Teaching Strategy

20 Minutes

Use Models to Count Faces, Edges, Vertices

OBJECTIVE Model and count faces, edges, and vertices

MATERIALS straws, string, tape, construction paper

Have students construct a rectangular prism, count the faces, edges, and vertices, and record the numbers.

Using the straws as edges, have students thread the string through the straws and knot them to hold the straws together.

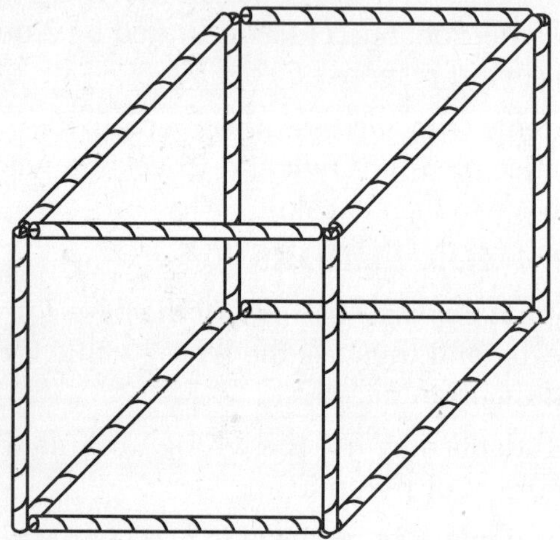

Ask: **How many straws did you use to build the rectangular prism?** (12)

Explain that the number of straws represents the number of edges in the rectangular prism. Have students record the number. Ask: **How many knots did you tie to hold the straws together?** (8)

Point out that the number of knots represents the number of vertices in the rectangular prism.

Distribute construction paper. Have the students tape a different color to each side to represent each face.

Ask: **How many different colors did you use to cover the rectangular prism?** (6)

Point out that the number of different colors used represents the number of faces on the rectangular prism.

Help students recognize that they recorded 12 edges, 8 vertices, and 6 faces for the rectangular prism.

When students show an understanding of how to count the faces, edges, and vertices of a rectangular prism, introduce the formulas below. Explain that instead of counting, they can use these formulas:

Let n = number of sides on the base.

$n + 2$ = number of faces
$n \times 2$ = number of vertices
$n \times 3$ = number of edges

Using the models the students made, demonstrate how the formulas represent the parts of the prism. Then use the formulas and compare the results to the totals they found by counting.

Name ______________________ Skill ______________________

Skill 79

Faces, Edges, Vertices

A polyhedron has faces that are polygons.
The line where two faces meet is called an **edge**.
The point where three or more edges meet is called a **vertex**.
You can find the number of faces, edges, and vertices on solid figures.

Observe and Count

Count the number of faces, edges, and vertices on each figure.

Rectangular Prism

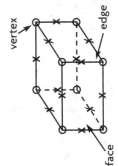

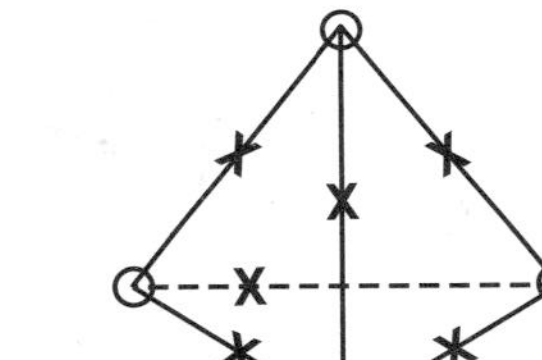

6 faces, 8 vertices, 12 edges

Triangular Pyramid

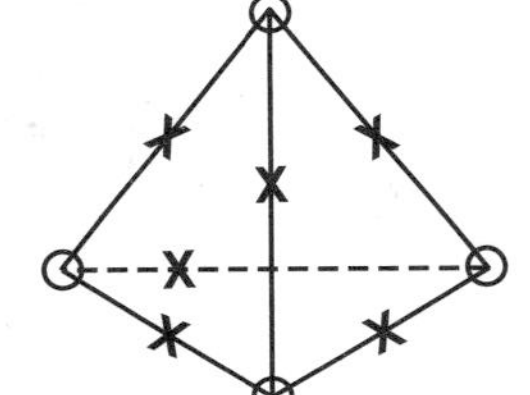

4 faces, 4 vertices, 6 edges

Remember: A prism is a solid figure with two congruent faces called *bases*.
A pyramid is a solid figure with one base and three or more triangular faces that share a common vertex.

Use a Formula

Use a formula to find the number of faces, edges, and vertices.

Prism

Let n = number of sides on the base.
$n + 2$ = number of faces
$n \times 2$ = number of vertices
$n \times 3$ = number of edges

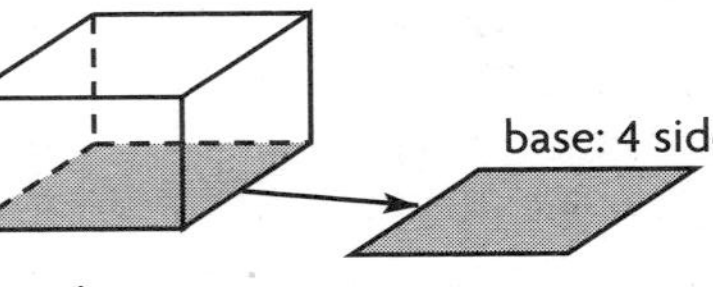

$n = 4$
Faces: $n + 2 = 4 + 2 = 6$
Vertices: $n \times 2 = 4 \times 2 = 8$
Edges: $n \times 3 = 4 \times 3 = 12$
So, a rectangular prism has 6 faces, 8 vertices, and 12 edges.

Pyramid

Let n = number of sides on the base.
$n + 1$ = number of faces
$n + 1$ = number of vertices
$n \times 2$ = number of edges

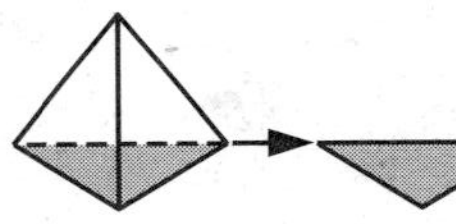

$n = 3$
Faces: $n + 1 = 3 + 1 = 4$
Vertices: $n + 1 = 3 + 1 = 4$
Edges: $n \times 2 = 3 \times 2 = 6$
So, a triangular pyramid has 4 faces, 4 vertices, and 6 edges.

Go to the next side.

Name ______________________ Skill ______________________

Practice on Your Own

Skill 79

Prism

Let $n = 3$.

Faces: $n + 2 = 3 + 2 = 5$

Vertices: $n \times 2 = 3 \times 2 = 6$

Edges: $n \times 3 = 3 \times 3 = 9$

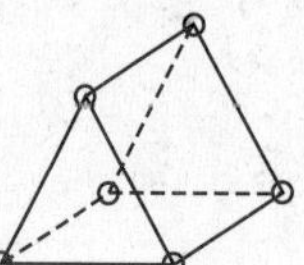

Pyramid

Let $n = 4$.

Faces: $n + 1 = 4 + 1 = 5$

Vertices: $n + 1 = 4 + 1 = 5$

Edges: $n \times 2 = 4 \times 2 = 8$

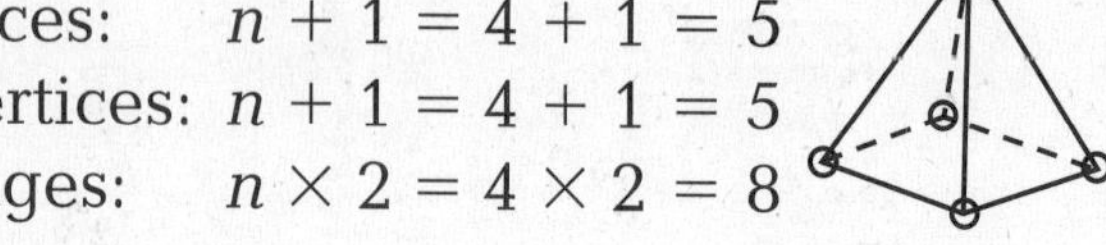

Write whether to use the formula for *prism* or *pyramid.*
Then use the formula to find the number of faces, vertices,and edges.

1. Use formula for ________

faces: ________
vertices: ________
edges: ________

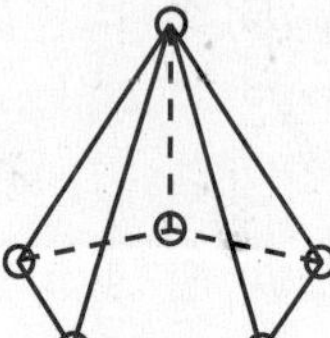

2. Use formula for ________

faces: ________
vertices: ________
edges: ________

Write the number of faces, vertices, and edges.

3. 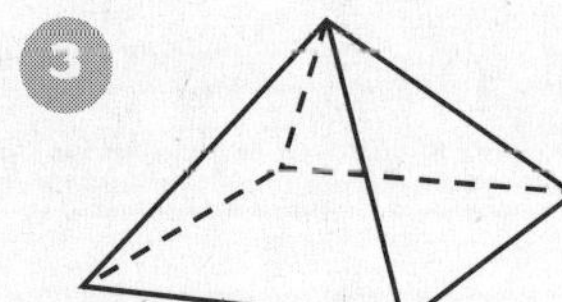

4. 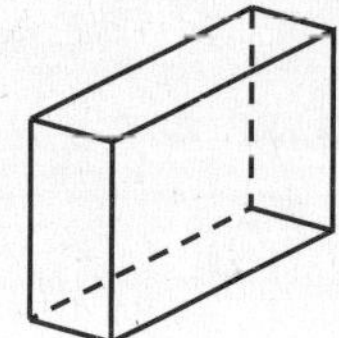

5. 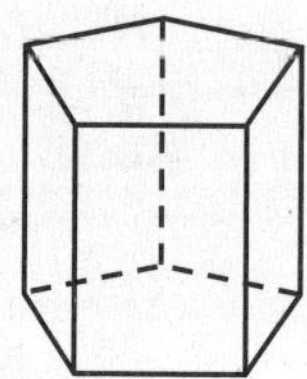

6. 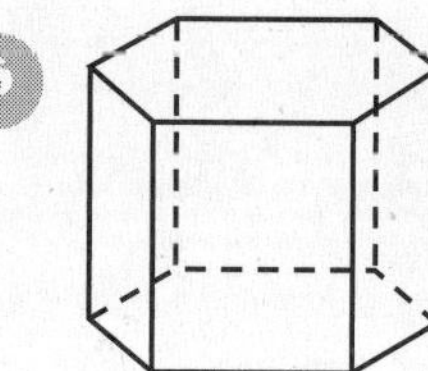

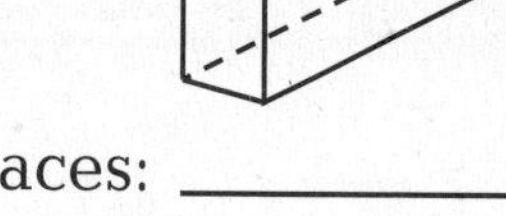

3. faces: ________ vertices: ________ edges: ________

4. faces: ________ vertices: ________ edges: ________

5. faces: ________ vertices: ________ edges: ________

6. faces: ________ vertices: ________ edges: ________

7. ________ ________ ________

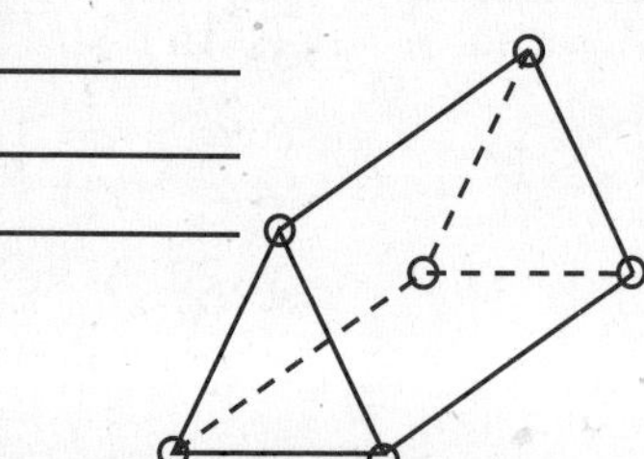

8. ________ ________ ________

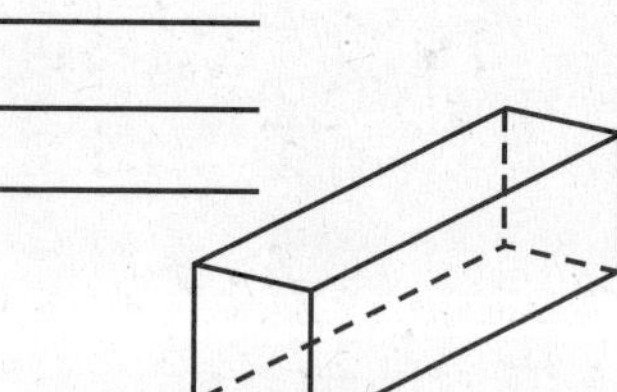

9. ________ ________ ________

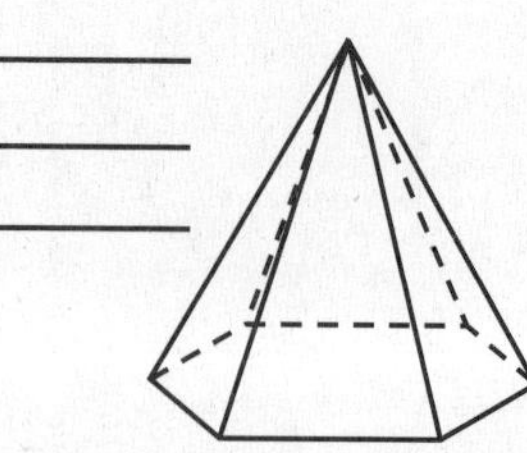

Check

Write the number of faces, vertices, and edges.

10. ________ ________ ________

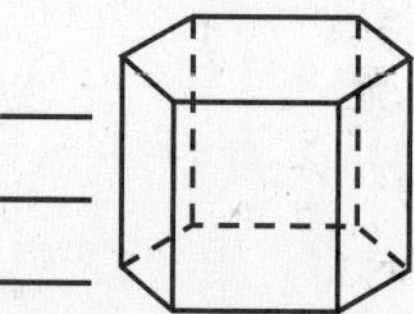

11. ________ ________ ________

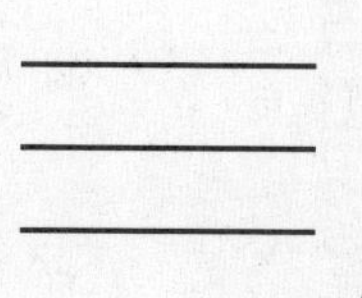

12. ________ ________ ________

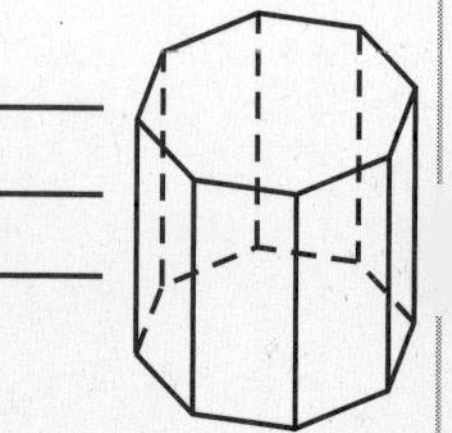

Skill 80 Classify Lines

Using Skill 80

OBJECTIVE Classify parallel lines, intersecting lines, and perpendicular lines

Look at the top of the page. Read about a line and how to read and write the names of lines. Point out to the students that a line containing the points *X* and *Y* can be read as line *XY* or line *YX*.

Refer to Example A.

Ask: **What are the names of the lines in the first example?** (line *CD* or line *DC*, and line *MN* or line *NM*) **If the lines were extended forever in both directions, would they ever intersect?** (no) **Would the distance between the lines ever change?** (no)

Tell students that lines that never intersect and are always the same distance apart are called *parallel lines.*

Ask: **What are some ways to name the first set of lines in the second example?** (line *XZ*, line *XY*, or line *ZY*; and line *UZ*, line *UV*, or line *ZV*) **What is the point where the two lines cross?** (point *Z*) **If two lines cross, how many points do they have in common**? (one point)

Compare and contrast the intersecting lines with the perpendicular lines in the next box. Students should understand that perpendicular lines are special intersecting lines. It is not wrong to call them intersecting lines, but describing them as perpendicular gives much more information about how the lines are related.

PRACTICE ON YOUR OWN Review the examples at the top of the page. As they work through the exercises, suggest that students recite the definition for each type of line.

CHECK Determine if students know that parallel lines never meet and perpendicular lines are special intersecting lines. Success is indicated by 3 out of 3 correct responses.

Students who successfully complete the **Practice on Your Own** and **Check** are ready to move to the next skill.

COMMON ERRORS

- Students may fail to distinguish perpendicular lines from ordinary intersecting lines.
- Students may rely on assumptions rather than given information to classify lines as perpendicular.

Students who made more than 4 errors in the **Practice on Your Own**, or who were not successful in the **Check** section, may benefit from the **Alternative Teaching Strategy** on the next page.

Optional

Alternative Teaching Strategy

Model Classifying Lines

OBJECTIVE Model classifying parallel, intersecting, and perpendicular lines

Have students point out pairs of things in the classroom that remind them of parallel lines. For example, they might mention the top edge of a wall and the bottom edge of the wall.

Ask: **Can you hold your arms so that they are parallel to each other?** (yes) Have students demonstrate how they can hold their arms parallel to each other.

Have students point out pairs of things in the classroom that remind them of intersecting lines. For example, they might mention an edge on the side of a wall and an edge at the top of the wall.

Ask: **Can you hold your arms so that they intersect each other?** (yes) Have students demonstrate how they can cross their arms. Have them identify the point where their arms cross.

Have students point out pairs of things in the classroom that remind them of perpendicular lines. For example, they might mention the corner of a math book.

Have students try to identify two lines in the room that intersect and form right angles. You may have to explain that right angles are angles that measure 90°. Encourage them to verify their assumptions by comparing to the corner of an index card.

Ask: **Where are there right angles in the room?** (the top edge of the wall with the side edge of the wall)

Have students identify other classroom examples of parallel lines, intersecting lines, and perpendicular lines.

Classify Lines

Skill 80

A **line** is a straight path that extends without end in opposite directions. Here are some ways to describe certain lines.

Read: line XY or line YX

Write: $\overleftrightarrow{XY}$ $\overleftrightarrow{YX}$

Example A

Parallel lines are lines in a plane that are always the same distance apart. They never intersect and have no common points.

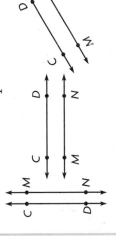

Intersecting lines cross at exactly one point.

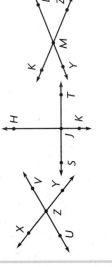

Perpendicular lines intersect to form right angles.

Example B

You can find examples of parallel, perpendicular, and intersecting lines in different geometric figures.

The figure at the right is a rectangular prism.

- These lines are parallel to $\overleftrightarrow{AB}$: $\overleftrightarrow{GC}$, $\overleftrightarrow{FH}$, $\overleftrightarrow{ED}$.

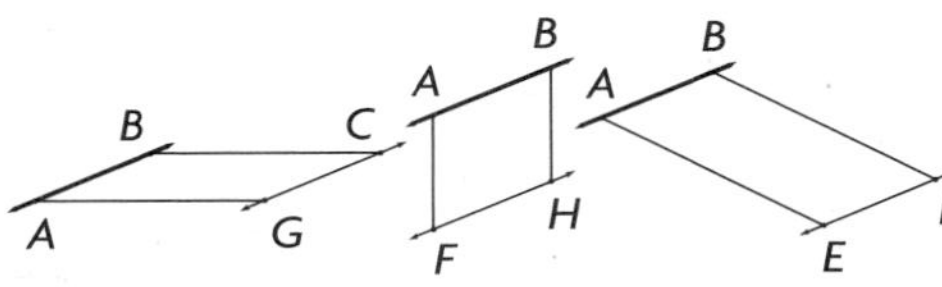

- These lines are perpendicular to and intersect $\overleftrightarrow{FE}$: $\overleftrightarrow{AF}$, $\overleftrightarrow{HF}$, $\overleftrightarrow{GE}$, $\overleftrightarrow{DE}$.

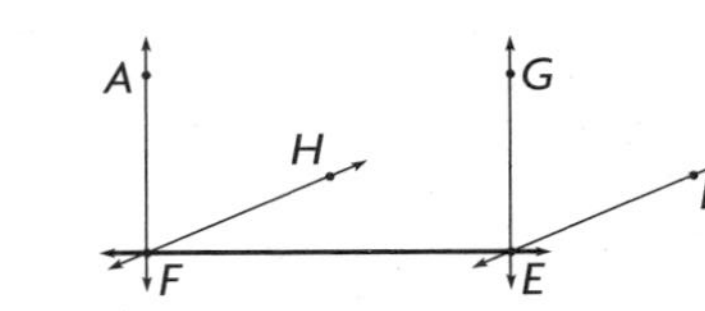

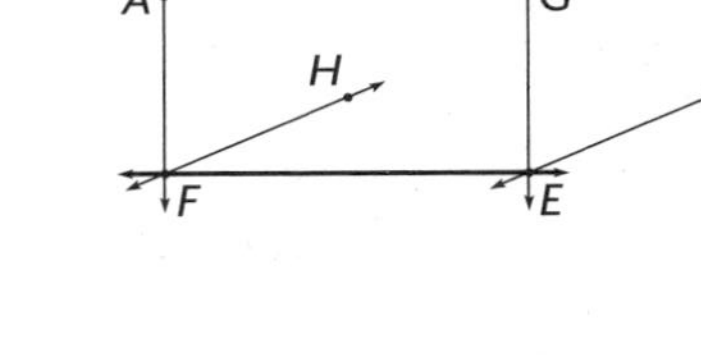

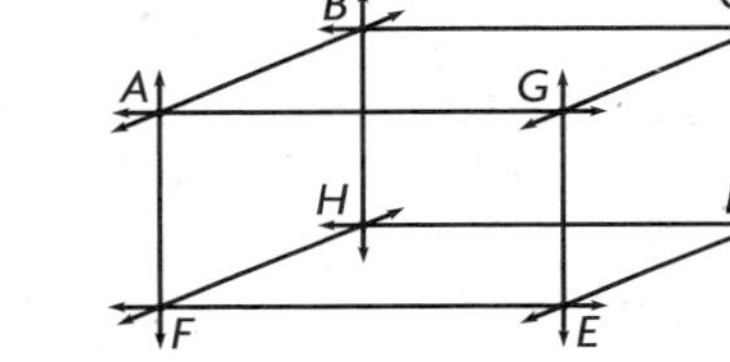

Go to the next side.

Name ______________________ Skill ______________________

Practice on Your Own

Skill 80

Parallel Lines	Intersecting Lines	Perpendicular Lines

Classify the lines. Choose parallel, intersecting, or perpendicular.

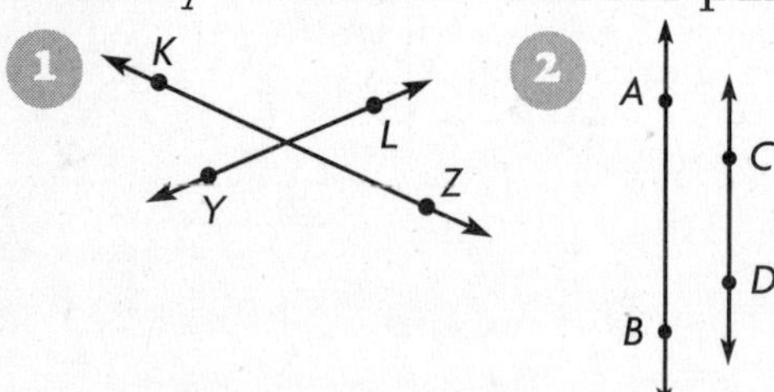

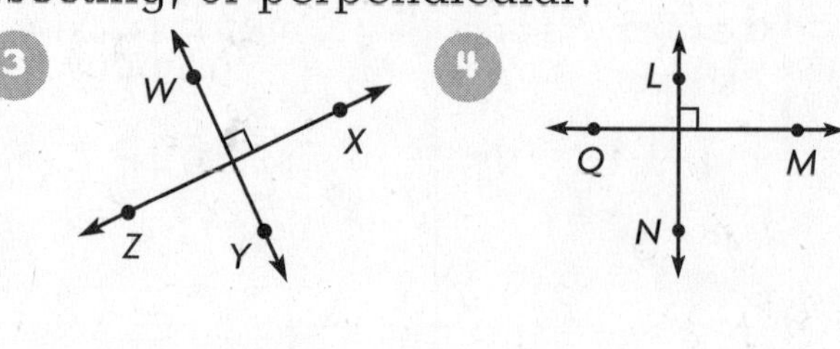

1. ______ 2. ______ 3. ______ 4. ______

Complete. Write parallel, perpendicular, or intersecting.

5. $\overleftrightarrow{AB}$, $\overleftrightarrow{GH}$ ______________

6. $\overleftrightarrow{AB}$, $\overleftrightarrow{CD}$ ______________

7. $\overleftrightarrow{AB}$, $\overleftrightarrow{FE}$ ______________

8. $\overleftrightarrow{AB}$, $\overleftrightarrow{AC}$ ______________

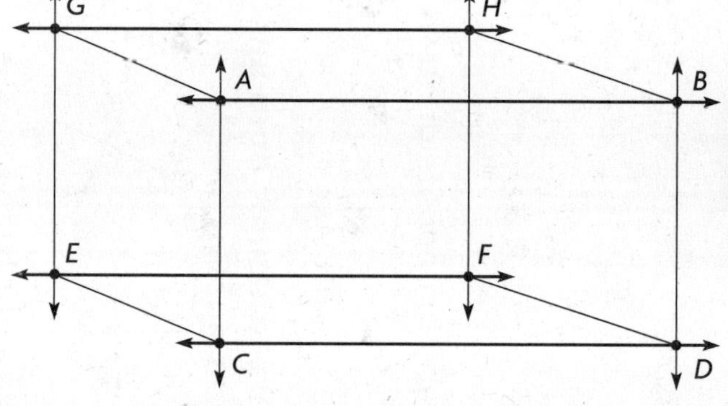

9. Name one line parallel to $\overleftrightarrow{LM}$. ______

10. Name two lines that intersect $\overleftrightarrow{RQ}$.
______ ______

11. Name one line that is perpendicular to and intersects $\overleftrightarrow{LS}$. ______

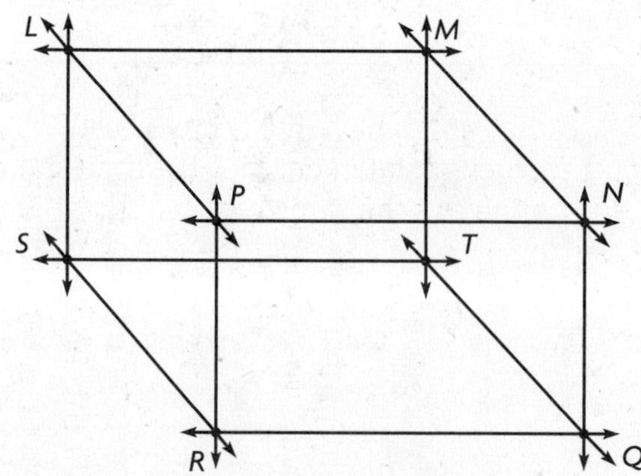

Check

Complete.

12. Name two lines that are parallel to $\overleftrightarrow{LM}$. ______ ______

13. Name two lines that intersect $\overleftrightarrow{SR}$. ______ ______

14. Name two lines that are perpendicular to and intersect $\overleftrightarrow{PR}$. ______ ______

Skill 81 Identify Congruent Figures

Using Skill 81

OBJECTIVE Identify congruent figures

Read about congruent figures at the top of the page. Explain to students that congruent figures have exactly the same size and shape.

Look at the first set of figures.

Ask: **What are the geometric figures?** (rectangles) **How long are the rectangles?** (12 cm, 12 cm) **How wide are the rectangles?** (6 cm, 6 cm) **If the figures are both rectangles and they are the same length and the same width, what can you conclude about the rectangles?** (They are congruent.)

Focus on the second set of geometric figures. Be sure students understand the definition of congruent. The figures must be the same shape *and* the same size.

Ask: **What are the geometric figures?** (squares) **Since the figures are both squares, can you conclude that they are congruent?** (No, they are not the same size.)

Look at the third set of geometric figures. Make sure students know that when two polygons are congruent, their corresponding parts have the same measure. A congruence statement lists the corresponding angles in the same order.

Ask: **How do you know that the triangles are congruent?** (By the congruence statement above the triangles.) **What angle does angle *C* correspond to?** (angle *M*) **How do you know?** (Because of the order of the congruence statement, *C* corresponds to *M*.) **What side length does *CD* correspond to?** (*MN*) **How do you know?** (Because of the order of the congruence statement, side *CD* corresponds to side *MN*.)

TRY THESE Exercises 1–2 require students to judge shape and size when deciding on congruence. Exercise 3 requires students to identify corresponding parts of congruent figures.

- **Exercise 1** Congruent
- **Exercise 2** Not congruent
- **Exercise 3** $\overline{AB} \cong \overline{QR}$; $\overline{BC} \cong \overline{RS}$; $\angle Q \cong \angle A$

PRACTICE ON YOUR OWN Review the examples at the top of the page. As they work through the exercises, remind students that the figures must be the same shape *and* size to be congruent.

CHECK Determine if students know how to identify corresponding parts.

Success is indicated by 3 out of 3 correct responses.

Students who successfully complete the **Practice on Your Own** and **Check** are ready to move to the next skill.

COMMON ERRORS

- Students may classify all squares as congruent because they are the same shape.
- Students may only look at one dimension when deciding whether shapes are the same size.
- Students might think that figures must have the same orientation to be congruent.

Students who made more than 2 errors in the **Practice on Your Own**, or who were not successful in the **Check** section, may benefit from the **Alternative Teaching Strategy** on the next page.

Optional

Alternative Teaching Strategy

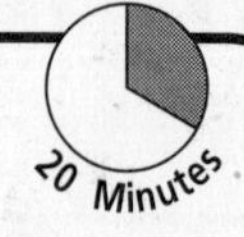

Model Congruent Figures

OBJECTIVE Model identifying congruent figures

MATERIALS scissors, worksheets with geometric figures, transparency of geometric figures

Distribute worksheets of geometric figures shown below to students.

TRIANGLES

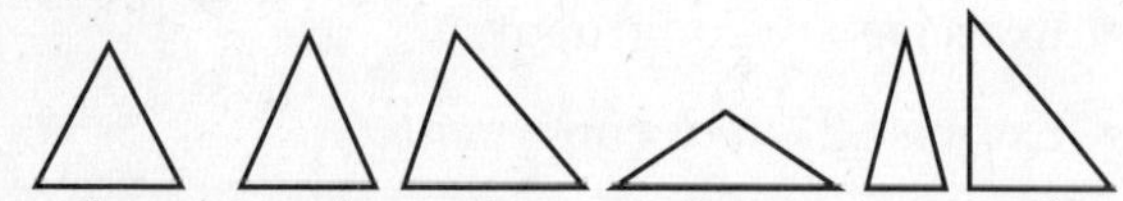

equilateral isosceles scalene obtuse acute right

QUADRILATERALS:

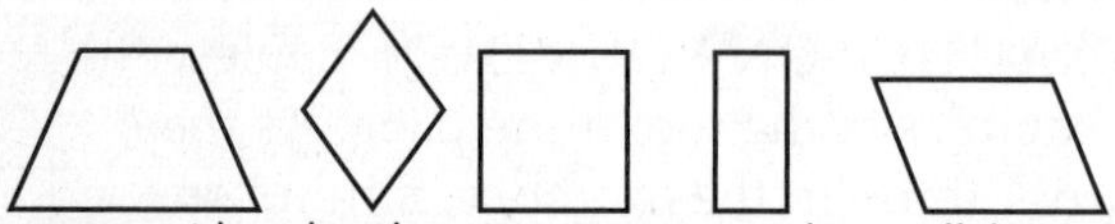

trapezoid rhombus square rectangle parallelogram

PENTAGONS

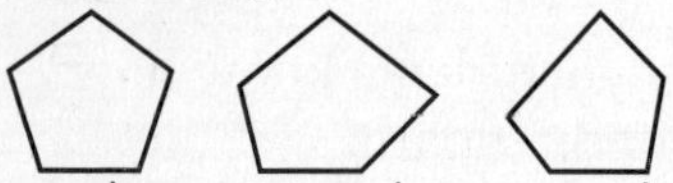

regular not regular not regular

HEXAGONS

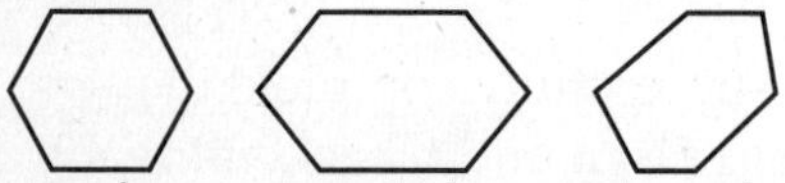

regular not regular not regular

OCTAGONS

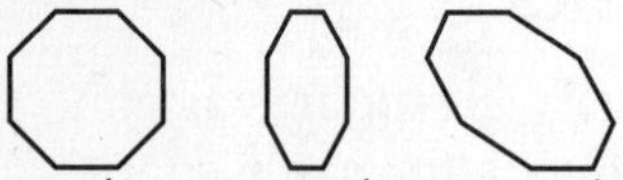

regular not regular not regular

Ask: **Which figures do you think are the same shape and the same size?** (Answers may vary.)

Cut one pair of congruent figures from the transparencies and demonstrate how to check for congruence by laying one on top of the other on an overhead projector. Repeat for a non-congruent pair.

Have the students cut out their figures and check to see which pairs are congruent and which are not.

Lead students to understand that the congruent figures are the same shape and size, and that the geometric figures that are not congruent are either not the same shape or not the same size.

Name ______________________ Skill ______________________

Skill 81

Identify Congruent Figures

Congruent figures have the same shape and the same size. Compare the shapes and the lengths of the sides to decide if the two figures are congruent.

These figures have the same shape and the same size.

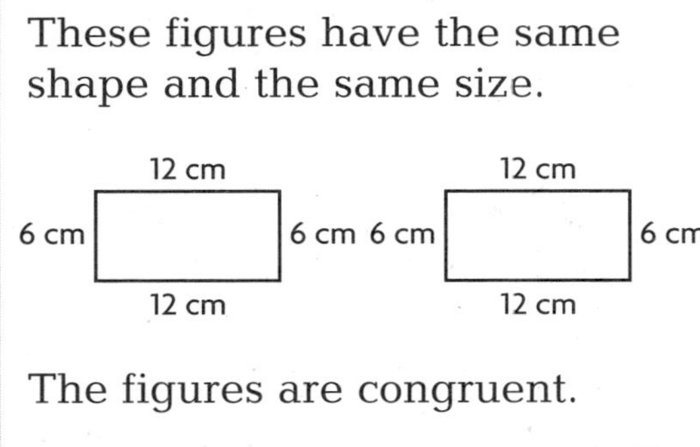

The figures are congruent.

These figures have the same shape, but do not have the same size.

8 m
8 m
8 m
8 m
6 m
6 m
6 m
6 m

The figures are *not* congruent.

$\Delta CDE \cong \Delta MNP$

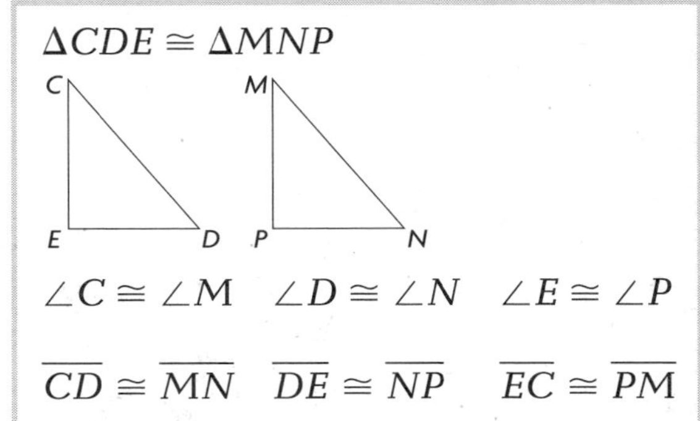

$\angle C \cong \angle M$ $\angle D \cong \angle N$ $\angle E \cong \angle P$

$\overline{CD} \cong \overline{MN}$ $\overline{DE} \cong \overline{NP}$ $\overline{EC} \cong \overline{PM}$

Try These

Complete. Decide if the two figures are congruent.

1.

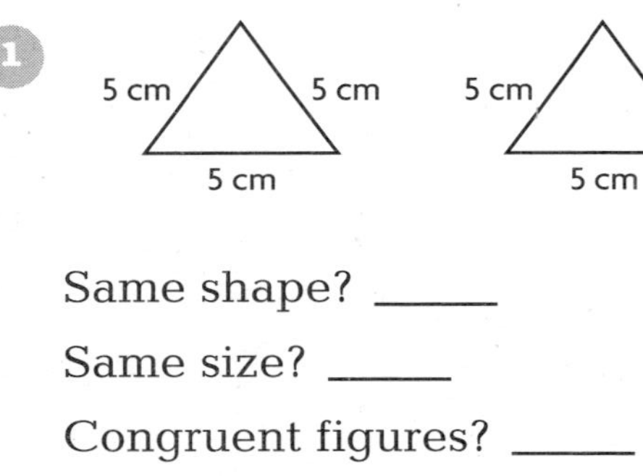

Same shape? ______

Same size? ______

Congruent figures? ______

2.

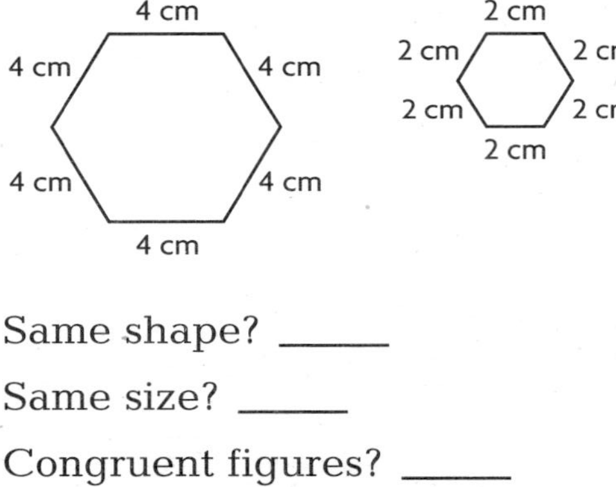

Same shape? ______

Same size? ______

Congruent figures? ______

3. Complete the congruence statements.
$\Delta ABC \cong \Delta QRS$

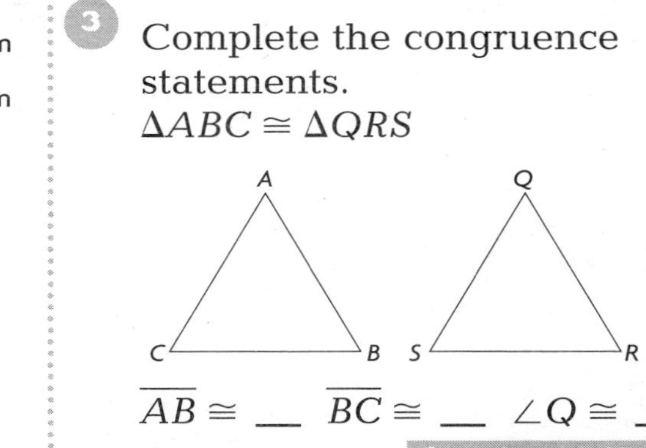

$\overline{AB} \cong$ ___ $\overline{BC} \cong$ ___ $\angle Q \cong$ ___

Go to the next side.

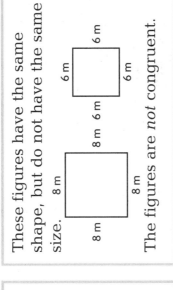

Name ______________________ Skill ______________________

Practice on Your Own

Skill 81

Think:
Congruent figures have the same shape and the same size.

Congruent

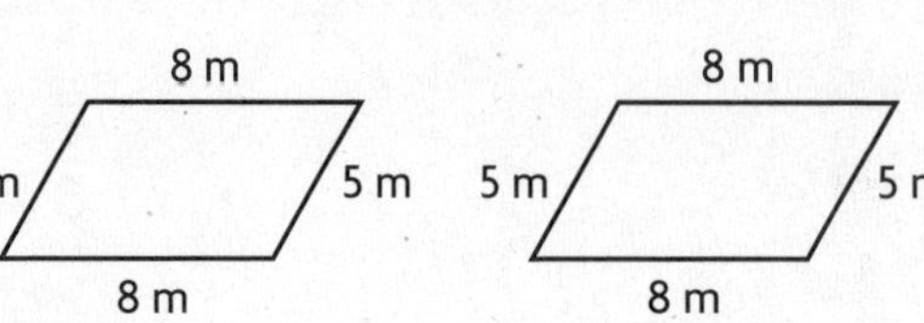

Not Congruent

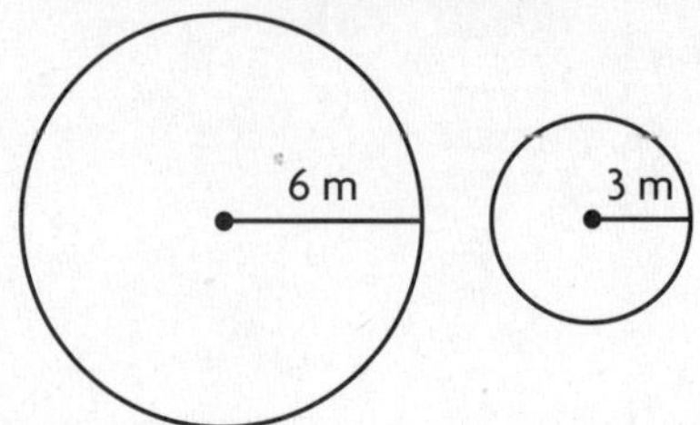

Complete. Decide if the two figures are congruent.

1
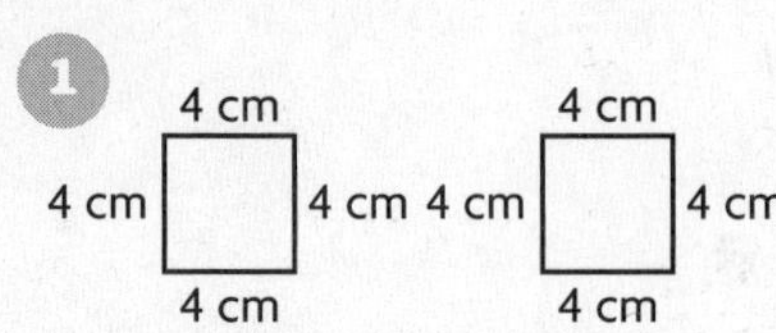

Same shape? _____
Same size? _____
Congruent figures? _____

2
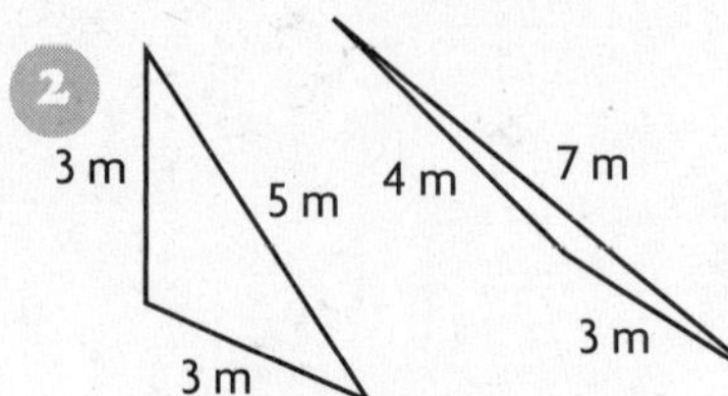

Same shape? _____
Same size? _____
Congruent figures? _____

3
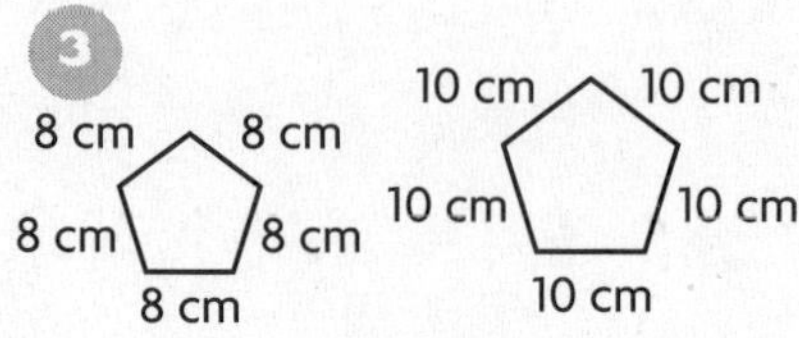

Same shape? _____
Same size? _____
Congruent figures? _____

4
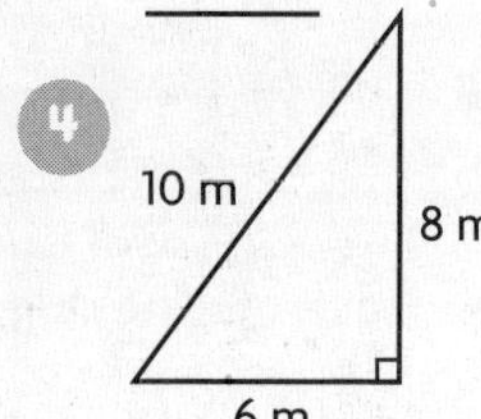

Congruent figures? _____

5
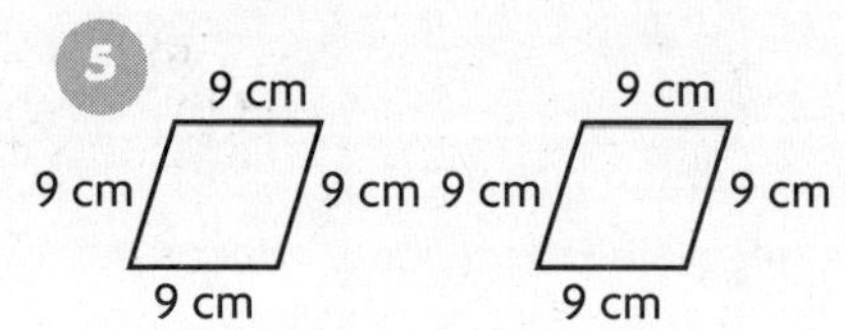

Congruent figures? _____

6
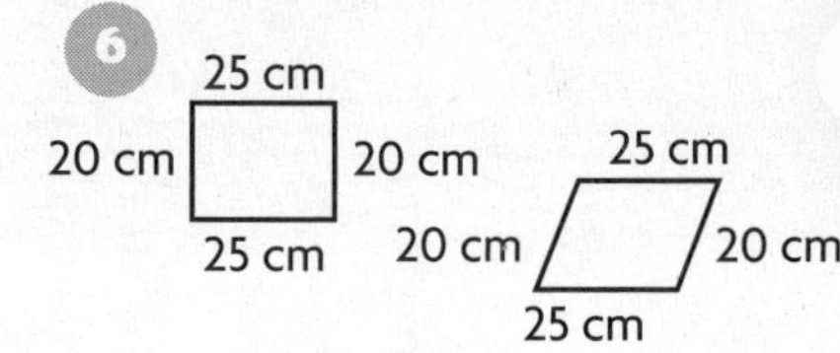

Congruent figures? _____

Complete the congruence statements.
$\Delta DEF \cong \Delta PRN$

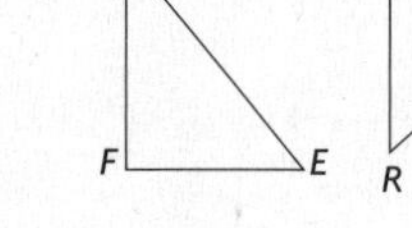

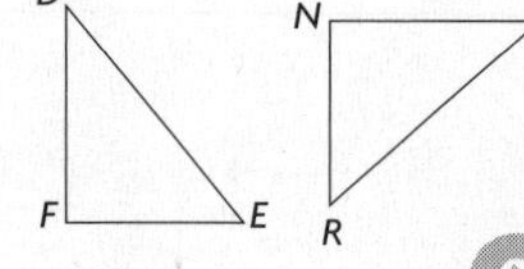

7 $\angle F \cong$ _____
8 $\angle D \cong$ _____
9 $\angle E \cong$ _____

10 $\overline{EF} \cong$ _____
11 $\overline{NP} \cong$ _____
12 $\overline{RN} \cong$ _____

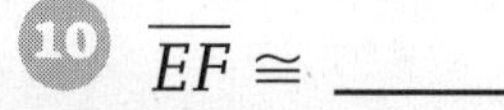

Check

13
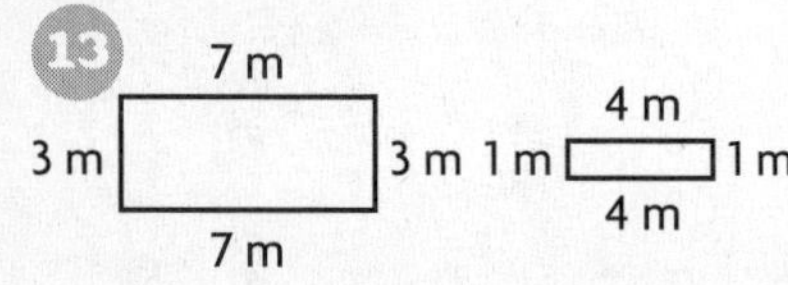

Congruent figures? _____

14
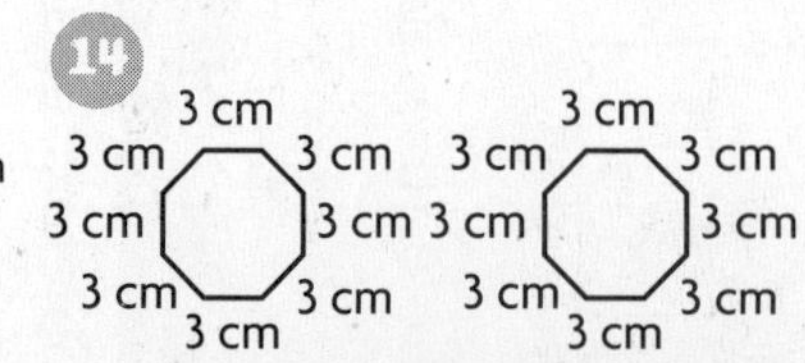

Congruent figures? _____

15 Given that $\Delta STU \cong \Delta JKL$:

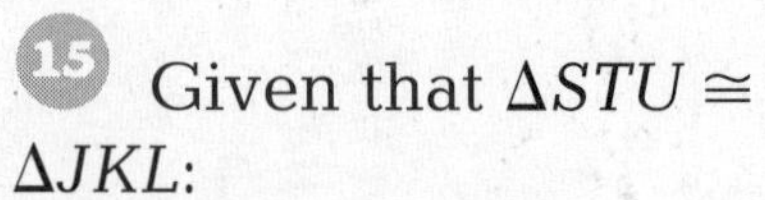

What corresponds to $\angle K$? _____
What corresponds to $\overline{LJ}$? _____

Skill 82 Similar Figures

Using Skill 82

OBJECTIVE Identify similar figures

Read about similar figures at the top of Skill 82. Stress that similar figures are always the same shape but can be different sizes.

Direct students' attention to the squares in the first frame. Ask: **Are all squares the same shape?** (yes) **Are all squares the same size?** (no)

Help students to conclude that any two squares are always similar.

Direct attention to the second frame. Ask: **What type of triangles are shown?** (right)

Say: **Look at the sides of each triangle. How does the length of each side of the larger triangle compare to the corresponding side of the smaller triangle?** (The sides of the larger triangle are twice as long as the sides on the smaller triangle.)

Explain that not all triangles are similar. Stress that in this case they are similar because if the dimensions of the smaller triangle are multiplied by 2, the results are the dimensions of the larger one. The dimensions are proportional. To emphasize this point, display a right triangle that is not similar to the other two.

Direct attention to the third frame. Ask: **What are the figures in the third example?** (rectangles) **How do the rectangles compare to each other?** (They are congruent.) Point out that congruence is a special case of similarity: same shape *and* same size.

For the final set of figures, help students recognize that although some sides are congruent, the figures are not similar because they are not the same shape.

TRY THESE Exercises 1–4 provide questions that help students identify similar figures.

- **Exercise 1** Similar rectangles of different sizes
- **Exercise 2** Similar triangles of different sizes
- **Exercise 3** Similar trapezoids of the same size
- **Exercise 4** Non-similar triangle and rhombus, sides of the same length

PRACTICE ON YOUR OWN Review the example at the top of the page. Have students focus first on comparing the shapes of the figures to determine if they are similar.

CHECK Determine if students can identify similar figures. Success is indicated by 3 out of 3 correct responses.

Students who successfully complete the **Practice on Your Own** and **Check** are ready to move to the next skill.

COMMON ERRORS

- Students may classify all triangles or all rectangles as similar without regard to shape.
- Students may confuse *congruent* and *similar,* and mark only congruent figures as similar.

Students who made more than 2 errors in the **Practice on Your Own**, or who were not successful in the **Check** section, may benefit from the **Alternative Teaching Strategy** on the next page.

Optional

Alternative Teaching Strategy
Model Similar Figures

OBJECTIVE Model identifying similar figures

MATERIALS centimeter grid paper

Have the students draw as many squares of different sizes as they can fit on their papers. Ask: **Do all squares have the same shape?** (yes) **How do you know they all have the same shape?** (They all have 4 sides that are the same length and 4 right angles.)

Help students understand that these squares of different sizes are similar because they are the same shape.

You may want to have the students cut out their squares and arrange them in a design such as the one shown below to help them see that the squares are similar to each other.

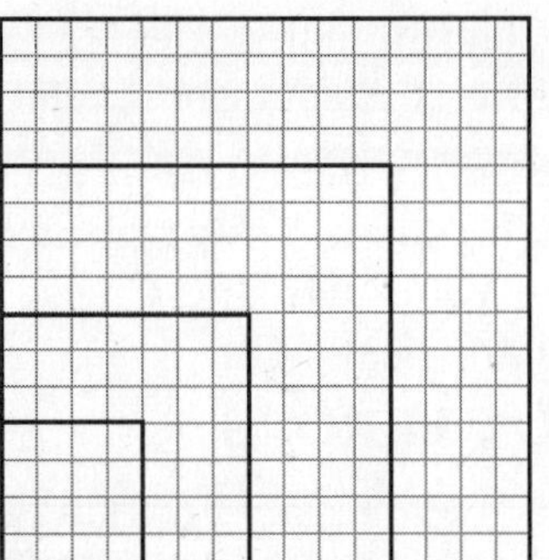

Have students draw two rectangles on grid paper. One should be 8 by 10 and the other should be 4 by 5.

Ask: **Do these figures appear to have the same shape?** (yes) **Look at the sides of the rectangles. How do they compare?** (The sides of the large rectangle are twice as long as the sides of the small rectangle.)

Explain that because the lengths of the sides of the large rectangle are twice the lengths of the sides of the small rectangle, the sides are proportional. Draw a rectangle that is 1 by 10 and compare it to the other two rectangles. Explain that the sides of this rectangle are not proportional to the sides of the other rectangles. This rectangle is not the same shape, and thus it is not similar to the other two.

When students show an understanding of similar figures, have students draw a figure on grid paper, exchange papers with a partner, and have the partner draw a similar figure. Then compare the drawings.

Similar Figures

Skill 82

Similar figures have the same shape and angles of the same measure.

The squares are similar. They have the same shape, but not the same size.

Since the lengths of all the sides on a square are equal, then the shape of any two squares is the same.

The triangles are similar. They have the same shape but not the same size.

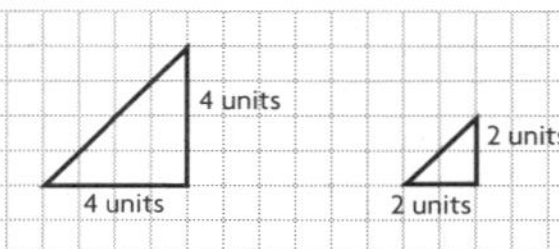

The triangle on the right appears to be half the size of the triangle on the left.

The rectangles are similar. They have the same shape and the same size.

The trapezoid and the parallelogram are not similar. They do not have the same shape.

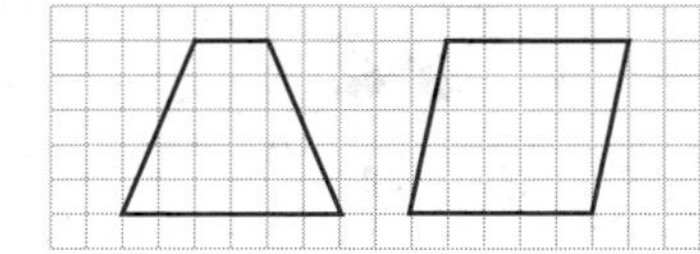

Try These

Tell if the figures have the same shape and if they appear to be similar.

1.

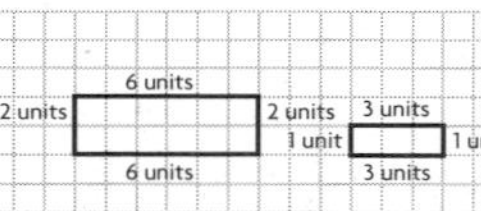

Same shape? ______

Similar figures? ______

2.

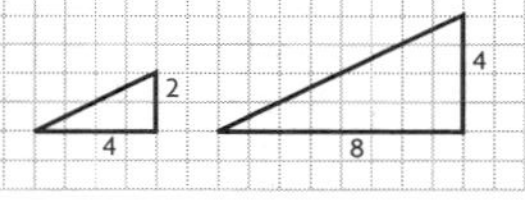

Same shape? ______

Similar figures? ______

3.

Same shape? ______

Similar figures? ______

4.

Same shape? ______

Similar figures? ______

Go to the next side.

Practice on Your Own

Skill 82

Think:
Similar figures
have the same shape,
but may be different sizes.

similar not similar

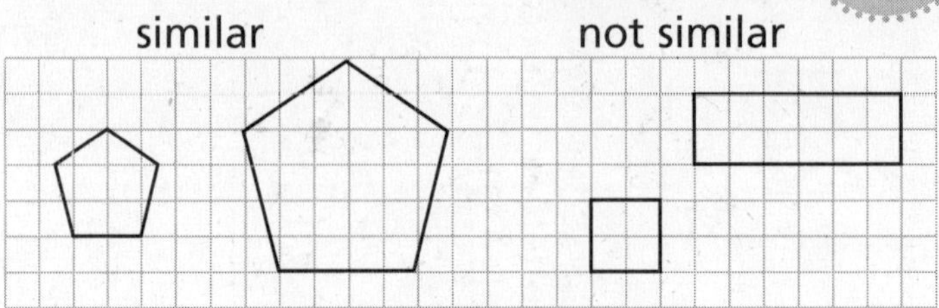

Complete. Tell whether the figures in each pair appear to be similar.

1. 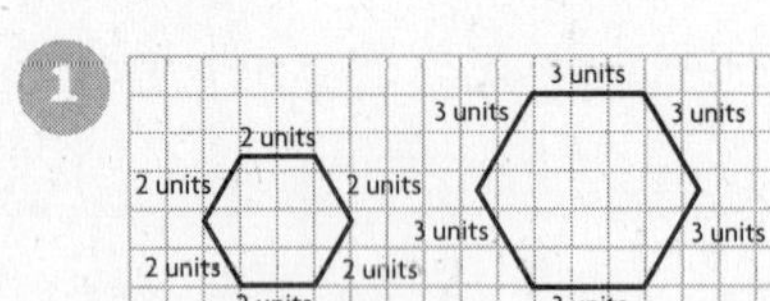

Same shape? ______

Similar figures? ______

2. 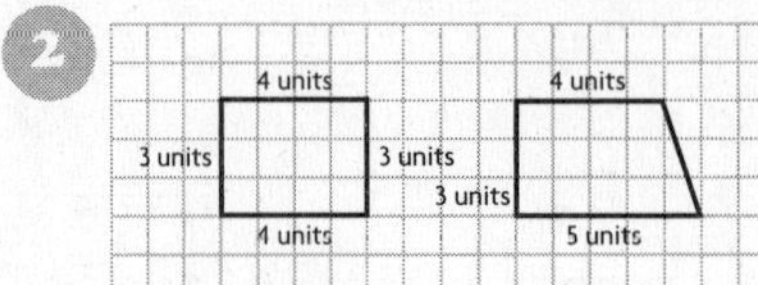

Same shape? ______

Similar figures? ______

3. 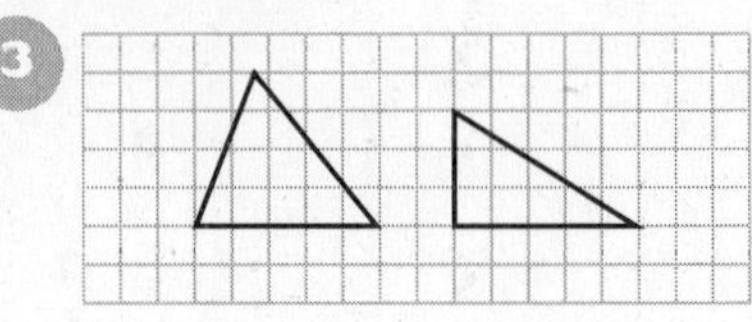

Same shape? ______

Similar figures? ______

4. 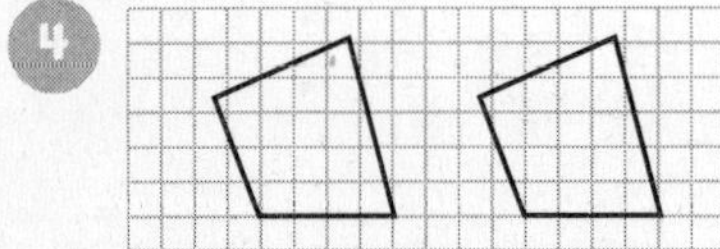

Similar figures? ______

5. 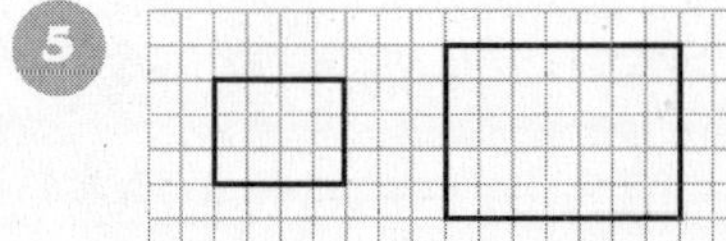

Similar figures? ______

6. 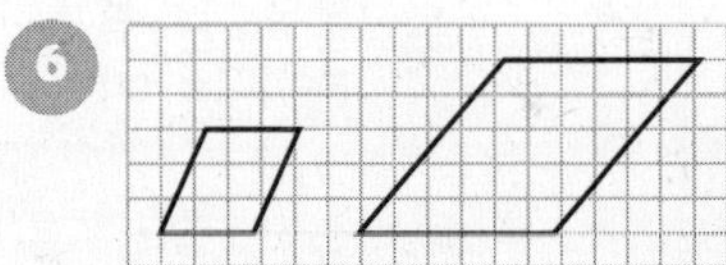

Similar figures? ______

7. 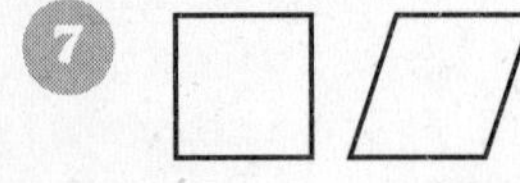

Similar figures? ______

8. 

Similar figures? ______

9. 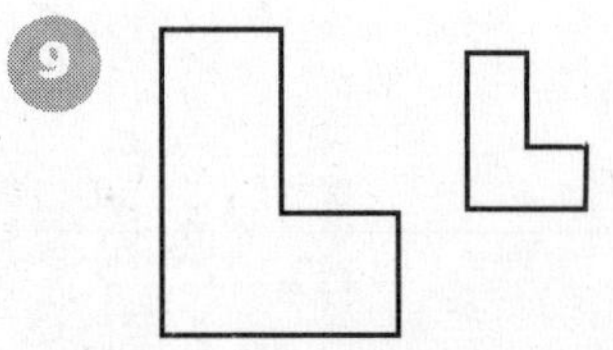

Similar figures? ______

 **Check**

Tell whether the figures in each pair appear to be similar.

 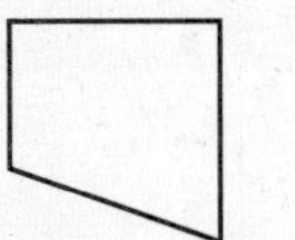 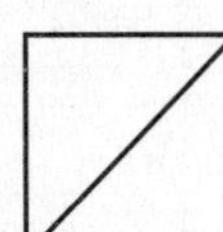

Similar figures? ______

 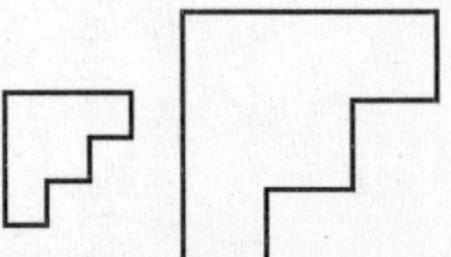

Similar figures? ______

 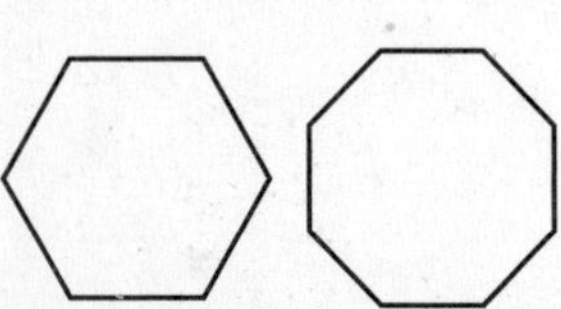

Similar figures? ______

Using Skill 83

OBJECTIVE Find the perimeter of a polygon by adding the lengths of the sides

You may wish to review addition strategies for multiple addends.

Draw attention to the triangle in Step 1.

Ask: **How many sides are there and what is the name of the figure?** (3; triangle) **What is the length of each side?** (3 cm) **What operation can we use to find the distance around?** (addition)

Draw attention to Step 2. Be sure students understand that an addition sentence is an equation.

Ask: **What equation is used to represent the perimeter?** ($P = 3 + 3 + 3$)

Draw attention to Step 3. Help students to see that, when they add numbers with the same units, they add the numbers and their sum has the same units.

Work through several other examples, using a rectangle, a pentagon, and a scalene triangle. Help students to see that the perimeter of *any* figure is the sum of the lengths of its sides.

TRY THESE Exercises 1–3 model the equation for perimeter.

- **Exercise 1** Scalene triangle
- **Exercise 2** Square
- **Exercise 3** Pentagon

PRACTICE ON YOUR OWN Review the example at the top of the page. Have students identify the lengths of all sides. Ask them how they can tell the name of the units in the perimeter.

CHECK Determine if students can find the perimeter.

Success is indicated by 3 out of 4 correct responses.

Students who successfully complete the **Practice on Your Own** and **Check** are ready to move to the next skill.

COMMON ERRORS

- Students might fail to include all sides when finding the perimeter.
- Students might not recall addition facts.
- Students might forget to include units in the final answer.

Students who made more than 4 errors in the **Practice on Your Own,** or who were not successful in the **Check** section, may also benefit from the **Alternative Teaching Strategy** on the next page.

Optional

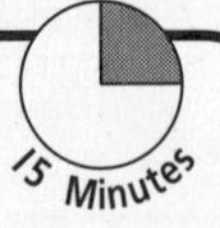

Alternative Teaching Strategy
Finding the Perimeter

OBJECTIVE Find the perimeter of objects

MATERIALS yardstick, ruler, or measuring tape, string or yarn, paper

Direct students to suggest five or six classroom objects they can use to find perimeter. They might suggest a desk top, a door frame, a flip chart, a chalkboard, the front of a fish tank, or an area rug.

Choose one of the suggested objects. Ask a volunteer to wrap yarn around the edge of that object.

Direct the volunteer to tie a knot to indicate the end of the measure. Extend the yarn against the yardstick. Record the measure.

Next, ask a second volunteer to make a sketch of the measured object. Then, using a yardstick or measuring tape, direct the first volunteer to find the length of each side of the object. They should record the measures on the sketch.

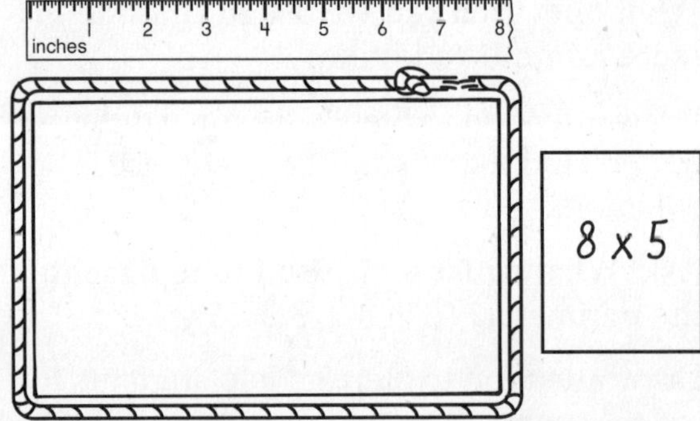

Ask students to find the sum of the measures. The sum should equal the length of the yarn.

Point out to students that the *perimeter* of any object is the distance around its outermost edge. On a circle, this distance is called the *circumference.*

Name ______________________ Skill ______________________

Find Perimeter

Skill 83

Perimeter is the distance around a figure. You can find the Perimeter (P) of a figure by adding the lengths of the sides. Find the perimeter of the triangle.

Step 1 Find the lengths of the sides.

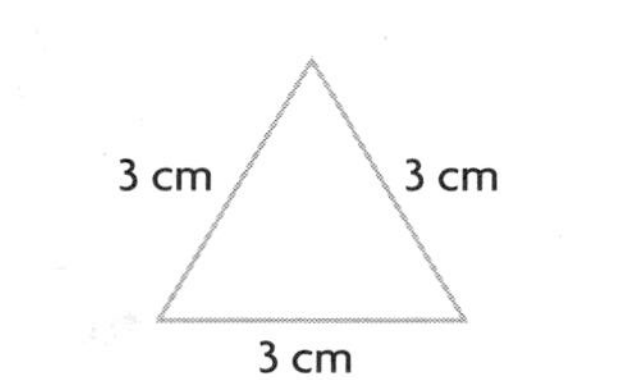

Perimeter (P) = length of side + length of side + length of side

Step 2 Write an equation.

$P = 3\text{ cm} + 3\text{ cm} + 3\text{ cm}$

Step 3 Add to find the value of P.

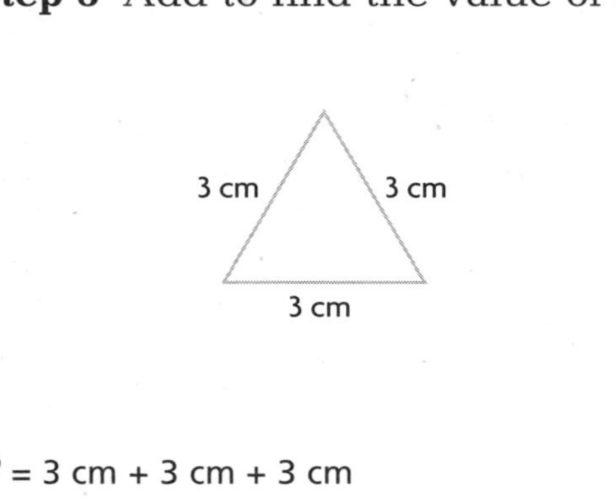

$P = 3\text{ cm} + 3\text{ cm} + 3\text{ cm}$

$P = 9\text{ cm}$

So, the perimeter of the triangle is 9 cm.

Try These

Find the perimeter of each polygon.

1. 3 cm, 2 cm, 4 cm

$P = 3\text{ cm} + 2\text{ cm} + 4\text{ cm}$

$P =$ _____ cm

2. 3 cm, 3 cm, 3 cm, 3 cm

$P =$ __ cm + __ cm + __ cm + __ cm

$P =$ _____ cm

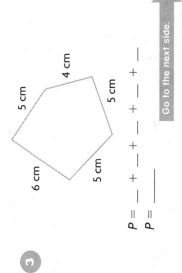

3. 6 cm, 5 cm, 4 cm, 5 cm, 5 cm

$P =$ __ + __ + __ + __ + __

$P =$ _____

Go to the next side.

Name ______________________ Skill ______________________

Practice on Your Own

Skill 83

Find the perimeter of the rectangle.

Think Add the lengths of all sides to find the perimeter of a polygon.	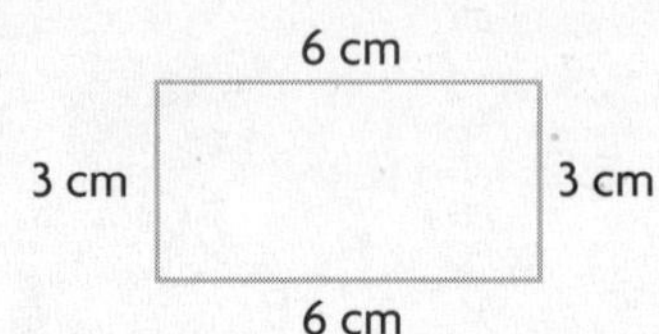 Perimeter $(P) = 3\text{ cm} + 6\text{ cm} + 3\text{ cm} + 6\text{ cm}$ $P = 18\text{ cm}$ The perimeter of the rectangle is 18 cm.

Find the perimeter of each polygon.

1

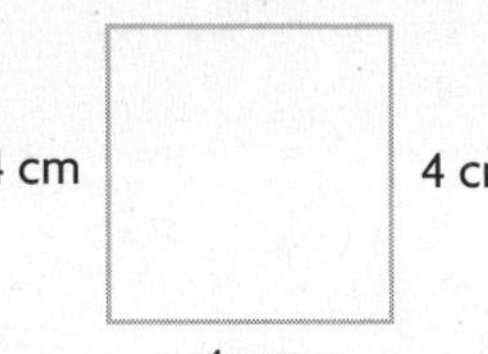

P = __ cm + __ cm + __ cm + __ cm

P = _____ cm

2

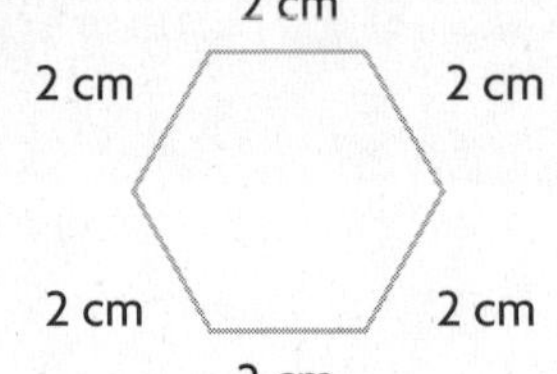

P = __ cm + __ cm + __ cm + __ cm + __ cm + __ cm

P = _____ cm

3

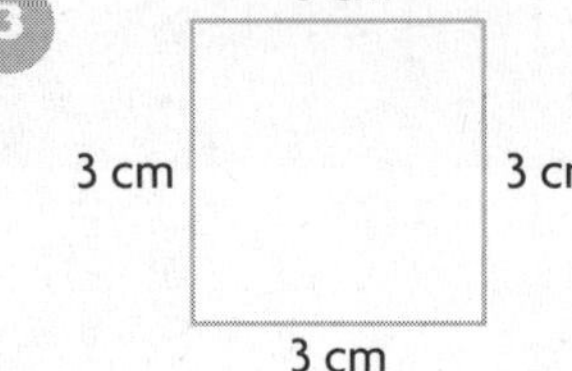

P = __ cm + __ cm + __ cm + __ cm

P = _____ cm

4

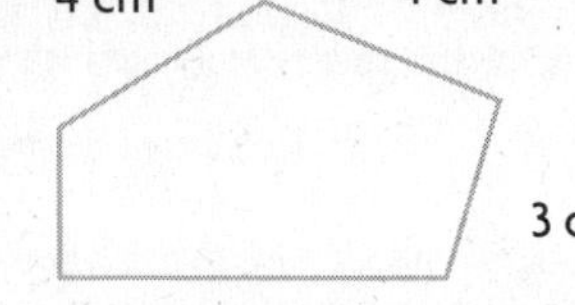

P = __ + __ + __ + __ + __

P = _____

5

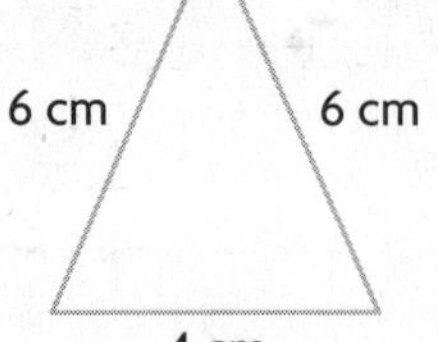

P = __ + __ + __

P = _____

6

4 cm

5 cm 3 cm

9 cm

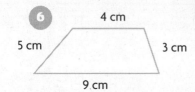

P = __ + __ + __ + __

P = _____

7

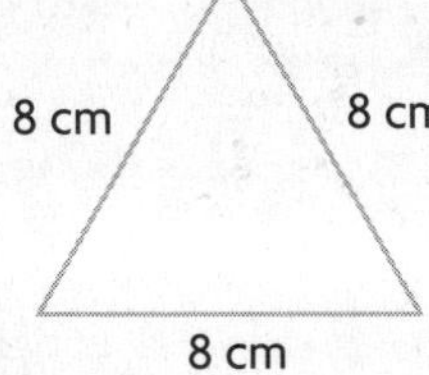

P = _____

8

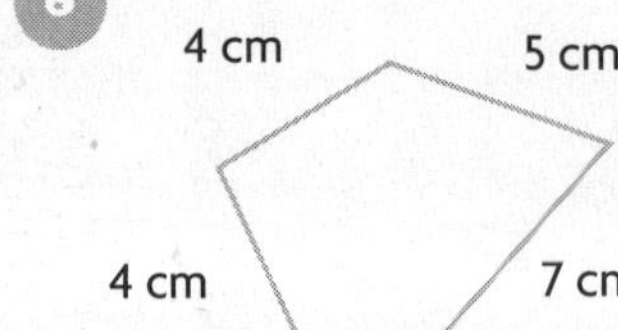

P = _____

9

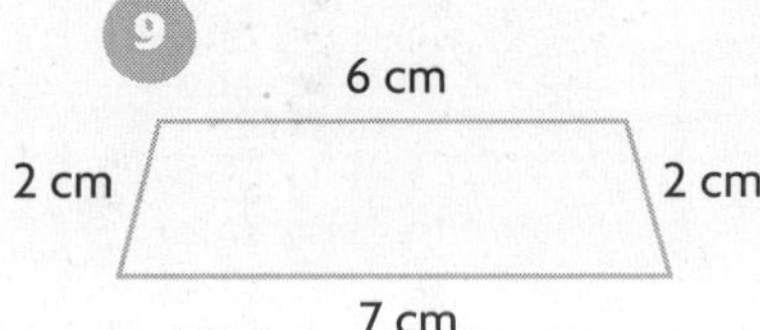

P = _____

Check

10

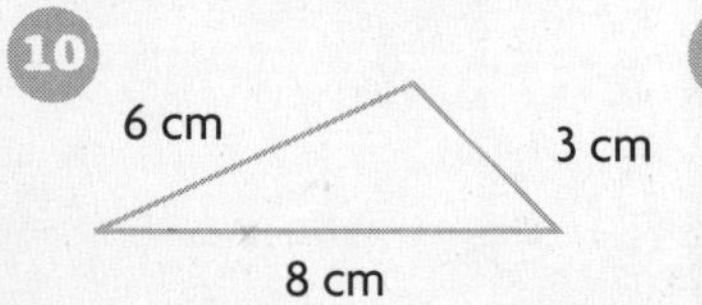

P = _____

11

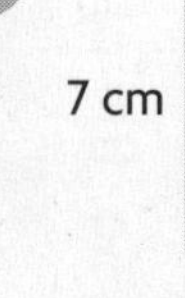

P = _____

12

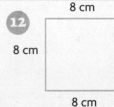

8 cm

8 cm 8 cm

8 cm

P = _____

13

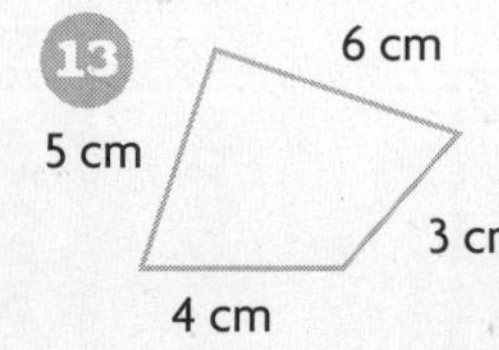

P = _____

Skill 84 Faces of Prisms and Pyramids

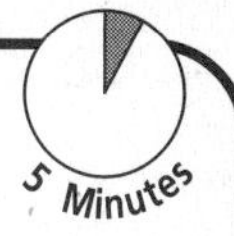

Using Skill 84

OBJECTIVE Name the polygon-shaped faces of prisms and pyramids

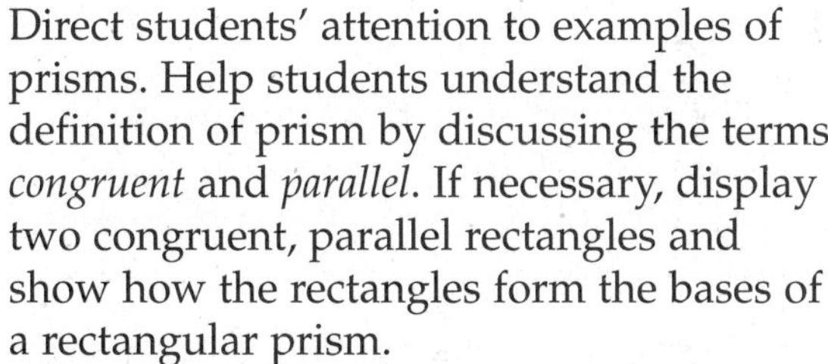

Direct students' attention to examples of prisms. Help students understand the definition of prism by discussing the terms *congruent* and *parallel*. If necessary, display two congruent, parallel rectangles and show how the rectangles form the bases of a rectangular prism.

Then, referring to Skill 84, ask: **How many faces does the prism have?** (6) Note that the faces on the bottom and on the top are called the bases. **What shape are the bases?** (rectangles) Continue: **The name of the prism is a *rectangular prism*. The prism is named for the shape of the base.** Ask: **What is the shape of all of the other faces of the rectangular prism?** (rectangles)

As you work through the example for the triangular prism, draw attention to the fact that there are 5 faces, the two bases are triangles, and the 3 other faces are rectangles. Review the examples of pyramids. Compare and contrast the properties of prisms and pyramids so students will be able to distinguish between the figures.

Have students notice that, other than the base, the faces of the pyramids are all triangles that always meet at a common vertex. Also note that a pyramid is named by the shape of its base.

TRY THESE Exercises 1–2 model the type of exercises students will find on the **Practice on Your Own** page.

- **Exercise 1** Faces of rectangular prism
- **Exercise 2** Faces of hexagonal prism

PRACTICE ON YOUR OWN Review the example of the hexagonal prism and square pyramid. As they work through the exercises, remind students to identify the polygon-shaped face that is the base of the prism and pyramid.

CHECK Determine if the students know that a prism has 2 congruent and parallel bases and that its other faces are rectangular; and, that a pyramid has one polygon-shaped face and that its other faces are triangles.

Success is indicated by 2 out of 2 correct responses.

Students who successfully complete the **Practice on Your Own** and **Check** are ready to move on to the next skill.

COMMON ERRORS

- Students may have trouble identifying the base.
- Students may identify triangular prisms as triangular pyramids.

Students who made more than 1 error in the **Practice on Your Own**, or who were not successful in the **Check** section, may benefit from the **Alternative Teaching Strategy** on the next page.

Optional

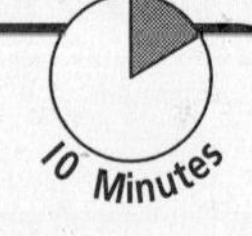

Alternative Teaching Strategy
Modeling Faces of Prisms and Pyramids

OBJECTIVE Use three-dimensional models to name the shape of the bases and faces of prisms and pyramids

MATERIALS three-dimensional models of prisms and pyramids, tracing paper, ruler

Distribute 2 prisms and 2 pyramids to each student and several sheets of tracing paper. Guide them to position the prisms and the pyramids so that the bases are on the bottom.

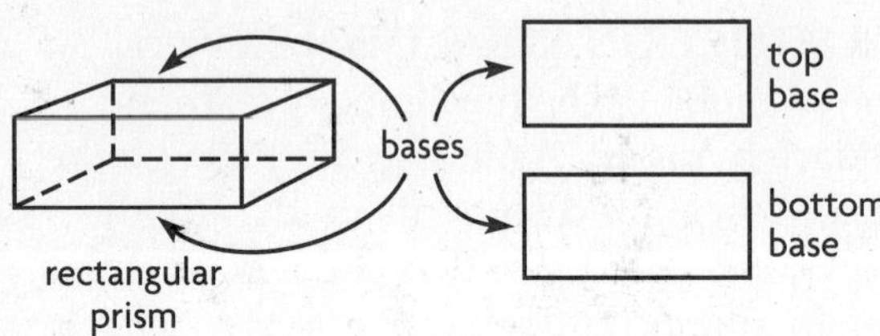

Begin by having students examine a rectangular prism. Say:
Trace the shape of the base of the prism on one sheet of paper. Then trace the other base on another sheet. Place one tracing on top of the other.

Ask: **Are the opposite sides congruent?** (yes) **Does the shape contain four right angles?** (yes) **What is the shape of the base?** (rectangle)

Have the students examine the bases on the model. Ask: **Are the opposite sides parallel?** (yes)

Have students trace the other faces on their paper and identify the shapes.

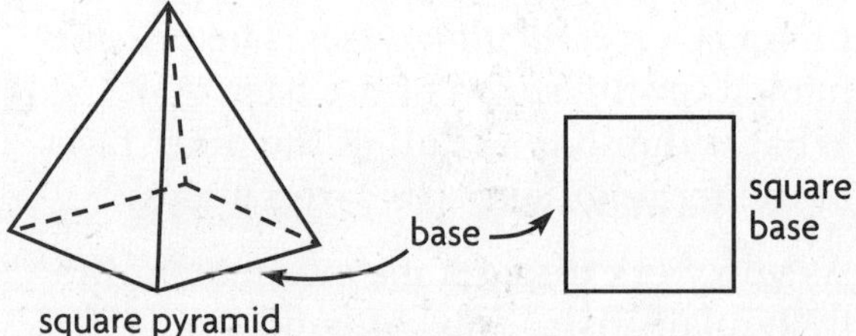

Then have the students take a square pyramid. Have them trace the base, measure the sides to confirm that they are of equal length, and identify the four right angles. Students should recognize that the base is a square. If necessary, have students trace the triangular faces to identify the shape of the faces on a pyramid.

Repeat this activity with the other three-dimensional models. When students show understanding, have them identify a 3-dimensional figure that you select at random.

Name ______________________ Skill ______________________

Faces of Prisms and Pyramids

Skill 84

Use the names of polygons to identify the faces of prisms and pyramids.

Prisms

A **prism** is a solid figure with two congruent, parallel polygon-shaped faces called **bases**. The other faces are rectangles. A prism is named for the shape of its bases.

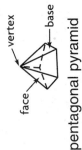

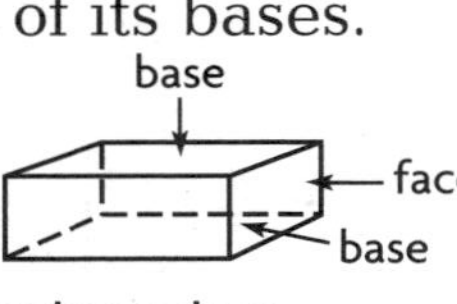

rectangular prism

There are 2 congruent bases. The 2 bases are rectangles. The 4 other faces are rectangles. There are 6 faces in all.

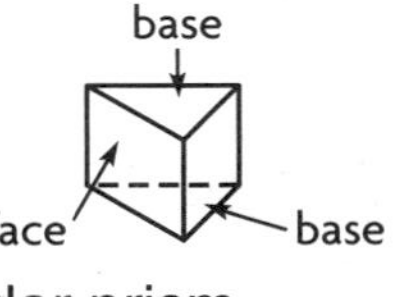

triangular prism

There are 2 congruent bases. The 2 bases are triangles. The 3 other faces are rectangles. There are 5 faces in all.

Pyramids

A **pyramid** is a solid figure with one polygon-shaped face for its base. Its other faces are triangles that meet at a common **vertex**. A pyramid is named for the shape of its base.

triangular pyramid

There is 1 base.
The base is a triangle.
The 3 other faces are triangles.
There are 4 faces in all.

pentagonal pyramid

There is 1 base.
The base is a pentagon.
The 5 other faces are triangles.
There are 6 faces in all.

Try These

Complete.

1.

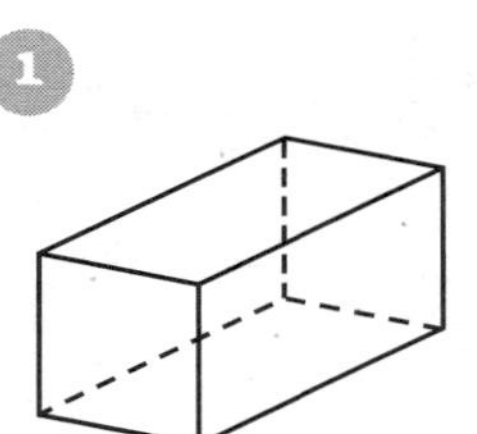

Number of bases____
Shape of base(s)______________
Number of other faces ____
Shape of other faces ___________
Total number of faces ____

2.

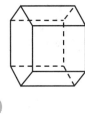

Number of bases____
Shape of base(s)______________
Number of other faces ____
Shape of other faces ___________
Total number of faces ____

Go to the next side.

Name ______________________ Skill ______________________

Practice on Your Own

Skill 84

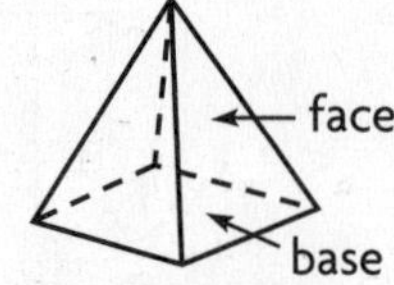

square pyramid

1 base is a square.
4 faces are triangles.
5 faces in all.

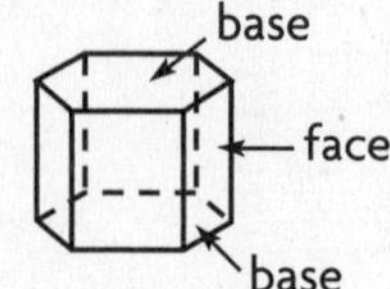

hexagonal prism

2 bases are hexagons.
6 faces are rectangles.
8 faces in all.

Complete.

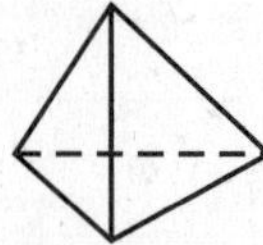

Number of bases ________
Shape of base(s) ________
Number of other faces ____
Shape of other faces ______
Total number of faces ____
Name of figure ______________

Number of bases ________
Shape of base(s) ________
Number of other faces ____
Shape of other faces ______
Total number of faces ____
Name of figure ______________

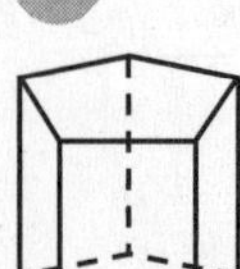

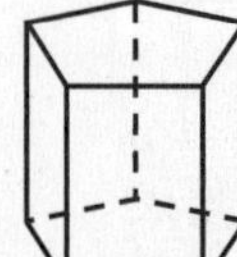

Number of bases ________
Number of other faces ____
Total number of faces ____
Name of figure ______________

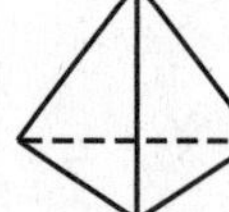

Number of bases ________
Number of other faces ____
Total number of faces ____
Name of figure ______________

Check

Complete.

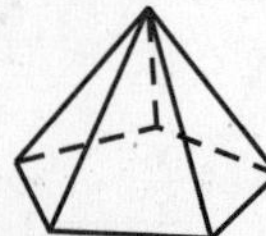

Number of bases ________
Number of other faces ____
Total number of faces ____
Name of figure ______________

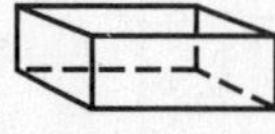

Number of bases ________
Number of other faces ____
Total number of faces ____
Name of figure ______________

Skill 85 Area of Squares, Rectangles, Triangles

15 Minutes

Using Skill 85

OBJECTIVE Use formulas to determine the area of squares, rectangles, and triangles

Read about area at the top of the page. Explain how the area of a figure is measured in square units. Have the students count the number of squares in the 3-by-5 rectangle. When multiplying two numbers whose units are the same, the product is square units. If the units are not the same, they must be adjusted so that they are the same.

Refer to the *Area of a Rectangle* section. Ask: **What is the length of the rectangle?** (2.5 cm) **What is the width of the rectangle?** (5.8 cm) **In the formula $A = \ell w$, what does each letter stand for?** (A is the area, ℓ is the length, and w is the width.)

Focus on how each variable is replaced by the value for that variable. Have the students do the multiplication. Explain that 14.50 = 14.5, so both 14.50 cm^2 or 14.5 cm^2 is the correct area.

Refer to the *Area of a Triangle* section. Ask: **In the formula $A = \frac{1}{2}bh$, what does each letter stand for?** (A is the area, b is the base, and h is the height.) **What operation is indicated in bh?** (multiplication) **In the rectangle that is 2.5 cm by 5.8 cm, which measure is the base and which is the height?** (base = 2.5 and height = 5.8, or base = 5.8 and height = 2.5) It is essential that students realize that, although these two measures are interchangeable in a rectangle, the height must be perpendicular to the side used as the base in a triangle.

TRY THESE Exercises 1–3 ask students to use formulas to find area.

- **Exercise 1** Area of a rectangle
- **Exercise 2** Area of a square
- **Exercise 3** Area of a triangle

PRACTICE ON YOUR OWN Review the examples at the top of the page. Focus on identifying the value for each variable in the formulas, and on writing the areas with correct units.

CHECK Determine if the students can use a formula to find area. Success is indicated by 3 out of 3 correct responses.

Students who successfully complete the **Practice on Your Own** and **Check** are ready to move to the next skill.

COMMON ERRORS

- Students may forget to express the area as square units.
- Students may forget to multiply the product of the base and height of a triangle by $\frac{1}{2}$.

Students who made more than 2 errors in the **Practice on Your Own**, or who were not successful in the **Check** section, may benefit from the **Alternative Teaching Strategy** on the next page.

Optional

Alternative Teaching Strategy

10 Minutes

Model Areas of Squares, Rectangles, Triangles

OBJECTIVE Model finding areas of squares, rectangles, and triangles

MATERIALS grid paper

Have the students draw a rectangle that is 4 units by 5 units.

Ask: **How many squares are inside the rectangle?** (20 squares) **How can you find the answer without counting the squares?** (multiply 4 by 5)

Have the students draw other rectangles with different dimensions and count the number of squares inside. Have them verify the number of squares by multiplying the dimensions. Be very consistent in requiring students to give area in square units.

Have the students draw a square that is 5 units by 5 units.

Ask: **How many squares are inside the square?** (25 squares) **How can you find the answer without counting the squares individually?** (multiply 5 by 5)

Have the students draw a rectangle that is 3 units by 6 units. Have them draw a diagonal line through the rectangle.

Ask: **How many squares are inside the rectangle?** (18 squares) **What part of the rectangle is each triangle formed by the diagonal?** (one half) **What is the area of each triangle?** (9 square units)

Draw students' attention to the fact that the triangle is half of the rectangle. You can divide the area of the rectangle in half or multiply the area by $\frac{1}{2}$ to find the area of one of the triangles.

Name ____________________ Skill ____________________

Area of Squares, Rectangles, Triangles

Skill 85

Area is the number of square units needed to cover a surface.
Use formulas to find the areas of rectangles, squares, and triangles.

5 units; 3 units; 1 square unit

3 units × 5 units = 15 square units

Area of a Rectangle
You can use this formula to find the area of a rectangle.

2.5 cm; 5.8 cm; 5.8 cm; 2.5 cm

Area of Rectangle
= length × width
$A = \ell \times w$
Then: Replace ℓ with 2.5.
$A = \ell \times w$ Replace w with 5.8.
$= 2.5 \times 5.8$
$= 14.5$ sq cm
So, the area of the rectangle is 15.5 cm².

Area of a Square
A square is a rectangle with sides all the same length.

$3\frac{1}{2}$ in.; $3\frac{1}{2}$ in.; $3\frac{1}{2}$ in.; $3\frac{1}{2}$ in.

So, you can use this formula to find the area of a square:
Area of square = side × side
$A = s \times s$ or $A = s^2$ Replace s with $3\frac{1}{2}$.
$= 3\frac{1}{2} \times 3\frac{1}{2}$
$= 12\frac{1}{4}$
So, the area of the square is $12\frac{1}{4}$ in².

Area of a Triangle
Use this formula to find the area of a triangle.
$A = \frac{1}{2}bh$
$= \frac{1}{2} \times (10 \times 6)$
$= \frac{1}{2} \times 60$
$= 30$ ft²

X; W; Y; 6ft; 10 ft

So, the area of triangle *WXY* is 30 ft².

Try These

Find the area.

1. $A = \ell \times w$
   = ____ × ____
   = ____
   Area is ____ in.²

   $15\frac{1}{2}$ in.; $6\frac{1}{2}$ in.

2. $A = s \times s$
   = ____ × ____
   = ____
   Area is ____ cm².

   1.5 cm; 1.5 cm

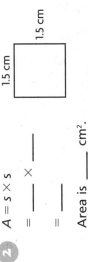

3. $A = \frac{1}{2}bh$
   $= \frac{1}{2} \times ($____ × ____$)$
   $= \frac{1}{2} \times$ ____
   = ____
   Area is ____ m².

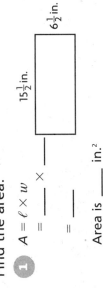

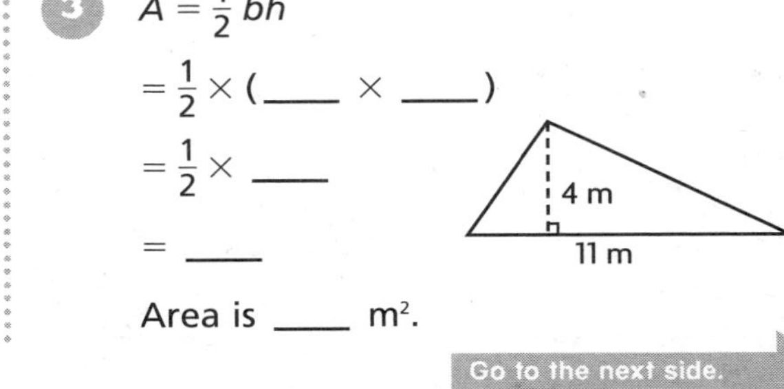

Go to the next side.

Name ______________________ Skill ______________________

Practice on Your Own

Skill 85

Think:

Remember to express the area in square units.

$A = \ell \times w$
$= 3 \times 12$
$= 36$

3 cm

12 cm

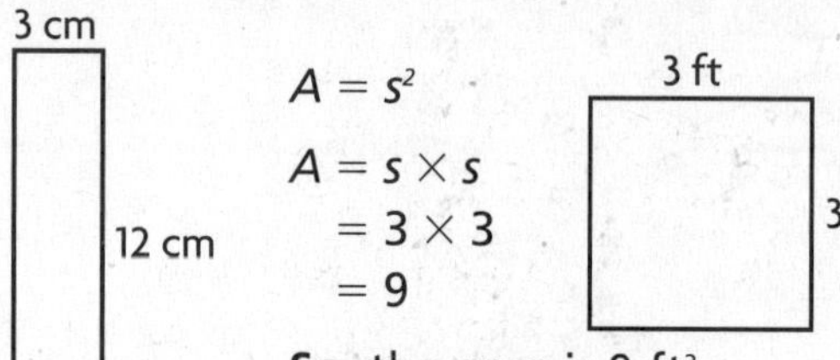

So, the area is $36\ cm^2$.

$A = s^2$

$A = s \times s$
$= 3 \times 3$
$= 9$

3 ft

3 ft

So, the area is $9\ ft^2$.

$A = \frac{1}{2}bh$
$= \frac{1}{2}(7 \times 3)$
$= \frac{1}{2}(21)$
$= 10\frac{1}{2}$

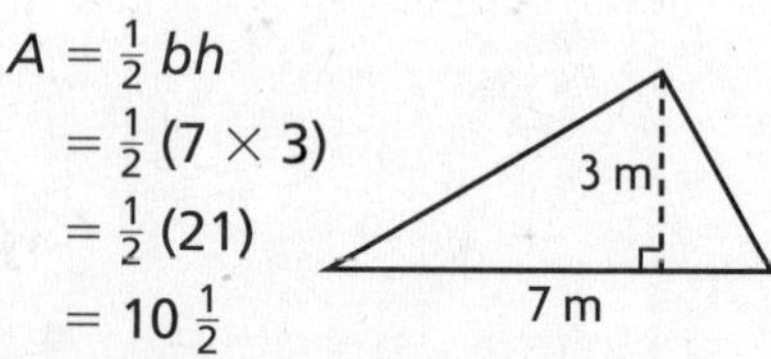

So, the area is $10\frac{1}{2}\ m^2$.

Find the area of each figure.

1 $A = \ell \times w$
$A =$ ____ $\times$ ____
$A =$ ____

$3\frac{3}{4}$ ft

$1\frac{1}{2}$ ft

2 $A = s \times s$
$A =$ ____ $\times$ ____
$A =$ ____

10 mi

10 mi

3 $A = \frac{1}{2}bh$
$A = \frac{1}{2} \times ($____ $\times$ ____$)$
$A = \frac{1}{2} \times$ ____
$A =$ ____

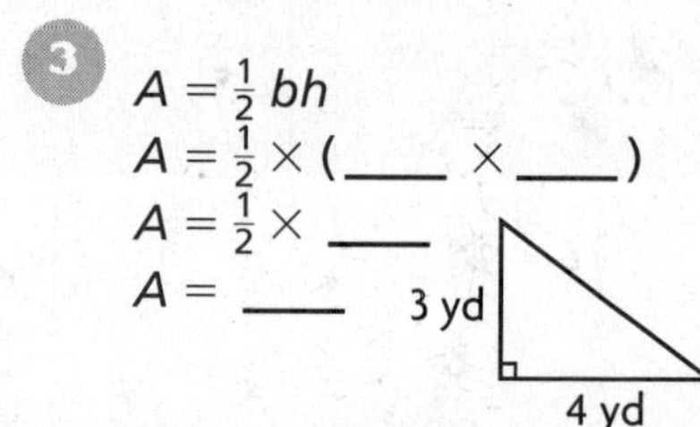

Write the formula. Find the area of each figure.

4 $A =$ ______
$A =$ ______

14 in.

$5\frac{1}{2}$ in.

5 $A =$ ______
$A =$ ______

6 ft

6 ft

6 $A =$ ______
$A =$ ______

3.5 cm

20 cm

Find the area of each figure.

7

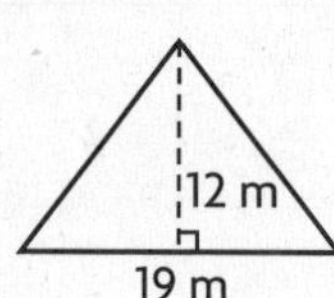

______

8

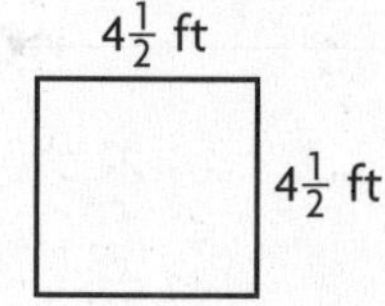

______

9

50 cm

10.2 cm

______

Check

Find the area of each figure.

10

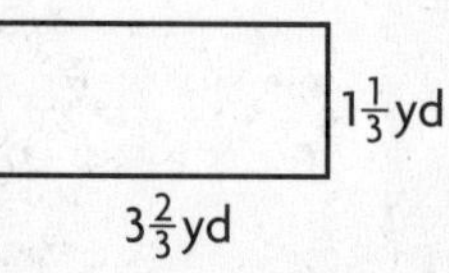

______

11

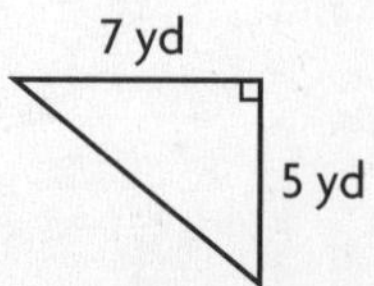

______

12

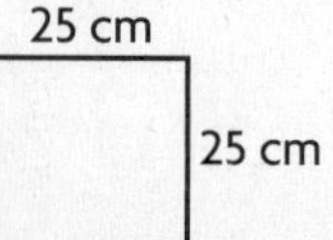

______

Skill 86 Area of Circles

Using Skill 86

OBJECTIVE Find the area of a circle by using a formula

Begin by reviewing the parts of a circle. Ask students to identify the radius (r) and circumference (C). Have them distinguish the radius from the diameter.

Display the formula to find the area of a circle, $A = \pi r^2$. Explain that just as students used formulas to find areas of rectangles, they can use a formula to find the area of a circle.

Read *Understanding the Formula.* Review the formula and have students identify each part. A is for area; π (*pi*) is approximately equal to 3.14 and also equals the ratio of the circumference to the diameter ($\frac{C}{d}$); r is the radius.

Look at *Find the area of each circle.* Ask: **What do you need to know to use the formula $A = \pi r^2$?** (the radius of the circle) **What is the radius of the circle?** (3 cm) **What do you do with the value for the radius?** (Substitute 3 for r)

In evaluating the formula, emphasize that the radius is squared and that the area will be approximate since $\pi \approx 3.14$. Ask: **What units are used to measure the area of the circle?** (square centimeters)

Point out that even though the circle is round, the area is still measured in square units.

For the second example, have students identify what the 12 feet represents. (diameter)

Ask: **How is the diameter of a circle related to the radius?** (The diameter is twice the radius.) **If the diameter is 12 feet, what is the radius?** (6 feet)

Point out to the students that $\frac{22}{7}$ is another way of approximating π. Have the students note that the area is in square feet.

TRY THESE Exercises 1–3 help the students step-by-step as they use the formula for finding the area of a circle.

- **Exercise 1** Use the radius and 3.14 for *pi.*
- **Exercise 2** Use the radius and $\frac{22}{7}$ for *pi.*
- **Exercise 3** Use the diameter and 3.14 for *pi.*

PRACTICE ON YOUR OWN Review the example at the top of the page. Have students focus on how to find the radius when given the diameter.

CHECK Determine if the students can use a formula to find the area of a circle. Success is indicated by 3 out of 3 correct responses.

Students who successfully complete the **Practice on Your Own** and **Check** are ready to move to the next skill.

COMMON ERRORS

- Students may multiply the radius by two instead of squaring it.
- Students may use the diameter instead of the radius.

Students who made more than 2 errors in the **Practice on Your Own**, or who were not successful in the **Check** section, may benefit from the **Alternative Teaching Strategy** on the next page.

Optional

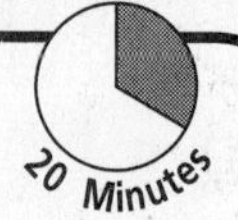

Alternative Teaching Strategy
Model Finding the Area of a Circle

OBJECTIVE Model finding the area of a circle using a formula

MATERIALS centimeter grid paper, compass, ruler

Have students draw a circle with a radius of 4 cm within an 8 cm by 8 cm square. Emphasize that every point on the circle is 4 cm from the center. Divide the square into fourths.

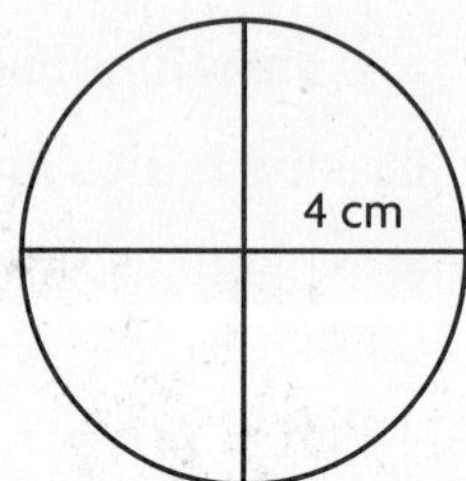

Explain to the students that they can use what they know about finding the area of a square, to estimate the area of a circle.

Guide students as they notice that the radius of the circle is also the length of one side of a square.

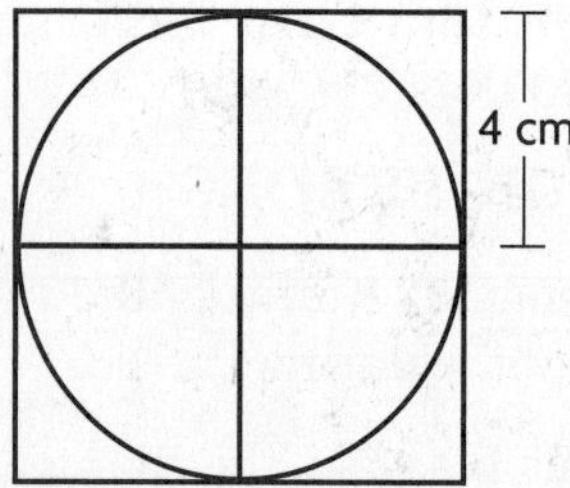

How can you use the radius to find the area of the small square? (If the radius is 4 cm long, then the side of the square is 4 cm. Think: $A = s^2$ or $A = r^2$; the area is 16 cm^2)

Suggest that since we can express the area of the small square as r^2, then we can say the area of the large square is $4 \times r^2$ or $4r^2$. Ask:

What is the area of the large square? ($4 \times 16 = 64$ cm^2)

Compare the area of the large square and the area of the circle.

Is the area of the large square greater than or less than the area of the circle? (greater than) **How do you know?** (The circle is inside the area of the 4 squares; the corners of the squares show outside the circle.)

Guide students to see that if the area of the large square is $4r^2$, they can estimate the area of the circle as about 3 small squares, or $3r^2$ ($3 \times 16 = 48$ cm^2).

Have students calculate the area of the circle using the formula. Guide them through each step. Remind them that $\pi \approx$ (is about equal to) 3.14. Compare $3r^2$ to the second step $A = 3.14\ (4)^2$

$A = \pi r^2$

$A \approx 3.14 \times (4)^2$

$A \approx 3.14 \times 16$

$A \approx 50.24$ square centimeters

Point out that the calculated area is close to the estimated area.

When students have completed the activity using the model, have students use the formula to find the area of other circles given the radius.

Area of Circles

Skill 86

Use the formula to find the area of each of the circles.

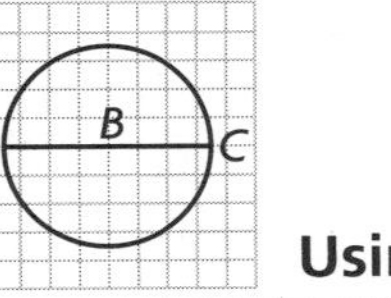

Understanding the Formula

Area is the number of square units needed to cover a surface. Remember: The ratio of the circumference to the diameter $(\frac{C}{d})$ is called pi. The value of *pi* is approximately 3.14 or $\frac{22}{7}$. To find the area, multiply the value of *pi* by the length of the radius squared. Express the area using the symbol $\approx$ which means approximately equal to.

Formula: $A = \pi r^2$

Using the Formula

Find the area of each circle.

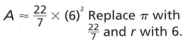

$A = \pi r^2$

$A \approx 3.14 \times (3)^2$ Replace π with 3.14 and r with 3.

$A \approx 3.14 \times 9$ Multiply.

$A \approx 28.26$

Rounded to the nearest centimeter, the area is about 28 cm^2.

First, find the radius.

$A = \pi r^2$

$A \approx \frac{22}{7} \times (6)^2$ Replace π with $\frac{22}{7}$ and r with 6.

$A \approx \frac{22}{7} \times 36$ $A \approx \frac{22}{7} \times \frac{36}{1}$

$A \approx \frac{792}{7}$

$A \approx 113.1428\ldots$

Rounded to the nearest foot, the area is about 113 ft^2.

Try These

Find the area. Round to the nearest whole number.

1. $A = \pi r^2$

   $A \approx 3.14 \times (\_\_)^2$

   $A \approx 3.14 \times \_\_$

   $A \approx$ ______ m^2

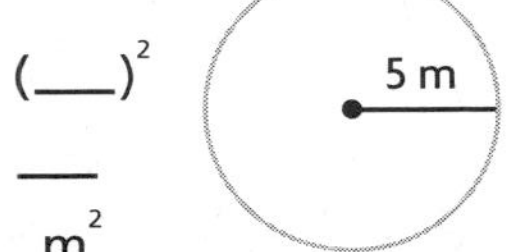

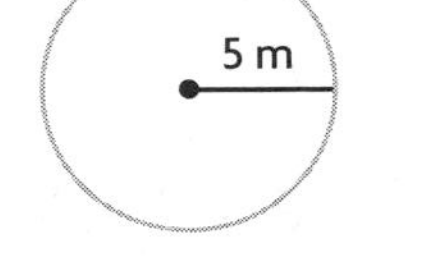

2. $A = \pi r^2$

   $A \approx \frac{22}{7} \times (\_\_)^2$

   $A \approx \frac{22}{7} \times \frac{\square}{1}$

   Simplify.

   $A \approx \_\_ \times \_\_$

   $A \approx$ ______ $in.^2$

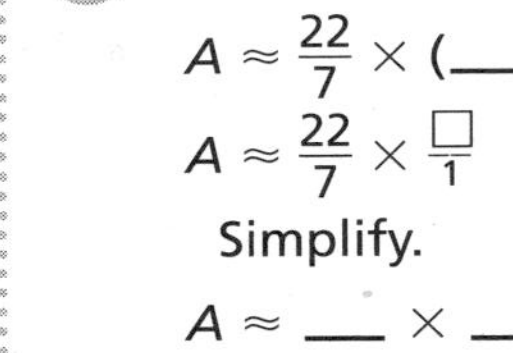

3. Find the radius.

   $r =$ ______

   $A = \pi r^2$

   $A \approx 3.14 \times (\_\_)^2$

   $A \approx 3.14 \times \_\_$

   $A \approx$ ______ cm^2

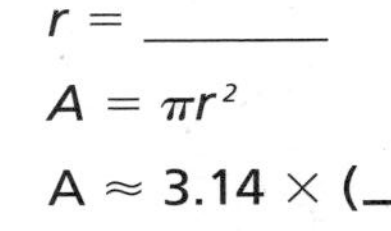

Go to the next side.

Name ____________________ Skill ____________________

Practice on Your Own

Skill 86

Think:
Use 3.14 for π.

Find the area to the nearest whole number.
The radius (r) is 19 m ÷ 2, or 9.5 m.

$A = \pi r^2$

$A \approx 3.14 \times (9.5)^2$

$A \approx 3.14 \times 90.25 \text{ m}^2$

$A \approx 283.385 \text{ m}^2$

Rounded to the nearest whole number, the area is about 283 m^2.

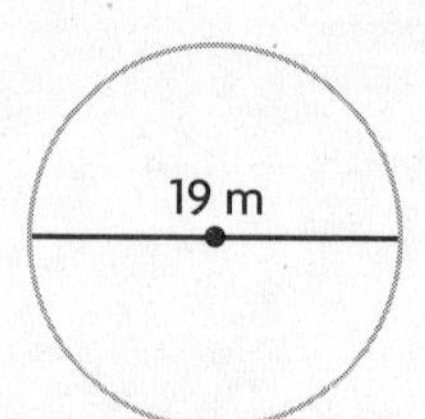

Find the area. Round to the nearest whole number.

1 6 cm

$A = \pi r^2$

$A \approx 3.14 \times (\_\_)^2$

$A \approx 3.14 \times \_\_$

$A \approx$ ________

Rounded to the nearest whole number, the area is ____.

2 14 yd

$A = \pi r^2$

$A \approx \frac{22}{7} \times (\_\_)^2$

$A \approx \frac{22}{7} \times \frac{\square}{1}$

Simplify.

$A \approx \_\_ \times \_\_$

$A \approx$ ________

Rounded to the nearest whole number, the area is ____.

3 9 m

$r =$ ______

$A = \pi r^2$

$A \approx 3.14 \times (\_\_)^2$

$A \approx 3.14 \times \_\_$

$A \approx$ ________

Rounded to the nearest whole number, the area is ____.

4 8 m

$A = \pi r^2$

$A \approx 3.14 \times (\_\_)^2$

____

____

Round: ________

5 15 ft

$A = \pi r^2$

$A \approx \frac{22}{7} \times (\_\_)^2$

____

____

Round: ________

6

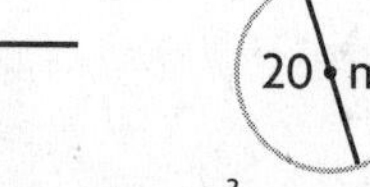

$r =$ ______

$A = \pi r^2$

$A \approx 3.14 \times (\_\_)^2$

____

____

7

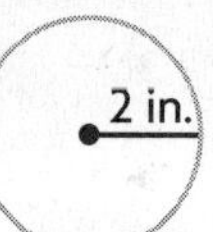

____

8

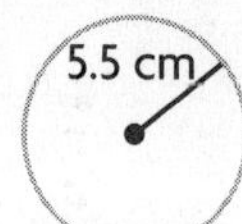

____

9

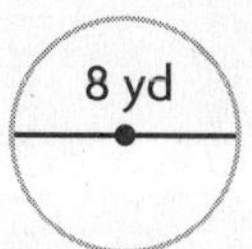

____

Check

Find the area. Round to the nearest whole number.

10

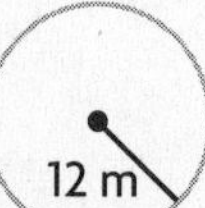

____

11

____

12

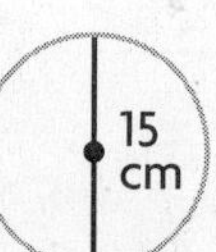

____

Using Skill 87

OBJECTIVE Identify whether a transformation is a translation, rotation, or reflection

Begin by explaining what transformations are. Explain to the students that today's lesson will be about translations, rotations, and reflections.

Have students look at the example for a translation. Point out that the dashed triangle is the original figure, and the arrow shows how it was moved to a new position.

Ask:
How do the triangles compare? (They look the same.)

Guide students to understand that when you translate a figure, the figure looks exactly the same, but it is in a new position.

Direct students to the example for a reflection.

Ask:
How does the triangle on one side of the line compare to the triangle on the other side of the line? (They look exactly the same, but they point in opposite directions.)

Point out to the students that when you reflect a figure over an imaginary line, both the position and the location of the figure change. The figure becomes the mirror image of itself.

In the example for rotation, the triangle turns around a point of rotation. Ask: **How does the transformation compare to its original figure?** (The two figures look exactly the same; they point in different directions.)

Lead students to conclude that when you rotate a figure, the figure rotates around a fixed point. Both the location and the position of the figure change. The point of rotation is fixed. It does not move.

TRY THESE In Exercises 1–3 students identify transformations.

- **Exercise 1** Identify a translation.
- **Exercise 2** Identify a reflection.
- **Exercise 3** Identify a rotation.

PRACTICE ON YOUR OWN Review the examples at the top of the page. Have students focus on the position of each shape.

CHECK Determine if students can identify the transformation of a figure as either a translation, a rotation, or a reflection. Success is indicated by 3 out of 3 correct responses.

Students who successfully complete the **Practice on Your Own** and **Check** are ready to move to the next skill.

COMMON ERRORS

- Students may confuse a reflection with a rotation.
- Students may think a rotation is a translation.

Students who made more than 2 errors in the **Practice on Your Own**, or who were not successful in the **Check** section, may benefit from the **Alternative Teaching Strategy** on the next page.

Optional

Alternative Teaching Strategy

Model Transformations

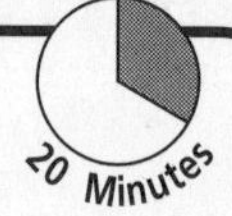

OBJECTIVE Model translations, rotations, and reflections

MATERIALS graph paper

Have students make a coordinate plane and then draw a triangle with coordinates *A*(0, 0), *B*(0, 3), and *C*(5, 0).

Have the students make a copy of the first triangle on another piece of paper by tracing and then cutting it out.

Have them label the inside of the second triangle with the letters of the vertices. The two triangles should be congruent.

Tell the students to place the triangle they cut out on top of the first triangle. Then have them move it horizontally 8 units on the coordinate plane.

Ask: **What are the coordinates of the new triangle?** (*A*(8, 0); *B*(8, 3); *C*(13, 0))

Have students translate the triangle and record the new coordinates. Focus on the fact that the orientation of the vertices of the triangle remains the same.

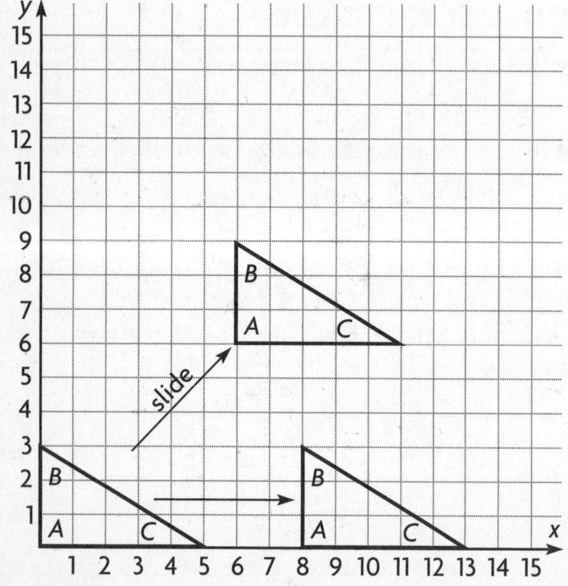

Repeat the activity using the coordinate grid for reflections and rotations. Have students record the coordinates for the figure in the original position, and then again after the transformation.

As students examine reflections and rotations, have them focus on the orientation of the vertices of the triangle.

A reflection over an imaginary line reverses the direction of the triangle. The reflected triangle becomes a mirror image.

A rotation changes the orientation of all points except for the fixed point of rotation.

Name ______________________ Skill ______________________

Skill 87

Transformations

Transformations are different ways to move a figure.
Three kinds of transformations are ***translations***, ***reflections***, and ***rotations***.

Translation
A **translation** slides a figure along a straight line.

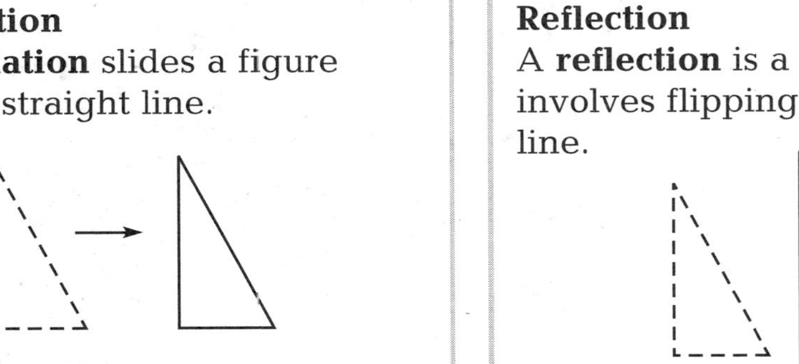

Reflection
A **reflection** is a movement that involves flipping a figure over a line.

Rotation
A **rotation** is a movement that involves rotating a figure around a point.

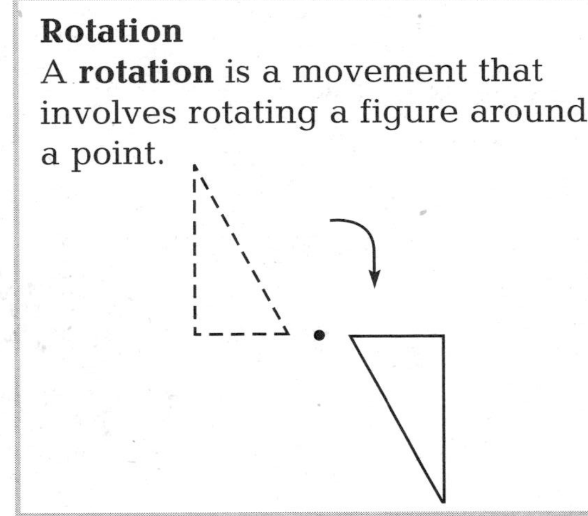

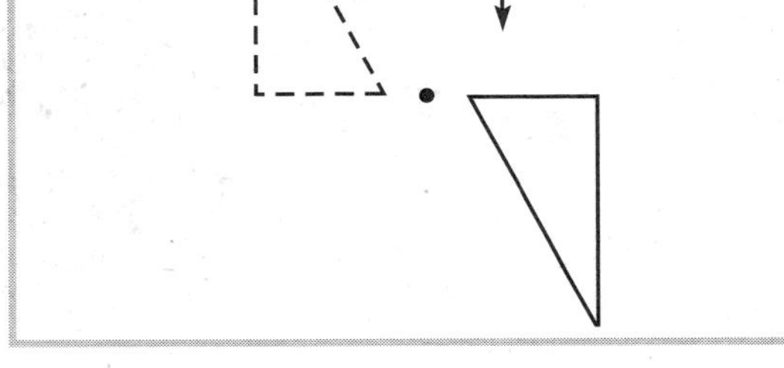

Try These

Identify the transformation as a *translation, reflection,* or *rotation.*

1. 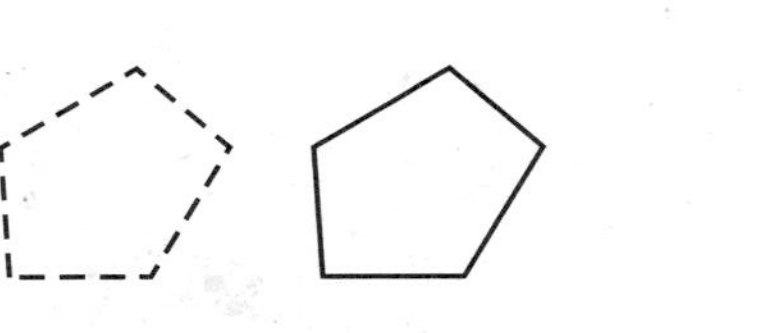
____

2. ______________

3. 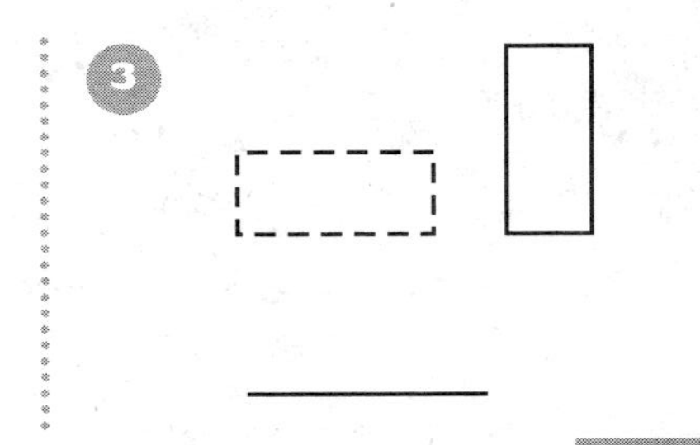
____

Go to the next side.

Name ____________________ Skill ____________________

Practice on Your Own

Skill 87

Think:
Transformations move figures in different ways.

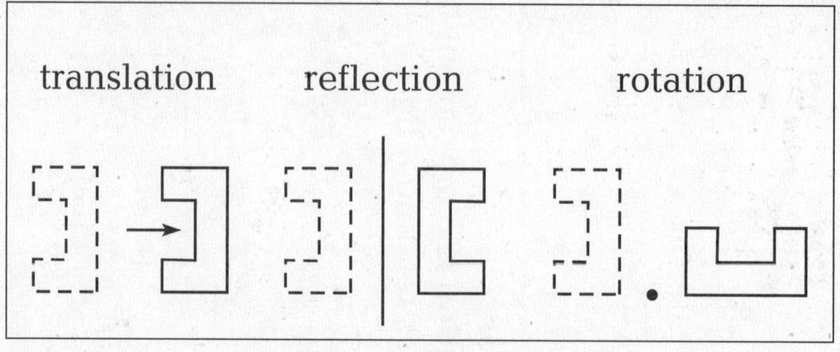

Identify the transformation as a *translation*, *reflection*, or *rotation*.

1  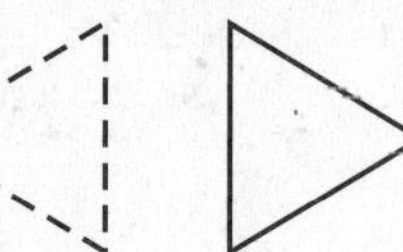

____

2  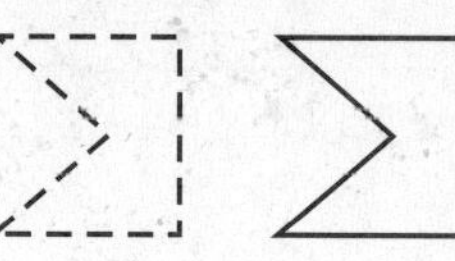

____

3  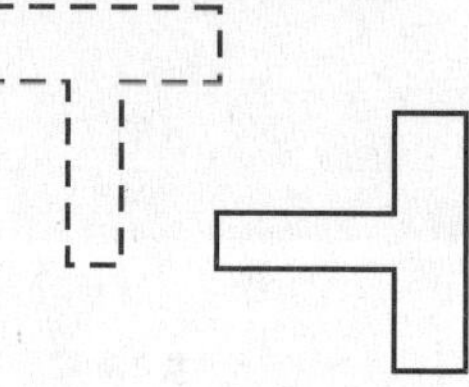

____

4 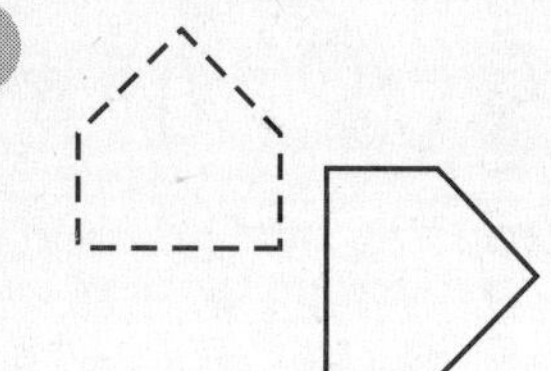

____

5 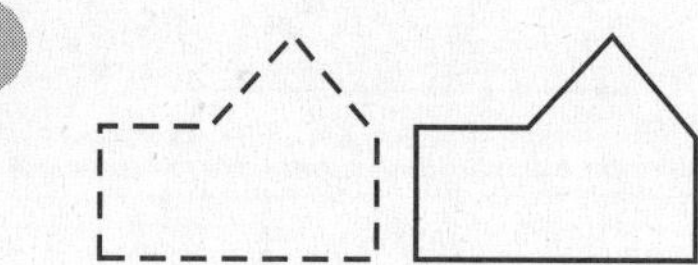

____

6 

____

7 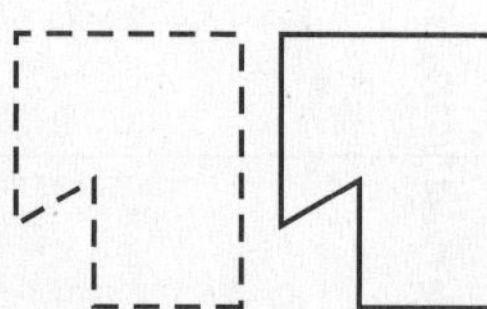

____

8 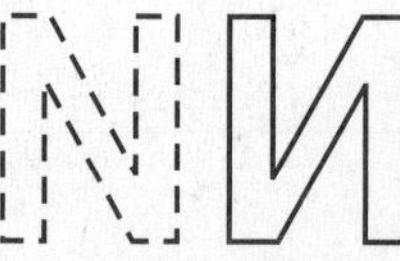

____

9 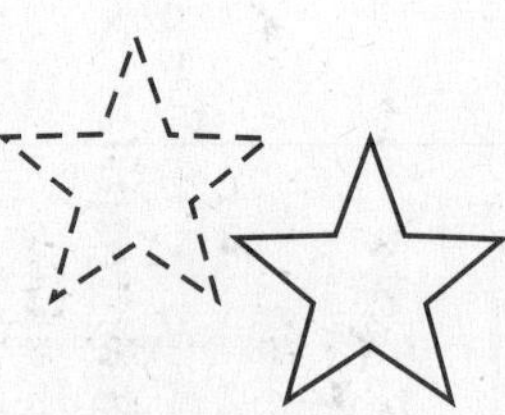

____

Check

Identify the transformation as a *translation*, *reflection*, or *rotation*.

10 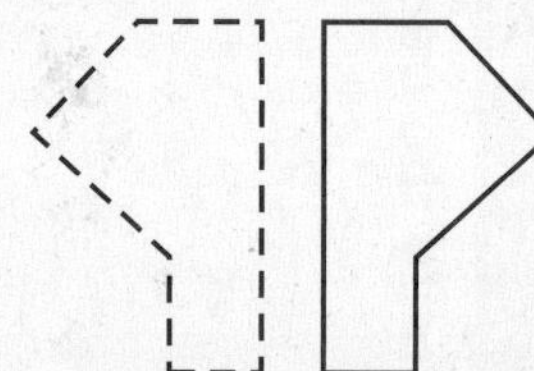

____

11 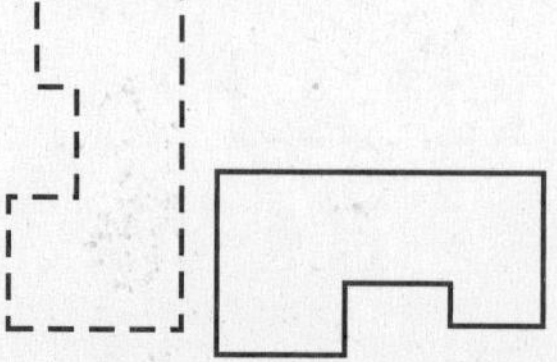

____

12 

____

Using Skill 88

OBJECTIVE Identify whether a figure has lines of symmetry

MATERIALS grid paper

You may wish to use grid paper to model the steps of the activity.

Begin by discussing how a figure with line symmetry can be folded to show that the parts are congruent. Recall that *congruent* means having the same shape and the same size.

Have students look at Step 1. Explain that grid paper makes it easy to copy some figures. Students can count the number of squares in each figure and then position the figures in the same way on the grid paper. Stress the importance of copying the figures precisely.

In Step 2, have students note that both dotted lines in the hexagon are lines of symmetry. Folding the figure along either line will show two matching halves.

The square has four lines of symmetry. Point out that the diagonal lines are lines of symmetry because both halves of the figure match.

Have students look at the third figure. Ask: **Why isn't each line a line of symmetry?** (Both parts of the figure do not match.) **Can you draw another line on the figure that is a line of symmetry?** (No, this figure has no line of symmetry.)

As students read the third step, conclude that some figures have more than one line of symmetry, while others have no lines of symmetry.

TRY THESE Exercises 1–4 present two congruent figures, each with different lines. Students determine whether or not a line is a line of symmetry.

- **Exercises 1, 3** The first line is a line of symmetry.
- **Exercise 2** The second line is a line of symmetry.
- **Exercise 4** Neither line is a line of symmetry.

PRACTICE ON YOUR OWN Review the examples at the top of the page. As students work through the exercises, encourage them to examine the two parts carefully, and determine if the parts are congruent before they write an answer.

CHECK Determine if students can identify one or more lines of symmetry. Success is indicated by 3 out of 4 correct responses.

Students who successfully complete the **Practice on Your Own** and **Check** are ready to move to the next skill.

COMMON ERRORS

- Students may identify diagonals in rectangles as lines of symmetry.

Students who made more than 2 errors in the **Practice on Your Own**, or who were not successful in the **Check** section, may benefit from the **Alternative Teaching Strategy** on the next page.

Optional

Alternative Teaching Strategy

Model Lines of Symmetry

OBJECTIVE Use models to identify lines of symmetry

MATERIALS mirrors, stencils of figures with and without lines of symmetry

Have the students use a stencil to draw a rectangle on their paper.

Review the definition of *line of symmetry*. Explain that a figure has a line of symmetry if it can be "reflected" or folded so that the two parts are congruent.

Suggest that students draw a line through the rectangle so the two halves will match.

Distribute the mirrors. Demonstrate how to test the line by putting the edge of the mirror along a line to see if the reflection in the glass matches the other side. If the reflection matches the other side, the line is a line of symmetry.

Have the students use the mirror to test the line they think is a line of symmetry. Ask: **Look at the rectangle again. Does the rectangle have another line of symmetry?**

Suggest that students look for another line of symmetry and test it with the mirror.

Repeat the activity by having students draw other figures and look for lines of symmetry. Discuss and compare the results.

When students are able to draw and recognize lines of symmetry, have them draw and test a circle. Guide them as they conclude that any line drawn through the center of the circle is a line of symmetry.

Name ______________________ Skill ______________________

Skill 88

Line Symmetry

A figure has **line symmetry** if it can be folded or reflected so that the two parts are congruent.

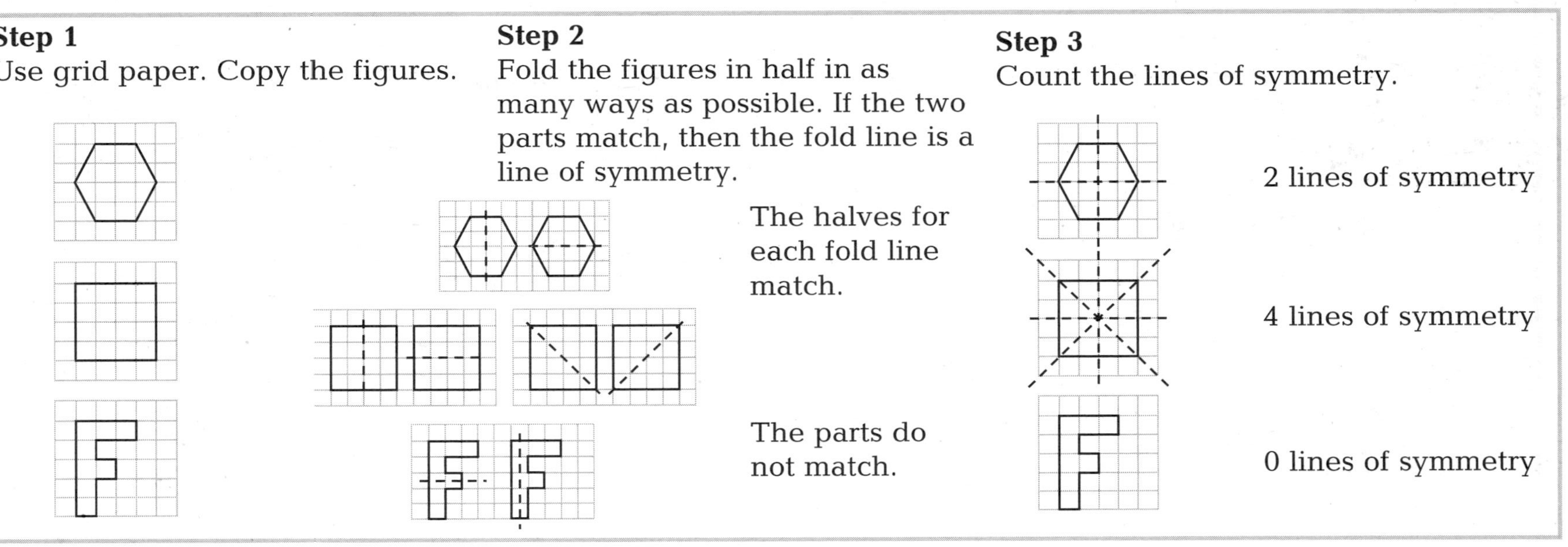

Step 1
Use grid paper. Copy the figures.

Step 2
Fold the figures in half in as many ways as possible. If the two parts match, then the fold line is a line of symmetry.

The halves for each fold line match.

The parts do not match.

Step 3
Count the lines of symmetry.

2 lines of symmetry

4 lines of symmetry

0 lines of symmetry

Try These

Tell whether the dashed line in each figure is a line of symmetry. Write yes or no.

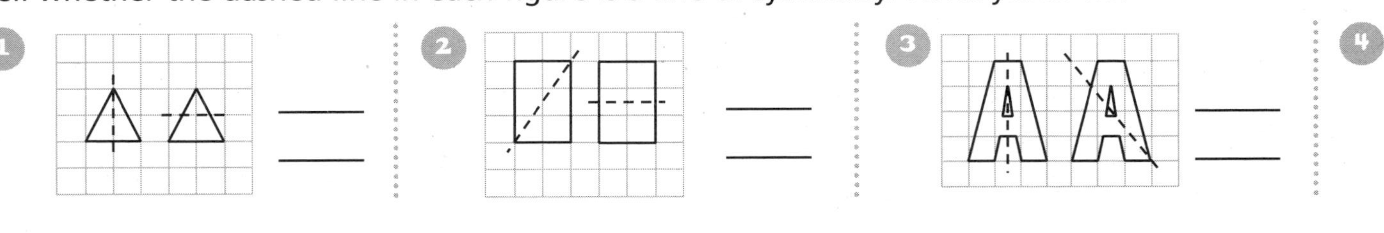

1. ______ ______

2. ______ ______

3. ______ ______

4. ______ ______

Go to the next side.

Name ______________________ Skill ______________________

Practice on Your Own

Skill 88

Think:
Do the parts match?
Are they the same size and shape?

1 line of symmetry
The parts are the same size and shape.

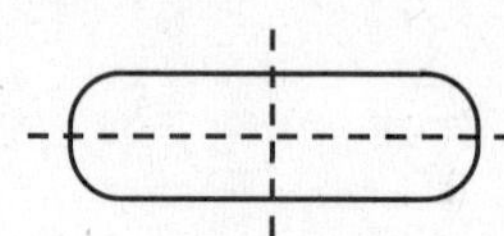

2 lines of symmetry
The parts are the same size and shape.

0 lines of symmetry
The parts are not the same size and shape.

Draw as many lines of symmetry as possible. Record the number you find.

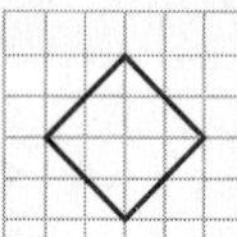

_____ lines of symmetry

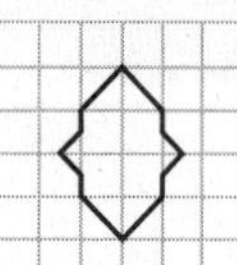

_____ lines of symmetry

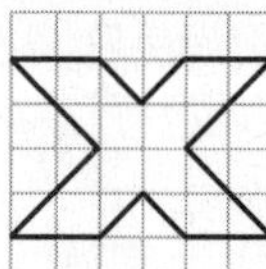

_____ lines of symmetry

4

_____ lines of symmetry

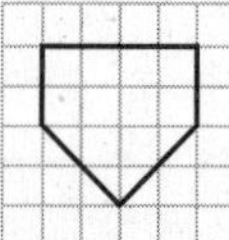

_____ lines of symmetry

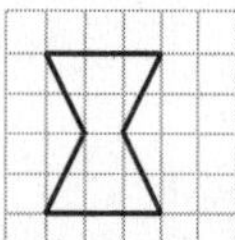

_____ lines of symmetry

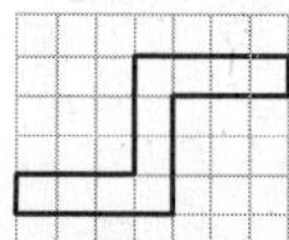

_____ lines of symmetry

_____ lines of symmetry

Check

Draw as many lines of symmetry as possible. Record the number you find.

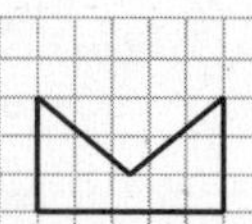

_____ lines of symmetry

10

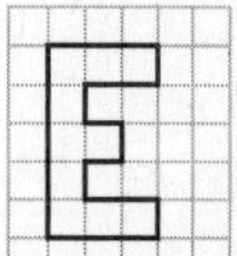

_____ lines of symmetry

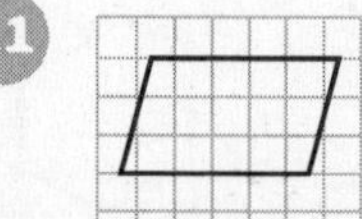

_____ lines of symmetry

_____ lines of symmetry

Using Skill 89

OBJECTIVE Use a protractor to find the measure of an angle

MATERIALS protractor

Begin Skill 89 by having students examine the protractor. Point out the center point and the one-degree intervals on the protractor's scale. Explain to students that they will be using a protractor to measure angles to the nearest degree

To guide students in Step 1, ask: **Do you think the angle will measure more than 90° or less than 90°?** (less because it is an acute angle) **Which point is the vertex of the angle?** (Point *B*) **What are the two rays that make up the angle?** (ray *BA* and ray *BC*)

Demonstrate how the center point of the protractor is placed at the vertex of the angle.

As students look at Step 2, caution them to place the horizontal line or base of the protractor along ray *BC* carefully, in order to get an accurate measurement. Note that since protractors differ in design, you may wish to check the placement of the protractor as each student measures.

In Step 3, have the students examine both scales and read the number on the bottom or inner scale to measure the angle. Ask: **With which number does ray *BA* align?** (30) **Angles are measured in degrees. What is the measure of $\angle ABC$?** (30°)

How can estimating the measure help you know which scale to use? (The choices on the protractor are either 30° or 150°. Since the angle measures less than 90°, the scale to use is the one showing 30°.)

TRY THESE In Exercises 1 and 2 students read the measure of an angle on a protractor.

- **Exercise 1** Angle of 90°
- **Exercise 2** Angle greater than 90°

PRACTICE ON YOUR OWN Review the example at the top of the page. Encourage students to turn the paper to measure the angle. Have them check their measurements by lining the protractor up on the ray opposite the one they used the first time.

CHECK Determine if students can use a protractor to measure an angle. Success is indicated by 3 out of 3 correct responses.

Students who successfully complete the **Practice on Your Own** and **Check** are ready to move to the next skill.

COMMON ERRORS

- Students may read the wrong scale when using the protractor.
- Students may not line up a ray of the angle on the protractor or may not place the vertex accurately.

Students who made more than 2 errors in the **Practice on Your Own**, or who were not successful in the **Check** section, may benefit from the **Alternative Teaching Strategy** on the next page.

Optional

Alternative Teaching Strategy

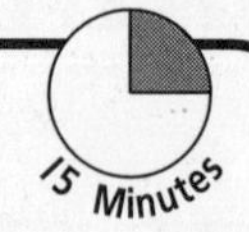

Model Measuring Angles

OBJECTIVE Model measuring angles using a protractor

MATERIALS protractor; angles measuring 30°, 60°, 90°, 120°, and 150°

Draw and label each angle on a separate piece of paper. Distribute angles and protractors to students. Have the students sort the angles from smallest to largest.

Discuss which angle is the smallest and which is the largest. Then sort the angles to show a 90° angle, angles greater than 90°, and angles less than 90°. Record these estimates on the back of the drawing.

Demonstrate the steps for measuring an angle with a protractor, and have each student show that they understand the procedure. Remind them that when they read the scale, they can use the relative size of each angle to help them decide which scale to use.

Have students take turns measuring the angles and recording the results. Then have them discuss and compare their results with each other, and with the estimates recorded on the back of the drawings.

When students show an understanding of the measuring process, suggest they use the protractor to draw an angle, exchange the angle with another student and measure it. Then have them compare their measurements.

Name ______________________ Skill ______________________

Skill 89

Measure Angles

Recall that an *angle* is formed by two rays with a common endpoint called a vertex. Measure angles with a protractor that has a scale in 1 degree intervals.

Measure the angle.

Step 1 Place the center point of the protractor on the vertex of the angle.

Step 2 Place the base of the protractor along ray BC.

Step 3 Read the same scale which has a ray passing through zero.

So, the measure of angle ABC is 30°.
Write: $m\angle ABC = 30°$

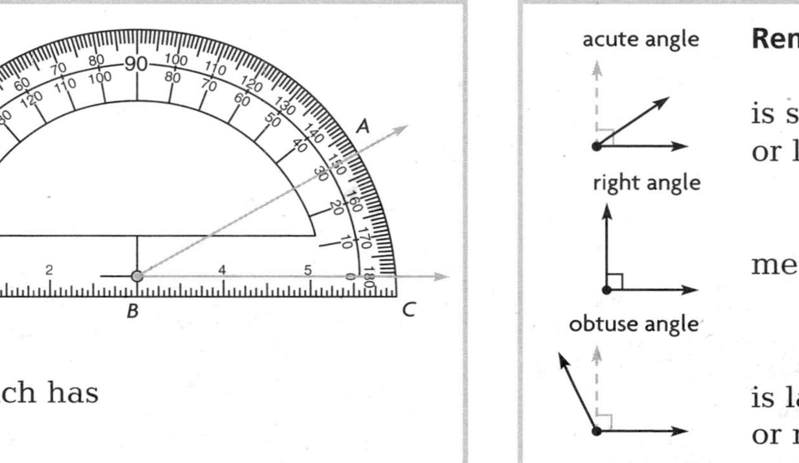

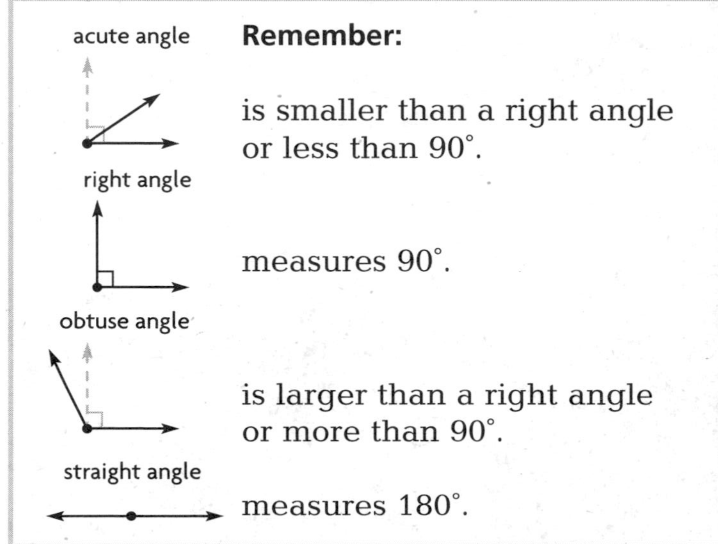

Remember:

acute angle: is smaller than a right angle or less than 90°.

right angle: measures 90°.

obtuse angle: is larger than a right angle or more than 90°.

straight angle: measures 180°.

Try These

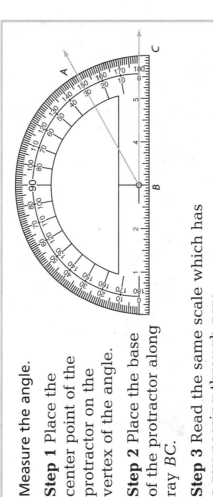

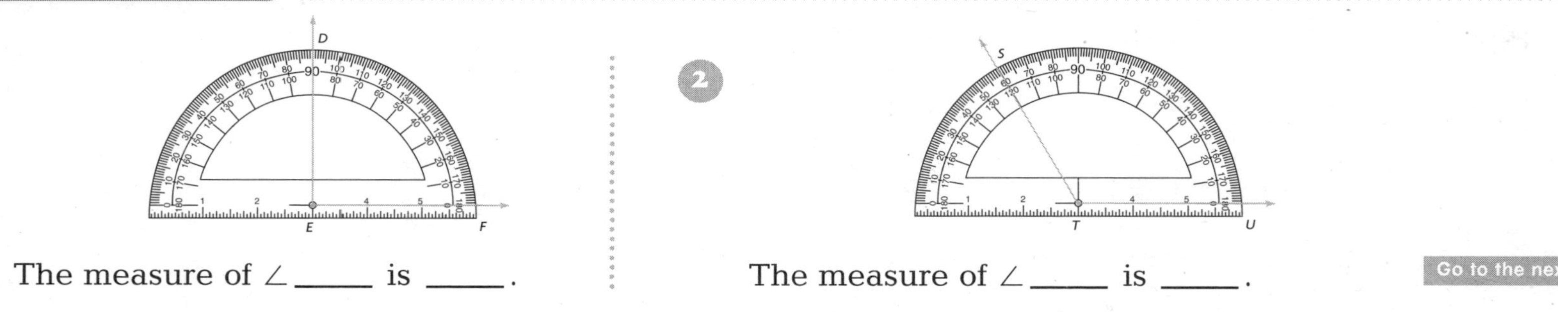

1. The measure of ∠ _____ is _____.

2. The measure of ∠ _____ is _____.

Go to the next side.

Name ______________________ Skill ______________________

Practice on Your Own

Skill 89

Think:
First place the center point of the protractor on the vertex of the angle.
Then align one ray with the base of the protractor.
Remember:
You can turn the page around to help you measure the angle.

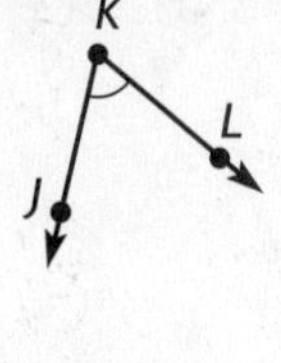

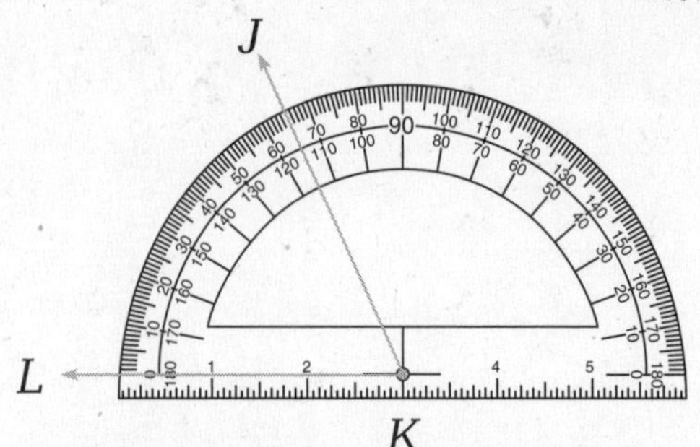

So, the measure of angle JKL is 65°.
$m\angle JKL = 65°$

Use a protractor. Measure the angle. Align the center point of the protractor with the vertex of the angle shown in blue.

1 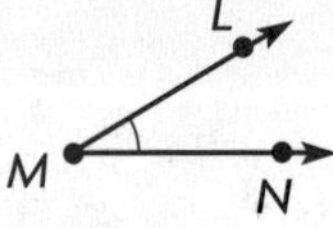

$m\angle LMN =$ ______°

2 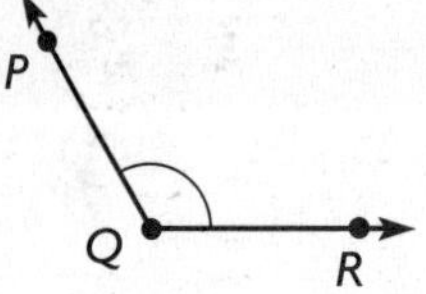

$m\angle PQR =$ ______°

3 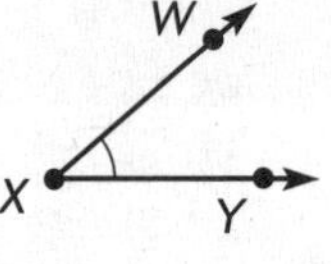

$m\angle WXY =$ ______°

4 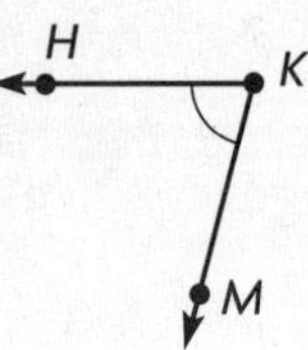

$m\angle$ _____ = _____

5 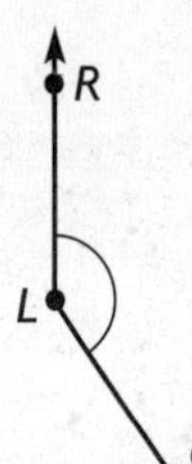

$m\angle$ _____ = _____

6 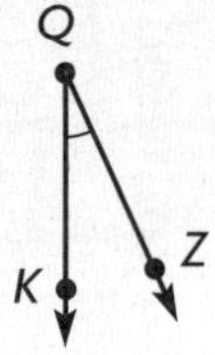

$m\angle$ _____ = _____

Use a protractor to measure each angle.

7 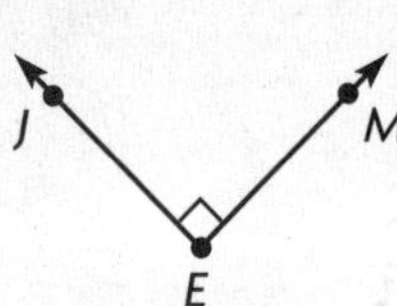

____

8 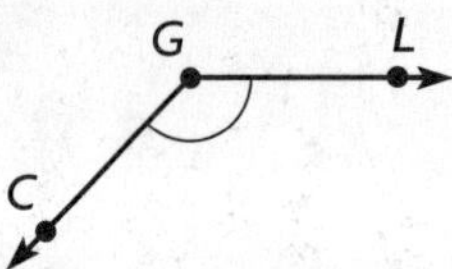

____

9 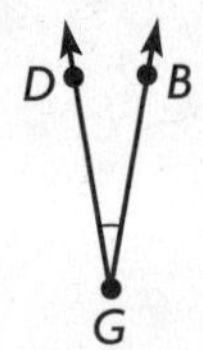

____

Check

Use a protractor to measure each angle.

10 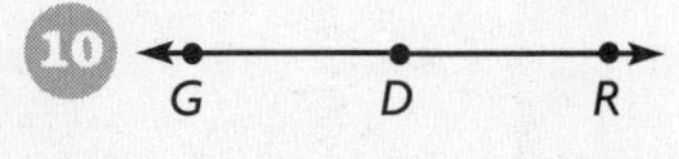

____

11 
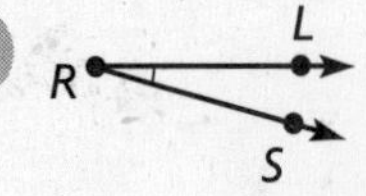

____

12 
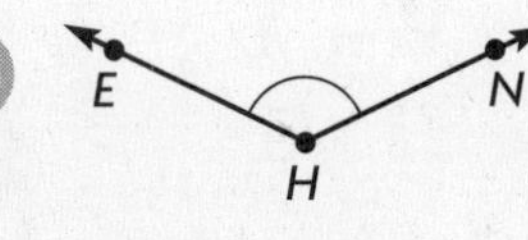

____

Skill 90 Read a Table

Using Skill 90

OBJECTIVE Read a table to find and compare data

Discuss the kind of data, or information, students can find in the table. Have students examine parts of the table.

Ask: **What is the title of the table?** *(Favorite Sports Activities)* **What activities does the table list?** (in-line skating, bicycling, hiking, climbing) **Whose favorite sports activities are these?** (boys' and girls')

Follow Steps 1–4 to determine the most popular sports activity among girls. Ask: **In which column will you look first?** (in the column for girls)

Guide students as they compare the numbers in the column for girls. Suggest that they find the greatest number of votes, then look in the same row under *Activity* to find the name of the sport.

What is the most popular sports activity among girls? (climbing)

Repeat the steps and have students find the least favorite sports activity among girls.

TRY THESE Exercises 1–3 provide practice in reading a table.

- **Exercises 1–2** Compare data.
- **Exercise 3** Find data.

PRACTICE ON YOUR OWN Examine the table at top of the page. As they work the exercises, some students may have difficulty focusing on the proper column or row. Guide them to underline the important words in the questions, then place their fingers on the row or column as they copy the data.

CHECK Determine if students can read a table to find and compare data.

Success is indicated by 2 out of 2 correct responses.

Students who successfully complete the **Practice on Your Own** and **Check** are ready to move to the next skill.

COMMON ERRORS

- Students may have difficulty tracking down a column or across a row.
- Students may add or subtract incorrectly.

Students who made more than 2 errors in the **Practice on Your Own**, or who were not successful in the **Check** section, may benefit from the **Alternative Teaching Strategy** on the next page.

Optional

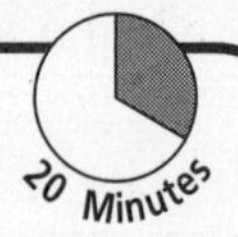

Alternative Teaching Strategy

Make and Read a Table

OBJECTIVE Make a table and record and compare data

MATERIALS containers, pattern pieces or paper figures

Prepare two containers. Label one container *A* and the other *B*. Into container *A*, place 18 circles, 4 squares, and 16 triangles. Into container *B*, place 17 circles, 5 squares, and 11 triangles.

Begin by explaining to students that in today's activity they will make a table. Point out that a table is a way to display data or information so that the data can be organized and compared easily.

Give out the containers and have two teams of students work together to sort the figures in each container. Then have them record the information about the contents of the containers in the table.

Guide students to see that since the information is about the types of figures in the containers, the title "Types of Figures" is appropriate.

Then discuss and record the contents of containers *A* and *B*. When the table is complete, ask:

Suppose you want to know which container has the greater number of circles, which column would you look at first?

Guide students to look at the column for circles, then have them compare the numbers. Since 18 is the greater number, have them look across the row to find that container *A* has the greater number of circles.

Continue asking questions and having students use the table to answer them. You may wish to have students make up questions and take turns answering them.

Types of Figures			
Container	○	■	▽
A	18	4	16
B	17	5	11

Name ______________________ Skill ______________________

Read a Table

Skill 90

Use the data in the table to answer the question.

What is the most popular sports activity among girls?

Favorite Sports Activities		
Activity	**Girls**	**Boys**
In-line skating	8	7
Bicycling	10	9
Climbing	12	13
Hiking	11	10

Step 1 Read the question. Underline the important words. It asks about *girls* and about their *most popular sports activity*.

Step 2 Look in the column labeled Girls. Find the greatest number in the column. The greatest number is 12.

Step 3 Look across the row to find the activity. The activity is climbing.

Step 4 Use the information to answer the question asked.

So, the most popular sports activity among girls is climbing.

Try These

Use the data in the table above to answer the questions.

1. What is the most popular sports activity among boys?
   Look in the column labeled ______.
   The greatest number is ______.
   The most popular sports activity among boys is ______________.

2. How many more girls than boys like bicycling the best?
   Look in the row labeled ________.
   ______ girls like bicycling.
   ______ boys like bicycling.
   ______ more girls than boys like bicycling the best.

3. How many girls like hiking or climbing the best?
   Look in the column labeled ______.
   ________ girls like hiking.
   ________ girls like climbing.
   ________ girls like hiking or climbing the best.

Go to the next side.

Name ______________________ Skill ______________

Practice on Your Own

Skill 90

Summerset Bowling League

	Game	Game	Game	
Bowlers	**1**	**2**	**3**	**Total**
Lucia	192	212	208	612
Theon	124	108	112	344
Jorge	205	218	198	621
Marina	137	122	140	399

Rows: across ⟷ Columns: up and down. ↕

Question:
Who had the highest score in Game 3?
Look for the column labeled Game 3.
Look down this column to find the greatest number. It is 208.
Look across the row to find the name. It is Lucia.
So, Lucia had the highest score in Game 3.

Use the data in the table to answer the questions.

1. What was Marina's highest score?
Look in the row labeled ________.
The greatest number is ________.
Marina's highest score was ________.

2. Who had the highest score in Game 1?
Look in the column labeled ________.
The highest score is ________.
________ had the highest score in Game 1.

3. In which game did Lucia score the least points?
Look in the row labeled ________.
The lowest number is ________.
Lucia scored the least points in ________.

4. How many more points did Jorge score in Game 2 than Lucia?
Look in the column labeled ________.
Lucia scored ________.
Jorge scored ________.
Jorge scored ________ more points than Lucia in Game 2.

5. What was Jorge's total score? ________

6. Who had the lowest total score? ________

Check

7. In which game did Theon score the highest? ________________

8. Who had the highest total score? ________________

Skill 91 Find Range

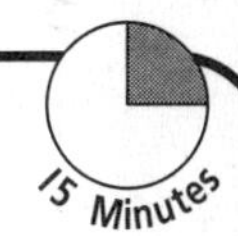

Using Skill 91

OBJECTIVE Find the range for a set of data

MATERIALS number line

Read the definition of range at the top of the skill page. Then proceed through Steps 1 and 2.

Ask: **How do you arrange the data?** (in order from least to greatest)

Remind students to compare the tens first when ordering 2-digit numbers. When the tens are the same, as in 17 and 19, and 22 and 25, you need to then compare the ones to put the numbers in order.

Have a student locate the numbers on a number line to check that the numbers are in order from least to greatest.

Ask: **How do you find the difference between two numbers?** (You subtract.)

Have students perform the subtraction vertically to check that 56 is the range of the data.

TRY THESE Exercises 1–3 provide practice in finding the range for a set of data.

- **Exercises 1–3** Order data, find the greatest number, the least number, and the range.

PRACTICE ON YOUR OWN Focus on the example at the top of the page. Students will notice that 183 appears twice in the set. Stress the importance of accounting for each piece of data. Point out how it is listed twice when the numbers are ordered.

CHECK Determine that students can identify the least and the greatest numbers. Success is indicated by 2 out of 2 correct responses.

Students who successfully complete the **Practice on Your Own** and **Check** are ready to move to the next skill.

COMMON ERRORS

- Students may arrange the data incorrectly.
- Students may subtract incorrectly when finding the range.

Students who made more than 2 errors in the **Practice on Your Own**, or who were not successful in the **Check** section, may benefit from the **Alternative Teaching Strategy** on the next page.

Optional

Alternative Teaching Strategy

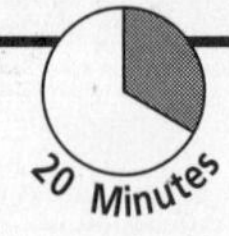

Find the Range

OBJECTIVE Order numbers from least to greatest

MATERIALS number line

Review the concept of order by having students stand in a line in order by the first letters of their names, starting with A. Then have them stand in a line in order by their birth months, starting with January.

Apply the concept to ordering numbers. Begin with 1-digit numbers. Have students locate the numbers on a number line and then list them in order from least to greatest.

Next, help students arrange the 2-digit numbers listed below in order from least to greatest.

38, 19, 75, 53, 21, 40, 96

Ask: **How do you put the numbers in order?** (compare tens) **What is the least number?** (19) **What is the greatest number?** (96)

Then show students these 2-digit numbers.

63, 46, 48, 86

Ask: **How do you put these numbers in order?** (compare tens) **What about 46 and 48?** (the tens are the same, so compare ones)

Have students incorporate the numbers into their ordered list of 2-digit numbers.

Display the numbers listed below.

579, 83, 423, 575, 91, 647

Ask: **How do you put the numbers in order?** (Order the 2-digit numbers first. Then order the 3-digit numbers by comparing hundreds.) **What about 575 and 579?** (The hundreds are the same, so compare tens; the tens are the same, so compare ones.) **What is the least number?** (83) **What is the greatest number?** (647)

You may wish to repeat the activity with other sets of 2- and 3-digit data.

Name ____________________ Skill ____________________

Find Range

Skill 91

The **range** of a set of data is the *difference* between the greatest number and the least number.
Find the range for this set of data:
73, 25, 17, 19, 68, 22, 54.

Step 1 Arrange the data in order from least to greatest.

least number ↓ ... greatest number ↓

17, 19, 22, 25, 54, 68, 73

Step 2 Find the difference between the greatest and least numbers.

$73 - 17 = 56$

So, the range of the data is 56.

Try These

Find the range for each set of data.

1. 6, 9, 8, 3, 2
   Order the data.
   ____
   Greatest number: ______
   Least number: ______
   Range: ______

2. 37, 52, 28, 19
   Order the data.
   ____
   Greatest number: ______
   Least number: ______
   Range: ______

3. 25, 54, 32, 71, 13, 60
   Order the data.
   ____
   Greatest number: ______
   Least number: ______
   Range: ______

Go to the next side.

Name ______________________ Skill ______________________

Practice on Your Own

Skill 91

Think:
The range is the *difference* between the greatest and the least numbers.

Find the range of this set of data:

183, 196, 172, 191, 183

172, 183, 183, 191, 196 ← Order the numbers from least to greatest.

$$\begin{array}{r} 196 \\ -172 \\ \hline 24 \end{array}$$

196 ← the greatest number
−172 ← the least number
24 ← the difference

The range is 24.

Find the range for each set of data.

1. 7, 6, 8, 4, 10
   Order the data.
   ____
   Greatest number: ________
   Least number: ________
   Range: ________

2. 77, 88, 81, 65, 79
   Order the data.
   ____
   Greatest number: ________
   Least number: ________
   Range: ________

3. 100, 98, 54, 102
   Order the data:
   ____
   Range: ________

4. 137, 137, 140, 195, 156
   Order the data:
   ____
   Range: ________

5. 86, 75, 42, 74, 75, 76, 30
   Range: ________

6. 168, 185, 170, 157, 188, 188
   Range: ________

Check

Find the range for each set of data.

7. 68, 87, 83, 74, 88
   Range: ________

8. 96, 105, 69, 84, 68, 93, 80
   Range: ________

Skill 92 Find Median and Mode

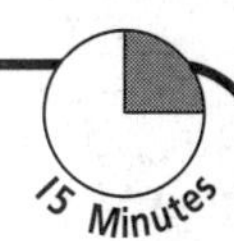

Using Skill 92

OBJECTIVE Find the median and mode for a set of data

Before you begin, present students with the list of data given at the top of the page. Have them arrange the numbers from least to greatest. You may wish to check that they have ordered the numbers correctly.

Lead students through the steps for finding the median. Stress care in accounting for each piece of data when they order the numbers and in locating the middle number. Ask: **How many middle numbers are there?** (one) **What is the median?** (88)

You may wish to present students with a list of data with two middle numbers and demonstrate how to find the average of the two middle numbers. Present 37, 99, 13, 29, 45, 99. Have students order the numbers and display the ordered numbers: 13, 29, 37, 45, 99, 99. Ask: **How many middle numbers are there?** (two—37 and 45) Work through the process of adding 37 and 45 and then dividing the sum to find the average. Ask: **What is the median?** (41) Students may notice that, when there is an odd number of items in the list of data, there is one middle number; when there is an even number of items, there are two middle numbers.

Lead students through the steps for finding the mode. Display the ordered list, but insert another 91. Ask: **How many modes are there now?** (two—83 and 91) Show the list again, but take out one 83 and one 91. Ask: **How many modes are there now?** (none)

TRY THESE Exercises 1–3 provide practice ordering data to find the median and the mode.

- **Exercise 1** Find the median and mode.
- **Exercise 2** Average two middle numbers to find the median; find the mode.
- **Exercise 3** Find the median and mode for a set of decimal numbers.

PRACTICE ON YOUR OWN Focus on the example at the top of the page. Have a student demonstrate adding and dividing to find the average of the two middle numbers.

CHECK Determine if students can order data and find the median and the mode. Success is indicated by 2 out of 2 correct responses.

Students who successfully complete the **Practice on Your Own** and **Check** are ready to move to the next skill.

COMMON ERRORS

- Students may not order data correctly.
- When finding the median, students may not correctly recognize the middle number or know how to average the two middle numbers.

Students who made more than 2 errors in the **Practice on Your Own**, or who were not successful in the **Check** section, may benefit from the **Alternative Teaching Strategy** on the next page.

Optional

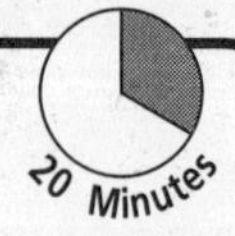

Alternative Teaching Strategy

Find the Median and the Mode

OBJECTIVE Find the median and the mode for a set of data

Present students with a few lists of data and have them practice arranging the numbers in order from least to greatest.

Lead students through finding the median of a set of data. Present the following list of numbers and have students arrange the numbers in order from least to greatest: 5, 3, 3, 9, 6. Display the ordered list: 3, 3, 5, 6, 9. Have a student underline the middle number. Ask: **How many items are to the left of 5?** (2) **How many items are to the right of 5?** (2) **How do you know that 5 is the middle number?** (There is the same number of items to the left of 5 as there is to the right of 5.)

$\underbrace{3, 3}_{\text{two items}}, \underline{5}, \underbrace{6, 9}_{\text{two items}}$

Again display the ordered list, but this time insert a 1. Have students try to locate the middle number. Ask: **Is there one middle number?** (no) **How many middle numbers are there?** (two—3 and 5) **What is the sum?** (8) **What is the sum divided by 2?** (4) **So, what is the median?** (4)

Lead students through finding the mode. Display the new ordered list: 1, 3, 3, 5, 6, 9. Ask: **Does any number in the list appear more than once?** (yes) **What number appears most often?** (3) **So, what is the mode?** (3)

Rewrite the ordered list, inserting another 6. Ask: **What number appears most often?** (both 3 and 6) **How many modes are there now?** (two—3 and 6)

Remove one 3 and one 6 from the ordered list. Ask: **Does any number appear more often than another?** (no) **How many modes are there now?** (none)

Name ____________________ Skill ____________________

Find Median and Mode

Skill 92

Find the median and the mode for this set of data: 83, 96, 72, 91, 83, 99, 88.

Find the median
The **median** is the *middle number* when the numbers are arranged in order. If there are two middle numbers, the median is the average of the two numbers.
Arrange the numbers in order from least to greatest.

72, 83, 83, 88, 91, 96, 99

Find the middle score.

72, 83, 83, **88**, 91, 96, 99

So, the median is 88.

Find the mode
The **mode** is the number that appears *most often*. A set of data may have no mode, or there may be more than one mode.
Identify the number, if any, that occurs most often.

72, **83**, **83**, 88, 91, 96, 99

So, the mode is 83.

The median is 88, and the mode is 83.

Try These

Find the median and the mode for each set of data.

1. 3, 8, 8, 7, 14
Order the data.
____
Median: ____________
Mode: ____________

2. 59, 75, 57, 60, 46, 57
Order the data.
____
Median: ____________
Mode: ____________

3. 1.4, 0.9, 1.4, 2.1, 6.5
Order the data.
____
Median: ____________
Mode: ____________

Go to the next side.

Name ______________________ Skill ______________________

Practice on Your Own

Skill 92

Think:
The **median** is the middle number or the average of the two middle numers. The **mode** is the number, if any, that appears most often. There may be no mode or more than one mode.

Find the median and the mode of this set of data: 96, 83, 91, 83, 94, 72.

72, 83, 83, 91, 94, 96 ← Arrange the data in order.

72, 83, **83**, **91**, 94, 96 ← There are two middle numbers. Find the average.

83 + 91 = 174
174 ÷ 2 = 87

The median is 87.

72, **83**, **83**, 91, 94, 96 ← 83 appears most often.

The mode is 83.

Find the median and the mode of each set of data.

1. 5, 7, 4, 5, 6
Order the data.
____
Median: ______
Mode: ______

2. 75, 80, 68, 82, 68
Order the data.
____
Median: ______
Mode: ______

3. 86, 95, 78, 90, 90, 82
Order the data.
____
Median: ______
Mode: ______

4. 4.4, 3.5, 3.0, 4.8, 4.6, 4.8
Order the data.
____
Median: ______
Mode: ______

5. 2.4, 1.8, 3.0, 2.2, 2.0, 2.6, 2.0
Median: _____ Mode: _____

6. 45, 35, 35, 55, 75, 25
Median: _____ Mode: _____

Check

Find the median and the mode of each set of data.

7. 95, 83, 95, 98, 87
Median: _____ Mode: _____

8. 4.8, 3.6, 4.4, 3.6, 3.8, 4.0
Median: _____ Mode: _____

Find Mean

Using Skill 93

15 Minutes

OBJECTIVE Find the mean or average of a set of data

MATERIALS examples from the newspaper of averages; the weather section for a week

Begin by discussing the term *average* since it may be more familiar to the students than the term *mean.*

Ask: **What are some ways that averages are used?** (sports, weather, attendance, etc.)

Have students look at the newspaper to find additional examples. Then, use the weather section from the newspaper to list the high temperatures for your location for one week.

Go over the procedure for finding the mean. Emphasize that if there is a 0 in the set, it must be counted as one of the members of the set.

Have a volunteer read the paragraph at the top of the page. Explain that for this activity *average* and *mean* have the same meaning.

Call students' attention to Step 1. Remind them of the importance of aligning numbers in a sum. Review Step 2.

TRY THESE In Exercises 1–3 students find the mean of a set of data

- **Exercises 1–2** Whole numbers
- **Exercise 3** Decimals

PRACTICE ON YOUR OWN Review the example at the top of the page. Remind students of the steps to be followed when finding the mean.

Ask: **What do you do first when finding the mean of a set of data?** (Find the sum of the numbers in the set.) **What is the next step?** (Divide the sum by the number of items.)

CHECK Determine if students can find the mean. Success is indicated by 3 out of 3 correct responses.

Students who successfully complete the **Practice on Your Own** and **Check** are ready to move to the next skill.

COMMON ERRORS

- Students may not count 0 as part of the set when counting the number of data items.
- Some students may have trouble with decimal computation.

Students who made more than 1 error in the **Practice on Your Own** section, or who were not successful in the **Check** section, may benefit from the **Alternative Teaching Strategy** on the next page.

Optional

Alternative Teaching Strategy

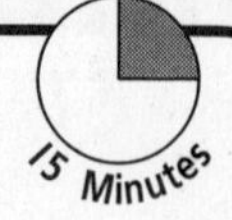

What's Your Mean?

OBJECTIVE Find a mean score

MATERIALS waste-paper baskets or boxes, crumpled pieces of paper, counters

Distribute 10 pieces of crumpled paper and a basket or box to each pair of students. Tell them that they are to stand 3 paces from the basket, which is the target, and toss the crumpled paper into it.

Students work in pairs. One partner stands 3 paces from the target and tries to throw 10 crumpled paper balls into it. The other partner is the recorder. Each basket is worth 4 counters, each miss is worth 0 counters.

After both partners have generated a data set, have them find the mean score for each partner by trying to move the accumulated counters into ten sets with the same number of counters in each set.

Now, have students use the formula for finding the mean: sum of numbers ÷ number of numbers for the same set of data. Remind students that a zero is still a member of the set of data and must be counted when finding the number of items. Help students realize that the mean is the number of points they would get for every attempt if they got the same score each time.

Repeat the activity from different distances and with different numbers of crumpled paper balls.

Name ______________________ Skill ______________________

Skill 93

Find Mean

Find the mean of the set of data: 80, 95, 85, 100, 90.

Find the mean or *average* of a set of data by first finding the sum of the numbers in the set. Then count the number of data items in the set and divide the sum by that number.

Step 1
Find the sum of the numbers in the set of data. Count the number of data items

```
   80
   95        5 data items
   85
  100
+  90
  450     ←sum of the numbers
```

Step 2
Divide the sum by that number.

```
    90     ←mean
 5)450     ←sum of the numbers
 - 45
    00
   - 0
     0
```

So, the mean of the set of data is 90.

Try These

Find the mean of each set of data.

1 8, 5, 7, 9, 6

```
  8
  5
  7
  9
+ 6
```

5)‾‾‾‾

Mean: ______

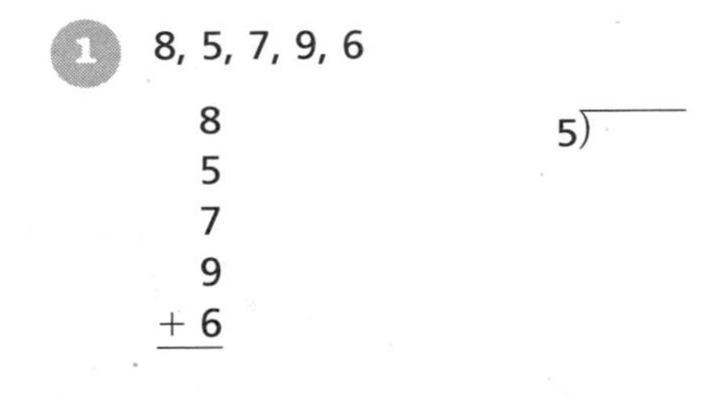

2 98, 75, 100, 96, 83, 88

```
   98
   75
  100
   96
   83
+  88
```

6)‾‾‾‾

Mean: ______

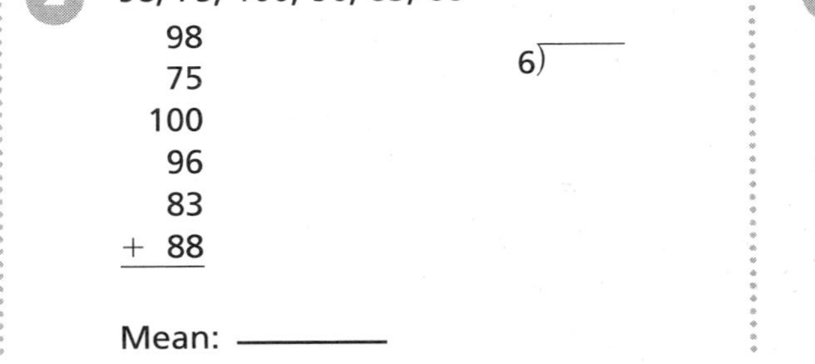

3 8.2, 7.8, 6.2, 8.0, 7.1, 8.3

```
  8.2
  7.8
  6.2
  8.0
  7.1
+ 8.3
```

6)‾‾‾‾

Mean: ______

Go to the next page.

Name ______________________ Skill ______________________

Practice on Your Own

Skill 93

Think:

To find the mean of a set of data, add all the numbers in the set of data. Then divide the sum by the number of data items.

```
  9.1
  8.0
  3.4
  6.7
+ 1.3
 28.5
```

```
                  5.7    ←mean
numbers→       5)28.5    ←sum of the
of data         −25        numbers
items             35
                 −35
                   0
```

Find the mean of each set of data.

1 8, 3, 5, 6, 8

```
  8
  3        5)‾‾‾
  5
  6
+ 8
```

Mean: ________

2 85, 70, 80, 93, 82

```
  85
  70       5)‾‾‾
  80
  93
+ 82
```

Mean: ________

3 9.5, 10.0 16.4, 8.8, 12.3

```
   9.5
  10.0     5)‾‾‾
  16.4
   8.8
+ 12.3
```

Mean: ________

4 46, 85, 79, 27, 13

Sum of the numbers: ________

Number of data items: ________

Mean: ________

5 79, 100, 25, 16, 43, 13

Sum of the numbers: ________

Number of data items: ________

Mean: ________

6 9.3, 8.2, 10, 7.7, 10, 10

Sum of the numbers: ________

Number of data items: ________

Mean: ________

7 78, 94, 31, 83, 59

Mean: ________

8 81, 83, 85, 87, 89, 91

Mean: ________

9 17.7, 12, 9.6, 18.7, 9.2, 8.4

Mean: ________

Check

Find the mean of each set of data.

10 8, 4, 9, 3, 5, 13

Mean: ________

11 93, 78, 97, 84, 98

Mean: ________

12 7.9, 9.5, 8, 6.6, 17.9, 12.5

Mean: ________

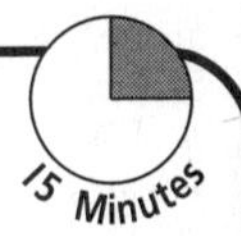

Using Skill 94

OBJECTIVE Use bar graphs to compare data

Direct students' attention to the horizontal bar graph. Ask: **How many animals are listed in the graph?** (5) **What is the title of the graph?** (Animal Lifespan) **What do the numbers along the horizontal axis represent?** (number of years) **What is the interval along the horizontal axis?** (10) **How can you read the age of an animal from the graph?** (Follow the vertical line from the end of the bar down to the horizontal axis and read the value where the vertical line crosses the horizontal axis.) **Which animal has the longest bar?** (elephant) **What does having the longest bar mean?** (The average life span for an elephant is longer than for the other animals.)

As you work through the second example, have the students use a ruler to align the end of the bar with the horizontal axis to estimate the average life span of the rhinoceros.

TRY THESE In Exercises 1–3 students read a bar graph to answer questions.

- **Exercise 1** Find the shortest average life span.
- **Exercise 2** Find an average life span.
- **Exercise 3** Compare two life spans.

PRACTICE ON YOUR OWN Review the example of a vertical bar graph at the top of the page. As they work through the exercise, remind students that the vertical scale is mass, as measured in grams.

CHECK Determine if students can find and compare data on a bar graph.

Success is indicated by 3 out of 3 correct responses.

Students who successfully complete the **Practice on Your Own** and **Check** are ready to move on to the next skill.

COMMON ERRORS

- Students may read the value from the wrong bar or may have difficulty tracking the top or end of a bar to the scale axis.
- Students may add the values of the bars when they want to know how much more one is than the other.

Students who made more than 2 errors in the **Practice on Your Own**, or who were not successful in the **Check** section, may benefit from the **Alternative Teaching Strategy** on the next page.

Optional

Alternative Teaching Strategy

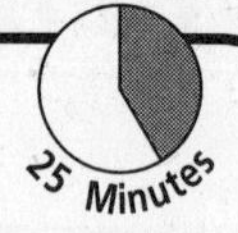

Modeling Bar Graphs

OBJECTIVE Use connecting cubes to model bar graphs

MATERIALS connecting cubes, grid paper

Distribute connecting cubes to each student. Survey the students to determine their favorite cube color. Record the results of the survey on the board in a tally table.

Color	Tallies
red	~~||||~~ ~~||||~~ ||
blue	|||
green	~~||||~~ ~~||||~~ |
purple	~~||||~~ ~~||||~~ ~~||||~~ |||

Mention to students that they will be making a 3-dimensional bar graph using the cubes.

Ask:

Which color will have the longest bar?

How many cubes long is the bar?

Have the students construct a bar for each color using the connecting cubes.

Continue to ask questions regarding the lengths of the bars in comparison to each other. Then ask students to use the grid paper to draw a bar graph of the data. Together, agree on a title, labels for the horizontal and vertical axes, and an interval.

Have students write and answer a question about their graphs.

Name ______ Skill ______

Skill 94

Read Bar Graphs

Use a bar graph to compare data.
Horizontal bar graphs have bars that go across.
The horizontal bar graph shows the average lifespan of animals.
The names of the animals are shown along the vertical axis of the graph.
Lifespan in number of years is shown along the horizontal axis.
The graph scale is in intervals of 10.

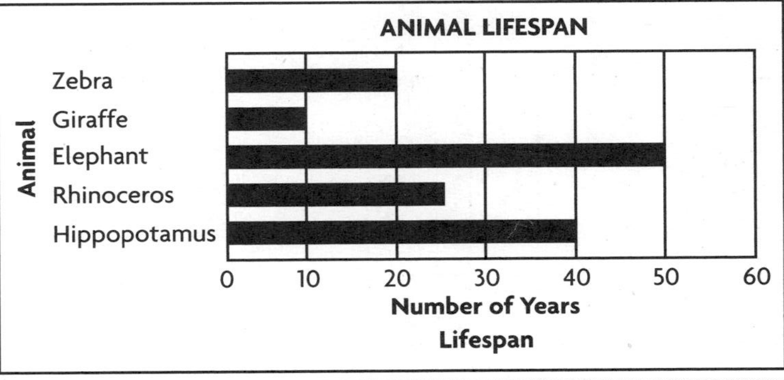

Example 1

- Which animal has the longest lifespan?

The bar for the elephant is the longest bar.
So, the elephant has the longest lifespan.

Example 2

- How much longer is the lifespan of an elephant than a rhinoceros?
  Find the bars labeled *Elephant* and *Rhinoceros*.
  The bar labeled *Elephant* stops at 50. So, an elephant lives an average of 50 years. The bar labeled *Rhinoceros* stops halfway between 20 and 30. So, a rhinoceros lives an average of 25 years. Find the difference: $50 - 25 = 25$.

So, an elephant has an average lifespan that is 25 years longer than that of a rhinoceros.

Try These

Use the bar graph shown above to answer the questions.

1. Which animal has the shortest average lifespan?
   ______

2. What is the average lifespan of a hippopotamus?
   ______

3. How much longer is the average lifespan of a zebra than that of a giraffe?
   ______

Go to the next side.

Name ______________________ Skill ______________________

Practice on Your Own

Skill 94

Vertical bar graphs have bars that go up. You can see from the vertical bar graph at the right that:

- a nickel has the greatest mass.
- the mass of an earring is 3 grams less than the mass of a nickel.

The combined mass of a paper clip and an earring is 3 grams. These two items together are equal to the mass of a finger ring.

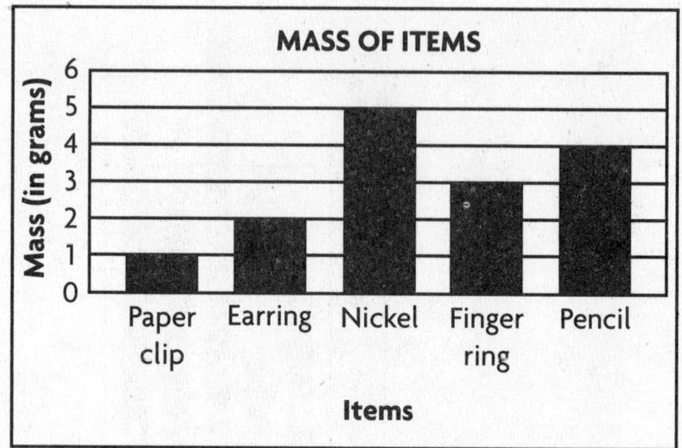

Use the bar graph shown above to answer the questions.

1. What is the mass of a nickel? ____________

2. Which has greater mass, a paper clip or a pencil? ____________

3. Which two items have a combined mass equal to the mass of a pencil? ____________

4. What is the mass of a paper clip? ____________

5. Which has less mass, a pencil or a nickel? ____________

6. Which two items have a combined mass equal to the mass of a nickel? ____________

Check

Use the bar graph shown above to answer the questions.

7. Which item has the least mass? ____________

8. What is the mass of an earring? ____________

9. Which two items have a combined mass equal to the mass of a finger ring? ____________

Skill 95 Read Circle Graphs

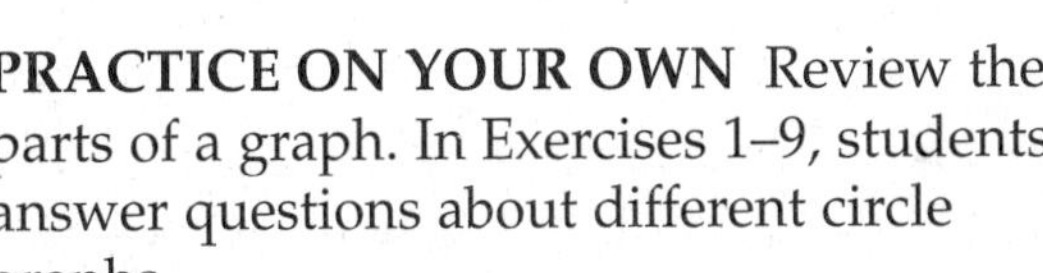

Using Skill 95

OBJECTIVE Reading circle graphs

15 Minutes

Direct students to the top of Skill 95. Stress that many different mathematical applications are related to graphs. There are many different types of graphs.
Ask: **Can you name some different types of graphs?** (bar, line, column, pictographs, coordinate plane) Being able to read a graph and identify the different parts of a graph can help to answer questions about a graph.

Ask: **What percent does the entire graph represent?** (100%) **What does each wedge represent?** (a part of the whole graph)

What is the title of the graph? (Favorite Camp Activities) **Which activities had more votes than archery?** (canoeing and swimming) **Which activities were least popular?** (music, archery and arts/crafts) **Which activity was the most popular?** (swimming) **About what percent of the students voted for swimming?** (50%)

TRY THESE In Exercises 1–6 students answer questions about the circle graph.

- **Exercise 1** Monthly Family Budget
- **Exercise 2** 6
- **Exercise 3** $1,200
- **Exercise 4** $700
- **Exercise 5** $600
- **Exercise 6** savings

PRACTICE ON YOUR OWN Review the parts of a graph. In Exercises 1–9, students answer questions about different circle graphs.

CHECK Verify that students can read information from a graph. Success is indicated by 4 out of 4 correct responses.

Students who successfully complete the **Practice on Your Own** and **Check** are ready to move on to the next skill.

COMMON ERRORS

- Students may read the wrong information.
- Students may read the legend incorrectly. Have students look carefully at the legend.

Students who made more than 3 errors in the **Practice on Your Own**, or who were not successful in the **Check** section, may benefit from the **Alternative Teaching Strategy** on the next page.

Optional

Alternative Teaching Strategy

Read Circle Graphs

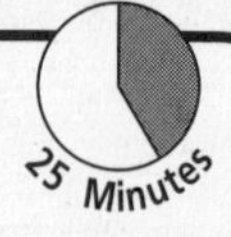

OBJECTIVE Read circle graphs

MATERIALS paper plate, colored cereal, string, scissors, ruler, pencil/pen

You may wish to have students work in pairs. Have students conduct a brief survey of their friends on different topics, such as favorite pizza toppings, favorite pet, favorite class, etc.

Have students tally their data into a table. Have students use different colors of cereal to represent each answer. Have students string the number of pieces of cereal for each answer. After all the cereal has been strung, tie the ends of the string together, forming a circle, and find the center. Have students lay the circle on the paper plate so that the centers of the paper plate and "cereal" coincide.

The students should use a ruler and draw a line dividing the paper plate into the different sized wedges based on the cereal colors.

The students should label each wedge with the appropriate name and tally.

Have students place the paper plates on a large sheet of paper and give the entire "graph" a title.

The students should then write 3 or 4 questions about their graph. When all students have completed this step have them pass their graph to another student to answer the questions they have written.

Name ______________________ Skill ______________________

Read Circle Graphs

Skill 95

A **circle graph** shows how parts of the data are related to the whole and each other.
Being able to analyze the information contained within a graph will help in making deductions and interpreting data.

The entire circle represents the whole.

Each wedge represents a part of the whole.

Being able to identify parts of the graph can help in answering questions about the graph.

What is the title of the graph?

Which activities had more votes than archery?

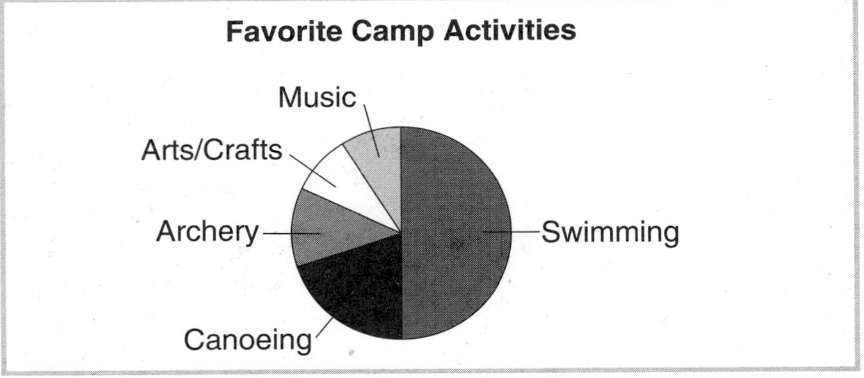

Try These

Use the circle graph.

1. What is the title of the graph?

____

2. How many different categories make up the budget?

____

3. How much was spent on housing? __________

4. How much was spent on food?

____

5. How much more is spent on transportation than clothing?

____

6. What is the least amount of money spent on? __________

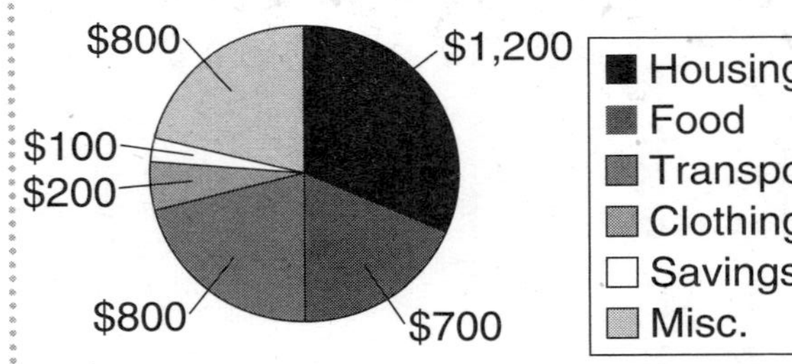

Go to the next side.

Name ______________________ Skill ______________________

Practice on Your Own

Skill 95

Circle graphs show how parts of the data are related to the whole and to each other.

Use the graph to answer each question.

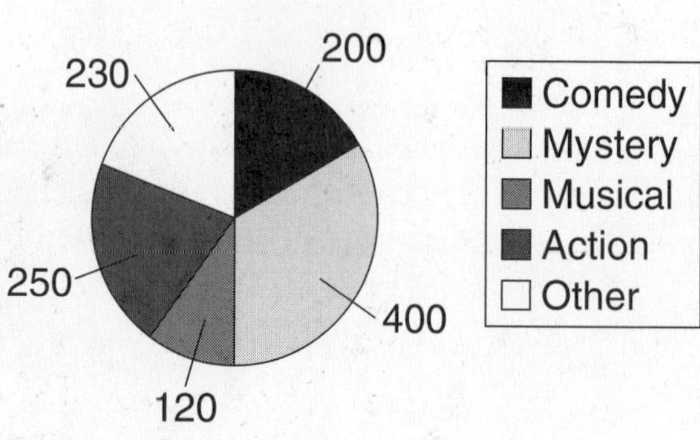

1. What is the title of the graph? ______________

2. What was the most popular type of movie? ______________

3. What type of movie was rented the least? ______________

4. Mysteries were twice as popular as what type of movie? ______________

5. Which two types of movies were rented about the same number of times? ______________

Use the graph to answer each question.

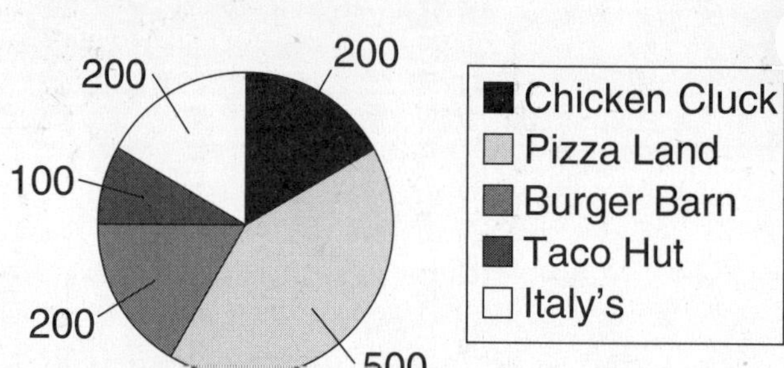

6. What is the title of the graph? ______________

7. Which restaurant is most popular? ______________

8. Which restaurant is least popular? ______________

9. Which restaurants had the same number of votes? ______________

Check

Use the graph to answer the questions.

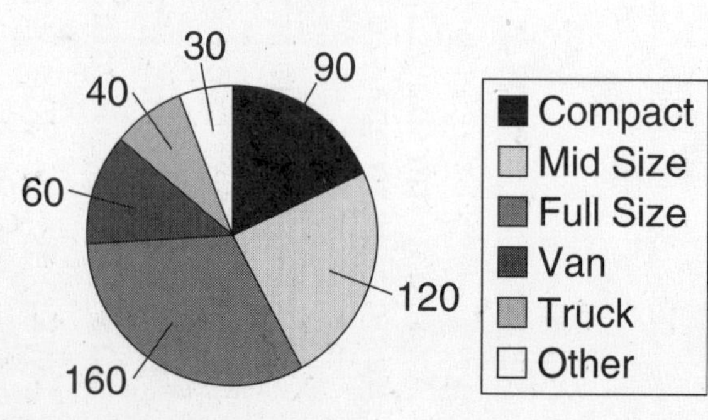

10. What is the title of the graph? ______________

11. What was the most popular vehicles rental in July? ______________

12. What was the least popular vehicles rental in July? ______________

13. There were twice as many mid-size car rentals as which vehicle? ______________

Skill 96 Read Stem-and-Leaf Plots

Using Skill 96

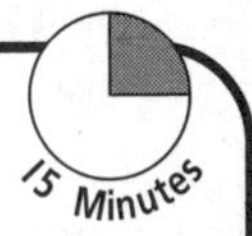

OBJECTIVE Read stem-and-leaf plots

Ask students to recall ways they have seen data organized. (They may suggest pictographs, bar graphs, line graphs and tables.) Then present stem-and-leaf plots as another way to organize data. Read about stem-and-leaf plots at the top of the page.

Ask: **What are the stems?** (tens digits) **What are the leaves?** (ones digits)

Have students say aloud some of the scores in the stem-and-leaf plot.

Direct students' attention to finding the range in Step 1.

Ask: **How do you find the least score?** (Look for the first stem and the first leaf.) **How do you find the greatest score?** (Look for the last stem and the last leaf.)

Have a student show the vertical subtraction and state the range.

Direct students' attention to finding the median in Step 2. Have a student use the stem-and-leaf plot to arrange the scores in order from least to greatest. Then have a student underline the middle score and state the median.

Direct students' attention to finding the mode in Step 3. Ask: **Do any scores other than 73 occur more than once?** (no)

TRY THESE Exercises 1–3 provide practice in reading stem-and-leaf plots.

- **Exercise 1** Find the range.
- **Exercise 2** Find the median.
- **Exercise 3** Find the mode.

PRACTICE ON YOUR OWN Review the example at the top of the page. Call out another stem-and-leaf and have students tell the score shown. Have students practice using ordinal numbers to call out a few more stems and leaves.

CHECK Determine if students can read data in a stem-and-leaf plot to find range, median, and mode. Success is indicated by 3 out of 3 correct responses.

Students who successfully complete the **Practice on Your Own** and **Check** are ready to move to the next skill.

COMMON ERRORS

- Students may confuse tens and ones digits.
- When finding the median, students may order the numbers incorrectly.

Students who made more than 2 errors in the **Practice on Your Own**, or who were not successful in the **Check** section, may benefit from the **Alternative Teaching Strategy** on the next page.

Optional

Alternative Teaching Strategy

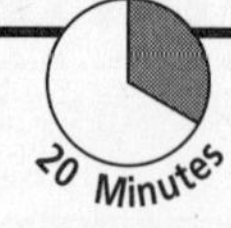

Read Stem-and-Leaf Plots

OBJECTIVE Read stem-and-leaf plots

MATERIALS place-value charts

Present the stem-and-leaf plot shown below. Show how to write the first score in a place-value chart. The tens digit is the stem 6; the ones digit is the leaf 5. Have students write all of the scores in order from least to greatest in a place-value chart. Then have a student read the scores aloud.

Stem	Leaves
6	5 7
7	2 8
8	5 5
9	0 4 8

Help students find the range of the scores. Remind them that the range is the difference between the least and the greatest scores. Ask: **What is the least score?** (65) **What is the greatest score?** (98) **How do you find the difference?** (subtract) Have students show the subtraction vertically. Ask: **What is the range?** (33)

To find the median, refer students to their place-value charts. Have students count the scores in both the chart and in the stem-and-leaf plot to be sure they have not left out any scores. You may suggest that, when they list scores to order them, students write a check mark next to them. Ask: **How many scores are there?** (9) **In what order are the scores arranged?** (from least to greatest) **What is the middle score? Explain.** (85; there are 4 items before 85 and 4 items after 85.)

To find the mode, refer students to the stem-and-leaf plot. Ask: **Does any score occur more than once?** (yes) **What is it?** (85) **Does any other score occur more than once?** (no) **Then what is the mode?** (85)

Name ________________ Skill ________________

Skill 96

Read Stem-and-Leaf Plots

A **stem-and-leaf plot** is a way to organize data.

These history test scores are shown in the stem-and-leaf plot to the right:
73, 86, 65, 91, 87, 55, 90, 71,
75, 82, 73, 74, 79, 63, and 81.

The tens digits are the stems.

HISTORY TEST SCORES

Stem	Leaves
5	5
6	3, 5
7	1, 3, 3, 4, 5, 9
8	1, 2, 6, 7
9	0, 1

The ones digits are the leaves.

Step 1: Find the range.
Think: The range is the difference between the least and greatest numbers in a set of data.

Find the least score.→ 55
Find the greatest score.→ 91
Find the difference.
$91 - 55 = 36$
So, the range is 36.

Step 2: Find the median.
Think: The median is the middle number in a group of numbers arranged in numerical order.
Count the total number of scores. Find the middle score.
When the scores are arranged in numerical order, the middle score is 75.
So, the median is 75.

Step 3: Find the mode.
Think: The mode is the number that occurs most often. Find the score that occurs most often.
73 occurs twice. No other score occurs more than once.
So, the mode is 73.

Try These

Use the stem-and-leaf plot at the right to answer the questions.

SPELLING TEST SCORES

Stem	Leaves
7	2, 9
8	0, 0, 5, 8
9	1, 4, 7

1. What is the range?
   Least score ____
   Greatest score ____
   Range ____

2. What is the median?
   Number of scores ____
   Median ____

3. What is the mode?
   Number that occurs most often ____ Mode ____

Go to the next side.

Name ______________________ Skill ______________________

Practice on Your Own

The stem-and-leaf plot shows math test scores.

The second stem's first leaf shows the score 60.

The fourth stem's sixth leaf shows the score 88.

MATH TEST SCORES

Stem	Leaves
5	8
6	0, 8
7	4, 6, 6, 8
8	2, 4, 4, 4, 6, 8
9	0, 4, 6, 8

↑ The tens digits are the stems.

↑ The ones digits are the leaves.

Use the stem-and-leaf plot above to answer the questions.

1. What is the score shown by the fourth stem and third leaf? ________

2. What is the score shown by the first stem and first leaf? ________

3. What is the score shown by the last stem and the last leaf? ________

4. What is the range of the set of data? ________

5. What is the median of the set of data? ________

6. What is the mode of the set of data? ________

Check

Use the stem-and-leaf plot at the right.

7. What is the range of the bowling scores? ________

8. What is the median of the bowling scores? ________

9. What is the mode of the bowling scores? ________

BOWLING SCORES

Stem	Leaves
5	0, 9, 9
6	4, 4, 4, 7
7	6, 8, 8
8	2, 3, 5, 5
9	7

Skill 97 Certain, Impossible, Likely, and Unlikely

Using Skill 97

OBJECTIVE Determine if an event is certain, impossible, likely, or unlikely

Discuss with students how they can judge the likelihood that an event will occur. Have students suggest events in life that are certain, impossible, likely, or unlikely. Define *likely* events as those that will *probably* happen; *unlikely* events may happen, but probably will not.

Guide students through Models 1–4 at the top of the page. Ask these questions about the spinners.

What is the only letter on the spinner in Model 1? (A) **Can the pointer stop on any other letter?** (no) **Then is it certain or impossible that the pointer will stop on A?** (certain)

What are the letters on the spinner in Model 2? (B, C, D, E) **Is there an A on the spinner?** (no) **Then is spinning an A possible?** (no) **What is the likelihood of spinning an A?** (impossible)

What are the letters on the spinner in Model 3? (A and B) **Are all the parts of the spinner equal in size?** (yes) **Are there the same number of parts labeled A as there are B? Explain.** (No. There are more parts labeled A than B.) **Are you likely to spin an A or a B?** (A)

What are the letters on the spinner in Model 4? (A and B) **Are all the parts equal in size?** (yes) **Are there the same number of parts labeled A as there are B? Explain.** (No, there are fewer parts labeled A.) **Is spinning an A likely or unlikely?** (unlikely)

TRY THESE Exercises 1–4 provide practice in determining if an event is certain, impossible, likely, or unlikely.

- **Exercise 1** Impossible event
- **Exercise 2** Likely event
- **Exercise 3** Certain event
- **Exercise 4** Unlikely event

PRACTICE ON YOUR OWN Review the spinners at the top of the page. For each spinner, ask how the spinner could be changed to make the opposite event occur.

CHECK Determine if students can relate *fewer* to *unlikely* and *more* to *likely* and can identify certain and impossible events. Success is indicated by 3 out of 3 correct responses.

Students who successfully complete the **Practice on Your Own** and **Check** are ready to move to the next skill.

COMMON ERRORS

- Students may not understand the meaning of the terms *likely* and *unlikely* and randomly apply the terms to events.

Students who made more than 1 error in the **Practice on Your Own**, or who were not successful in the **Check** section, may benefit from the **Alternative Teaching Strategy** on the next page.

Optional

Alternative Teaching Strategy

20 Minutes

Certain, Impossible, Likely, and Unlikely

OBJECTIVE Model an event that is certain, impossible, likely, or unlikely

MATERIALS blue and yellow counters, two 4-section spinners: one with circles in each section, the other with 2 squares, 1 diamond and 1 triangle, two 8-section spinners: one with 6 circles, 1 square, 1 triangle, the other with 2 circles, 2 squares, 2 diamonds, 2 triangles

Display 10 blue counters.

Ask: **How many counters are there?** (10) **What color are they?** (blue)

To model an event that is *certain*, have each student select a counter. *Be sure that each time a counter is selected, it is put back before it is the next student's turn.* Students will see that blue is always selected.

Ask: **Why is selecting a blue counter certain?** (All of the counters are blue.)

To model an event that is *impossible,* show students 10 yellow counters. Have each student select a counter.

Ask: **Did anyone select a blue counter?** (no) **Why is selecting a blue counter impossible?** (There are no blue counters.)

To model an event that is *likely,* display 8 blue counters and 2 yellow counters. Have students select 6 counters and tally the results. They will probably select more blue counters than yellow ones.

Ask: **Why is selecting a blue counter likely?** (There are more blue counters than yellow counters.)

To model an event that is *unlikely,* display 8 yellow counters and 2 blue counters. Have students select 6 counters and tally the results. They will probably select more yellow counters than blue ones.

Ask: **Why is selecting a blue counter unlikely?** (There are more yellow counters than blue counters.)

Follow the same procedure, using spinners this time. Have students determine if spinning a circle is certain, impossible, likely, or unlikely.

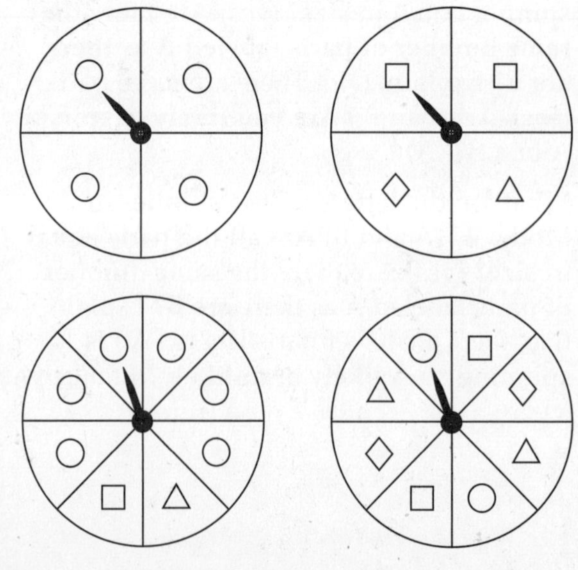

Name ____________________ Skill ____________________

Certain, Impossible, Likely, and Unlikely

Skill 97

Determine if the event is certain, impossible, likely, or unlikely.

Model 1
Spinning an **A** on this spinner.

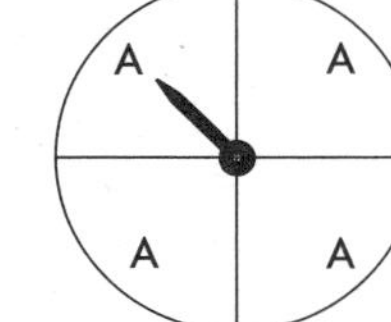

The pointer will always stop on an **A**.
So, the event is certain.

Model 2
Spinning an **A** on this spinner.

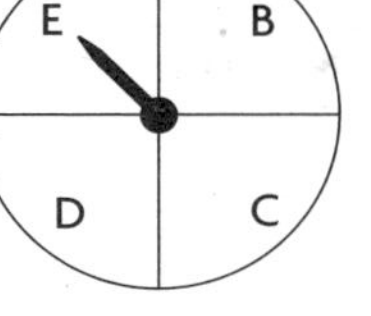

There is no **A** on the spinner.
So, the event is impossible.

Model 3
Spinning an **A** on this spinner.

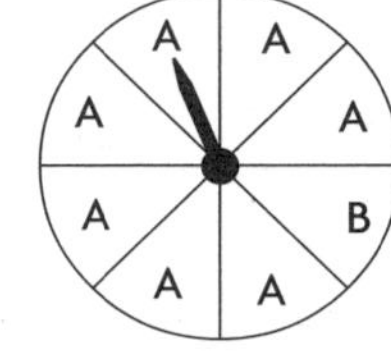

It is possible to spin an **A** in 7 out of 8 spins.
So, the event is likely.

Model 4
Spinning an **A** on this spinner.

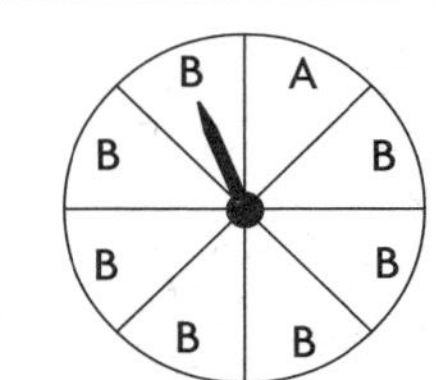

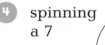

It is possible to spin an **A** in only 1 out of 8 spins.
So, the event is unlikely.

Try These

Write if the event is certain, impossible, likely, or unlikely.

1. spinning a 7

Think: How many 7s do you see?

____

2. spinning a 7

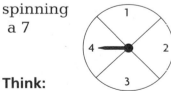

Think: Are there more or fewer 7s than there are other numbers?

____

3. spinning a 7

Think: How many numbers other than 7 do you see?

____

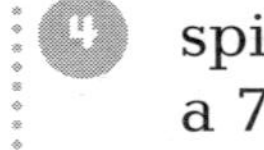

4. spinning a 7

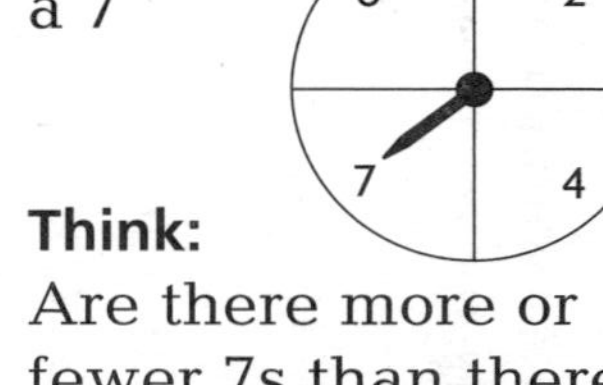

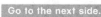

Think: Are there more or fewer 7s than there are other numbers?

____

Go to the next side.

Name ______________________ Skill ______________________

Practice on Your Own

Skill 97

Tell whether spinning a star is certain, impossible, likely, or unlikely for each spinner.

Spinner 1

Think: Are there all stars, no stars, more stars than diamonds, or **fewer stars than diamonds**?

unlikely

Spinner 2

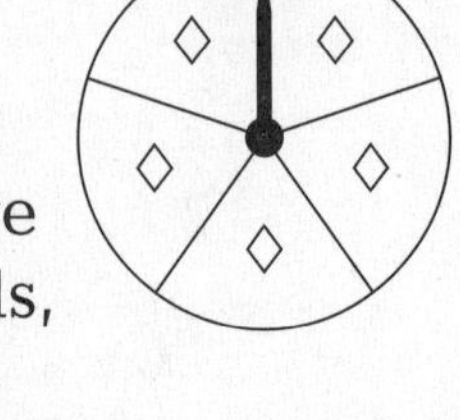

Think: Are there all stars, **no stars**, more stars than diamonds, or fewer stars than diamonds?

impossible

Spinner 3

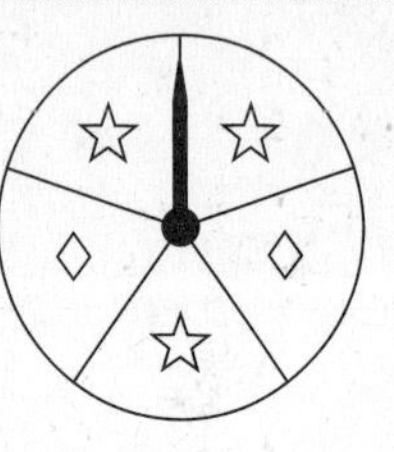

Think: Are there all stars, no stars, **more stars than diamonds**, or fewer stars than diamonds?

likely

Spinner 4

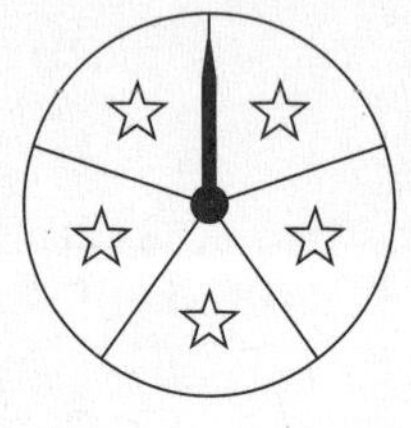

Think: Are there **all stars**, no stars, more stars than diamonds, or fewer stars than diamonds?

certain

Write if the event is certain, impossible, likely, or unlikely.

1. spinning a star

____

2. spinning a star

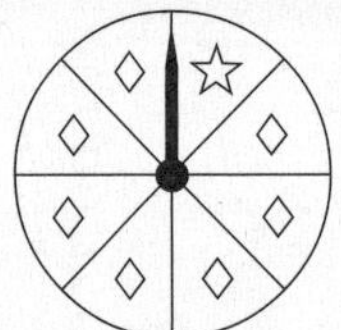

____

3. spinning a star

____

4. spinning a diamond

____

5. spinning a diamond

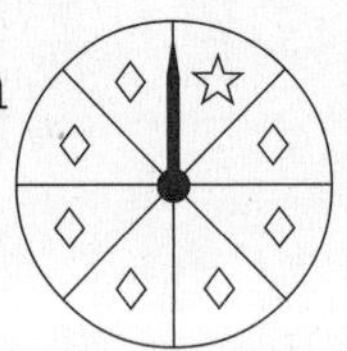

____

6. spinning a diamond

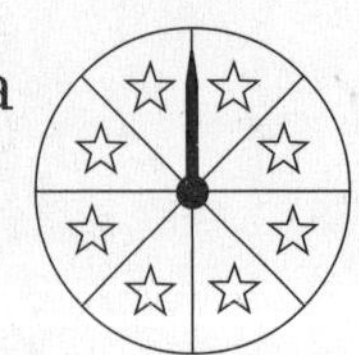

____

Check

Write if the event is certain, impossible, likely, or unlikely.

7. spinning a star

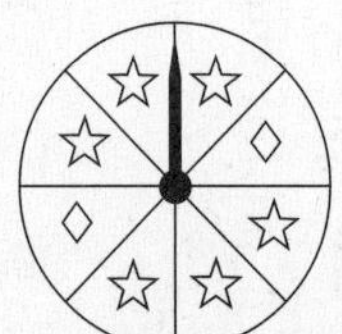

____

8. spinning a star

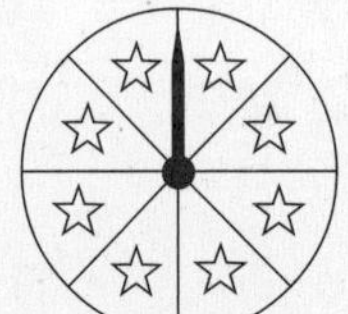

____

9. spinning a star

____

Skill 98 Analyze Data

Using Skill 98

OBJECTIVE Analyze data in line graphs and circle graphs

Have students read the information at the top of the page about data and graphs. Point out that graphs show data that can be read at a glance.

Have students examine the line graph in Example A. Discuss the fact that line graphs show data that changes over time. Focus on the title and the labels on the horizontal and vertical axes.

Ask: **What does this graph show?** (changes in theater attendance during one week) **What does each point show?** (one item of data) **By just looking at the graph, how can you tell when attendance rises?** (The line connecting the points goes up.) **How can you tell when attendance falls?** (The line goes down.)

Have students examine the circle graph in Example B. Discuss the fact that the circle represents 1 whole. Add the fractions on the graph to verify this. Read the title and all of the labels. Point out that the first bulleted item shows how parts of the data relate to the whole; the second bulleted item shows how parts of the data relate to each other.

TRY THESE Exercises 1–4 provide practice in analyzing data.

- **Exercises 1–2** Use a line graph.
- **Exercises 3–4** Use a circle graph.

PRACTICE ON YOUR OWN Be sure that students understand the difference between line graphs and circle graphs: line graphs show how data changes over time; circle graphs show how parts of data relate to the whole and to each other.

CHECK Determine if students can use line and circle graphs to compare data. Success is indicated by 4 out of 4 correct responses.

Students who successfully complete the **Practice on Your Own** and **Check** are ready to move to the next skill.

COMMON ERRORS

- On line graphs, students may not read the data that falls between intervals correctly. Also, they may not be able to visually track up or across the graph.
- On circle graphs, students may have trouble comparing fractional parts.

Students who made more than 2 errors in the **Practice on Your Own**, or who were not successful in the **Check** section, may benefit from the **Alternative Teaching Strategy** on the next page.

Optional

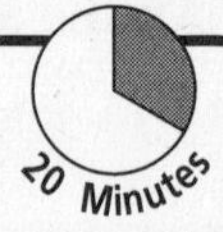

Alternative Teaching Strategy

Analyze Data

OBJECTIVE Use models of graphs

MATERIALS models of graphs prepared on large sheets of tag board, pushpins, yarn, double-stick removable poster tape

Prepare the line graph shown below using yarn and push pins to create the line.

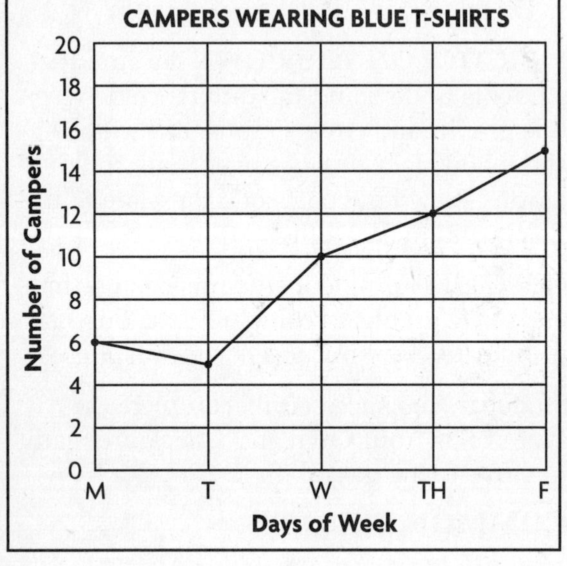

Ask: **What does the graph show?** (change in number of campers wearing blue T-shirts) **What period of time does the graph cover?** (1 school week, Monday-Friday) Have students identify the trend. (More students wore blue T-shirts as the week progressed.)

Have students analyze the data to answer questions similar to those in the lesson. Students may need help reading data that falls between the intervals.

Then pose a "what if" situation. For example, *What if the graph showed a downward trend for the week. What would the line look like?* Have a student adjust the pushpins and yarn to show a downward trend. Continue with other situations, having students change the graph to match each situation.

Then display a large blank circle. Have available different cut-out parts that are in tenths, some labeled and some unlabeled.

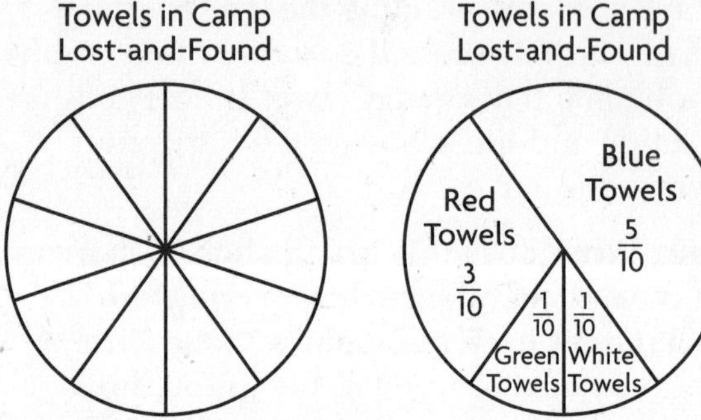

To begin, attach the labeled parts with double-stick poster tape.

Ask: **What does the graph show?** (the colors of the towels in the camp lost-and-found) **What is the whole?** (all the towels) **What are the parts?** (blue towels, red towels, green towels, white towels) **What fractional parts are represented?** ($\frac{5}{10}$, $\frac{3}{10}$, $\frac{1}{10}$, and $\frac{1}{10}$) **What is the sum of the parts?** ($\frac{5}{10} + \frac{3}{10} + \frac{1}{10} + \frac{1}{10} = \frac{10}{10} = 1$) Point out that the sum is equal to 1 whole.

Have students compare parts to answer questions about the data.

Have students remove the parts on the graph and label new parts to change the relationships in the graph. Have students ask and answer questions about the new graph.

Name ______________________ Skill ______________________

Skill 98

Analyze Data

Graphs are used to display data visually.

Example A
Line Graphs

A *line graph* shows how data changes over time.

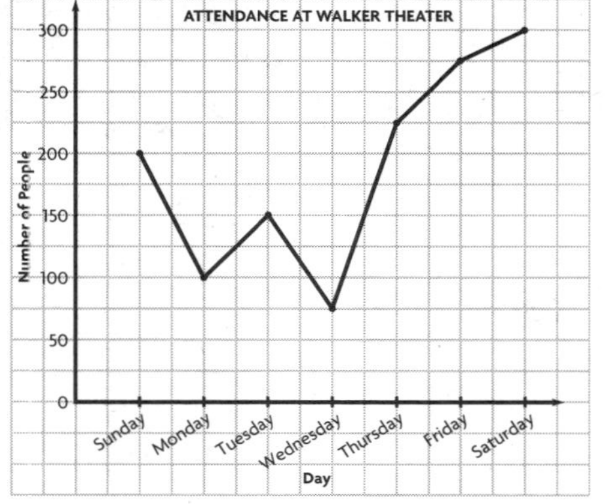

- Attendance fell during the beginning of the week.
- Attendance rose toward the end of the week.
- Attendance was greatest on Saturday, when 300 people went to the theater.

Example B
Circle Graphs

A *circle graph* shows how parts of the data are related to the whole and to each other.

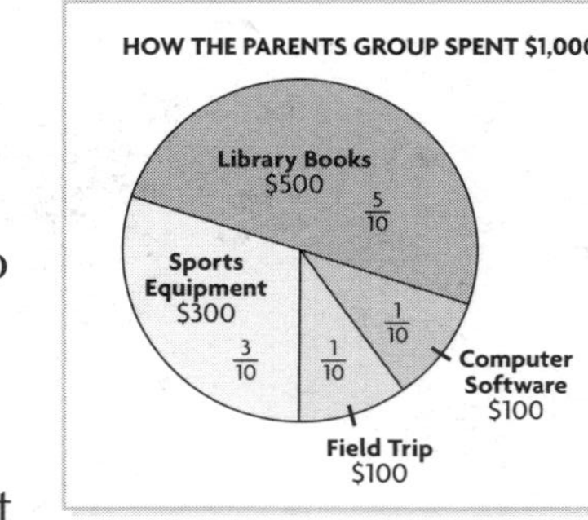

- Half of the total was spent on library books.
- The Parents Group spent three times as much on sports equipment as they did on a field trip.

Try These

Use the line graph.

1. How many people attended the theater on Monday? ________

2. How many more people attended the theater on Friday than on Thursday?
   Thursday ________
   Friday ________
   Answer ________

Use the circle graph.

3. Compare the amount spent on software to that spent on the field trip. Use >, <, or =.
   ________ ○ ________
   computer software   field trip

4. What part of the whole does sports equipment represent? ________

Go to the next side.

Name ______________________ Skill ______________________

Practice on Your Own

Skill 98

- Line graphs show how data changes over time.
- Circle graphs show how parts of the data are related to the whole and to each other.

The line graph at the right shows the sales of bottled water for a small refreshment stand.

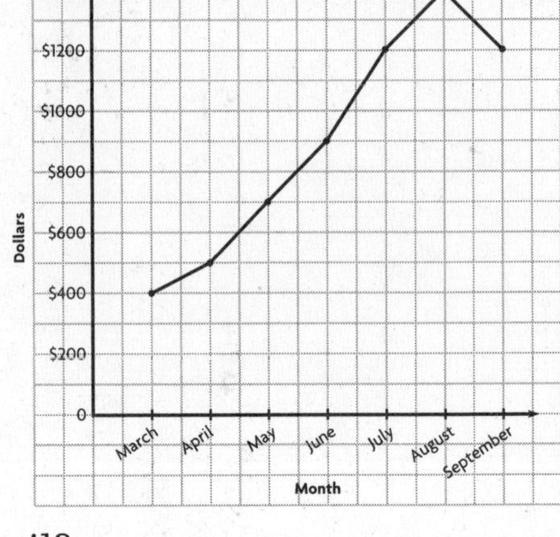

1. What was the amount of sales for March? ________

2. Were sales greater in August or September? ________

3. In which two months were sales the same? ________________

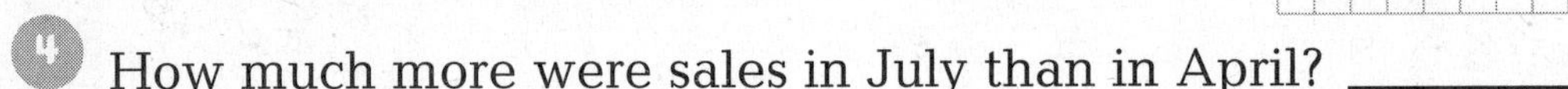

4. How much more were sales in July than in April? ________

The circle graph shows the amount of water used by average households in the United States.

HOW WATER IS USED BY THE AVERAGE HOUSEHOLD

Washing Machine $\frac{7}{25}$; Baths $\frac{2}{25}$; Faucets $\frac{3}{25}$ — including drinking water, cooking, toothbrushing, etc.; Other Uses $\frac{7}{25}$; Shower $\frac{5}{25}$; Dishwasher $\frac{1}{25}$

5. What part of the whole does the use of washing machines represent? ________

6. What part of the whole does the use of washing machines and other uses represent? ________

7. Is the amount of water used for dishwashers greater or less than the amount used for faucets? ________

8. Which two parts together equal the amount of water used by faucets? ________________

Check

Use the line and circle graphs above.

9. During which two months were sales of bottled water the least? ____________

10. How much greater were sales in May than in March? ________

11. In the average household, is more water used by showers or by baths? ________

12. Which activity uses the least amount of water? ________

Name ________________________________

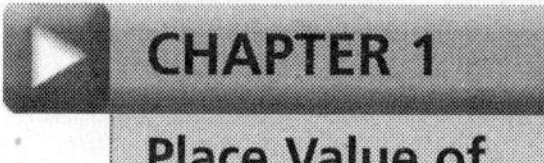

Place Value of Whole Numbers

ENRICHMENT

Place-Value Places

For 1–4, use the clues to circle the correct year for each event.

1. There was an 8 in the hundreds place in the year Colorado became a state. What year was it?

   1786 1796 1876

2. There was a 7 in the ones place in the year Michigan became a state. What year was it?

   1793 1837 1871

3. In the year New York became a state, the hundreds digit was 6 greater than the thousands digit. What year was it?

   1788 1872 1827

4. There was a 0 in the tens place in the year Oklahoma became a state. What year was it?

   1066 1890 1907

4,369,862	4,778,332	3,960,825	20,044,141
7,650,789	15,111,244	5,250,446	3,316,154

The table above lists the populations of eight states in 1999. Use the clues to find the correct population of each state.

5. The population of Arizona has an 8 in the thousands place.

   ____

6. The population of Texas has a 4 in the ten thousands place.

   ____

7. The population of North Carolina has the same digit in the millions place and hundreds place.

   ____

8. The population of Oregon has the same digit in its ten thousands place and hundreds place.

   ____

9. The population of Florida has a 1 in the ten millions place.

   ____

10. The population of Alabama has a 9 in the thousands place.

    ____

11. For the population of Kentucky, the sum of the millions digit and the ten thousands digit equals the digit in the hundred thousands place.

    ____

12. The population of Wisconsin has the same digit in the millions place and ten thousands place.

    ____

Use your answers from 5–12 to solve.

13. What is the value of the 2 in Wisconsin's population? ________________

14. What is the value of the 4 in Arizona's population? ________________

15. What is the value of the 6 in Oregon's population? ________________

Name ____

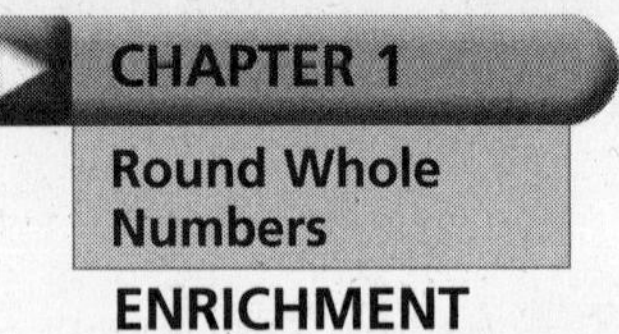

ENRICHMENT

Coming to Our Census

Every ten years, a census is taken in the United States to count the population. The table shows the United States population from 1800 to 1990. Round each number as indicated.

	YEAR	POPULATION	POPULATION ROUNDED TO THE NEAREST THOUSAND
1.	1800	5,308,483	
2.	1810	7,239,881	
3.	1820	9,638,453	
4.	1830	12,860,702	
5.	1840	17,063,353	
6.	1850	23,191,876	
7.	1860	31,443,321	
8.	1870	38,558,371	
9.	1880	50,189,209	
10.	1890	62,979,766	

	YEAR	POPULATION	POPULATION ROUNDED TO THE NEAREST TEN THOUSAND
11.	1900	76,212,168	
12.	1910	92,228,496	
13.	1920	106,021,537	
14.	1930	123,202,624	
15.	1940	132,164,569	
16.	1950	151,325,798	
17.	1960	179,323,175	
18.	1970	203,302,031	
19.	1980	226,542,203	
20.	1990	248,709,873	

Name ______________________________

Words and Equations/ Mental Math

ENRICHMENT

Mystery Numbers

Write an equation to represent each situation. Then solve your equation to find the mystery number.

1. Luce is thinking of a number. When 10 is multiplied by this number, the product is 70. What is Luce's number?

   Equation: ____________________

   Mystery Number: __________

2. Chaz is thinking of a number. When this number is divided by 9, the quotient is 6. What is Chaz's number?

   Equation: ____________________

   Mystery Number: __________

3. Al is thinking of a number. The product of this number and 11 is 99. What is Al's number?

   Equation: ____________________

   Mystery Number: __________

4. Yvette is thinking of a number. The quotient of this number divided by 12 is 8. What is Yvette's number?

   Equation: ____________________

   Mystery Number: __________

5. Ricardo is thinking of a number. When 49 is divided by this number, the quotient is 7. What is Ricardo's number?

   Equation: ____________________

   Mystery Number: __________

6. Inga is thinking of a number. Five times this number is 95. What is Inga's number?

   Equation: ____________________

   Mystery Number: __________

7. Paulina is thinking of a number. This number divided by 15 is 2. What is Paulina's number?

   Equation: ____________________

   Mystery Number: __________

8. Jeremy is thinking of a number. When 48 is divided by this number, the quotient is 6. What is Jeremy's number?

   Equation: ____________________

   Mystery Number: __________

9. Bea is thinking of a number. When 30 is multiplied by this number, the product is 6,000. What is Bea's number?

   Equation: ____________________

   Mystery Number: __________

10. Felo is thinking of a number. The quotient of this number divided by 4 is 9. What is Felo's number?

    Equation: ____________________

    Mystery Number: __________

Name ____________________

CHAPTER 2
Evaluate Expressions
ENRICHMENT

Triangle Expressions

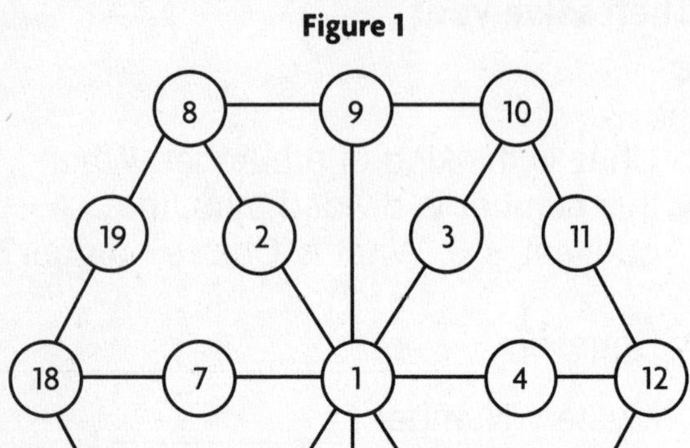

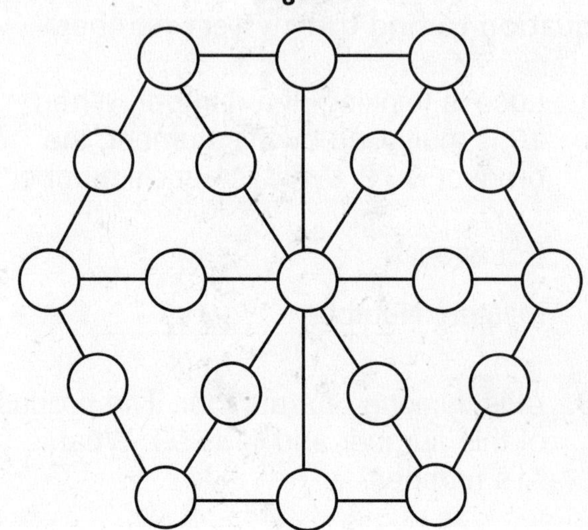

Evaluate each expression for the given value of each variable. Then find the exercise number in Figure 1 and write the answer for that exercise in the corresponding circle of Figure 2.

1. $\frac{x}{4}$ for $x = 24$

2. $7n$ for $n = 2$

3. $3ab$ for $a = 5$ and $b = 1$

4. $2m - 3$ for $m = 8$

5. $6y - 5z$ for $y = 14$ and $z = 15$

6. $fg - 11$ for $f = 6$ and $g = 3$

7. $1.6d$ for $d = 10$

8. $\frac{1}{3}u + 1$ for $u = 6$

9. $1.6 + 0.4w$ for $w = 41$

10. $pd - p - d$ for $p = 2$ and $d = 4$

11. $\frac{c}{5} + 5$ for $c = 60$

12. $4q$ for $q = 1$

13. $0.5k - 1$ for $k = 24$

14. $2xy$ for $x = 2$ and $y = 2$

15. $\frac{1}{6}m + \frac{1}{4}n$ for $m = 18$ and $n = 8$

16. $1 + 3s$ for $s = 3$

17. $10z + 2$ for $z = 1$

18. $p - m$ for $p = 7$ and $m = 6$

19. $9 + 0.1v$ for $v = 100$

20. Find the sum of the three numbers that form each side of a triangle in Figure 2.

____

Name ________________________________

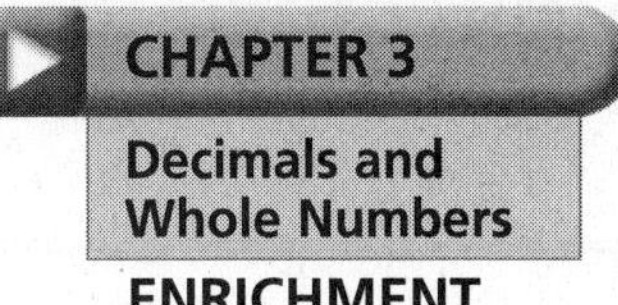

ENRICHMENT

Check That Decimal

For 1–4, draw a line from each decimal square to the decimal it models.

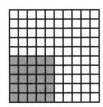

1. **2.** **3.** **4.**

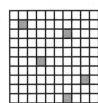

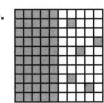

0.05 0.50 0.55 0.25

When you write a check to pay for something, the amount is written as a decimal and in words. Complete each check below by writing the correct amount next to the dollar sign.

5.

Samantha Stine
466 North Street
Smallville, PA 12005

1002

Pay to the order of Harwell Industries $ ______

Sixty-three and 67/100 dollars

SunnyBank
1000 Real Avenue
Smallville, PA 12116

Samantha Stine

⑈000255⑈ 063550054⑆06400005⑈

6.

Samantha Stine
466 North Street
Smallville, PA 12005

1003

Pay to the order of A. Curley $ ______

One hundred twenty-five and 44/100 dollars

SunnyBank
1000 Real Avenue
Smallville, PA 12116

Samantha Stine

⑈000255⑈ 063550054⑆06400005⑈

Name ___________________________

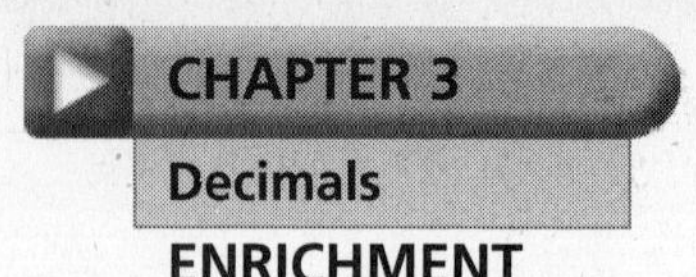

Check It Out!

Complete each check below by writing the correct amount in words.

1.

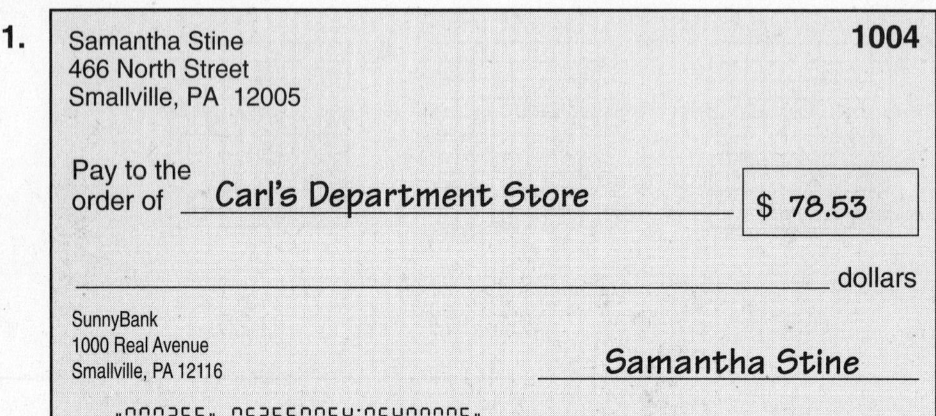
Samantha Stine
466 North Street
Smallville, PA 12005

1004

Pay to the order of Carl's Department Store $ 78.53

_______________ dollars

SunnyBank
1000 Real Avenue
Smallville, PA 12116

Samantha Stine

⑈000255⑈ 063550054⑆06400005⑈

2.

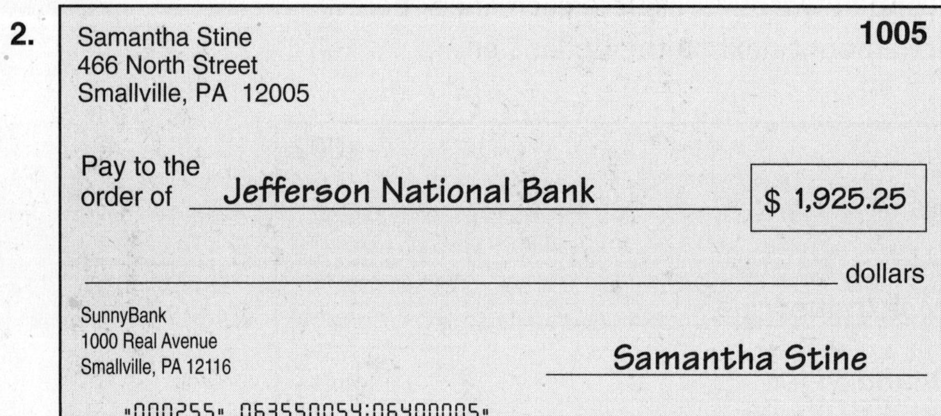
Samantha Stine
466 North Street
Smallville, PA 12005

1005

Pay to the order of Jefferson National Bank $ 1,925.25

_______________ dollars

SunnyBank
1000 Real Avenue
Smallville, PA 12116

Samantha Stine

⑈000255⑈ 063550054⑆06400005⑈

Round each of the check amounts to the nearest tenth of a dollar.

3. The check to Harwell Industries ______________

4. The check to A. Curley ______________

5. The check to Carl's Department Store ______________

6. The check to Jefferson National Bank ______________

Round each of the check amounts to the nearest dollar.

7. The check to Harwell Industries ______________

8. The check to A. Curley ______________

9. The check to Carl's Department Store ______________

10. The check to Jefferson National Bank ______________

Name ________________________________

CHAPTER 4
Prime and Composite
ENRICHMENT

Diamond Primes

The diamond diagram below contains 36 numbers.

1. Place a small circle around each prime number.
2. Place a small square around each composite number.
3. Use line segments to make a path connecting each of the prime numbers in ascending order.
4. Use line segments to make a path connecting each of the composite numbers in ascending order.
5. How many prime numbers are there in the diagram? _____
6. How many composite numbers are there in the diagram? _____
7. How many times do the two paths cross? _____

3

45 5

42 11 50

23 17 57 63

29 38 25 21 77

36 37 43 47 20 93

33 30 27 53 14

32 61 59 9

83 71 6

89 4

97

Name ____________________

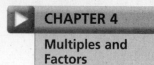

Factor and Multiple Trees

Each exercise shows a tree with a number written on its trunk. Fill in the factors of that number on the ends of the tree's roots.

1.

2.

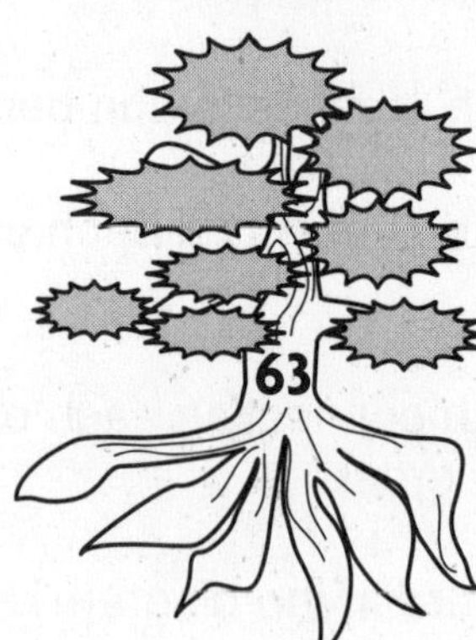

3.

Each exercise shows a tree with a number written on its trunk. Fill in the first five multiples of the number on the tree's fruit.

4.

5.

6.

Each exercise shows a tree with a number written on its trunk. Fill in the factors of that number on the ends of the tree's roots. Then fill in the first five multiples of the number on the tree's fruit.

7.

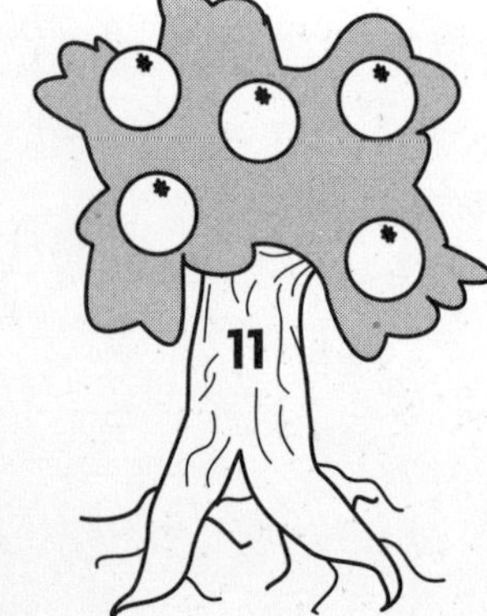

8.

9.

Name ______________________________

Name That Math

Name four special types of mathematics.

To decode the answer, solve each exercise. Then put the corresponding letter on the line(s) above the exercise number.

1. $\frac{2}{3} \bullet \frac{1}{5}$
2. $\frac{3}{7} \bullet \frac{14}{15}$
3. $3\frac{3}{4} \bullet \frac{4}{5}$
4. $1\frac{1}{2} \bullet 5\frac{2}{3}$
5. $\frac{11}{15} \div \frac{3}{5}$
6. $\frac{3}{5} \div 3$
7. $2\frac{2}{9} \div 1\frac{1}{9}$
8. $\frac{5}{6} + \frac{11}{12}$
9. $\frac{3}{4} + \frac{1}{2}$
10. $\frac{5}{9} - \frac{1}{3}$
11. $3\frac{3}{5} + \frac{2}{5}$
12. $6\frac{1}{4} + 2\frac{1}{2}$
13. $10\frac{8}{9} - 9\frac{1}{3}$
14. $3\frac{1}{5} - 2\frac{3}{5}$
15. $5 - 4\frac{1}{4}$

A. $1\frac{1}{4}$	**B.** $1\frac{2}{9}$	**C.** $\frac{2}{9}$	**E.** 3	**G.** $\frac{3}{5}$	**I.** $\frac{2}{15}$	**L.** 2	**M.** 4
N. $8\frac{1}{2}$	**O.** $1\frac{5}{9}$	**R.** $1\frac{3}{4}$	**S.** $\frac{3}{4}$	**T.** $\frac{2}{5}$	**U.** $8\frac{3}{4}$	**Y.** $\frac{1}{5}$	

__ __ __ __ __ __ __, __ __ __ __ __ __ __ __,
9 7 14 3 5 8 9 14 3 13 11 3 2 8 6

__ __ __ __ __ __ __ __ __ __ __ __ and
2 8 1 14 13 4 13 11 3 2 8 6

__ __ __ __ __ __ __ __
10 9 7 10 12 7 12 15

Name ______________________________

Puzzling Fractions

Evaluate the expressions in each clue to complete the crossword puzzle.

ACROSS

3. $5\frac{2}{5} \cdot 3\frac{1}{3} =$ ______

5. $3\frac{3}{4} \cdot 1\frac{1}{2} =$ 5 and ______ eighths

6. $3\frac{1}{5} + 6\frac{4}{5} =$ ______

7. $2\frac{1}{3} \div 1\frac{2}{5} =$ 1 and two ______

10. $\frac{5}{12} - \frac{1}{4} =$ one ______

12. $\frac{3}{5} \cdot \frac{1}{2} =$ ______ tenths

14. $\frac{7}{9} \div \frac{1}{4} =$ 3 and one ______

15. $4\frac{3}{10} - 3\frac{1}{4} =$ 1 and ______ twentieth

16. $\frac{9}{10} - \frac{1}{4} =$ thirteen ______

DOWN

1. $\frac{2}{7} \cdot \frac{1}{2} =$ one ______

2. $\frac{7}{24} \div \frac{7}{8} =$ one ______

4. $\frac{2}{3} \cdot \frac{5}{6} =$ five ______

5. $11\frac{5}{7} + 3\frac{6}{7} =$ 15 and ______ sevenths

8. $\frac{3}{8} \div 2 =$ three ______

9. $11\frac{1}{2} - \frac{9}{16} =$ 10 and ______ sixteenths

11. $\frac{1}{2} + \frac{2}{5} =$ ______ tenths

12. $\frac{1}{2} + \frac{1}{6} =$ ______ thirds

13. $6\frac{4}{5} - 2\frac{1}{5} =$ 4 and ______ fifths

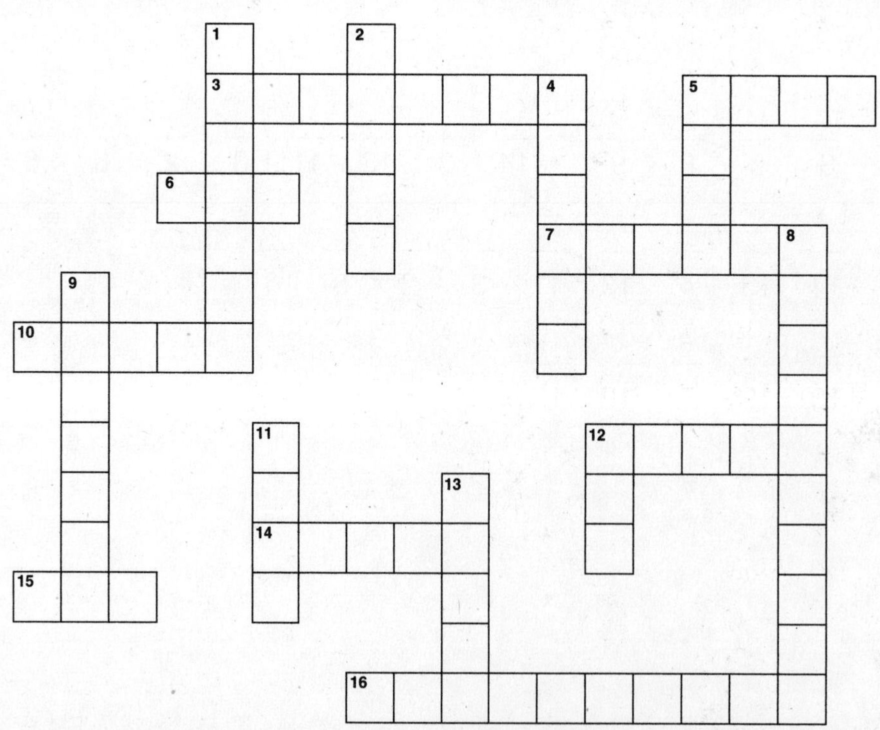

Name ______________________________

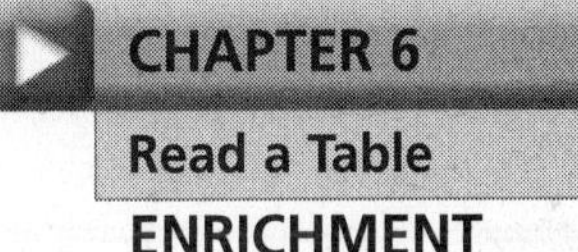

ENRICHMENT

Baby Numbers

The number of babies born in the United States in 1997 was close to the number of babies born in 1965. The table below shows those numbers according to how old the babies' mothers were. For 1–10, use the table.

BABIES BORN IN THE UNITED STATES			
	Mother's Age		
Year	Under 30	30–39	40 or older
1965	2,860,000	810,000	90,000
1997	2,500,000	1,300,000	80,000

1. How many babies born in 1965 had mothers age 40 or older?

____

2. How many babies born in 1997 had mothers under age 30?

____

3. How many babies born in 1997 had mothers age 30 or older?

____

4. How many babies born in 1965 had mothers under age 40?

____

5. How many babies were born in 1965?

____

6. How many babies were born in 1997?

____

7. How many more babies were born to mothers under 30 in 1965 than in 1997?

____

8. How many more babies were born to mothers 40 or older in 1965 than in 1997?

____

9. How many more babies were born to mothers age 30–39 in 1997 than in 1965?

____

10. How many more babies were born in 1997 than in 1965?

____

Name ________________________________

Missing Data

Each group of exercises begins with a data set that has one number missing. A clue is then given to help you solve each exercise.

2, 2, 56, 58, _____
The range is 60.

1. Find the missing data. _____

2. Find the median. _____

3. Find the mode. _____

4. Find the mean. _____

100, 106, 101, 106, _____
The median is 104.

5. Find the missing data. _____

6. Find the range. _____

7. Find the mode. _____

8. Find the mean. _____

83, 85, 80, 67, _____
The mean is 80.

9. Find the missing data. _____

10. Find the range. _____

11. Find the mode. _____

12. Find the median. _____

7, 11, 9, 9, 7, 10, 4, 8, _____
The mode is 7.

13. Find the missing data. _____

14. Find the range. _____

15. Find the mean. _____

16. Find the median. _____

Name ______________________________

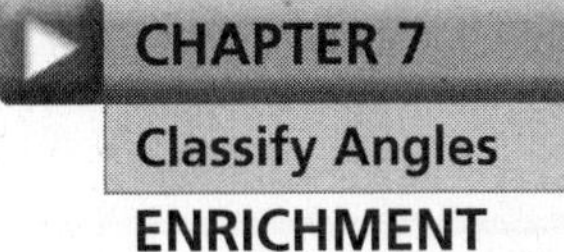

Eye Chart Angles

Inspect each letter below and place an "a" inside any acute angle, an "o" inside any obtuse angle, and an "r" inside any right angle. If no angles are present, write "No angles."

1. W	2. A	3. V	4. Y
5. T	6. H	7. E	8. M
9. S	10. L	11. O	12. X
13. N	14. F	15. Z	16. J

Name ________________________________

Time Zones

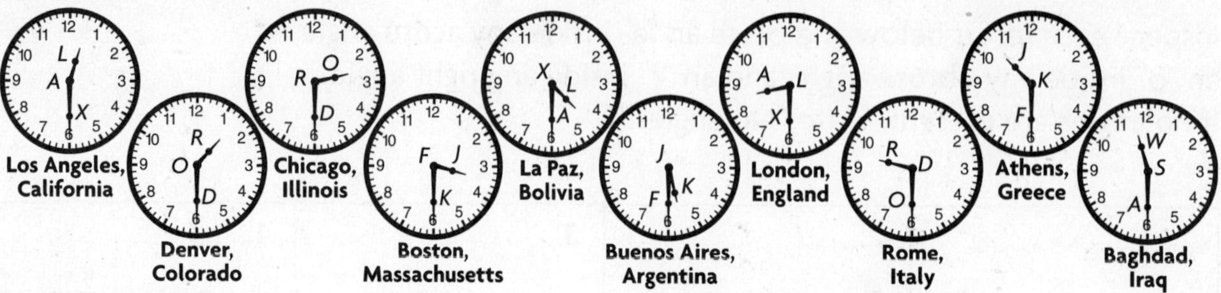

As you travel around the world, you pass through different time zones. The first clock above shows that it is 12:30 in Los Angeles, California. The other clocks show what time it then is in nine other cities around the world. Use the clocks to solve the problems below.

1. Name the angle formed by the hands of the clock in London, England.

   ____

2. Name the angle formed by the hands of the clock in Buenos Aires, Argentina.

   ____

3. Name the angle formed by the hands of the clock that shows 11:30.

   ____

4. Name the angle formed by the hands of the clock that shows 12:30.

   ____

5. Name the angle formed by the hands of the clock in Boston, Massachusetts.

   ____

6. For which city does the clock show $\angle ORD$?

   ____

7. For which city does the clock show $\angle LXA$?

   ____

8. What time does $\angle JKF$ represent?

   ____

9. What time does $\angle DOR$ represent?

   ____

10. What time does $\angle RDO$ represent?

    ____

11. When it is 12:30 P.M. in Los Angeles, California, it is 4:30 A.M. in Beijing, China. Draw hands that represent Beijing's time on the clock below. Label the angle $\angle B$.

12. When it is 12:30 P.M. in Los Angeles, California, it is 6:30 A.M. in Melbourne, Australia. Draw hands that represent Melbourne's time on the clock below. Label the angle $\angle M$.

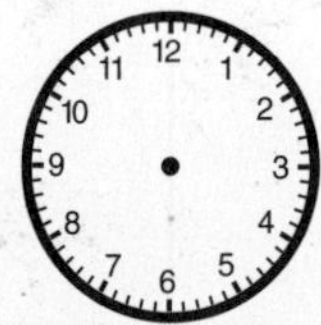

Name ______________________________

Conversion Riddles

Solve each set of exercises by using the choices in the far right column. Then write the letter above the corresponding exercise number to solve the riddle.

For 1–11, choose the letter of the equivalent customary measurement.

1. 4 yd	**A.** 12 ft
2. 48 oz	**B.** 6 lb
3. $3\frac{1}{4}$ lb	**E.** 5 yd
4. 2 gal	**G.** 8 qt
5. 30 ft	**H.** 360 in.
6. 20 qt	**I.** 52 oz
7. 144 in	**L.** 112 oz
8. $\frac{1}{2}$ gal	**N.** 2 qt
9. 16 pt	**R.** 3 lb
10. 7 lb	**S.** 3 gal
11. 15 ft	**T.** 40 pt

Which geometric figure is always correct?

__   __ __ __ __ __   __ __ __ __ __
1   2 3 4 5 6   7 8 9 10 11

For 12–21, chose the letter of the equivalent metric measurement.

12. 4,000 mm	**A.** 400 cm
13. 3 kg	**C.** 4,000 m
14. 4 m	**D.** 7 kg
15. 12,000 mL	**I.** 0.5 kg
16. 7,000 g	**K.** 500 mL
17. 40 cm	**R.** 12 L
18. 8 L	**S.** 400 mm
19. 500 g	**T.** 8,000 mL
20. 4 km	**U.** 40 km
21. 0.5 L	**Y.** 3,000 g

What has three feet, but cannot walk or run?

__   __ __ __ __ __ __ __ __ __
12   13 14 15 16 17 18 19 20 21

Name ____________________

Lucky Numbers

Solve the proportion in the center of the four-leaf clover. Circle the correct solution.

1.

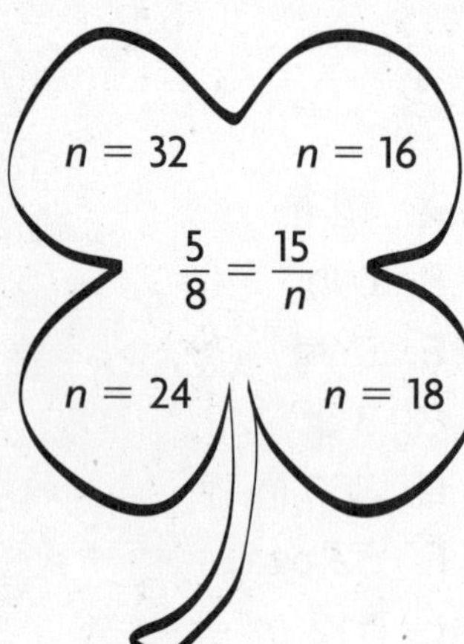

2.

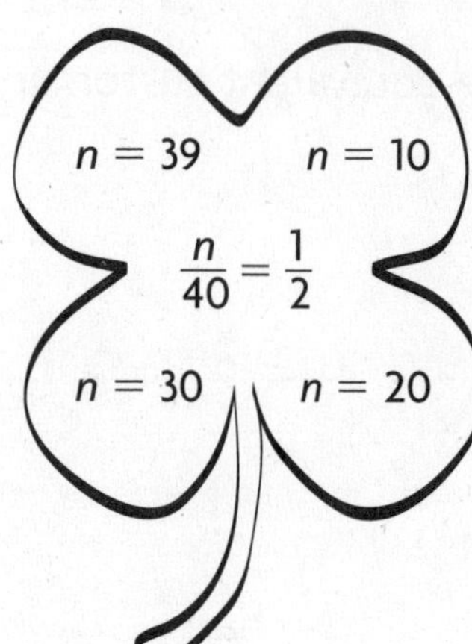

3.

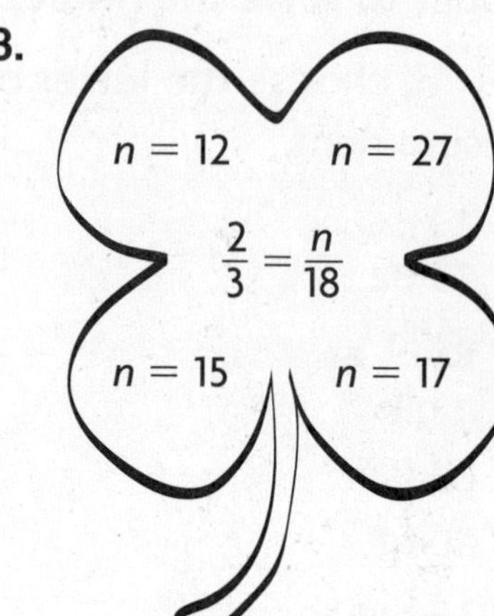

4.

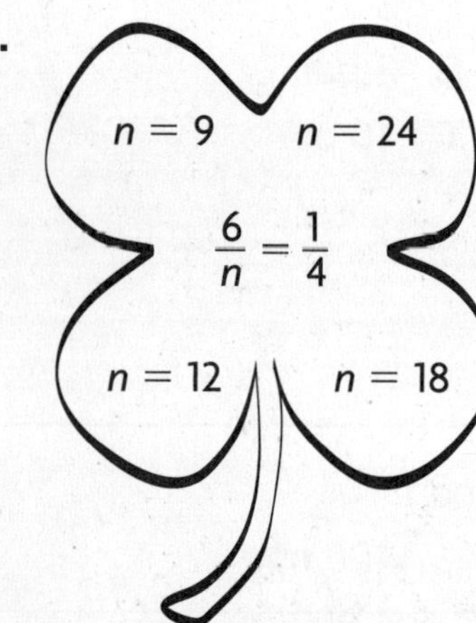

5.

$n = 40$ $n = 60$

$$\frac{7}{10} = \frac{42}{n}$$

$n = 45$ $n = 50$

6.

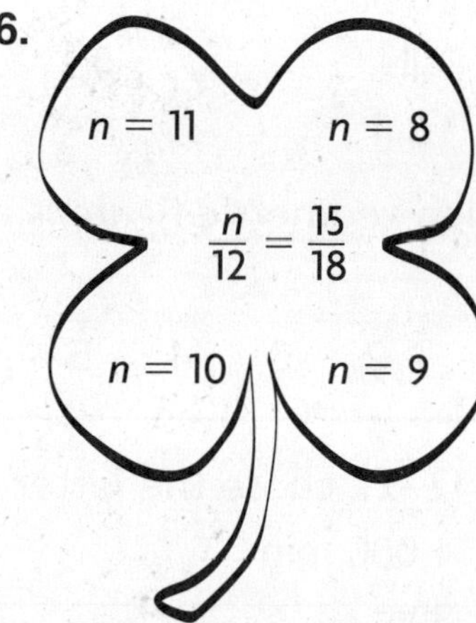

7.

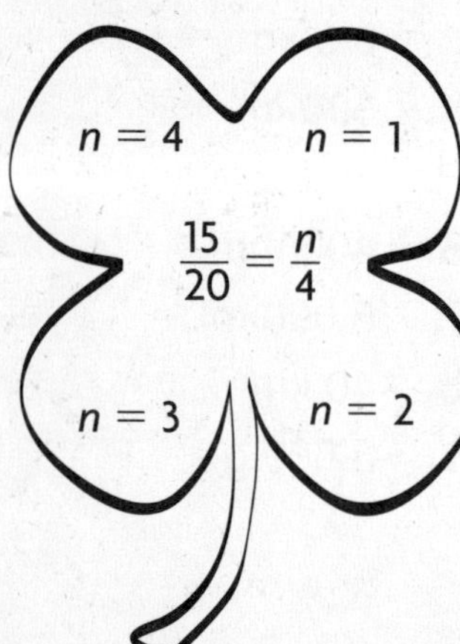

8.

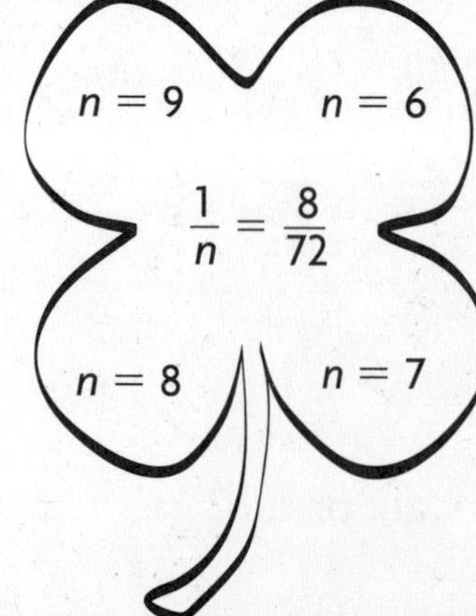

9.

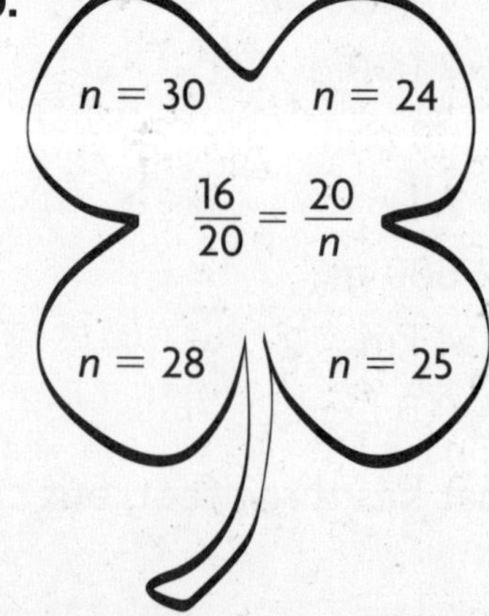

Name ______________________________

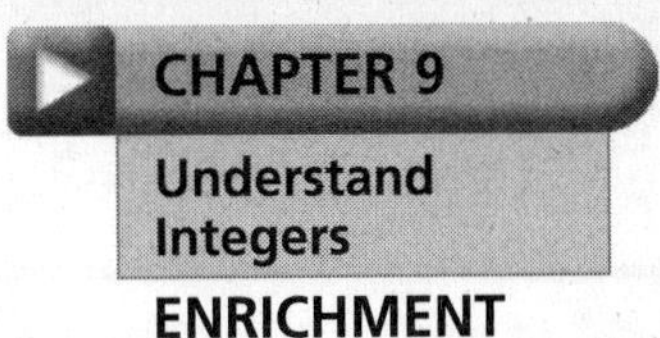

ENRICHMENT

One More Integer Riddle

Match each situation in Column 1 with the correct integer in Column 2. Then write the letter above the corresponding exercise number to solve the riddle.

Column 1

1. The submarine was traveling at a depth of 200 feet below sea level. _____
2. On a sale of a stock, Martin had a gain of $300. _____
3. The temperature was 28 degrees below zero. _____
4. Jack's golf score was 6 strokes under par today. _____
5. A baseball player's weight increased by 28 pounds. _____
6. A tree grew 12 feet in one year. _____
7. There were 300 fewer people at the annual ball this year. _____
8. There were 30 more days of rain this year than last year. _____
9. A hot-air balloon floated by at a height of 200 feet. _____
10. On a running play, a halfback lost 12 yards. _____
11. Six more students joined the Drama Club. _____
12. Jason lost $30 when he accidentally left his wallet at the beach. _____

Column 2

A. −300

E. −28

I. −30

H. +300

N. −6

O. −12

R. +6

S. +200

T. +28

V. +30

W. −200

Y. +12

When are buildings like books?

__ __ __ __   __ __ __ __
1 2 3 4   5 2 3 6

__ __ __ __   __ __ __ __ __ __ __
2 7 8 3   9 5 10 11 12 3 9

Name ________________________________

Number Puzzles

For 1–6, use the number line below to help solve each number puzzle.

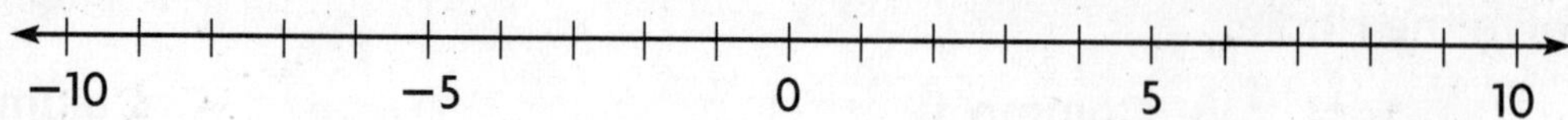

1. I am 3 units to the right of −9. ____
2. I am 8 units to the left of +5. ____
3. I am 2 units to the left of −1. ____
4. I am 6 units to the right of +2. ____
5. I am 5 units from −3 and 6 units from +8. ____
6. I am 7 units from 3 and 5 units from −9. ____

Find three numbers across or down that form a number sentence involving multiplication or division. Circle the numbers and write the operation and equal sign. You may use a number more than once. One has been done for you. Find the other 16 number sentences.

9	4	8 ×	9 =	72	10	3
5	12	60	4	6	11	66
45	2	6	2	12	110	10
7	3	10	11	3	48	20
40	5	8	22	44	4	11
4	15	8	12	96	12	3
10	9	3	3	8	24	12

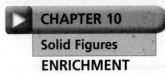

What Figure Am I?

Use the information to name each solid figure.

1. All my faces are squares. I have six faces in all.

   ____

2. All my faces are triangles. I have four faces in all.

   ____

3. I have two circular bases.

   ____

4. Basketballs and soap bubbles are examples of me.

   ____

5. Breakfast cereal is sold in boxes shaped like me.

   ____

6. I have a circular base and a point at my other end.

   ____

7. I have a square face and four triangular faces.

   ____

8. Two of my faces have eight sides. I also have eight rectangular faces.

   ____

9. I have a face with five sides and five faces with three sides.

   ____

10. You can buy soup, vegetables, and soda in containers shaped like me.

    ____

11. Some people like to eat ice cream from a cup. Others order it in a container they can eat that is shaped like me.

    ____

12. Two of my faces have six sides. I also have six rectangular faces.

    ____

13. Three of my faces are rectangles and two of my faces are triangles.

    ____

14. I have six rectangular faces.

    ____

Name ______________________________

Figure It Out

Match each statement in Column 1 with the figure it describes in Column 2. Then write the letter above the corresponding exercise number to solve the riddle.

Column 1

1. This figure has 6 edges.

2. This figure has 2 bases but no faces.

3. This figure has 4 vertices.

4. This figure has 18 edges.

5. This figure has 6 faces.

6. This figure has 8 vertices.

7. This figure has 8 edges.

8. This figure has no faces and no bases.

9. This figure has 4 more edges than vertices.

10. This figure has 5 vertices.

11. This figure has 12 vertices.

12. This figure has 7 faces.

Column 2

C. 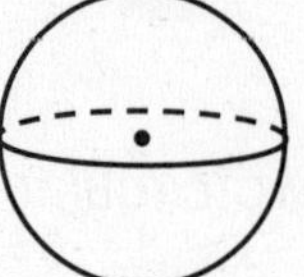

E. 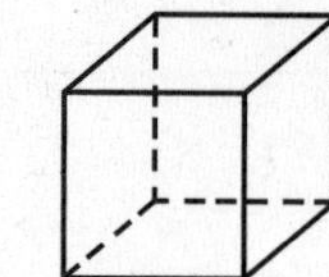

F. 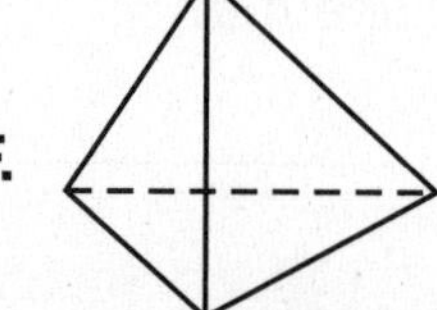

I. 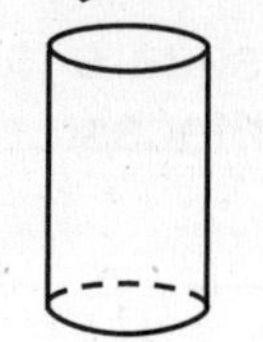

N. 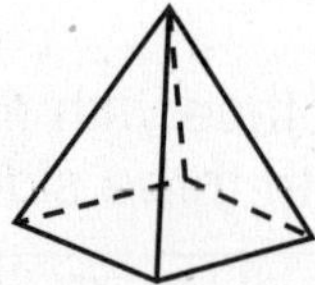

S. 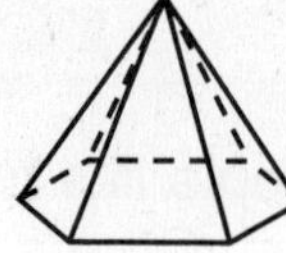

T. 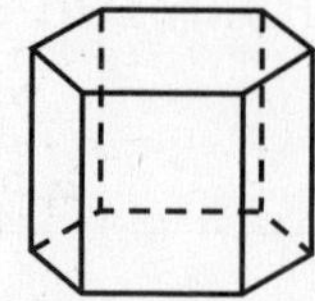

What is the difference between a brand new quarter and a very old dime?

___	___	___	___	___	___	___		___	___	___	___	___
1	2	3	4	5	6	7		8	9	10	11	12

Name ______________________________

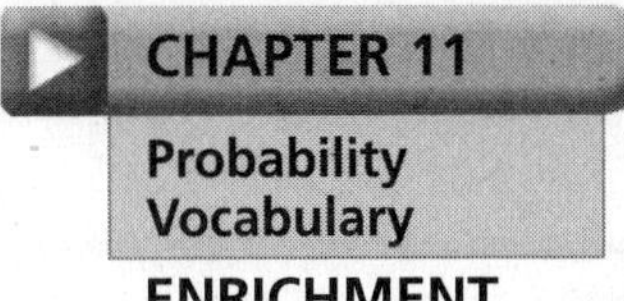

ENRICHMENT

Peek-a-Boo Probability

Write the definition beside each word. Then find the word in the seek-and-find.

1. Probability ______________________________
2. Experiment ______________________________
3. Outcomes ______________________________
4. Sample Space ______________________________
5. Experimental Probability ______________________________
6. Theoretical Probability ______________________________
7. Equally Likely ______________________________
8. Fair ______________________________
9. Compound Event ______________________________
10. Prediction ______________________________
11. Odds ______________________________

```
E T T V N O X A L M R E V A D Z C L O M W Q E
S O U D G B H E T Y L O W N E J S S T N R I Q
A J U E E C Q A B O K Q B V N O O N N L Z C U
M Z A T N E V E D N U O P M O C E S D G Q E A
P P O I C Y T R E W Q A S D F M G H L Z C M L
L R E W P O F K F R Y S H U I F D K R A A E L
E X P E R I M E N T A L P R O B A B I L I T Y
S G R V E Z M E Y L A Q E R A S L F A F U R L
P H T F D K L D S D H P I O O P F D F K Q E I
A J D I I E R J P A X A H O Q E R Z S K A I K
C E Q U C A L L N E T T A S D H N K B A E L E
E A R F T H O L P I Q S R T Y U O L T R Q E L
G S E V I Y I M S K A X P R O B A B I L I T Y
N Z D B O U K P D L Z D F G H J I P G F E L S
T X C N N J M U D M W E C B N M K N H A Q U A
Y T I L I B A B O R P L A C I T E R O E H T L
```

Name ______________________________

Hank's Homers

How many homeruns did Hank Aaron hit in his baseball career? To discover the answer, solve each problem. Then shade in the sections of the digital display that contain the answers. Read the number from the digital display.

1. You roll a die and write down the outcome. What is the sample space? ________
2. You roll two dice and record the sum of the numbers. How many possible outcomes are there? ________
3. There are 2 blue, 3 green and 5 black marbles in a bag. If you reach in and pick one marble, what is the probability of picking a green one? ________
4. What is the probability of getting an even number when you roll a die? ________
5. There are 6 girls and 4 boys in a class. If the teacher chooses one student to work a problem at the board, what is the probability that a girl is chosen? ________
6. Sally has shot 50 free throws and made 32 of them. What is the probability that she will make her next shot? ________
7. Jamie is a good skateboard rider and can "stick" the landing on 85% of his jumps. Write the probability that he does not "stick" his next landing as a decimal. ________
8. What is the probability of getting a 5 or a 6 when rolling a die? ________
9. There are 7 red, 10 blue, and 8 black cars in the parking lot of a baseball stadium. Barry Bonds hits a homerun and the ball hits one of the cars. What is the probability that the ball hits a red or a blue car? ________
10. You flip a coin and roll a die and record your findings. How many possible outcomes are there? ________
11. You can order a hotdog or a hamburger on a wheat or white bun, with either ketchup or mustard. If you choose one meat, one bun and one condiment, how many different choices are there? ________
12. There are 30 marbles in a bag and 11 of them are red. What are the odds of picking a red marble from the bag? ________
13. Bobby has 34 baseball cards and 21 of them have Red Sox players on them. If you close your eyes and pick one, what are the odds of not choosing one with a Red Sox player? ________

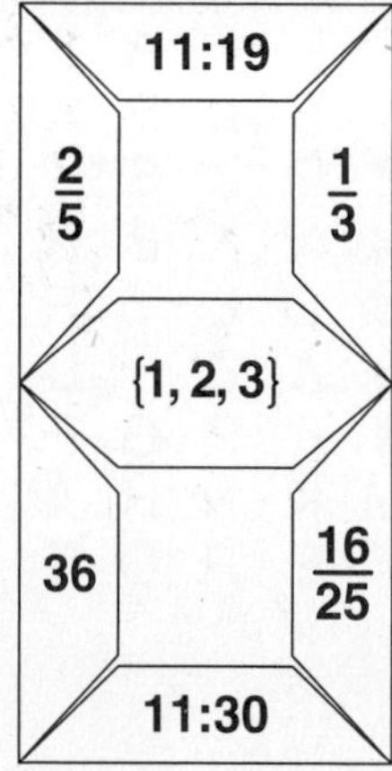

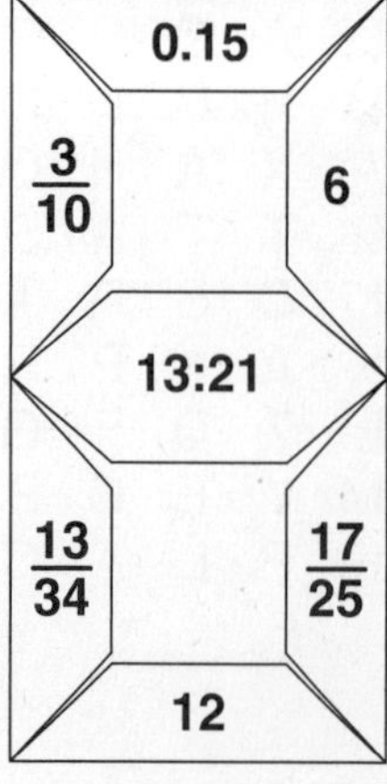

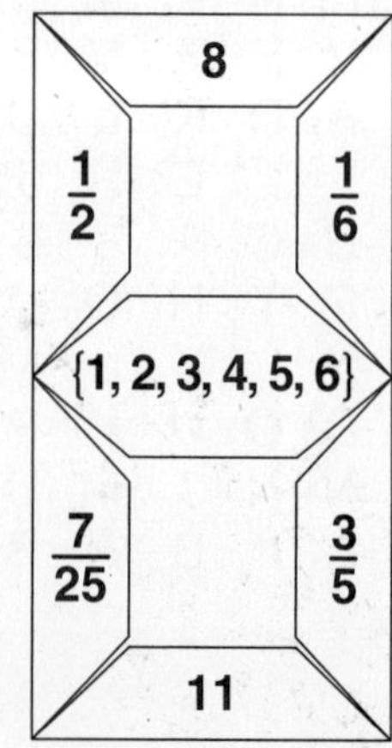

Name ______________________________

Hidden Message, Hidden Designs

Sue and her friends are playing a game in which each person takes turns hiding a bag of marbles and the others try to find it. Use the letters for each number below to solve Exercises 1–7.

A -3	**B** -12	**C** -5	**D** 2.5	**E** 0.1	**G** $5\frac{1}{3}$	**H** 0.05
I $\frac{9}{4}$	**N** $\frac{12}{5}$	**R** $\frac{3}{8}$	**S** $-\frac{1}{4}$	**T** 0	**U** 1%	

1. Compare E, S, and U. ______ < ______ < ______
2. Compare D, H, and I. ______ < ______ < ______
3. Compare E, H, and T. ______ < ______ < ______
4. Compare A, B, and G. ______ < ______ < ______
5. Compare I and N. ______ < ______
6. Compare E, H, and R. ______ < ______ < ______
7. Compare A, C, and R. ______ < ______ < ______
8. Examine your answers to Exercises 1–7. Use the ordered letters to find out where Sue hid the bag of marbles.

_ _ _   _ _ _   _ _ _   _ _ _   _ _   _ _ _   _ _ _.

Graph the ordered pairs for each exercise and connect the points in the order they are listed. Then connect your last point to your first point to discover the hidden design.

9. (−2, −2), (0, 4), (2, −2), (−2, 2), (2, 2)

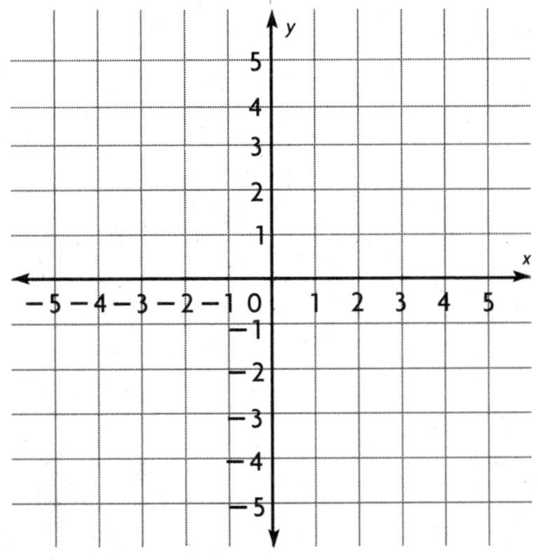

10. (0, 1), (0, 3), (2, 3), (2, 4), (4, 2), (2, 0), (2, 1)

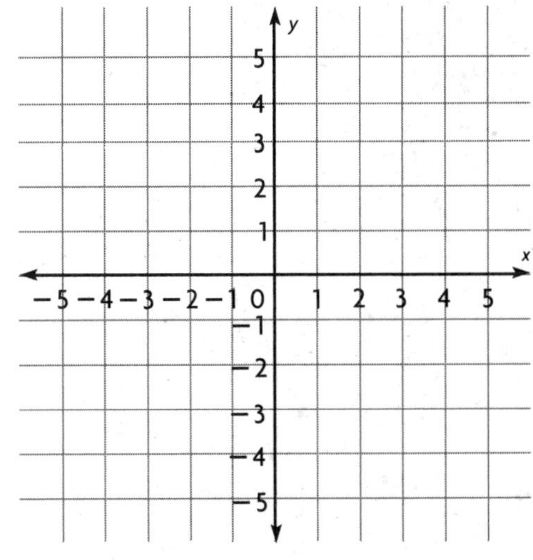

Name ____

Flip It

Draw the reflection of the figure after it is flipped across the line.

1. 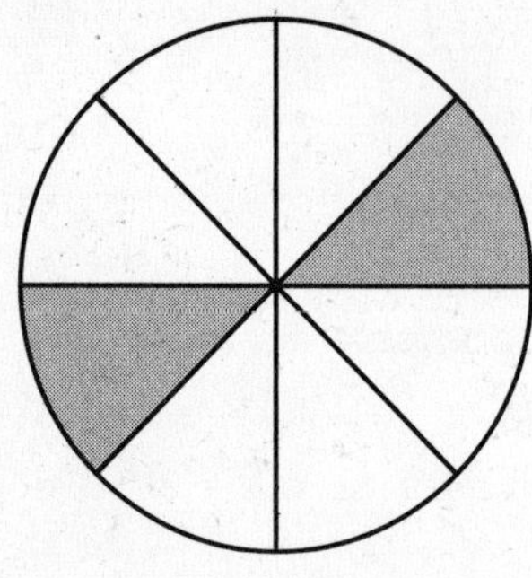

2. 

3. 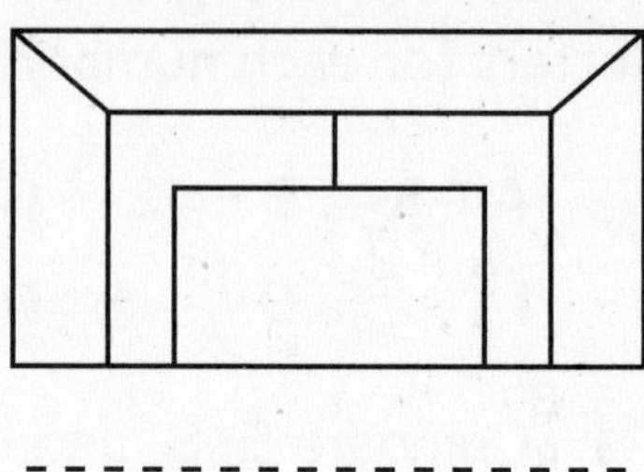

4. 

5. 

6. 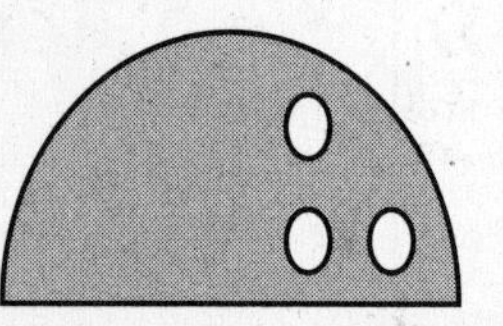

7. 

Diagnostic Assessment
Answers

Number and Quantitative Reasoning

1. D
2. G
3. C
4. G
5. B
6. G
7. B
8. G
9. D
10. H
11. D
12. H
13. B
14. J
15. B
16. G
17. A
18. H
19. D
20. F
21. B
22. G
23. C
24. G
25. A
26. H
27. A
28. H
29. C
30. H
31. D
32. G
33. A

Operations

34. H
35. B
36. H
37. B
38. J
39. B
40. F
41. C
42. J
43. B
44. F
45. B
46. F
47. A

Algebra

48. H
49. D
50. G
51. D
52. J
53. A
54. G
55. C
56. H
57. C
58. H
59. A
60. H
61. B
62. G
63. A
64. H
65. C
66. G
67. B
68. J
69. C

Measuring

70. F
71. B
72. H
73. D

Geometry

74. F
75. A
76. G
77. C
78. J
79. D
80. F
81. A
82. G
83. B
84. H
85. C
86. H
87. A
88. H
89. A

Statistics and Data Analysis

90. J
91. A
92. G
93. D
94. H
95. B
96. H
97. C
98. G

Answers

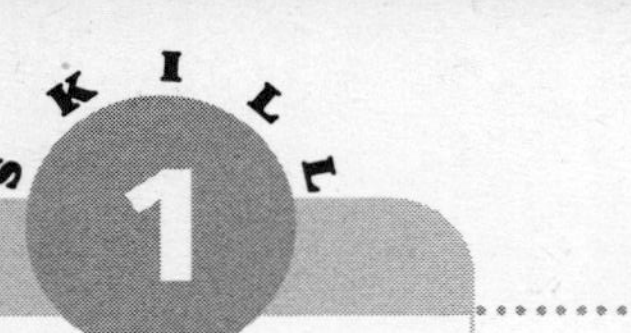

TRY THESE

1. thousands, hundreds, 3 hundred thousands or 300,000
2. millions, tens, 2 ten millions or 20,000,000
3. billions, ones, 1 billion, or 1,000,000,000

PRACTICE

1. ones, hundreds, 7 hundreds or 700
2. millions, ones, 0 millions or 0
3. billions, ones, 2 billions, or 2,000,000,000
4. 4 hundreds, or 400
5. 6 hundred thousands or 600,000
6. 8 hundred millions or 800,000,000
7. 7 tens or 70

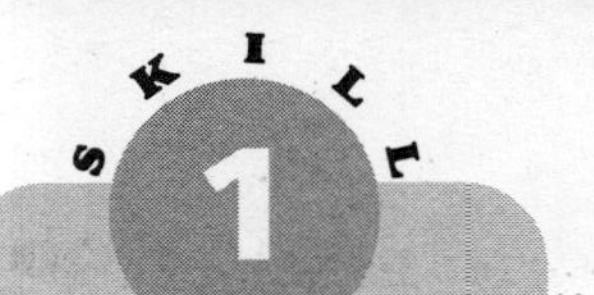

8. 1 billion or 1,000,000,000
9. 0 ten thousands or 0

CHECK

10. 6 ten thousands or 60,000
11. 1 hundred million or 100,000,000
12. 5 million or 5,000,000

TRY THESE

1. billions; millions; 2,000,525,452
2. millions; ones; 8,415,000
3. billions, thousands; 18,200,000,672

PRACTICE

1. billions; millions
2. millions, none
3. billions; thousands and ones
4. 7,250,916
5. 30,000,485,129
6. 216,026,000,000
7. 85,760,000

CHECK

8. 216,893,012
9. 15,634,000

SKILL 3

TRY THESE

1. 4,700
2. 2,000
3. 20,000
4. 305,100

PRACTICE

1. 350
2. 2,390
3. 9,320
4. 87,040
5. 800
6. 1,500
7. 9,300
8. 57,100
9. 9,000
10. 5,000
11. 11,000
12. 32,000
13. 20,000
14. 40,000
15. 220,000
16. 420,000

CHECK

17. 364,600
18. 435,000
19. 680,000
20. 817,020

Answers

Skill 4

TRY THESE

1. <, hundreds place
2. >, none
3. <, tens place

PRACTICE

1. < , hundreds place
2. < , thousands place
3. >, none
4. > , ten thousands place
5. 0, 1, 2, 3, 4, 5,and 6
6. 7, 8, and 9

CHECK

7. =
8. >
9. <
10. >

Skill 5

TRY THESE

1. 379, 258, 251; Order 251, 258, 379
2. 591, 586, 514; Order 591, 586, 514
3. 1,204, 635, 501, 499; Order 499, 501, 635, 1,204

PRACTICE

1. 182, 175, 115; Order 115, 175, 182
2. 1,025, 876, 867; Order 867, 876, 1,025
3. 352, 62; Order 352, 279, 251, 62
4. 2,405, 507; Order 2,405, 2,345, 624, 507

CHECK

5. 3,896, 3,215, 584
6. 5,109, 4,876, 4,116, 823
7. 316, 327, 348
8. 835, 1,218, 1,401, 1,409

Skill 6

TRY THESE

1. 5
2. 8
3. 10
4. 13

PRACTICE

1. counting numbers, whole numbers, even numbers
2. counting numbers, whole numbers, odd numbers
3. counting numbers, whole numbers, odd numbers
4. counting numbers, whole numbers, even numbers

For Exercises 5-12, 4 choices each exercise. Possible answers given.

5. numbers 1 through 19

Skill 6

CHECK

6. numbers 0 through 19
7. 2, 4, 6, 8, 10, 12, 14, 16, 18
8. 1, 3, 5, 7, 9, 11, 13, 15, 17, 19
9. 40, 41, 42, 43, 44, 45, 46, 47, 48, 49, 50
10. 40, 41, 42, 43, 44, 45, 46, 47, 48, 49, 50
11. 40, 42, 44, 46, 48, 50
12. 41, 43, 45, 47, 49

Answers

Skill 7

TRY THESE

1. 3, 6, 9, 12, 15; 3, 6, 9, 12, 15
2. 2, 4, 6, 8, 10; 2, 4, 6, 8, 10
3. 6, 12, 18, 24, 30; 6, 12, 18, 24, 30

PRACTICE

1. 8, 16, 24, 32, 40; 8, 16, 24, 32, 40
2. 10, 20, 30, 40, 50; 10, 20, 30, 40, 50
3. 22, 33, 44, 55, 1, 2, 3, 4, 5
4. 24, 36, 48, 60, 1, 2, 3, 4, 5
5. 40, 60, 80, 100
6. 60, 90, 120, 150
7. 28, 32, 36
8. 42, 49, 56

CHECK

9. 60, 75, 90
10. 100, 125, 150

Skill 8

TRY THESE

1. 1 × 6, 2 × 3, 1, 2, 3, 6
2. 1 × 10, 2 × 5, 1, 2, 5, 10
3. 1 × 16, 2 × 8, 4 × 4, 1, 2, 4, 8, 16

PRACTICE

1. 1 × 9, 3 × 3, 1, 3, 9
2. 1 × 14, 2 × 7, 1, 2, 7, 14
3. 1 × 20, 2 × 10, 4 × 5, 1, 2, 4, 5, 10, 20
4. 1 × 12, 2 × 6, 3 × 4, 1, 2, 3, 4, 6, 12
5. 1 × 15, 3 × 5, 1, 3, 5, 15
6. 1 × 11, 1, 11
7. 1, 17
8. 1, 2, 3, 4, 6, 8, 12, 24
9. 1, 3, 13, 39

CHECK

10. 1, 2, 3, 6, 9, 18
11. 1, 2, 4, 7, 14, 28
12. 1, 13

Skill 9

TRY THESE

1. yes, 3, yes, prime
2. no, not prime
3. yes, yes, prime

PRACTICE

1. 2, no, not prime
2. 2, yes, 3, yes, 4, yes, 5, yes, prime
3. 2, no, not prime
4. 2, no, not prime
5. 2, no, not prime
6. 2, yes, prime
7. not prime
8. prime
9. not prime

CHECK

10. not prime
11. prime
12. not prime

Skill 10

TRY THESE

1. yes, 3, no, 3, 5, yes
2. 2, no, 2, 5, yes
3. 2, yes, 3, yes, 1, 7, no

PRACTICE

1. 2, no, 1, 52, 2, composite
2. 2, yes, 3, no, 1, 27, 3, composite
3. 2, yes, 3, yes, 4, yes, 1, 17, not composite
4. 2, yes, 3, no, 1, 21, 3, composite
5. 1, 37, not composite
6. 1, 28, 2, composite
7. 1, 5, 45, composite

CHECK

8. 1, 34, 2, composite
9. 1, 29, not composite
10. 1, 63, 3, composite

Answers

Skill 11

TRY THESE

1. 225; 3,375
2. 400; 8,000
3. $\frac{4}{9}$

PRACTICE

1. 324
2. 196
3. $\frac{1}{16}$
4. 15, 625
5. 1,728
6. 4,096
7. 2,304
8. $\frac{25}{64}$
9. 1,600
10. 4,913
11. 27,000
12. 9,261

CHECK

13. 144
14. 484
15. $\frac{1}{9}$
16. 1,331
17. 125,000
18. 64,000

Skill 12

TRY THESE

1. second, 6 × 6, 36
2. third, 4 × 4 × 4, 64
3. fourth, 3 × 3 × 3 × 3, 81

PRACTICE

1. second, 8 × 8, 64
2. third, 3 × 3 × 3, 27
3. fifth, 2 × 2 × 2 × 2 × 2, 32
4. 7 × 7, 49
5. 10 × 10 × 10, 1,000
6. 2 × 2 × 2 × 2, 16
7. 25
8. 343
9. 8
10. 100,000

CHECK

11. 81
12. 10,000
13. 125

Skill 13

TRY THESE

1. add 4 or + 4, 23, 27, 31
2. multiply by 3 or x 3, 81, 243, 729
3. subtract 2 or − 2, 17, 15, 13

PRACTICE

1. subtract 4 or − 4, 34, 30, 26
2. add 8 or + 8, 40, 48, 56
3. divide by 4 or ÷ 4; 16, 4, 1
4. 21, 14, 7
5. 256, 1,024, 4,096
6. 80, 75, 70
7. 67, 77, 87
8. 48, 60, 72
9. 10,000, 100,000, 1,000,000

CHECK

10. 22, 11, 0
11. 100, 125, 150
12. 25, 5, 1

Skill 14

TRY THESE

1. $\frac{4}{10}$, 0.4
2. $\frac{75}{100}$, 0.75
3. $1\frac{1}{10}$, 1.1
4. $1\frac{35}{100}$, 1.35

PRACTICE

1. $\frac{3}{10}$, 0.3
2. $\frac{7}{10}$, 0.7
3. $\frac{1}{10}$, 0.1
4. $1\frac{5}{10}$, 1.5
5. $\frac{17}{100}$, 0.17
6. $\frac{70}{100}$, 0.70
7. $\frac{4}{100}$, 0.04
8. $1\frac{65}{100}$, 1.65

CHECK

9. $\frac{9}{10}$, 0.9
10. $1\frac{6}{10}$, 1.6
11. $\frac{82}{100}$, 0.82
12. $1\frac{37}{100}$, 1.37

Answers

Skill 15

TRY THESE

1. 826.3; 826 and 3 tenths
2. 4,351.22; 4 thousand, 351 and 22 hundredths

PRACTICE

1. 23.57; 23 and 57 hundredths
2. 177.68, 177 and 68 hundredths
3. 890.3; 890 and 3 tenths
4. 106,434.19; 106 thousand, 434 and 19 hundredths
5. 169.45
6. 2,165.5

CHECK

7. 6 thousand, 489 and 9 tenths
8. 123 thousand, 690 and 56 hundredths

Skill 16

TRY THESE

1. 7, 6, yes, 8
2. 1, 1, no, 13.1
3. 4, 7, yes, 28.535

PRACTICE

1. 7, 4, no, 37
2. 1, 2, no, 83.1
3. 2, 5, 63
4. 7, 6, 52.488
5. 8, 4.8
6. 4, 27.595
7. 2
8. 57.1
9. 0.812

CHECK

10. 62
11. 47.5
12. 35.613

Skill 17

PRACTICE

1. $>$
2. $<$
3. $>$
4. $<$
5. $>$
6. $=$
7. 0.89, 0.91, 3.42
8. 0.03, 0.5, 2.4, 2.65
9. 1.3, 1.27, 1.18, 1.11

CHECK

10. $>$
11. $<$
12. 2.83, 2.48, 2.38, 1.7
13. 0.5, 1.18, 1.38, 1.83

Skill 18

TRY THESE

1. 2, 3, $\frac{2}{3}$
2. 1, 4, $\frac{1}{4}$
3. 2, 5, $\frac{2}{5}$

PRACTICE

1. 1, 4, $\frac{1}{4}$
2. 3, 4, $\frac{3}{4}$
3. 1, 2, $\frac{1}{2}$
4. $\frac{5}{8}$
5. $\frac{5}{7}$
6. $\frac{2}{3}$
7. $\frac{3}{6}$
8. $\frac{3}{8}$
9. $\frac{9}{9}$

CHECK

10. $\frac{5}{6}$
11. $\frac{7}{8}$
12. $\frac{6}{10}$

Answers

Skill 19

TRY THESE

1. $3, 3, \frac{3}{3}, \frac{4}{5}$
2. $4, 4, \frac{4}{4}, \frac{1}{3}$
3. $2, 2, \frac{2}{2}, \frac{4}{5}$

PRACTICE

1. $3, 3, \frac{3}{3}, \frac{3}{4}$
2. $3, 3, \frac{3}{3}, \frac{2}{5}$
3. $3, 3, \frac{3}{3}, \frac{1}{6}$
4. 1, 2, 3, 4, 6, 12; 1, 2, 7, 14; 2, $\frac{6}{7}$
5. 1, 2, 3, 5, 6, 10, 15, 30; 1, 2, 4, 5, 8, 10, 20, 40; 10, $\frac{3}{4}$
6. 1, 2, 3, 6, 9, 18; 1, 3, 5, 15; 3, $\frac{6}{5}$ or $1\frac{1}{5}$
7. $\frac{2}{3}$
8. $\frac{3}{1}$ or 3
9. $\frac{3}{5}$

CHECK

10. $\frac{2}{5}$
11. $\frac{1}{2}$
12. $\frac{3}{2}$ or $1\frac{1}{2}$

Skill 20

TRY THESE

1. 0
2. 1
3. $\frac{1}{2}$

PRACTICE

1. $\frac{1}{2}$
2. $\frac{1}{2}$
3. 1
4. $\frac{1}{2}$
5. 0
6. 1
7. 1
8. 0
9. 1
10. $\frac{1}{2}$

CHECK

11. 1
12. 0
13. $\frac{1}{2}$
14. 1

Skill 21

TRY THESE

1. $1, 1\frac{1}{2}$
2. $1, 1\frac{2}{3}$
3. $1, 1, 2\frac{3}{4}$

PRACTICE

1. $2, 2, 2, 2, 1, 1, 1, 1, 1, \frac{1}{2}, 4, \frac{1}{2}, 4\frac{1}{2}$
2. $3, 3, 2, 1, 1, \frac{2}{3}, 2, \frac{2}{3}, 2\frac{2}{3}$
3. $4, 4, 4, 3, 1, 1, 1, \frac{3}{4}, 3, \frac{3}{4}, 3\frac{3}{4}$
4. $\frac{5}{5}, \frac{5}{5}, \frac{3}{5}, 1, 1, \frac{3}{5}, 2, \frac{3}{5}, 2\frac{3}{5}$
5. $\frac{2}{2}, \frac{2}{2}, \frac{2}{2}, \frac{1}{2}, 1, 1, 1, \frac{1}{2}, 3, \frac{1}{2}, 3\frac{1}{2}$
6. $\frac{3}{3}, \frac{3}{3}, \frac{3}{3}, \frac{2}{3}, 1, 1, 1, \frac{2}{3}, 3, \frac{2}{3}, 3\frac{2}{3}$
7. $1\frac{7}{8}$
8. $4\frac{4}{5}$
9. $3\frac{1}{6}$

CHECK

10. $3\frac{1}{8}$
11. $2\frac{7}{10}$
12. $4\frac{1}{4}$

Skill 22

TRY THESE

1. 3, 3, 7
2. $4, 4, 4, \frac{15}{4}$
3. $5, \frac{9}{5}$

PRACTICE

1. $2, 2, 2, 2, \frac{9}{2}$
2. $4, 4, \frac{11}{4}$
3. $3, 3, 3, \frac{11}{3}$
4. $1 + 1 + 1 + \frac{2}{5}, \frac{5}{5} + \frac{5}{5} + \frac{5}{5} + \frac{2}{5}, \frac{17}{5}$
5. $1 + 1 + \frac{1}{8}, \frac{8}{8} + \frac{8}{8} + \frac{1}{8}, \frac{17}{8}$
6. $1 + 1 + 1 + \frac{5}{6}, \frac{6}{6} + \frac{6}{6} + \frac{6}{6} + \frac{5}{6}, \frac{23}{6}$
7. $\frac{23}{4}$
8. $\frac{44}{5}$
9. $\frac{20}{3}$

CHECK

10. $\frac{23}{4}$
11. $\frac{49}{8}$
12. $\frac{23}{5}$

Answers

TRY THESE

1. 10: 10, 20, 30, 40, 50, 60, 70, 80, 90, …
   8: 8, 16, 24, 32, 40, 48, 56, 64, 72, 80, …
   The LCM is 40.
2. 4: 8, 12, 16, 20, …
   16: 16, 32, 48, …
   The LCM is 16.
3. 4: 4, 8, 12, 16, 20, 24, 28, …
   5: 5, 10, 15, 20, 25, …
   The LCM is 20.

PRACTICE

1. 2, 4, 6, 8, 10, 12, …; 5, 10, 15, 20; … 10
2. 3, 6, 9, 12, …; 6, 12, 18, … 6
3. 7, 14, 21, …; 14, 21, 28, … 14
4. 10
5. 24
6. 15
7. 48
8. 30

CHECK

9. 72
10. 30
11. 32
12. 56

SKILL 24

TRY THESE

1. 4
2. 6
3. 6
4. 1

PRACTICE

1. 2
2. 2
3. 10
4. 6
5. $\frac{1}{2}$, $\frac{1}{2}$, 3, 3
6. $\frac{3}{4}$, $\frac{3}{4}$, 9, 9
7. $\frac{2}{2}$, 2, 2
8. $\frac{3}{3}$, 6, 6
9. 3, 3
10. 4, 4
11. $\frac{2}{2}$, 1, 1
12. $\frac{4}{4}$, 1, 1
13. 8
14. 1
15. 3
16. 7

CHECK

17. 5
18. 4
19. 1
20. 14

SKILL 25

TRY THESE

1. no, $<$, $<$
2. yes, no, 4, $>$, 3, $>$
3. $<$
4. 2, =, 2

PRACTICE

1. no, 10, $>$, $>$
2. yes, no, 6, $<$, $<$
3. $<$
4. no, 6, $>$, $>$
5. $<$
6. $>$, 2
7. yes, no, 12, $<$, 15, $<$
8. $<$
9. $>$, 3
10. $<$
11. $>$
12. $<$

CHECK

13. $>$
14. $>$
15. $<$

Answers

Skill 26

TRY THESE

1. 20, 0, 4
2. 20, 100, 100, 0, 5
3. 300, 0, 6

PRACTICE

1. 40, 0, 8, 0.8
2. 8, 20, 20, 0, 25, 0.25
3. 120, 100, 100, 0, 65, 0.65
4. 0.7
5. 0.2
6. 0.625
7. 0.5
8. 0.48
9. 0.875

CHECK

10. 0.45
11. 0.375
12. 0.08

Skill 27

TRY THESE

1. 4, 3, 4 to 3, $\frac{4}{3}$, 4:3
2. 6, 5, 6 to 5, $\frac{6}{5}$, 6:5
3. 6, 11, 6 to 11, $\frac{6}{11}$, 6 to 11

PRACTICE

1. 2, 6, 2 to 6; 2:6; $\frac{2}{6}$
2. 5, 2, 5 to 2; 5:2; $\frac{5}{2}$
3. 6, 13, 6 to 13; 6:13; $\frac{6}{13}$
4. 25 to 15; 25:15; $\frac{25}{15}$
5. 13 to 12; 13:12; $\frac{13}{12}$
6. 24 to 11; 24:11; $\frac{24}{11}$
7. 9 to 13; 9:13; $\frac{9}{13}$
8. 15 to 7; 15:7; $\frac{15}{7}$
9. 12 to 7; 12:7; $\frac{12}{7}$

Skill 27

CHECK

10. 4 to 4; 4:4; $\frac{4}{4}$
11. 15 to 21; 15:21; $\frac{15}{21}$
12. 9 to 2; 9:2; $\frac{9}{2}$

Skill 28

TRY THESE

1. 3, $\frac{2}{5}$
2. 6, 6, 6, $\frac{3}{2}$
3. 2, 2, 2, $\frac{16}{45}$

PRACTICE

1. 5, 5, 5, $\frac{2}{1}$
2. 3, 3, 3, $\frac{7}{9}$
3. 10, 10, 10, $\frac{3}{2}$
4. 8: 1, 2, 4, 8
10: 1, 2, 5, 10
GCF = 2
$\frac{4}{5}$
5. 12: 1, 2, 3, 4, 6, 12
8: 1, 2, 4, 8
GCF = 4
$\frac{3}{2}$
6. 24: 1, 2, 3, 4, 6, 8, 12, 24
30: 1, 2, 3, 5, 6, 10, 15, 30
GCF = 6
$\frac{4}{5}$
7. $\frac{8}{7}$

Answers

Skill 28

8. $\frac{5}{3}$
9. $\frac{17}{3}$

CHECK

10. $\frac{1}{4}$
11. $\frac{3}{1}$
12. $\frac{4}{3}$

Skill 29

TRY THESE

1. 24, 24
2. 35, 35
3. 68, 68
4. 81, 81

PRACTICE

1. 19, 19
2. 65, 65
3. 82, 82
4. 45, 45
5. 58, 58
6. 94, 94

CHECK

7. 23
8. 64
9. 87

Skill 30

TRY THESE

1. 30, 30, 0.3
2. 9, 9, 0.09
3. 40, 40, 40%
4. 1, 25, 125, 125%

PRACTICE

1. 37, 37, 0.37
2. 60, 60, 0.6
3. 2, 2, 0.02
4. 75, 75, 0.75
5. 55, 55, 55%
6. 8, 8, 8%
7. 40, 40, 40%
8. 2, 45, 245, 245%
9. 0.99
10. 0.2
11. 0.05
12. 1
13. 86%
14. 1%
15. 30%
16. 210%

CHECK

17. 0.03
18. 0.42
19. 70%
20. 150%

Skill 31

TRY THESE

1. 25, 25, 75, 75, 0.75, 75%
2. 20, 20, 20, 20, 0.20, 20%
3. 00, 90, 0, 90, 0.90, 90%
4. 00, 25, 50, 50, 0, 12, 0.12, 12%

PRACTICE

1. 50, 50, 50, 50, 0.50, 50%
2. 20, 20, 60, 60, 0.60, 60%
3. 5, 5, 30, 30, 0.30, 30%
4. 00, 200, 200, 200, 0, 55, 0.55, 55%
5. 00, 18, 20, 18, 2, 66, $0.\overline{6}$, $66.\overline{6}$%
6. 000, 48, 20, 16, 40, 40, 0, 625, 0.625, 62.5%
7. 0.80, 80%
8. 0.84, 84%
9. 0.125, 12.5%

Answers

CHECK

10. 0.50, 50%
11. 0.66, 66%
12. 0.44, 44%

SKILL 32

TRY THESE

1. $<$, 30, 0.30
2. $<$, 0.87
3. $>$, 75, 0.75, 0.71

PRACTICE

1. $>$ 80, 0.80, 0.77
2. $<$ 0.32
3. $=$ 28, 0.28, 0.28
4. $>$ 60, 0.60

CHECK

5. $=$
6. $>$
7. $<$
8. $<$
9. $>$
10. $>$

SKILL 33

TRY THESE

1. positive, $^{+}20$
2. negative, $^{-}15$
3. negative, $^{-}12$

PRACTICE

1. positive
2. positive
3. negative
4. negative
5. $^{-}12$
6. $^{+}125$
7. $^{-}4$
8. $^{-}25$
9. $^{-}17$
10. 0
11. $^{+}45$
12. $^{-}33$
13. $^{-}110$
14. $^{+}35$
15. $^{+}12$
16. $^{-}40$
17. $^{+}10$
18. $^{+}6$
19. $^{-}5$
20. $^{+}13$

CHECK

21. $^{+}9$
22. $^{-}36$
23. $^{-}2$
24. $^{-}6$

SKILL 34

TRY THESE

1. 1, 455
2. 6, 15, 249
3. 186; 6,510; 6,696
4. 464, 34, 8 r 34

PRACTICE

1. 1, 75
2. 1, 1, 313
3. 566
4. 275
5. 6, 13, 28
6. 3, 12, 18, 369
7. 488
8. 553
9. 360; 2,880; 3,240
10. 768; 3,840; 4,608
11. 35,583
12. 13,680
13. 115, 184, 184, 0, 58
14. 16, 34, 32, 2, 24 r 2
15. 33
16. 324 r 4

CHECK

17. 421
18. 739
19. 7,245
20. 75

Answers

Skill 35

TRY THESE

1. 4
2. 4, 2, 8
3. 4, 8, 16
4. 4, 8, 16, 32

PRACTICE

1. 16, 64
2. 25, 125, 625
3. 9, 27, 81, 243
4. 100, 1,000, 10,000
5. 81, 729
6. 36, 216
7. 125
8. 343
9. 1,024
10. 512
11. 6,561
12. 1,331

CHECK

13. 4,096
14. 1,000
15. 64

Skill 36

TRY THESE

1. 16, 16, 24, 27
2. 10, 20, 30, 40, 50, 60

PRACTICE

1. 32, 36
2. 40, 45
3. 48, 54
4. 15; 18
5. 10; 12
6. 12; 16
7. 50, 60, 70, 80
8. 33, 44, 55, 66
9. 48, 60, 72, 84
10. 56
11. 90
12. 99
13. 96

CHECK

14. 28
15. 36
16. 30
17. 77
18. 50
19. 63
20. 55
21. 132

Skill 37

TRY THESE

1. 70, 700, 7,000, 70,000
2. 9.2, 0.92, 0.092, 0.0092

PRACTICE

1. 50; 500; 5,000
2. 120; 1,200; 12,000
3. 1,520; 15,200; 152,000
4. 0.3; 0.03; 0.003
5. 2.4; 0.24; 0.024
6. 57.4; 0.574; 0.0574
7. 170,000; 4; right
8. 0.0017; 4; left
9. 700; 2, right
10. 0.068; 3; left
11. 90; 1; right
12. 1.18; 2; left
13. 98,000
14. 0.0034
15. 12,400

Skill 37

CHECK

16. 28,000
17. 2,500
18. 1,360
19. 0.018
20. 1.97
21. 0.14

Answers

SKILL 38

TRY THESE

1. 8, 8, 8
2. 9, 9, 9
3. 11, 11, 11
4. 7, 7, 7

PRACTICE

1. 28, 4
2. 63, 7
3. 40, 10
4. 48, 4
5. 30, 6
6. 49, 7
7. 36, 12
8. 90, 10
9. 7
10. 11
11. 6
12. 6
13. 4
14. 4
15. 11
16. 12
17. 4
18. 8
19. 9
20. 8
21. 7
22. 9
23. 6
24. 4

SKILL 38

CHECK

25. 7
26. 2
27. 11
28. 5

SKILL 39

TRY THESE

1. 24, 2, 6 r 2
2. 12, 30, 24, 6, $12\frac{1}{2}$
3. 00, 24, 27, 24, 30, 24, 60, 60, 0, 22.25

PRACTICE

1. 45, 2, 9 r 2
2. 11, 80, 77, 3, 17 r 3
3. 16, 34, 32, 21, 16, 5, 121 r 5
4. 32, 2, $8\frac{1}{2}$
5. 32, 84, 80, 4, $25\frac{1}{4}$
6. 111, 189, 185, 4, $35\frac{4}{37}$
7. 00, 24, 30, 28, 20, 20, 0, 6.75
8. 75, 33, 30, 30, 0, 52.2
9. 0, 36, 189, 180, 90, 72, 180, 180, 0, 152.5

CHECK

10. 12 r 5
11. $15\frac{1}{3}$
12. 20.5

SKILL 40

TRY THESE

1. 71.62
2. 20.7
3. 5.076, 2, 1, 3
4. 9.4

PRACTICE

1. 95.63
2. 0.868, 2, 1, 3
3. 3.7
4. 13.418
5. 75.63
6. 5.375
7. 9.225
8. 22.57
9. 0.425

CHECK

10. 18.41
11. 3.6
12. 45.41
13. 6.484
14. 3.075
15. 6.657

Answers

Skill 41

TRY THESE

1. 4, 40, 400
2. 0.6, 6, 60
3. 15, 150, 1,500

PRACTICE

1. 5, 50, 500
2. 1.8, 18, 180
3. 76, 760, 7,600
4. 9, 1
5. 20, 2
6. 1,900, 3
7. 240, 2
8. 5,080, 3
9. 6.1, 1
10. 5,700
11. 12.3
12. 7

CHECK

13. 89
14. 40
15. 538
16. 16
17. 8,390
18. 270

Skill 42

TRY THESE

1. $\frac{9}{10}$
2. $\frac{1}{2}$
3. $\frac{1}{9}$
4. 4

PRACTICE

1. $\frac{2}{8}, \frac{3}{8}, \frac{5}{8}$
2. $\frac{15}{36}, \frac{28}{36}, \frac{43}{36}$ or $1\frac{7}{36}$
3. $\frac{12}{15}, \frac{10}{15}, \frac{2}{15}$
4. $\frac{22}{30}, \frac{18}{30}, \frac{2}{15}$
5. $\frac{3 \times 1}{5 \times 6} = \frac{3}{30}, \frac{1}{10}$
6. $\frac{5 \times 3}{8 \times 10} = \frac{15}{80}, \frac{3}{16}$
7. $\frac{4 \times 3}{9 \times 1} = \frac{12}{9}, 1\frac{1}{3}$
8. $\frac{9 \times 6}{10 \times 3} = \frac{54}{30}, 1\frac{4}{5}$

CHECK

9. $1\frac{2}{9}$
10. $\frac{5}{16}$
11. $\frac{1}{7}$
12. $\frac{9}{20}$

Skill 43

TRY THESE

1. yes, $\frac{4}{5}$, yes
2. yes, $\frac{2}{7}$, yes
3. yes, $\frac{4}{8}$, no, $\frac{4 \div 4}{8 \div 4} = \frac{1}{2}$

PRACTICE

1. yes, $\frac{2}{6} + \frac{3}{6} = \frac{5}{6}$, yes
2. yes, $\frac{4}{5} - \frac{3}{5} = \frac{1}{5}$, yes
3. yes, $\frac{7}{10} + \frac{1}{10} = \frac{8}{10}$, no, $\frac{8 \div 2}{10 \div 2} = \frac{4}{5}$
4. $\frac{3}{5}$, yes
5. $\frac{4}{8}$, no, $\frac{4 \div 4}{8 \div 4} = \frac{1}{2}$
6. $\frac{2}{10}$, no, $\frac{2 \div 2}{10 \div 2} = \frac{1}{5}$
7. $\frac{2}{7}$
8. $\frac{4}{9}$
9. $\frac{1}{2}$
10. 1

Skill 43

CHECK

11. $\frac{1}{3}$
12. $\frac{7}{8}$
13. $\frac{1}{3}$
14. $\frac{4}{5}$

Answers

Skill 44

TRY THESE

1. $\frac{1}{12}$
2. $\frac{3}{8}$
3. $\frac{6}{20}, \frac{3}{10}$

PRACTICE

1. $\frac{1}{4}$
2. $\frac{3}{16}$
3. $\frac{6}{15}, \frac{2}{5}$
4. $\frac{1 \times 1}{4 \times 5}, \frac{1}{20}$
5. $\frac{2 \times 1}{3 \times 6}, \frac{2}{18}, \frac{1}{9}$
6. $\frac{4 \times 5}{5 \times 6}, \frac{20}{30}, \frac{2}{3}$
7. $\frac{1}{35}$
8. $\frac{1}{16}$
9. $\frac{1}{3}$

CHECK

10. $\frac{1}{27}$
11. $\frac{1}{8}$
12. $\frac{1}{4}$

Skill 45

TRY THESE

1. 15, 2
2. 5, 5, 1, $\frac{75}{5}$, 15

PRACTICE

1. 42, 1
2. 30, 2
3. 100, 2
4. $\frac{21}{5}$
5. 30
6. 20
7. 124.8
8. 1,287
9. 30.16

CHECK

10. 57
11. 323.7
12. 72

Skill 46

TRY THESE

1. 0.15, 9
2. 0.65, 26
3. 0.75, 3

PRACTICE

1. 0.10, 8
2. 0.45, 27
3. 0.90, 45
4. 4
5. 6
6. 24
7. 40
8. 140
9. 13.5

CHECK

10. 4
11. 4.2
12. 45

Skill 47

TRY THESE

1. 107, different
2. −226, same
3. 98, same
4. −26, different

PRACTICE

1. −5, different
2. 27, different
3. −25, same
4. −18, different
5. −80, different
6. 12, same
7. 84, same
8. −15, different

CHECK

9. 24
10. −68
11. −23
12. 17

Answers

TRY THESE

1. 6×7
2. $2 \times (8 \times 5)$
3. 1
4. 0

PRACTICE

1. Commutative Property
2. Property of Zero
3. Property of One
4. Associative Property
5. 0; Property of Zero
6. 1; Property of One
7. 32; Commutative Property
8. 5; Associative Property
9. 2; Associative Property
10. 4; Commutative Property

SKILL 48

CHECK

11. 0; Property of Zero
12. 5; Associative Property
13. 15; Commutative Property
14. 52; Property of One

SKILL 49

TRY THESE

1. 80 + 16; 96
2. 70 + 35; 105
3. 50 + 45; 95

PRACTICE

1. $4 \times 16 =$
   $(4 \times 10) + (4 \times 6)$
   $= 40 + 24$
   $= 64$
2. $6 \times 22 =$
   $(6 \times 20) + (6 \times 2)$
   $= 120 + 12$
   $= 132$

In Ex. 3–6, factors may vary. Sample answer given.

3. $5 \times 15 =$
   $(5 \times 10) + (5 \times 5)$
   $= 50 + 25$
   $= 75$
4. $5 \times 21 =$
   $(5 \times 20) + (5 \times 1)$
   $= 100 + 5$
   $= 105$

SKILL 49

CHECK

5. $8 \times 16 =$
   $(8 \times 10) + (8 \times 6)$
   $= 80 + 48$
   $= 128$
6. $7 \times 24 =$
   $(7 \times 20) + (7 + 4)$
   $= 140 + 28$
   $= 168$

Answers

Skill 50

TRY THESE

1. 8, 17
2. 6, 24
3. $a = 2$

PRACTICE

1. 10, 13
2. 6, 12
3. 6, 42
4. 3, 9
5. 17
6. 1
7. 150
8. 40
9. $c = 4$
10. $a = 2$
11. $p = 6$
12. $b = 7$
13. $y = 1$
14. $c = 11$

CHECK

15. 50
16. 0
17. 7

Skill 51

TRY THESE

1. $8 \div 2 = 4; 3 + 4 = 7; 7$
2. $5 + 3 = 8; 8 \times 7 = 56; 56$
3. $12 - 3 = 9; \frac{9}{3} = 3; 3 \times 8 = 24; 24$
4. $10 - 6 = 4; 5 \times 5 = 25; 25 - 4 = 21; 21$

PRACTICE

1. $10 \div 5 = 2; 7 + 2 = 9; 9$
2. $18 - 6 = 12; \frac{12}{4} = 3; 3 \times 2 = 6; 6$
3. $15 - 6 = 9; 4 \times 4 = 16; \frac{9}{3} = 3; 3 + 16 = 19; 19$
4. $5^2 \div 5$
$25 \div 5$
5
5. $36 \div 3^2$
$36 \div 9$
4
6. $\frac{9}{3} \times 8$
3×8
24

Skill 51

CHECK

7. $10 + 5$
15
8. $4^2 - 8$
$16 - 8$
8
9. $\frac{9}{9} + 6^2$
$\frac{9}{9} + 36$
$1 + 36$
37

Skill 52

TRY THESE

1. multiply $\frac{1}{2}$ by 6, multiply 3 by 3, 9
2. multiply 2 by 3.14, multiply 6.28 by 14, 87.92
3. add 4 and 7, multiply $\frac{1}{2}$ by 8 then multiply 4 by 11, 44

PRACTICE

1. square 6, 54
2. add 2 and 6, 40
3. square 4, 150.72
4. square 5, 235.5
5. multiply $\frac{1}{2}$ by 6, 17.25
6. add 3 and 7, 80

CHECK

7. 47.1
8. 252
9. 66

Answers

Skill 53

TRY THESE

1. addition; $5 + t$ or $t + 5$
2. subtraction; $12 - p$

PRACTICE

1. multiplication; $2m$
2. subtraction; $x - 8$
3. division; $\frac{24}{c}$ or $24 \div c$
4. addition; $4 + s$ or $s + 4$
5. multiplication; $5b$
6. subtraction; $r - 11$
7. d
8. a
9. b
10. c
11. addition, multiplication, $3 + 8p$ or $8p + 3$
12. subtraction, multiplication, $7n - 4$

Skill 53

13. division, subtraction $\frac{a}{4} - 6$

CHECK

14. addition, $17 + x$ or $x + 17$
15. multiplication, subtraction, $29y - 8$
16. b
17. a

Skill 54

TRY THESE

1. 5; $20 - 6$; 14, 14
2. 4; 4; $2 + 1$; 3, 3
3. 3; $2 \cdot 7^2$; $2 \cdot 49$; 98; 98

PRACTICE

1. 5, 2; $70 - 3$; 67; 67
2. $^-8$, $5 \cdot 2^2$; $5 \cdot 4$; 20; 20
3. $\frac{3 \times 24}{4} + 8$; $\frac{72}{4} + 8$; $18 + 8$; 26
4. $3(^-4 + 8)^2$; $3 \cdot 4^2$; $3 \cdot 16$; 48
5. $7 \cdot {}^-3 + 12$; $^-21 + 12$; $^-9$
6. 45
7. $^-9$
8. 243

CHECK

9. 10
10. 15
11. 144

Skill 55

TRY THESE

1. $3x$, $-x$, 7, -4, $2x + 3$
2. $2a$, 5, -7, $2a - 2$
3. $-7x$, $-2x$, $8y$, 4, 9, $-9x + 8y + 13$

PRACTICE

1. $6n$, $-3n$, 2, $3n + 2$
2. $5y$, y, 4, -6, $6y - 2$
3. $2a$, $-a$, $-5b$, $-b$, $a - 6b$
4. $-y$, $4y$, 26, 4, $3y + 30$
5. $-x$, $-4x$, $7y$, 6, $-5x + 7y + 6$
6. $3a$, $-4b$, $-b$, 6, 7, $3a - 5b + 13$

CHECK

7. $7y + 5$
8. $2a + 6b + 2$
9. $-7n + 5$

Answers

Skill 56

Variables may vary.

TRY THESE

1. addition; $12 + x = 17$
2. subtraction; $x - 1 = 2$
3. multiplication; $3x = 15$
4. division; $\frac{24}{x} = 6$

PRACTICE

1. addition; $x + 8 = 19$
2. subtraction; $x - 6.8 = 1.1$
3. division; $\frac{x}{3} = 9$
4. multiplication; $2x = 30$
5. addition; $31 = x + 8$
6. division; $\frac{x}{16} = \frac{3}{8}$
7. $x + 12 = 45$
8. $x - 16 = 5$
9. $7x = -35$
10. $28.9 = x + 7.2$
11. $3x = 33$
12. $\frac{8}{x} = {}^{-}2$ or $8 \div x = {}^{-}2$

Skill 56

CHECK

13. $7x = 84$
14. $19.2 - x = 6.7$
15. $\frac{x}{6} = \frac{2}{3}$
16. $x + 12 = 67$
17. $x - 15 = 82$
18. $3x = -36$

Skill 57

TRY THESE

1. addition; $2 + 7 = n$; 9
2. subtraction; $7 - 3 = n$; 4
3. multiplication; $4 \times n = 24$; 6
4. division; $12 \div 6 = n$; 2

PRACTICE

1. $n = 2 + 7$; 9
2. $25 - 12 = n$; 13
3. $8 \times n = 32$; 4
4. $30 \div 5 = n$; 6
5. $11 + n = 18$; 7
6. $27 - 12 = n$; 15
7. $9 \times n = 63$; 7
8. $81 \div 9 = n$; 9
9. 39
10. 43
11. 45
12. 6
13. $11 \times 20 = 220$
14. $388 - 253 = 135$ or $388 - 135 = 253$
15. $480 \div 32 = 15$ or $480 \div 15 = 32$
16. $176 + 172 = 348$

Skill 57

CHECK

17. 15
18. 13
19. 9
20. 26
21. $151 + 78 = 229$
22. $126 \div 9 = 14$ or $126 \div 14 = 9$
23. $287 - 109 = 178$ or $287 - 178 = 109$
24. $18 \times 12 = 216$

Answers

Skill 58

TRY THESE

1. 7, 7, 7, 16, 16
2. 10, 10, 10, 15, 15
3. 4, 4, 4, 28, 28
4. 80, 80, 80, 10, 10

PRACTICE

1. 4, 4, 4, 16, 16
2. 36, 36, 36, 12, 12
3. 18, 18, 18, 10, 10
4. 2, 2, 2, 14, 14
5. 0.4, 0.4, 0.4, 1.2, 1.2
6. 7.5, 7.5, 7.5, 1.5, 1.5
7. 1.8
8. 0.6
9. 12.6

CHECK

10. 14.5
11. 8
12. 63

Skill 59

TRY THESE

1. $1n = 7$
   $n = 7$
   Check 7; 14
2. $1t = 70$
   $t = 70$
   Check 70; 3.5

PRACTICE

1. $6 \div \frac{2}{3} = 1c$
   $6 \bullet \frac{3}{2} = c$
   $9 = c$
   Check 9; 6
2. $15 \div \frac{3}{4} = 1y$
   $15 \bullet \frac{4}{3} = y$
   $20 = y$
   Check 20; 15
3. 4; $n = 4$
4. 12; $6 = h$
5. 0.2; $x = 25$
6. 0.3; $b = 70$
7. 5
8. 30
9. 8
10. 13

CHECK

11. 20
12. 54
13. 12
14. 13

Skill 60

TRY THESE

1. −8, −2, −2, −5, −5
2. 3, 9
3. $7 + y$; $x = \frac{7 + y}{3}$

PRACTICE

1. 18, 3
2. 12, 3
3. $5x - 2$; $m = \frac{5x - 2}{3}$
4. 2, 12
5. 15, 6
6. $12x - 4$; $y = \frac{12x - 4}{6}$

CHECK

7. −2
8. 28
9. $c = \frac{8 - a}{5}$

Skill 61

PRACTICE

For 1. to 7. Check number lines

1. left
2. positive, 0, right
3. negative, 0, left
4. right
5. negative, left
6. positive, right
7. negative, left
8. check number lines
9. check number lines
10. check number lines
11. check number lines

Answers

Skill 62

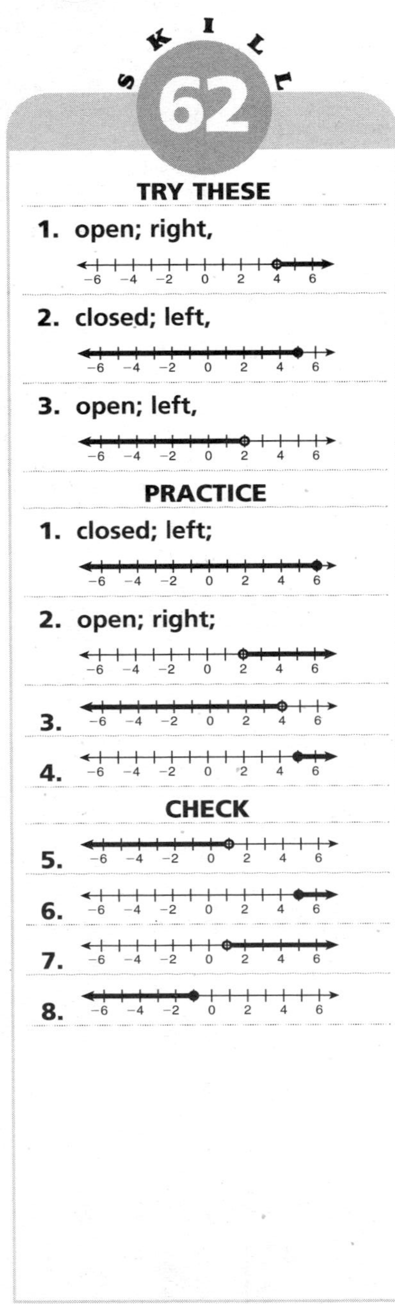

TRY THESE

1. open; right,
2. closed; left,
3. open; left,

PRACTICE

1. closed; left;
2. open; right;
3.
4.

CHECK

5.
6.
7.
8.

Skill 63

TRY THESE

1. −4, open, left, $a < -4$
2. −2, closed, right, $a \geq -2$
3. 3, closed, left, $a \leq 3$

PRACTICE

1. −3, closed, left, $a \leq -3$
2. 1, closed, right, $a \geq 1$
3. $a < 0$
4. $a < -5$

CHECK

5. $a < 6$
6. $a \geq -6$
7. $a \leq 2$
8. $a < 1$

Skill 64

TRY THESE

1.

x	$x + 2$	y	(x, y)
−2	−2 + 2	0	(−2, 0)
−1	−1 + 2	1	(−1, 1)
0	0 + 2	2	(0, 2)
1	1 + 2	3	(1, 3)

PRACTICE

1.

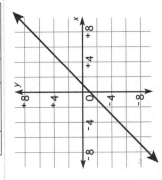

x	$x - 1$	y	(x, y)
−2	−2 − 1	−3	(−2, −3)
−1	−1 − 1	−2	(−1, −2)
0	0 − 1	−1	(0, −1)
1	1 − 1	0	(1, 0)

Answers

2.

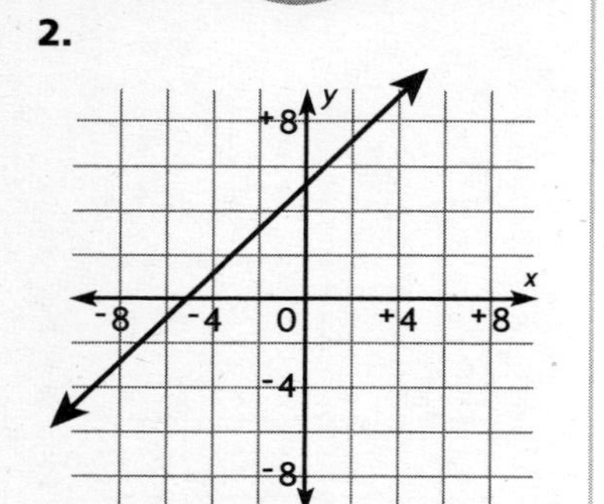

3.

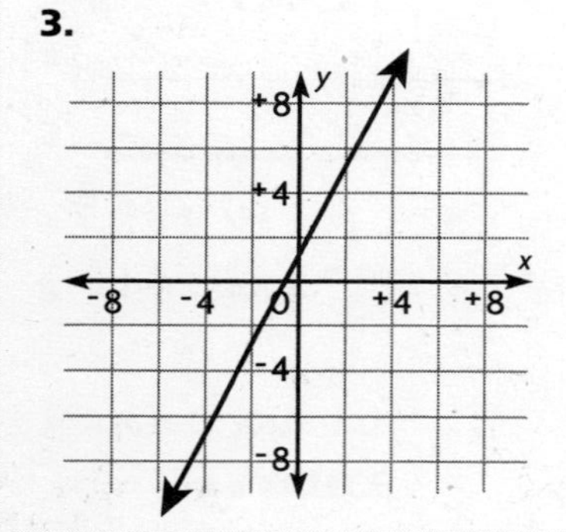

CHECK

4.

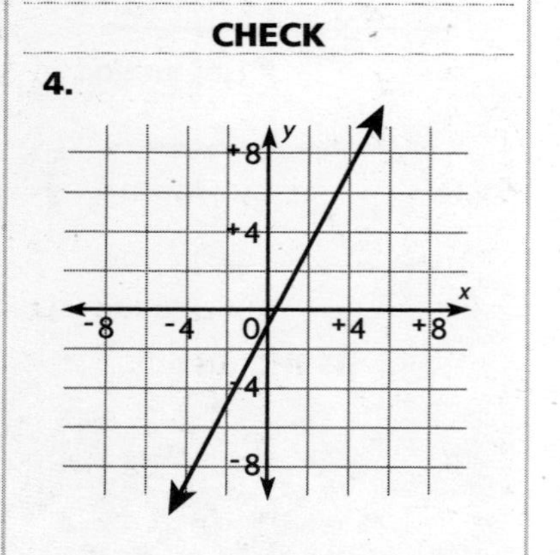

SKILL 65

TRY THESE

1. 9; 108; 108; 54
2. 6; 72; 72; 9
3. 27; 135; 135; 15

PRACTICE

1. 4; 80; 5; $\frac{80}{5}$; 16; Check: 80 = 80
2. 8; 72; 6; $\frac{72}{6}$; 12; Check: 72 = 72
3. 3; 63; 7; $\frac{63}{7}$; 9
4. 3; 45; $\frac{45}{9}$; 9; 5
5. 63
6. 4

CHECK

7. 8
8. 6
9. 3

SKILL 66

TRY THESE

1. yards, 3, 18
2. inches, 12, 6
3. meters, 100, 400
4. centimeters, 100, 7

PRACTICE

1. Multiply; 7,040
2. Multiply; 80
3. Multiply; 21
4. Divide; 4
5. Divide; 0.007
6. Divide; 3
7. 24
8. 6,000
9. 4,000
10. 5
11. 3
12. 9
13. 45
14. 300
15. 5
16. 9

CHECK

17. 8,800
18. 830
19. 4
20. 0.004

Answers

Skill 67

TRY THESE

1. 10; 11
2. 1.1; 3.3

PRACTICE

1. 21; 42
2. 4; 6
3. 10.1 + 11.8, 21.9; 12.3 + 11.8, 24.1; 14.1 + 11.8, 25.9
4. 5.9 − 3.5, 2.4; 13.1 − 3.5, 9.6; 15.6 − 3.5, 12.1
5. 15 • 5, 75; 24 • 5, 120; 37 • 5, 185
6. 84 ÷ 12, 7; 108 ÷ 12, 9; 132 ÷ 12, 11

CHECK

7. 29.8 − 6.7, 23.1; 42.9 − 6.7, 36.2; 58.3 − 6.7, 51.6
8. 3 • 14, 42; 7 • 14, 98; 11 • 14, 154

Skill 68

TRY THESE

1. 4; 1; *F*
2. 5; 2; *E*
3. 6; 5; (6, 5)

PRACTICE

1. 1; right; 3; up; (1, 3)
2. 5; right; 0; up; (5, 0)
3. 3; left; 4; down; ($^{-}3$, $^{-}4$)
4. ($^{-}5$, 4)
5. ($^{-}2$, $^{-}3$)
6. (0, 1)
7. (5, 4)
8. ($^{-}6$, 0)
9. (5, $^{-}4$)

CHECK

10. (2, $^{-}2$)
11. (0, $^{-}6$)
12. ($^{-}3$, 5)
13. (4, 0)

Skill 69

TRY THESE

1. 1, 4, (1, 4)
2. 6, 5, (6, 5)
3. Video Store

PRACTICE

1. 1, 5, (1, 5)
2. 2, 1, (2, 1)
3. 3, 7, (3, 7)
4. (5, 4)
5. (6, 9)
6. (7, 3)

CHECK

7. (1, 6)
8. (2, 3)
9. (4, 5)
10. (6, 7)

Skill 70

TRY THESE

1. 80, 90, up, 80, 88
2. 90, 100, up, 90, 94
3. 0, $^{-}10$, down, 0, $^{-}6$
4. 20, 30, up, 20, 22

PRACTICE

1. $^{-}10$
2. 0, 10, down, 10, 8
3. $^{-}10$, $^{-}20$, up, $^{-}20$, $^{-}18$
4. 20, 30, up, 20, 22
5. 0, 4
6. $^{-}20$, $^{-}18$
7. 10, 12
8. 20, 22
9. $^{-}8$
10. 62
11. $^{-}12$
12. 44
13. 30
14. 10
15. 0
16. $^{-}20$

Answers

Skill 70

CHECK

17. $^{-}4$
18. 28
19. 42
20. 56
21. $^{-}6$
22. 60
23. 10
24. $^{-}10$

Skill 71

TRY THESE

1. multiply, 3; 36
2. gallons, multiply, 4; 128
3. ounces, multiply, 16; 400

PRACTICE

1. yards, multiply; 27
2. gallons, multiply; 100
3. pounds, multiply; 640
4. inches, divide; 9
5. cups, divide; 15
6. ounces, divide; 12
7. multiply, 81
8. multiply, 300
9. multiply, 1,920
10. divide, 20
11. divide, 45
12. divide, 36
13. 54
14. 240
15. 1,152
16. 12

Skill 71

17. 28
18. 7

CHECK

19. 162
20. 144
21. 432
22. 10
23. 13
24. 8

Skill 72

TRY THESE

1. multiply, 100; 40,000
2. liters, multiply, 1,000; 7,000
3. milligrams, multiply, 1,000; 25,000

PRACTICE

1. 3,000
2. multiply; 200,000
3. multiply; 6,000
4. 7
5. divide; 4
6. divide; 25
7. 2,700
8. 75,000
9. 12,000
10. 24
11. 1
12. 1

CHECK

13. 1,800
14. 71,000
15. 72,000
16. 27
17. 54
18. 18

Answers

Skill 73

TRY THESE

1. $\frac{3}{8}$ in.
2. $4\frac{1}{2}$ cm
3. $2\frac{1}{8}$ in.

PRACTICE

1. $7\frac{1}{2}$ in.
2. $2\frac{1}{2}$ cm.
3. 11 in
4. will vary
5. will vary
6. will vary

CHECK

7. will vary
8. will vary
9. will vary

Skill 74

TRY THESE

1. right
2. acute
3. obtuse
4. straight

PRACTICE

1. acute
2. right
3. obtuse
4. straight
5. right
6. acute
7. obtuse
8. straight
9. right

CHECK

10. acute
11. obtuse
12. right

Skill 75

TRY THESE

1. *GHK; KHG; H*
2. *d*
3. *BGD; DGB*

PRACTICE

1. *GCN; NCG; C*
2. *a*
3. *RQE; EQR*
4. *DEW; WED; E*
5. *g*
6. *SOP; POS*
7. 3
8. *OPL; LPO*
9. *TAP; PAT*

CHECK

10. *CDA; ADC*
11. *R*
12. *PDQ; QDP*

Skill 76

PRACTICE

1. isosceles triangle
2. equilateral triangle
3. right triangle
4. obtuse triangle
5. rectangle
6. parallelogram
7. rhombus
8. trapezoid
9. pentagon
10. hexagon
11. octagon
12. scalene triangle

CHECK

13. rhombus or square
14. isosceles triangle
15. rectangle
16. parallelogram

SKILL 77

TRY THESE

1. *HGJ; GJK; JKH; KHG*; all right
2. *MPN; PNM; NMP*; all acute
3. obtuse; acute; right; right

PRACTICE

1. *ABC; BCA; CAB*
2. *DEF; EFG; FGD; GDE*
3. *VWX; WXY; XYZ, YZV; ZVW*
4. acute; acute; acute
5. right; right; right; right
6. acute; obtuse; right; right
7. *FGH* - acute; *GHF* - right; *HFG* - acute
8. *WXY* - acute; *XYZ* - obtuse; *YZW* - obtuse; *ZWX* - acute
9. *MNP* - acute; *NPQ* - obtuse; *PQR* - right; *QRM* - right; *RMN* - obtuse

SKILL 77

CHECK

10. *ABC* - right *BCD* - right; *CDA* - right; *DAB* - right
11. *XYZ* - acute; *YZX* - acute; *ZXY* - obtuse
12. *MNP* - obtuse; *NPQ* - acute; *PQM* - acute; *QMN* - obtuse

SKILL 78

PRACTICE

1. 2; triangular; triangular prism
2. 1; pentagonal; pentagonal pyra-mid
3. 2; circular; cylinder
4. 2; rectangular; rectangular prism
5. 1; circular; cone
6. 1; triangular; triangular pyramid
7. sphere
8. square pyramid
9. hexagonal prism
10. cylinder

CHECK

11. cone
12. pentagonal prism
13. sphere
14. hexagonal pyramid

SKILL 79

PRACTICE

1. pyramid; 6, 6, 10
2. prism; 6, 8, 12
3. 5, 5, 8
4. 6, 8, 12
5. 7, 10, 15
6. 8, 12, 18
7. 5 faces, 6 vertices, 9 edges
8. 6 faces, 8 vertices, 12 edges
9. 7 faces, 7 vertices, 12 edges

CHECK

10. 8 faces, 12 vertices, 18 edges
11. 9 faces, 9 vertices, 16 edges
12. 10 faces, 16 vertices, 24 edges

Answers

Skill 80

PRACTICE

1. intersecting lines
2. parallel lines
3. perpendicular and intersecting lines
4. perpendicular and intersecting lines
5. parallel
6. parallel
7. parallel
8. intersecting and perpendicular
9. $\overleftrightarrow{PN}$, $\overleftrightarrow{ST}$, $\overleftrightarrow{RQ}$
10. $\overleftrightarrow{PR}$, $\overleftrightarrow{NQ}$, $\overleftrightarrow{TQ}$, $\overleftrightarrow{SR}$
11. $\overleftrightarrow{ML}$, $\overleftrightarrow{TS}$ $\overleftrightarrow{PL}$, $\overleftrightarrow{RS}$

CHECK

12. $\overleftrightarrow{ST}$, $\overleftrightarrow{RQ}$, $\overleftrightarrow{PN}$
13. $\overleftrightarrow{LS}$, $\overleftrightarrow{PR}$, $\overleftrightarrow{RQ}$, $\overleftrightarrow{TS}$
14. $\overleftrightarrow{PN}$, $\overleftrightarrow{RQ}$, $\overleftrightarrow{LP}$, $\overleftrightarrow{SR}$

Skill 81

TRY THESE

1. yes; yes; yes
2. yes; no; no
3. $\overline{QR}$; $\overline{RS}$; $\angle A$

PRACTICE

1. yes; yes; yes
2. no; no; no
3. yes; no; no
4. no
5. yes
6. no
7. $\angle N$
8. $\angle P$
9. $\angle R$
10. $\overline{RN}$
11. $\overline{FD}$
12. $\overline{EF}$

CHECK

13. no
14. yes
15. $\angle T$; $\overline{US}$

Skill 82

TRY THESE

1. yes; yes
2. yes; yes
3. yes; yes
4. no; no

PRACTICE

1. yes; yes
2. no; no
3. no; no
4. yes
5. no
6. no
7. no
8. yes
9. yes

CHECK

10. no
11. yes
12. no

Skill 83

TRY THESE

1. 9
2. 3, 3, 3, 3; 12
3. 6 cm, 5 cm, 5 cm, 4 cm, 5 cm; 25 cm

PRACTICE

1. 4, 4, 4, 4; 16
2. 2, 2, 2, 2, 2, 2; 12
3. 3, 3, 3, 3; 12
4. 4 cm, 4 cm, 3 cm, 5 cm, 2 cm; 18 cm
5. 6 cm, 6 cm, 4 cm; 16 cm
6. 5 cm, 4 cm, 3 cm, 9 cm; 21 cm
7. 24 cm
8. 23 cm
9. 17 cm

CHECK

10. 17 cm
11. 20 cm
12. 32 cm
13. 18 cm

Answers

Skill 84

TRY THESE

1. 2, rectangle, 4, rectangle, 6
2. 2, hexagon, 6, rectangle, 8

PRACTICE

1. 1, triangle, 3, triangle, 4, triangular pyramid
2. 1, rectangle, 4 triangle, 5, rectangular pyramid
3. 2, 5, 7, pentagonal prism
4. 1, 3, 4, triangular pyramid

CHECK

5. 1, 5, 6, pentagonal pyramid
6. 2, 4, 6, rectangular prism

Skill 85

TRY THESE

1. $15\frac{1}{2}$; $6\frac{1}{2}$; $100\frac{3}{4}$; $100\frac{3}{4}$;
2. 1.5; 1.5; 2.25; 2.25
3. 11; 4; 44; 22; 22

PRACTICE

1. $3\frac{3}{4}$ ft; $1\frac{1}{2}$ ft; $5\frac{5}{8}$ ft^2
2. 10, 10; 100 mi^2
3. 4, 3; 12; 6 yd^2
4. $A = \ell \times w$ or $5\frac{1}{2} \times 14$; 77 in^2
5. $A = s \times s$ or 6×6; 36 ft^2
6. $A = \frac{1}{2}bh$, $\frac{1}{2} \times (20 \times 3.5)$, $\frac{1}{2} \times 70$, 35 cm^2
7. $A = 114\ m^2$
8. $A = 20\frac{1}{4}\ ft^2$
9. $A = 510\ cm^2$

CHECK

10. $A = 4\frac{8}{9}\ yd^2$
11. $A = 17.5\ yd^2$
12. $A = 625\ cm^2$

Skill 86

TRY THESE

1. 5, 25, 78.5
2. 7, 49, $\frac{22}{7} \times \frac{49}{1}$, $\frac{1,078}{7}$ or 154
3. 9 cm, 9, 81, 254.34

PRACTICE

1. 6, 36, 113.04 cm^2, 113 cm^2
2. 14, 196, $\frac{22}{7} \times \frac{196}{1}$, $\frac{4,312}{7}$, 616 yd^2, 616 yd^2
3. 4.5 m, 4.5, 20.25, 63.585 m^2, 64 m^2
4. 8, $A \approx 3.14 \times 64$; $A \approx 200.96\ m^2$, $A \approx 201\ m^2$
5. 15^2, $A \approx \frac{22}{7} \times \frac{225}{1}$, $A \approx \frac{4,950}{7}$, $A \approx 707.14\ ft^2$, $A \approx 707\ ft^2$
6. 10 m, 10, $A \approx 3.14 \times 100$, $A \approx 314.00\ m^2$, $A \approx 314\ m^2$
7. $A \approx 13\ in^2$

Skill 86

8. $A \approx 95\ cm^2$
9. $A \approx 50\ yd^2$

CHECK

10. $A \approx 452\ m^2$
11. $A \approx 1,385\ in^2$
12. $A \approx 177\ cm^2$

Answers

Skill 87

TRY THESE

1. translation
2. reflection
3. rotation

PRACTICE

1. reflection
2. translation
3. rotation
4. rotation
5. translation
6. reflection
7. translation
8. reflection
9. translation

CHECK

10. reflection
11. rotation
12. translation

Skill 88

TRY THESE

1. yes, no
2. no, yes
3. yes, no
4. no, no

PRACTICE

1. 4
2. 2
3. 2
4. 0
5. 1
6. 2
7. 0
8. 2

CHECK

9. 1
10. 1
11. 0
12. 1

Skill 89

TRY THESE

1. *DEF*, 90°
2. *UTS*, 120°

PRACTICE

1. 30
2. 120
3. 40
4. *HKM*, 75°
5. *RLO*, 145°
6. *KQZ*, 25°
7. $m\angle JEM = 90°$
8. $m\angle CGL = 135°$
9. $m\angle DGB = 20°$

CHECK

10. $m\angle GDR = 180°$
11. $m\angle LRS = 15°$
12. $m\angle EHN = 130°$

Skill 90

TRY THESE

1. Boys, 13, climbing
2. Bicycling, 10, 9, 1
3. Girls, 11, 12, 23

PRACTICE

1. Marina, 140, 140
2. Game 1, 205, Jorge
3. Lucia, 192, Game 1
4. Game 2, 212, 218, 6
5. 621
6. Theon

CHECK

7. Game 1
8. Jorge

Answers

Skill 91

TRY THESE

1. 2, 3, 6, 8, 9; 9; 2; 7
2. 19, 28, 37, 52; 52; 19; 33
3. 13, 25, 32, 54, 60, 71; 71; 13; 58

PRACTICE

1. 4, 6, 7, 8, 10; 10; 4; 6
2. 65, 77, 79, 81, 88; 88; 65; 23
3. 54, 98, 100, 102; 48
4. 137, 137, 140, 156, 195; 58
5. 56
6. 31

CHECK

7. 20
8. 37

Skill 92

TRY THESE

1. 3, 7, 8, 8, 14; 8; 8
2. 46, 57, 57, 59, 60, 75; 58; 57
3. 0.9, 1.4, 1.4, 2.1, 6.5; 1.4; 1.4

PRACTICE

1. 4, 5, 5, 6, 7; 5; 5
2. 68, 68, 75, 80, 82; 75; 68
3. 78, 82, 86, 90, 90, 95; 88; 90
4. 3.0, 3.5, 4.4, 4.6, 4.8, 4.8; 4.5; 4.8
5. 2.2, 2.0
6. 40, 35

CHECK

7. 95, 95
8. 3.9, 3.6

Skill 93

TRY THESE

1. 35, $\begin{array}{r}7\\5\overline{)35}\end{array}$, 7
2. 540, $\begin{array}{r}90\\6\overline{)540}\end{array}$, 90
3. 45.6, $\begin{array}{r}7.6\\6\overline{)45.6}\end{array}$, 7.6

PRACTICE

1. 30, $\begin{array}{r}6\\5\overline{)30}\end{array}$, 6
2. 410, $\begin{array}{r}82\\5\overline{)410}\end{array}$, 82
3. 57.0, $\begin{array}{r}11.4\\5\overline{)57.0}\end{array}$, 11.4
4. 250, 5, 50
5. 276, 6, 46
6. 55.2, 6, 9.2
7. 69
8. 86
9. 12.6

CHECK

10. 7
11. 90
12. 10.4

Skill 94

TRY THESE

1. giraffe
2. 40 years
3. 10 years

PRACTICE

1. 5 grams
2. pencil
3. finger ring and paper clip
4. 1 gram
5. pencil
6. Possible answers: pencil and paper clip; finger ring and earring

CHECK

7. paper clip
8. 2 grams
9. earring and paper clip

Answers

Skill 95

TRY THESE

1. Monthly Family Budget
2. 6
3. $1,200
4. $700
5. $600
6. savings

PRACTICE

1. Number and Type of Movies Rented
2. mystery
3. musical
4. comedy
5. action and other
6. Favorite Restaurant Votes
7. Pizza Land
8. Taco Hut
9. Chicken Cluck, Burger Barn and Italy's

CHECK

10. Number and Type of Vehicles Rented in July
11. full size
12. other
13. van

Skill 96

TRY THESE

1. 72, 97, 25
2. 9, 85
3. 80, 80

PRACTICE

1. 84
2. 58
3. 98
4. 40
5. 84
6. 84

CHECK

7. 47
8. 76
9. 64

Skill 97

TRY THESE

1. impossible
2. likely
3. certain
4. unlikely

PRACTICE

1. likely
2. unlikely
3. certain
4. unlikely
5. likely
6. impossible

CHECK

7. likely
8. certain
9. impossible

Skill 98

TRY THESE

1. 100
2. 225, 275, 50
3. $100 = $100
4. $\frac{3}{10}$ or 30%

PRACTICE

1. $400
2. August
3. July, September
4. $700
5. $\frac{7}{25}$ or 28%
6. $\frac{14}{25}$ or 56%
7. less
8. baths and dishwashers

CHECK

9. March, April
10. $300
11. showers
12. dishwasher

Enrichment Answers

CHAPTER 1: Place Value of Whole Numbers:

1. 1876 **2.** 1837 **3.** 1788 **4.** 1907 **5.** 4,778,332 **6.** 20,044,141 **7.** 7,650,789 **8.** 3,316,154 **9.** 15,111,244 **10.** 4,369,862 **11.** 3,960,825 **12.** 5,250,446 **13.** 200,000 **14.** 4,000,000 **15.** 6,000

CHAPTER 1: Round Whole Numbers:

1. 5,308,000 **2.** 7,240,000 **3.** 9,638,000 **4.** 12,861,000 **5.** 17,063,000 **6.** 23,192,000 **7.** 31,443,000 **8.** 38,558,000 **9.** 50,189,000 **10.** 62,980,000 **11.** 76,210,000 **12.** 92,230,000 **13.** 106,020,000 **14.** 123,200,000 **15.** 132,160,000 **16.** 151,330,000 **17.** 179,320,000 **18.** 203,300,000 **19.** 226,540,000 **20.** 248,710,000

CHAPTER 2: Words and Equations/Mental Math:

1. Possible Equation: $10n = 70$, Mystery Number: 7
2. Possible Equation: $\frac{n}{9} = 6$, Mystery Number: 54
3. Possible Equation: $11n = 99$, Mystery Number: 9
4. Possible Equation: $\frac{n}{12} = 8$, Mystery Number: 96
5. Possible Equation: $\frac{49}{n} = 7$, Mystery Number: 7
6. Possible Equation: $5n = 95$ Mystery Number: 19
7. Possible Equation: $\frac{n}{15} = 2$, Mystery Number: 30
8. Possible Equation: $\frac{48}{n} = 6$ Mystery Number: 8
9. Possible Equation: $30n = 6{,}000$, Mystery Number: 200
10. Possible Equation: $\frac{n}{4} = 9$, Mystery Number: 36

CHAPTER 2: Evaluate Expressions:

1.–19.

Figure 2

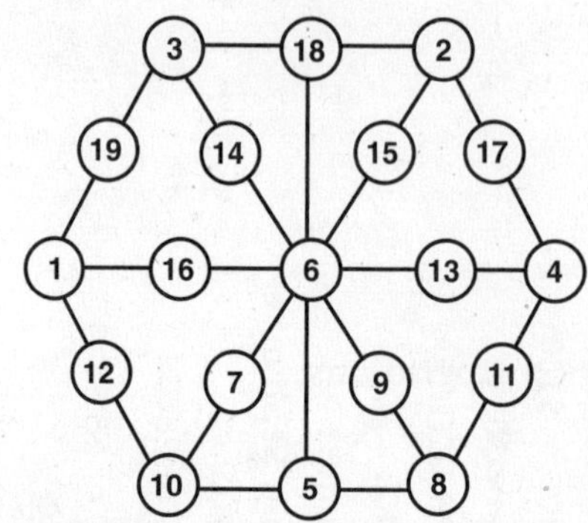

The sum is 23.

CHAPTER 3: Decimals and Whole Numbers:

1. 0.50 **2.** 0.25 **3.** 0.05 **4.** 0.55 **5.** $63.67 **6.** $ 125.44

CHAPTER 3: Decimals:

1. Seventy-eight and 53/100 **2.** One thousand, nine hundred twenty-five and 25/100 **3.** $63.70 **4.** $125.40 **5.** $78.50 **6.** $1,925.30 **7.** $64 **8.** $125 **9.** $79 **10.** $1,925

CHAPTER 4: Prime and Composite:

1.–4.

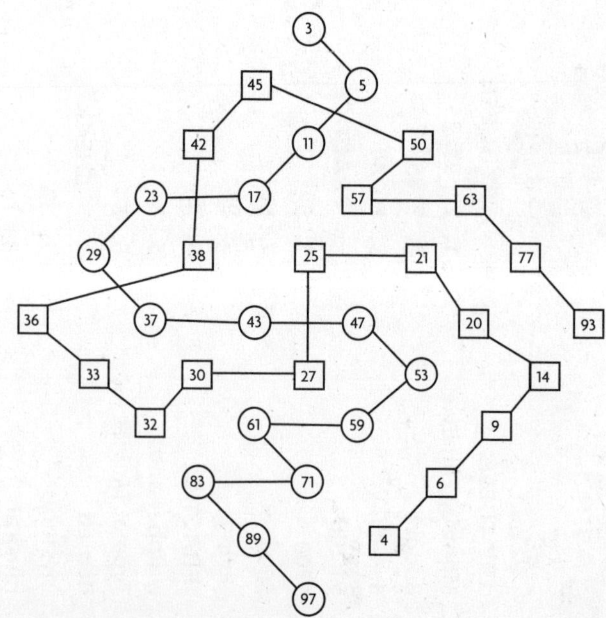

5. 16 **6.** 20 **7.** 4

CHAPTER 4: Multiples and Factors:

1. 1, 3, 5, 15 **2.** 1, 3, 7, 9, 21, 63 **3.** 1, 2, 3, 4, 6, 9, 12, 18, 36 **4.** 6, 12, 18, 24, 30 **5.** 7, 14, 21, 28, 35 **6.** 10, 20, 30, 40, 50 **7.** Factors: 1, 11, Multiples:11, 22, 33, 44, 55 **8.** Factors: 1, 3, 9, Multiples: 9, 18, 27, 36, 45 **9.** Factors: 1, 2, 3, 4, 6, 12, Multiples: 12, 24, 36, 48, 60

CHAPTER 5: Fraction Operations:

1. I **2.** T **3.** E **4.** N **5.** B **6.** Y **7.** L **8.** R **9.** A **10.** C **11.** M **12.** U **13.** O **14.** G **15.** S
Solution: ALGEBRA, GEOMETRY, TRIGONOMETRY, and CALCULUS

CHAPTER 5: Fraction Operations:

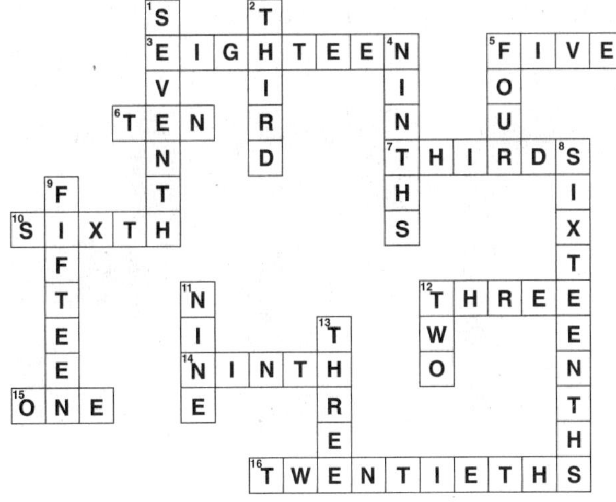

CHAPTER 6: Read a Table:

1. 90,000 **2.** 2,500,000 **3.** 1,380,000 **4.** 3,670,000 **5.** 3,760,000 **6.** 3,880,000 **7.** 360,000 **8.** 10,000 **9.** 490,000 **10.** 120,000

CHAPTER 6: Mean, Median, Mode, Range:

1. 62 **2.** 56 **3.** 2 **4.** 36 **5.** 104 **6.** 6 **7.** 106 **8.** 103.4 **9.** 85 **10.** 18 **11.** 85 **12.** 83 **13.** 7 **14.** 7 **15.** 8 **16.** 8

CHAPTER 7: Classify Angles:

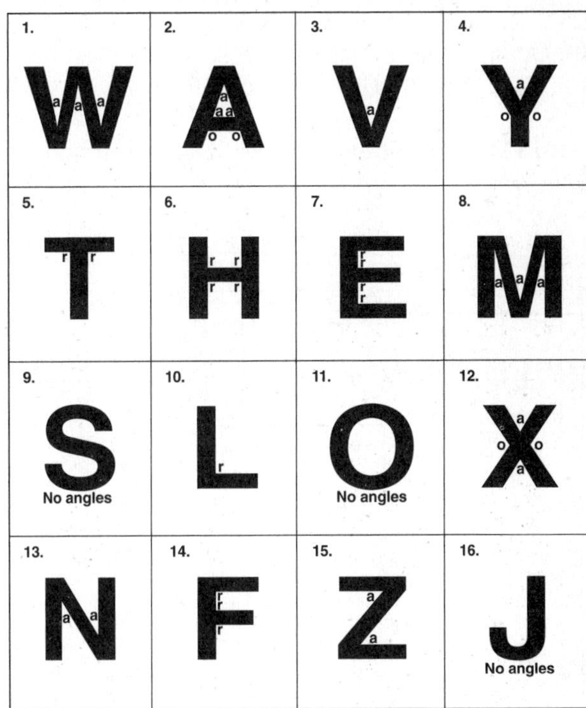

CHAPTER 7: Name Angles:

1. $\angle L$, $\angle ALX$, or $\angle XLA$ **2.** $\angle J$, $\angle KJF$, or $\angle FJK$ **3.** $\angle S$, $\angle WSA$, or $\angle ASW$ **4.** $\angle A$, $\angle LAX$, or $\angle XAL$ **5.** $\angle F$, $\angle JFK$, or $\angle KFJ$ **6.** Chicago, Illinois **7.** La Paz, Bolivia **8.** 10:30 **9.** 1:30 **10.** 9:30
11. **12.**

CHAPTER 8: Customary and Metric Units:

1. A **2.** R **3.** I **4.** G **5.** H **6.** T **7.** A **8.** N **9.** G **10.** L **11.** E
Solution: A RIGHT ANGLE
12. A **13.** Y **14.** A **15.** R **16.** D **17.** S **18.** T **19.** I **20.** C **21.** K
Solution: A YARDSTICK

CHAPTER 8: Solve Proportions:

1. $n = 24$ **2.** $n = 20$ **3.** $n = 12$ **4.** $n = 24$ **5.** $n = 60$ **6.** $n = 10$ **7.** $n = 3$ **8.** $n = 9$ **9.** $n = 25$

Enrichment
Answers

CHAPTER 9: Understand Integers:

1. W **2.** H **3.** E **4.** N **5.** T **6.** Y **7.** A **8.** V **9.** S **10.** O **11.** R **12.** I
Solution: WHEN THEY HAVE STORIES

CHAPTER 9: Number Lines/ Multiplication and Division:

1. −6 **2.** −3 **3.** −3 **4.** +8 **5.** +2 **6.** −4

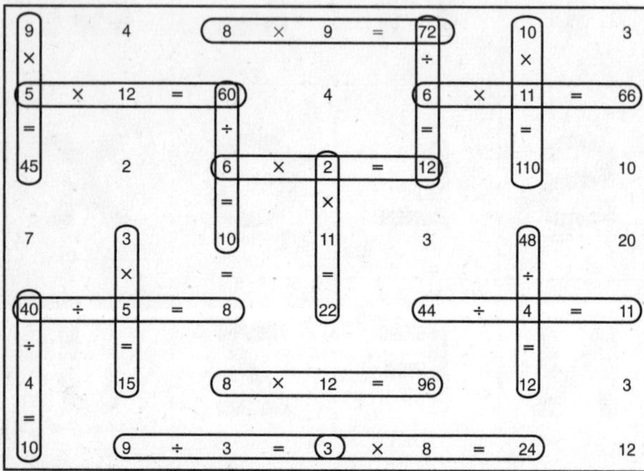

9 4 8 × 9 = 72 10 3
× ÷ ×
5 × 12 = 60 4 6 × 11 = 66
= ÷ = =
45 2 6 × 2 = 12 110 10
= ×
7 3 10 11 3 48 20
× = = ÷
40 ÷ 5 = 8 22 44 ÷ 4 = 11
÷ = =
4 15 8 × 12 = 96 12 3
=
10 9 ÷ 3 = 3 × 8 = 24 12

CHAPTER 10: Solid Figures:

1. a cube **2.** a triangular pyramid **3.** a cylinder **4.** a sphere **5.** a rectangular prism **6.** a cone **7.** a square pyramid **8.** an octagonal prism **9.** a pentagonal pyramid **10.** a cylinder **11.** a cone **12.** a hexagonal prism **13.** a triangular prism **14.** a rectangular prism

CHAPTER 10: Solid Figures:

1. F **2.** I **3.** F **4.** T **5.** E **6.** E **7.** N **8.** C **9.** E **10.** N **11.** T **12.** S
Solution: FIFTEEN CENTS

CHAPTER 11: Probability Vocabulary:

1.–11.

```
E T T V N O X A L M R E V A D Z C L O M W Q E
S O U D G B H E T Y L O W N E J S S T N R I Q
A J U E E C Q A B O K Q B V N O O N N L Z C U
M Z A T N E V E D N U O P M O C E S D G Q E A
P P O I C Y T R E W Q A S D F M G H L Z C M L
L R E W P O F K F R Y S H U I F D K R A A E L
E X P E R I M E N T A L P R O B A B I L I T Y
S G R V E Z M E Y L A Q E R A S L F A F U R L
P H T F D K L D S D H P I O O P F D F K Q E I
A J D I I E R J P A X A H O Q E R Z S K A I K
C E Q U C A L L N E T T A S D H N K B A E L E
E A R F T H O L P I Q S R T Y U O L T R Q E L
G S E V I Y I M S K A X P R O B A B I L I T Y
N Z D B O U K P D L Z D F G H J I P G F E L S
T X C N N J M U D M W E C B N M K N H A Q U A
Y T I L I B A B O R P L A C I T E R O E H T L
```

CHAPTER 11: Outcomes and Sample Space:

1. {1, 2, 3, 4, 5, 6} **2.** 11 **3.** $\frac{3}{10}$ **4.** $\frac{1}{2}$ **5.** $\frac{3}{5}$ **6.** $\frac{16}{25}$ **7.** 0.15 **8.** $\frac{1}{3}$ **9.** $\frac{17}{25}$ **10.** 12 **11.** 8 **12.** 11:19 **13.** 13:21

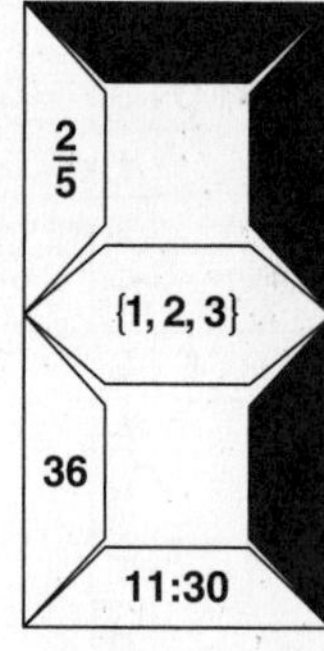

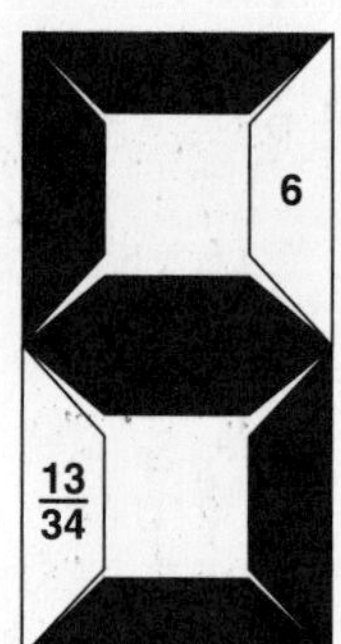

Hank Aaron hit 755 homeruns during his baseball career.

CHAPTER 12: Compare Numbers/Ordered Pairs:

9.

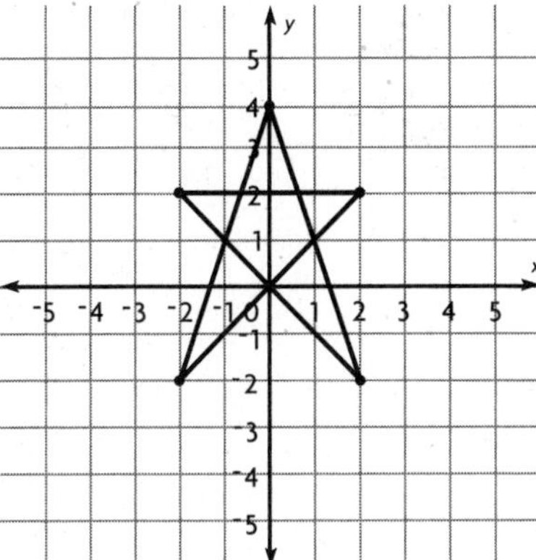

10.

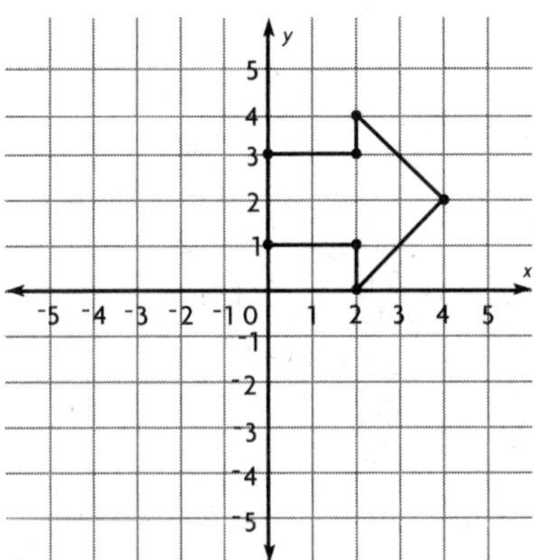

CHAPTER 12: Transformations:

1.

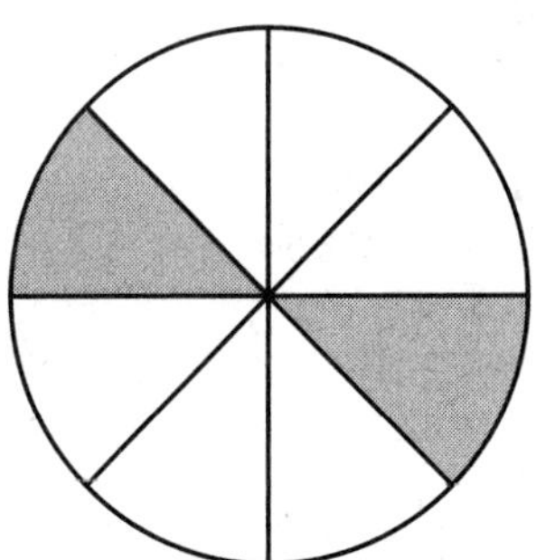

2.

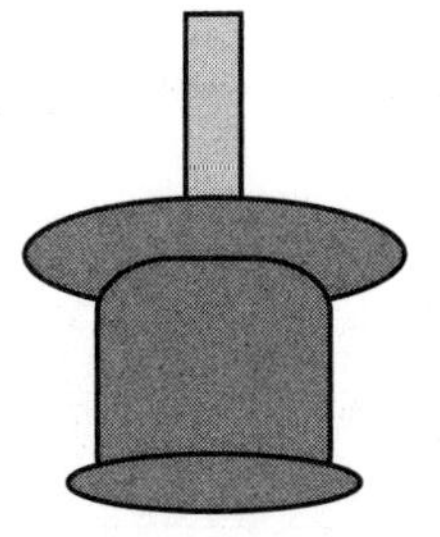

3.

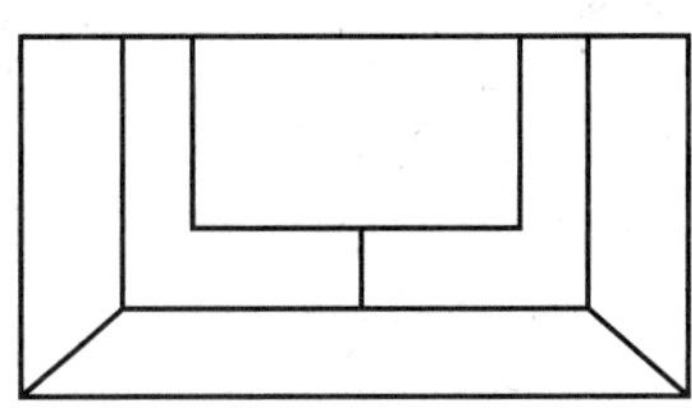

4.

5.

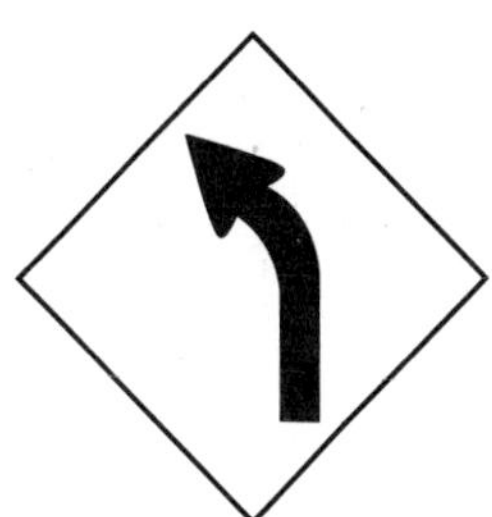

6.

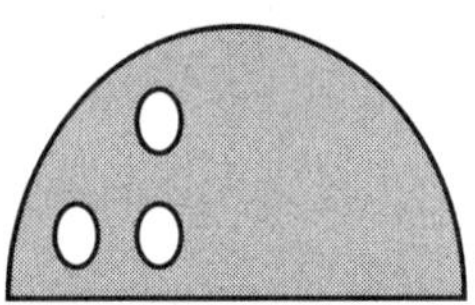

7.

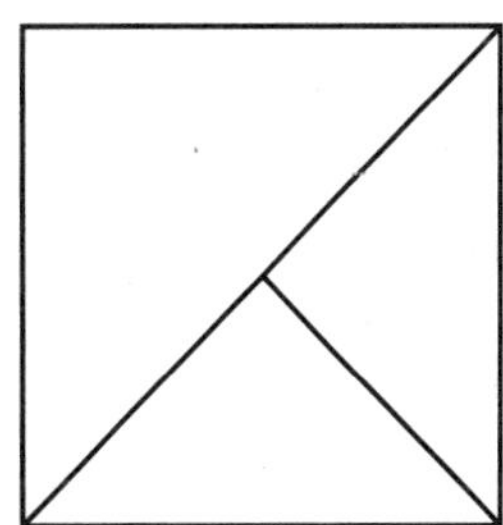